THE ENCYCLOPEDIA OF
EARTH
A Complete Visual Guide

THE ENCYCLOPEDIA OF
EARTH
A Complete Visual Guide

WELDON
OWEN

Conceived and produced by
Weldon Owen Pty Ltd
59–61 Victoria Street, McMahons Point
Sydney NSW 2060, Australia
Copyright © 2008 Weldon Owen Pty Ltd

WELDON OWEN GROUP
Chairman John Owen

WELDON OWEN PTY LTD
Chief Executive Officer Sheena Coupe
Creative Director Sue Burk
Vice President, International Sales Stuart Laurence
Vice President, Sales and Business Development Amy Kaneko
Vice President Sales: Asia and Latin America Dawn Low
Administration Manager, International Sales Kristine Ravn
Publishing Coordinator Mike Crowton

Managing Editor Jennifer Taylor
Project Editor Carol Natsis
Development Editor Jasmine Parker
Senior Designer Hilda Mendham
Designers Gabrielle Green, Kathryn Morgan
Jacket Design John Bull
Picture Research Joanna Collard, Hilda Mendham
Copy Editors Annette Carter, Nathalie Nuijens
Art Manager Trucie Henderson

ISBN-13: 978-1-74089-779-2
ISBN-10: 1-74089-779-X

16 15 14 13 12 11 10 09 08
10 9 8 7 6 5 4 3 2 1

Colour reproduction by Chroma Graphics (Overseas) Pte Ltd
Printed by Tien Wah Press
Manufactured in Singapore

A WELDON OWEN PRODUCTION

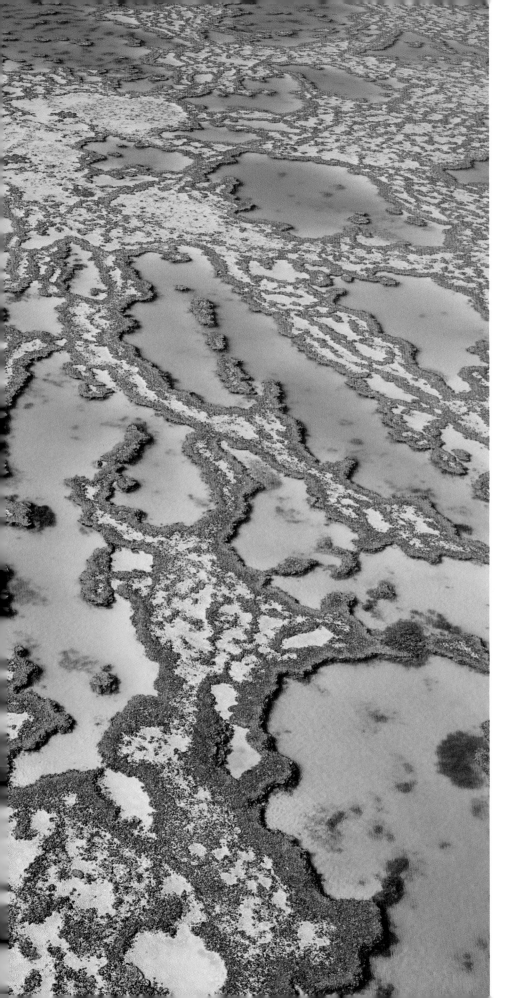

AUTHORS

Michael Allaby
Science Writer
West Highlands, Scotland

Dr. Robert R. Coenraads
Lecturer
Gemmological Association of Australia
Sydney, Australia

Dr. Stephen Hutchinson
Visiting Senior Research Fellow
National Oceanography Centre
Southampton, U.K.

Karen McGhee
Science Writer
Sydney, Australia

Dr. John O'Byrne
Senior Lecturer and Director of
Academic Programs, School of Physics
University of Sydney
Sydney, Australia

Dr. Ken Rubin
Professor, Department of Geology
and Geophysics
University of Hawaii
Hawaii, U.S.A.

CONSULTANTS

Ronald C. Cohen
Associate Professor,
Chemistry and Earth
and Planetary Sciences;
Director, Berkeley
Atmospheric Science Center
University of California,
Berkeley, U.S.A.

Frank W. Davis
Professor,
Landscape Ecology,
Conservation Planning
Donald Bren School of
Environmental Science
and Management
University of California
Santa Barbara, U.S.A.

Douglas Dreger
Associate Professor
of Geophysics
University of California,
Berkeley, U.S.A.

Lisa Tauxe
Professor of Geophysics
Scripps Institution
of Oceanography,
California, U.S.A.

Chi-Yuen Wang
Professor of Geophysics
University of California,
Berkeley, U.S.A.

CONTENTS

FOREWORD

One could make the case that geology, the science of Earth, is the most critical of all the sciences for the 21st century. Certainly chemistry and physics can improve the way we do things, and biomedical science can lengthen and improve the quality of our lives. But humanity has only one planet and we are stressing its ability to sustain us. If we wreck Earth, none of those other improvements will do us much good. Geology is the science that allows us to understand the one planet we can live on—to know how it works, to learn its history, and to make reasonable projections of what it might be like in times to come. Geology is, quite literally, vital for our future.

But geology is also a science of great beauty. Its practitioners live and work in all parts of the globe, in mountains, deserts, plateaus, canyons, and beneath the sea. In those places we are surrounded by scenery ranging from the intimate to the majestic, and back home in the university or the laboratory we often do our research using images that are also aesthetically attractive, ranging in scale from the microscopic constituents of Earth's rocks to views of the entire planet. Even the images geologists construct on computers to display information about hidden realms, such as the interior of our planet, have an artistic character.

In this remarkable book, one can find both these aspects of geology in abundance—the knowledge of Earth and its past, which we need in order to be wise stewards of our home planet, together with those visually appealing images that make the study of geology so agreeable. The authors of this volume have done a fine service in bringing together so much beauty and understanding.

WALTER ALVAREZ
*Professor of Geology in the Department of Earth and Planetary Science
at the University of California, Berkeley, U.S.A.*

HOW TO USE THIS BOOK

This book is divided into six sections: Birth, Fire, Land, Air, Water, and Humans. Birth provides an overview of Earth's 4,600-million-year history and the evolution of life through the ages. Fire explains the inner workings of our dynamic planet, its structure, and the tectonic forces that have molded its landscape. Land surveys rocks, minerals, and habitats; Air covers weather, including extreme weather events; and Water describes the planet's oceans, rivers, and lakes. The final section, Humans, provides a portrait of our relationship with Earth, including our management of resources and threats to our world. Each section is broken down into chapters devoted to particular subjects. Each chapter begins with an introduction to the subject (right), providing a general overview, then the subject is broken down in detail in the pages that follow (examples are below). Special features, called "Insights" (far right), explore the evolution of our knowledge about Earth through text, photographs, and a timeline of key developments through the ages.

INTRODUCTORY FEATURE

Section and chapter heading
This indicates the broad theme and specific area under discussion.

Global locator map
This pinpoints the location of the specific examples discussed below it.

Charts and graphs
These group data and present statistics and forecasts in an easy-to-understand format.

Fact file
This panel explains processes or profiles several examples of the subject under discussion.

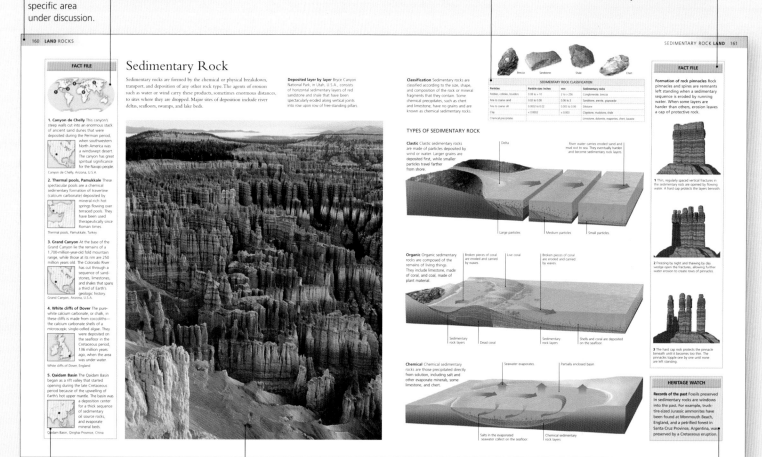

Location map
Regional maps show the locations of key examples from around the world.

Photograph
An evocative photograph shows a landform or feature that is representative of the subject matter under discussion.

Heritage Watch box
This provides information about World Heritage sites, as well as about regions that are threatened or potentially at risk.

INSIGHTS

Diagrams
Where appropriate, diagrams are included to illustrate complex concepts.

Introductory text
This provides a general overview of the subject.

World map
This shows the global distribution of a feature being profiled, and is accompanied by text that discusses the feature in more detail.

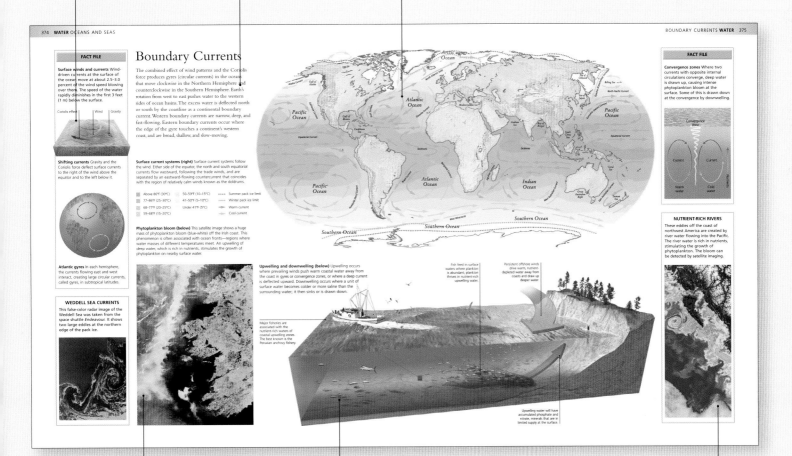

Satellite photography
Images taken from space provide unique perspectives on Earth.

Illustration
A graphic cutaway illustration shows the inner workings of a physical phenomenon.

Feature box
Photographs or illustrations, and text, highlight an interesting aspect of the topic being explored.

BIRTH

BIRTH

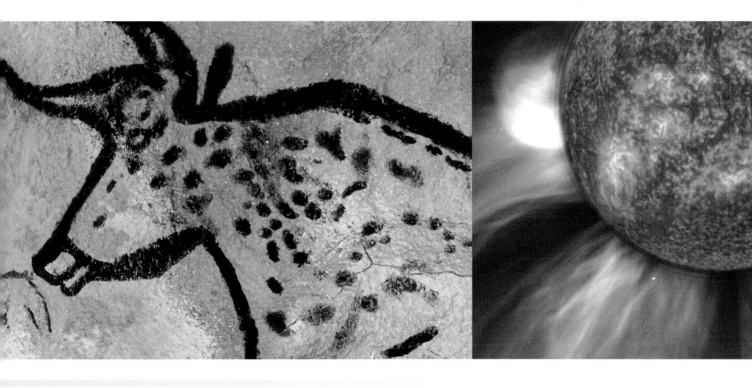

THE EMERGENCE OF LIFE 42

EARTH'S PLACE IN THE UNIVERSE

Our view of Earth's place in the universe has changed. Once regarded as being the center of everything, Earth is now seen as an infinitesimal fragment circling an obscure star in one of billions of galaxies scattered through the visible universe. While determining our place in the entire universe, astronomers have also realized that we—the Sun, Earth and all things that live on it, including humans—are products of the stars. Many of the atoms that make up the world around us were made during generations of massive stars, which themselves were built from the debris of the explosion of space and time that created the universe.

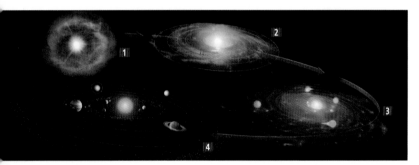

A star is born (left) Star formation occurs in cold, dense clouds of gas and dust. The clouds may collapse when a density wave sweeps around the galaxy or when a nearby massive star blows itself up (**1**). Once the collapse begins, dense cores in the cloud heat up to become protostars enshrouded in the cloud (**2**). Each is surrounded by a disk of material accreting onto the forming star (**3**). After several million years, the star "turns on," dispersing the disk and the surrounding cloud, perhaps to reveal a newly formed planetary system (**4**).

STELLAR ORIGINS

Around 13.7 billion years ago, the universe began in an expansion of time and space that we call the Big Bang. Exactly how and why it occurred is unknown. Within a tiny fraction of a second it began to evolve in ways that we can describe, leading to the formation of stars, galaxies, and ultimately Earth.

The universal expansion, which began the instant the Big Bang occurred, suddenly accelerated for a brief phase of inflation. This ended after just 10^{-32} seconds, but in that instant the universe expanded dramatically, with the result that the universe we can see today is only a tiny subset of the whole.

As the expansion continued, the super-hot universe gradually cooled, allowing particles to form, only to annihilate again within an instant. However, not every particle disappeared—a few survived as matter. Within a few minutes, some of the hydrogen nuclei reacted together to synthesize the helium nuclei that make 25 percent of the matter in the universe today.

Some 380,000 years after the Big Bang, expansion had made it cool enough for the hydrogen and helium nuclei to couple with electrons to form stable atoms. This lifted the universal fog and allowed the universe to become transparent for the first time. The radiation streaming from that time is the cosmic microwave background radiation we still see today.

Within a few hundred million years of the Big Bang, clouds of gas began to collapse into the first stars, lighting up the universe. These stars processed hydrogen and helium into heavier elements, which in turn were fed to successive generations of stars. Massive stars reprocessed the gas and dispersed it back into the interstellar medium when they died as supernovas.

Large systems of stars and gas congregated around clumps of mysterious dark matter to form galaxies. Some galaxies collided and formed more massive galaxies, many with huge central black holes that powered tremendous energy output.

Still, the universe expanded and cooled. About 4.6 billion years ago, the Sun and many companion stars were formed. As usually happens, the infant stars were surrounded by disks of gas and dusty debris. Within the Sun's disk a system of small planets formed. The innermost were small rocky objects that, perhaps unusually, were left undisturbed by their larger giant neighbors. Each of the inner planets survived a turbulent early history of massive impacts and volcanic mayhem. The result in each case was different, creating the planets we see today.

Nebulas (right) Glowing clouds of gas and dust such as the Tarantula Nebula are the birthplace of stars. Massive stars light up the nebula, but smaller stars like the Sun are also present. The Sun-like stars outlast the colorful light show of their short-lived bigger brothers. However, it is the brightness of the young stars and their glowing gas and dust clouds that light up many galaxies. They trace out the spiral arms in the Milky Way, while the Sun adds a gentle background glow.

Planets and water (right) Rocky planets like Mars (above right) are expected to form close to the warm glow of their parent stars. For a few, conditions will allow water to flow across the surface, carving channels as shown here on the rim of a Martian crater, eroding the surface and possibly allowing life to take hold.

The Big Bang

The Big Bang theory explains the origin of the universe as a sudden rapid expansion of space that began 13.7 billion years ago. Space expanded, but matter and radiation declined from their incredibly hot, dense beginnings to form the cooler, sparser universe of today. In the far distant future, accelerating expansion will lead to a very cold, dark universe.

A model of the expanding universe Expansion of the universe in three dimensions is a difficult concept. It may be more easily understood by taking the simpler model of a two-dimensional universe and comparing it to the surface of an expanding balloon.

Stretching As the surface stretches, this universe expands, increasing the distance between galaxies—as measured on the surface.

Moving apart Galaxies appear to move away from one other at a speed that increases with their distance apart. Nowhere on the surface is special and there is no center to the expansion.

Measuring expansion Astronomers can measure how fast galaxies move away from one other and how long it is since expansion began, which is estimated to be about 13.7 billion years ago.

FUTURE OF THE UNIVERSE

As the universe ages, galaxies will fade and die as more and more gas is tied up in dark stellar remnants—white dwarfs, neutron stars, and black holes. Even the smallest stars will eventually cool and fade away after perhaps 100 trillion years. By then, the universal expansion will have carried even the nearest galaxies far apart and the universe will be cold and dark.

Expansion and evolution from the Big Bang to the present (below)
The foggy glow that existed before the universe became transparent concealed the formation of matter and the origins of the structure we see today.

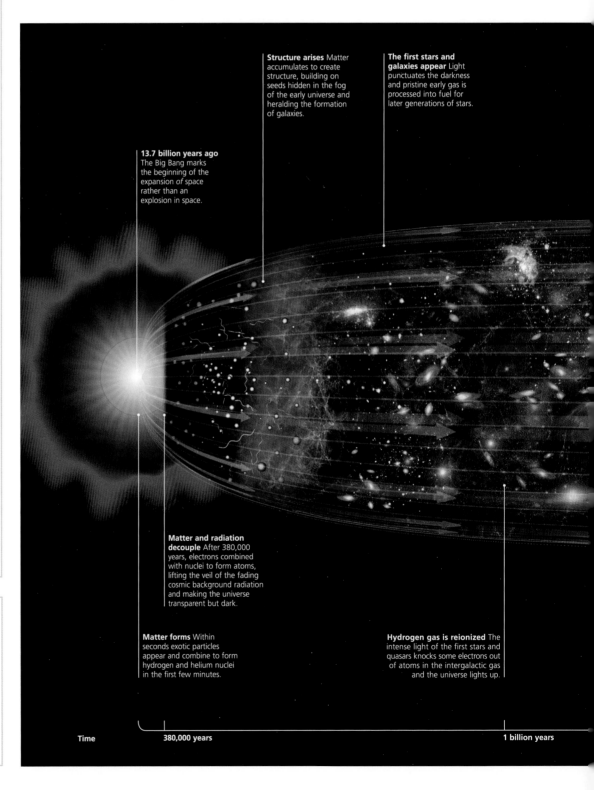

Structure arises Matter accumulates to create structure, building on seeds hidden in the fog of the early universe and heralding the formation of galaxies.

The first stars and galaxies appear Light punctuates the darkness and pristine early gas is processed into fuel for later generations of stars.

13.7 billion years ago The Big Bang marks the beginning of the expansion *of* space rather than an explosion in space.

Matter and radiation decouple After 380,000 years, electrons combined with nuclei to form atoms, lifting the veil of the fading cosmic background radiation and making the universe transparent but dark.

Matter forms Within seconds exotic particles appear and combine to form hydrogen and helium nuclei in the first few minutes.

Hydrogen gas is reionized The intense light of the first stars and quasars knocks some electrons out of atoms in the intergalactic gas and the universe lights up.

Time   380,000 years   1 billion years

Dark matter (left) This is the hidden factor behind the structure of the universe today. Galaxies trace out a filamentary structure (seen in this simulation) largely because of the gravitational dominance of unseen dark matter.

Cosmic evolution The structure of the universe evolved from tiny fluctuations in the fog of the early universe to the clusters and superclusters of galaxies that we can see today.

1 The early glow reveals faint ripples in the cosmic background radiation.

2 Background ripples grow to be fluctuations in the density of matter.

3 The densest clouds of matter form massive stars and protogalaxies.

4 Gravity piles matter up, and galaxies grow by accumulating other galaxies.

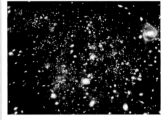

5 Today, galaxies form a filamentary structure of clusters and voids.

Stars and galaxies evolve
Generations of massive stars are born and galaxies gradually take on the appearance they have today.

Solar system is born
About 9 billion years after the Big Bang, the solar system appears, building on countless generations of earlier stars.

Dark energy This will drive the universe into an accelerating expansion in the far distant future.

9 billion years

Stars and Galaxies

Galaxies These huge groupings of stars, up to trillions (10^{12}), are bound together by gravity. Some types are permeated by gas and dust that provide the raw material for new generations of stars.

Elliptical Yellow and dustless, these contain aging stars, and lack new generations of massive stars.

Irregular In these small hotbeds, stars actively form, like the massive blue stars lighting up this galaxy.

Spiral Older yellow stars are encircled by a disk whose spiral arms are traced by brilliant blue-white young stars.

Barred spiral The blue-white arms of a spiral galaxy hang from a bar of older stars across the nucleus.

Hydrogen and helium from the Big Bang are the main components of the Sun. The heavier building blocks of Earth and our solar system—carbon, oxygen, silicon, iron, and other elements—were produced in many generations of massive stars. Clues to the origin of these elements abound in star formation and evolution, as seen in our galaxy and others.

Where stars are born Giant clouds of gas and dust are often the birthplace of stars. In the Orion Nebula, massive newborn stars light up part of the cloud with a pink glow, while younger stars still lie concealed.

Stellar life cycle A massive blue-white star (**1–6**) and a yellow Sun-like star (**1, 7–10**) have similar lives but end very differently. Both kinds of star take shape in a disk of interstellar gas and dust (**1**) and pass stable lives consuming their hydrogen fuel (**2** and **7**). A massive star runs short of fuel within a few million years and swells to become a red supergiant (**3**), before exploding spectacularly as a supernova (**4**) and leaving a black hole (**5**) or neutron star (**6**) as a remnant. The Sun-like star has a more leisurely life (**7**), before expanding as a red giant (**8**) and then puffing off its outer layers to form a short-lived planetary nebula (**9**) around the cooling ember of a white dwarf (**10**).

FACT FILE

Star death Mass determines the fate of stars and their influence on succeeding star generations. Only a massive star returns processed material to the interstellar medium to enrich the next generation.

Small star The Cat's Eye Nebula formed when a small star puffed off its outer layers of gas at the end of its life, over perhaps 100,000 years.

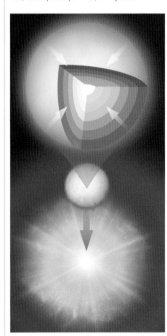

Massive star The core of a red supergiant develops layers of progressively heavier elements, then suddenly collapses and rebounds outwards as a supernova explosion.

ETA CARINAE

The supermassive Eta Carinae, around 7,500 light years from Earth, is the closest candidate most likely to die in a supernova explosion in the next million years.

The Milky Way Galaxy

The Milky Way is Earth's home galaxy. Buried in its disk, the Sun is a middle-aged star lost among innumerable similar stars. All the stars, star clusters, and nebulae familiar to astronomers can be found within a few thousand light years of the Sun—well short of the 26,000 light years from the solar system to the center of the galaxy.

Composition (below) A spiral galaxy with at least 200 billion stars, the Milky Way has a central bar and four major arms traced by massive blue stars. The Sun orbits the center in 220–250 million years, so far completing at least 20 orbits in its life.

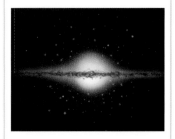

Side view In cross section, the Milky Way is bisected by a thin layer of gas and dust, its central region surrounded by a halo of globular star clusters.

Alpha Centauri The two Sun-like stars on the right and their red dwarf companion are the Sun's nearest neighbors in the Milky Way.

OTHER STARS WITH PLANETS

Recent observations have revealed the Sun is not unique in having planets. More than 200 planets have been discovered orbiting nearby stars. Most of these planets, like the one seen orbiting the star 70 Virginis in this artist's impression, are giants—as large as Jupiter and often larger. They may be circled by moons, silhouetted here, that are similar to Earth in size.

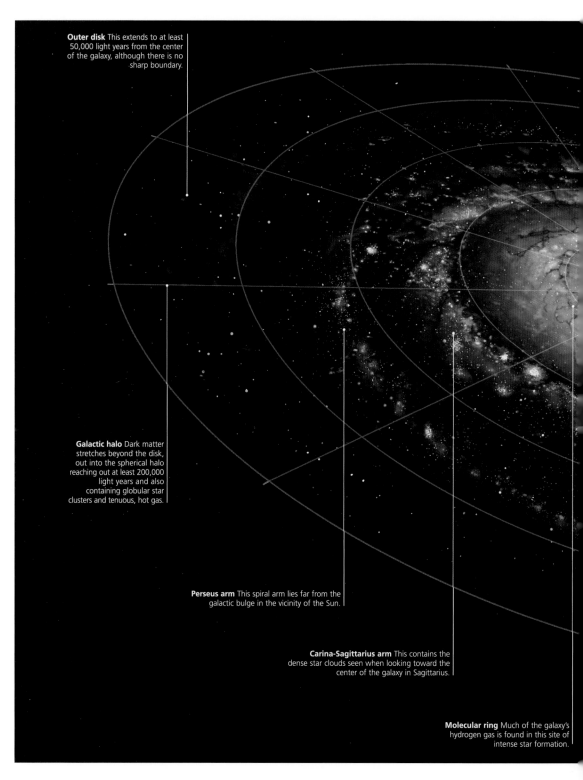

Outer disk This extends to at least 50,000 light years from the center of the galaxy, although there is no sharp boundary.

Galactic halo Dark matter stretches beyond the disk, out into the spherical halo reaching out at least 200,000 light years and also containing globular star clusters and tenuous, hot gas.

Perseus arm This spiral arm lies far from the galactic bulge in the vicinity of the Sun.

Carina-Sagittarius arm This contains the dense star clouds seen when looking toward the center of the galaxy in Sagittarius.

Molecular ring Much of the galaxy's hydrogen gas is found in this site of intense star formation.

The heart of the Milky Way (left)
Infrared light allows us to peer through intervening dust clouds to see the dense swirls of dust and gas at the galaxy's bright center.

Nebula These visible portions of the interstellar gas and dust range from tiny, dark globules to huge, glowing clouds powered by massive stars.

Central bulge and bar About 27,000 light years long, these are made up of old stars.

Cygnus-Norma arm This can be seen among the stars of the constellation Norma near the bulge and the stars of Cygnus farther out.

Crux-Scutum arm Visible in the constellation of Centaurus, this is sometimes called the Centaurus arm.

10 000

20 000

30 000

40 000

50 000

Solar system The Sun and our solar system lie about 26,000 light years from the galaxy's center.

The Orion arm or local spur This contains the Sun and many of the well-known stars, clusters, and nebulas of the night sky.

Open star clusters Found in the disk of the galaxy, these are loosely bound groups of hundreds of young stars, like the Pleiades cluster shown here.

Globular clusters Omega Centauri is the largest example of a globular cluster, with perhaps a million stars found in the galaxy's spherical halo.

UNDERSTANDING THE UNIVERSE

The word cosmology comes from the Greek words *cosmos* (world or order) and *logos* (plan). It is the science that asks big questions: What does the universe look like? How old is it? How did it begin? What does the future hold? Until about 500 years ago, prevailing cosmology had Earth at its center. The blossoming of scientific investigation and observation displaced this view. Now Earth is only a tiny piece in the Big Bang model of the universe. Nevertheless, explaining Earth's existence, with its abundance of living things, remains vital to any model of the cosmos.

Aztec calendar (left) This massive stone, 12 feet (3.6 m) in diameter, records the calendar and cosmological beliefs of the Aztecs. The center represents the current age of the world, surrounded by four previous ages, in turn surrounded by the 20 days of the Aztec month.

Egyptian cosmology (right) Shafts in the Great Pyramid of Giza are thought to point to stars as they were positioned in the sky almost 5,000 years ago. A more controversial theory matches the locations of the three Giza pyramids to stars in the "belt" of the constellation Orion.

Sky survey (above) In this map produced by the Wilkinson Microwave Anisotropy Probe (WMAP) spacecraft, tiny fluctuations in the smooth glow of the cosmic background radiation are revealed. Color represents the variations in temperature and density of the early universe that led to the formation of galaxy clusters. WMAP surveys the sky from its orbit about 1 million miles (1.6 million km) from Earth.

AN EMERGING SCIENCE

Ancient civilizations around the world practiced cosmology based on observations by eye. They focused on trying to understand the movements of the stars, Sun, and planets, and used a mix of logic, tradition, and religion.

About 400 years ago, perception of the world dramatically changed as a modern, experimental approach to science was developed. Nicolaus Copernicus' Sun-centered model was beginning to take hold, with refinements introduced by Johann Kepler and Isaac Newton. In the early 17th century, Galileo used the first optical telescopes to reveal a universe of stars and planets.

Telescopes grew in size over time, but in the middle of the 19th century spectroscopy began to revolutionize the field. It allowed astronomers to move beyond merely positions and motions to understand the composition of the stars, planets, and faint clouds of gas and dust between the stars. Physical theory developed alongside the new developments to explain these observations.

In the early 20th century, theory took a leap ahead with Einstein's general theory of relativity. He described how the universe works on the largest scales, but left many possible models to describe the details. Choosing the right model requires hard-won observations. During the 20th century, the window for these observations broadened from visible light to radio, infrared rays, ultraviolet rays, X-rays, gamma rays, and even neutrinos.

By around 1970, the Big Bang model of an expanding universe had emerged as the accepted picture. This model was built on three key observations: the expansion of the universe, the detection of the all-pervading cosmic background radiation, and the correct prediction of the relative abundance of the lightest elements making up the universe.

More recently, large telescopes with new detectors have allowed surveys of the distribution of galaxies on the largest scales within the universe. Other surveys have revealed distant exploding stars, which indicate the Big Bang is not as simple as we thought—universal expansion is accelerating. Putting all the observations together reveals that our "best fit" model of the universe is one in which ordinary matter is dominated by unseen "dark matter" and even more mysterious "dark energy." The explanation of this model awaits new theories and many more observations.

THROUGH THE AGES

4th century B.C. Greek philosopher Aristotle described an Earth-centered model of the universe that dominated cosmology for almost 2,000 years.

Ca A.D. 150 In the *Almagest*, Greek-Egyptian astronomer Ptolemy summarized ancient observations and gave a mathematical treatment of Earth-centered cosmology.

1609 Italian astronomer Galileo learned of the invention of the telescope and began observing the sky. He published his results and consequently launched a revolution in astronomy.

1687 Sir Isaac Newton published *Philosophiae Naturalis Principia Mathematica*, describing a universal theory of gravity.

1915, 1916 Albert Einstein presented his general theory of relativity, which allowed various possible models of the universe.

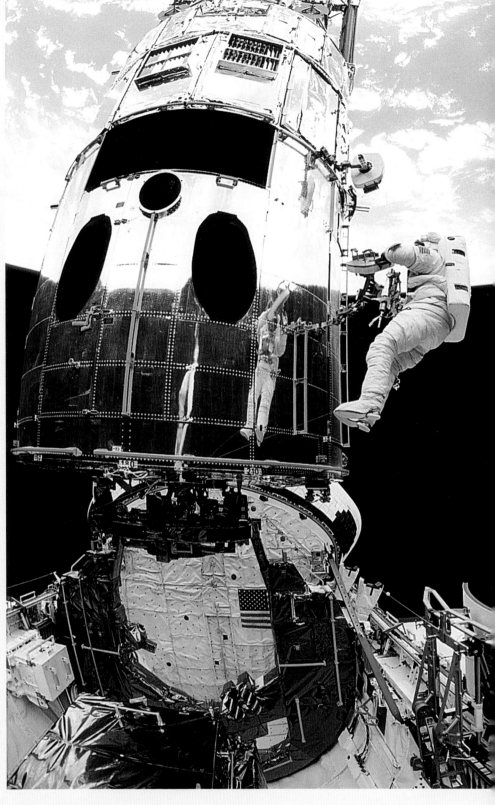

Space telescope (right) Serviced by astronauts working from a space shuttle, the Hubble Space Telescope takes advantage of its position outside Earth's atmosphere to probe the universe in unprecedented detail. It is unaffected by the blurring that the atmosphere causes with Earth-based telescopes.

Radio telescopes (below) The 27 antennas of the Very Large Array (VLA) in New Mexico form the world's largest array of radio telescopes. Their power lies in the ability to form images, with a resolution equivalent to a single large radio telescope, that are up to 22 miles (36 km) across.

1929 Edwin Powell Hubble published the claim that the speed of recession of relatively nearby galaxies is proportional to distance, consistent with an expanding universe.

1948 Ralph Alpher and George Gamow presented a paper in which they calculated the relative abundances of the light elements produced in the hot Big Bang.

1965 Arno Penzias and Robert Wilson discovered the cosmic microwave background radiation, providing clear evidence for the hot Big Bang theory.

1992 The COBE satellite detected tiny irregularities in the cosmic microwave background radiation that mark the seeds of the universe's structure today.

1998 Research teams led by Saul Perlmutter, Adam Riess, and Brian Schmidt announced the discovery that universal expansion is accelerating.

The Solar System

Earth's immediate place in space is the solar system, one of the many planetary systems orbiting stars in the Milky Way. In the last 50 years the direct exploration of the universe has begun with spacecraft, but our reach is limited to this local neighborhood. Our understanding of the origin and history of Earth is intimately linked to our knowledge of the solar system.

Composition The eight planets orbiting the Sun are the solar system's primary members. However, the solar system extends much farther—past the dwarf planets and smaller objects of the Kuiper Belt to the cold outer reaches of the Oort Cloud.

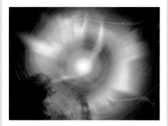
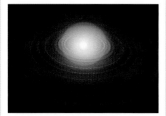

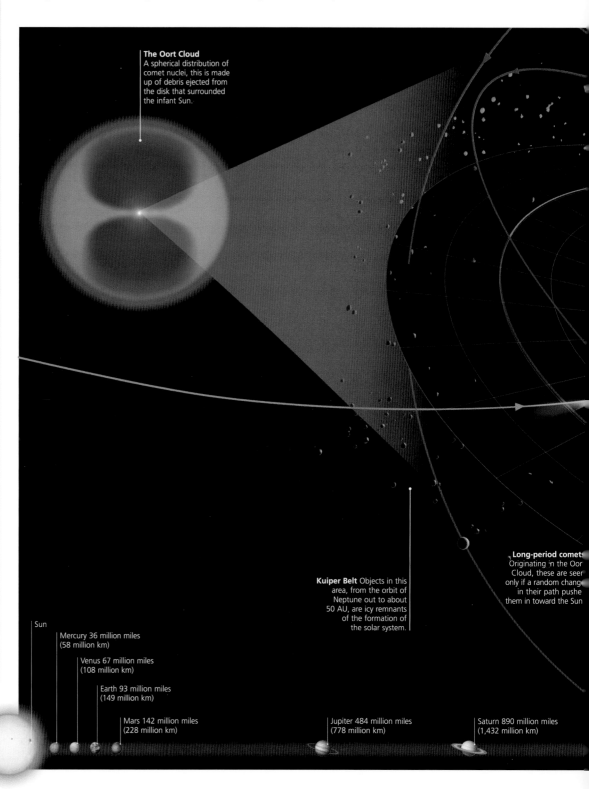

The Oort Cloud
A spherical distribution of comet nuclei, this is made up of debris ejected from the disk that surrounded the infant Sun.

Long-period comets Originating in the Oort Cloud, these are seen only if a random change in their path pushes them in toward the Sun

Kuiper Belt Objects in this area, from the orbit of Neptune out to about 50 AU, are icy remnants of the formation of the solar system.

Sun

Mercury 36 million miles (58 million km)

Venus 67 million miles (108 million km)

Earth 93 million miles (149 million km)

Mars 142 million miles (228 million km)

Jupiter 484 million miles (778 million km)

Saturn 890 million miles (1,432 million km)

INNER PLANETS

☿ Mercury
♀ Venus
⊕ Earth
♂ Mars

OUTER PLANETS

♃ Jupiter
♄ Saturn
♅ Uranus
♆ Neptune

ORBITS

—— Inner planetary orbit
—— Outer planetary orbit
—— Minor planet orbit
—— Short-period comet
—— Long-period comet

AU Astronomical Unit, the average distance from Earth to the Sun, used to measure distances in the solar system.

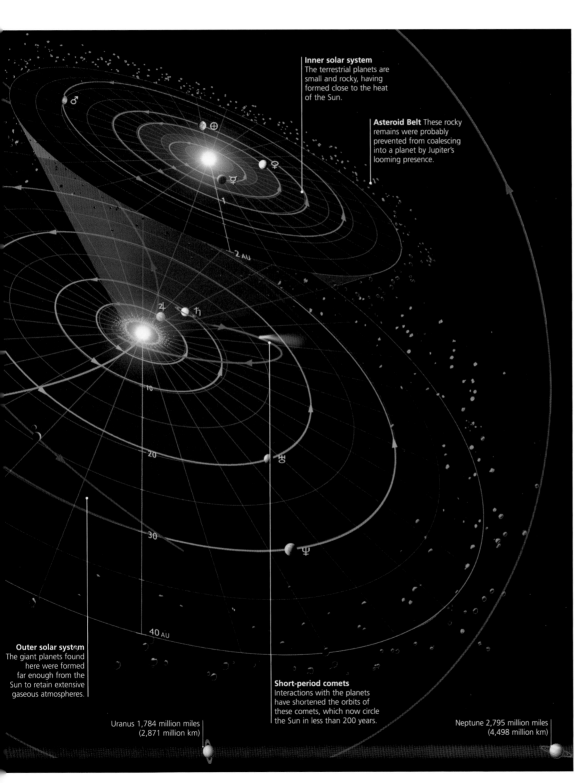

Inner solar system
The terrestrial planets are small and rocky, having formed close to the heat of the Sun.

Asteroid Belt These rocky remains were probably prevented from coalescing into a planet by Jupiter's looming presence.

Outer solar system
The giant planets found here were formed far enough from the Sun to retain extensive gaseous atmospheres.

Short-period comets
Interactions with the planets have shortened the orbits of these comets, which now circle the Sun in less than 200 years.

Uranus 1,784 million miles (2,871 million km)

Neptune 2,795 million miles (4,498 million km)

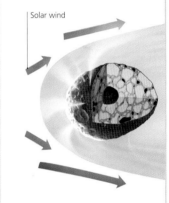
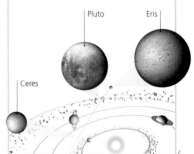

The Sun

Although it is only a very ordinary star, the Sun dominates the solar system in size and mass, and its gravity dictates the motions of the objects that orbit it. The energy that it produces drives many of the processes on the surfaces and in the atmospheres of the planets—and sustains almost all life on Earth.

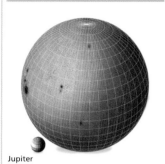
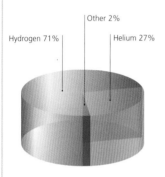
Coronal mass ejections (right) Eruptions of hot gas (shown as white) arise from instabilities in the Sun's magnetic field. If this material reaches Earth, it causes a geomagnetic storm in Earth's magnetosphere.

STRUCTURE OF THE SUN

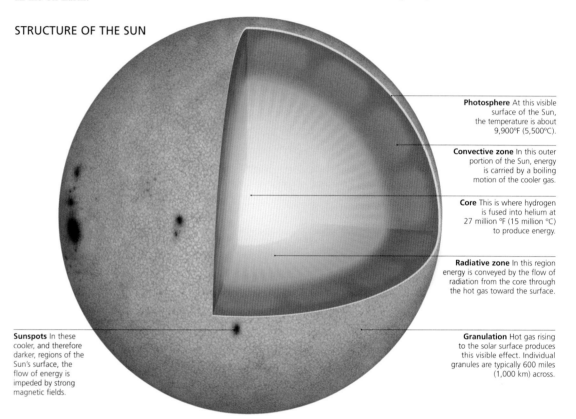

Photosphere At this visible surface of the Sun, the temperature is about 9,900°F (5,500°C).

Convective zone In this outer portion of the Sun, energy is carried by a boiling motion of the cooler gas.

Core This is where hydrogen is fused into helium at 27 million °F (15 million °C) to produce energy.

Radiative zone In this region energy is conveyed by the flow of radiation from the core through the hot gas toward the surface.

Sunspots In these cooler, and therefore darker, regions of the Sun's surface, the flow of energy is impeded by strong magnetic fields.

Granulation Hot gas rising to the solar surface produces this visible effect. Individual granules are typically 600 miles (1,000 km) across.

ECLIPSE OF THE SUN

The corona, the tenuous outer atmosphere of the Sun, becomes visible during a solar eclipse. This happens when the Moon is just big enough to cover the Sun's photosphere, as viewed from Earth.

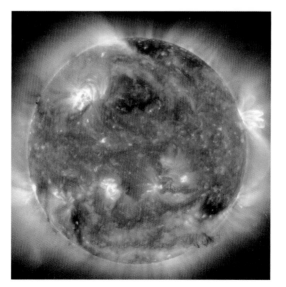

Corona The gases of the corona, viewed here under ultraviolet light, reach extremely high temperatures (shown in false color): blue—1.8 million °F (1.0 million °C); green—2.7 million °F (1.5 million °C); and red—3.6 million °F (2.0 million °C).

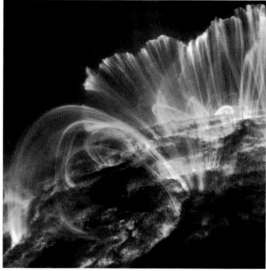

Coronal loops Created by hot gas that is channeled by magnetic field lines above an active region on the solar surface, these loops are over 125,000 miles (200,000 km) high—more than 15 times the diameter of Earth.

FACT FILE

Sunspots These are the visible markers of magnetic activity in an active region on the solar surface. The spots have a dark umbra merging into a slightly brighter penumbra.

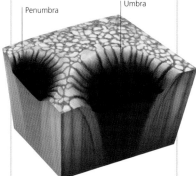

Penumbra | Umbra

Sunspot cycle The sunspot activity on the solar surface varies over a cycle of about 11 years and is evident in the number and location of spots.

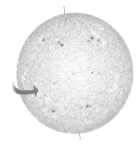

Year 1 Early in the cycle sunspots are rare and typically occur at high latitudes.

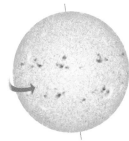

Year 5 Around solar maximum, the sunspots are spread across the Sun's surface.

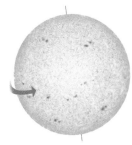

Year 9 Near the cycle's end, sunspots decline in numbers and spots from the new cycle appear.

Earth's Nearest Neighbors

The rocky inner planets of the solar system are often called the terrestrial planets because their basic characteristics are similar to those of Earth. Each is a small rocky ball with a thin veneer of atmosphere. These planets share the common history of the inner solar system, yet are remarkably different in many ways.

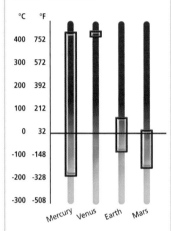
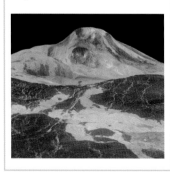
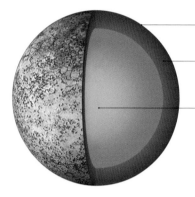

Crust Between 60 and 120 miles (100–200 km) thick, the crust is heavily cratered.

Mantle This relatively thin blanket of silicate rocks is perhaps 400 miles (600 km) thick.

Core Rich in iron, the core dominates the planet, occupying 75% of the diameter. The innermost portion may be liquid.

Mercury The smallest of the inner planets, Mercury is nevertheless very dense, perhaps because an early impact stripped away much of its outer layers. Its heavily cratered surface resembles that of the Moon, but with distinctive ridges, which may be cracks that formed as the planet cooled and contracted. Like the Moon, it has virtually no atmosphere.

Venus The surface of Venus cooks under an oppressively hot, thick atmosphere. Smooth volcanic plains surround massive volcanoes and cover most of the surface, obliterating much of the record of ancient cratering. Venus rotates very slowly and backward compared to all the other planets.

Crust Punctuated by volcanoes, the crust may be relatively thin, perhaps only 30 miles (50 km) deep.

Mantle This is thick, occupying some 50% of the planet's diameter.

Core Filling the inner half of the planet, the core is partly, or perhaps completely, solid.

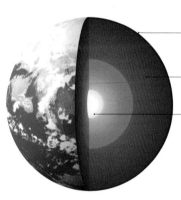

Crust Thin and mobile, the crust is broken into plates that continually change the surface over millions of years.

Mantle This comprises 84% of the planet's volume, reaching 1,800 miles (2,900 km) below the surface.

Core Earth is the only terrestrial planet that has a liquid outer core surrounding the solid inner core, both of them hot and under tremendous pressure.

Earth Liquid water covers 71% of Earth's surface, and ice extends over some of the remainder. The planet is wrapped in an atmosphere reaching at least 100 miles (160 km) into space, rich in oxygen and flecked with white clouds of water. Life proliferates in every niche of the surface.

Mars This small, cratered world is marked by several enormous volcanoes and a canyon system that cuts a great gash across the planet. The surface shows intriguing evidence of a wetter past, yet the cold, thin atmosphere permits only a little ice and no liquid water to remain on the surface today.

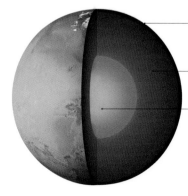

Crust Perhaps 75 miles (120 km) thick, the crust does not move, allowing huge volcanoes to grow.

Mantle This thick shell of rock comprises the bulk of the planet.

Core A relatively small and light core gives Mars the lowest average density of all the terrestrial planets.

Water on Mars Looking for water is one of the main objects of Mars exploration. Evidence of the existence of water in the past abounds. This image from the Mars Global Surveyor spacecraft shows what appear to be recently formed gullies on the weathered wall of a crater. Similar gullies on Earth would have been cut by surface water. A light frost coats the walls in this winter view.

Mars exploration Since their landing in January 2004, Rovers Spirit and Opportunity have together covered more than 11 miles (18 km), exploring two locations on opposite sides of Mars.

Ice on Mars In a crater near the Mars north pole, water ice is seen in an image taken by the European Space Agency's Mars Express spacecraft in 2005. Frost is also apparent on the crater walls.

FACT FILE

Atmospheres Earth's oxygen-rich atmosphere is unique among the inner planets. Mercury is the only other planet that has any oxygen, but its atmosphere is thin, nearly non-exsistent. On Venus and Mars carbon dioxide predominates.

MERCURY

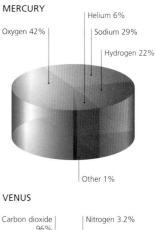

Oxygen 42%
Helium 6%
Sodium 29%
Hydrogen 22%
Other 1%

VENUS

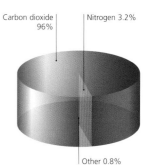

Carbon dioxide 96%
Nitrogen 3.2%
Other 0.8%

EARTH

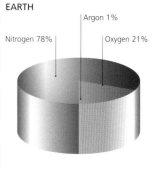

Nitrogen 78%
Argon 1%
Oxygen 21%

MARS

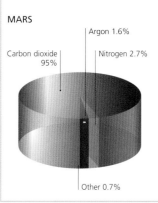

Carbon dioxide 95%
Argon 1.6%
Nitrogen 2.7%
Other 0.7%

Earth's Distant Companions

The giant planets of the outer solar system are quite unlike the terrestrial planets. The visible "surface" of each is not solid, but made up of cloud layers in the atmosphere. All have families of satellites, the largest of which are complex worlds born when the planets themselves formed. Others are little more than debris captured by their host's powerful gravitational grip.

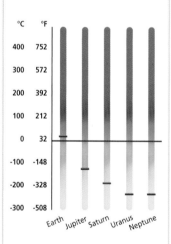
LAKES ON TITAN

Radar imaging of Saturn's largest moon by the Cassini spacecraft seems to have confirmed that huge lakes (color-coded blue), probably methane, exist near its north pole.

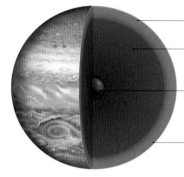

Outer mantle This is a broad transition zone, dominated by liquid hydrogen.

Inner mantle The pressure of this extensive layer is so high that hydrogen is compressed into a liquid metallic state.

Core This rock and ice ball several times the mass of Earth is under enormous pressure from the overlying bulk of Jupiter.

Atmosphere This outer skin, 600 miles (1,000 km) deep, has at least three cloud layers, forming the visible features.

Jupiter The giant of the solar system, Jupiter has more than three times the mass of its nearest rival, although it is only 20% larger. Despite its size, Jupiter rotates in under 10 hours, driving dynamic weather in its turbulent atmosphere. Around the planet are a retinue of at least 63 satellites, a faint ring, and an enormous magnetic field.

Saturn Next in size to Jupiter, Saturn is almost twice as far from the Sun, and the deepening cold of the outer solar system results in less colorful atmospheric patterns. Saturn also has a family of satellites, but its fame rests with its extensive, intricately structured ring system, visible from Earth even with small telescopes.

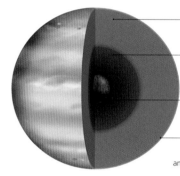

Outer mantle This region of liquid hydrogen occupies half the planet's diameter.

Inner mantle Like Jupiter liquid metallic hydrogen predominates, but this region covers a smaller zone because the less massive planet has lower pressure.

Core The rock and ice heart of the planet has as much as 20 times the mass of Earth.

Atmosphere This is like Jupiter's but colder, with more widely spaced cloud layers of ammonia, ammonium hydrosulfide, and water.

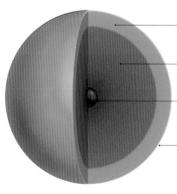

Outer mantle Consisting of liquid hydrogen and other compounds, this is about 6,000 miles (10,000 km) deep.

Inner mantle Quite different from those of Jupiter or Saturn, this is a slushy layer of water, methane, and ammonia ices.

Core This is likely to be a mixture of rock and ice several times the mass of Earth.

Atmosphere So far only methane ice clouds have been detected in the planet's bland skin.

Uranus Less than half the size and one-sixth the mass of Saturn, Uranus is quite different—and not just because the planet, its satellite system, and dark rings are all tipped on their side. Uranus is sometimes called an ice giant because of the importance of the icy compounds of water, methane, and ammonia.

Neptune Uranus' twin in many ways, Neptune has almost the same size and mass. Like its companion, it has a thin, dark ring system and a set of satellites. However, it is surprisingly different in appearance, probably because internal heat keeps it a bit warmer than its wintry location in the outer solar system would suggest.

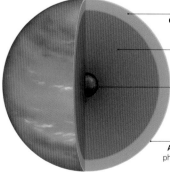

Outer mantle A rigid liquid mix of hydrogen and icy compounds, this is similar to the corresponding layer in Uranus.

Inner mantle This is dominated by ices, leading to Neptune's description as an ice giant.

Core This is believed to be a mix of rock and ice at high temperature, but under enormous pressures.

Atmosphere Remarkably dynamic, its atmosphere has methane ice clouds at high altitudes, casting shadows on the deeper cloud layers.

Saturn's rings Seen up close, these are broken into thousands of ringlets. This color-coded image from the Cassini spacecraft gives information about the density and size of the icy and dusty ring particles. White zones are packed most tightly with particles. All the colored zones have particles as big as boulders, but some are swept clear of smaller particles the size of stones or sand.

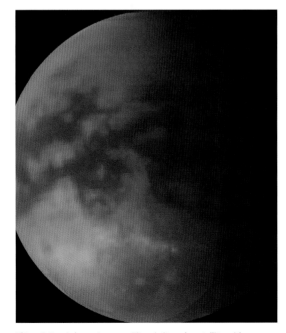

Titan Saturn's largest moon, Titan is its only satellite with a substantial atmosphere. In this image taken by the Cassini spacecraft, pinkish clouds may be methane rain clouds.

Smaller satellite Epimetheus, one of Saturn's many smaller moons, is an irregular rocky fragment 60 miles (100 km) across. It is shown here with Titan and a portion of Saturn's ring system.

FACT FILE

Atmosphere Hydrogen and helium, the main elements in the Sun, dominate the outer atmospheres of the giant planets. Methane becomes more than a trace in the colder Uranus and Neptune.

JUPITER

Hydrogen 90%

Helium 10%, with traces of ammonia and methane

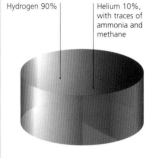

SATURN

Hydrogen 96%

Helium 4%

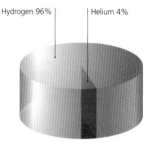

URANUS

Methane 2%

Hydrogen 83%

Helium 15%

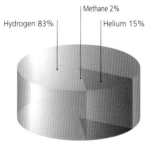

NEPTUNE

Methane 3%

Hydrogen 79%

Helium 18%

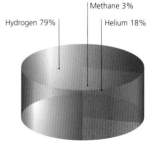

THIRD PLANET FROM THE SUN

Earth's early history must be read from the few remaining rocks of its early crust. Most early rocks have been destroyed by weathering or forced down below the surface by motion of the crust, to be melted once again. As a result, the oldest rocks on Earth are 3.8 billion years old, though single zircon crystals have been dated to 4.4 billion years. Because of the lack of weathering and geologic activity, many rocks from the Moon's highlands preserve an older history that is as much as 4.5 billion years old. This epoch marks the common origin of Earth and the Moon in the birth of the solar system, about 4.6 billion years ago.

TIME OF TURBULENCE

The birth of the Sun was accompanied by the birth of the planets in a surrounding disk of gas and dust. Close to the infant Sun, small planets formed from rocky material that could condense in the hot environment. Farther away, lower temperatures allowed larger planets to grow from elements that preferred the cooler surroundings.

The early history of the planets was a turbulent time, with collisions between planetary-sized objects smashing some protoplanets and throwing others out of the solar system. Earth suffered just such a collision. An object perhaps as large as Mars crashed into Earth, throwing debris from the impactor and Earth's outer layers into orbit. Some of this accumulated to form the Moon. This was not the end of the tumult for either object. Heavy bombardment by smaller debris from the formation of the solar system lasted for over 500 million years, with some large impacts occurring for a billion years more.

The record of this era is plain to see on the Moon, with the lava plains marking large impact basins and the lunar highlands saturated with impacts of smaller objects. The evidence of the early bombardment of Earth's surface is long since gone, overwritten by millennia of activity.

While the Moon cooled off to become a dead world, Earth's internal temperature remained high, driving volcanic activity that produced new rocks to overlie the older ones. It also drove the process of plate tectonics, in which new crust is created where plates move apart, and old crust is destroyed when plates come together.

In addition, Earth found itself at just the right distance from the Sun to allow liquid water to condense on its surface and collect into deep oceans. Its size also allowed it to keep sufficient atmosphere to retain this water and sustain a cycle of water moving from the oceans to the atmosphere and returning to the surface as rain, frost, or snow. The smaller planet Mars was not so lucky in its combination of circumstances. While evidence of water is clear, that water is now lost or locked away in the surface. As a result, the recent impact record is clearer on the Martian surface.

Despite Earth's turbulent early history, primitive life emerged remarkably quickly in its oceans. It was not until around 2.3 billion years ago that primitive life began to exert its influence by pumping oxygen into the atmosphere. This led to the unique oxygen–rich atmosphere that distinguishes Earth from the other planets today.

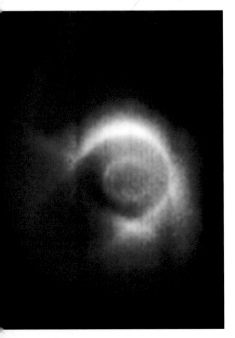

Protective blanket (below) Earth is enshrouded in a magnetic blanket called the magnetosphere. Within this lies a zone of ionized gas called the plasmasphere— seen as purple in this ultraviolet image— extending out to a distance of about four Earth radii. The brighter glow all around the sunward side of Earth is air glow.

Comparison (above) The Moon is often said to be a very large satellite compared to Earth. The Moon is only about one-quarter the diameter of Earth and only about one-eightieth of Earth's mass, but it has a profound effect on Earth. For example, tidal forces currently increase the length of the day by 0.002 seconds per century. This rate varies over time, but it does imply that the day is now hours longer than it was hundreds of millions of years ago when complex life-forms first appeared in Earth's oceans.

Impact scar (right) Meteor, or Barringer, Crater in Arizona, U.S.A., seen here snow-covered, is perhaps the best known of about 120 impact craters on Earth's surface. Measuring 0.7 miles (1.1 km) across, the crater survives because it is only 50,000 years old. Weathering will eventually remove all signs of the impact that the 160-foot (50 m) diameter object made on the land.

Lunar surface (far right) In stark contrast to Earth, the Moon's surface is pockmarked with millions of craters of all sizes. Unlike on Earth, there is no weathering to remove them. This image centers on the crater Aristarchus, 25 miles (40 km) in diameter, on the lava floor of Oceanus Procellarum. With an estimated age of 450 million years, it is one of the youngest large craters on the Moon.

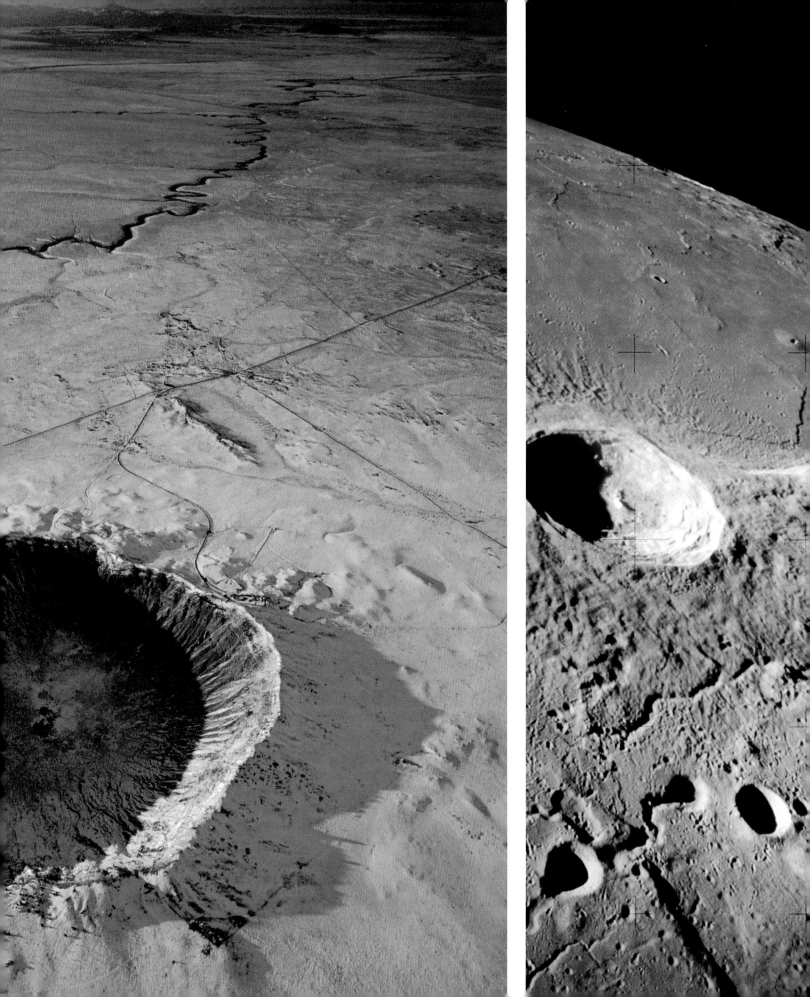

Earth's Moon

The Moon is Earth's closest neighbor in space and the only place beyond Earth's orbit visited by explorers. Its heavily cratered surface records the early history of the inner solar system, which has been erased on Earth's rapidly evolving surface. Without the Moon, Earth's axis would wobble erratically over time, with profound effects on Earth's climate.

Nearside of the Moon (below) Tidal forces are slowing Earth's rotation. They have already slowed the Moon's rotation until this matches the orbital period. The Moon is tidally "locked" and always presents the same face to Earth.

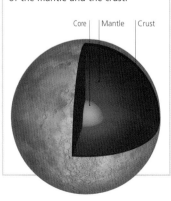
APOLLO LANDING SITES

- **Apollo 11** July 20, 1969
- **Apollo 12** November 19, 1969
- **Apollo 14** February 5, 1971
- **Apollo 15** July 30, 1971
- **Apollo 16** April 20, 1972
- **Apollo 17** December 11,1972

Montes Jura
SINUS IRIDUM
(Bay of Rainbows)
Plato
MARE FRIGORIS
(Sea of Cold)
Aristoteles
Eudoxus
Hercules
Atlas
MARE IMBRIUM
(Sea of Showers)
Cassini
Montes
Aristillus
Euler
Archimedes
Timocharis
APOLLO 15
LANDING SITE
MARE SERENITATIS
(Sea of Serenity)
Posidonius
Cleomedes
Montes Apenninus
Montes Haemus
Macrobius
APOLLO 17
LANDING SITE
MARE
CRISIUM
(Sea of Crises)
Eratosthenes
Kepler
Copernicus
OCEANUS PROCELLARUM
(Ocean of Storms)
MARE
TRANQUILLITATIS
(Sea of Tranquility)
MARE
FECUNDITATIS
(Sea of Fertility)
APOLLO 12
LANDING SITE
APOLLO 14
LANDING SITE
APOLLO 11
LANDING SITE
Letronne
MARE
COGNITUM
(Sea of Knowledge)
Ptolemaeus
APOLLO 16
LANDING SITE
Albategnius
Theophilus
Gassendi
Alphonsus
MARE NECTARIS
(Sea of Nectar)
MARE
HUMORUM
(Sea of Moisture)
Arzachel
MARE
NUBIUM
(Sea of Clouds)
Catharina
Pitatus
Purbach
Fracastorius
Deslandres
Piccolomini
Tycho

Phases of the Moon (below) These result from the Moon's motion around Earth over about 28 days. While we always see the same side of the Moon, varying amounts of it are in sunlight.

FACT FILE

Moon missions Exploration of the Moon using spacecraft began in 1959 with the impact of Luna 2 on the Moon. Just ten years later, Apollo 11 landed the first men on the Moon.

First image Earthrise over the edge of the Moon is a unique view of Earth. First seen from Apollo 8's lunar orbit in 1968, this image has been described as "the most influential environmental photograph ever taken."

Lunar landscape (above) Typical of the Moon's surface, this desolate, boulder-strewn scene was photographed next to Camelot Crater, near the Sea of Serenity, during the Apollo 17 mission.

Earth's tides (below) These occur not only in Earth's surface water but also in its rocks and atmosphere. The tides in the rock can reach heights of more than 20 inches (50 cm).

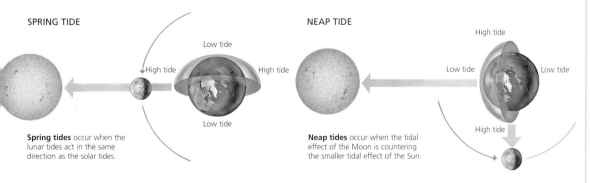

SPRING TIDE

Low tide

High tide   High tide

Low tide

Spring tides occur when the lunar tides act in the same direction as the solar tides.

NEAP TIDE

High tide

Low tide   Low tide

High tide

Neap tides occur when the tidal effect of the Moon is countering the smaller tidal effect of the Sun.

First landing Neil Armstrong's photograph of Buzz Aldrin on the Moon during the historic Apollo 11 mission is undoubtedly one of the most famous images of the 20th century.

Earth's Infancy

About 4.6 billion years ago, Earth and the other planets condensed from a disk of debris spinning around the Sun. As it grew, Earth became hotter. Its gravity pulled the heavier elements, like iron, toward its center, while the lighter ones—aluminum and silicon—rose upward. Three separate layers took shape, and the core, mantle, and eventually a hard crust were formed.

Harsh beginnings During the so-called "Eon of Hell," or the Hadean, infant Earth was a heavily bombarded inferno. Any thin crust that began to form was quickly shattered by incoming debris as the planet continued to grow in size.

Growth Under continuous bombardment, Earth grew to its present size by accretion, and then its crust hardened. Gases from volcanoes and impacting comets made up its early atmosphere.

4.6–4.2 billion years ago Earth grew as a result of heavy planetary bombardment.

4.2–3.8 billion years ago Bombardment slowed, and the crust and oceans formed

OXYGEN

About 2.3 billion years ago, when unoxidized elements such as iron and sulfur had been fully satisfied, oxygen levels in the primitive atmosphere began to increase.

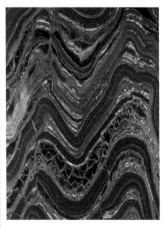

Red and gray layers in banded ironstone indicate seasonal cycles of oxygen build-up.

Seething oceans (above) Beneath heavy, poisonous skies, water vapor condensed in massive storm clouds. Pouring rains lashed the planet's surface and torrents of water ran across the hot landscape to collect in boiling oceans. Land and sea were born.

Time of turbulence (below) Lava from erupting volcanoes and issuing from deep impact fractures cooled to form a thin crust, but it was rapidly recycled and destroyed by vigorous plate tectonic activity. Very few rocks remain from the Hadean eon.

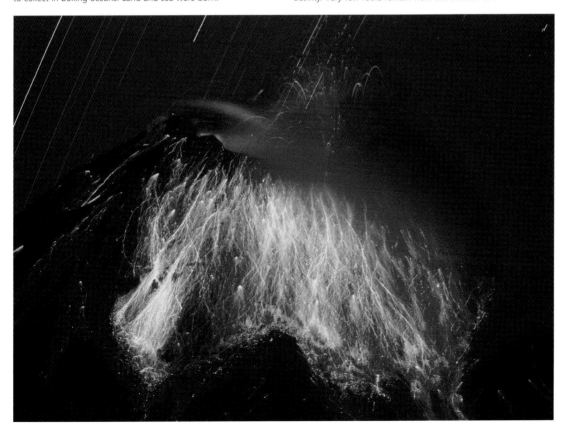

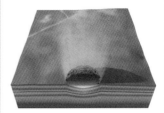
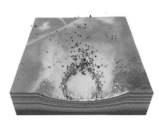
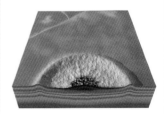
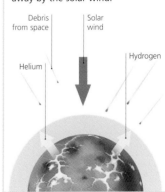

First oceans and land Toward the end of the Hadean, the infant Earth began to cool. A crust formed, the oceans grew, and by 3.8 billion years ago the oldest continental rocks had appeared.

1 As meteorite bombardment became less intense, a thin, brittle crust began to harden on the surface of the molten ball that was Earth.

2 Volcanic activity continued to pump out water vapor and other gases. As cooling continued, the vapor condensed as rain to feed the oceans.

3 Silica- and aluminum-rich granite rocks, formed in volcanoes, were pushed together by tectonic forces into the first continents.

Atmosphere A poisonous mix of gases and water vapor from countless volcanoes contributed to Earth's early atmosphere.

Filling the oceans Water vapor condensed into clouds and fell as torrential rain on the volcanoes' flanks. Erosion began and the ancient oceans filled with water and sediment.

Red rivers of lava Flowing down volcanoes' sides, basalt lava cooled into a block-like or ropy form on land but took the shape of pillows under water.

Growing volcanoes Molten magma rose from below Earth's first thin crust and erupted at the surface to build volcanoes.

The Landscape Takes Shape

As heavy meteor bombardment of Earth slowed, a permanent crust formed. Huge slabs, or plates, were driven around by convection heat. Continual melting and re-crystallization concentrated the lightest elements into quartz and feldspar, which formed the first permanent landmasses. These are the ancient centers, or shields, of today's large continents.

Lines of volcanoes The movement of Earth's plates recycled the early crust to form lines of volcanoes in the oceans.

Land is born The very first land appeared as Earth's surface solidified and cooled. Countless volcanoes ruptured the thin crust, emitting gases and building a primitive oxygen-less atmosphere. Volcanic water vapor condensed into vast oceans.

Salty water Oceans became more salty as soluble elements from the volcanic gases and ash dissolved in the seawater.

Pillow lava As lava flowed beneath the sea, it cooled quickly and a skin formed. When pressure built up inside, new "pillows" burst through ruptures in the skin.

Layers Volcanoes grew as alternating layers of lava and explosive ash built up.

Landmasses Over several hundred million years, supercontinents broke up and re-formed in cycles. Rising heat from Earth's interior drove the continents across the globe at the speed of a growing fingernail.

Rodinia The first known supercontinent, Rodinia broke apart about 750 million years ago.

Pangea Earth's last supercontinent formed 275 million years ago and broke up from 200 million years ago.

90 million years ago Pangea's broken fragments were moving toward their present-day arrangements.

EARTH'S OLDEST ROCKS

Earth's earliest rocks are found in the ancient "shields" of the continents. At 3.8 billion years old, the oldest known of these are the altered metamorphic and igneous rocks in Greenland's Isua Greenstone Complex. Organic carbon indicates these were once sedimentary rocks harboring Earth's first primitive life. Other examples of rocks that are nearly as old are found in shields of the Americas, southern and western Africa, western Australia, Siberia, and India.

THE EMERGENCE OF LIFE

The story of the appearance and evolution of life on Earth is truly amazing. It is a story that would be totally unbelievable if we were not able to follow it in the fossil record—the hundreds of millions of fossil specimens in the world's museums that paleontologists study to follow the development of life through geological time. It is as if Earth is a giant seed growing toward maturity, evolving its own consciousness and increasingly able to influence its own destiny the more it develops. Today, freed from the early time-consuming and risky tasks of hunting and gathering food, humans have more time than ever before to use their powerful brains to reflect on and influence their own future.

Crinoids (left) Also called sea lilies, these cup-like filter feeders proliferated during the Ordovician period on the sea bottom from the tropics to the Poles, but were decimated by the Permian mass extinction. Today a much-reduced number survive, mostly short-stemmed mobile types.

Primitive life (right) The rainbow colors in the waters of Grand Prismatic Hot Springs, Yellowstone National Park, U.S.A., are caused by different bacteria. These single-celled organisms can live in extremes of temperature and are unchanged since they first evolved 3.8 billion years ago.

AN AMAZING STORY

A massive 4,600 million years of geologic time has seen Earth change from a cooling, lifeless ball to the complex networked global economy that we live in today. Like a slowly rising but unstoppable tide, single-celled life gradually evolved, not only adapting to the surrounding environment, but also contributing to it by building up oxygen levels in the primitive atmosphere. Stromatolite reefs dominated the Neoarchean coastlines.

By the end of the Proterozoic eon, cells were more complex, having developed a nucleus. This paved the way for an explosion of different forms of multicellular life during the Ediacaran and Cambrian periods. Evolution of "hard parts"

left a clearly visible trail for scientists to study in the fossil record. The evolutionary "arms race" had begun. Predatory life-forms developed more sophisticated means of tracking and capturing prey, such as eyesight, teeth, and clawed appendages. Prey species countered with more sophisticated defense strategies, such as armored plates, shells, spines, and toxins.

Life evolved and adapted on Earth's ever-shifting continents, driven onwards by the natural selection of forms that were better suited to conditions at the time. Armor-plated fishes and sharks ruled the Devonian seas, while plants and amphibians colonized the bare land, opening the way for reptiles.

Occasional calamities struck the planet, sometimes killing as much as 95 percent of existing species, and clearing space for the rapid spread of those that survived. For 200 million years, dinosaurs evolved, only to be wiped out

by the giant meteorite strike that terminated the Cretaceous period. Mammals appeared and diversified after this extinction, heralding the arrival of primates, our human ancestors, and eventually anatomically modern humans some 200,000 years ago in Africa. It was the rise of flowering plants and grasses that permitted the evolution of the grazing plains herbivores and their predators, and finally of the intelligent *Homo*, the hunter. Starting out from northeast Africa humans moved north into the Arabian Peninsula, then farther north into Europe and east into Asia, reaching parts of Oceania as recently as 1,000 years ago.

Life on Earth (below) This timeline covers geological time from the appearance of the first prokaryote cells 3.8 billion years ago to the evolution of anatomically modern humans 200,000 years ago, which comparatively is no more than a blip at the very end of the line. Geological time is divided into eons and then subdivided into eras, periods, and epochs, which mark significant stages in the evolution of Earth and its life-forms. These changes were noted in the fossil record long before it was realized that the closure of a stage often corresponded to a calamitous extinction event, such as the one at the end of the Permian period 251 million years ago when nearly all land and sea life on the planet disappeared.

Early leaves These strange-looking *Annularia* fossils are actually the central portions of the leaves of spore-bearing horsetails, which were huge trees on a river delta during the Carboniferous, and predate evolution of the flowering plants. They are preserved in the 300-million-year-old shale at Mazon Creek in Illinois, U.S.A.

TIMELINE   ◯ Mass extinctions

| Eoarchean era Before 3,800 mya | Paleoarchean era 3,600 mya | Mesoarchean era 3,200 mya | Neoarchean era 2,800 mya | Paleoproterozoic era 2,500 mya | Mesoproterozoic era 1,600 mya | Neoproterozoic era 1,000 mya | Ediacaran period 630 mya | Cambrian period 542 mya | Ordovician period 488 mya | Silurian period 444 mya | Devonian period 416 mya | Carboniferous period 359 m |

| ARCHEAN EON | PROTEROZOIC EON | PALEOZOIC ERA |

Soft-bodied life *Mawsonia spriggi* is one of the earliest forms of soft-bodied multicellular life, perhaps an algae holdfast, jellyfish, filter feeder, or microbial colony. It lived during the Ediacaran, 570 to 542 million years ago, a period that takes its name from the Ediacara Hills in Australia's Flinders Ranges, where this specimen was found.

Sea creatures This Jurassic ammonite was fossilized when its hard and soft body parts were replaced by pyrite after it was buried in an oxygen-poor and sulfur-rich seafloor environment. This location is now the Holzmaden oil shales in Germany, where a variety of marine life has been preserved with all its delicate detail.

All-purpose mollusk Some 12,000 years ago, this Van Hyning's cockle was one of a number of mollusks used by the Calusa Indians, or "Shell People," of southwest Florida for food and other purposes such as fishing-net weights. They even used shells to build their own island, known as Mound Key.

Permian period 299 mya	Triassic period 251 mya	Jurassic period 200 mya	Cretaceous period 146 mya	Paleogene period 65.5 mya		55.8 mya		33.9 mya		Neogene period 23.0		5.3	Quaternary period 1.8		11,800
				Paleocene epoch		Eocene epoch		Oligocene epoch		Miocene epoch		Pliocene epoch	Pleistocene epoch		Holocene epoch

MESOZOIC ERA   CENOZOIC ERA

Fossilization Fossils are preserved in sedimentary rocks only if organisms are protected from destruction or decay. To become fossils, plants and animals must undergo rapid burial, like the dinosaurs below.

1 Two battling dinosaurs were buried by collapsing sand 70 million years ago. Soft tissue disappeared, leaving only the bones.

2 The interlocked skeletons were compressed beneath layers of hardening sediments and the bones were replaced by other minerals.

3 When movements of Earth's crust produced new mountains in an ice age 20,000 years ago, the fossil layer was uplifted.

4 Erosion exposed the fossilized bones, giving paleontologists a rare insight into the life that existed at that place in the past.

The Fossil Record

Layers of sedimentary rock are like the pages of a giant stone book that tells the story of Earth's living history. Opening the pages allows us to travel back in time to different geological periods. Preserved between the layers of sand and mud are the fossilized imprints or remains, such as bones or shells, of animals and often-bizarre communities of organisms.

Important evidence Within the layers of Butterloch Canyon, Italy, are preserved the fossil remains from a natural disaster that wiped out almost all of Earth's land and sea life, and marked the close of the Permian period.

Trilobites First seen in the oceans of the Cambrian period, these arthropods (right) evolved into many types before dying out in the Permian mass extinction. Their fossils (below) often reveal the environment and age of the rock containing them.

Lichida kettneraspis

Agnostida pagetia

Proetida carolinites

FACT FILE

Fossil types Plants and animals fossilize in various ways. They can be thin carbon impressions between sedimentary layers, embalmed in tree resin, turned to stone (petrified) cell by cell, frozen in ice, or mummified in dry deserts.

Mudstone This crinoid, or sea lily, was preserved in Silurian mudstone. A long stalk attached its feeding arms and cup-like body to the seafloor.

Ammonites These intelligent squid-like marine carnivores (right), related to the modern nautilus, evolved rapidly, some growing larger than a truck tire. Ammonites preserved in limestone at Lyme Regis, England, (below) date this rock to the Jurassic period.

Paratexanites

Tumulites

Nostoceras

Carbon copy Stems and berries preserved as an imprint and thin carbon film between layers of siltstone record the life cycle of the Basswood tree.

Amber Wasps entombed in the sticky resin of a conifer tree are preserved intact. Insects in amber are valued as gemstones.

HERITAGE WATCH

Conserving our past Fossil sites that allow unique insight into the past are protected. The Cambrian Burgess Shale in Canada's Yoho National Park, for example, preserves whole communities of bizarre life-forms. Controversy erupts when people dig up and sell such fossils for their personal gain.

1822 It was shown as a reptile on all fours with a horned snout.

Early 1900s It was viewed as a giant bipedal iguana, propped up by its tail.

Today It is seen as having an outstretched tail and using either four or two legs.

REASSEMBLY

Paleontologists put evidence together like a jigsaw puzzle in a long and painstaking process. Bones are labeled and removed from the rock. In the laboratory, missing pieces are interpreted, and the whole skeleton is reassembled.

Clues to Earth's Past

Whole living communities may be fossilized by some natural disaster, as were Pompeii and its people beneath Mount Vesuvius' volcanic ash in A.D. 79. Such circumstances are rare, but the enormity of geological time has left many spectacular, well-preserved fossil sites, known as lagerstätten, that provide informative snapshots of long-forgotten past life.

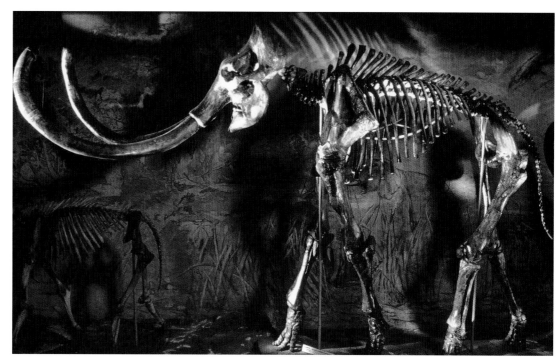

Ice-age relic (above) A well-preserved woolly mammoth skeleton with huge curved tusks provides us with clues about ice age life. Mammoths became extinct 10,000 years ago.

Herbivorous dinosaur (below) The fossilized bones of the long-necked *Phuwiangosaurus sirindhornae* from the early Cretaceous were discovered in Thailand in 1982 and later reassembled.

Solnhofen (above left) This lizard, which lived some 190 million years ago, is one of the 400 fossils of marine and terrestrial species preserved by the finely layered limestones at Solnhofen, Germany.

Karoo Beds (above right) The fossils at this site span a 70-million-year period and include amphibians, reptiles, and dinosaurs. These impressions decorate bedding surfaces in the South African Swartberg Mountains.

Major lagerstätten Earth's significant fossil sites provide a picture of the evolution of life, from the 2,300-million-year-old stromatolites at Cochabamba in the Bolivian Andes to the 40,000-year-old vertebrates of the La Brea Tar Pits.

Dinosaur eggs In Henan, China, duck-billed hadrosaur eggs from the Cretaceous left these impressions.

Feces This fossilized fish and turtle dung may provide information about each animal's diet and lifestyle.

Tracks These show if a dinosaur walked on two or four legs, as well as its size, weight, and hunting methods.

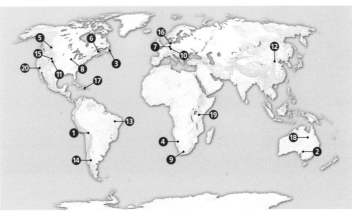

KEY TO MAP			
Site	**Location**	**Age**	**Types of fossils**
1. Cochabamba	Eastern Andes, Bolivia	2,300 mya	Stromatolites
2. Ediacara Hills	Flinders Ranges, South Australia, Australia	570–542 mya	Soft-bodied marine organisms
3. Mistaken Point	Avalon Peninsula, Newfoundland, Canada	565 mya	Soft-bodied marine organisms
4. Driedoornvlagte Reef Complex	Near Rietoog, southern Namibia	549 mya	Ediacaran *Cloudina* fossils
5. Burgess Shale	Yoho National Park, British Columbia, Canada	505 mya	Soft-bodied and arthropod-like forms
6. Miguasha National Park	Gaspé Peninsula, Québec, Canada	375–350 mya	Lobe-finned fishes
7. Hunsrückschiefer	Bundenbach, Wissenbach, Gemünden, Germany	370 mya	Trilobites, arthropods, cephalopods, sea stars
8. Mazon Creek	Illinois, U.S.A	300 mya	Ferns, mosses, mollusks, arthropods, fish, amphibians
9. Karoo Beds	Karoo Basin, South Africa	280–210 mya	Reptiles, early mammal-like reptiles
10. Holzmaden Solnhofen	Bavaria, Germany Bavaria, Germany	190 mya 190 mya	Ichthyosaurs, pliosaurs, plesiosaurs Feathered dinosaurs, pterosaurs
11. Dinosaur National Monument	Near Vernal, Utah/Colorado, U.S.A.	150 mya	Duck-billed and horned dinosaurs
12. Liaoning Province	China	125 mya	Bird-like dinosaurs
13. Romualdo Member	Santana Formation, Brazil	108–92 mya	Dinosaurs, fishes, pterosaurs, reptiles, amphibians, invertebrates, plants
14. Auca Mahuevo	Patagonia, Argentina	80 mya	Sauropod dinosaur eggs
15. Bridger Formation	Green River, Colorado/Utah/Wyoming, U.S.A.	50–48 mya	Primitive mammals, fishes, boas, flamingos, crocodiles
16. Grube Messel	Darmstadt, Germany	40 mya	Fish, crocodile, tapir, bat, turtle, horse
17. Dominican Amber	La Cordillera Septentrional, Bayaguana, and Sabana de la Mar, Dominican Republic, Caribbean	30–10 mya	Insects in amber
18. Riversleigh	Northwest Queensland, Australia	25–15 mya	Vertebrates, including mammals
19. Olduvai Gorge	Eastern Serengeti plains, Tanzania	2.1–0.015 mya	Hominids
20. Rancho La Brea Tar Pits	Los Angeles, California, U.S.A.	40,000 ya to present	Large mammals, including bison, sabertooth cats

Precambrian Pioneers

Evolving 3.8 billion years ago in the warm Archean seas, photosynthetic prokaryotes exploded in number to become the dominant life-form of Earth's oceans. These simple single cells without a nucleus used sunlight to feed themselves. The vast quantity of oxygen that they produced in this process contributed to Earth's early atmosphere.

Black smokers Mineral-rich plumes pouring out of hydrothermal vents on the ocean floor support communities based on thermophile bacteria.

Alternative energy Simple anaerobic archaea around a thermal spring in New Zealand use the yellow sulfur as an energy source instead of oxygen.

EARTH'S FIRST OZONE LAYER

As it reacted with oxygen in the early atmosphere, sunlight formed an ozone layer that protected Earth's surface from harmful radiation. This paved the way for the evolution of more complex life.

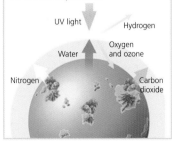

UV light
Hydrogen
Oxygen and ozone
Water
Nitrogen
Carbon dioxide

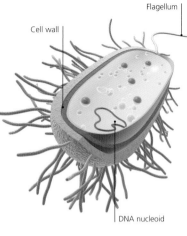

Flagellum
Cell wall
DNA nucleoid

Prokaryotes (above) These simple cells have no nucleus, only a nucleoid of DNA. Some have a rotating tail, or flagellum.

Earliest life-form (left) Single-celled prokaryotes were like this 10-million-year-old bacterial cell fossilized in seafloor chert.

Cyanobacteria Prokaryotes containing chlorophyll, like these cyanobacteria on a rock, produce oxygen by photosynthesis.

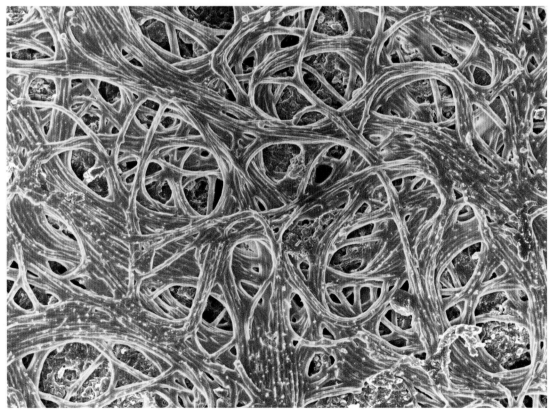

TIMELINE

Eoarchean era	Paleoarchean era	Mesoarchean era	Neoarchean era
Before 3,800 mya	3,600 mya	3,200 mya	2,800 mya

ARCHEAN EON

STROMATOLITE STRUCTURE

Growth The mat of cyanobacteria filaments continues to grow upward and clear of the accumulating sediment.

Cement Calcium carbonate secretions from the cyanobacterial mat trap and bind sediment to form darker layers.

Interior Older, curved, concentric growth layers make up the interior of the upward- and outward-growing stromatolite.

Base At its base, the stromatolite mound is firmly attached to the substrate.

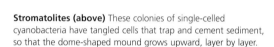

Stromatolites (above) These colonies of single-celled cyanobacteria have tangled cells that trap and cement sediment, so that the dome-shaped mound grows upward, layer by layer.

Living reefs (below) Once abundant, most stromatolite reefs have been displaced by modern corals. The best living stromatolites still thrive in Hamelin Pool, Shark Bay, Western Australia.

Paleoproterozoic era	Mesoproterozoic era	Neoproterozoic era	Ediacaran period	
2,500 mya	1,600 mya	1,000 mya	630 mya	542 mya

PROTEROZOIC EON

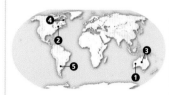

1. Apex Chert Prokaryote-like imprints in this 3.5-billion-year-old formation in Western Australia have been interpreted as the oldest Archean fossil bacterial and cyanobacterial structures found on Earth to date, but this is disputed by some researchers.

Apex Chert, Western Australia, Australia

2. Gunflint deposits These contain 2-billion-year-old stromatolites beautifully preserved in gem-quality red, yellow, and gray chert layers. Thousands of minute spheres, flasks, and segmented filaments reveal the diversity of Precambrian single-celled life.

Gunflint deposits, Minnesota and Ontario, North America

3. Bitter Springs At this site, early eukaryotes (cells with a nucleus), a type of single-celled marine plankton, were found in the 1.2- to 1.4-billion-year-old chert, which also contains diverse bacteria and cyanobacteria, including stromatolites.

Bitter Springs, Central Australia

4. Mistaken Point This Canadian site is known worldwide for its deep-sea fossil community of multicellular soft-bodied creatures dating back 565 million years. These include leaf-like forms with stems, bush-like or branching tree-like networks, and long, pointed spindle shapes.

Mistaken Point, Avalon Peninsula, Newfoundland, Canada

5. Rio de la Plata Craton On the eastern edge of this craton 900–800 million years ago, stromatolites built a huge carbonate reef, which continued growing into the early Cambrian. In Uruguay it is the Nico Perez Terrane; in Argentina the Tandilia System.

Rio de la Plata Craton, Uruguay and Argentina

FACT FILE

Endosymbiosis The eukaryote cell evolved by endosymbiosis, in which one cell is captured alive within another. In this way respiratory and photosynthetic prokaryotic bacteria became chloroplasts and mitochondria that supplied energy to the host cell.

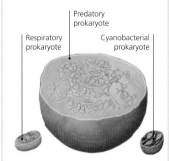

1 In primitive cyanobacterial, respiratory, and larger predatory prokaryotes, DNA is not surrounded by a nuclear membrane.

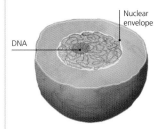

2 The larger primitive prokaryote evolves a nuclear envelope that encloses and protects its DNA.

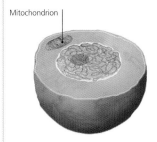

3 The larger cell engulfs the smaller respiratory prokaryote alive, which becomes the mitochondrion of a eukaryotic animal cell.

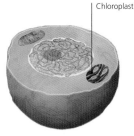

4 The larger cell engulfs the smaller cyanobacterial prokaryote, which becomes the chloroplast of a eukaryotic plant cell.

Complex Life Arises

By the end of the Proterozoic eon, cells with a nucleus, or eukaryotes, had already evolved into complex multicellular life. The Ediacaran was a period of major evolutionary change, during which soft-bodied life appeared around the globe. Life-forms were increasing rapidly in abundance, size, complexity, and diversity well before the onset of the Cambrian period.

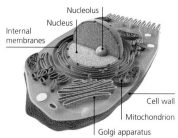

Eukaryotes (above) These cells have a true nucleus and complex structures, such as mitochondria and the Golgi apparatus, bound by internal membranes.

***Dickinsonia* (left)** This soft-bodied animal is preserved in 570–542-million-year-old sandstone in South Australia's Ediacara Hills.

***Grampania spiralis* (below)** These spiral-shaped photosynthetic algae are the earliest-known eukaryote cells.

Algae (bottom) Seaweeds are marine algae that are very similar to the simple eukaryotes that evolved in the early oceans.

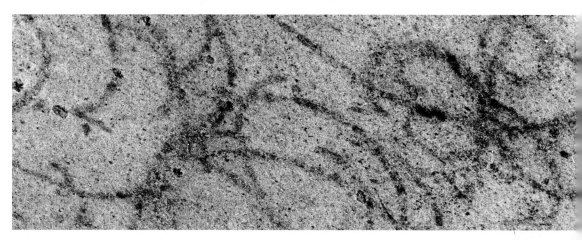

TIMELINE

Eoarchean era	Paleoarchean era	Mesoarchean era	Neoarchean era
Before 3,800 mya	3,600 mya	3,200 mya	2,800 mya

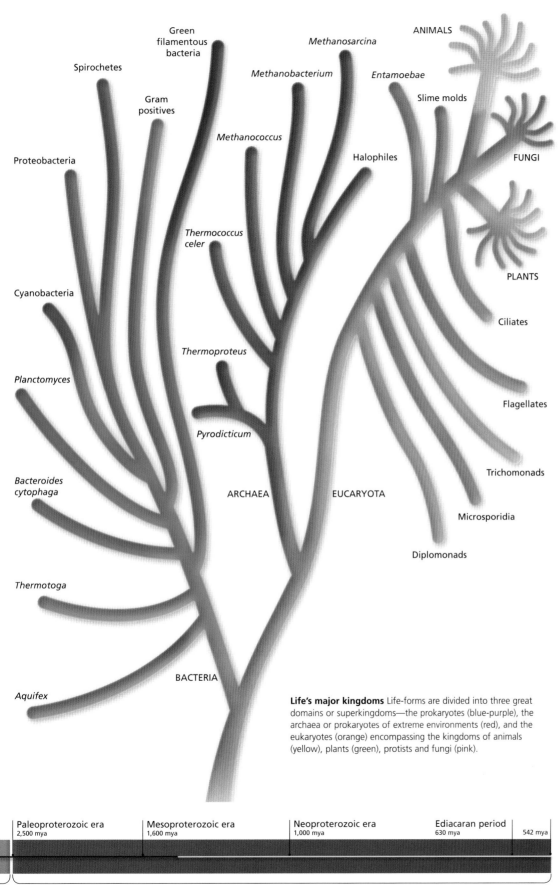

Spirochetes

Green filamentous bacteria

Methanosarcina

ANIMALS

Gram positives

Methanobacterium

Entamoebae

Proteobacteria

Slime molds

Methanococcus

FUNGI

Halophiles

Cyanobacteria

Thermococcus celer

PLANTS

Planctomyces

Thermoproteus

Ciliates

Bacteroides cytophaga

Pyrodictium

Flagellates

ARCHAEA

EUCARYOTA

Trichomonads

Microsporidia

Thermotoga

Diplomonads

BACTERIA

Aquifex

Life's major kingdoms Life-forms are divided into three great domains or superkingdoms—the prokaryotes (blue-purple), the archaea or prokaryotes of extreme environments (red), and the eukaryotes (orange) encompassing the kingdoms of animals (yellow), plants (green), protists and fungi (pink).

FACT FILE

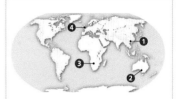

1. Doushantuo Formation Dating back 590–565 million years, this site in China's Guizhou Province is one of the earliest Ediacaran fossil beds, with phosphatized microfossils of cyanobacteria, algae, seaweeds, acritarchs, sponges, and early corals.

Doushantuo Formation, Guizhou, China

2. Ediacara Hills This site in the Flinders Ranges, South Australia, features fossils of bizarre-shaped giant soft-bodied life-forms. They resembled flatworms, soft corals, and jellyfish, and lived in tropical seas between 570 and 550 million years ago.

Ediacara Hills, South Australia, Australia

3. Rietoog, Namibia *Cloudina*, the first animal with a hard shell, was discovered near Rietoog in southern Namibia, and has since been found widely. It resembled a nested stack of tiny cones and lived 549 million years ago, becoming extinct at the start of the Cambrian period.

Rietoog, southern Namibia

4. Charnwood Forest The Ediacaran frond-like marine life-form, *Charnia*, was discovered in 1957 in Charnwood Forest, Leicestershire, U.K. At around 575 and 560 million years old, it was one of the most widespread complex life-forms.

Charnwood Forest, Leicestershire, U.K.

EARLIEST SEXUAL REPRODUCTION

Bangiomorpha pubescens was found in the 1,200-million-year-old Hunting Formation on Somerset Island in northern Canada, making it the earliest complex multicellular eukaryote that displayed sexual reproduction using spores. It resembled filamentous red algae growing from the seafloor.

Paleoproterozoic era 2,500 mya	Mesoproterozoic era 1,600 mya	Neoproterozoic era 1,000 mya	Ediacaran period 630 mya	542 mya

PROTEROZOIC EON

THEORIES OF EVOLUTION

Living populations pass on inherited traits from one generation to the next via genes that are copied during reproduction. Mutations in these genes can produce new traits, leading to heritable differences between organisms. Migrating populations also carry different traits around the world. Scientists speculate that evolution occurs when the differences become distinctly more common in a population, either randomly through genetic drift, or pushed by "natural selection." Charles Darwin recognized that natural selection would favor those attributes that allow a species to survive and help individuals to reach reproductive age.

DRIVE AND ADAPTATION

During a five-year voyage around the world on the *Beagle*, Charles Darwin observed that animals of the same species isolated on different islands had become distinctly different over time. For example, finches living on different Galápagos islands had developed different beaks through adaptation to a variety of food sources.

M. le CHEVALIER de LAMARCK.
Professor of Botany of the National Institute.

Theory pioneer (left) As early as 1800, Jean-Baptiste Lamarck proposed that evolution followed natural laws and that inheritance of certain characteristics helped species to adapt. This "use it or lose it" model set the tone for evolutionary biology.

***The Animals Entering the Ark* (below)** Conventional wisdom in Darwin's time was that God created all species in their present form and that the animals and plants of the day were essentially those that survived the Biblical Flood on Noah's Ark.

This led him to his theory of natural selection, building on Jean-Baptiste Lamarck's earlier conclusion that life had a natural "driving force" that allowed modification to suit the environment. This evolutionary drive helps predators to become more efficient at sourcing food, making them stronger, more agile, aggressive, or intelligent. It also helps prey species to avoid capture by developing speed, good eyesight, or camouflage. Circumstances may push traits in opposite directions: for example, bright colors that attract mates may also attract predators, or mark an inedible species. Successful traits become more common.

In 1858 Alfred Russel Wallace emphasized that this was a slow, involuntary process, for "Neither did the giraffe acquire its long neck by desiring to reach the foliage of the more lofty shrubs, and constantly stretching its neck for that purpose," but because "those with a longer neck than usual at once secured a fresher range of pasture than their shorter-necked companions, and at the first scarcity of food were thereby enabled to outlive them." Earth is thus an evolutionary battlefield, with different traits jostling for ranking in a statistical hierarchy that constantly changes as surrounding conditions change. Earth itself drives that change as its internal heat engine pushes continents from the tropics to the Poles, tearing some communities apart and forcing others to collide.

During the 1930s and 1940s, the more complex aspects of evolution finally came together as "The Modern Synthesis of Evolution and Genetics," founded on the works of biologists such as R.A. Fisher, J.B.S. Haldane, and S. Wright.

More recent developments in gene mapping allow the amount of genetic variation, or biochemical individuality, to be studied. The differences are surprisingly small: any two humans differ in about 0.1 percent of their genomes; humans and chimpanzees differ in only about 5 percent. These genetic differences will eventually reveal when and where species' divergence began as a result of genetic drift, gene flow, or natural selection.

THROUGH THE AGES

1802 French naturalist Jean-Baptiste Lamarck published the first comprehensive theory of evolution, proposing that an innate drive pushes species to acquire characteristics to help them adapt to local conditions.

1855 British naturalist Alfred Russel Wallace published a paper on the origin of species. With no formal higher education, he based his ideas on extensive field experience.

1859 Charles Darwin published his history-changing book *On the Origin of Species by Means of Natural Selection,* subtitled *The Preservation of Favored Races in the Struggle for Life.*

1866 Austrian biologist Gregor Johann Mendel published "Experiments on Plant Hybridization," based on his pea crossbreeding experiments, which showed that inheritance of traits follows set laws.

Brave new work (left) Darwin was lampooned by the popular press because his new theory of evolution was so different from conventional wisdom and upset the religious authorities of the time. They believed that life was in static balance and humans were divinely set apart from the animal kingdom. The public was particularly outraged by what Darwin's work insinuated about human origins.

Journey of discovery (below) Darwin was the naturalist on the H.M.S. *Beagle*'s second voyage from 1831 to 1836. The chance to observe and collect life-forms from different continents and islands helped him develop his theory of evolution. He collected scientific evidence relating to competition for resources among organisms, with their survival dependent on their varied forms and the passing of favorable traits through generations.

Evolutionary patterns (right) The spiraling deoxyribonucleic acid (DNA) molecule contains a cell's entire genetic information. Comparing DNA of different species can show relationships that provide clues to a potential shared ancestor.

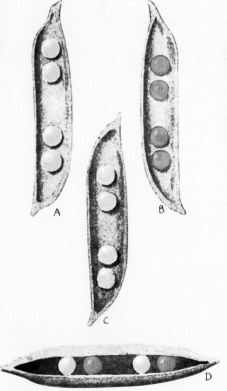

Mendel's peas (right) Gregor Mendel used peas to conduct experiments on heredity between 1856 and 1863. He crossbred yellow (**A**) and green (**B**) peas to produce a generation of yellow peas (**C**), concluding that some traits dominate others. The third generation (**D**) had both colors, again proving that certain genes are recessive, or hidden.

Survival of the fittest tortoise (left) The giant Galápagos tortoise provided important inspiration for Charles Darwin's developing thoughts on evolution and adaptation. The vice–governor of the Galápagos Islands informed Darwin that simply by looking at a tortoise, or even tasting it, he could identify exactly which island it came from.

1930 British geneticist Ronald A. Fisher published *The Genetical Theory of Natural Selection*, showing Mendelian genetics was consistent with the main elements of neo-Darwinism.

1936–1947 Evolutionary biologists reached a consensus known as "The Modern Synthesis of Evolution and Genetics," which includes genetic drift and gene flow in addition to natural selection.

1960s The modern synthesis was further developed to include newer scientific discoveries such as DNA and genetics, allowing analyses of phenomena such as kin selection, altruism, and speciation.

1990–2003 The human genome project mapped the 20,000 to 25,000 genes in human DNA. Interestingly, chimpanzees and humans differ by less than 5 percent of their genomes.

FACT FILE

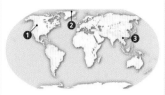

1. Burgess Shale This 505-million-year-old Canadian Rockies site gives the best snapshot of the unusual Cambrian life-forms, preserved when a shallow marine community was swept off the continental shelf and rapidly buried. Over 140 species have been found, including *Anomalocaris* specimens larger than a dinner plate.

Burgess Shale, British Columbia, Canada

2. Sirius Passet Sponges, arthropods, *Olenellus* trilobites, blind relatives of *Anomalocaris*, and *Halkieria* have been found at this fossil site in Greenland, which dates back to 518 million years ago. With its large shellplate at either end, *Halkieria* belongs to the group from which both mollusks and brachiopods may have stemmed.

Sirius Passet, Greenland

3. Yunnan, China From 525 to 520 million years old, this Maotianshan shale contains lower Cambrian marine assemblages termed the Chengjiang fauna, preserved beneath sediment avalanches. All animal groups found in the Burgess Shale are present, plus important chordates that appear to be primitive jawless fishes.

Chengjiang, Yunnan Province, China

TRILOBITE FOSSILS

These arthropods flourished in the Cambrian as predators, scavengers, or filter feeders. They declined during the Devonian and finally perished in the Permian mass extinction, 251 million years ago.

Into the Paleozoic

The Paleozoic era began with the Cambrian period, when life in Earth's oceans exploded in diversity. Shelled invertebrates flourished among sponge reefs, and chordates evolved, followed by jawless fishes. Creatures acquired weapons of attack such as teeth, matched by defensive strategies such as hard exoskeletons. The Cambrian ended with a mass extinction.

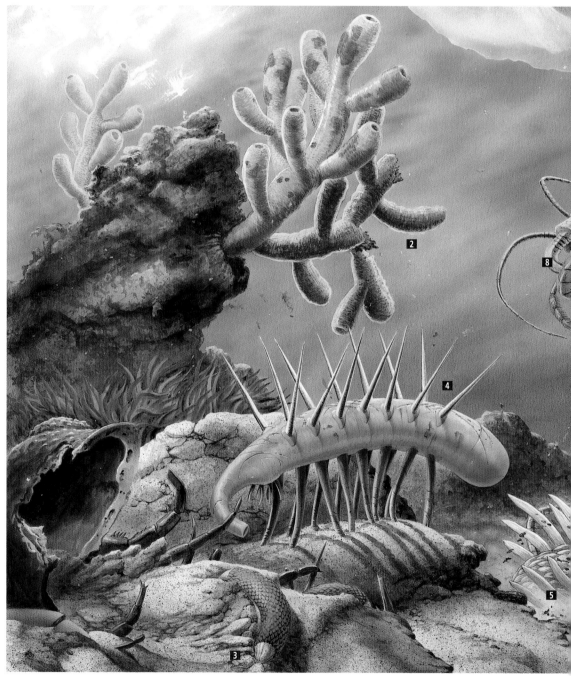

TIMELINE ◯ Mass extinctions

| Cambrian period 542 mya | Ordovician period 488 mya | Silurian period 444 mya | Devonian period 416 mya | Carboniferous period 359 mya |

PALEOZOIC ERA

Late Cambrian seas Life struggles for survival as the glacial ice that eventually brought the period to a close encroaches on the continental shelves. The reef-forming archaeocyathids (**1**) and sponges such as *Vauxia* (**2**) are dying back. The sightless armored *Halkieria* (**3**), *Hallucigenia* (**4**), and *Wiwaxia* (**5**) forage for food among the green algae and trilobite remains on the seafloor.

Sensing danger nearby, the 14-legged, spiny *Hallucigenia* (**4**) pauses and turns. A trilobite (**6**) attempts to overturn the spiked *Wiwaxia* (**5**) and attack its unprotected underbelly. Meanwhile, *Anomalocaris* (**7**), a predatory segmented arthropod, ensnares a passing *Marella* lace crab (**8**). *Pikaia* (**9**), one of the earliest animals to evolve a spinal chord, cruises along while filter feeding.

After the Cambrian Following the mass extinction, marine communities rebuilt, and many new invertebrates appeared, such as corals, mollusks, graptolites, crinoids, and brachiopods.

Sea scorpions New giant arthropods known as sea scorpions, some larger than humans, thrived in the seas from the Ordovician to the Permian periods.

Evaporite. As sea levels fell, great evaporite deposits formed in huge landlocked basin lakes, such as Australia's Lake Eyre.

JAWLESS RELIC

Early jawless cartilaginous fishes sucked their food from the seafloor. Jaws later evolved during the Devonian, leading to an explosion in diversity. One of the few jawless fishes that remain today is the hagfish (below), which sucks the blood of other fishes.

Permian period 299 mya	Triassic period 251 mya	Jurassic period 200 mya	Cretaceous period 146 mya 65.5 mya

MESOZOIC ERA

First land plants Because primitive land plants had no structures for conducting water, they were unable to grow large or survive away from moist environments. They appeared as early as the Ordovician period.

Mosses The first non-vascular plants to colonize moist areas near the coast were mosses.

Cooksonia This earliest vascular plant appeared in the mid-Silurian. It had spore sacs, but no leaves or flowers.

LUNGFISH

Like prehistoric *Panderichthys*, the Australian lungfish can breathe using either its gills or its single lung. Mostly it lives in quiet or slow-flowing rivers using its gills to absorb oxygen. During dry periods when streams stagnate, or when its gills are clogged with mud, it surfaces to breathe with its lung.

Lung (modified swim bladder)　Gills

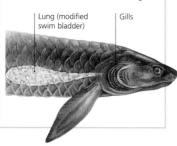

Life Moves onto the Land

Mosses, which evolved from near-shore green algae, were the first plants to colonize the barren coasts. True leaves, stems, and roots developed by the late Silurian period, followed by the appearance of mites, spiders, and centipedes. Amphibians pushed onto the land in the Devonian and thrived in the Carboniferous swamps. Later, reptiles dominated the drier Permian.

Carboniferous period (right) Club mosses, tree ferns, horsetails, and non-flowering trees dominated the warm forests and swamps, which were alive with giant insects thriving in the oxygen-enriched atmosphere. Much carbon was locked away in vast coal beds.

From fishes to amphibious tetrapods (below) The Devonian, between 385 and 360 million years ago, saw the gradual evolution of four weight-supporting limbs, lungs that were initially used along with gills, and a tough skin.

1 *Eusthenopteron* **(about 385 mya)** An open ocean fish with fleshy limb-like fins and a tetrapod-like skull

2 *Panderichthys* **(about 385 mya)** A lungfish adapted to breathe while submerged in mud

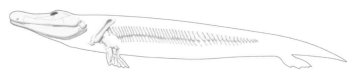

3 *Tiktaalik* **(375 mya)** A creature between *Panderichthys*-like fishes and *Acanthostega*-like tetrapods that lived in oxygen-poor shallow water

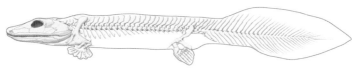

4 *Acanthostega* **(about 365 mya)** The first tetrapod genus having recognizable limbs with digits

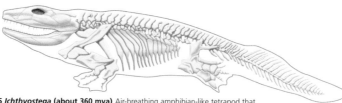

5 *Ichthyostega* **(about 360 mya)** Air-breathing amphibian-like tetrapod that used its legs to wade through the swamps

TIMELINE　◎ Mass extinctions

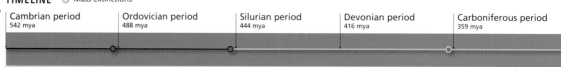

Cambrian period 542 mya	Ordovician period 488 mya	Silurian period 444 mya	Devonian period 416 mya	Carboniferous period 359 mya

FACT FILE

Coal formation Coal is formed by compaction of vegetation. The process drives off moisture and organic gases, and progressively boosts carbon content. Anthracite, the highest-grade coal, has less than 15 percent water.

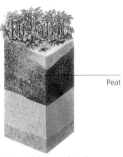

Peat

1 Dead plant material accumulates in swamps where, protected from decay beneath the anoxic waters, it is compressed into peat.

Lignite, or brown coal

2 As compaction continues lignite, or brown coal, is formed. This still contains about 45 percent water.

Black, or bituminous, coal

3 Further compaction forms bituminous or black coal, which contains less than 20 percent water.

PLACODERMS

The placoderm fishes first appeared in the Silurian and thrived in the Devonian, dying out in the mass extinction at its end. Placoderms evolved the first jaw, probably from the front gill arches, and had heads protected by armored plates.

Permian period	Triassic period	Jurassic period	Cretaceous period	
299 mya	251 mya	200 mya	146 mya	65.5 mya

MESOZOIC ERA

Lost species The very fact that numerous plants and animals have evolved over time and then disappeared in major mass extinctions helps geologists to match up and classify fossil-bearing sedimentary rocks.

Calymene One of many different trilobites, *Calymene* lived during the Ordovician and Silurian and could roll itself up for protection.

Dicranuras This Lower Devonian trilobite had large spines for protection, or perhaps to prevent it from sinking in the soft mud.

Rugosa These large, horn-shaped corals dominated mid-Silurian reefs but, like tabulate corals, died out in the Permian extinction.

Glossopteris This seed-bearing conifer-like tree grew widely on Permian continents, but disappeared in the Permian extinction.

The Permian Catastrophe

Around the world, fossil "death beds" mark the end of the Permian period 251 million years ago, which followed the most catastrophic event ever witnessed on Earth. Up to 95 percent of marine species and 70 percent of all terrestrial species were wiped out after extensive volcanic eruptions triggered severe climate change.

TIMELINE ◎ Mass extinctions

Cambrian period 542 mya	Ordovician period 488 mya	Silurian period 444 mya	Devonian period 416 mya	Carboniferous period 359 mya

The Permian extinction scene After explosive volcanic eruptions in Siberia, skies glow purplish red, and volcanic dust and greenhouse gases block sunlight. Global temperatures are falling quickly. There is little to eat in the dying araucaria forests (**1**), where a pair of saber-toothed mammal-like therapsids (**2**) attack a group of bony-plated scutosaur reptiles (**3**). In the sea, a large whorl-toothed shark (**4**) moves in to attack a smaller shark-like ray (**5**), stirring up the seabed and attracting three ray-finned bony fish (**6**). On the seafloor, *Phillipsia*, the last of the trilobites (**7**), feed among the long-stemmed crinoids, or sea lilies (**8**, **9**), growing on the soon-to-be extinct tabulate coral reef (**10**). The filter-feeding brachiopods (**11**, **12**, **13**) will soon also give way to the evolving mollusks.

FACT FILE

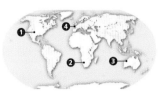

1. Wellington Formation Since this site's discovery in the early 1900s near Elmo, Kansas, its limestones have produced a treasure trove of well-preserved early Permian insect fossils. The site was once a tropical coastal plain along an inland sea.
Wellington Formation, Kansas and Oklahoma

2. Karoo Beds This South African site contains an unbroken sequence of fossils that range from 280 to 210 million years old. It records the rise of early mammals from their reptilian ancestors, and the first dinosaurs toward the end of the Triassic.
Karoo Beds, South Africa

3. Canning Basin The barrier reefs of the Canning Basin, Australia, fringed an ancient Devonian landmass 375–350 million years ago, when the now-dry basin contained a tropical sea. Deep gorges have created the world's best cross sections of a Devonian reef.
Canning Basin Reef, Australia

4. Hunsrück slates This 370-million-year old formation in Germany has fossils of cephalopods, sea stars, trilobites, and other arthropods such as *Mimetaster*, a bottom feeder with eyes on stalks, spectacularly preserved as golden pyrite in black slates.
Hunsrückschiefer, Germany

HERITAGE WATCH

Guadaloupe Mountains National Park This U.S. national park was World-Heritage-listed in 1995 because it contains the world's most extensive and significant Permian limestone fossil reef. The reef was formed by the growth and accumulation of invertebrate skeletons of algae, sponges, and tiny colonial animals known as bryozoans.

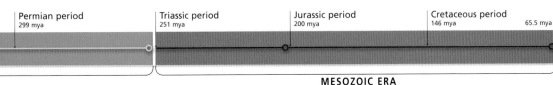

| Permian period
299 mya | Triassic period
251 mya | Jurassic period
200 mya | Cretaceous period
146 mya | 65.5 mya |

MESOZOIC ERA

Extinction survivors Another extinction at the end of the Triassic killed off a quarter of all terrestrial and marine life, particularly the large amphibians, the mammal-like reptiles, and the non-dinosaurian reptiles.

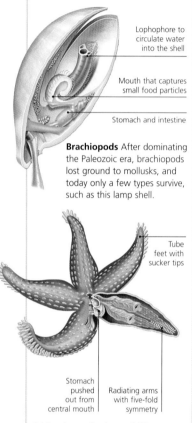

Lophophore to circulate water into the shell

Mouth that captures small food particles

Stomach and intestine

Brachiopods After dominating the Paleozoic era, brachiopods lost ground to mollusks, and today only a few types survive, such as this lamp shell.

Tube feet with sucker tips

Stomach pushed out from central mouth

Radiating arms with five-fold symmetry

Echinoderms Survivors of this group are represented today by sea stars (above), sea urchins, sand dollars, feather stars, and sea cucumbers.

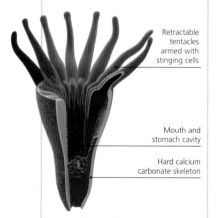

Retractable tentacles armed with stinging cells

Mouth and stomach cavity

Hard calcium carbonate skeleton

Corals After the Permian extinction primitive corals were replaced by hard corals, which are the reef builders of today's tropical seas.

Dawn of the Mesozoic

The Mesozoic era was a new beginning after the near-total Permian mass extinction. It opened with the Triassic, a period of rebuilding and radiation of life. Reptiles dominated the land, took to the sea as nothosaurs and ichthyosaurs, and ruled the skies as pterosaurs. Modern coral reefs took shape, the first dinosaurs arose, and true mammals appeared.

TIMELINE ○ Mass extinctions

Cambrian period 542 mya	Ordovician period 488 mya	Silurian period 444 mya	Devonian period 416 mya	Carboniferous period 359 mya

The Triassic landscape Reptiles are the dominant land predators. An armored *Postosuchus* (**1**) hunting along the river flats has spotted a herd of tusked mammal-like reptiles (**2**), despite their camouflage. On the other bank an *Ornithosuchus* (**3**) is devouring a small reptile, and a horned herbivorous reptile (**4**) continues to graze quietly. By the water's edge a giant amphibian (**5**) lies partially hidden by the horsetails (**6**) and cycads (**7**). Nearby, *Lariosaurus* (**8**), an aquatic reptile, hunts fish. Pterosaurs (**9**) dominate the skies, while lizards (**10**) glide through the Triassic forest of araucarias (**11**), maidenhair trees (**12**), conifers (**13**), and giant ferns (**14**). In the foreground, a pair of small, fast-moving theropod carnivores (**15**) are precursors to the dinosaurs.

FACT FILE

Other survivors Life that survived the end-of-Triassic mass extinction evolved into the life-forms of the Jurassic and Cretaceous. The extinction made the rise of the dinosaurs possible.

Conifers Cone-bearing seed plants survived alongside the newly emerging flowering trees and plants, and still dominate Earth's cooler and wetter regions.

Moths Insects such as moths that evolved in the Silurian were first into the air in the Carboniferous, and then became pollinators of flowering plants.

Insect-eaters Creatures like the echidna adapted to an abundant food source by developing a long snout, a sticky tongue, and strong claws.

Early mammals Small rodent-like creatures, the first mammals, evolved in the Triassic and survived the Triassic and Cretaceous extinctions.

HERITAGE WATCH

Ancients at risk Many species that have successfully come through several mass extinctions are now threatened by human activity. The coelacanth, for example, existed before life emerged from the sea. Sea turtles are the tlast of the giant marine reptiles. Both are at risk from overfishing and habitat loss.

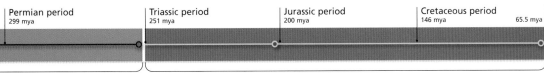

| Permian period 299 mya | Triassic period 251 mya | Jurassic period 200 mya | Cretaceous period 146 mya | 65.5 mya |

MESOZOIC ERA

Dinosaur hips Evolution of hip bones allowed dinosaurs to stand upright with their legs beneath their bodies. They used less energy, traveling farther and running faster than any reptile, allowing them to dominate and reach huge sizes.

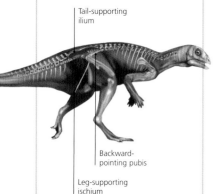

Tail-supporting ilium

Backward-pointing pubis

Leg-supporting ischium

Bird-hipped The pubis bone pointed backward, making space for the enormous large intestines needed by plant-eaters to digest their food.

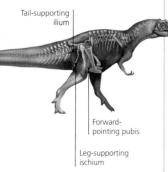

Tail-supporting ilium

Forward-pointing pubis

Leg-supporting ischium

Lizard-hipped The pubis bone pointed forward, providing strong support for the leg muscles and allowing these dinosaurs to run fast.

Therapods The forward-pointing pubis bone, sharp teeth, and claws of these tiny-to-huge carnivores made them fast, efficient hunters.

When Dinosaurs Ruled

The Jurassic and Cretaceous were periods of great evolution and diversity. On land dinosaurs flourished, both herbivores and carnivores attaining enormous sizes, while early mammals remained in the background. More efficient marine reptiles—ichthyosaurs, plesiosaurs, and pliosaurs—evolved in the tropical seas to prey on fish, sharks, rays, and invertebrates.

TIMELINE   ◎ Mass extinctions

Cambrian period 542 mya	Ordovician period 488 mya	Silurian period 444 mya	Devonian period 416 mya	Carboniferous period 359 mya

The Cretaceous landscape Life is thriving just before Earth's second largest extinction event, 65 million years ago. Pterosaurs (**1**), including the largest of all time, *Quetzalcoatlus* (**2**), soar above gymnosperm forests of kauri (**3**), bunya (**4**), and *Metasequoia* (**5**). Below, giant *Tyrannosaurus* dinosaurs (**6**) and some small bird-like *Troodon* scavengers (**7**) follow a herd of duck-billed, long-crested hadrosaurs (**8**). Nearby a *Carnotaurus* (**9**) feasts on a carcass, while armor-plated (**10**) and horned (**11**) herbivores continue browsing. In the seas, long-necked plesiosaurs (**12**) and mosasaurs (**13**) dive for fishes, cephalopods (**14**), ammonites (**15**), and other marine invertebrates. *Hesperornis* (**16**), the tooth-beaked flightless bird, also dives in the sea for its food.

FACT FILE

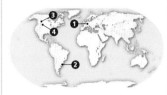

1. Heroldsberg The first *Plateosaurus* specimen was discovered at Heroldsberg, Germany, in 1837. The largest dinosaur of its time, it roamed

Triassic Europe in herds 216–200 million years ago. It was a herbivore with a long neck and powerful limbs.

Heroldsberg, Germany

2. Rio Grande do Sul A 228-million-year-old fossil, *Unaysaurus tolentinoi*, was found by Tolentino Marafiga in Rio Grande do Sul Province, Brazil, which

is known for its dinosaur bone beds. This herbivore is one of the earliest dinosaurs known to science.

Rio Grande do Sul Province, South Brazil

3. Drumheller In Dinosaur Provincial Park, near Drumheller in Alberta, Canada, 75-million-year-old bones of duck-billed and horned dinosaurs can

be seen eroding out of the rocks. These dinosaurs roamed North America in great herds in search of food.

Drumheller, Alberta, Canada

4. Hells Creek Rivers deposited the Hells Creek Formation, Montana, 65 million years ago. Near its top, the Cretaceous extinction boundary is

visible. Invertebrate, plant, mammal, fish, reptile, amphibian, bird, and pterosaur fossils are found at Hells Creek.

Hells Creek region, Montana, U.S.A.

HERITAGE WATCH

Chalk Most of Earth's chalk was deposited in the Cretaceous, a name derived from *creta*, Latin for chalk. Black shale formed when feeding anaerobic archeotes produced carbon dioxide and hydrogen sulphide. Excess carbon dioxide and calcium allowed marine algae to produce chalk.

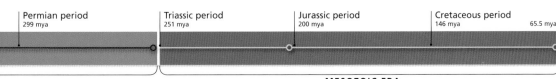

| Permian period 299 mya | Triassic period 251 mya | Jurassic period 200 mya | Cretaceous period 146 mya | 65.5 mya |

MESOZOIC ERA

Flowers and Birds Appear

Flowering plants, or angiosperms, appeared in Southeast Asia some time before the Late Jurassic and became more widespread toward the end of the Cretaceous, gradually displacing the non-flowering conifers, cycads, and ferns. Pollinating insects and nectar-drinking birds evolved alongside flowering plants to achieve the symbiotic partnership they enjoy today.

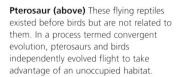

Pterosaur (above) These flying reptiles existed before birds but are not related to them. In a process termed convergent evolution, pterosaurs and birds independently evolved flight to take advantage of an unoccupied habitat.

Earliest flower (left) The water lily may be the closest modern relative of *Archaefructus sinensis,* the earliest-known fossil flowering plant. The water lily grows in calm, shallow waters, with flowers and seeds above the surface.

Magnolia (below) Today's magnolia tree may be one of the most direct descendants of the first flowering plants. The earliest fossils of the magnolia-like *Archaeanthus,* found in North America, are 100 million years old.

FACT FILE

First flowers There is much debate about the link between modern flowering plants and the fossil water plant *Archaefructus sinensis.* Genetic evidence suggests that *Amborella trichopoda,* extant in New Caledonia, is also a contender.

Archaefructus Growing in river shallows, it extended thin stems above the water. Its seeds dropped into the water and germinated near the shore.

Amborella Genetically the most primitive flowering plant, this species does not have any vessels to transport water from the ground into its leaves.

Welwitschia This unique gymnosperm, a living fossil with both male and female flowers, is considered the closest link to primitive angiosperms.

TIMELINE ○ Mass extinctions

| Cambrian period 542 mya | Ordovician period 488 mya | Silurian period 444 mya | Devonian period 416 mya | Carboniferous period 359 mya |

FEATHERED FOSSIL

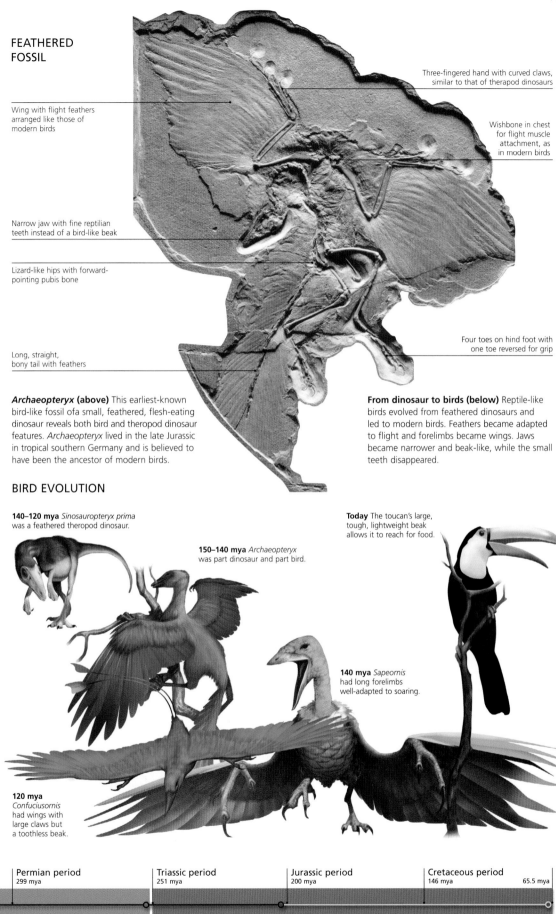

Wing with flight feathers arranged like those of modern birds

Narrow jaw with fine reptilian teeth instead of a bird-like beak

Lizard-like hips with forward-pointing pubis bone

Long, straight, bony tail with feathers

Three-fingered hand with curved claws, similar to that of therapod dinosaurs

Wishbone in chest for flight muscle attachment, as in modern birds

Four toes on hind foot with one toe reversed for grip

***Archaeopteryx* (above)** This earliest-known bird-like fossil of a small, feathered, flesh-eating dinosaur reveals both bird and theropod dinosaur features. *Archaeopteryx* lived in the late Jurassic in tropical southern Germany and is believed to have been the ancestor of modern birds.

From dinosaur to birds (below) Reptile-like birds evolved from feathered dinosaurs and led to modern birds. Feathers became adapted to flight and forelimbs became wings. Jaws became narrower and beak-like, while the small teeth disappeared.

BIRD EVOLUTION

140–120 mya *Sinosauropteryx prima* was a feathered theropod dinosaur.

150–140 mya *Archaeopteryx* was part dinosaur and part bird.

Today The toucan's large, tough, lightweight beak allows it to reach for food.

140 mya *Sapeornis* had long forelimbs well-adapted to soaring.

120 mya *Confuciusornis* had wings with large claws but a toothless beak.

| Permian period 299 mya | Triassic period 251 mya | Jurassic period 200 mya | Cretaceous period 146 mya | 65.5 mya |

MESOZOIC ERA

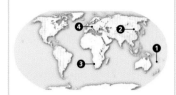

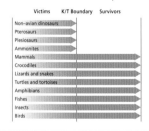
The Rise of Mammals

After the Cretaceous extinction, mammals took advantage of vacated habitats to diversify. The Paleocene tropical forests gave way to drier open woods and grasslands by the end of the Eocene, allowing the grazing herbivores to thrive. Predators, such as cats, dogs, and bears, soon followed. Mammals also adapted to life in the sea—as whales.

Diversity (right) During the Pleistocene, mammalian diversity reached its peak, heralding the rise of early human hunters. Today's African plains are the last pockets of such abundance.

Tar victims (below) Fossils from the 40,000-year-old La Brea Tar Pits are witness to the many animals that died in the sticky tar. Saber-toothed cats, lured by an easy meal, were also trapped.

Rodhocetus (bottom) About 50–40 million years ago, mammals like this took to the sea and became whales. Their hind limbs gradually shrank and disappeared, and flipper-like forelimbs developed.

TIMELINE ◎ Mass extinctions

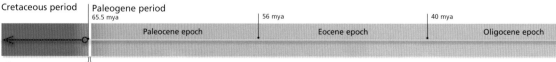

Cretaceous period | Paleogene period
65.5 mya | 56 mya | 40 mya
Paleocene epoch | Eocene epoch | Oligocene epoch

Neogene period		Quaternary period		
23 mya	5.3 mya	1.8 mya	11,800 mya	Present
Miocene epoch	Pliocene epoch	Pleistocene epoch	Holocene epoch	

FACT FILE

1. Whale Valley Fossils from the World-Heritage-listed Wadi Al-Hitan, known as "Whale Valley," in the Western Desert of Egypt, tell the story of whale evolution—a transition from land-based to ocean-dwelling mammal—that took place in a shallow bay 40 million years ago. The numerous fossils record the gradual loss of the small hind limbs, feet, and toes, as well as the streamlining of body form to one typical of modern whales.

Wadi Al-Hitan, Western Desert, Egypt

2. Grube Messel This old oil shale quarry near Darmstadt, Germany, contains 40-million-year-old fossils of fishes, crocodiles, sharks, bats, horses, turtles, and plants. Delicate details of the skin, fur, feathers, internal organs, and even stomach contents have been preserved. The quarry provides unique information about the evolution of mammals, and in 2005 it was listed as a World Heritage site.

Grube Messel, Germany

3. Bridger Formation The organic rich oil shales and coal beds of the Bridger Formation, Green River, Wyoming, U.S.A., were laid down during the Eocene, 50–48 million years ago, when luxuriant forests grew around the lakes of the Green River Basin. These rocks contain abundant fossils of many different primitive mammals as well as fossils of fishes, boas, flamingos, and crocodiles.

Bridger Formation, Wyoming, U.S.A.

HERITAGE WATCH

Unique record World-Heritage-listed Riversleigh, Queensland, Australia, provides a singular insight into the evolution of mammals. Its record begins 25 million years ago with now-extinct mammals such as the marsupial lion, and goes through to ancestors of today's marsupial moles and feather-tailed possums.

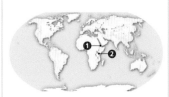

1. Hadar The most important fossil finds from the 3.3-million-year-old Hadar site in Ethiopia are the skeletons of a 20-year-old female, "Lucy," and a 3-year-old Dikika girl.

The earliest *Homo* fossil with stone tools, dating to 2.3 million years, has also been found.

Hadar, Ethiopia

2. Laetoli Apart from the tracks found by Mary Leakey in 1978, Laetoli has also produced remains—mostly jaws and teeth—of 13 *Australopithecus afarensis*, as well as fossils of antelope,

baboons, birds, boars, buffalo, cats, elephants, giraffes, gazelles, hares, hipparion, hyenas, and rhinos.

Laetoli, Tanzania

PRIMATE FORERUNNERS

Our mammalian ancestors already existed in the Cretaceous, evolving into the primates. Branches from this line became lemurs, monkeys, apes, and humans.

Lower primate skull

Higher primate skull

Human skull

The ring-tailed lemur, a lower primate found only in Madagascar

The bonobo, a higher primate relative of the chimpanzee with DNA over 95 percent identical to that of *Homo sapiens*

Early Human Ancestors

Humans evolved from lemur-like primates, driven by a need to survive on the sparsely wooded plains as Earth's climate dried. Adaptations involved development of bipedal movement, upright posture, reduction in tooth and jaw size, loss of body hair, and increase in brain size accompanied by changes in skull shape. Speech and the use of tools also developed.

Ash record (above) Layers of ash from the now-extinct Sadiman volcano in Tanzania have preserved hominid remains and artifacts that tell the story of human evolution and cultural development.

Hominid tracks (below) At Laetoli, Tanzania, volcanic ash has preserved the footprints of two adults and a child, left 3.7 million years ago by an *Australopithecus* family who walked upright.

Origins of humans Several ape-like creatures evolved in Africa, leading to the first *Homo* species 2.3 million years ago. Later *Homo* species migrated north in waves to the Mediterranean Sea, and then spread out in all directions.

- ○ The earliest hominids
- ● Australopithecines
- ● Early *Homo*
- ● *Homo ergaster/erectus*
- ● *Homo antecessor, Homo heidelbergensis*, archaic *Homo sapiens*
- ▨ Neanderthal settlement
- ▨ Earliest known *Homo* fossils
- ✎ Path of diffusion
- **BP** Before present

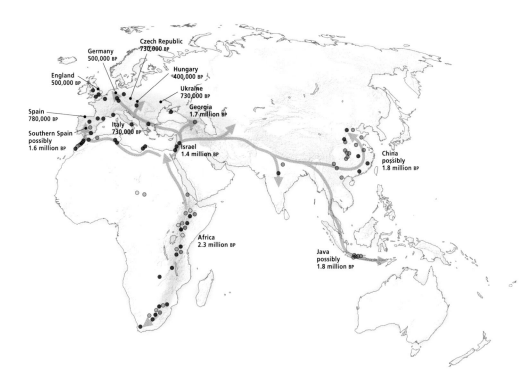

Brain development The primitive hominid skulls named *Adapis*, *Proconsul*, and *Australopithecus africanus* show a gradual increase in size, with the cranial cavity becoming higher-domed over time to accommodate the evolving larger brain.

Adapis, 50 mya

Proconsul, 23–15 mya

Australopithecus africanus, 3.0–1.8 mya

LUCY'S BABY

The earliest near-complete skeleton of *Australopithecus afarensis* found so far dates to 150,000 years before Lucy. The 3-year-old, nicknamed "Lucy's Baby" and found in sandstone at Dikika, in Ethiopia, was probably killed and buried by a sudden flood. The skull shows how *A. afarensis* individuals developed and reveals a longer childhood compared to higher primates.

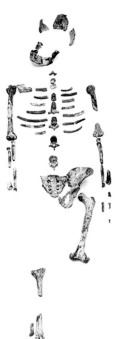

Homo floresiensis The most recently living non-modern human was discovered on the Indonesian island of Flores in 2003. An adult, but no taller than a child, it was nicknamed "the Hobbit."

"Lucy" The near-complete skeleton (above left) of a 20-year-old female *Australopithecus afarensis*, nicknamed "Lucy," has shed much light on human evolution. Lucy's body size, brain size, and skull shape resemble those of a chimpanzee. However, her hip and pelvis show that she walked upright like a human. A reconstruction (above right) shows how Lucy may have looked when she lived 3.3 million years ago.

***Homo* skulls** The *Homo* genus evolved from early human ancestors such as *Australopithecus*. The first anatomically modern human appeared at least 195,000 years ago and was distinguished by a larger cranium and a smaller jaw.

Homo habilis (*H. rudolfensis*), 3.0 to 1.8 mya

Homo erectus (*H. ergaster*), 1.8 to 0.3 mya

Early *Homo sapiens*, 92,000 ya

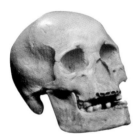

Homo sapiens (Cro-Magnon), 40,000 ya

Homo sapiens, present day

The Advance of Humans

Different hominid groups left Africa in waves. It is not clear, however, whether modern *Homo sapiens* evolved independently from different groups of *Homo erectus* that left Africa about one million years ago, or whether modern humans evolved in Africa and then migrated out of the continent about 200,000 years ago. Recent genetic and archaeological evidence tends to favor the latter option, known as the single origin theory.

Olduvai Gorge, Tanzania (below) Known as "The Cradle of Mankind," this area has produced human ancestor fossils that are 2.5 million years old, as well as stone tools dating from 2 million years ago.

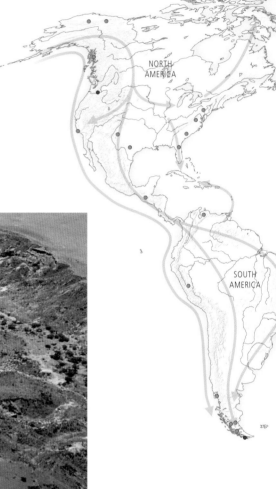

Stone tools Over two million years ago early *Homo* began to make stone tools out of flakes of local basalt and quartz from river beds. This toolmaking tradition was named "Olduwan" after tools found at Olduvai, Tanzania.

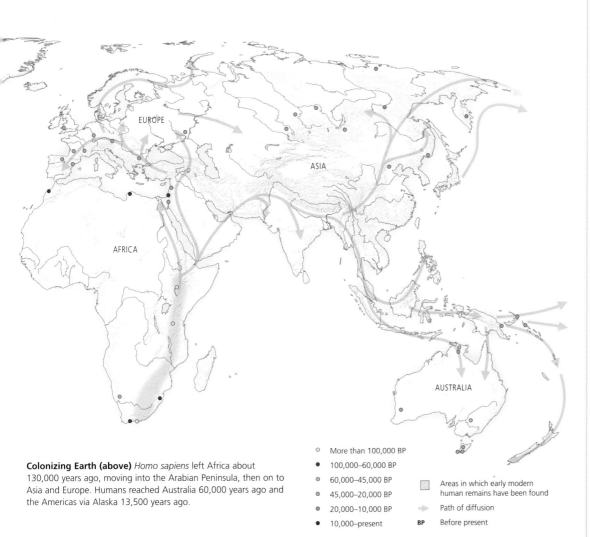

Colonizing Earth (above) *Homo sapiens* left Africa about 130,000 years ago, moving into the Arabian Peninsula, then on to Asia and Europe. Humans reached Australia 60,000 years ago and the Americas via Alaska 13,500 years ago.

○ More than 100,000 BP
● 100,000–60,000 BP
◉ 60,000–45,000 BP
◉ 45,000–20,000 BP
◉ 20,000–10,000 BP
● 10,000–present

▢ Areas in which early modern human remains have been found

➔ Path of diffusion

BP Before present

Homo ergaster An early type of *Homo erectus*, this hominid lived in eastern and southern Africa from about 1.9 to as recently as 0.3 million years ago. *Homo ergaster* was skilled in using advanced hunting tools and knew about fire for cooking.

FACT FILE

Peopling the Pacific Even after the relatively recent spread of humans from Asia into the Pacific region 3,500–1,000 years ago, ethnic and cultural differences evolved and are reflected in artifacts found on various Pacific islands.

New Zealand This Maori war club was carved in the shape of a stylized, curved body with a mythical head.

Papua New Guinea The Lapita peoples produced intricately decorated pottery, as shown in this fragment found in Papua New Guinea.

Fijian Islands These ancient stone axes and pottery fragments were found at a Fijian archaeological site.

HERITAGE WATCH

Early hominid sites The following are World Heritage listed: Willandra Lakes, Australia; Peking Man Site, Zhoukoudian, China; Omo and Awash valleys, Ethiopia; Sangiran Early Man Site, Indonesia; Lake Turkana National Parks, Kenya; Sterkfontein, Swartkrans, Kromdraai, South Africa; Ngorongoro Conservation Area, Tanzania.

1. Le Moustier At Le Moustier Cave in southwestern France, the near-complete skeleton of a four-month-old Neanderthal baby was discovered in

1914. The baby had died about 40,000 years ago and its body had been placed in a small rock shelter.

Le Moustier, France

2. Shanidar Cave At this site in the Zagros Mountains, Iraq, the remains of nine Neanderthals were found. They lived 60,000 to 80,000 years ago in

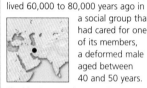

a social group that had cared for one of its members, a deformed male aged between 40 and 50 years.

Shanidar Cave, Kurdistan, northern Iraq

3. Neander Valley The first bones of Neanderthals were discovered in 1856 in this valley in Germany. Workers digging for lime thought they had found ancient cave bear bones.

The bones were later attributed to *Homo neanderthalensis,* until that time an unknown human species.

Neander Valley, Germany

TRANSITIONAL STAGE

In 1971 a 450,000-year-old skull was found in Arago Cave in the French Pyrenees. Known as Tautavel Man, it records a transitional stage between *Homo erectus* and *Homo neanderthalensis.*

Lost Cousins

Our lost cousins, the Neanderthals (*Homo neanderthalensis*), lived 200,000 years ago. Short, strong-boned, and robust, they were suited to the colder northern European climate. Neanderthals coexisted with *Homo sapiens*, but it is not known if there was interbreeding. As modern humans increased, Neanderthals declined and eventually became extinct 24,000 years ago.

Neanderthal life Neanderthals had brains as large as ours. They lived in social groups, used stone tools and fire, took care of their sick and aged, had funeral ceremonies, used simple language, and made ornaments out of teeth and ivory.

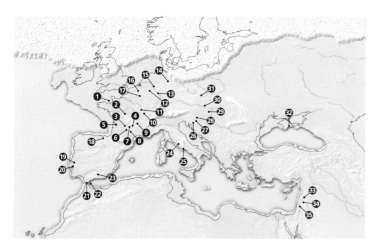

1	La Cotte de St. Brelade	18	El Castillo
2	Angles-sur-l'Anglin	19	Columbeira
3	La Quina	20	Salemas
4	Regourdou	21	Forbes Quarry
5	St. Césaire	22	Devil's Tower
6	Le Moustier	23	Carigüela
7	Pech-de-l'Azé	24	Saccopastore
8	La Ferrassie	25	Circeo
9	La Chapelle-aux-Saints	26	Veternica
10	Genay	27	Krapina
11	Arcy-sur-Cure	28	Velika Pécina
12	Fonds-de-Forêt	29	Tata
13	Wildscheuer	30	Šal'a
14	Salzgitter	31	Kulna Cave
15	Neander Valley	32	Kilk-Koba
16	Spy	33	Wadi Amud
17	La Naulette	34	Qafzeh
		35	Mount Carmel: Skhul, Tabun, Kebara Cave

Neanderthal sites (above) Living mainly in Eurasia, Neanderthals began to be displaced 45,000 years ago by modern humans and eventually became extinct as the last ice age peaked.

Gorham Cave, Gibraltar (below) Remains of the last-known Neanderthal population were found in this cave. Other findings showed they cooked and ate deer, tortoises, and various plants.

Spears Neanderthals knapped their spear points from a core stone and used animal skin to tie them to wooden spear shafts.

Stone point

Animal skin

Wooden shaft

Technique Hunting in Pleistocene Europe needed skill, practice, and cooperation between group members.

Prehistoric Rock Art

Rock markings and carvings as old as 500,000 years predate the first appearance of *Homo sapiens*. However, art as a form of symbolic representation flourished 40,000–50,000 years ago with the arrival of modern humans in Europe. The creation of art indicates an ability to think beyond basic survival needs, or may be linked to early forms of worship.

Realism (below) World-Heritage-listed Lascaux Caves in southwestern France preserve 17,000-to-15,000-year-old rock art. Animals known from fossil evidence to have lived in the area at the time have been drawn in realistic perspective.

FACT FILE

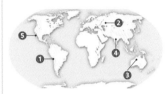

1. Parque Nacional Lauca This site in the dry Atacama Desert of northern Chile has 800-year-old geoglyphs of animals in pack trains, human figures, and geometric patterns. Geoglyphs are a type of rock art created on hillsides by laying or clearing stones.

Parque Nacional Lauca, Chile

2. Kapova Cave This Paleolithic rock art site in Bashkortostan, in Russia's southern Ural Mountains, was occupied from 13,900 to 14,680 years ago. It features a long gallery with over 40 paintings of mammoths, rhinoceroses, bison, and horses.

Bashkortostan, Ural Mountains, Russia

3. Koonalda Cave This Nullarbor Plain cave in South Australia contains Aboriginal rock art and a workshop where tools were made from the limestone cave walls. The parallel geometric finger engravings in soft cave mud, called "meanders," are 19,000 to 20,000 years old.

Koonalda Cave, Nullarbor Plain, South Australia, Australia

4. Bhimbetka Caves In these Madhya Pradesh caves, superimposed paintings in red, white, yellow, and green ochers are up to 30,000 years old. They portray dancing, hunting, riding, religious symbols, and animals such as bison, boars, crocodiles, dogs, elephants, lions, and tigers.

Bhimbetka Caves, Madhya Pradesh, India

5. Baja California Rock shelters in the mountains of Baja California, Mexico, contain the "Great Murals," larger-than-life rock art that is up to 7,500 years old. Depictions of humans, deer, rabbits, sheep, birds, fishes, and snakes use single colors, or combinations of red, black, white, pink, orange, and green.

Baja California, Mexico

Hall of the Bulls (left) The walls of the Great Hall of the Bulls in Lascaux Cave are decorated with images of animals that include early horses, bulls, and stags. Painted dots may even represent maps of the night sky.

FACT FILE

Early art The development of art is thought to reflect the flowering of the human mind. The Lascaux paintings and other Cro-Magnon ice age art represent the emergence of a new, distinctly human consciousness.

28,000–24,000 years ago Carved Venus figurine, Willendorf, Austria

24,000–22,000 years ago Mammoth, Rouffignac, France

18,000 years ago Deer, Les Trois Frères, France

15,000 years ago Hoofed animal, Le Portel, France

12,000 years ago Bison, Altamira, Spain

DISCOVERING THE PAST

Archaeology is the scientific study of ancient cultures, based on clues and traces that they left behind. Like detectives, archaeologists use this evidence to reconstruct the story of how humans of the past interacted with their environment—how long ago they lived, what they ate, what tools they used, how they built their homes, and what finally became of them. This knowledge is preserved for future generations. Archaeologists use field techniques such as remote sensing, surveying, geophysics, coring, and excavation. Laboratory procedures include compositional analysis, age dating, and statistical analyses. In North America, archaeology is one of the four branches of anthropology, alongside cultural anthropology, linguistics, and physical anthropology.

ARCHAEOLOGY

Archaeology had its beginnings in the 15th century with the antiquarians—enthusiasts interested in ancient objects and the study of disused languages. Italian Flavio Biondo is often considered to be the earliest antiquarian for his documentation of the ancient Roman Forum. By the 19th century, antiquarianism had split into the academic disciplines of archaeology and linguistics. Even today, however, most people still associate archaeology with the search for lost treasures rather than with the reconstruction of past societies. This "treasure-hunter" attitude is embodied in popular fiction, such as *Raiders of the Lost Ark* and *King Solomon's Mines*.

The turning point in 19th-century archaeology was Napoleon Bonaparte's Egyptian campaign. He took with him about 150 artists, scientists, scholars, engineers, and technicians to study Egypt's monuments and ancient relics. Their findings were published in *Description de l'Égypte* in 1809. The trilingual inscription on the Rosetta Stone, discovered in 1799, provided the key to deciphering the ancient hieroglyphs on the monuments.

Tutankhamen's tomb, containing the Egyptian king's sarcophagus and thousands of artifacts, was considered to be the most important find of the 20th century. Also significant were the discoveries of Pompeii and Herculaneum, Roman cities buried by volcanic ash during the eruption of Mount Vesuvius in A.D. 79 and stumbled upon 15 centuries later by a hydraulics engineer. In 1974 an amazing collection of more than 8,000 terracotta warriors were found in Xi'an, China. The figures had been buried in the tomb complex of China's first emperor, completed in 210 B.C. These sites are still being excavated, revealing much about the life of those times.

Archaeology's most important tool, radiocarbon dating, was only invented in 1949. It allowed the age of organic artifacts such as bone, teeth, wood, and fabric to be determined accurately.

Discovery of a lifetime (left) In 1922 British archaeologist Howard Carter discovered King Tutankhamen's tomb, where the king's mummy lay in a gold mummy case, the third in a nest of coffins. Based on an earlier discovery by Theodore Davis, Carter had suspected that the tomb lay in the Valley of the Kings. Asked if he could see anything as he peered into a room untouched for almost 3,300 years, he replied, "Yes, wonderful things!"

Ancient power house (right) The Forum was the religious and political center of ancient Rome, and extensive archaeological reconstruction work makes it a site that is still much visited today. The ruins lay buried beneath soil and were overgrown with vegetation until the mid-1400s, when Flavio Biondo began to excavate and document the ancient architecture. This sparked a revival of interest in the former capital of the Roman Empire.

THROUGH THE AGES

1444–1446 Flavio Biondo became the first archaeologist with his three-volume work on the reconstruction of ancient Roman topography around the Forum, entitled *De Roma Instaurata* ("Rome Restored").

1572 A society for the preservation of national antiquities—a forerunner of the London Society of Antiquities—was founded in England by Bishop Matthew Parker, Sir Robert Cotton, and William Camden.

1599 Architect and engineer Domenico Fontana accidentally discovered Pompeii and Herculaneum while digging a water conduit. The long-lost cities were buried by an eruption of Vesuvius in A.D. 79.

1648 At the age of 22 John Aubrey recognized the significance of the Stonehenge earthworks while hunting with friends in Wiltshire. He later described them in "Monumenta Britannica," based on his notes.

1784 The third U.S. president, Thomas Jefferson, supervised the systematic excavation of a Native American burial mound on his land in Virginia, U.S.A.

1798 France's Napoleon Bonaparte led an expedition to Egypt, later known as the "Birth of Egyptology." It led to a careful and detailed depiction of the monuments as well as the discovery of the Rosetta Stone.

Ancient monoliths (left) Archaeologists believe that the Stonehenge complex (far left) was built in several stages over at least 3,000 years, with the earliest circular ditch dated to 3,100 B.C. In 1648 English archaeologist John Aubrey (inset) was the first to realize the importance of the stoneworks, which he described in *Monumenta Britannica* with a plan of the earthworks and standing stones.

Radiocarbon dating (below) The linear accelerator shown here is part of an accelerator mass spectrometer, which is used to count the carbon-14 atoms in organic samples such as bones, wood, and cloth. The ratio of carbon-14 atoms, which decay at a set rate over time, to carbon-12 atoms, which are stable, determines the sample's radiocarbon age. When Willard Libby introduced this tool in 1949, he revolutionized the field of archaeology.

1821 Sir Richard Colt Hoare, English archaeologist, published *Ancient Wiltshire*, a book about the hundreds of barrows (burial mounds) and other sites that he excavated on Salisbury Plain in southern England.

1829 Eduard Gerhard founded the Institute for Archaeological Correspondence (Instituto di Corrispondenza Archeologica) in Rome under supervision of the Prussian ambassador, Christian von Bunsen.

1896 Professor Sir William Matthew Flinders Petrie, pioneer of systematic methodology in archaeology, discovered the the Merneptah Stele, originally commissioned by the Egyptian king Amenhotep III.

1911 The Inca city of Machu Picchu in the Peruvian Andes was revealed to the outside world by American explorer Hiram Bingham.

1922 English archaeologist Howard Carter discovered the tomb of Tutankhamen in the Valley of the Kings, Egypt.

1949 American chemist Willard Libby introduced the world to radiocarbon dating. Based on the decay of carbon-14, it is used to calculate the age of plant-based artifacts up to 45,000 years old.

1974 At Xi'an in China a local farmer digging a well discovered Emperor Qin's terracotta army. Excavation of this site continues.

FIRE

FIRE

EARTH FROM THE INSIDE OUT 82

HEAT FROM WITHIN   106

EARTH FROM THE INSIDE OUT

One legacy from Earth's birth in the hot inner region of the solar nebula is the great amount of heat still stored in the planet's interior. The conduction of this heat from the core into the mantle drives the slow but continual convection of mantle rocks. This in turn causes the great tectonic plates of Earth's surface to rift, glide past, sink beneath, and collide with each other. Mantle convection and its surface manifestation as plate tectonics continually renew Earth's surface, and drive material and heat transfers between the planetary interior and the surface.

Convection currents Heat from molten core churns overlying layers.

Crust The outer rocky shell is thin under oceans and thick under continents.

Volcanoes These occur at tectonic plate boundaries and within plate interiors.

Mantle Rock and molten material move slowly but constantly.

Lithosphere Tectonic plates are made of solid uppermost mantle and crust.

Earth's mantle (above) The mantle accounts for the largest part of Earth's interior. It is made from hot, dense rock and accounts for about 84 percent of Earth's volume and 68 percent of its mass. It is predominantly solid and overlies Earth's iron-rich core. Melting of shallow parts of the mantle has produced a thin crust near the surface, upon which we live.

ACTIVE PLANET

The theory of plate tectonics holds that slow-moving, nearly rigid rafts of rock move about Earth's surface. This accounts for much of the volcanic and seismic activity, mountain building, crustal structure, and patterns of rock type and fossil distribution within the crust. Earth scientists currently view the theory as a general model for how Earth has operated for most of its history, because it has been exceptionally successful at explaining a wide number of observations. Evidence suggests that a few dozen plates and perhaps an equal number of microplates cover Earth today. Some of the major plates are described in the following pages.

The so-called "Plate Tectonics Revolution" of the 1960s heralded the general acceptance of the theory by geologists and geophysicists, following an intensive decade of discoveries from the geological record. Yet the overall idea took many years and many modifications before it became generally accepted.

Before plate tectonic theory had been given a name, many notable scientists noticed the "fit" of the coastlines of the continental landmasses bordering the Atlantic Ocean. Scientists who included the possibility of continental drift in their work centuries before the hypothesis was proven include Flemish mapmaker Abraham Ortelius with his 1596 publication *Thesaurus geographicus*, English natural philosopher Sir Francis Bacon in 1620, American scientist and diplomat Benjamin Franklin in 1782, and Italian geographer Antonio Snider-Pellegrini in his 1858 book *La Création et ses mystères dévoilés*.

The first complete statement of the theory was written by German meteorologist Alfred Wegener. He presented his theory in lectures in 1912, and published it in full in 1915 in his most important work, *Die Entstehung der Kontinente und Ozeane*. In this publication Wegener postulated that roughly 200 million years ago the continents had been one large landmass, which he named Pangea. This landmass subsequently rifted apart in a process he named continental drift, a term that is still in use today.

Wegener's theory was not well-accepted, even though it explained much of what was known about Earth at the time. The difficulty involved explaining how the continents might plow through the seemingly rigid ocean basin crust. His theory sank into obscurity until its resurrection in the 1960s.

In 1929, Arthur Holmes suggested that thermal convection of the mantle could break apart and move continental landmasses. Observations in the 1950s by Russ Raitt and Maurice Ewing showed that the upper structural unit of Earth was lithosphere, an up to 80 miles (130 km) thick packet of mantle and crust. Soon thereafter, geophysicists Robert Deitz, in 1961, and Harry Hess, in 1962, hypothesized that the lithosphere carried the continents astride the mantle convection, unifying continental drift with the idea of seafloor spreading at ocean ridges into the idea of plate tectonics.

Volcanic glass (right) Spherical pieces of rock made of volcanic glass, such as this Philippine tektite, are produced during asteroid and meteorite impact events on Earth's crust. An immense amount of energy is released during those large impacts, and sometimes it can even melt the crust of the impact zone. Droplets of molten material are shot high into the atmosphere, where they cool and attain aerodynamic shapes before dropping back onto the ground. Tektites occur in sediment layers that sometimes also record mass extinctions.

Energy release (above) Pressurized water bursting forth from a geyser in Yellowstone National Park, U.S.A., is one of the many manifestations of energy release and material transfer on our geologically active planet.

Heat transfer (left) Incandescent volcanic cinders and lava shoot up from a radial fissure during the 1979 eruption of Cerro Azul volcano on the Galápagos Islands. Volcanism transfers heat from Earth's core to the surface.

Elements inside Earth The dense metallic core separated early in Earth's history. The remaining silicate rock differentiated into the crust and mantle. The charts below show percent (by weight) of elements in Earth's core, and of element-oxides in the crust and mantle.

CORE

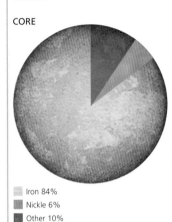

- Iron 84%
- Nickle 6%
- Other 10%

CRUST

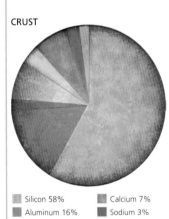

- Silicon 58%
- Aluminum 16%
- Iron 8%
- Magnesium 4%
- Calcium 7%
- Sodium 3%
- Potassium 2%
- Other 2%

MANTLE

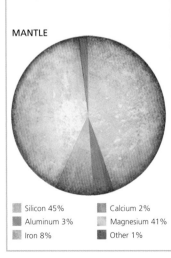

- Silicon 45%
- Aluminum 3%
- Iron 8%
- Calcium 2%
- Magnesium 41%
- Other 1%

Earth's Core

The largely iron core formed in the earliest days of Earth's formation. The core plays a major role in shaping the surface of our living planet, from the geomagnetic field to the internal heat source that drives plate movement and volcanic activity.

Earth's layers Very soon after Earth formed, it separated into layers: a dense, iron-rich core encased within a rocky mantle, surrounded by a hot gaseous atmosphere. With time, a crust formed and water condensed to make oceans.

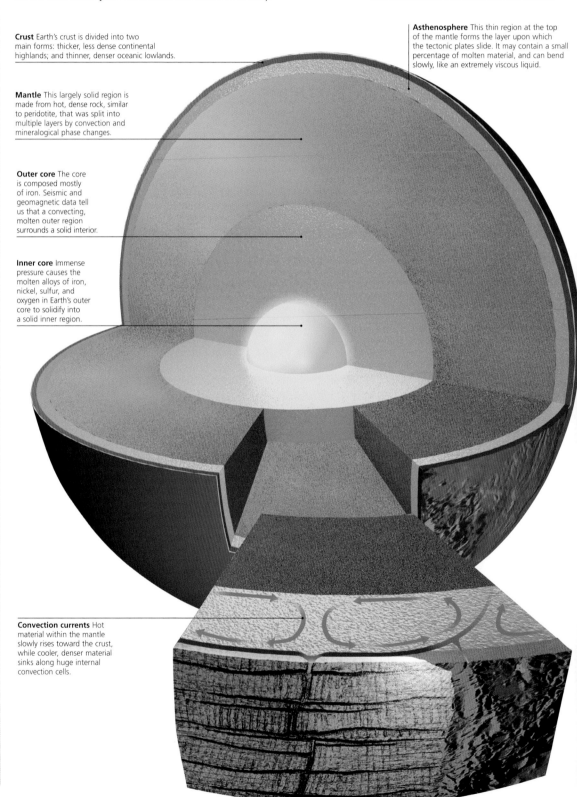

Crust Earth's crust is divided into two main forms: thicker, less dense continental highlands; and thinner, denser oceanic lowlands.

Mantle This largely solid region is made from hot, dense rock, similar to peridotite, that was split into multiple layers by convection and mineralogical phase changes.

Outer core The core is composed mostly of iron. Seismic and geomagnetic data tell us that a convecting, molten outer region surrounds a solid interior.

Inner core Immense pressure causes the molten alloys of iron, nickel, sulfur, and oxygen in Earth's outer core to solidify into a solid inner region.

Asthenosphere This thin region at the top of the mantle forms the layer upon which the tectonic plates slide. It may contain a small percentage of molten material, and can bend slowly, like an extremely viscous liquid.

Convection currents Hot material within the mantle slowly rises toward the crust, while cooler, denser material sinks along huge internal convection cells.

Iron meteorites These pure metal rocks come from the cores of exploded planets. They often contain some nickel or troilite (iron-sulfide), and they help to define the composition of Earth's core.

Olivine nodules Chunks of the upper mantle are occasionally carried to the surface by volcanic eruptions. Besides olivine they can contain the minerals pyroxene, spinel, and occasionally garnet.

FACT FILE

Seismic tomograms These images from inside Earth are constructed from the way that earthquake waves pass through the interior. The San Andreas Fault at Parkfield, California, U.S.A., is shown at different depths in the tomograms below.

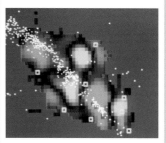

Layer 1 Between 1.5 and 2 miles (2.5–3.5 km) deep

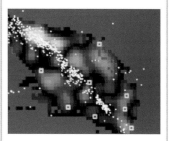

Layer 2 Between 2 and 3.7 miles (3.5–6 km) deep

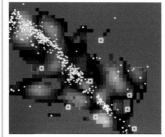

Layer 3 Between 3.7 and 5.5 miles (6–9 km) deep

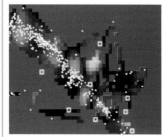

Layer 4 Between 5.5 and 9 miles (9–15 km) deep

Restless planet Heat released from Earth's interior drives eruptions at the surface. In the last century, the Arenal Volcano in Costa Rica was one of the world's most persistently active volcanoes.

Earth's Crust

The outer rocky layers of Earth consist of large blocks of rock that rest on the mantle. Asteroid and meteorite bombardment, volcanism, and plate tectonics have largely erased evidence of rocks that formed in Earth's first 500 million years. However, isolated pockets of rocks nearly 4 billion years old, some with mineral grains almost 300 million years older, have been found.

Dolomite Mountains, Italy These mountains are limestone and dolomite beds that formed in an ancient ocean. They were uplifted and sculpted by slow-moving glaciers. Today, their flanks expose cross sections of a Triassic coral reef community.

Arches National Park, Utah, U.S.A. (above) Carved by wind and water, the formation of these sandstone arches was aided by the subsidence of the underlying salt beds of an ancient inland sea.

Killbear Provincial Park, Ontario, Canada (below) This bedrock is part of the Canadian Shield, formed from continental crust. It has been undisturbed by tectonic activity for at least 600 million years.

Plate boundaries Heat that rises by convection from Earth's mantle causes plate movement. Plates spread apart, collide, or slide past each other, forming three general classes of plate boundaries.

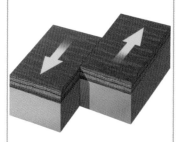

Transform fault boundary Where plates slide past each other with little or no convergent or divergent motion, they form a transform fault boundary.

Divergent boundary When plates move apart, the crust thins and new seafloor forms at oceanic spreading centers, or rifts, in continental crust.

Convergent boundary Mountain building and volcanism are common where plates collide. Often the denser plate is subducted back into the mantle.

Earth's Plates

The lithosphere, Earth's uppermost solid layer, is broken into strong, rigid plates about 60 miles (100 km) thick. The plates move across the surface on a malleable part of the upper mantle called the asthenosphere. The 12 major plates, and a number of smaller ones, account for nearly all of Earth's most prominent geological features.

The world's plates (below) Earth's surface is made up of plates moved by forces deep within the planet. They are in constant motion, shaping and rearranging the continents and ocean basins as they move against one another.

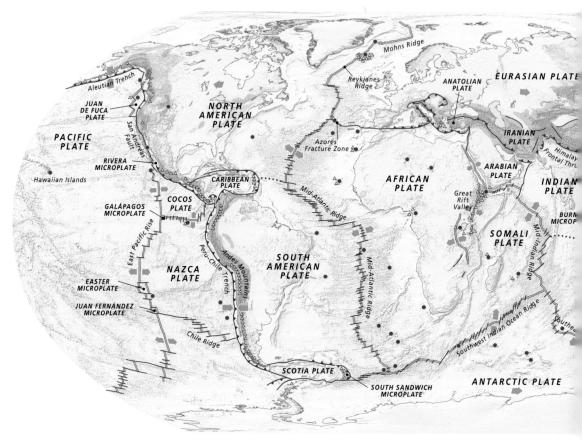

Geological features (below) Earth's constantly moving tectonic plates are responsible for many of its large-scale geological features.

Undersea collision
Arcs of volcanic islands occur where two ocean plates collide and one subducts beneath the other.

Mid-ocean ridge
New ocean crust is formed by volcanic activity at divergent plate boundaries, fed by the upwelling mantle underneath.

Hot-spot volcanoes
Volcanic activity away from plate boundaries is caused by the unusually hot mantle in spots beneath the interiors of the plates.

Coastal collision
Arcs of volcanic mountains occur where an oceanic plate collides with a continent and subducts beneath it.

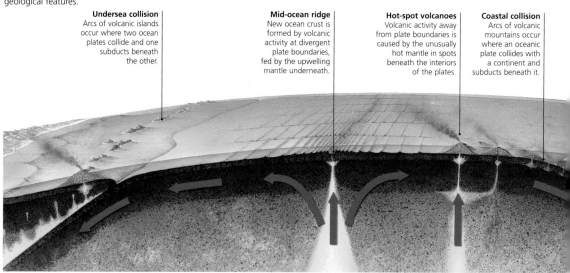

Collision and subduction (right) Where moving continents collide, the plates crumple like a tablecloth pushed together from two ends. When an ocean basin collides with a continent, sedimentary rocks on the seabed are thrust upward.

Ocean-to-ocean subduction This kind of plate movement forms a deep trench where one plate descends, and an arc of volcanic islands on the overriding plate.

Fijian Islands

Tongan Islands

Deep-ocean trench

Indo–Australian Plate

Pacific Plate

Continent-to-continent boundary When continental plates collide, they cause Earth's crust to thicken and fold, uplifting the land into great mountain ranges.

Himalayas

Tarim Basin

Plateau of Tibet

Bay of Bengal

Eurasian Plate

Indo–Australian Plate

Ocean-to-continent boundary Colliding oceanic and continental plates form a deep trench where the more dense oceanic plate descends, and a line of subduction volcanoes on the continental plate.

Chimborazo volcano

Amazon Basin

The Andes

Galápagos Islands

South American Plate

Peru–Chile Trench

Nazca Plate

Sliding plates Transform faults occur where plates move past each other. Zones that slide poorly occasionally stick, then unfreeze and produce earthquakes.

Continental rift The pulling apart of a continental mass forms a deep valley that sometimes continues to thin, until seafloor spreading forms a new ocean basin.

Folding crust Colliding continental plates cause great thickening and crumpling of the crust, which results in high mountains.

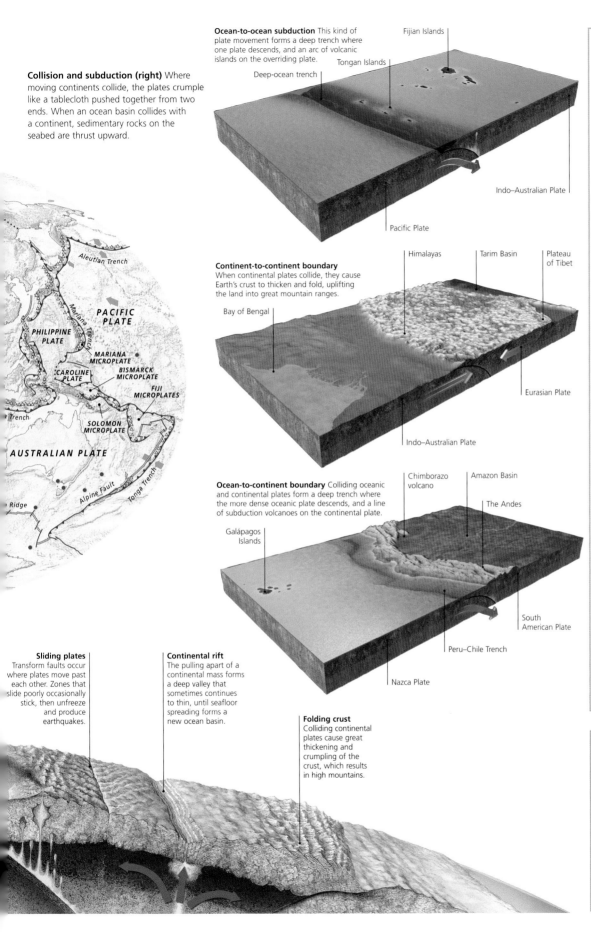

Aleutian Trench

PACIFIC PLATE

Mariana Trench

PHILIPPINE PLATE

MARIANA MICROPLATE

CAROLINE PLATE

BISMARCK MICROPLATE

FIJI MICROPLATES

SOLOMON MICROPLATE

AUSTRALIAN PLATE

Trench

Ridge

Alpine Fault

Tonga Trench

The Pacific Plate

Most of the Pacific Ocean is floored by this giant plate. It is home to thousands of volcanic isles, islets, atolls, and submerged mountains, or seamounts. Early Melanesian, Polynesian, and Chinese seafarers steered their course among these features, followed by Europeans seeking a sea route around the globe.

1. Challenger Deep Formed by the subduction of the Pacific Plate, this deepest part of the world's oceans is in the Mariana Trench and extends nearly 36,000 feet (11,000 m) below

sea level. In 1960, a two-man crew inside the U.S. Navy's submersible Trieste descended into Challenger Deep.

Challenger Deep, Mariana Trench

2. Hawaii–Emperor chain This linear volcanic chain stretches across more than 3,040 miles (4,900 km) of the North Pacific seafloor. It records 85 million years of volcanism at an almost

fixed spot in the Pacific Plate, currently near the Big Island of Hawaii, where the youngest and largest islands sit.

Hawaii-Emperor island and seamount chain

3. San Francisco–La Paz A thin sliver of continent running from La Paz to San Francisco forms the largest contiguous landmass above sea level on the Pacific Plate. It formed about

5 million years ago when the East Pacific Rise began to dissect a margin of the North American plate.

San Francisco–La Paz, North and South America

4. East Pacific Rise Earth's fast-spreading ocean ridge system lies just south of Easter Island, where the Pacific and Nazca plates are pulling apart at a rate of more than 8 inches (20 cm)

per year. Volcanism is very frequent with new lava flows being mapped by marine scientists on repeat visits.

East Pacific Rise at 30° south

5. Mauna Loa volcano This is Earth's largest and most active volcano. In the past 200 years, Mauna Loa has erupted 39 times—most recently in 1984. This

huge shield volcano is 60 miles long by 30 miles wide (95 x 50 km), and covers half Hawaii's Big Island.

Mauan Loa volcano, Hawaii, U.S.A.

Mauna Kea Thin air and low light pollution at the 13,700-foot-(4,200-m)-high summit of this dormant volcano in Hawaii, U.S.A., make it an ideal location for the world's largest astronomical observatories.

South Pacific The western and central tropical portions of the Pacific Plate contain many volcanic islands fringed by coral reefs and calm marine lagoons that have inspired writers and painters with their tranquillity.

Mitre Peak Rising 5,540 feet (1,692 m), this mountain has one of the many tall and sheer rock faces that line the 9 miles (15 km) of Milford Sound on New Zealand's Tasman Sea coast.

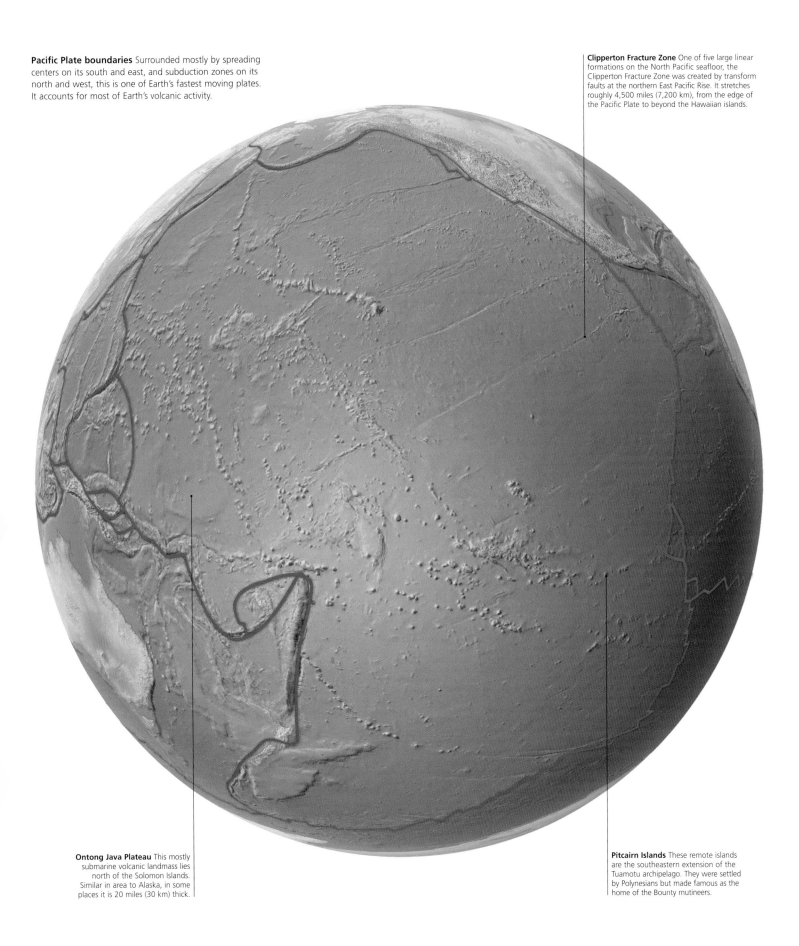

Pacific Plate boundaries Surrounded mostly by spreading centers on its south and east, and subduction zones on its north and west, this is one of Earth's fastest moving plates. It accounts for most of Earth's volcanic activity.

Clipperton Fracture Zone One of five large linear formations on the North Pacific seafloor, the Clipperton Fracture Zone was created by transform faults at the northern East Pacific Rise. It stretches roughly 4,500 miles (7,200 km), from the edge of the Pacific Plate to beyond the Hawaiian islands.

Ontong Java Plateau This mostly submarine volcanic landmass lies north of the Solomon Islands. Similar in area to Alaska, in some places it is 20 miles (30 km) thick.

Pitcairn Islands These remote islands are the southeastern extension of the Tuamotu archipelago. They were settled by Polynesians but made famous as the home of the Bounty mutineers.

The African Plate

The continental half of this plate is comprised of several peviously stable elements (cratons) brought together about 550 million years ago when the Gondwana supercontinent formed. The plate is rifting in the east along the Great Rift Valley, possibly because of underlying hot material rising through the mantle—a mantle plume.

Red Sea Separating Africa and Arabia, the Red Sea is part of the Great Rift Valley, which runs north and south of this sea. It is one of three places where the African and Eurasian plates are moving apart. As they continue to separate, the sea may eventually become an ocean the size of the Atlantic.

Baobab trees These trees are native to the African and Australian plates. The greatest number of species occurs in Madagascar. Baobabs can store large quantities of water in their trunks, and only lose their leaves in the driest season of the year.

African savanna This vast tropical grassland, scattered with shrubs and occasional trees, stretches across central Africa and along its east side. It supports many unique plants and animals.

African Plate boundaries This plate is made up of continental crust in Africa and oceanic crust in the Indian, Atlantic, and Southern oceans. It is slowly moving northward. The northern boundary contains transform and convergent margins.

The Arabian Plate This is a relatively small feature whose collision with the Eurasian Plate is causing the uplift of Iran's Zagros Mountains. It was part of the African Plate until rifting of the Red Sea in the Oligocene epoch, some time between 33 and 23 million years ago.

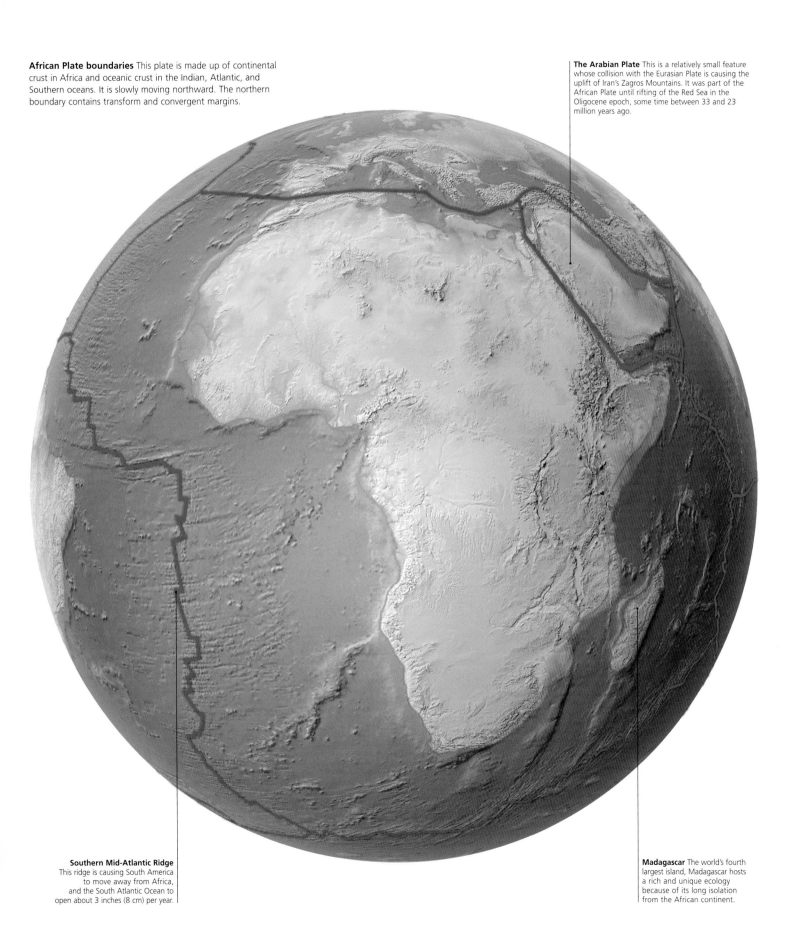

Southern Mid-Atlantic Ridge This ridge is causing South America to move away from Africa, and the South Atlantic Ocean to open about 3 inches (8 cm) per year.

Madagascar The world's fourth largest island, Madagascar hosts a rich and unique ecology because of its long isolation from the African continent.

The Eurasian Plate

This vast continental landmass stretches from Western Europe to the middle of Siberia, and from the Arctic Ocean to tropical Indonesia. It has experienced a widely variable natural and geological history, and supports the largest number of Earth's human inhabitants.

The Himalayas
Earth's tallest mountain system was formed during the collision of the Indian subcontinent and Asia, between 50 and 70 million years ago. The mountains here experience the full range of climate zones, from tropical habitats at their base to arctic regions at the highest elevations.

Guilin Karst
Strange limestone peaks and hills rise from the landscape in China's Guangxi Zhuang Autonomous Region. Formed of heavily eroded marine carbonate sediments, now exposed on land, karst landscapes have many caverns, caves, and sinkholes.

Mosel River Although formally a tributary of the Rhine, this river flows for 340 miles (545 km) through France, Luxembourg, and Germany. It winds through one of Europe's richest wine-growing regions.

Eurasian Plate boundaries This plate extends eastward from Iceland and the Mid-Atlantic Ridge to the Pacific Ocean. It touches the North American Plate across its entire northern boundary, and multiple other plates across its southern boundary.

Siberian Traps Earth's largest known continental flood basalt province was formed from extensive volcanic eruptions that took place over a few million years between the Permian and Triassic periods. Today, they cover some 770,000 square miles (2 million km²).

Mediterranean Sea
The Mediterranean Sea and its bordering mountain ranges were shaped by the collision of the Eurasian and African plates.

South China Sea This oil-rich marginal sea formed about 45 million years ago. It holds large amounts of sediment deposited by the Mekong, Pearl, and Red rivers.

The Australian Plate

The Australian Plate includes the Australian continent, islands to the north and west, parts of New Zealand, and a vast area of the Indian Ocean south of the Java Trench. Some of Earth's oldest rocks and oldest-known fossils are found in Australia.

The Pinnacles These limestone formations in Western Australia were created by the erosion of sand dunes made from marine fossil-bearing sediments. Plants once lived on the dunes and contributed to calcite cementation of interior columns, which have since been exposed by the erosion of softer dune material.

Uluru Also known as Ayers Rock, this large formation of coarse-grained sandstone is the last remaining piece of a huge alluvial fan that was produced by the erosion of predominantly granite terrain. It stands as an isolated remnant eroded from an initially much larger structure.

Tasman Sea This large body of water between Australia and New Zealand is part of the South Pacific Ocean. It includes the Lord Howe Island group, Ball's Pyramid, and Norfolk Island.

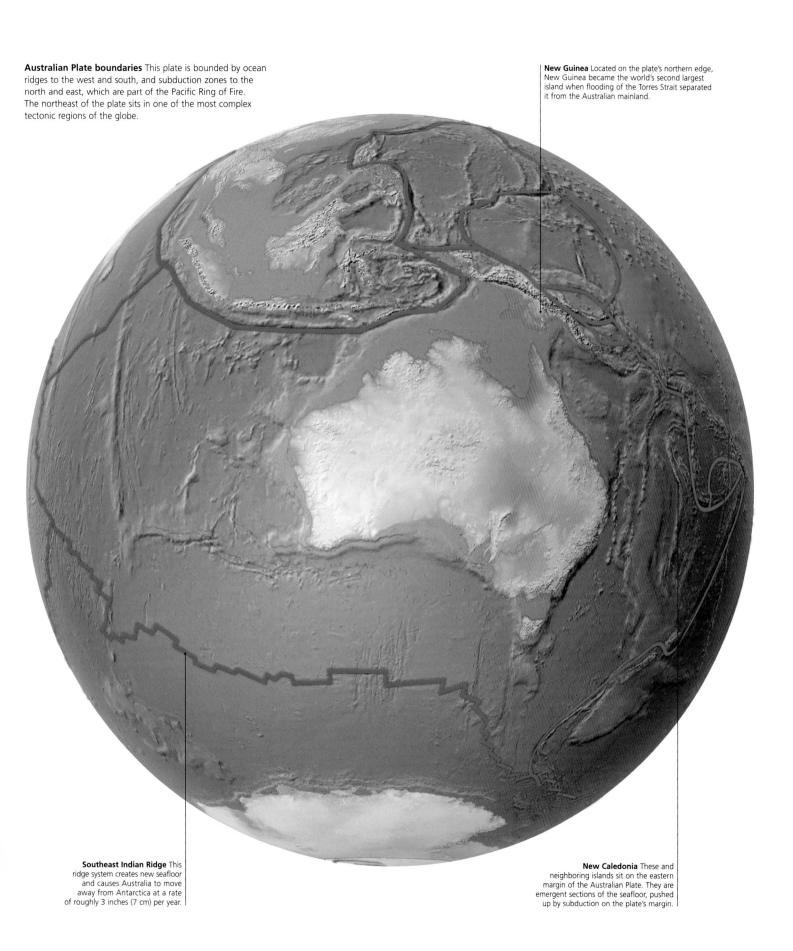

Australian Plate boundaries This plate is bounded by ocean ridges to the west and south, and subduction zones to the north and east, which are part of the Pacific Ring of Fire. The northeast of the plate sits in one of the most complex tectonic regions of the globe.

New Guinea Located on the plate's northern edge, New Guinea became the world's second largest island when flooding of the Torres Strait separated it from the Australian mainland.

Southeast Indian Ridge This ridge system creates new seafloor and causes Australia to move away from Antarctica at a rate of roughly 3 inches (7 cm) per year.

New Caledonia These and neighboring islands sit on the eastern margin of the Australian Plate. They are emergent sections of the seafloor, pushed up by subduction on the plate's margin.

The Antarctic Plate

The South Pole, Antarctic continent, and the surrounding seas of the Southern Ocean are all located on this plate. Rocks with fossils of tropical flora have been found here, proof of the plate's former location in a pleasant climate zone. Today, a thick ice sheet covers roughly 98 percent of the Antarctic continent and is Earth's largest single continuous ice mass.

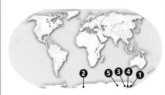

Icebergs These large chunks of freshwater ice are calved from the marine ice shelves that surround Antarctica. Icebergs float freely in the open ocean. Most of their mass sits below seawater, but the tip of an iceberg emerges because its density is lower than that of seawater.

Weddell Sea This sea is part of the Southern Ocean and is a huge bay bounded by the Antarctic Peninsula and Coats Land. It is an important part of the deep global ocean circulation system, as cool saline surface waters sink here.

McMurdo Station This is the largest human settlement in Antarctica, and is operated by the U.S. National Science Foundation to promote scientific study of the region. It sits on the southern tip of Ross Island and can house more than 1,200 residents at a time.

Antarctic Plate boundaries This tectonic plate is almost surrounded by rifting plate boundaries. It is moving slowly, at about 0.5 inch (1.5 cm) per year, toward the Atlantic Ocean. In the middle of the Cretaceous period, it began to rift from Australia and opened up the Tasman Sea.

Southwest Indian Ridge The super slow- spreading Southwest Indian Ridge forms the boundary between the Antarctic and African plates. Its unusual structure includes areas where deep crustal rocks and shallow mantle rocks occur at the surface.

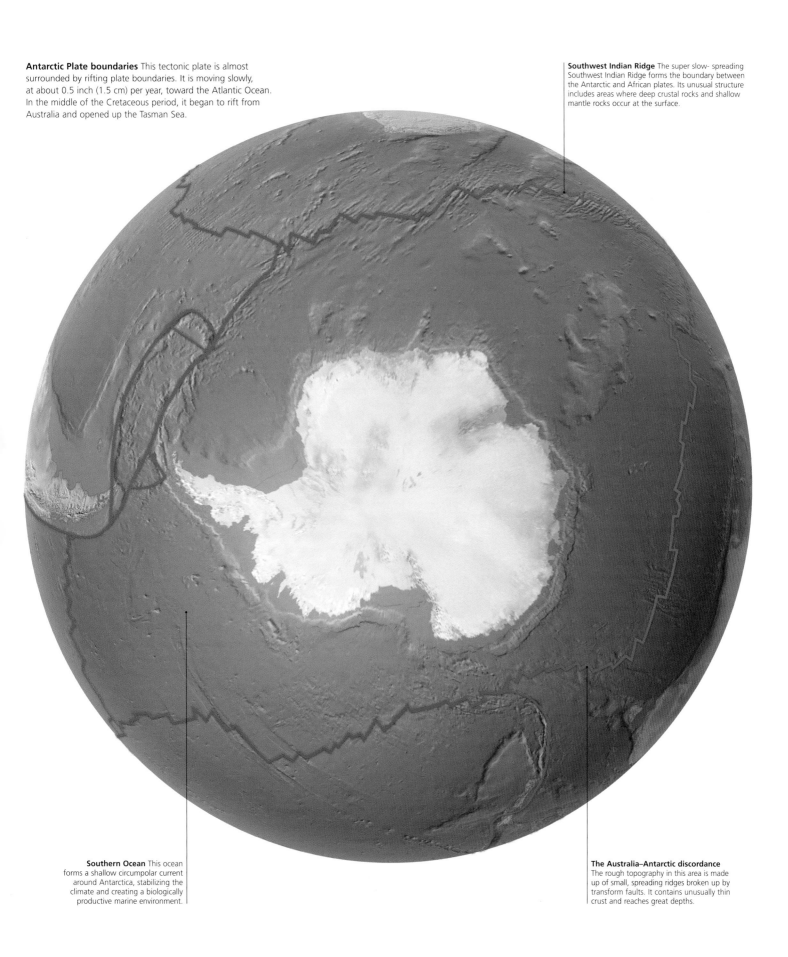

Southern Ocean This ocean forms a shallow circumpolar current around Antarctica, stabilizing the climate and creating a biologically productive marine environment.

The Australia–Antarctic discordance The rough topography in this area is made up of small, spreading ridges broken up by transform faults. It contains unusually thin crust and reaches great depths.

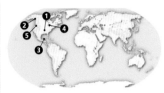
1. Mississippi River Including its tributaries, this is North America's longest river system. It stretches from the center of the continent to the Gulf of Mexico. The complete Jefferson-

Missouri-Mississippi river system is 3,900 miles (6,275 km) long and drains the world's third-largest river catchment.

Mississippi River, U.S.A.

2. Western Cordillera These almost continuous mountain ranges and basins extend along the western boundary of the North American plate. With its sister ranges in South America,

the Cordillera makes up the eastern side of the Pacific Ring of Fire, which accounts for much of Earth's active volcanism.

Western Cordillera, Canada and U.S.A.

3. Yucatán Peninsula This formation of deeply eroded limestone is riddled with caves, sinkholes, and groundwater, although it has no rivers or lakes. A crater in the north of the peninsula, dated to

65 million years old, is believed to be the site of an ancient asteroid impact that led to the extinction of the dinosaurs.

Yucatán Peninsula, Mexico

4. The Great Lakes Together, these five lakes represent almost 25 percent of Earth's surface fresh water and are the largest group of freshwater lakes on Earth. The Great Lakes

formed about 10,000 years ago, at the end of the last ice age, as the Laurentide Ice Sheet receded.

The Great Lakes, Canada and U.S.A.

5. Columbia River flood basalt One of the largest preserved flood basalts, this igneous province covers about 63,000 square miles (164,000 km²).

It formed during 10 to 15 million years of volcanism, related to the same hot spot that now sits near Yellowstone Caldera.

Columbia River flood basalt, Washington, Oregon, and Idaho, U.S.A.

The North American Plate

From Central America to Greenland, Canada, and eastern Siberia, the North American Plate presents a great variety of geologic and geographic features. Its eastern margin bears the marks of ancient continental collisions and contains Earth's oldest rocks, while mountains on the west are evidence of more than 100 years of boundary collisions and volcanic activity.

Bryce Canyon
The multihued rocks of this large amphitheater in Utah, U.S.A., record the geologic history of sedimentary deposition by wind and water during the Cretaceous period and Cenozoic era. Different rock types and extensive erosion have created unique rock forms.

Death Valley
This deep valley in California and Nevada includes the lowest elevation in North America—282 feet (86 m) below sea level. It owes its great depth and topography to basin (valley) and range (mountain) extension that dominates much of the region.

Mount McKinley
Also known as Denali, this Alaskan mountain is North America's tallest at 20,320 feet (6,194 m). It is composed mostly of granite and sits within a band of exotic terrain that became attached to the continent during the Cenozoic era.

North American Plate boundaries This large plate covers North America and part of the northwest Atlantic Ocean. It includes some of Earth's oldest rocks and the current position of the magnetic North Pole.

Greenland Ice Sheet This thick continental glacier accounts for 5 percent of the fresh water on Earth. The weight of the ice sheet depresses the landmass beneath it as deep as 1,000 feet (300 m) below sea level.

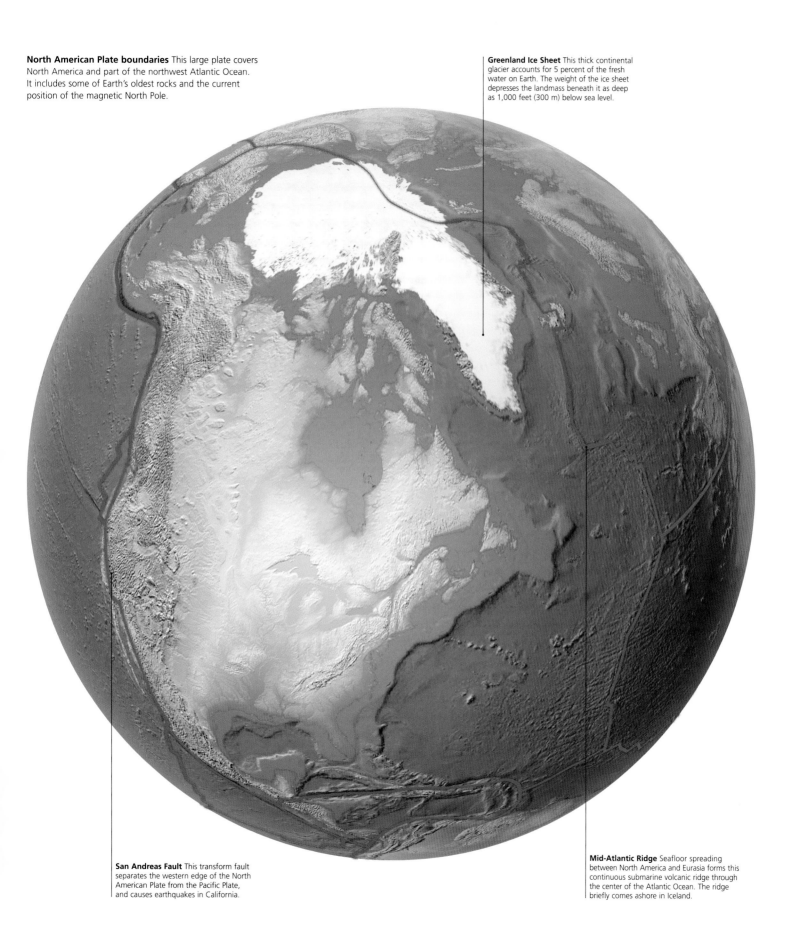

San Andreas Fault This transform fault separates the western edge of the North American Plate from the Pacific Plate, and causes earthquakes in California.

Mid-Atlantic Ridge Seafloor spreading between North America and Eurasia forms this continuous submarine volcanic ridge through the center of the Atlantic Ocean. The ridge briefly comes ashore in Iceland.

The South American Plate

The continental half of the South American Plate stretches from the tropical Caribbean Sea to its southern tip at Cape Horn, where icy waters are just 620 miles (1,000 km) from the Antarctic Circle, and includes the full range of Earth's climate zones. The other half of the plate lies under the Atlantic Ocean.

Mount Aconcagua
This is the world's highest peak outside the Himalayas. Located in the Argentine Andes, it was built from multiple kinds of rocks, which were tectonically uplifted to their present elevation.

Patagonian glacier
Hundreds of mountain glaciers in southern Argentina carve deep valleys into the eastern Andes as they make their way to the lowlands.

Torres del Paine This national park in Chile is part of the Andes mountain chain and contains glaciers, lakes, rivers, and extensive wildlife. At the center of the park is the Paine Massif, which consists of granite and metamorphosed sedimentary rocks.

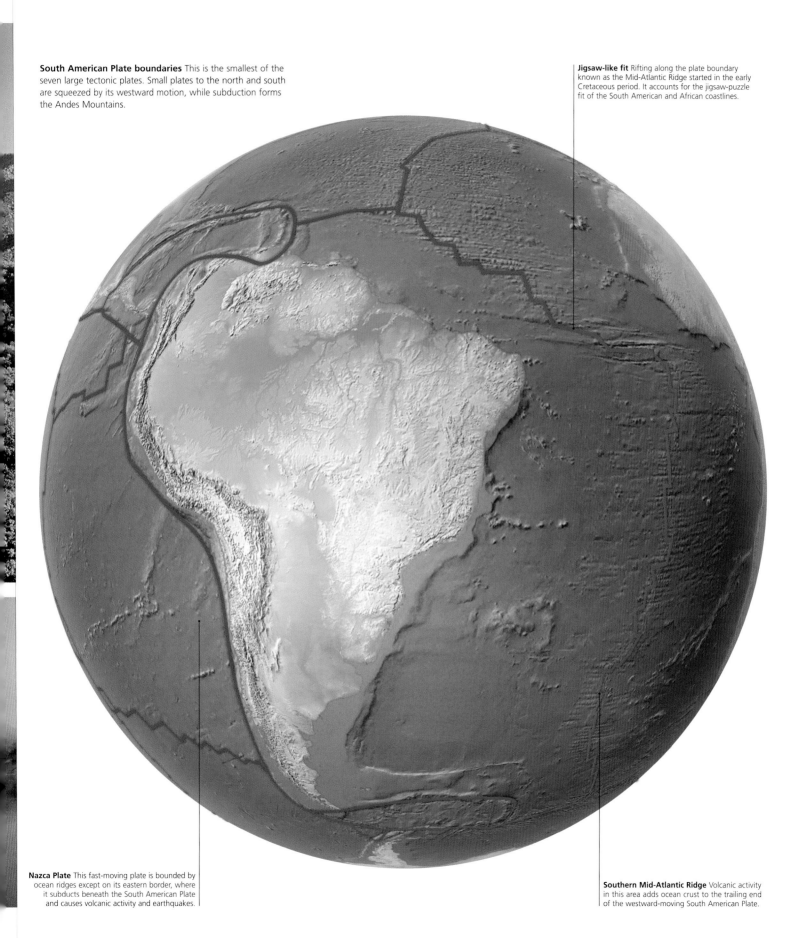

South American Plate boundaries This is the smallest of the seven large tectonic plates. Small plates to the north and south are squeezed by its westward motion, while subduction forms the Andes Mountains.

Jigsaw-like fit Rifting along the plate boundary known as the Mid-Atlantic Ridge started in the early Cretaceous period. It accounts for the jigsaw-puzzle fit of the South American and African coastlines.

Nazca Plate This fast-moving plate is bounded by ocean ridges except on its eastern border, where it subducts beneath the South American Plate and causes volcanic activity and earthquakes.

Southern Mid-Atlantic Ridge Volcanic activity in this area adds ocean crust to the trailing end of the westward-moving South American Plate.

HEAT FROM WITHIN

Earth is an energetic planet. Heat rising from its interior causes volcanic activity, and stresses its crust until the energy is suddenly released, resulting in earthquakes and tsunamis. Constant upheaval within the hot mantle forms new crust on the seafloor at spreading centers, and drives the movement of continental crust over the surface. Heat that builds up as plates scrape together during subduction is disssipated by volcanoes and earthquakes in zones where material returns to the mantle. All this action constantly changes the landforms and rock masses found on the surface.

BELOW THE SURFACE

One look at a physical map of the globe shows that there is a certain order in the arrangement of large-scale features. Mountains generally line up in belts that protrude through the otherwise gently sloping continental plains, while most volcanoes are arranged in lines or along curved paths. Where a continent meets the sea, either thick accumulations of sediment descend to the seafloor or there are narrow seabed trenches parallel to the coast, with a line of volcanoes on the adjacent continents. Running through each ocean basin is a great, yet mostly submerged, mountain range with long, wide, parallel cracks moving away from it.

Since the advent of the plate tectonics theory, Earth scientists have understood that all these features share a common characteristic: they all mark the present or former boundaries of the great lithospheric plates that move over the planet's surface. These are the zones where most of Earth's volcanic and earthquake activity, or seismicity, is concentrated. The Pacific Ocean is surrounded by such active plate margins, forming what is often called the Pacific Ring of Fire.

There are no plate boundaries on the continental coasts of the Atlantic Ocean, making these continental margins for the most part volcanically and seismically inactive. Yet volcanoes and earthquakes do sometimes occur away from the plate boundaries, either as a response to built-up stress in the plates, or as a result of the upwelling of hot mantle from below at "hot spots."

All the geologically active sites on the planet demonstrate that Earth is doing its best to get rid of excess heat. In fact, one possible future could see Earth as a cold, inactive rock after all its heat is disssipated. Today there are no signs that the internal convection is slowing down, but almost certainly the churnings and rumblings were greater in the distant past, when there was even more interior heat within the planet.

Molten rock (below) This glowing, red-hot mass is lava flowing down the slopes of Mount Etna, a volcano in Italy. Nearly every day, molten lava pours out of one of Earth's many active volcanoes on land, or beneath the sea. It initiates a process that renews the surface of the planet, and brings matter and heat out of the planet's interior.

Skylight (right) Surrounded by insulating solid rock, lava flows through lava tubes, such as this one at Kilauea volcano, Hawaii, U.S.A. Breaks in the tube's upper crust, called skylights, offer volcanologists opportunities to observe the flowing lava.

South American Plate boundaries This is the smallest of the seven large tectonic plates. Small plates to the north and south are squeezed by its westward motion, while subduction forms the Andes Mountains.

Jigsaw-like fit Rifting along the plate boundary known as the Mid-Atlantic Ridge started in the early Cretaceous period. It accounts for the jigsaw-puzzle fit of the South American and African coastlines.

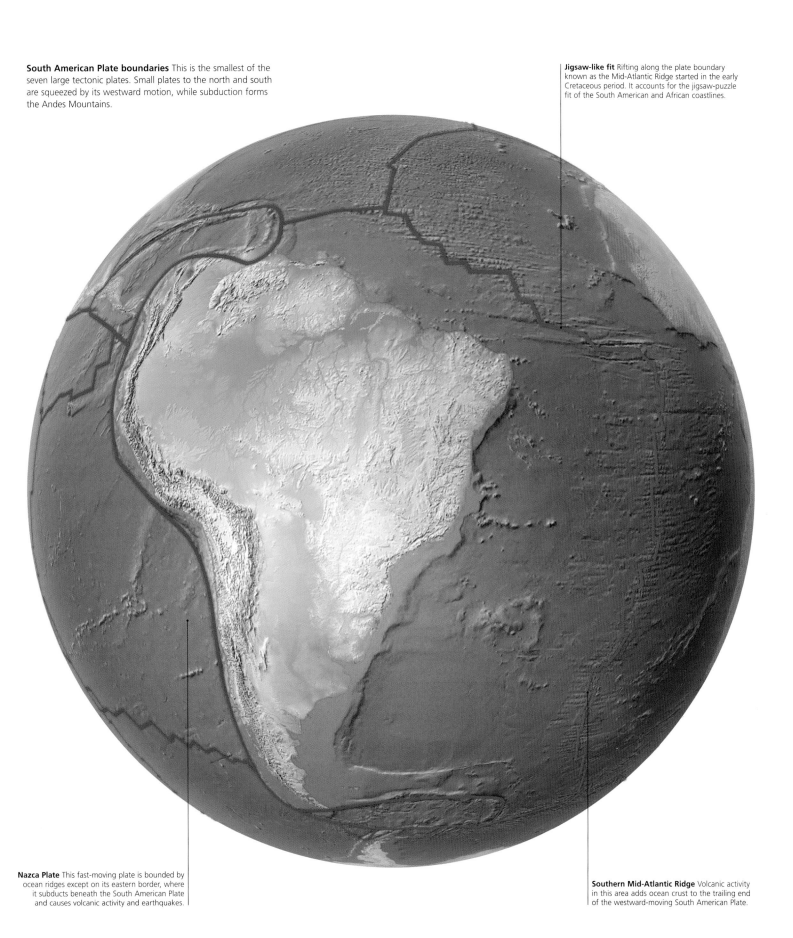

Nazca Plate This fast-moving plate is bounded by ocean ridges except on its eastern border, where it subducts beneath the South American Plate and causes volcanic activity and earthquakes.

Southern Mid-Atlantic Ridge Volcanic activity in this area adds ocean crust to the trailing end of the westward-moving South American Plate.

Drift and the Living World

The term continental drift refers to the theory that the continents have not always been in their present positions. Its origins go back at least five centuries, but it was widely accepted only in the 1960s as part of the broader theory of plate tectonics, which provides an explanation for the slow rearrangement of the lithosphere throughout Earth's history.

Glossopteris Similar fossils of this tree-like plant, which grew on the ancient supercontinent Gondwana, have been found on both the east coast of South America and the west coast of Africa.

Cycads The three families of distinctively coned cycads are now widely distributed throughout tropical and temperate Australia, Malaysia, South Africa, and the Americas.

Coral trees The presence of these trees in both the Americas and Africa is sometimes cited as evidence of continental drift.

A land apart (below) Australia drifted away from Antarctica 40 million years ago and has been isolated ever since. Australia's separation from other major landmasses is a major reason why its flora and fauna are so different from those of other regions.

Wallace Line In the 19th century, naturalist Alfred Russel Wallace identified a boundary dividing the Indonesian archipelago into eastern and western regions. Fauna in the west were similar to those in continental Asia, while the eastern islands had species that resembled Australian animals.

Land bridge The ebb and flow of global climate over the past two million years has caused the polar ice caps to grow and shrink repeatedly. This in turn has caused sea levels to rise and fall, sometimes flooding and sometimes exposing a land bridge from Australia to New Guinea.

130,000 years ago

90,000 years ago

20,000 years ago

Today

Ancient collision (above and left)
Two ancient continents drifted toward each other and collided 500 million years ago. They formed a mountain range that extended north from the Adirondacks in the eastern U.S.A. through Nova Scotia, Canada, Greenland, Britain, and Norway. Remnants of this once-majestic range have been left in each of these lands. They include the Great Smoky Mountains of Tennessee, U.S.A., (above) and the cool arctic peaks on the island of Spitsbergen, Norway (left).

FACT FILE

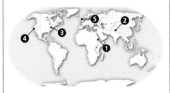

1. Keraf Suture This major fault zone represents the collision of two continental fragments 650 to 600 million years ago, as Gondwana formed. The mountains that were

built probably rivaled today's Himalayas in size. Part of the Nile River now flows along this zone.

Keraf Suture, Sudan

2. Himalayas These mountains resulted from the buckling and thickening of continental crust that started when India drifted into Asia some 50 million years ago. Because

continental crust is too light to subduct back into the mantle, collisions like this cause it to pile into huge mountain belts.

Himalayas, Bhutan, China, India, Nepal, Pakistan, and Afghanistan

3. Appalachian Mountains
Roughly 350 to 300 million years ago, Gondwana and North America collided to form the supercontinent Pangea, creating a huge mountain belt. Today

the deeply eroded Appalachians contain rocks that betray the huge forces involved in continental collisions.

Appalachian Mountains, Pennsylvania, U.S.A.

4. San Francisco The rocks of California's coastal ranges are typical of accreted terrain—formed by pieces of rock uplifted in a collision between continental and oceanic plates. The mix

of marine sediment, volcanic rock, and metamorphosed rock was plastered here as recently as 40 million years ago.

San Francisco, California, U.S.A.

5. Grenville remnant A continental collision during the formation of the supercontinent Rodinia, some 1.3 to 1 billion years ago, produced a

mountain belt that once extended from Scotland, through Newfoundland, Canada, to North Carolina, U.S.A.

Grenville remnant, West Scotland

HEAT FROM WITHIN

Earth is an energetic planet. Heat rising from its interior causes volcanic activity, and stresses its crust until the energy is suddenly released, resulting in earthquakes and tsunamis. Constant upheaval within the hot mantle forms new crust on the seafloor at spreading centers, and drives the movement of continental crust over the surface. Heat that builds up as plates scrape together during subduction is disssipated by volcanoes and earthquakes in zones where material returns to the mantle. All this action constantly changes the landforms and rock masses found on the surface.

BELOW THE SURFACE

One look at a physical map of the globe shows that there is a certain order in the arrangement of large-scale features. Mountains generally line up in belts that protrude through the otherwise gently sloping continental plains, while most volcanoes are arranged in lines or along curved paths. Where a continent meets the sea, either thick accumulations of sediment descend to the seafloor or there are narrow seabed trenches parallel to the coast, with a line of volcanoes on the adjacent continents. Running through each ocean basin is a great, yet mostly submerged, mountain range with long, wide, parallel cracks moving away from it.

Since the advent of the plate tectonics theory, Earth scientists have understood that all these features share a common characteristic: they all mark the present or former boundaries of the great lithospheric plates that move over the planet's surface. These are the zones where most of Earth's volcanic and earthquake activity, or seismicity, is concentrated. The Pacific Ocean is surrounded by such active plate margins, forming what is often called the Pacific Ring of Fire.

There are no plate boundaries on the continental coasts of the Atlantic Ocean, making these continental margins for the most part volcanically and seismically inactive. Yet volcanoes and earthquakes do sometimes occur away from the plate boundaries, either as a response to built-up stress in the plates, or as a result of the upwelling of hot mantle from below at "hot spots."

All the geologically active sites on the planet demonstrate that Earth is doing its best to get rid of excess heat. In fact, one possible future could see Earth as a cold, inactive rock after all its heat is disssipated. Today there are no signs that the internal convection is slowing down, but almost certainly the churnings and rumblings were greater in the distant past, when there was even more interior heat within the planet.

Molten rock (below) This glowing, red-hot mass is lava flowing down the slopes of Mount Etna, a volcano in Italy. Nearly every day, molten lava pours out of one of Earth's many active volcanoes on land, or beneath the sea. It initiates a process that renews the surface of the planet, and brings matter and heat out of the planet's interior.

Skylight (right) Surrounded by insulating solid rock, lava flows through lava tubes, such as this one at Kilauea volcano, Hawaii, U.S.A. Breaks in the tube's upper crust, called skylights, offer volcanologists opportunities to observe the flowing lava.

Volcanoes

Volcanoes dot the landscape of every continent and ocean basin, and are often impressive mountains of fire. No two volcanoes or eruptions are exactly alike, but all active volcanoes spew hot material from one or more vents that connect their interiors with the surface. This material can include molten lava, gas, ash, and solidified rocks called blocks and bombs.

Mount Fuji (inset, below left) At 12,388 feet (3,776 m), this beautiful, cone-shaped stratovolcano is Japan's highest mountain. The dormant volcano last erupted in 1708. Five lakes, including the popular Lake Kawaguchi, surround the volcano.

Cinder cone Mildly explosive eruptions build up cone-shaped hills of volcanic cinders around a central vent. Such eruptions sometimes end with lava flows that can fill the crater.

Composite or stratovolcano These tall, steep-sided volcanoes are formed when multiple eruptions deposit alternating layers of ash and lava. They are admired for their conical shape.

Shield When lava flows radially from a central vent, it creates a shield volcano. These broad volcanoes can form from a single eruption or from many thousands of them.

Fissure and rift A fissure volcano is formed from a linear fracture through which magma has erupted. A rift volcano forms from a combination of eruptions and the spreading of solid rock away from a fissure.

Eruption Hot and viscous magma forms when heat deep inside Earth melts rocks. The magma rises and collects in large, pressurized subterranean chambers (**1**), from which it occasionally erupts. Small crystals begin to form, and water and gas bubbles increase the magma pressure until it pushes open a conduit to the surface (**2**), where it erupts from a central (**3**) or satellite volcanic vent (**4**). Fissure eruptions feed a series of vents aligned with stress cracks in the volcano (**5**). All three types of vents are fed by magma-filled cracks, called dikes (**6**). Eruptions can produce lava flows (**7**) or pyroclastic material (**8**). Steam, gas, and rocks create clouds of smoke during eruptions. Magma that does not reach the surface cools to form a laccolith (**9**).

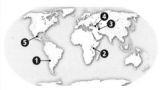
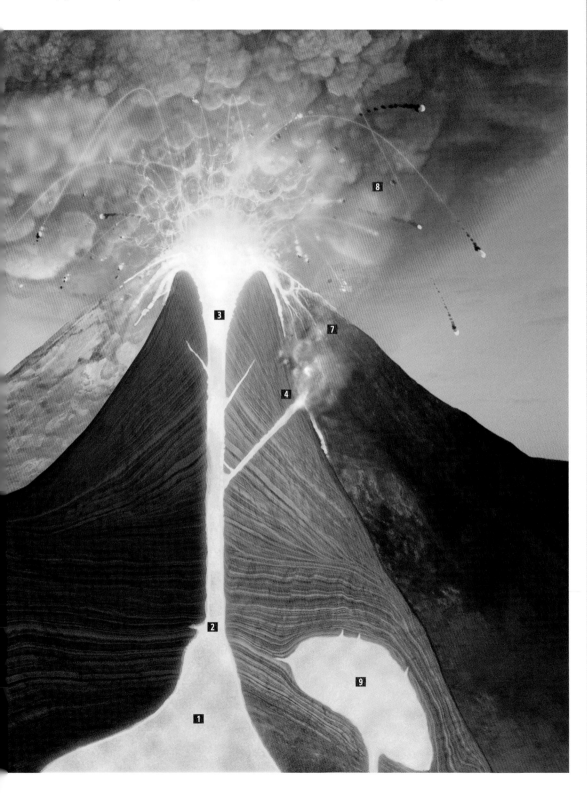

Hawaiian After a gas-rich opening stage that can produce fire fountains up to 3,000 feet (1 km) high, these eruptions produce mainly lava flows and lakes of hot, runny magma. They are named for the Hawaiian Islands.

Strombolian Named for the Italian volcano Stromboli, these eruptions produce explosions of glowing rock that reach up to 600 feet (200 m) in the air, then fall to Earth near the vent.

Vulcanian Named for the Italian volcano Vulcano, these small-volume eruptions can shoot ash and cinders up to an altitude of 15 miles (20 km), dispersing material over a greater area than Strombolian-type eruptions.

Long eruption (right) A fiery lava fountain shoots out in 1983, during early stages of the to date 25-year-long eruption of the Pu'u O'o vent on Kilauea, Hawaii.

Types of Eruptions

Many factors contribute to the diversity of volcanic eruption types, yet all eruptions emit gas, lava, and/or fragmented rock particles, known as pyroclasts, from single or multiple vents along a volcanic fissure. Volcanologists recognize two main eruption types: effusive, when lava flows gently from the volcano; and explosive, when volcanic particles fall out from huge clouds shot violently from the volcano.

Measuring eruptive volume The amount of material ejected by a volcano is often a good indicator of the overall strength of the eruption. The Volcanic Explosivity Index (VEI) is a logarithmic scale used to categorize the size and power of eruptions.

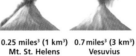

0.25 miles³ (1 km³)	0.7 miles³ (3 km³)	2.4 miles³ (10 km³)	4.25 miles³ (18 km³)	19 miles³ (80 km³)	24 miles³ (100 km³)	670 miles³ (2,800 km³)
Mt. St. Helens	Vesuvius	Pinatubo	Krakatau	Tambora	Taupo	Toba
VEI: 5	VEI: 5	VEI: 6	VEI: 6	VEI: 7	VEI: 8	VEI: 9

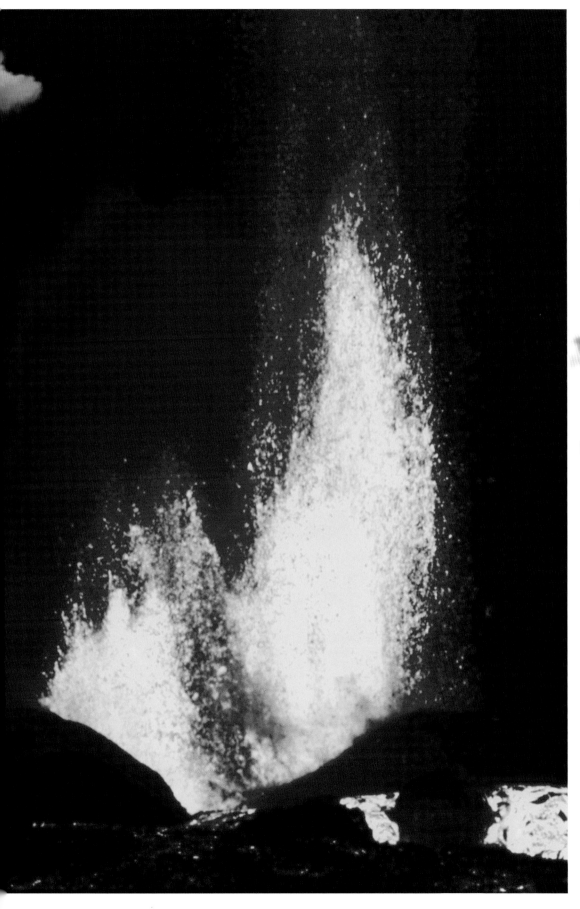

Peleean Named for Mount Pelée on the island of Martinique, these eruptions produce large, fast-moving, gravity-driven flows of hot gas, rock, and ash from the collapse of viscous lava domes.

Plinian These eruptions take their name from Pliny the Younger, a Roman scholar who described the A.D. 79 Mount Vesuvius eruption. Material can shoot up 30 miles (45 km) and disperse widely.

Kilauea (left) The world's most active and studied volcano, in Hawaii, U.S.A., erupted almost 50 times in the last century and has been erupting nearly continuously since 1983.

SURTSEYAN

This type of eruption is named for Surtsey, the Icelandic island formed in 1963. Large quantities of shallow seawater interact with hot magma to build a cone of rock fragments. Sometimes this culminates in less violent activity as the vent is isolated from seawater.

Volcanic Landscapes

Volcanoes have shaped Earth's crust since its birth, producing dramatic mountains, craters, and plateaus, as well as rolling hills, islands, and fertile farmlands. Erupting or recently erupted volcanoes are easy to spot, yet hundreds of millions to billions of years after eruptions have ceased, volcanism still leaves its mark on the landscape.

Ol Doinyo Lengai (right) This steep-sided, African Rift Valley volcano produces an unusual magma type. It is low in temperature, under 1,100°F (600°C), and low in silica, but high in water and carbonate salts of alkali metals.

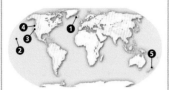

Volcanic island Volcanoes formed under the sea can grow into islands. Seamounts are volcanoes that stop growing before they reach the surface.

Dormant volcano Volcanoes can lie quiet for many centuries between eruptions, allowing plants, animals, and people to live on the rich land in the mountain's shadow. However, volcanoes that awaken infrequently are some of the most dangerous.

Crater lake Volcanic craters and calderas often fill with water. They sometimes take unusual colors and chemistries from volcanic gases and geothermal water that discharge into them.

Volcanic dike These dramatic structures are monuments to long-dead volcanoes whose softer outer layers have eroded away, exposing harder rock from their interior.

Volcanic features (above) The distinctive shapes of young volcanoes, or their eruption deposits, are commonly recognized. Volcanic landforms also occur far from active volcanoes. This imaginary landscape depicts many of the features to be found in ancient and modern volcanic terrains worldwide.

Klyuchevskaya Volcano This tall, steep, symmetrical cone volcano on Russia's Kamchatka Peninsula has been erupting almost continuously since its first detected eruption in 1697. It is one of the most active volcanoes of the region.

Formation of a caldera Calderas develop on the summits of some volcanoes above the eruptive vent. They are large subsidence structures bound by concentric ring faults, along which huge portions of the volcano's summit collapse into the empty magma chamber below.

1 Magma fed into the crust produces a large subterranean magma chamber that erupts when internal pressure is sufficient to crack the overlying rock.

2 A composite volcano forms above the crustal magma chamber after repeated eruptions of ash and/or lava.

3 A powerful eruption evacuates a large portion of the chamber volume, leaving a void below the heavy volcanic cone.

4 A caldera forms when the magma chamber roof collapses along ring faults into this void, leaving a flat-floored depression.

UNDERSTANDING VOLCANOES

The history of volcano observation is as long as the history of human culture. Volcanic eruptions represent one of the most immediate and recognizable manifestations of the internal life of our restless planet, yet volcanoes can remain dormant for tens of thousands of years between eruptions. Volcanic eruptions can be both beautiful and devastating displays of natural force. For a short while after an eruption, volcanic landscapes can seem lifeless, but with time they often develop into fertile oases. Mountains built of volcanic ejecta are places of natural grandeur, but they present multiple hazards, even when not erupting. For all these reasons, volcanoes are worthy of our constant attention.

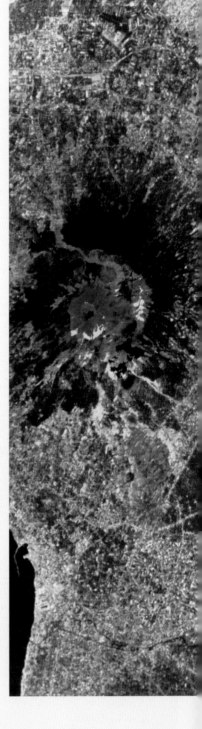

Early thinking Jesuit scholar Athanasius Kircher's *Mundus Subterraneus*, published in 1665, offered one of the earliest theories on the cause of volcanism. He theorized that a great fiery chamber lay at Earth's core and was connected to numerous other such chambers. He formulated his ideas after observing active volcanoes in Italy, including mounts Vesuvius and Etna.

Hazard mapping (right) Volcanologists map volcano hazards by comparing land-use patterns with the distribution and age of volcanic products, such as lava flows, ash flows, pyroclastics flows, and lahars. This false-color, infrared aerial view of Vesuvius and its surroundings shows volcanic ash (purple), lavas (pink and light blues), and vegetation and towns.

MYTHS AND SCIENCE

Humans have been living with volcanoes for countless millenia. Some cave paintings, such as the 6000 B.C. example at Çatal Höyük in Turkey, depict volcanic eruptions. Along with danger, volcanoes provided our distant ancestors with fertile soils and useful materials such as obsidian, which was highly valued by some Stone Age cultures for making tools, weapons, mirrors, and jewelry.

For most of human history, cultures as diverse as the Sumerians, Egyptians, Polynesians, and Norse had only religious explanations for volcanic activity. The ancient Greeks were the first people known to seek natural explanations for volcanoes. But it was not until the "Age of Reason," in the 17th century, that scientific thinking began to play a major role in Western discourse on volcanism. By the 19th century the science of volcanology had taken hold among many geologists and naturalists.

However, it was only midway through the 20th century that volcanology took on significant

predictive power. Scientists began to understand how frequently and with what style a particular volcano might erupt, and why volcanoes do or do not occur in different parts of the world. The latter question was only satisfactorily answered by plate tectonics theory in the 1960s.

Twenty-first century volcanology involves the real-time monitoring of volcanoes with instrument observatories and satellites, and the microbeam geochemical analysis of microscopic pieces of volcanic rocks and crystals. Specialists can date an eruption from the close examination of samples of hardened magma, as well as discover the temperature, pressure, and chemical variations in the magma just before eruption. Sophisticated computer modeling allows the modern volcanologist to understand the interplay between the wide array of physical and chemical phenomena that contribute to the unique qualities of each volcano on the planet. All of this information adds to our understanding of the different volcanic hazards, which in turn helps to protect human life.

Vesuvius erupts again (below) The high fountain of lava when Mount Vesuvius erupted on August 8, 1779, is depicted in this image. It was the culmination of an eruptive episode that began in 1770. Ash and bombs were deposited on the city of Ottaviano, just northeast of the volcano.

THROUGH THE AGES

A.D. 79 Accounts of a Vesuvius eruption were written in a letter by Pliny the Younger to the historian Tacitus. They described the eruption cloud and pyroclastic flows that buried Pompeii and Herculaneum.

1763 French geologist Desmarest discovered the volcanic origin of basalt lavaflows in Auvergne by tracing them to nearby ancient volcanoes—disproving the theory that such rocks were formed by sedimentation in primeval oceans.

1804 Scottish geologist Gregory Watt's studies on the cooling of melted basalt showed that the transition from a solid with a glassy, vitreous texture to one with a crystalline texture depends on the rate of cooling.

1805 Scottish natural scientist James Hutton's *Theory of Earth*, presented the idea that volcanism and volcanic intrusion created some surface rocks, including granite found penetrating metamorphic rocks.

1840–50s From his observations during the 1830s *Beagle* expedition, Charles Darwin proposed that as a volcanic island ages the volcano sinks, and the island's coral reef changes from fringing to barrier reef, then to atoll.

1849 American geologist James Dana wrote extensively on Hawaiian volcanoes, proposing that erosion and subsidence reflect age progression along linear volcanic island groups—more than a century before hot spot theory.

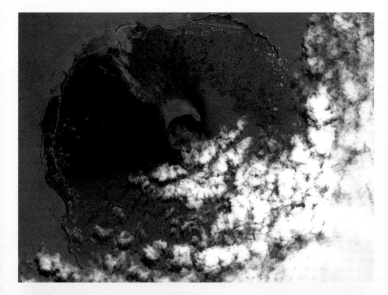

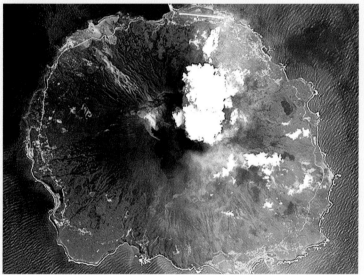

Ash deposition (above) These thermal emission and reflection images were collected by satellite 48 days apart during an eruption of Mount Oyama in the summer of 2000. They show the Japanese island volcano's heavily vegetated slopes (red), becoming increasingly coated in volcanic ash (dark gray). The caldera of the stratovolcano is visible in the earlier (top) image, but is mostly obscured by a steam plume (white) in the image below it. These images help volcanologists study ash deposition patterns so that they can better understand eruption hazards.

Into the fire (right) Many studies of erupting volcanoes are conducted at a distance, but it is sometimes necessary to make observations closer to the action. Here, a volcanologist in heat-protective clothing approaches an active fire fountain at Italy's Mount Etna, a persistently active volcano that emits lava and pyroclastics from at least one of three summit craters, and from flank vents. In the past, lava has flowed down all sides of the volcano and reached the sea on the southeastern flank. Measuring lava temperature, effusion rates, and gas content is a way to understand evolving hazards.

1928 Experiments on the pressure and temperature of magma and crystal formation were conducted by Norman Bowen and colleagues at the Carnegie Geophysical Lab, and published in *Evolution of the Igneous Rocks*.

1944 Icelandic volcanologist Sigurdur Thorarinsson completed his doctoral thesis showing how layers of volcanic ash linked to specific eruptions can be used to date nearby volcanic and other strata.

1950s–80s British volcanologist G.P.L. Walker pioneered the use of quantitative field measurements and mathematical studies of volcanic deposits to understand hazards, lava flows, and ash dispersal from volcanic explosions.

1969–72 Scientists studied moon rocks returned to Earth by Apollo missions 11 to 17, and determined that the mostly volcanic rocks were 3.5 to 4.5 billion years old.

1980 The USGS Volcano Hazards Program took its pioneering earthquake-monitoring program of Hawaiian volcanoes to Mount St. Helens, and to other volcanoes thereafter, improving early warning capability.

1990s Earth-orbiting satellites became important tools for monitoring active volcanoes, including eruption cloud tracking, measuring volcanic hot zones, studying ground movements, and measuring volcanic gas emission.

Volcanoes, Past and Present

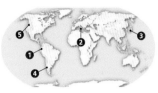

At once beautiful, dangerous, life-giving, and mysterious, volcanoes have captured the interest of many of the world's civilizations, and form the basis of many society-changing events throughout history and prehistoric mythology. Many civilizations were born in the fertile soils of a volcanic landscape. Although some volcanoes are active only once, the vast majority have experienced hundreds, if not thousands, of eruptions during their geological histories. The stories written in their volcanic deposits allow volcanologists to understand the size,

1. Cotopaxi This stratovolcano near Quito has experienced 50 eruptions since 1738, the latest confirmed one ending in 1904. Between 1975 and 1976 there were enhanced steam emissions and small quakes, and in 1877 a summit eruption melted snow and ice, and mud flowed for 60 miles (100 km).

Cotopaxi, Ecuador

2. Stromboli This volcano forms one of the Aeolian Islands, rising 2,900 feet (900 m) above the Tyrrhenian Sea. It is one of Earth's most active volcanoes, erupting nearly continuously for at least 2,000 years. Most eruptions involve frequent, small gas explosions that throw lava bombs out of the summit crater.

Stromboli, Italy

3. Mount Fuji Stunningly conical, this stratovolcano has experienced 16 moderate or larger-sized eruptions since A.D. 781. The most recent in 1707–08 created a noticeable flank crater. This and four other eruptions have damaged nearby structures, but no fatalities have been recorded.

Mount Fuji, Japan

4. Villarrica This active Andean basaltic stratovolcano is a known killer, having produced four fatal eruptions in 1949, 1963, 1964, and 1971. In each case the fatalities were from hot mud-flows that raced down the volcano flanks. The first of 55 small-to-moderate-sized historical eruptions occured in 1558.

Villarrica, Chile

5. Mount Rainier This highest volcano of the Cascade Range is deeply covered in ice and snow. Although erosion has been greater than volcano growth in the last 100,000 years, and its last eruption was about 2,200 years ago, it is still thought to be potentially dangerous.

Mount Rainier, Washington, U.S.A.

style, and frequency of eruptions, as well as the general hazards associated with a particular volcano—information that becomes increasingly important as the world's burgeoning population inches closer and closer to these mountains of fire.

Pinatubo explosion During the 1991 eruption of this volcano in the Philippines, searing clouds of gas and rock, called a pyroclastic flow, rushed down its flanks. The highly explosive eruption occurred nearly 500 years after the last-known eruption. Many local residents did not know the volcano was still active.

Famous volcanoes Volcanoes that capture the attention of visitors and residents are spread throughout the world. They come in a large variety of shapes and sizes, yet all share a common birth from fire.

Mayon, the Philippines This classically shaped conical stratovolcano has erupted 47 times since 1616, making it the Philippines' most active volcano. Twelve eruptions have caused fatalities.

Torres del Paine, Chile This 12-million-year-old complex represents the starkly beautiful eroded remnants of slowly cooled magma intrusions in Patagonian Chile.

Mount St. Helens, Washington, U.S.A. This conical stratovolcano was forever changed after a cataclysmic 1980 eruption blasted away a huge portion and killed 57 people.

Santorini, Greece The small volcanic archipelago of Santorini is the remains of a tremendous volcanic eruption 3,500 years ago that decimated the population of a once larger island.

Volcanoes, Past and Present
continued

Earth would not be the planet we know without volcanoes. From ancient times volcanism has played a role in defining attributes of local and global environments, including rock and soil types, valuable mineral deposits, and the composition of the ocean and atmosphere. Volcanism may also have provided conditions favorable to the development of life on the young planet.

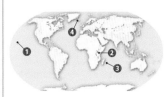

Mount Etna This frequently active volcano towers over Catania, the second-largest city in Sicily, Italy. Mount Etna erupts effusively and explosively, shooting out fiery lava from vents inside the craters of its horseshoe-shaped caldera, called Valle del Bove, and from vents on its flanks.

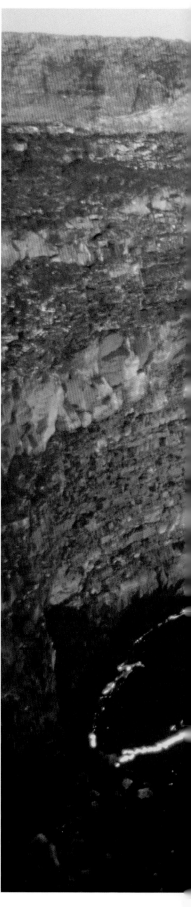

Erta Ale This isolated Ethiopian basaltic shield volcano erupts effusively and forms a low, broad rise in the Danakil depression, which lies below sea level. Its summit caldera has supported one, and occasionally two, persistently active lava lakes over the last 100 years.

FACT FILE

1. Bora Bora This volcanic hotspot island in the Society Islands group is heavily eroded, but a well-preserved caldera can still be seen in its three-to-four-million-year-old rocks. Crystal-clear lagoons lie within its coral barrier.

Bora Bora, French Polynesia

2. Lord Howe Island This crescent-shaped island is the eroded remnant of a six-to-seven-million-year-old shield volcano, 370 miles (600 km) east of Australia. It is part of the Lord Howe seamount chain, believed to have formed from a hot spot beneath the Australian Plate.

Lord Howe Island, Australia

3. Mariana Islands This group of volcanic islands owe their existence to subduction-zone volcanism, where the Pacific Plate descends under the Philippine Plate. The islands include active stratovolcanoes and seamounts.

Mariana Islands, North Pacific, near Guam

4. Kazan Retto Islands This volcanic island group, which includes the World War II battle site at Iwo Jima island, is part of the Bonin Island group, a northerly extension of the Marianas volcanic arc system.

Kazan Retto Islands, Japan

Volcanic Islands

Warm and lush, arid and remote, cold and barren—these are all terms that apply to the great variety of volcanic islands that dot the globe. Grown from infancy on the seafloor, these volcanoes rise above the waves to make islands at intraplate hot spots and divergent and convergent plate boundaries.

Hot spot and collision map (below) Most plate collision zones, highlighted in red, ring the Pacific Ocean or stretch from Australia to Europe along the margins of the ancient Tethys sea. Earth's prominent hot spots are indicated by red dots.

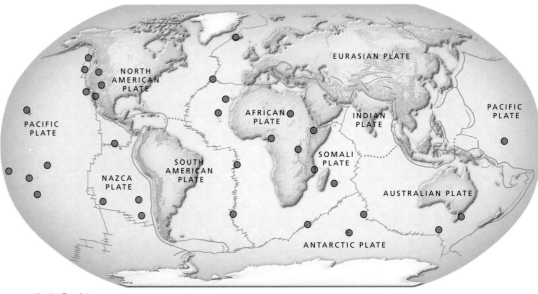

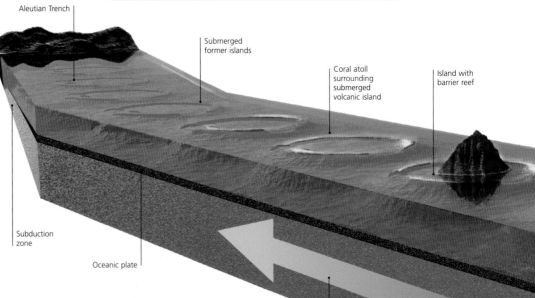

The Hawaiian chain (above) Hot-spot volcanic chains like the archetypal Hawaiian Islands were formed by volcanic activity related to hot, easy-to-melt rocks at a nearly stationary hot spot in the mantle. Volcanoes grow with magma supplied from below, then shut down as they are rafted away from the hot spot by motion of the tectonic plate on which they sit. The number and size of active volcanoes depends on the strength of the hot spot, whereas the age differences among islands along the chain depend on the speed of the underlying plate.

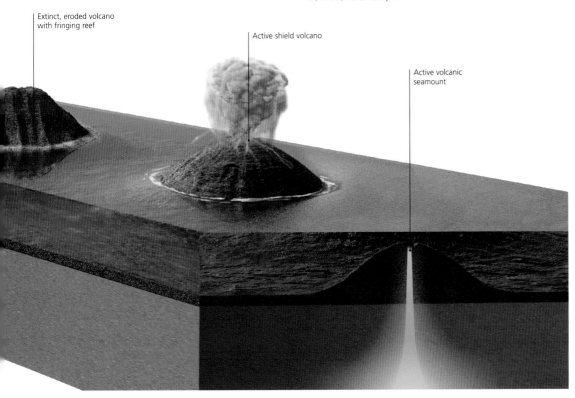

View from space (above) The main Hawaiian Islands spread out along a linear swath in the Pacific Ocean, seen in this NASA space image. The largest and youngest island is Big Island, formed from five volcanoes, of which three are still active.

Extinct, eroded volcano with fringing reef

Active shield volcano

Active volcanic seamount

FACT FILE

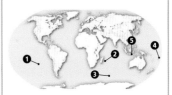

1. Easter Island This lonely island in the southeastern Pacific Ocean is formed of three extinct volcanoes. Settled by Polynesians as the eastern outpost of a huge triangle that extended to New Zealand and Hawaii, Easter Island is now a territory of Chile. The island is famous for its huge moai statues.

Easter Island (Rapa Nui)

2. Réunion This French island in the Indian Ocean was created by the same intraplate hot spot that produced the Mauritius and Rodrigues islands. The island is formed of two great volcanoes, Piton des Neiges and Piton de la Fournaise. The latter is one of the world's most active volcanoes.

Réunion, Indian Ocean

3. Heard Island This remote volcanic island is 2,500 miles (4,000 km) south-west of Australia. Mountainous and barren, the island is heavily glaciated. Its active volcano last erupted in 1993, and the island has experienced multiple subglacial eruptions in the past. In 1997, it became a World Heritage site.

Heard Island, Southern Ocean

4. Tutuila This third-largest Samoan island was formed at a hot spot under the Pacific Plate. The inactive, eroded volcanic island is famous for its huge, cashew-shaped natural harbor, which snakes deep into the island's interior. It is surrounded by high volcanic peaks and supports a large tuna fleet.

Tutuila, Samoa

5. Bali This popular island has a long volcanic history. Its most active volcano is the stratovolcano Batur. Much of Bali's famous bas-relief sculpture is carved into ignimbrites, pumice-dominated deposits from eruptions 30,000 years ago.

Bali, Indonesia

Thermal Springs

Temperatures gradually increase with depth nearly everywhere in the crust, more so near volcanoes or other internal heat sources. Hot water issuing from the crust onto the surface constitutes a thermal spring. Some countries use this hot water to heat homes and to generate electricity. It is one of the cleanest ways of generating power because the main by–product is steam.

Thermal pools The relatively gentle outflow of non-pressurized hydrothermal waters can produce thermal springs at sites of active or dormant volcanoes, and at non-volcanic sites where fractures help warm waters rise from great depths.

Champagne Pool, New Zealand
Carbon dioxide that bubbles up with 165°F (74°C) water gives this pool in the Wai-O-Tapu geothermal area its name.

Mineral deposits Unusual formations of mud riddled with gas bubbles form on the floor of the almost circular Champagne Pool, North Island, New Zealand.

HERITAGE WATCH

Yellowstone The U.S. Congress established Yellowstone National Park in 1872 to preserve the area's "geothermal marvels." These are home to a variety of micro-organisms that can withstand high water temperatures. The organisms were unknown to 19th-century conservationists, who sought to protect the visible flora and fauna. Protecting the organisms from commercial exploitation is a future challenge.

Hydrothermal landscape (below) Hydrothermal areas occur on land and beneath the sea. Temperatures of the chemical-rich waters range from hot tap water to beyond the point of water boiling at sea-level atmospheric pressure.

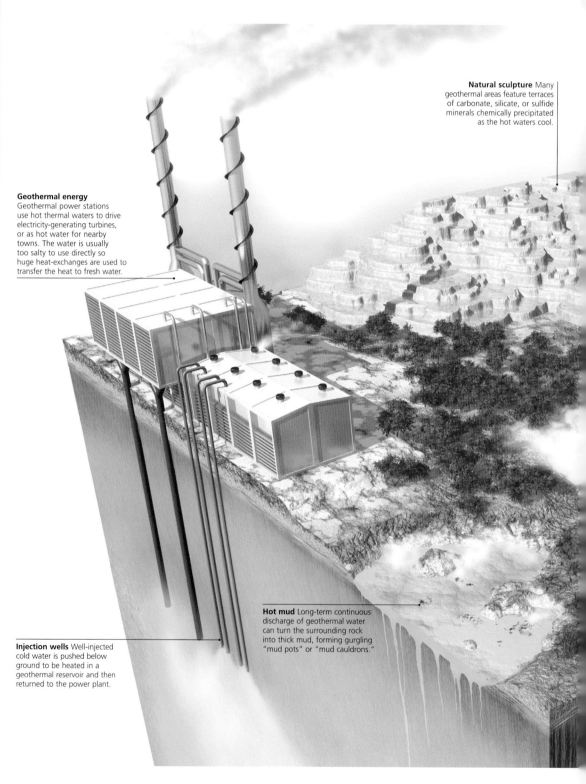

Natural sculpture Many geothermal areas feature terraces of carbonate, silicate, or sulfide minerals chemically precipitated as the hot waters cool.

Geothermal energy Geothermal power stations use hot thermal waters to drive electricity-generating turbines, or as hot water for nearby towns. The water is usually too salty to use directly so huge heat-exchanges are used to transfer the heat to fresh water.

Hot mud Long-term continuous discharge of geothermal water can turn the surrounding rock into thick mud, forming gurgling "mud pots" or "mud cauldrons."

Injection wells Well-injected cold water is pushed below ground to be heated in a geothermal reservoir and then returned to the power plant.

Travertine pools (left) Rims and crusts precipitated from hot, mineral-rich waters at thermal pools are sedimentary deposits. Fine layers of calcium carbonate produce travertine along the raised edges of these terraced Turkish thermal pools.

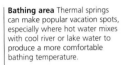

Bathing area Thermal springs can make popular vacation spots, especially where hot water mixes with cool river or lake water to produce a more comfortable bathing temperature.

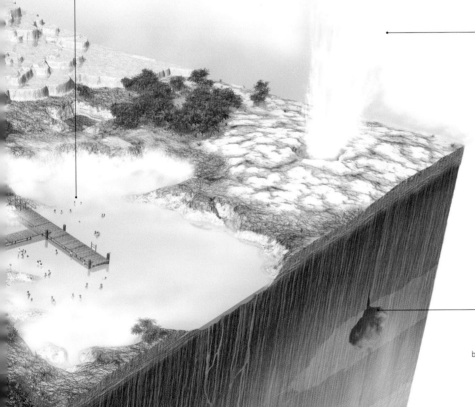

Force of nature Geysers are periodic explosions of pressurized, gas-rich geothermal water from beneath the surface.

Pressure chamber Below every geyser is one or more subterranean cavities that fill up with water and gases between each geyser eruption.

Infiltrating water Cool water percolates along cracks and fissures in the "recharge zone" in order to resupply the geyser source.

FACT FILE

Features of thermal springs Geothermal activity takes multiple forms and can produce a range of associated mineral deposits, depending on the temperature and chemical composition of the waters and surrounding rocks.

Sulfur crystals Thermal water usually exits the crust as stream rich in sulfur and other minerals. Much sulfur crystallizes around the vent.

Boiling mud Hot, usually acidic thermal waters can rapidly weather rock near a thermal spring, producing viscous, wet pools of hot mud.

Mineral deposits Mineral precipitates form around vents because temperature and pressure drop suddenly as the water or steam enters the atmosphere.

WINTER WARMTH

Japanese macaque monkeys have learned to keep warm in the winter by bathing in the hot water of the thermal springs that are associated with active volcanoes on the Japanese island of Honshu.

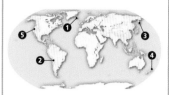

FACT FILE

1. Geysir This location, from which the English word for geyser was taken, can offer a spectacular spray of water 200 feet (60 m) high. Its neighbor, Strokkur, spouts water jets 60–100 feet (13-30 m) high every five minutes. Both geysers are on the eastern flank of Iceland's Western Volcanic Rift Zone.

Geysir, Iceland

2. El Tatio At roughly 13,700 feet (4,200 m) elevation in the Andes sits Los Géiseres del Tatio, the largest geyser field in the Southern Hemisphere, and the third-largest field in the world. More than 80 active geysers eject water here, some as high as 18 feet (6 m).

El Tatio, Chile

3. Valley of Geysers Nearly 90 geysers strech 4 miles (6 km) along Eurasia's only geyser field. Discovered in 1941, it is the world's second largest, after Yellowstone, U.S.A. Some of its geysers gush forth every 10 to 12 minutes, while others erupt only once in five hours. In June 2007, a landslide in this active terrain buried two of the geysers.

Valley of Geysers, Kamchatka Peninsula, Russia

4. Taupo Geysers and thermal springs dot the active volcanic landscape of New Zealand's Taupo volcanic zone, They include two at Tokaanu, south of Lake Taupo; boiling springs and geysers in Geyser Valley at Wairakei; and a few that are scattered along the Waikato River banks at Orakeikorako.

Taupo,North Island, New Zealand

5. Steamboat Springs Geothermal drilling and resource exploitation in 1987 destroyed this once accessible geyser area in a small volcanic field of rhyolitic lava domes. Twenty-one geysers observed as recently as 1984 no longer spout. The area still has thermal springs.

Steamboat Springs, Nevada, U.S.A.

Thermal Springs continued

Groundwater circulating through hot rock picks up heat, becomes less dense, and works its way to the surface with varying degrees of force and dissolved gas content. This leads to a range of exit behaviors at thermal springs. Occasionally, subterranean chambers become filled and pressurized with hot water that bursts forth on the surface in an explosion of water called a geyser.

Geyser explosion Superheated water and steam are ejected from the Pohutu (right), and Prince of Wales Feathers (left), geysers at Whakarewarewa, New Zealand. Hot water leaves the subterranean geothermal reservoir, expands and boils as it travels to the surface, and suddenly erupts.

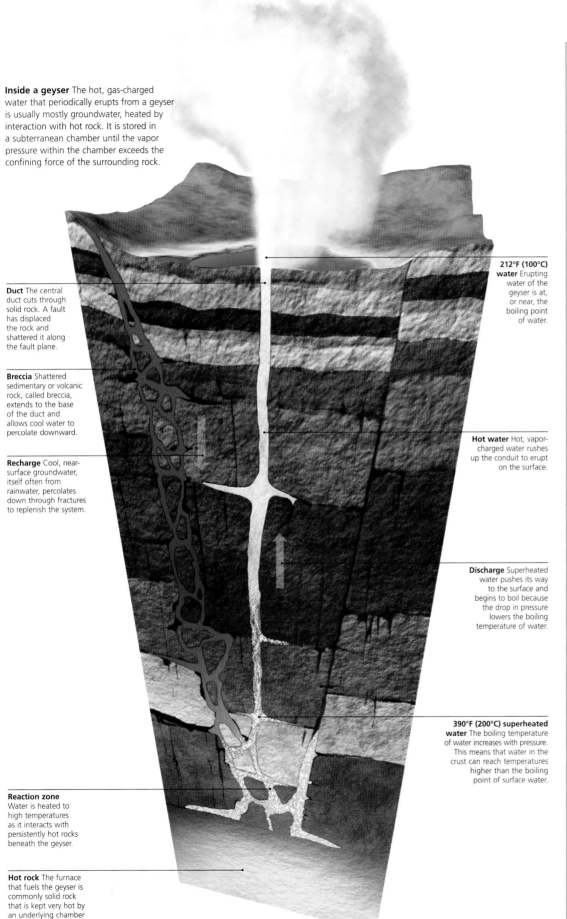

Inside a geyser The hot, gas-charged water that periodically erupts from a geyser is usually mostly groundwater, heated by interaction with hot rock. It is stored in a subterranean chamber until the vapor pressure within the chamber exceeds the confining force of the surrounding rock.

Duct The central duct cuts through solid rock. A fault has displaced the rock and shattered it along the fault plane.

Breccia Shattered sedimentary or volcanic rock, called breccia, extends to the base of the duct and allows cool water to percolate downward.

Recharge Cool, near-surface groundwater, itself often from rainwater, percolates down through fractures to replenish the system.

Reaction zone Water is heated to high temperatures as it interacts with persistently hot rocks beneath the geyser.

Hot rock The furnace that fuels the geyser is commonly solid rock that is kept very hot by an underlying chamber of molten magma.

212°F (100°C) water Erupting water of the geyser is at, or near, the boiling point of water.

Hot water Hot, vapor-charged water rushes up the conduit to erupt on the surface.

Discharge Superheated water pushes its way to the surface and begins to boil because the drop in pressure lowers the boiling temperature of water.

390°F (200°C) superheated water The boiling temperature of water increases with pressure. This means that water in the crust can reach temperatures higher than the boiling point of surface water.

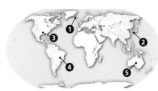

Faults

The ground beneath your feet is probably not as solid as it seems, but is riddled with cracks, zones of weakness, and areas of differential stress in the underlying mile or two of rocky crust. Faults are unevenly distributed cracks in the crust that experience relative movement between opposing rock faces, as either slow creep or sudden, earthquake-producing jolts.

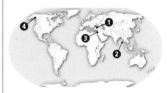
1. Anatolian Fault This major transform fault crosses Turkey from east to west and runs just 12 miles (20 km) south of Istanbul. It has been the site

of many high-energy earthquakes, which in the 20th century alone caused more than 50,000 fatalities.

Anatolian Fault, Turkey

2. Andaman Fault This Australian Plate subduction-zone fault is in the strait that separates Burma and Sumatra. It ruptured along roughly

1,000 miles (1,600 km) of fault line in two close pulses in 2004. This produced a huge earthquake and tsunamis.

Andaman Fault, Andaman Sea

3. Dead Sea Fault Zone Connecting to the Red Sea spreading center in the south, this transform fault allows sliding between the Arabian and African plates.

Over the last 20 million years, the eastern flank moved 60 miles (96 km) north of the western side, creating the Dead Sea.

Dead Sea Fault Zone, Dead Sea

4. Denali Fault Compressive stress from the subducting Pacific Plate drives the right-lateral slip on this long transform fault, which has slid an

estimated 250 miles (400 km) since the late Mesozoic era. It produced a magnitude 7.9 earthquake in 2002.

Denali Fault, Alaska, U.S.A.

Thingvellir, Iceland (top) Houses dot the picturesque shoreline of Lake Thingvallavatn, just downslope of a huge normal fault line. The lake sits in a fault-bounded valley where the world's first parliament, the Althing, was founded in A.D. 930.

Kunlun Fault, Tibet (bottom) This image of the strike-slip fault zone on Tibet's north side shows two fault splays crossing from east to west. The upper juxtaposes reddish sedimentary rocks against alluvium, and the lower cuts through the alluvium itself.

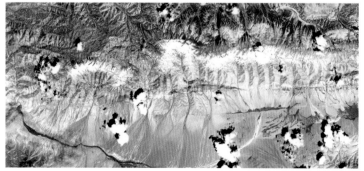

Types of faults Faults are classified by the direction of motion of their opposing faces. Movement can occur slowly and continuously, or in large, sudden shifts that can deform or rupture the land surface.

Normal fault Rocks on one side of the fault slump below the other side, usually accompanied by mild extension across the fault plane.

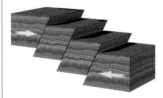

Reverse fault The rocks on one side of the fault are pushed up above those on the other side, usually accompanied by compression across the fault plane.

Thrust fault The action is similar to that of a reverse fault, but at low angles. Such faults can stack like rock units and can greatly thicken the crust locally.

Transform, or strike-slip, fault Rocks on either side of the fault slide past each other with little or no vertical component to the motion.

San Andreas Fault This fault zone bounding the Pacific and North American tectonic plates is clearly visible as it crosses southern California's Carrizo Plains. The transform fault slips 0.8 to 1.4 inches (2–3.5 cm) per year. Some parts slide relatively uninhibitedly; others are locked and ripe for an earthquake.

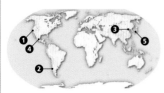

1. San Francisco, 1906 In one minute, an earthquake destroyed this city, with the most extensive ground rupturing ever witnessed. Huge differences in the shaking of ground on sedimented rock versus bedrock gave geologists a new understanding of earthquake hazards. Up to 6,000 people were killed.

San Francisco, U.S.A.

2. Valdivia, 1960 This magnitude 9.5 earthquake is the strongest ever recorded. Severe ground shaking caused massive damage, and generated a tsunami with waves up to 38 feet (11.5 m) high. It caused hundreds of deaths in Chile, Hawaii, Japan, and the Philippines.

Valdivia, Chile

3. Tangshan, 1976 At least a quarter of a million people died in what was the most deadly earthquake of the 20th century. Centered in Hebei Province, it occurred early in the morning and lasted only 10 to 15 seconds. The early hour and an intense aftershock 16 hours later contributed to a high death toll.

Tangshan, China

4. Mexico City, 1985 This magnitude 8.1 subduction-zone earthquake devastated Mexico City, even though the epicenter was offshore 220 miles (350 km) away. Three to four minutes of shaking hit the city hard, particularly in areas built over silty sediments of the dry Lake Texcoco. About 9,000 people died.

Mexico City, Mexico

5. Kobe, 1995 This fierce subduction-zone earthquake first struck near Awaji Island, where the ground heaved up 9 feet (3 m). Seismic waves propagated through the crust to Kobe, 12 miles (20 km) away. They caused extensive damage to the city, making this one of the world's most expensive disasters.

Kobe, Japan

Earthquakes

Earthquakes occur whenever rocks on either side of faults in Earth's crust suddenly break and slide past each other, causing the ground to shake, bounce, or rock. The strength and duration of earthquakes depend on many factors, such as the depth of the rupture, the stress state of rocks before the fault slip, and the kinds of rocks involved.

Atacama Fault (right) This satellite photo shows the Atacama Fault—a major structural feature that runs parallel to the west coast of Chile. It cuts through the Paleozoic and Mesozoic metamorphic rocks of the Chilean coastal mountain ranges.

Low risk
Medium risk
High risk
Very high risk

Earthquake risk (above) In some places earthquakes may never occur, while in others tremors are regular and the risk of a destructive earthquake is always present.

Rift zone (below) The North American and European plates separate at a rift zone that traverses Iceland. Ravines and cliffs mark the fault at Thingvellir, where the land sank 20 inches (50 cm) during an earthquake in 1789.

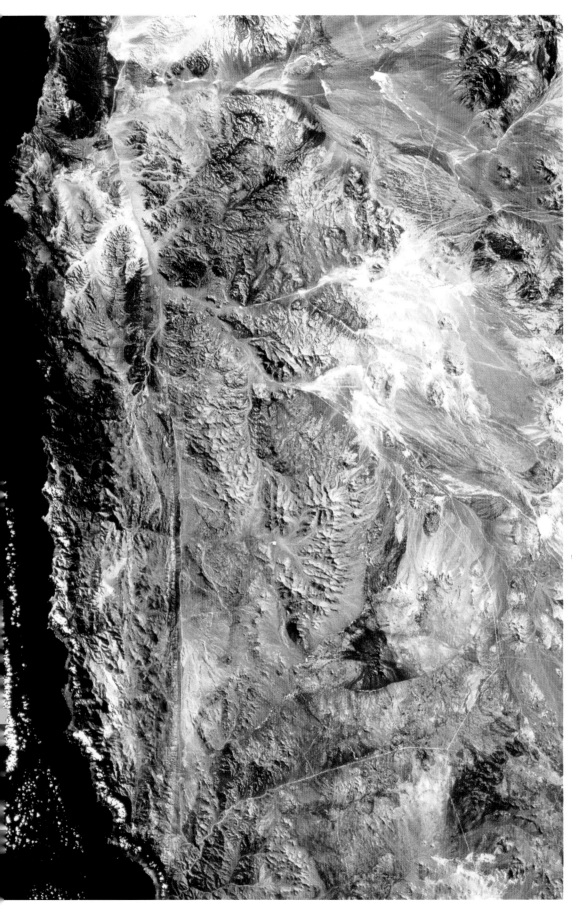

Seismic waves Earthquakes release four types of energy waves that travel through the surrounding rock. Two of these travel through Earth's interior, and two slower, more destructive waves travel just beneath Earth's surface.

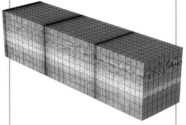

P-waves Primary, or pressure, waves pulse quickly through Earth's interior to the surface. These are the first waves felt in an earthquake.

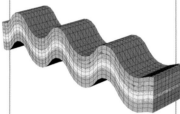

S-waves Secondary, or shear, waves shift material sideways as they propagate through Earth's interior at about half the speed of P-waves.

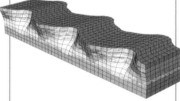

Love waves These waves are side-to-side shearing motions of Earth's surface. Love waves move more slowly than P- or S-waves.

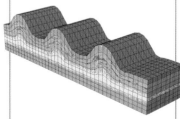

Rayleigh waves Rayleigh waves cause the ground surface to deform like waves on the ocean. These are the slowest of the four seismic wave types.

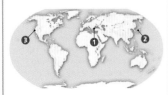

Seismic Destruction

Tremors and earthquakes disrupt Earth's crust many times each day. Most events are too small for humans to feel, but occasionally large earthquakes release huge amounts of energy, causing widespread destruction of buildings and heavy loss of human life. On the Mercalli scale, the strength of an earthquake is measured according to the amount of movement and damage.

From above (right) A rare photo taken during an earthquake shows dust and dirt being thrown violently into the air, as the magnitude 5.9 "Whittier Narrows" earthquake rocked Los Angeles, U.S.A., in 1987.

Search for survivors (below) Rescue workers clear rubble from the collapsed Margala Towers in Islamabad, Pakistan, in the wake of an early-morning magnitude 7.6 earthquake in 2005. More than 87,000 people were killed and 3 million people were made homeless.

Mercalli intensity (right) (**1**) People feel no movement. (**2**) Those on upper floors of tall buildings notice movement. (**3**) Vibration, as of a passing truck, is felt by people indoors. (**4**) Dishes, windows, and doors rattle; parked cars rock. People outdoors may feel movement. (**5**) Sleeping people wake. Doors swing. Dishes break. (**6**) Everyone feels movement. Walking is difficult. Furniture moves. Pictures fall. Trees shake. Slight damage in poorly built structures. (**7**) Standing is difficult. Cars shake. Loose bricks fall. Slight damage to well-built buildings, worse in weak buildings. (**8**) Driving is difficult. Tree branches break. Heavy furniture overturns. (**9**) Well-built buildings considerably damaged. Ground cracks, pipes break. (**10**) Most buildings and foundations destroyed. Dams seriously damaged. Large cracks in the ground and landslides. (**11**) Most buildings collapse. Some bridges are destroyed. Underground pipes destroyed. (**12**) Total destruction. Objects thrown in air as the ground moves in waves.

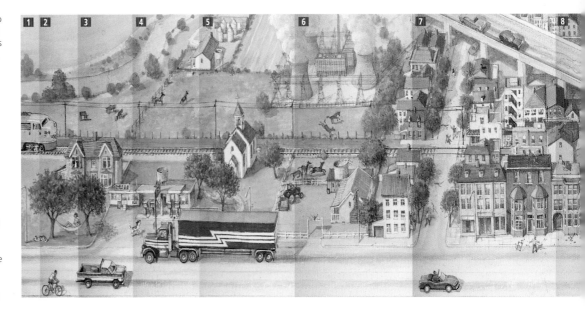

Disaster stages In 1959, the ground shook for 30–45 seconds in a magnitude 7.5 quake at Hebgen Lake, Montana, U.S.A. In a few moments, 28 human lives were lost and the landscape was radically altered.

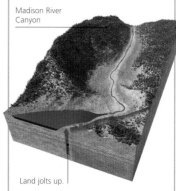

Madison River Canyon

Land jolts up.

1 As the earthquake struck, the land north of Hebgen Lake moved upward in a sudden jolt, creating a fault scarp 20 feet (6 m) high.

Rock avalanche

2 A massive face of a mountain at the side of Madison Canyon broke free, sending an avalanche of rocks down to the river below.

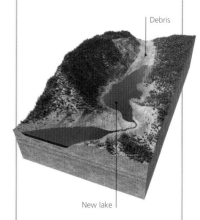

Debris

New lake

3 Landslide debris came to rest on the canyon floor, damming the Madison River and forming a new lake.

Tsunamis

Sudden motion of the seabed from an earthquake, volcanic eruption, or landslide can generate giant waves that may travel for thousands of miles across the open ocean. The rise in seafloor near a coastline slows the tsunami, and causes it to rush upward into one or more towering walls of water that flood the coast.

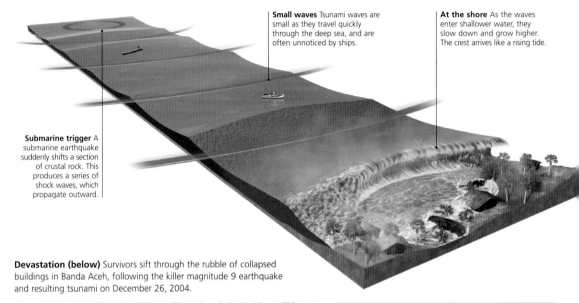

Tsunami wave trains (below) Tsunamis are groups of waves that form as energy is released from shifts in an unstable portion of the seabed. They rapidly spread from their source to the surrounding ocean.

Small waves Tsunami waves are small as they travel quickly through the deep sea, and are often unnoticed by ships.

At the shore As the waves enter shallower water, they slow down and grow higher. The crest arrives like a rising tide.

Submarine trigger A submarine earthquake suddenly shifts a section of crustal rock. This produces a series of shock waves, which propagate outward.

Devastation (below) Survivors sift through the rubble of collapsed buildings in Banda Aceh, following the killer magnitude 9 earthquake and resulting tsunami on December 26, 2004.

TEN WORST TSUNAMIS			
	Year	Place	Deaths (approx.)
1.	2004	Indian Ocean	300,000
2.	1883	Krakatau, Indonesia	36,000
3.	1896	Sanriku Coast, Japan	20,000
4.	1771	Okinawa, Japan	12,000
5.	1792	Kyushu, Japan	5,000
6.	1976	Mindanau, Philippines	5,000
7.	1933	Sanriku Coast, Japan	3,000
8.	1960	Chile	2,000
9.	1998	Papua New Guinea	2,000
10.	1944	Tonankai, Japan	1,200

Tsunami disasters The locations of the ten most destructive tsunamis, listed above, are plotted on this map. The area around Japan is shown in detail because half of the tsunamis listed occurred in this region.

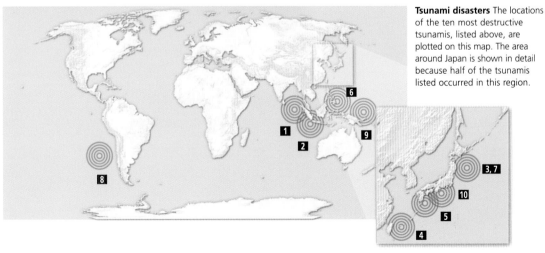

Before and after (left) Satellite images of southwestern coastal Thailand, before (top), and after (bottom), show the devastating effect of the 2004 tsunami. Tourist resorts and areas that were previously covered in lush vegetation near Pankarang Cape were inundated. Most of the beaches were destroyed. The death toll in Thailand exceeded 5,000; half of those were tourists.

FACT FILE

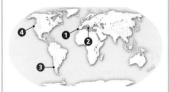

1. Lisbon, 1755 One of history's deadliest seismic disasters was caused by an earthquake rupture of the seafloor 120 miles (190 km) offshore from Lisbon. The earthquake and following

 tsunami destroyed much of the city. This disaster marked the beginning of modern earthquake science.

Lisbon, Portugal

2. Messina–Reggio, 1908 A late December earthquake struck both coasts of the Straits of Messina, causing one of Italy's worst natural disasters. Moments after the earthquake, tsunami

 waves 40 feet (10 m) high hit the coast. Up to two-thirds of Messina's 150,000 residents may have perished.

Messina–Reggio, Italy

3. Pacific, 1960 The seabed lurched up as much as 60 feet (20 m) when this magnitude 9.5 earthquake ruptured a Pacific seafloor fault zone. A Pacific-wide tsunami event struck Chile

 almost immediately. It also caused loss of life and major destruction in Hawaii and Japan, 15 and 22 hours later.

Pacific Ocean

4. Crescent City, 1964 An earthquake off Anchorage, Alaska, on Good Friday produced a tsunami that raced down the west coast of North America. Crescent City was particularly hard hit.

 Four giant waves struck in an hour and a half, killing 12 people and damaging the harbor city.

Crescent City, California, U.S.A.

STUDYING EARTHQUAKES

Earthquakes are sustained movements of Earth's crust, such as shaking, trembling, and undulating of the ground underfoot. Most earthquakes are too small to be sensed or detected by humans, even at the epicenter, but movements that are large enough to be felt occur daily somewhere on Earth. Occasionally, very large earthquakes release tremendous amounts of energy and can have devastating effects on local residents and their property. Most earthquakes are caused by sudden shifts of rock across a fault surface. The collapse of a subterranean cavern (or mine), an explosion, or the impact of a meteorite on the planet are some of the other events that can trigger an earthquake.

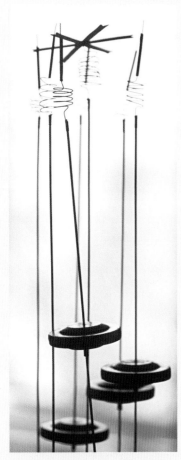

Early seismometer (above) Sophisticated instruments to record ground motions from earthquakes and other causes became available for the first time at the end of the 19th century. Inertial seismometers, such as the one pictured above, recorded the motion of an inertial mass, such as a pendulum, relative to the instrument, which was mechanically coupled to the ground.

GATHERING INFORMATION

Earthquakes are a fact of life on our planet. Generally, they are caused by the release of accumulated stresses in rock masses within the crust, a result of plate-tectonic action. Large changes in the distribution of mass on the crust over a geologically short period of time—for instance, rapid growth or collapse of a volcano, glacier, or other landmass—can also cause earthquakes.

Modern science has provided seismologists with extensive information about earthquake activity, such as where most active faults on Earth lie, how frequently they experience earthquakes, and how big these have been or are likely to be. Most earthquakes occur at or near the boundaries of the tectonic plates, although there are also risk zones that are located well away from the plate edges. This kind of information is invaluable for urban planners wishing to know the seismic risks in their region.

Seismologists continually monitor seismic activity and can make estimates of the probability of earthquakes for a particular spot over the next 50 to 100 years. However, this is nothing like earthquake prediction, which, as yet, is an unattained goal for these scientists.

As anyone who has experienced a moderately large earthquake can attest, the sudden shaking of the ground is a disarming experience, particularly when the shaking lasts for a long time. Early civilizations often considered a large earthquake to be a sign of displeasure from a deity, or the result of some other supernatural force. Although some early thinkers, such as Aristotle and Pliny the Elder, viewed earthquakes as natural phenomena—they thought that winds inside Earth caused occasional shaking at the surface—most Western thinkers continued to attribute earthquakes to supernatural forces well into the Renaissance.

The 1755 earthquake and tsunami at Lisbon, Portugal, signaled a major shift in earthquake thinking. Scientists and even church clergy began to realize that studies of the times and places where earthquakes occurred, and the effects that they wrought, would be useful for understanding why they occurred.

Expressway collapse (above right)
An earthquake in January 1995 nearly leveled the city of Kobe in Japan. Ground displacements as large as 9 feet (3 m) occurred at the surface rupture zone. The elevated Hanshin Expressway was hard hit, with damage to half of its concrete piers, and the collapse of ten separate spans.

Willmore seismometer (right)
This portable seismometer measures the velocity of ground movement by allowing copper wire coils to move around a fixed magnet. This induces an electric current in the coils that is proportional to the size of the earthquake. This type of seismometer is very good at measuring rapid vibrations of less than three seconds' frequency, also known as short-period waves.

THROUGH THE AGES

1831 B.C. The earliest written accounts of earthquakes we know of were made in China's Shandong Province. Carefully maintained records of earthquakes began in 780 B.C. during the Zhou Dynasty.

A.D. 132 Chinese scientist Zhang Heng invented an elaborate seismometer. When disturbed, a pendulum within a bronze chamber opened a dragon's mouth and dropped a ball into the mouth of a toad.

1703 French physicist Jean de la Hautefeuille proposed a device to measure the direction of earthquake motion. His device was based on mercury spilling out of a bowl into containers on the sides.

1755 After the earthquake in Lisbon, Portugal, the Catholic Church conducted the first recorded surveys of survivors' accounts and localized levels of destruction. This led to new quake-resistant building methods.

1844 James Forbes designed an inverted-pendulum seismometer by mounting a pendulum on a stiff wire. The stable inverted pendulum returned to an upright position after being disturbed.

Aftermath (below left) Fire raged through the Mission District of San Francisco, California, U.S.A., the day after the 1906 earthquake. This color-enhanced photograph shows fires burning out of control. The city lies on the San Andreas Fault, one of Earth's longest and most active fault lines. The earthquake and three days of fire destroyed the city center and much of the nearby residential areas.

Andrija Mohorovicic (below center) Studying seismic wave patterns from a 1909 Balkan earthquake, this Croatian geophysicist observed a sharp boundary beneath Earth's outer rocky shell through which earthquake waves traveled more rapidly than at the surface. He deduced that this boundary formed the top of a much thicker and stronger layer underneath the crust. The boundary is called the Mohorovicic Discontinuity, and is now known to lie between 3 and 40 miles (5–65 km) below the surface.

Charles Richter (below) In 1935, this seismologist and physicist created the Richter scale for measuring earthquake magnitude. The scale is logarithmic. An increase of 1 represents a tenfold increase in earthquake power. The Richter scale was originally designed to be used with a specific type of seismometer, but became widely used by seismologists. Richter was also involved with designing building codes for earthquake-prone areas.

1880 John Milne invented an early version of the modern pendulum seismograph after the Yokohama, Japan, earthquake. The same year he helped to found the world's first seismological society.

1906 Analysis of the San Francisco earthquake showed differences in the severity of ground shaking between soft sediment and bedrock areas. This led to a new understanding of earthquake hazards.

Early 20th century Seismographic stations were established in active earthquake zones, measuring frequency and size. They used Mercalli's intensity and Richter's magnitude scales.

1996 onward Seismic monitoring plays an important role in checking for disallowed nuclear explosions under the UN's Comprehensive Test Ban Treaty.

2001–02 Borehole seismometers (very sensitive measuring devices) were installed along the San Andreas Fault in the greater San Francisco Bay, U.S.A., to monitor seismic activity.

Earth's Folding Crust

Perhaps no other structure on Earth depicts the enormous geological forces that shape our world better than the crinkled, wrinkled folds of solid rock that are now exposed in many great mountain belts. High pressure and temperature force rocks to deform in response to collisions between the great tectonic plates.

Intense folding (below) Crustal shortening, intense folding, and high rates of uplift and erosion have formed high mountains and deep valleys in the Himalayas, currently Earth's fastest-rising mountain chain.

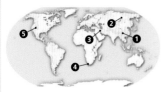

Types of folding Folding occurs when forces compress rock layers of differing strengths, causing the rocks to buckle. The layers deform in response to pressure gradients. Domes form by active upwarping, whereas adjustment of rock layers to multiple directions of force twists them into a variety of shapes.

Monocline This is the simplest type of fold. It involves bending of rock layers, which causes the once-horizontal layers to be inclined downward. The dip of the layers is highest at the fold axis.

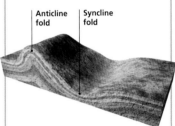

Anticline fold   Syncline fold

Anticline and syncline folds An anticline fold arches upward, with the youngest rock layer on top of the arch. A fold that bends downward to form a basin, with the youngest rocks on top of the bend, is a syncline fold.

Recumbent fold This type of fold involves nearly parallel limbs. Highly directed pressure gradients lay the fold over to an almost horizontal axial plane. Some geologists restrict the term to folds that dip no more than 10 degrees.

Ancient folds The Alps in central Europe represent some of the earliest and most-studied folded rock structures on Earth. A wide range of metamorphic rock types have been exposed in this majestic mountain belt.

Fault-Block Mountains

Fold mountain genesis Slow squeezing motions at plate collision zones cause rocks to behave like soft plastic as they are pushed into folds and troughs, in the same way that a rug crumples.

Periods of crustal stretching and extension cause vertical motion along normal faults, breaking the crust into blocks and allowing upward or downward motion. Tilting may accompany faulting, and create ranges with steep escarpments on one side and more gentle ramps on the other. These ranges dominate the Basin and Range region of the western United States, and part of northern Europe.

Lake Louise and Valley of Ten Peaks (right) This scenic valley in Banff National Park is surrounded by peaks that form the high points of predominantly carbonate-bearing fault-block mountains in the Canadian Rockies of southwestern Alberta.

1 The original flat-lying layers are uplifted and folded by strong, compressional mountain-building forces.

2 Folded rock belts become eroded. The tops of the folds (anticlines) go first as they have been weakened by the folding.

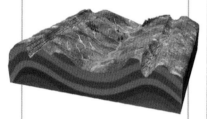

3 Streams localize on the eroded anticlines, rapidly gouging out deep valleys. Glaciations can further erode high mountain valleys.

4 This process can ultimately lead to inverted topography, where valleys become mountains or vice versa.

Franklin Mountains State Park, Chihuahuan Desert These tilted fault-block mountains rise to 7,192 feet (2,192 m) behind El Paso, and contain the oldest (Precambrian) rocks in Texas. The block was lifted 60 to 70 million years ago.

1. Sierra Nevada This mountain range is 400 miles (650 km) long. Triassic and younger rocks began to be uplifted on a westward-tilting fault block just

 four million years ago, which, with recent glaciations, accounts for its rugged relief and spectacular scenery.

Sierra Nevada, California, U.S.A.

2. Carpathian Mountains This long mountain chain stretches 930 miles (500 km) across eastern Europe—primarily Romania. It was formed during the mountain-building event related to the collision of the African

 and Eurasian plates. Several separate ranges were heaved up along thrust faults during the Paleocene and Eocene epochs.

Carpathian Mountains, Europe

3. Jura Mountains This small range north of the Alps separates the Rhine and Rhône rivers. The heavily folded rocks were uplifted on north-trending normal faults during fault-block

 extension in the Eocene to Pliocene—the same series of events responsible for the Alps and Carpathians.

Jura Mountains, Europe

4. Wasatch Range These mountains stretch 160 miles (260 km) through central Utah to Idaho at the western edge of the Rocky Mountains. They were lifted along the Wasatch fault

 zone during regional uplift in the Miocene epoch. Salt Lake City, in Utah, sits along the range's western front.

Wasatch Range, Utah, U.S.A

5. Sierra Nacimiento Range Rising up from near the city of Albuquerque, this small mountain range formed between 80 and 35 million years

 ago. It is the southernmost part of the Rockies, and the western boundary of the Rio Grande Rift.

Sierra Nacimiento Range, New Mexico, U.S.A.

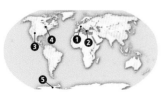
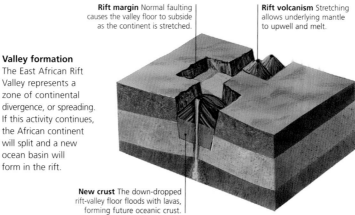
1. Rhine Graben This continental rift is related to the same period of extension that led to the opening of the western Mediterranean Sea. The Rhine Graben was important for early human

development, as it was inhabited by Neanderthals 100,000 years ago, and Cro-Magnon *Homo sapiens* until 7,600 years ago.

Rhine Graben, Germany, France, and The Netherlands

2. The Gulf of Corinth Active continental rifting is separating the Peloponnese from the western Greek mainland, forming this deep inlet of the

Ionian Sea. Rifting at about 1 inch (2.5 cm) per year makes this one of Europe's most seismically active locations.

The Gulf of Corinth, Greece

3. Rio Grande Rift This inactive rift valley was formed during a period of crustal thinning that started about 35 million years ago. The rift appears to have been pulled apart slowly and evenly, allowing underlying mantle

to rise up and melt, which produced rift-margin volcanism. The deepest parts of the rift have been filled with alluvium.

Rio Grande Rift, U.S.A.

4. Keewenawan Rift This ancient rift system was active 1,100 million years ago. It poured out voluminous basaltic lava flows in the area now occupied by Lake Superior. Geologists hypothesize

that the rift formed from a hot spot that was impinging on the underside of the North American continental landmass.

Keewenawan Rift, Great Lakes region, U.S.A.

5. West Antarctic Rift The active rift valley between West and East Antarctica forms the shallow Ross Sea, and a part of West Antarctica. The area is opening

at about 0.1 inch (0.25 cm) per year. All recent volcanism occurring in Antarctica is related to this rift.

West Antarctic Rift, Antarctica

Rifting

Episodes of continental drift can begin with continental rifting, during which extension of the crust splits and thins a continental block into two parts, forming a central, linear down-dropped fault segment. Divergence of land on either side of the rift can cause crustal thinning, sedimentary basin formation, thermal water springs development, and volcanic activity.

The Great Rift Valley (below) The Great Rift Valley reaches 50 miles (80 km) wide as it passes through Kenya and Tanzania, where great volcanoes, boiling pools, geysers, and trough lakes dominate the landscape.

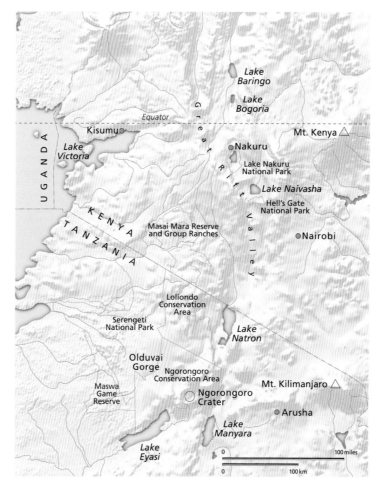

Valley formation
The East African Rift Valley represents a zone of continental divergence, or spreading. If this activity continues, the African continent will split and a new ocean basin will form in the rift.

Rift margin Normal faulting causes the valley floor to subside as the continent is stretched.

Rift volcanism Stretching allows underlying mantle to upwell and melt.

New crust The down-dropped rift-valley floor floods with lavas, forming future oceanic crust.

Rift-valley lakes Stretching and thinning of Earth's continental lithosphere creates depressions in the landscape. These depressions often host lakes or ephemeral wetlands in the enclosed basins.

Salton Trough This area of ongoing rifting in California is dominated by the Salton Sea, a hypersaline lake about 220 feet (65 m) below sea level.

Lake Baikal This southern Siberian lake fills an ancient rift valley. At more than 1 mile (1.5 km) deep, it is the deepest lake in the world today.

Great Rift Valley landscape (left) Running north to south from the Dead Sea to Mozambique, this valley is the longest crack on Earth. It is home to numerous lakes and wetlands, and boasts a mild climate and rich biodiversity.

Cradle of mankind Rich deposits of early hominid fossils have been found in Africa's Great Rift Valley. At Olduvai Gorge Louis and Mary Leakey unearthed artifacts and fossils of our early ancestors, while at Laetoli homid footprints are preserved in 3.7-million-year-old volcanic rock.

Mountain Ranges

Nowhere on Earth are the effects of plate tectonics more evident than in its modern and ancient mountain ranges, formed by the shifting of continental landmasses over time. The primary processes accounting for most of Earth's highlands include folding, block faulting, and volcanism. Erosion by wind, water, and ice enhance dramatic mountainscape relief.

Andes (right) South America's longest mountain range stretches 4,400 miles (7,000 km) along the west coast. The mountains are formed of eastern and western cordilleras, separated in most places by a central valley.

The Rockies (above) These grand cordilleran mountains of western North America stretch more than 3,000 miles (4,800 km) from British Columbia to New Mexico. Their highest point is at Mount Elbert, Colorado, U.S.A., 14,440 feet (4,400 m) above sea level.

Great Dividing Range The largest mountain belt in Australia stretches more than 2,200 miles (3,500 km) along the eastern coastline. Its complicated geological history is told in multiple ranges, uplands, plateaus, and escarpments that now dominate the region's landscape.

Formation of the Himalayas Earth's highest and youngest mountain range—the Himalayas—was created from a slow but mighty collision between the Indian subcontinent and Asia.

1 About 200 million years ago the ancient supercontinent Pangea broke up, and India began to move northward.

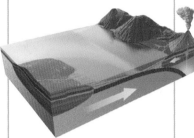

2 Indian Ocean crust of the Australian Plate was subducted beneath Eurasia, while the ocean basin of the Tethys Sea shortened.

3 India rammed into Asia about 50 to 40 million years ago as the last of the Tethys Sea was subducted. The Himalayan uplift began.

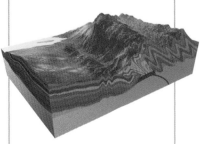

4 The uplift reached full intensity 10 million years ago, but continues today. As India cannot subduct, the process will one day jam to a stop.

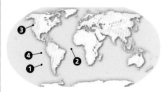

Seafloor Spreading

Deep beneath the ocean, new crust is born and spreads apart at undersea mountain ranges, called mid-ocean ridges. Rapid plate divergence usually produces broad, rounded mountains, termed a rise. Slower spreading produces a ridge with a deep valley along its top. Ridges were discovered in the early 20th century, but they were not recognized as volcanic until the 1960s.

Red Sea (right) This satellite photo shows the northern end of the Red Sea (center). As new seafloor fills the area between the diverging Arabian and African plates, the Red Sea is growing wider.

Pulled apart (below) New seafloor in the South Atlantic Ocean is formed by volcanism and rifting along the Mid-Atlantic Ridge, in a process that continually moves the South American and African continents apart.

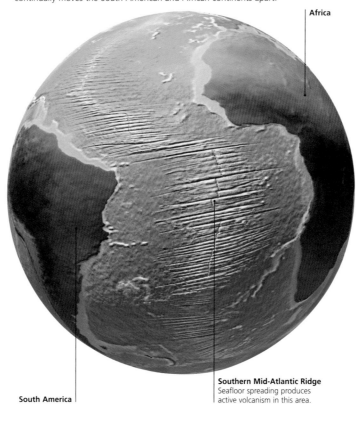

Africa

South America

Southern Mid-Atlantic Ridge Seafloor spreading produces active volcanism in this area.

How an ocean forms (below) Seafloor spreading begins with cracking and stretching of the lithosphere in response to divergent plate motion. The rift crust drops along normal faults, and thins sufficiently for the underlying mantle to upwell and melt, producing rift volcanism. The process continues as the sea invades the ever-spreading, volcanic-floored valley.

CRACKING   UPLIFT AND COLLAPSE   CONTINUED RIFTING

Expansion cracks   Inward-facing faults   New seafloor   Upwelling basalt

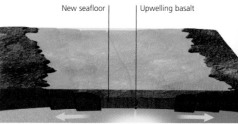

MATURE OCEAN

Transform fault offset | Mid-ocean ridge rift valley

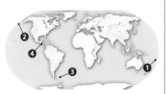
1. Tonga Trench This western Pacific trench and its southerly continuation called the Kermadec Trench form at the site where the Pacific Plate subducts beneath the Australian Plate. Horizon Deep, the trench's deepest point, is 35,702 feet (10,882 m) below sea level. Recent Global Positioning Satellite (GPS) measurements indicate that the

convergence rate is currently 0.85 feet (0.2 m) per year, making this the fastest plate convergence rate ever recorded.

Tonga Trench, Pacific Ocean

2. Aleutian Trench This trench runs to the south of Alaska's Aleutian Islands. It marks part of the boundary at which the Pacific Plate is being subducted beneath the North American Plate. Moving westward through the trench system, it changes from continental to oceanic subductions which makes it an

interesting site for scientific research. At its deepest, the trench is 25,194 feet (7,679 m) below sea level.

Aleutian Trench, Pacific Ocean

3. Scotia Trench This small island arc system, also known as the South Sandwich Arc, is in the extreme south of the Atlantic Ocean. It marks the subduction of the South American Plate's oceanic crust beneath the Antarctic Plate. The trench is a relatively young and primitive

feature, making it a good locality to study the early stages of subduction and arc-related volcanism.

Scotia Trench, Atlantic Ocean

4. Middle America Trench This plate subduction system runs 1,700 miles (2,750 km) from central Mexico to Costa Rica. It marks the convergence of four tectonic plates, where the Pacific and Cocos plates subduct east-ward beneath the North American and

Caribbean plates. Its depth of 21,880 feet (6,669 m) is limited by sediment runoff from North America.

Middle America Trench, Pacific Ocean

Undersea Trenches

Oceanic trenches mark the spot where oceanic crust subducts beneath less dense continental or oceanic crust. The seafloor reaches great depths, up to nearly 2 miles (3 km), as it plunges into the mantle. This produces volcanism, earthquakes, and uplift of the overriding plate. Trenches and arcs mark Earth's greatest topographic relief over small surface distances.

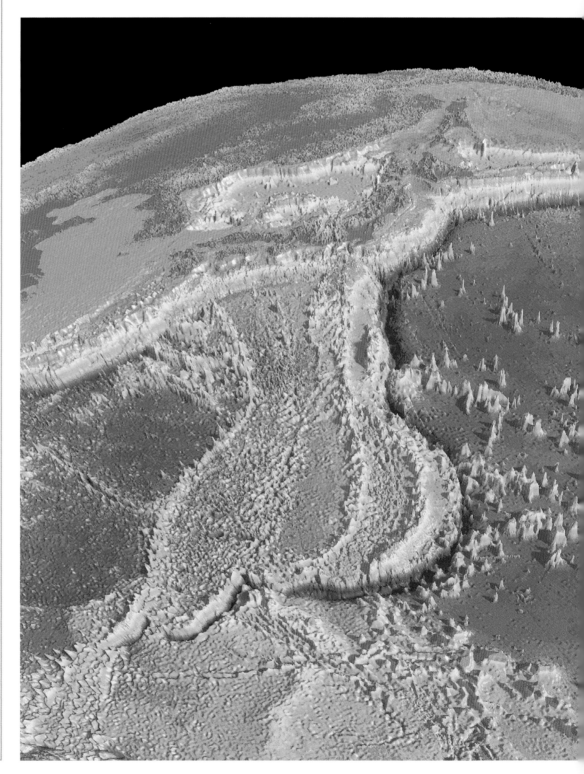

Marianas Trench (below) The Marianas Trench is colored purple in this computer model of the region's topography. It marks the spot where the Pacific Plate sinks beneath the Philippine Plate, and contains Challenger Deep, which at 35,798 feet (10,911 m) below sea level is the lowest point on Earth. Discovered in 1951, it was visited in 1960 by Don Walsh and Jacques Piccard in the bathyscaphe Trieste.

Peru–Chile Trench (below) The Nazca Plate of the Eastern Pacific Ocean subducts beneath the South American Plate at the Peru–Chile Trench, which runs parallel to both the western coastline of the continent and the subduction-related Andes Mountains. At 3,670 miles (5,900 km), it is one of the longest trenches that form the ocean basin encircling the Pacific Ring of Fire.

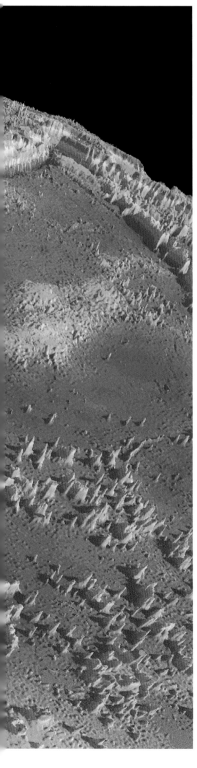

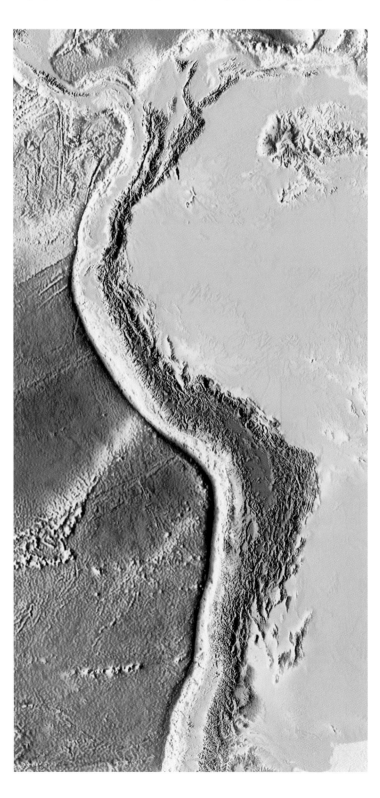

FACT FILE

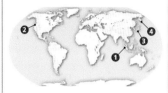

1. Sunda-Banda Arc Subduction of the Australian Plate beneath the far eastern edge of the Eurasian Plate occurs along the Sunda-Banda Arc system, also know as the Java Trench. Some of Earth's most explosive volcanoes occur in this zone.

Sunda-Banda Arc, Indian Ocean

2. Cascadia Subduction of the small Juan de Fuca and Gorda plates beneath western North America forms the majestic volcanoes of the Cascade chain. Today's chain was once part of a larger, continuous arc system that stretched all the way to Mexico.

Cascadia, Pacific Ocean

3. Nankai Trough Subduction of the Philippine Plate beneath the Eurasian Plate produced the Nankai Trough, which fronts one of Earth's most active earthquake zones. Plate convergence rates are relatively slow but have produced many violent, large-scale earthquakes.

Nankai Trough, Pacific Ocean

4. Kamchatka Also called the Kuril-Kamchatka Trench, this system forms the locus of Pacific Plate subduction in the northeast Pacific Ocean, and causes significant volcanism on the Kamchatka Peninsula and Kurile Islands. It connects to the Aleutian Trench in the north.

Kamchatka Trench, Pacific Ocean

HERITAGE WATCH

Solomon Islands rain forests These low volcanic islands, formed by subduction of the Australian Plate beneath the Pacific Plate, host tropical rainforests of unusual biological diversity, including species that are endemic to single islands, and 69 unique bird species. Despite the biological richness, there is only one protected area in the entire islands ecoregion.

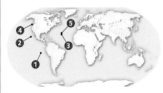
1. Rose Garden In 1977 the first submarine hydrothermal systems were found on the spreading center located just north of the Galápagos Islands. None of the vents were emitting superhot water, yet the chimney structures and associated vent biota found there were completely new to science.

Rose Garden, Pacific Ocean

2. 21°N East Pacific Rise This location near the Gulf of California's mouth is famous for the 1979 discovery of black-smoker hydrothermal chimneys. A large array of unusual life-forms, thriving at the interface of waters up to 750°F (400°C) and the near-freezing surrounding seawater, were seen here for the first time.

21°N East Pacific Rise, Pacific Ocean

3. TAG hydrothermal field Extending at least 3 square miles (5 km²), this is one of the largest-known vent fields. Its active low- and high-temperature vents and inactive deposits may have formed 100,000 years ago. Today, high-temperature venting is restricted to a mound 650 feet (200 m) in diameter.

TAG hydrothermal field, Mid-Atlantic Ridge

4. Endeavour field Strong hydrothermal venting occurs at five sites along the Endeavour segment of the Juan de Fuca Ridge; at locales known as Sasquatch, Salty Dawg, High Rise, Mothra, and Main Endeavour. The first to be discovered was Main Endeavour, in 1984.

Endeavour field, Juan de Fuca Ridge

5. Lost City Most known hydrothermal systems are powered by volcanic heat, but Lost City is fueled by the interaction of seawater and mantle rocks beneath the site. This entirely new type of vent was discovered in 2000. Its towering limestone chimneys emit 190°F (88°C) fluids, supporting a unique ecosystem.

Lost City, Mid-Atlantic Ridge

Undersea Vents

Hot, smoky waters containing energy-rich minerals spew from the seafloor at deep-sea volcanoes, building tall "chimney" structures and supporting rich communities of strange and beautiful life-forms that are dependent on the chemicals in these waters. The chimneys have exotic minerals with high concentrations of lead, copper, zinc, barium, and other elements.

Black smoker (right) Black smokers get their color from particles that contain mostly sulfide minerals of iron, zinc, copper, and lead, with lesser amounts of rare metals, such as cobalt and silver. The plumes' mineral composition changes from vent to vent and over time. White smokers produce streams of water rich in gypsum, barite, and silica.

Inside a black smoker (below) Seawater forces its way deep into the crust through cracks near active submarine volcanoes. Water heated by contact with hot rocks dissolves surrounding minerals and rises to the surface. Its temperature is up to 750°F (400°C), more than three times hotter than boiling water at atmospheric pressure, but high pressures on the deep-sea floor prevent it from becoming steam as it emerges. Contact with cold, ambient seawater causes minerals to be deposited in chimneys around the main and secondary vents.

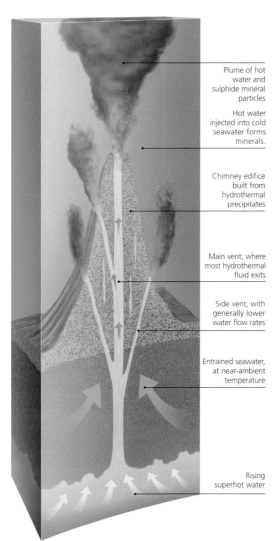

Plume of hot water and sulphide mineral particles

Hot water injected into cold seawater forms minerals.

Chimney edifice built from hydrothermal precipitates

Main vent, where most hydrothermal fluid exits

Side vent, with generally lower water flow rates

Entrained seawater, at near-ambient temperature

Rising superhot water

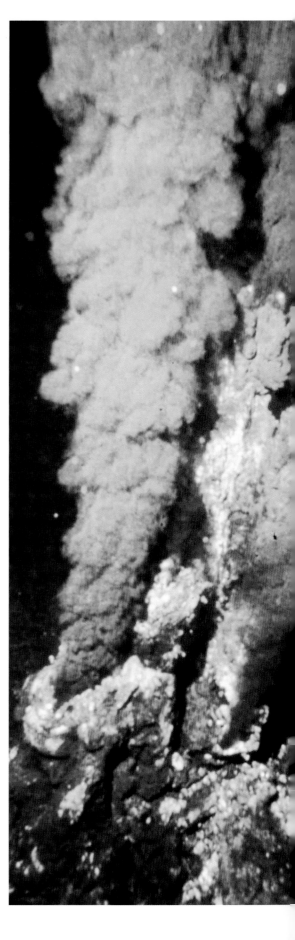

Creatures of the deep Colonies of microscopic bacteria feed off energy-rich mineral waters and support a rich ecosystem of exotic animals. The food chain depends on these chemicals in the way that plants and animals on the surface need light energy from the sun.

Monster mussels Like giant tube worms, the huge mussels of vent communities are "fed" by bacteria that live in their flesh.

Eelpout Slim, eel-like fish called eelpouts prey on other members of the vent community, such as crabs and amphipods.

Tube worms (top left) Giant tube worms can be up to 8 feet (2 m) tall. They live around vents and are generally found in large groups, forming a microhabitat for a number of smaller animals, such as small crabs that use the tubes for shelter and feed on organic debris from the worms. Vent clams and mussels are often found in association with tube worms.

White crabs (bottom left) Not all vents are large chimneys surrounded by giant tube worms. The water from this crack, 3 feet (90 cm) wide, in the East Pacific Rise contains sulfides and other minerals that feed a mat of bacteria. In turn, innumerable white crabs and other animals that live around the fissure graze on the bacteria.

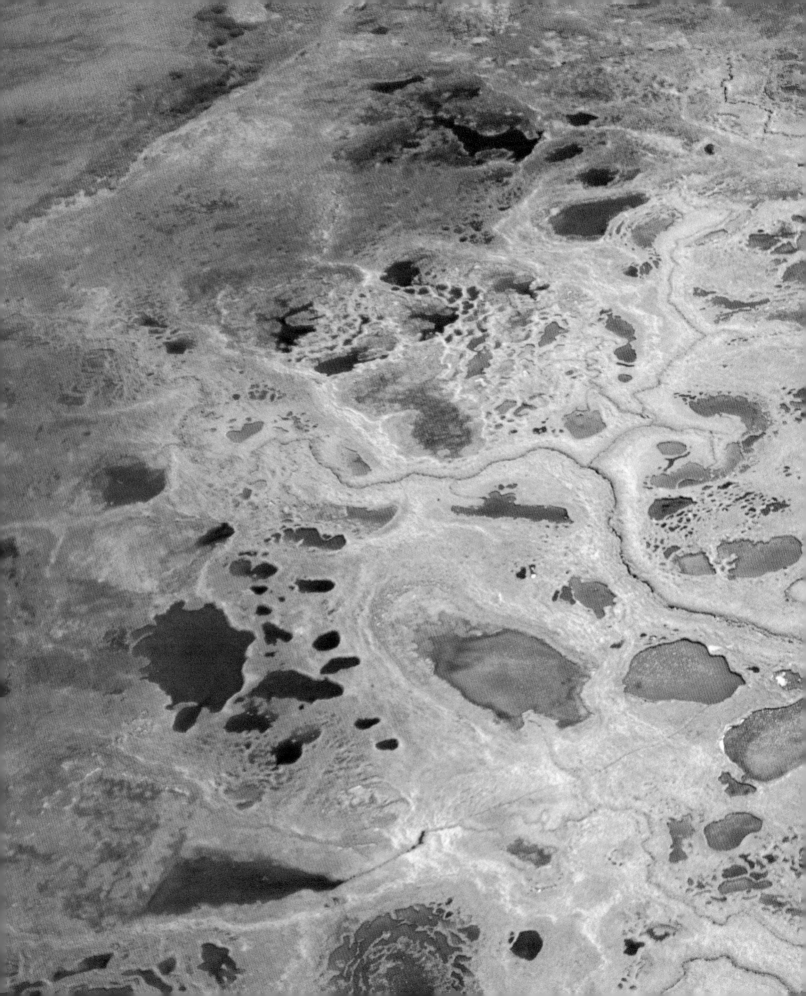

LAND

LAND

ROCKS

Earth's rocks are constantly forming and changing. At the beginning of geologic time, igneous rocks began to form as a solid crust on the cooling planet. Basaltic in composition, these were quickly recycled and recrystallized until permanent granitic continents formed. Sedimentary rocks soon followed as new land surfaces were lashed by rain and wind, and swollen rivers carried the debris into the sea. Metamorphic rocks also began to form with the heat and pressure created as mobile landmasses, or continents, collided with one another. These collisions crumpled and buckled rocks around the continental edges into high mountain chains.

ANALYZING ROCKS

Rocks are everywhere we look, and have been central to our very existence since humans evolved on the planet. We began by living in rock caves, painting on rocks, using them for spear tips and stone tools, and starting fires with them. Today, we still rely on them. All the clay for bricks, sand for cement and glass, and metals, coal, oil, and gas for our building, transportation, and energy needs are derived from rocks in Earth's crust.

Rocks are defined as being composed of one or more minerals: for example, calcite is a metamorphic, or heated, rock formed from interlocking crystals of the mineral calcite; granite is an igneous rock made up predominantly of quartz and feldspar, with some mica. Once placed in one of three major rock categories—igneous, sedimentary, or metamorphic—rocks are classified according to the composition, shape, size, and orientation of their constituent minerals. This is done by the trained eye of geologists working in the field. The more interesting, or potentially useful or valuable samples, are sent to the laboratory for further analysis. Rocks are sliced up and mounted on glass slides, ground down to less than paper-thin wafers, and then viewed on a petrologic microscope, which clearly shows their internal structure and allows their origin to be determined. The composition of difficult-to-identify crystals can be found using an electron microprobe, while other samples are crushed and analyzed for their economic metal content.

Rocks in the landscape (right) The eroded volcanic peaks, Paine Grande and Cuernos del Paine, glow in an orange sunrise in Torres del Paine National Park, Chile. Now heavily carved by glacial erosion, they form part of the Andes mountain chain that lines the Pacific coast of South America and was formed when the Pacific oceanic plate pushed beneath the continental Americas.

Even the age of a rock can be calculated if it contains certain mineral crystals, such as potassium, feldspar, and zircon. These have radiogenic elements that break down to more stable elements over a set time, which can be measured using an ion microprobe. The galleries on the following pages show some common igneous, metamorphic, and sedimentary rocks found in Earth's crust.

Rock cycle In a never-ending cycle, rocks transform from one type into another. Molten magma that erupts from volcanoes or cools underground hardens into igneous rocks (**1**). These rocks erode, providing sediments for rivers to carry into the sea, where they are cemented into sedimentary rocks (**2**). Recycled beneath Earth's crust or squeezed against a continental edge, rocks are heated and deformed into metamorphic rocks (**3**). When they re-melt into magma (**4**), the rock cycle is complete.

Igneous Rocks that have crystallized from molten magma or lava are called igneous rocks. Those that cool slowly, deep underground, have time to grow large crystals, such as the granite above. Rocks that cool quickly have crystals that are too fine to see with the naked eye. Igneous rocks still form today, in major volcanic belts and along the mid-oceanic ridges.

Sedimentary Minerals or pieces of any rock type that are cemented together are called sedimentary rocks. They begin life as loose sediment of different consistencies, ranging from coarse types, such as in the conglomerate above, to fine clays that have been eroded by water, wind, or ice. Sedimentary rocks occur in basins, such as those forming beneath Earth's major river deltas.

Metamorphic Any rock type, such as the gneiss above, that has been heated or compressed, or both, is a metamorphic rock. These rocks are found in Earth's continental collision zones, such as the Himalayas. Under pressure, mineral crystals form in the solid state. They grow with a preferred alignment due to the directional stress, giving many high-pressure rocks a "banded" look.

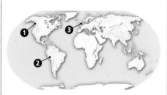

BATHOLITH FORMATION

As temperature rises, molten liquid moves up between rock crystals and begins to collect in layers. Being lighter, the liquid rises upward in balloon-shaped bodies. These push the overlying rocks out of the way and accumulate as batholiths.

Igneous Rock

Igneous rocks are those that crystallize from molten magma below Earth's surface, or from lava erupting from volcanoes. Today, igneous rocks are forming along the edges of Earth's tectonic plates in areas where they interact with one another—either rifting apart along mid-oceanic rifts or colliding and slipping over one other.

Classification Igneous rocks are classified according to the size and composition of the their mineral crystals. For example, granite has large, light-colored crystals including quartz, while basalt has small, dark-colored crystals and usually no quartz.

Top line Fine crystals < 0.04 inch (< 1 mm)

Middle line Medium 0.04–0.2 inch (1–5 mm)

Bottom line Coarse > 0.2 inch (> 5 mm)

INCREASING SILICA CONTENT

Basalt	Andesite	Obsidian
Dolerite	Microdiorite	Microgranite
Gabbro	Diorite	Granite

BASIC   INTERMEDIATE   SILICIC

Basalt stairway (right) The Giant's Causeway near Antrim, Ireland, is a natural stairway of perfectly formed basalt columns. As the lava flow cooled, it shrank and cracked into polygonal shapes, in the same way that mud cracks form when a lake bed dries out.

Formations Molten igneous rock intrudes into the landscape and molds its shape. A magma dome rises creating a batholith (**1**), a huge bottomless mass that pushes rock layers upward. A smaller mass of magma escapes from the batholith to form a stock (**2**). From the stock, a neck (**3**), or circular vertical channel, feeds magma into the volcano (**4**). Some magma forced between cracks pushes rock layers aside and accumulates in different shapes. A sill (**5**) is a horizontal sheet-like mass, a dike (**6**) is a vertical sheet-like mass, while a laccolith (**7**) is a dome-shaped mass. The large saucer-shaped mass is a lopolith (**8**), which can be several hundreds of miles in diameter.

FACT FILE

Column formation Columns are the ancient, hard skeletal remains of now-unrecognizable old volcanic cones and their lava flows. They emerge in erosional landscapes when softer surrounding rock types weather more rapidly.

1 A lava flow cools and shrinks as it loses heat to the air from its top surface, and to the ground from its bottom.

2 Tension cracks begin to develop and grow, forming a network over the cooling surfaces. The center remains hot.

3 Columns form as the cracks spread from the top and bottom, and join up in the center.

BASALT SANDS

Some black beach sands, such as those in Dyrhólaey Beach, Iceland, (below) are formed when hot basalt lava flows into the sea and is shattered into fragments as it suddenly chills. Basalt is typically the first lava to flow out of a volcano.

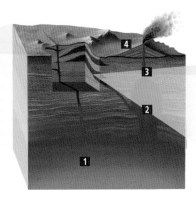

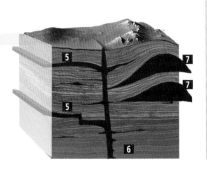

Igneous Rock Gallery

Igneous rocks display a wide variety of textures, crystal sizes, and colors because of variation in their composition and the different rates at which they cooled. Slow cooling underground allows minerals to grow into large, well-formed crystals, while rapid cooling means that minerals might be microscopic in size, or even become glass.

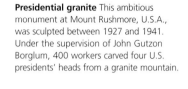

Presidential granite This ambitious monument at Mount Rushmore, U.S.A., was sculpted between 1927 and 1941. Under the supervision of John Gutzon Borglum, 400 workers carved four U.S. presidents' heads from a granite mountain.

FACT FILE

Comparing composition Rocks can be compared by studying their chemical compositions. In both basalt and granite, the main oxide is silica. Granite has more silica, potassium, and sodium oxide than basalt, but less aluminum, iron, magnesium, and calcium oxide.

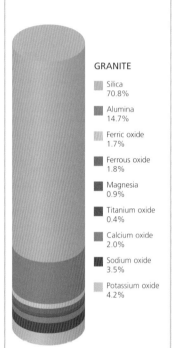

GRANITE

Silica
70.8%

Alumina
14.7%

Ferric oxide
1.7%

Ferrous oxide
1.8%

Magnesia
0.9%

Titanium oxide
0.4%

Calcium oxide
2.0%

Sodium oxide
3.5%

Potassium oxide
4.2%

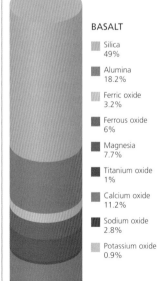

BASALT

Silica
49%

Alumina
18.2%

Ferric oxide
3.2%

Ferrous oxide
6%

Magnesia
7.7%

Titanium oxide
1%

Calcium oxide
11.2%

Sodium oxide
2.8%

Potassium oxide
0.9%

Basalt Basalt lava is associated with rifting continents and shield volcanoes. Basalt rock is composed of tiny feldspar, pyroxene, and olivine crystals, and is often dotted with gas cavities. It is used as a building material and for road bases.

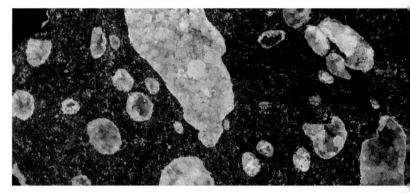

Granite Granite is made up of large crystals of quartz, pink and white feldspar, and mica. It cools slowly underground and is exposed by erosion as batholiths along subduction zones. Polished granite is used for buildings and monuments.

Pegmatite Pegmatite is a coarse quartz and feldspar rock. It often contains giant gemstone crystals such as topaz, aquamarine, and tourmaline—a result of very slow cooling. In this sample, black tourmaline crystals stand out from lighter quartz and feldspar.

Obsidian Obsidian is a glassy rock formed when silica-rich lava cools so quickly that individual crystals do not have time to grow. It is often black or brown. Some rocks that display a rainbow iridescence in the sunlight are prized by native American cultures.

Rhyolite Rhyolite is similar in composition to granite but fine-grained due to rapid cooling. In this magnified image, fine, elongated white crystals of feldspar and black minerals are visible in a glassy, reddish groundmass.

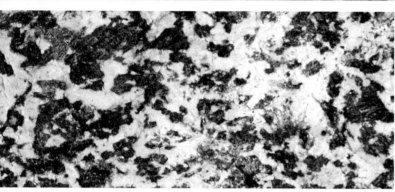

Gabbro Gabbro is composed of coarse crystals of white feldspar and dark pyroxene and olivine, which grew in slow-cooling magma deep below Earth's surface. Gabbro polishes well and is used for benches, tables, building facings, and monuments.

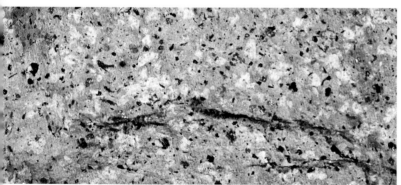

Dacite Dacite is a fine-grained lava that contains more quartz than andesite, but not as much as rhyolite. It is often associated with explosive subduction-zone volcanoes. In this sample, light and dark crystals are visible in a fine-grained gray matrix.

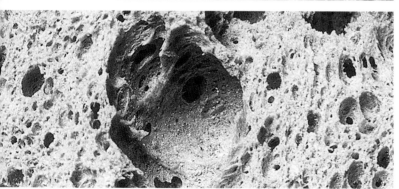

Pumice Pumice is a light-colored, silica-rich rock that forms during explosive volcanic eruptions when highly gas-charged lava cools so rapidly that the gas cannot escape. The light, frothy-looking rock is so full of bubbles that it can float on water.

Thin sections Studied under a microscope, paper-thin slices of rock, known as "thin sections," reveal a myriad of internal features. Minerals in the rock are easy to identify and provide vital clues to the rock's origin.

Basalt The combination of colorful olivine crystals and elongated white feldspar crystals, set against a fine, dark background, is typical of basalt lava.

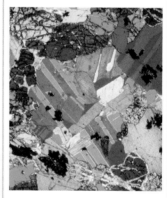

Gabbro Large, intergrown crystals of olivine and striped feldspar make up this rock. Their large size shows that it has cooled slowly, deep inside Earth.

Andesite These long, rectangular crystals of feldspar all have the same orientation because of the direction in which the lava flowed as it cooled.

Sedimentary Rock

Sedimentary rocks are formed by the chemical or physical breakdown, transport, and deposition of any other rock type. The agents of erosion such as water or wind carry these products, sometimes enormous distances, to sites where they are dropped. Major sites of deposition include river deltas, seafloors, swamps, and lake beds.

Deposited layer by layer Bryce Canyon National Park, in Utah, U.S.A., consists of horizontal sedimentary layers of red sandstone and shale that have been spectacularly eroded along vertical joints into row upon row of free-standing pillars.

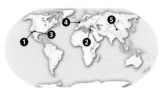

Breccia

Sandstone

Shale

Chert

Classification Sedimentary rocks are classified according to the size, shape, and composition of the rock or mineral fragments that they contain. Some chemical precipitates, such as chert and limestone, have no grains and are known as chemical sedimentary rocks.

SEDIMENTARY ROCK CLASSIFICATION

Particles	Particle size: inches	mm	Sedimentary rocks
Pebbles, cobbles, boulders	0.08 to > 10	2 to > 256	Conglomerate, breccia
Fine to coarse sand	0.02 to 0.08	0.06 to 2	Sandstone, arenite, graywacke
Fine to coarse silt	0.0002 to 0.02	0.003 to 0.06	Siltstone
Clay	< 0.0002	< 0.003	Claystone, mudstone, shale
Chemical precipitates			Limestone, dolomite, evaporites, chert, bauxite

TYPES OF SEDIMENTARY ROCK

Clastic Clastic sedimentary rocks are made of particles deposited by wind or water. Larger grains are deposited first, while smaller particles travel farther from shore.

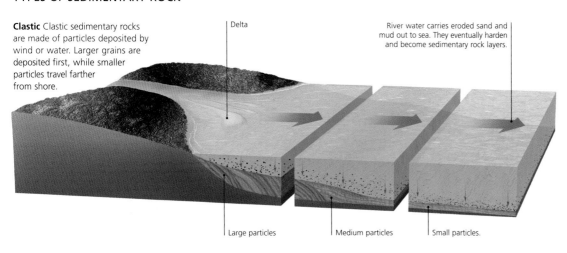
Delta

River water carries eroded sand and mud out to sea. They eventually harden and become sedimentary rock layers.

Large particles

Medium particles

Small particles.

Organic Organic sedimentary rocks are composed of the remains of living things. They include limestone, made of coral, and coal, made of plant material.

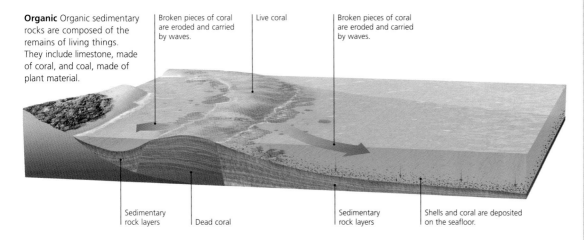
Broken pieces of coral are eroded and carried by waves.

Live coral

Broken pieces of coral are eroded and carried by waves.

Sedimentary rock layers

Dead coral

Sedimentary rock layers

Shells and coral are deposited on the seafloor.

Chemical Chemical sedimentary rocks are those precipitated directly from solution, including salt and other evaporate minerals, some limestone, and chert.

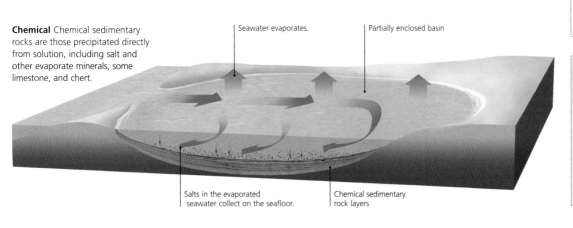
Seawater evaporates.

Partially enclosed basin

Salts in the evaporated seawater collect on the seafloor.

Chemical sedimentary rock layers

Sedimentary Rock Gallery

Types of unconformities Breaks in the geologic record, during which time either no deposition took place or deposited rocks were eroded away, are known as unconformities. Some are easier to recognize than others.

Disconformity The deposition of rock layers is followed by uplift, erosion of the older layers, and then deposition of newer layers on top.

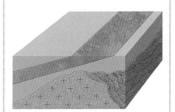

Nonconformity Sedimentary rocks are deposited on an older, eroded surface of igneous or metamorphic rocks.

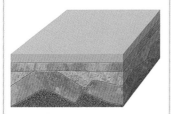

Angular conformity Older rocks are uplifted, folded, or folded and tilted. They erode before younger layers are deposited on top.

Paraconformity Overlying younger rocks are parallel to the older rocks beneath. In this case, it is not easy to recognize the time gap between them.

Sedimentary rocks show a variety of grain sizes, shapes, and colors depending on the type of rocks that they were eroded from and how far the rock fragments were carried by the transporting medium. Powerful currents can carry larger pieces, and the farther a sedimentary fragment is carried, the rounder it becomes.

Created by force Cross beds are layers at an angle in otherwise flat-lying sandstone. Like the steep front face of a migrating sand dune or river sand bar, cross beds indicate the strength and direction of the forces that created them.

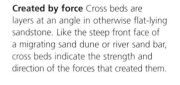

Sandstone Sandstone is made of sand grains that were deposited in a river delta, desert, or on a beach and have been cemented together by calcite, quartz, or iron oxide. Quartz grains are common and resistant to weathering.

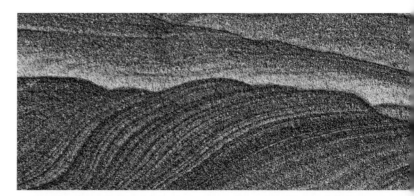

Shale Shale is a finely layered gray rock made up of clay. It is deposited in calm locations, such as a lagoon, floodplain, or marine environment far from the coast. Shale splits easily into layers, which often contain a treasure trove of fossils.

Conglomerate Conglomerate is a cemented mixture of sand, gravel, pebbles, and cobbles or even boulders—depending on the energy of the rivers or waves that deposit them. Each piece, or "clast," tells the story of its igneous, metamorphic, or sedimentary origin.

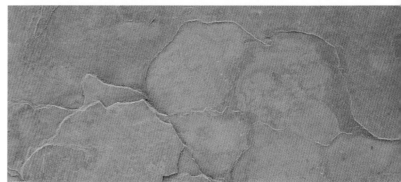

Chert Chert is tough and finely crystalline. It is chemically or organically deposited, and occurs in a variety of colors including white, gray, brown, green, red (jasper), and black. It also occurs as flint nodules in chalk, which were traditionally worked into stone tools and weapons.

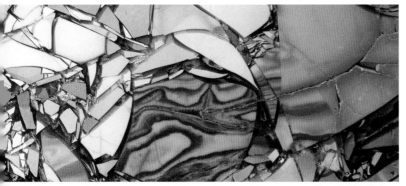

Breccia Breccia is made up of poorly sorted angular fragments, carried a minimal distance from a nearby source. They include cemented scree (also known as talus), debris thrown from a volcanic blast, or debris from the collapse of limestone caves.

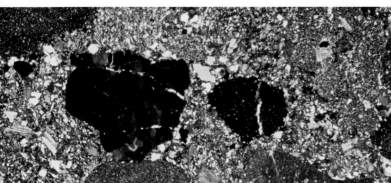

Graywacke Graywacke consists of poorly sorted fragments of rock or mineral that are coarse to fine, and angular to sub-angular. The fragments were deposited around active volcanic belts, and are cemented by clay—giving the rock a gray or greenish appearance.

Ironstone Earth's oldest sedimentary formations, dating back to three billion years, are ironstones deposited as banded iron layers on the ocean floor. The name "ironstone" describes hard, red sandstone in which the grains are cemented by iron oxide.

Coal Coal forms from accumulated plant material in an oxygen-poor swamp. The organic material changes from peat to brown coal, to black coal, and finally to anthracite as it becomes compacted, loses water, and increases in energy content.

What lies within Polished slices of sedimentary rock can reveal much about their fragmentary grains, including their composition, where they were eroded from, how far they have traveled, and what cements them together.

Grains of stone A microscope reveals the fine details of this sandstone. It is made of a well-packed cemented framework of angular mineral grains.

Ripple marks Fossilized ripple marks tell us that in ancient times rocks were deposited by similar processes to those seen today at beaches and in rivers.

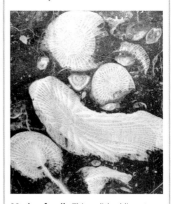

Marine fossils This polished limestone reveals white coral fossils in a fine-grained black calcareous matrix, the ancient remains of reef-building corals.

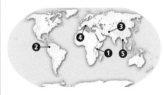
1. Longido Ruby-zoisite is a spectacular apple green, epidote-rich regional metamorphic rock, studded with bright red ruby crystals. Known as anyolite or Tanganyika artstone, it is carved and polished into statues and other elaborate works of art by skilled local artisans.

Longido, Tanzania

2. Emerald Belt Most of the world's emeralds are mined from the Muzo, Coscuez, and Chivor deposits in Colombia. They occur as intense green hexagonal crystals in a shiny black matrix of low-grade schist. The rare trapiche emerald has a six-pointed star pattern.

Emerald Belt, Boyaca, Colombia

3. Sar-e-Sang Lapis lazuli is a beautiful contact metamorphic rock composed of blue lazurite and white calcite, peppered with golden pyrite. This rare azure-blue gem was originally used to produce ultramarine blue pigment. It is prized for jewelry and carvings.

Sar-e-Sang, Kokcha Valley, Afghanistan

4. Carrera This is where the famous Carrera marble is found. Fine-grained and pure white, it is well known by the world's sculptors for its excellent carving qualities, and is the same Italian marble used by Michelangelo for his Pietà in St. Peter's basilica, Rome, and for many other sculptures.

Carrera, Italy

5. Mogok The granulites and marbles of the Mogok metamorphic belt in Myanmar have been formed by the same regional compressive forces that pushed up the Himalaya Mountains. For thousands of years, these high-grade metamorphic rocks have been mined by the locals for their crystals of precious gemstones, such as ruby and sapphire.

Mogok, Myanmar

Metamorphic Rock

Metamorphic rocks form when other rocks are changed—metamorphosed—by heat or pressure. There are many types of metamorphic rocks, but those formed from high pressure are easily recognized because their minerals have all been forced to line up in one direction. As the amount of metamorphism—known as the metamorphic grade—increases, the minerals grow larger until they finally melt.

Striped quartzite (right) These resistant quartzite outcrops in Utah's High Unitas Wilderness, U.S.A., have been carved smooth by glacial activity and stained in a rusty purple-and-white striped pattern by the passage of iron-bearing groundwater.

Metamorphosis in action (far right) The Himalaya mountains are still being pushed up by intense, directed pressure from the collision of the Indian and Asian continents. Gneisses, granulites, and marbles are common, containing a wealth of gem minerals.

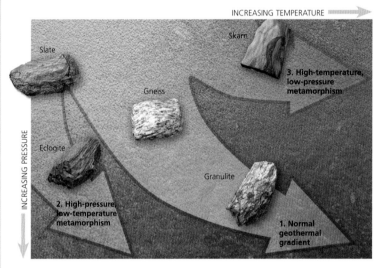

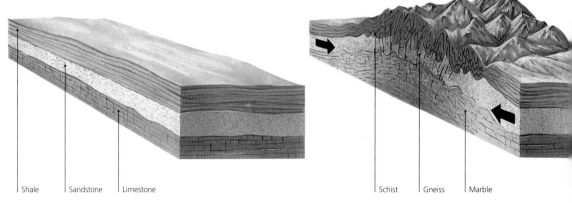

Classification (above) Metamorphic rocks are classified according to the size, shape, and composition of their minerals. The different metamorphic pathways depend on whether a rock is subject to intense heat, intense pressure, or both of these at once.

REGIONAL METAMORPHISM

Shale | Sandstone | Limestone

Schist | Gneiss | Marble

1 When two continental landmasses collide, large sections of the crust are subjected to intense, crushing pressure, as though being squeezed in a giant vice. This pressure can metamorphose rocks. Initially, the sedimentary layers lie flat and straight.

2 The intense pressure pushes the layers up into high fold-mountain ranges. Existing minerals break down and metamorphose into new minerals that "foliate" or grow in one direction. These rocks follow the high temperature and pressure pathway (see the classification chart, no.1).

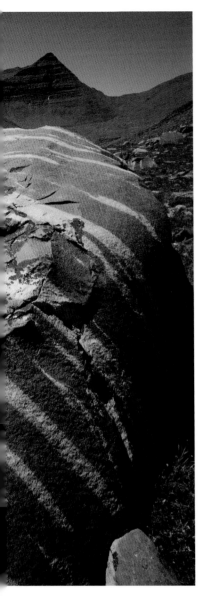

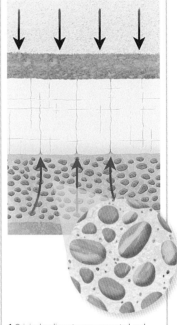

Marble When Earth's tectonic plates crash together, they often push up mountains. The pressure squeezes minerals in rocks, such as limestone, and they recrystalize into a solid mass to become marble.

1 Original sediments are compacted and solidify. Water between the grains is driven off by the overlying weight and escapes through fissures.

CONTACT METAMORPHISM

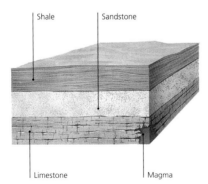

Shale   Sandstone

Limestone   Magma

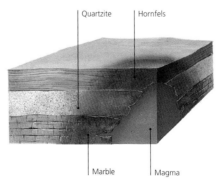

Quartzite   Hornfels

Marble   Magma

1 When magma rises to the surface, the intense heat bakes surrounding rocks, as though they were cooked by a blowtorch. The heat hardens the rocks and causes the minerals inside them to change.

2 New contact metamorphic rocks form from parent rocks of different composition. These rocks follow high-temperature, low-pressure pathway (see the classification chart, no.3).

2 Squeezing deforms and folds the sedimentary rocks. The grains grow together into a close-packed formation with no spaces left between them.

Metamorphic Rock Gallery

There is a rich and abundant variety of metamorphic rocks, including some colorful rocks that are rare and highly sought after. Hidden within the rocks is evidence of the different processes that formed them and the nature of the parent rocks. However, as a rock's metamorphic grade increases, it becomes increasingly difficult to interpret this information.

Gneiss Gneiss consists of coarse, light bands of quartz and feldspar, and dark bands made up of biotite. It forms when quartz-rich sedimentary or igneous rocks are subjected to high temperatures and pressures, such as during plate collisions when mountain belts are uplifted.

Slate Slate forms by low-grade metamorphism of clay-rich rocks. Small, platy crystals of mica and chlorite grow at right angles to the maximum pressure, giving the rock a perfect slaty cleavage, which is ideal for slate roofs.

Schist Schist forms by medium-grade metamorphism of clay-rich rocks. Its foliation is caused by the alignment of mica minerals under regional stress. Schists are part of a sequence of increasing metamorphic grade, which starts with slate and phyllite.

Hornfels Hornfels is a fine-grained rock that is produced by baking, or thermal metamorphism, of shales that surround an igneous intrusion. This tough rock breaks into irregular splintery or blocky fragments across its original sedimentary banding.

Slate roofs Traditional roofing materials are still used in many parts of the world, such as in Dublin, Ireland. Slate is easily split into large, strong, but thin sheets.

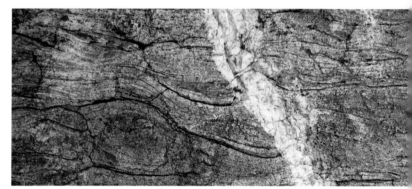

Quartzite Quartzite is a hard, tough, white-to-gray rock that is formed by metamorphism of quartz-rich sandstone. Original quartz grains and cement recrystallize to form an interlocking crystal mosaic. Quartzite is crushed for road and railway aggregate.

Marble Marble forms during the mountain-building process when limestone is subject to heat or pressure, or to both these forces. Pure marble is a tightly interlocking mosaic of white calcite crystals, and is highly sought after for carving into statues and decorative objects.

Amphibolite Amphibolite is a medium-grade rock formed by the regional metamorphism of basalt or gabbro. Pressure-oriented, elongated amphibole crystals give the rock a black shiny appearance. It is speckled with plagioclase and minor quartz, epidote, ilmentie, and magnetite.

Phyllite Phyllite is an intermediate-grade rock between slate and schist. Composed of quartz, mica, and chlorite, it is formed from the metamorphism of sandy to clayey sedimentary rocks. The aligned micaceous minerals give phyllite its layered appearance.

Foliation In metamorphic rocks, foliation is caused by an alignment of newly growing platy minerals, such as mica and chlorite, at right angles to the direction of maximum regional compressive stress.

Myonlite This rock is formed by movement along major fault lines. It shows distinct layers of coarse, recrystallized quartz and fine mica.

Gneiss This is a typical metamorphic texture of black, white, and gray quartz grains that interlock with oriented, slender, brown mica grains.

Phyllite Microscopic detail of pressure-contorted phyllite layers reveals that new minerals have segregated into dark mica and chlorite-rich layers and lighter-colored, quartz-rich layers.

MINERALS

Rocks are made up of minerals, which are in turn formed by the chemical combination of one or more of Earth's 92 naturally occurring elements. There are more than 4,000 known minerals, although only a handful are commonly seen in rocks. These are calcite, olivine, pyroxene, amphibole, mica, feldspar, and quartz, and are known collectively as the rock-forming minerals. For the amateur collector, rock-forming minerals are the perfect way to start a collection. Minerals that are particularly attractive are used as gemstones. Their names are often well known because of their long history as treasures, and for their use in jewelry and ornaments.

Rare gems These gems are all diamonds displaying different "fancy" colors that many people, being accustomed to white diamonds, are not even aware exist. Many more times as expensive and rare as their colorless equivalents, these diamonds illustrate the difficulty in relying on a single property to make a positive identification. These are perfect gems—attractively colored, transparent, and free from flaws, with a beautiful polish.

Semiprecious stones (right) Minerals and rocks that are beautiful, yet commonplace, such as the quartz varieties and other rocks shown here, are called semiprecious or ornamental gemstones. Being more abundant, they are used for statues, tiles, tabletops, and other utilitarian purposes. For example, lapis lazuli and malachite were used in the interior of St. Isaac's Cathedral, in St. Petersburg, Russia.

IDENTIFYING MINERALS

Minerals have fixed physical, chemical, and optical properties that reflect the way their constituent elements have combined at the atomic level. The most common properties are illustrated in the side panels on the following pages: color (172), luster (176), crystal systems (180), hardness (182), transparency (184), cleavage (186), habit (188), sheen (190), fluorescence (192), and inclusions (194). To make a positive identification several properties must usually be considered together, using destructive or non-destructive tests.

Destructive tests involve scratching a mineral to determine its hardness; breaking it to look for cleavage—obvious planes of weakness; or crushing it to make a chemical analysis or to determine the streak—the color of the mineral in fine powder form. Naturally, these tests are not carried out on valuable specimens or gems.

A host of non-destructive tests can also be used. The specific gravity or weight of a piece of a mineral can be measured, simply by comparing its weight in air with its weight when submerged in water. Optical properties can also be measured, such as a mineral's refractive index—how much it bends a ray of light passing through it; dispersion—how much a mineral splits white light into its rainbow color spectrum; fluorescence and phosphorescence—the different colors that a mineral may show under ultraviolet light; and dichroism—the different colors seen when a mineral is viewed from different angles. Some minerals display a unique luster which may lead them to be used as gems. Examples are precious moonstone, with its distinctive bluish haze; cat's eye stones, lit by a bright ray of light; and others with multiple rays, such as star sapphire and ruby. Most non-destructive tests are suitable for identifying gems, even when they are set in gold or silver.

Minerals are usually studied with a microscope or hand lens to find characteristic surface features, or to search their interiors for tiny inclusions of other minerals.

The minerals on the following pages are split into elemental minerals and compound minerals. The elemental minerals are made up of single elements, such as native copper. There are about ten geologically significant native elements. The compound minerals consist of a chemical combination of two or more elements. They are divided, depending on the combining elements, into recognized mineralogical groups: sulfides; silicates and silica; oxides and hydroxides; phosphates, arsenates, and vanadates; sulfates; carbonates; halides; borates and nitrates; molybdates, chromates, and tungstates.

Opal Precious opals display play-of-color sheen that changes as they are moved in the light—this specimen displays blue and green. The unique opal sheen is produced by rays of light reflecting from the ordered internal arrangement of silica spheres.

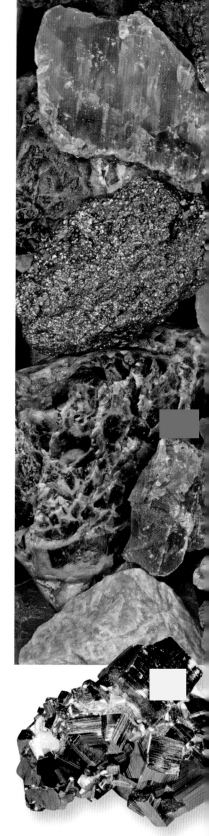

Pyrite Iron sulfide, known as pyrite, has an unmistakable brassy-yellow metallic luster that enables it to be used as a gemstone. Metallic luster is one of the typical properties displayed by sulfide minerals, as well as a heavy feel and low transparency to light.

Anglesite This sulfate mineral is also called "lead spar," because it was used as an ore of lead. It has the unusual property of being transparent with an adamantine (diamond-like) luster, yet it is heavy. With a hardness of only 3, it is not a very useful gemstone.

Magnetite Also known as lodestone, magnetite shows the unusual property of strong magnetism. When pure, this oxide contains about 72 percent iron metal and is an important ore of iron. It is usually black or gray, distinctly heavy, and opaque.

Barite This sulfate of barium is also known as "heavy spar" because of its weight, although it is not as heavy as lead spar. Barite is found in sedimentary and hydrothermal deposits. It fluoresces white to blue-green under ultraviolet light.

Geode A geode forms when mineral crystals grow inward from the walls of an open rock cavity. These tiny treasure caves, such as the one above filled with purple amethyst, often weather out of their host volcanic rocks and are eagerly sought by collectors.

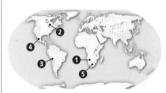

Elemental Minerals

Elemental minerals are those naturally occurring minerals that are made up entirely of single elements from the periodic table. Compared to other minerals they are not common, but despite their rarity, elemental mineral deposits were quickly discovered and utilized by humankind. They include minerals such as gold, silver, copper, diamond, graphite, and sulfur.

Native elements (below) The elements listed in the chart below are those that can be found as minerals in the "native," or uncombined, state. Less reactive elements such as gold are far more common than reactive elements such as zinc.

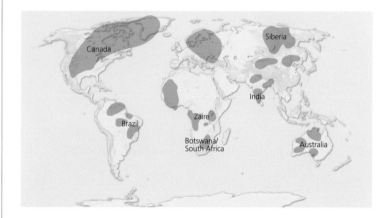

Diamond distribution (above) Diamonds are found in Earth's oldest continental rocks or cratons (shaded purple). Explosive volcanic eruptions, known as diatremes, carry diamond crystals to the surface from their high-temperature and high-pressure origins in the mantle.

NATIVE ELEMENTS		
Metals	**Semimetals**	**Nonmetals**
Gold (Au)	Arsenic (As)	Sulfur (S)
Silver (Ag)	Bismuth (Bi)	Diamond (C)
Copper (Cu)	Tellurium (Te)	Graphite (C)
Platinum	Antimony (Sb)	
Group (Pt)	Selenium (Se)	
Iron-nickel	Silicon (Si)	
(Fe–Ni)		
Cadmium (Cd)		
Chromium (Cr)		
Aluminum (Al)		
Lead (Pb)		
Mercury (Hg)		
Tin (Sn)		
Titanium (Ti)		
Zinc (Zn)		

Gold Buddha head (above) Gold is a popular medium in many cultures because it is soft, malleable, easy to work with, and beautiful. Gold objects do not tarnish or deteriorate.

Traditional jewelry (above right) This jewelry from Gioielli Tuareg, in the southwest Libyan Desert, North Africa, is fashioned from silver and gemstones in traditional style.

Copper connection (right) The excellent electrical conductive properties of copper, its flexibility, and its resistance to corrosion have led to this metal's important role in modern society.

Lead uses Lead is a soft, heavy, malleable metal. Although rare as a native element, lead is easy to smelt and was discovered early, along with important Bronze Age metals such as copper and tin.

Lead weights Lead is used in the weight belts that scuba divers wear to compensate for the buoyancy they experience in the water.

Typesetting Lead was used for hot-metal typesetting. It was injected into letter-shaped molds, which were used to press ink onto paper.

Sulfur mountain (left) Elemental sulfur is stockpiled in huge yellow mountains at this mine site in Western Australia. Sulfur plays an important role in the production of fertilizer, sulfuric acid for car batteries, paper, and rubber products.

Mine waste dumps Environmentally toxic and polluting chemicals in mine dumps have long given the mining industry a bad name. Today, mine waste is strictly controlled, and technological advances have allowed dumps to be reprocessed to recover valuable elements.

Different colors Fluorite occurs in a variety of colors. The different colors are caused by trace amounts of impurities. It is, however, recognizable by its perfect octahedral cleavage and its fluorescence.

Sulfur   Rhodochrosite

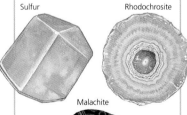

Malachite

One color Minerals colored by the elements in their chemical formula are always the same color. Sulfur is always yellow, rhodochrosite is always pink, and malachite is always green.

Elemental Minerals Gallery

These examples of elemental minerals include copper, vital in the rise of early civilization; diamond, cherished as a precious gemstone; gold and silver, both precious metals and important for coinage and jewelry; graphite, used for pencil leads and as a lubricant; and sulfur, used for fertilizer, paper, and acid production.

Diamond crystal trigons The octahedral crystal face of a diamond is immediately recognizable under the microscope by the geometrically arranged, triangular-shaped pits. These were etched by corrosive chemicals during the diamond's journey to Earth's surface.

SULFUR S

Elemental sulfur is recognizable as bright yellow deposits associated with volcanic fumaroles or hot spring activity. It is soft and brittle, melts easily, and is inflammable. It burns with a blue flame, releasing pungent sulfur dioxide gas.

Properties Yellow color; adamantine luster; orthorhombic crystal system; hardness 1.5–2; translucent; conchoidal-to-uneven brittle fracture; crystalline-to-earthy habit.

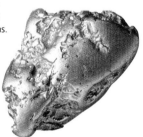

COPPER Cu

Native copper occurs as tree-like forms or heavy masses weighing up to several hundred tons. Surfaces are copper pink when fresh but typically coated with green tarnish. The world's largest deposit was on the Keweenaw Peninsula, U.S.A.

Properties Light red color; metallic luster; cubic crystal system; hardness 2.5–3; opaque; rough fracture; malleable; arborescent, dendritic (tree-like)-to-massive habit.

PLATINUM Pt

Platinum is a prized and extremely rare element in Earth's crust. It can become enriched in low silica mantle intrusions, and concentrated in nearby alluvial river systems. Small amounts of iron can make it magnetic.

Properties Gray-to-white color; metallic luster; cubic crystal system; hardness 4–4.5; opaque; rough fracture; malleable; crystalline-to-granular habit.

GOLD Au

Gold is a rare mineral in hydrothermal deposits, and can be concentrated in alluvial deposits because of its high density. This golden yellow metal never tarnishes and has been the source of many a "gold rush."

Properties Yellow color; metallic luster; cubic crystal system; hardness 2.5–3; opaque; rough fracture; malleable; crystalline, nuggetty-to-massive habit.

GRAPHITE C

Dark-gray-to-black elemental carbon occurs in veins or high temperature metamorphic deposits. Graphite is immediately recognizable by its soft, slippery feel, making it an ideal lubricant. It is a good conductor of electricity.

Properties Dark-gray color; metallic luster; hexagonal crystal system; hardness 1–1.5; opaque; greasy feel; perfect cleavage; scaly-to-earthy habit.

SILVER Ag

Native silver often occurs in wiry or dendritic (tree-like) shapes, with its silvery surfaces coated in black tarnish. It is a good electrical conductor and is found in hydrothermal deposits. Major localities include the U.S.A., Canada, Chile, and Germany.

Properties Silver-white color; metallic luster; cubic crystal system; hardness 2.5–3; opaque, rough fracture; ductile; crystalline, wiry-to-massive habit.

ELECTRUM Au, Ag

Electrum is a naturally occurring alloy of gold and silver. Gold content varies anywhere between 80 percent to under 50 percent. Electrum was used to make ancient drinking vessels and coins, and was known as white gold.

Properties Pale yellow or yellowish-white color; conducts electricity; metallic; opaque; harder and more durable than either gold or silver.

DIAMOND C

Diamonds are a transparent, high-pressure form of carbon, the hardest mineral known. Their rarity and ability to split white light up into a rainbow spectrum makes them the most prized of precious gems.

Properties Colorless-to-pale colors; adamantine luster; cubic crystal system; hardness 10; transparent to translucent; perfect cleavage; octahedral habit.

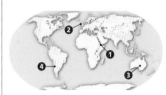
1. Mineral spires The jagged mineral spires rising from the desert floor in Djibouti, east Africa, are made of calcium carbonate. They were formed when mineral-laden spring water percolated up to the surface through faults. As the water evaporated, it left deposits of concentrated minerals.

 With time, as the surrounding land has been eroded, these mineral spires have become prominent desert features.

Mineral spires, Djibouti

2. Chalk cliffs "White Rocks" is the name given to the chalk cliffs near Portrush, in County Antrim, Ireland. The chalk layers were formed by the build-up of calcium carbonate skeletons from tiny, single-celled marine organisms called coccoliths, which lived in the

 Cretaceous period. These organisms died and fell to the seafloor between 142 and 65 million years ago.

Chalk cliffs, County Antrim, Ireland

3. Lake Eyre saltpan Lake Eyre Basin is the world's largest evaporite saltpan, covering about one-sixth of the Australian continent. All the basin's riverbeds lead inland toward Lake Eyre, which in most years is completely dry. Shimmering white flats of salt extend as far as the eye can see. On the dry

 lake, zones of different minerals can be observed, with the first to crystallize being the least soluble.

Lake Eyre saltpan, Australia

4. Rhodochrosite caves In this cave in Catamarca Province, Argentina, there is rare abundance of dissolved manganese in the groundwater. As the water dripped down from the cave ceiling, precipitation has led to the growth of delicately banded, pink-and-white stalactites. These formations

 are made of the gem-quality manganese mineral rhodochrosite, rather than the more typical white calcite.

Rhodochrosite caves, Catamarca Province, Argentina

Compound Minerals

Compound minerals are naturally occurring crystalline substances, which are formed by the chemical combination of two or more of the periodic table's 90 naturally occurring elements. Almost all the 4,000-plus known minerals in the rocks around us are compounds. They fall into classes such as oxides, sulfides, silicates, and so on, depending on the combining elements.

Minerals of Earth's crust The silicates are by far the biggest compound mineral class, making up about 90 percent of the rocks in Earth's crust. Of these, feldspar is the most abundant mineral group, at a massive 77 percent, and is present in almost every rock.

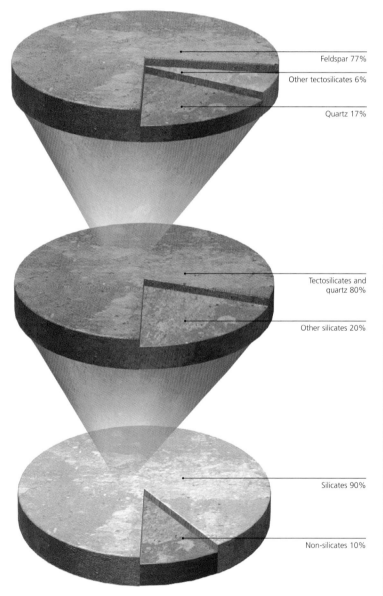

Feldspar 77%

Other tectosilicates 6%

Quartz 17%

Tectosilicates and quartz 80%

Other silicates 20%

Silicates 90%

Non-silicates 10%

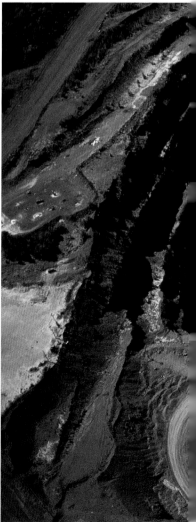

Iron mining (right) The Empire Iron Mine is a large, deep open pit in Ishpeming, Michigan, U.S.A. The iron occurs as an oxide (the minerals magnetite and hematite) and must be smelted with coking coal to remove the oxygen and recover the iron metal.

EVAPORITE DEPOSITION

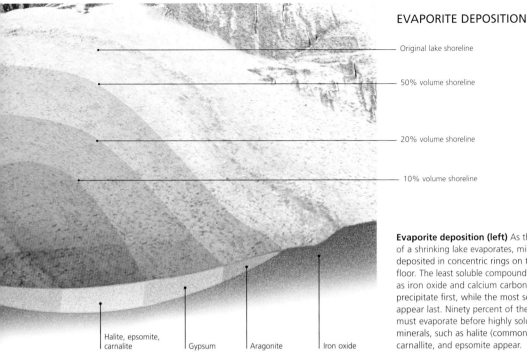

Original lake shoreline

50% volume shoreline

20% volume shoreline

10% volume shoreline

Halite, epsomite, carnalite

Gypsum

Aragonite

Iron oxide

Evaporite deposition (left) As the water of a shrinking lake evaporates, minerals are deposited in concentric rings on the lake floor. The least soluble compounds, such as iron oxide and calcium carbonate, precipitate first, while the most soluble appear last. Ninety percent of the water must evaporate before highly soluble minerals, such as halite (common salt), carnallite, and epsomite appear.

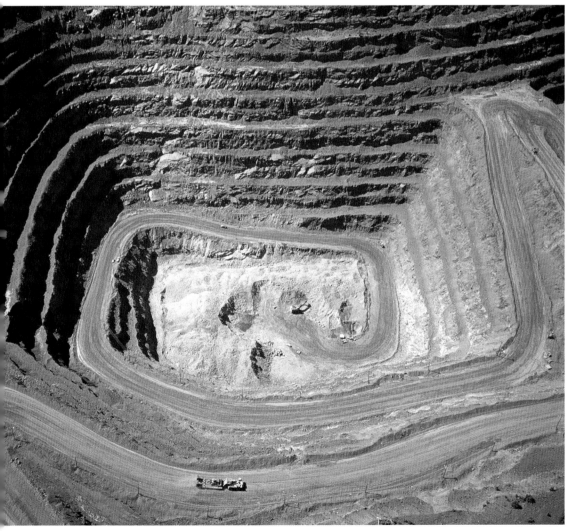

FACT FILE

Beautiful minerals Brightly colored, transparent, hard, or shiny minerals have long attracted people's interest. Gem minerals have been used for barter and trade, or as a form of ornamentation, by many different cultures.

Blue jewels Turquoise is a compound of copper, phosphorous, and oxygen. Here it has been fashioned into earrings, worn by the upper class in Lhasa, Tibet.

Red and green gems The 14th-century Hylle Jewel forms the letter "M." It is studded with rubies, diamonds, emeralds, and pearls.

FACT FILE

Lapis lazuli A compound of sodium, calcium, aluminum, silicon, oxygen, sulfur, and chlorine gives this rare gem its blue color. Originally mined at Sar-e-Sang, Afghanistan, it was one of the first gems used for jewelry and carving. In Europe, it was crushed for blue pigment.

Sulfides

The sulfides are an important mineral group in which different metallic elements have combined chemically with sulfur. Sulfide minerals are neither widespread nor common, but are sought for their strategically important metals such as copper, lead, zinc, nickel, and tin. These minerals are typically heavy, opaque, and display a metallic luster.

Fool's gold Pyrite (FeS_2) or "iron pyrites" is also known as "fools gold" because of the people who find it and believe they have made their fortune. Compared to gold, pyrite is brassy and brittle not malleable, and has a green-black streak rather than a metallic yellow one.

CHALCOCITE Cu_2S

Chalcocite is formed by the combination of two copper atoms with one sulfur atom and is an ore of copper. It has been mined at Redruth, in Cornwall, England, associated with other hydrothermal copper minerals.

Properties Dark-gray color with blue-green tint; metallic to dull luster; hardness 2.5–3; opaque; uneven fracture; brittle; crystalline-to-earthy habit.

CHALCOPYRITE $CuFeS_2$

Chalcopyrite is a brassy yellow ore of copper—a combination of one copper, one iron, and one sulfur atom. It is often found with black sphalerite (ZnS), an important zinc ore.

Properties Yellow color, black streak; metallic luster; tetragonal crystal system; hardness 3.5–4; opaque; conchoidal fracture; brittle; crystalline-to-massive habit.

ACANTHITE Ag_2S

Acanthite is rare. It is the principal ore of silver and commonly occurs with galena (lead ore). Associated with hydrothermal veins in subduction zones, major deposits are in Bolivia, Peru, Mexico, and Honduras.

Properties Gray-to-black color, black streak; metallic luster; hardness 2; opaque; uneven to conchoidal fracture; malleable; dendritic (tree-like) crystalline-to-massive habit.

STIBNITE Sb_2S_3

Stibnite is the principal ore of antimony, used for metal alloys, fireworks, and in the rubber and textile industry. Major hydrothermal deposits occur in Hunan and Kwantung provinces, China, and beautiful crystals are found in Ichinokawa, Japan.

Properties Steel-gray color, gray streak; metallic luster; orthorhombic crystal system; hardness 2; opaque; perfect cleavage; flexible; columnar-to-fibrous habit.

PENTLANDITE $(Fe,Ni)_9S_8$

Pentlandite is the principal source of nickel. It is associated with low silica rocks that are, perhaps, the result of meteorite impacts. Major deposits are mined at Sudbury, Canada, and the Bushveld Complex, Transvaal, in South Africa.

Properties Bronze-brown color, green-black streak; metallic luster; cubic crystal system; hardness 3.5–4; opaque; one good cleavage; brittle; massive habit.

CINNABAR HgS

Cinnabar is a heavy, red, principal ore of mercury. It evaporates readily when heated, leaving metallic mercury droplets. Cinnabar forms in a low-temperature hydrothermal environment and was once used as the pigment vermilion.

Properties Red color, scarlet streak; adamantine luster; trigonal crystal system; hardness 2-2.5; opaque; perfect cleavage; brittle; crystalline-to-massive habit.

GALENA PbS

Galena, or "lead glance," is the principal ore of lead. It is associated with the zinc ore, sphalerite, in medium-temperature hydrothermal environments. The U.S.A., Australia, England, and Mexico have major mines.

Properties Lead-gray color, gray streak; metallic luster; cubic crystal system; hardness 2.5; opaque; perfect cubic cleavage; brittle; granular-to-massive habit.

MARCASITE FeS$_2$

Marcasite or "spear pyrites" and its cubic cousin pyrite are mined to produce sulfuric acid. When struck with a hammer, they produce a sulfureous odor. Both can be polished into bright metallic yellow gemstones.

Properties Brass-yellow or dark tarnish color, gray-green streak; metallic luster; orthorhombic crystal system; hardness 6–6.5; opaque; "spearhead" crystals, concretionary habit.

Silicates and Silica

The silicates are the most abundant group of minerals, in which metallic elements combine with different ratios of silicon and oxygen. Common members are called the "rock forming minerals," as at least one of them occurs in virtually every rock. These are olivine, pyroxene, amphibole, mica, feldspar, and quartz (silica, an oxide of silicon).

Chiastolite This variety of aluminum silicate grows in metamorphic rocks. Its crystals have fine black carbonaceous inclusions, which result in a striking cross-shaped pattern popular in religious jewelry. This specimen comes from Alconie Hill, South Australia.

FELDSPAR, VARIETY AMAZONITE

Amazonite is a jungle-green variety of potassium feldspar found in pegmatite rocks, shown here in a cluster with a prismatic, smoky quartz crystal. Amazonite has been used for cabochons and beads since ancient times.

Properties Green-to-blue-green color, white streak; vitreous luster; triclinic crystal system; hardness 6; translucent to opaque; brittle; prismatic habit.

QUARTZ, VARIETY AMETHYST

Amethyst is a purple variety of quartz found as crystals growing in cavities in volcanic rocks. When huge deposits were discovered in Brazil in the 19th century, this once-royal gem became generally affordable.

Properties Light-to-intense purple color, white streak; vitreous luster; trigonal crystal system; hardness 7; transparent to translucent; short pyramidal habit.

DIOPTASE

Dioptase is a beautiful green copper mineral popular with collectors and sometimes cut as a gemstone. It occurs as a rare secondary mineral in the oxidized zone of copper orebodies, and is mined in Namibia and Chile.

Properties Dark-green color, green streak; vitreous luster; cubic crystal system; hardness 5; translucent to transparent; good cleavage; blocky, aggregate habit.

BERYL, VARIETY MORGANITE

Morganite is a rare, rose-pink-to-red beryl variety, colored by trace amounts of manganese. Non-gem beryl is mined for the element beryllium, which is used in the production of light metal alloys.

Properties Pink-to-red color, white streak; vitreous luster; hexagonal crystal system; hardness 7.5–8; translucent to transparent; brittle; columnar prismatic habit.

BERYL, VARIETY AQUAMARINE

Aquamarine is a popular, sea-blue-to-green-blue gem beryl, colored by traces of iron. In general, beryl crystals of all colors grow in pegmatites, with some non-gem crystals from Brazil weighing several hundred tons.

Properties Light-blue-to-green-blue color, white streak; vitreous luster; hexagonal crystal system; hardness 7.5–8; transparent; brittle; columnar, flat-topped, prismatic habit.

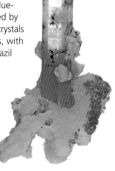

BERYL, VARIETY EMERALD

Emerald is the best-known and most precious of all gem beryls. It was appreciated for its beauty by ancient Egyptian and Native American cultures. Its intense green color is caused by traces of chromium.

Properties Deep-green color; white streak; vitreous luster; hexagonal crystal system; hardness 7.5–8; transparent; often heavy inclusions; brittle; columnar, prismatic habit.

HEULANDITE

Heulandite is a member of the zeolite group that usually occurs in secondary, mineral-filled cavities in basalt, associated with calcite. The open structure of zeolites' mineral framework makes them ideal chemical filters.

Properties White-to red-color; pearly luster; monoclinic crystal system; hardness 3.5–4; translucent to transparent; perfect cleavage; fibrous; stellate (starry) habit.

OLIVINE

Olivine is well known as the olive-green gemstone peridot. It is the main constituent of Earth's mantle and is carried to the surface in basaltic volcanic eruptions. Rare large crystals are found in Russia and Egypt.

Properties Green color; vitreous luster; orthorhombic crystal system; hardness 6.5–7; translucent to transparent; stubby, prismatic habit or granular aggregates.

Oxides and Hydroxides

The oxide minerals are a chemical combination of metallic elements with oxygen. Some of the minerals in this group are fairly common and include the principal ores of metals such as iron (hematite), titanium (rutile), aluminum (bauxite), and uranium (uraninite). Hydroxides are formed by combination with water in the near–surface environment.

Magnetite Magnetism is the most diagnostic property of magnetite, an iron oxide. Known by ancient civilizations as "lodestone," it was suspended by a string to form a primitive compass and used for navigation. This specimen shows magnetite (black), calcite and quartz crystals (white), and epidote (green).

FACT FILE

Hardness A mineral's hardness is determined by scratching it with an object or another mineral of known hardness. It is placed on Moh's Hardness Scale from 1 to 10, ranging between talc, the softest, and diamond, the hardest known.

1 Talc

2 Gypsum

3 Calcite

4 Fluorite

5 Apatite

6 Orthoclase

7 Quartz

8 Topaz

9 Corundum

10 Diamond

SPINEL $MgAl_2O_4$

Gem-quality spinel is variously colored and transparent, while common spinel is black and nearly opaque. Being hard and heavy, spinel is concentrated in river deposits and associated with sapphires, rubies, and zircons.

Properties All colors; vitreous luster; cubic crystal system; hardness 8; translucent to transparent; brittle, conchoidal fracture; octahedral habit.

TANTALITE $(Mn, Fe)(Ta, Nb)_2O_6$

Tantalite occurs in granite pegmatites and, being heavy, is concentrated in river deposits. It is the principal ore of the rare metals tantalum and niobium, which are used for heat-resistant alloys, stainless steel, and superconductors.

Properties Black-brown color; sub-metallic luster; orthorhombic crystal system; hardness 6–6.5; opaque; striated, tabular crystals or aggregates; weakly radioactive.

SAPPHIRE Al_2O_3

Blue sapphire is believed to be the world's most important colored gemstone. This tough, hard, and heavy oxide of aluminum grows in metamorphic and basaltic volcanic rocks and is concentrated in river deposits, such as those mined in Australia and Sri Lanka.

Properties Blue, yellow, and green colors, vitreous luster; trigonal crystal system; hardness 9; transparent; pyramidal or prismatic crystals; needle-like rutile inclusions.

HEMATITE Fe_2O_3

Hematite is the world's principal source of iron. It formed in massive sedimentary deposits in Earth's ancient continental shield areas. It is immediately distinguishable by its cherry-red streak, heaviness, and weak attraction to a magnet.

Properties Brown, gray, and black colors, red streak; metallic-to-dull luster; hexagonal crystal system; hardness 6.5; opaque; reniform to massive habit; magnetic.

LIMONITE $FeOOH \cdot_nH_2O$

Limonite is a hydrated iron oxide formed by the weathering of other iron-rich minerals. It is sometimes used as an ore of iron and, in its soft, earthy form, as a yellow ochre pigment.

Properties Brown-yellow color, brown streak; sub-vitreous to dull luster; amorphous; hardness 5–5.5; opaque; crusty, oolitic (small spheres), botryoidal (grape-like), stalactitic habit.

CHRYSOBERYL $BeAl_2O_4$

Chrysoberyl can occur as a green transparent gem, or as cymophane—a cat's eye variety. The rare Alexandrite variety changes color from green in daylight to red at night.

Properties Yellow, green colors, vitreous luster; orthorhombic crystal system; hardness 8.5; transparent to translucent; tabular twinned crystals; green luminescence.

RUBY Al$_2$O$_3$

"Pigeon-blood" red rubies are prized—large stones are worth more than equivalent-sized white diamonds. Metamorphic "Burmese" rubies, some with magnificent asterism, or "stars," are mined in Mogok Valley, Myanmar.

Properties Pink-to-red color; vitreous luster; trigonal crystal system; hardness 9; transparent; tabular or prismatic crystals; acicular (needle-like) rutile inclusions.

RUTILE TiO$_2$

Oxides of titanium (rutile), iron (hematite), and silicon (quartz) have grown together in this radiating crystal arrangement. The delicate orange-red rutile crystals display classic acicular (needle-like) habit.

Properties Black, brown, and red colors; adamantine to sub-metallic luster; tetragonal crystal system; hardness 6–6.5; translucent to opaque; striated, prismatic-to-needle-like habit.

FACT FILE

Transparency Transparency, or diaphaneity, describes how easily light is able to pass through a mineral. Many minerals are transparent when pure, but they can be rendered translucent or opaque by inclusions or cracks.

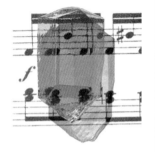

Transparent Minerals such as quartz are completely see-through.

Semitransparent Minerals such as moonstone show a blurred image.

Translucent Minerals such as chrysoprase allow only a little light.

Opaque Minerals such as malachite do not allow any light to pass through.

Phosphates, Arsenates, and Vanadates

This mineral class is the combination of metal atoms with negatively charged groups of phosphate, arsenate, and vanadate. Phosphate minerals are often used for corrosion control and fertilizers, while arsenates and vanadates are sources of arsenic and vanadium.

Turquoise $CuAl_6(PO_4)_4(OH)_8 \bullet 4H_2O$ Formed by the weathering of aluminum and copper-rich rocks in arid areas, turquoise is a sky-blue copper phosphate. Inferior specimens are treated with dyes, oils, and resins to improve their appearance.

VANADINITE ON BARITE $Pb_5(VO_4)_3Cl$

Vanadinite is a rare secondary mineral and ore of the metal vanadium, used as an alloy to make speciality steel products. Vanadinite is found in Argentina, Austria, Morocco, Namibia, South Africa, and Zambia.

Properties Reddish orange color; adamantine-to-resinous luster; hexagonal crystal system; hardness 3; brittle; translucent; short hexagonal prismatic habit.

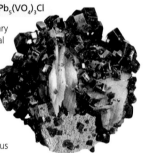

APATITE $Ca_5(PO_4)_3(F,OH)$

Apatite is used in the production of phosphate fertilizer, phosphoric acid, and phosphorous. It is mostly mined from chemical sedimentary deposits in Naru, Egypt, and northern Africa. Transparent colored igneous crystals are cut as gemstones.

Properties All colors; vitreous; greasy luster; hexagonal crystal system; hardness 5; brittle; transparent to translucent; prismatic, oolitic (small spheres), earthy habit.

CHILDRENITE $(Fe,Mn)Al(PO_4)(OH)_2 \bullet H_2O$

Childrenite was discovered in the secondary alteration zone of the George and Charlotte Mine at Tavistock, in Devon, England. It was identified by mineralogist John George Children in 1823. It is only of interest to collectors.

Properties Brown and yellow colors; vitreous luster; orthorhombic crystal system; hardness 4.5–5; brittle; translucent; short hexagonal prismatic habit.

PYROMORPHITE $Pb_5(PO_4)_3Cl$

Pyromorphite is a rare secondary mineral found in the oxidized zone of lead deposits in Germany, the Czech Republic, England, Australia, and Mexico. Also known as "green lead ore," it can show green luminescence under ultraviolet light

Properties Yellow-green color; adamantine resinous luster; hexagonal crystal system; hardness 3.5–4; brittle; translucent; short barrel-shaped prisms, reniform crusty habit.

HERDERITE $CaBe(PO_4)(F,OH)$

Herderite is a rare ore of phosphorous and beryllium, a lightweight metal used for aerospace applications. Identifying features are its deep blue fluorescence under ultraviolet light, and its tabular fishtail or pseudo-hexagonal twinned crystals.

Properties White, yellowish, bluish color; vitreous luster; monoclinic crystal system; hardness 5–5.5; brittle; transparent to translucent; tabular cyclic twinned habit.

PHOSPHOPHYLLITE $Fe(PO_4) \bullet 2H_2O$

Phosphophyllite is quite soft, yet this rare iron phosphate is sometimes cut as a gemstone. The best fine, transparent crystals come from Potosi, in Bolivia. It is luminescent and soluble in most acids.

Properties Blue-green color; vitreous luster; monoclinic crystal system; hardness 3.5; perfect cleavage; brittle; transparent; tabular-to-columnar habit; violet luminescence.

LIROCONITE Cu$_2$Al(AsO$_4$)(OH)$_4$•4H$_2$O

Liroconite is a rare hydrated copper aluminum arsenate. Colored light blue to green by copper, it forms from the oxidation of copper ores and is associated with other secondary copper minerals, such as malachite and chalcophyllite.

Properties Blue-to-green color, blue streak; vitreous luster; monoclinic crystal system; hardness 2–2.5; brittle; transparent to translucent; flattened pseudo-octahedral habit.

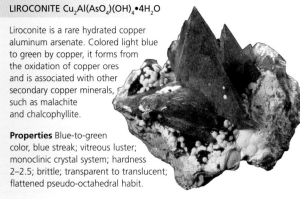

VIVIANITE Fe$_3$(PO$_4$)$_2$•8H$_2$O

Vivianite, or "blue iron earth," displays the remarkable property where its color and streak change from white to dark green or blue on exposure to light. It cleaves perfectly into flexible plates. When heated it turns red and fuses into a magnetic bead.

Properties Dark blue and green colors; vitreous, pearly luster; monoclinic crystal system; hardness 2; translucent; radiating prismatic-to-tabular habit.

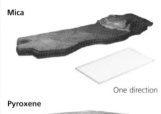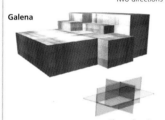
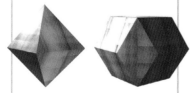
Sulfates

Sulfate minerals form when metals combine with the negatively charged SO_4^{2-} group, made up of one sulphur atom and four oxygen atoms. There are about 200 sulfate minerals. Some, such as anhydrite and gypsum, are common, but most are rare and occur locally. Sulfates are mostly transparent to translucent, soft, heavy, and soluble in water to some degree. They are a source for fertilizer or different metals.

Copper sulfate Chalcanthite $CuSO_4 \bullet 5H_2O$ is a naturally occurring copper sulfate, and major ore of copper. Specimens must be kept in an airtight container or they lose water and crumble. Chalcanthite occurs in the oxidized zone of copper deposits.

LINARITE $PbCu(SO_4)_2(OH)_2$

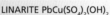

Linarite is a rare secondary mineral that occurs as encrustations in the oxidation zone of lead deposits. It was named in 1832 after being found in Linares, Spain. It is soluble in dilute nitric acid.

Properties Blue color, blue streak; vitreous luster; monoclinic crystal system; hardness 2.5; heavy; perfect cleavage; brittle; translucent; columnar; platy habit.

GYPSUM $CaSO_4 \bullet 2H_2O$

This common desert evaporite mineral occurs as transparent crystals, fibrous aggregates called selenite, or flower-like sandy clusters called desert roses. Gypsum is soluble in hot water and used in plaster and cement.

Properties Colorless; vitreous, pearly luster; monoclinic crystal system; hardness 2; perfect cleavage; slightly flexible; transparent; tabular habit; spearhead-shaped crystals.

CELESTITE $SrSO_4$

Celestite grows in cavities in volcanic rocks and also in evaporate deposits. It is the principal ore of strontium, used in the manufacture of television tubes and flares. Despite its softness, celestite is sometimes cut as a gemstone.

Properties White, blue, yellow, and red colors; pearly luster; orthorhombic crystal system; hardness 3–3.5; perfect cleavage; transparent to translucent; columnar, platy habit.

BARITE $BaSO_4$

Barite, or "heavy spar," occurs as crystals, rosettes, and stalactitic or concretionary masses. It forms in hydrothermal veins with lead and silver sulfides, hot springs, or sedimentary deposits. Barite is the principal ore of barium.

Properties Colorless; vitreous, pearly luster; orthorhombic crystal system; hardness 3–3.5; perfect cleavage; transparent to translucent; platy, radiating fibrous habit; luminescent.

ETTRINGITE $Ca_6Al_2(SO_4)_3(OH)_{12} \bullet 26H_2O$

Ettringite takes its name from Ettringen, Rhineland-Palatinate, Germany. It is slightly soluble in water and readily soluble in dilute acids. It crystallizes from hydrothermal solutions and is light because of its high water content.

Properties Colorless; yellow, vitreous luster; monoclinic crystal system; hardness 2–2.5; perfect cleavage; brittle; translucent; short prismatic, acicular (needle-like) habit.

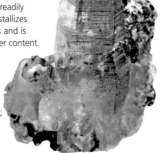

CREEDITE $Ca_3Al_2SO_4(F,OH)_{10} \bullet 2H_2O$

Creedite was first described in 1916 at the Creed Quadrangle in Mineral County, Colorado, U.S.A. It forms during intense oxidation of ore deposits and is associated with fluorite. Creedite is found in Bolivia, Mexico, and the U.S.A.

Properties White and purple colors; vitreous luster; monoclinic crystal system; hardness 4; perfect cleavage; transparent to translucent; prismatic, radiating acicular (needle-like) habit.

BROCHANTITE $Cu_4(SO_4)(OH)_6$

Brochantite is rare outside of Chuquicamata, Chile, where it is an important copper ore. It occurs in arid areas in the oxidized zones of copper deposits. It was named after the French mineralogist, André Brochant de Villiers.

Properties Green color, green streak; vitreous, pearly luster; monoclinic crystal system; hardness 3.5–4; good cleavage; transparent to translucent; platy, fibrous habit.

ANGLESITE $PbSO_4$

Anglesite, or "lead spar," is a lead ore formed by alteration of galena in the oxidized zone of lead deposits. Fine crystals come from Tsumeb in Namibia, Westphalia in Germany, and Pennsylvania in the U.S.A. These are sometimes cut as gems.

Properties Colorless; silky adamantine luster; orthorhombic crystal system; hardness 3; transparent to translucent; very heavy; platy, prismatic, stalactitic habit; luminescent.

PRECIOUS GEMS AND METALS

Gemstones and precious metals have been used and admired by many different cultures throughout the ages. For a mineral to be considered a precious gemstone it must satisfy the three fundamental criteria of beauty, rarity, and durability. A truly precious gemstone must be attractive to the beholder, not be so commonplace that it is easy to find, and be long-wearing so that it can be handed down from generation to generation, increasing its historic and sentimental value. Many beautiful minerals are too fragile to be gemstones. Attractive rocks and minerals that are too commonplace to be precious are known as ornamental gemstones.

PERCEPTION AND USE

The appreciation of stones purely for their beauty, and not simply for their functionality, began at least 25,000 years ago during the upper Paleolithic, accompanying the explosion in Europe of the use of art for symbolic representation. The aesthetic appreciation of non-functional objects and art indicates the ability to think beyond the needs of basic survival—perhaps indicative of an emerging spirituality or an early form of worship.

Egyptian jewelry This vulture pendant belongs to a necklace found in the tomb of Tutankhamen and was made between 1370 and 52 B.C. It demonstrates exquisite craftsmanship in lapidary and metalworking, with polished blue lapis lazuli from ancient Afghan mines and red carnelian set in gold. Such treasures from royal tombs are priceless today.

About 6,000 years ago in Mesopotamia, some of the earliest gemstones used included turquoise, lapis lazuli, and a red type of quartz known as carnelian. Later, jade was used in China. The discovery of gold and silver meant these stones could be set together in larger objects of art or wearable jewelry.

Precious metals are rare. Expensive metallic chemical elements, such as gold and silver, are best known for their historic use in coinage, jewelry, and art. Lesser-known and more recently discovered precious metals include rhenium, ruthenium, rhodium, palladium, osmium, iridium, and platinum. Rhodium is the most expensive of these.

Gemstones are mentioned throughout the Bible. In Exodus 28:17–21, the Lord instructed Moses to engrave the names of the 12 sons of Israel on

Aztec treasure (right) This pectoral ornament, crafted between 1400 and 1521, is in the form of a double-headed serpent and represents Tlaloc, the feared Aztec god of rain, fertility, and water. Tiny polished squares of blue turquoise with orange and white shell are encrusted on a wooden base. Worn by an Aztec high priest, it was part of the treasure given to Hernán Cortés by emperor Montezuma, who believed the Spanish conquistador to be a returning god. Native Mexican cultures traded gold, turquoise, jade, obsidian, onyx, shell, and bone for use in ceremonial and decorative works.

Symbolism (below right) Jewelry can be a sign of wealth or status, and may be unique to a region or indigenous group. In the city of Mopti, in the West African country of Mali, this Fulah woman wears ornate hair decorations made of amber, gold, and other materials. "Mali garnet" is also found in the region, and when cut displays a remarkable brilliance, luster, and dispersion.

12 stones in the breastplate of the high priest, stating the exact order, arrangement, and type of each stone to be used. Today, the best-known precious gemstones are rubies, diamonds, sapphires, emeralds, and opals. Diamonds are the most popular because of the success of global marketing campaigns.

The imitation of precious gemstones has been attempted for as long as there was a profit to be made from deceit and trickery. Common minerals or glass are early examples. The first synthetic gemstone was a sapphire made by French chemist Auguste Victor Louis Verneuil in 1902. Today, synthetics are commonplace. These laboratory-created stones have identical physical and chemical characteristics to the natural gem, but are far less expensive. Jewelry stores are bound by laws and ethics to disclose synthetic gemstones to their customers.

THROUGH THE AGES

25,000–12,000 B.C. Upper Paleolithic peoples used stones and other objects for personal adornment.	**6000 B.C.** Ceremonial objects and jewelry in royal tombs were made from bone, seashell, limestone, quartz, turquoise, lapis lazuli, carnelian, and copper.	**4000 B.C.** Jade was finely crafted in China. Lapis lazuli beads and pendants were used for currency by the Assyrians, and gold jewelry appeared in ancient Mesopotamia.	**3000 B.C.** A belt set with agate, carnelian, jade, jasper, and lapis lazuli was placed in an Indian tomb, revealing that gemstone use and trade was widespread by this time.	**2600 B.C.** King Tushratta of the Mitanni said gold was "more plentiful than dirt" in Egyptian hieroglyphs. Egypt and Nubia became gold-producing areas.	**2000 B.C.** Baltic amber was traded by the Phoenicians in the Mediterranean area. Gemstones were esteemed for magical properties, as well as their attractive colors.	**296 B.C.** The earliest diamond references appeared in the Budo text *Anguttara Nikaya* and in the Sanskrit text *Arthashastra*.

Modern metal (below) Bright, light aluminum is glorified by 15,000 spun disks that cover the Selfridges department store in Birmingham, England. Designed by Future Systems, the modern building contrasts strikingly with the Gothic-style St. Martin's Church in the foreground. Aluminum was once rare and considered a precious metal until 1886, when chemists Charles Martin Hall (inset left) and Paul Louis-Toussaint Héroult (inset right) independently invented a cheap, electrolytic process for refining it. The technique involves dissolving aluminum oxide (bauxite) in molten cryolite flux.

200 B.C. Distinctively styled turquoise was extensively used by southwestern U.S. Native Americans and by many Indian tribes in Mexico.

A.D. 1512 Hernán Cortés arrived in the New World and found that indigenous Mexican cultures placed a higher value on jade and turquoise than on gold.

1557 The first European reference was made to platinum, "the mysterious metal found in the Central American mines" and "impossible to melt."

1802–1844 Precious metals iridium, rhodium, osmium, palladium, and ruthenium were discovered.

1886 The Hall-Héroult process was developed for the easy production of aluminum, causing a collapse in the price of the metal.

1902 The first artificial gemstone, synthetic sapphire, was made by French chemist Auguste Victor Louis Verneuil using the "flame-fusion" method.

1905 The largest gem-quality rough diamond, the Cullinan, weighing 3,106.75 carats, was found by Frederick Wells in South Africa.

1954 Howard Tracy Hall grew the first synthetic diamond while working for General Electric, using a high-pressure and high-temperature apparatus.

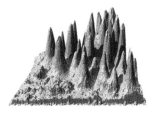

Carbonates

Carbonate minerals form when metal atoms combine with carbonate groups. They are common in near–surface sedimentary environments. Carbonates usually display well-developed cleavage, and are soft and transparent. They are light colored, except when colored by copper, manganese, iron, or lead. Carbonates are soluble in acid and effervesce carbon dioxide gas.

Aurichalcite $(Zn,Cu)_5(CO_3)_2(OH)_6$ This attractive light-blue-to-green carbonate mineral forms in the oxidized zone of copper and zinc-ore bodies. Aurichalcite occurs habitually as crusts, or as delicate radiating arrangements of needle-like monoclinic crystals, as seen here.

WITHERITE $BaCO_3$

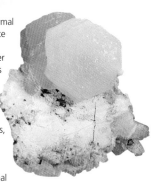

This low-temperature hydrothermal mineral is associated with barite and galena. It is fluorescent and phosphorescent blue under ultraviolet light and effervesces in dilute acid. It is a barium source and is used in glassmaking.

Properties White color; vitreous, resinous luster; orthorhombic crystal system; hardness 3.5; perfect cleavage; transparent to translucent; pseudo-hexagonal twinned habit; luminescent.

ARAGONITE $CaCO_3$

Aragonite has the same chemistry as calcite, but it has different structures and properties. The popular pseudo-hexagonal cyclic twin crystals were discovered in Aragon, Spain. A layered sedimentary variety, "Mexican Onyx," is often carved.

Properties All colors; vitreous, dull luster; orthorhombic crystal system; hardness 3.5–4; transparent to translucent; pseudo-hexagonal prismatic; acicular (needle-like), stalactitic habit; luminescent.

MALACHITE $Cu_2CO_3(OH)_2$ ON SHATTUCKITE

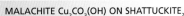

Malachite (green) and shattuckite (a blue copper silicate) occur in the oxidized zone of copper deposits. Malachite was an important copper ore and pigment (mountain green) but is now prized as an ornamental gemstone.

Properties Green color, green streak; vitreous, silky luster; monoclinic crystal system; hardness 3.5–4; opaque; botryoidal habit; luminescent; effervescent.

SMITHSONITE $ZnCO_3$

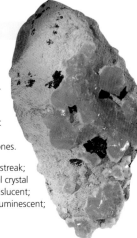

Smithsonite is an ore of zinc commonly found in the weathered (oxidized) zone of lead-zinc ore bodies. It is identifiable by its blue or green fluorescence and effervescence in hydrochloric acid. Colored or banded specimens are cut as gemstones.

Properties All colors, white streak; vitreous, pearly luster; trigonal crystal system; hardness 5–5.5; translucent; botryoidal, stalactitic habit; luminescent; effervescent.

SIDERITE $FeCO_3$ ON FLUORITE

Siderite (brown iron carbonate), here on fluorite (lavender calcium fluoride), is an important iron ore because it is free of sulfur. Siderite is heavy, effervesces in hot hydrochloric acid, and becomes black and magnetic when heated.

Properties Yellow, brown color; white streak; vitreous, pearly luster; trigonal crystal system; hardness 4; opaque; rhombohedral, botryoidal, oolitic (small spheres) habit; effervescent.

CALCITE $CaCO_3$

Calcite is an important rock-forming mineral found in all environments, but probably best known for its stalactitic cave formations. Transparent calcite, or "Iceland spar," shows the doubling of images viewed through the crystal.

Properties Colorless; vitreous, pearly luster; trigonal crystal system; hardness 3; transparent; perfect rhombohedral cleavage; concretionary, stalactitic habit; luminescent; effervescent.

CERUSSITE PbCO₃

Cerussite, or "white lead ore," is common in the oxidized zone of lead–zinc ore bodies. It forms from the chemical alteration of galena. Cerussite is heavy and effervesces strongly in nitric acid, but not in hydrochloric acid.

Properties White to colorless; adamantine luster; orthorhombic crystal system; hardness 3–3.5; transparent to translucent; heavy; heart-shaped twinned habit; luminescent; effervescent.

RHODOCHROSITE MnCO₃

Rhodochrosite forms in hydrothermal veins or secondary deposits associated with sulfide. It was mined for manganese. Beautiful pink rhodochrosite crystals are sought after by collectors; its stalactitic form is polished as a gemstone.

Properties Pink color; vitreous luster; trigonal crystal system; hardness 4; translucent; heavy; prismatic, platy, stalactitic habit; luminescent; effervescent.

Halides

Halide minerals form when metals combine with the halogen elements fluorine, chlorine, bromine, and iodine. The few common halide minerals include halite (salt) and the colorful gem mineral fluorite. Halide minerals are typically soft, transparent, generally not heavy, display good cleavage, and are often brightly colored.

Salt deposits, Dead Sea Evaporite minerals, most commonly halite, grow in crystal clusters on the rocky shoreline of the Dead Sea. Salt has long been considered commercially important as a food additive and preservative, and is extracted from seawater or mined from ancient evaporite deposits.

CRYOLITE Na_3AlF

Cryolite was used as flux for refining aluminum, but has been replaced by synthetic fluorine salts. Used for pottery glazes and in the manufacture of optical glass, cryolite is a rare mineral of fluorine-rich pegmatites.

Properties White and gray colors; vitreous to pearly luster; monoclinic crystal system; hardness 2.5–3; transparent to translucent; pseudo-cubic habit arranged in tessellated patterns.

HALITE $NaCl$

Halite, or common "rock salt," is formed by the evaporation of saline waters. It is commonly white, but impurities produce a variety of colors such as violet, yellow, and red. Halite is highly soluble in water.

Properties White color; vitreous, greasy luster; cubic crystal system; hardness 2; transparent to translucent; crystalline; compact, crusty habit; salty taste.

PSEUDOBOLEITE $Pb_5Cu_4Cl_{10}(OH)_8 \cdot 2H_2O$

Pseudoboleite is a rare halide and minor ore of lead and copper. It is found closely associated with boleite. Both take their name from their type locality, the Boleo Mine, Baja California, Mexico. Specimens are difficult to find.

Properties Indigo blue color, blue streak; vitreous, pearly luster; tetragonal crystal system; hardness 2.5; transparent to translucent; blocky, pseudo-cubic habit.

ATACAMITE $Cu_2Cl(OH)_3$

Atacamite forms as an alteration product of copper sulfide minerals in arid environments. It is found as large masses in Chile's Atacama Desert, where it is mined as an important ore of copper.

Properties Green color; green streak; vitreous, pearly luster; orthorhombic crystal system; hardness 3.5; translucent; radiating, vertically striated acicular (needle-like) habit.

BOLEITE $Pb_{26}Cu_{24}Ag_9Cl_{62}(OH)_{48} \cdot 3H_2O$

Boleite is a rare lead, copper, and silver chloride. It is found in blue, dice-sized cubes in the unusual sedimentary copper deposits at Boleo Mine, Baja California, Mexico. Boleite is often intergrown with pseudoboleite.

Properties Light-to-dark-blue color, blue streak; vitreous, pearly luster; tetragonal crystal system; hardness 3.5; translucent; blocky, pseudo-cubic habit.

SYLVITE KCl

Sylvite is an evaporite mineral found in salt lakes. It dissolves in water but has a more bitter, salty taste than halite. Sylvite is used as a source of potassium and in the preparation of fertilizer.

Properties White-to-pale colors; vitreous luster; cubic crystal system; hardness 2; translucent; perfect cleavage; blocky, cubic, octahedral habit; soluble in water.

MENDIPITE $Pb_3Cl_2O_2$

Mendipite is a secondary oxy-halide that occurs in the oxidized zone of lead ore bodies. It was named after its type locality in the Mendip Hills, Somerset, England. Specimens must be kept in a dark, dry place.

Properties White-to-pale colors; resinous, adamantine luster; orthorhombic crystal system; hardness 2.5; transparent to translucent; perfect cleavage; radiating fibrous habit.

FLUORITE CaF_2

Fluorite occurs in hydrothermal veins or sedimentary deposits and is identifiable by its fluorescence and perfect octahedral cleavage. Beautifully colored and transparent, fluorite has been used as a carving material since the time of the ancient Greeks.

Properties All colors, white streak; vitreous luster; cubic crystal system; hardness 4; transparent; perfect octahedral cleavage; cubic octahedral habit; blue luminescence.

Borates and Nitrates

Borate minerals are numerous, but rare due to the scarcity of boron in Earth's crust. Borax is the most common mineral in this group. Borates generally have an alkaline taste and form in evaporite deposits. Most nitrate minerals are stable only in arid conditions, and readily dissolve in water or absorb atmospheric moisture, described as "deliquescence."

Borax $Na_2B_4O_7 \cdot 10H_2O$ Also known as sodium tetraborate, borax is soluble in water. It is crushed and sold for numerous applications, such as cleaners, fluxes, and insecticides. Viewed under a polarizing light microscope, the nondescript white powder takes on all the colors of the rainbow.

Strontianite Radiating crystals of white strontianite (strontium carbonate) display a bright, greenish-blue fluorescence under ultraviolet light. This mineral is a source of strontium, used for the production of fireworks.

Fluorite The classic fluorescent mineral is fluorite (calcium fluoride), luminescing a strong, blue-violet color under ultraviolet light, and phosphorescing when heated. It is used as a flux in the metal and glass industry.

Willemite In this "polka dot" zinc ore, translucent red willemite (zinc silicate) fluoresces bright green, and white calcite (calcium carbonate) fluoresces red. Willemite can be cut as a gemstone.

RHODIZITE $(K,Cs)Be_4Al_4(B,Be)_{12}O_{28}$

Found only in Madagascar and the Ural Mountains, Russia, rhodizite specimens are too rare to be used as gemstones. The name comes from the Greek "rhodezein," (to be rose-colored) because it burns with a rose-colored flame.

Properties White-to-pale-yellow color; vitreous, adamantine luster; cubic crystal system; hardness 8; transparent to translucent; dodecahedral habit.

COLEMANITE $CaB_3O_4(OH)_3 \cdot H_2O$

Colemanite is a common borate mined from evaporite lake basins in the U.S.A., Turkey, Chile, and Russia. It is one of the main ores of boron, and is used for the production of chemicals, paints, glass, flux, and rocket fuel.

Properties White color; vitreous luster; monoclinic crystal system; hardness 4.5; transparent to translucent; perfect cleavage; equant (blocky) habit; luminescent; phosphorescent.

BORAX $Na_2B_4O_7 \cdot 10H_2O$

Borax occurs in saline lakes in desert regions, where crystals grow to enormous size. Specimens dehydrate easily and become chalky white. Borax is soluble in water and is used for fertilizers and cleaning chemicals.

Properties White color; greasy luster; monoclinic crystal system; hardness 2–2.5; translucent to transparent; perfect cleavage; short prismatic, crusty, earthy habit; sweetish taste.

JEREMEJEVITE $Al_6(BO_3)_5(F,OH)_3$

Jeremejevite is a rare mineral in boron-rich pegmatites, named after the Russian mineralogist Pavel Jeremejev. Extremly rare bicolored pale-blue-to-colorless terminated crystals come from the Erongo Mountains, Namibia. It can be cut as a gemstone.

Properties White to pale blue or yellow; vitreous luster; hexagonal crystal system; hardness 7; transparent; conchoidal fracture; columnar prismatic habit.

NITRATITE $NaNO_3$

Nitratite, or soda niter, is a nitrates source for fertilizer and fireworks. It grows in arid conditions, precipitating in soda lakes. Specimens absorb water from the atmosphere and must be kept in airtight containers.

Properties White color; vitreous to dull luster; trigonal crystal system; hardness 1.5–2; translucent; perfect cleavage; rhombohedral habit; sweetish taste.

KERNITE $Na_2B_4O_6(OH)_2 \cdot 3H_2O$

Kernite was discovered in 1926 in Kern County, California, U.S.A. This location was the only source of kernite for many years. An evaporite mineral, kernite is soluble in water, so it must be kept in an airtight container.

Properties White color; vitreous, pearly luster; monoclinic crystal system; hardness 2.5; elastic; translucent to transparent; perfect cleavage; columnar, fibrous, massive habit.

ULEXITE NaCaB$_5$O$_6$(OH)$_6$•5H$_2$O

Ulexite is known as "television stone" for its unusual ability to transmit images through its crystal fibers from one of its polished surfaces to another. It forms in boron-rich evaporite lakes in the deserts of Chile and the U.S.A.

Properties White color; silky luster; triclinic crystal system; hardness 1; transparent; perfect cleavage; fibrous, radiating habit; white luminescence.

SINHALITE MgAlBO$_4$

Sinhalite is a rare borate, first found in the gem gravels of Sri Lanka and originally mistaken for peridot. Its name comes from the Sanskrit for "Island of Ceylon." Good hardness and color favor its use as a gemstone.

Properties Brown, greenish-yellow color; vitreous luster; orthorhombic crystal system; hardness 6.5; transparent to translucent; distinct cleavage; blocky habit; strongly pleochroic (changes color when viewed from different angles).

Amethyst Remnants of the "mother liquor" in which this amethyst crystal grew are preserved as tiny frozen droplets within the crystal.

Ruby Tiny oriented needles of the mineral boemite lie at 120° to one another in a ruby crystal. They create a three-rayed star.

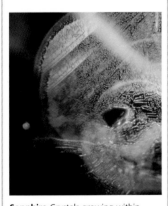

Sapphire Crystals growing within another crystal often cause tension cracks, creating tiny haloes known as "fingerprints," as in this sapphire.

Molybdates, Chromates, and Tungstates

The combination of one or more metal atoms with negatively charged groups of molybdate, chromate, and tungstate forms the minerals in this class. Several are important ores of molybdenum, chromium, and tungsten.

Wolframite $(Fe^{2+})WO_4$ to $(Mn^{2+})WO_4$ This mineral is intermediate in composition between iron-rich ferberite and manganese-rich hübnerite. Wolframite takes its name from the German *Wolfram*, (tungsten). It is an important ore of tungsten—a metal alloyed with iron that is used for dense tool steels.

CROCOITE $PbCrO_4$

Crocoite, or "red lead ore," was once a lead ore, but because of its beauty and rarity it is now a highly sought collector's mineral. Crocoite forms when primary lead minerals are altered by chrome-rich hydrothermal solutions.

Properties Orange-red color; greasy adamantine luster; monoclinic crystal system; hardness 2.5–3; translucent; good cleavage; prismatic, acicular (needle-like) habit; brown luminescence.

POWELLITE $CaMoO_4$

Powellite is a rare secondary molybdate. It is formed when hydrothermal solutions react with primary sulfide ore bodies. Powellite is named after the former director of the U.S. Geological Survey, John W. Powell.

Properties Yellow, yellowish-green color; greasy adamantine luster; tetragonal crystal system; hardness 3.5–4; transparent; platy, pyramidal, scaly habit; golden-yellow luminescence.

SCHEELITE $CaWO_4$

Scheelite is an ore of tungsten metal used in the manufacture of toughened steel and filaments. Named after the discoverer of tungsten, Carl W. Scheele, it occurs in high-temperature hydrothermal veins, pegmatites, and metamorphic rocks.

Properties Yellow, brown, red colors; greasy adamantine luster; tetragonal crystal system; hardness 4.5–5; transparent to translucent; platy, pyramidal, pseudo-octahedral habit; blue luminescence.

HÜBNERITE $MnWO_4$

Hübnerite is the rare manganese tungstate end member of the wolframite series. Wolframite is the principal ore of tungsten. It grows in pegmatite or high-temperature hydrothermal veins, and is concentrated in alluvial deposits.

Properties Brownish, red, black colors; brown, gray streak; sub-metallic, greasy luster; monoclinic crystal system; hardness 5; translucent to opaque; platy, prismatic habit.

FERBERITE $FeWO_4$

Ferberite is the iron end-member of the wolframite series. Iron makes ferberite denser, heavier, and magnetic compared to the manganese end-member hübnerite. Ferberite and hübnerite are found in Bolivia, Peru, Germany, and the U.S.A. They are rarer than wolframite.

Properties Black color; brown, black streak; sub-metallic, dull luster; monoclinic crystal system; hardness 5.5; opaque; platy, prismatic habit; weakly magnetic.

WULFENITE $PbMoO_4$

Wulfenite, or "yellow lead ore," is a minor ore of lead and molybdenum. It is a secondary mineral that occurs in the oxidized zone of lead deposits, often as a replacement for cerussite. Wulfenite is highly sought after by collectors.

Properties Yellow-orange color; greasy adamantine luster; tetragonal crystal system; hardness 3; transparent to translucent; platy, square tabular habit.

SOILS

Soil is the medium that supports plants as well as a huge variety of animals, fungi, and microorganisms. As determined by Hans Jenny in 1941, soil development, or pedogenesis, is regulated by five factors: climate, living organisms, parent material, topography, and time. Climate plays a major role in regulating soil formation, which is more developed in areas with high rainfall and temperatures. It also determines which organisms are present, affecting the soil chemically and physically. Over time, decomposing vegetation recycles nutrients that are essential for plant growth, dissolving and moving them through the soil.

SOILS OF THE WORLD

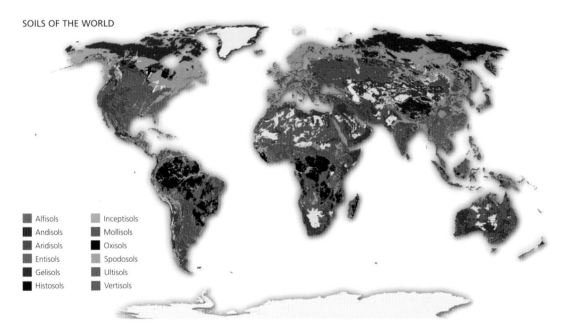

- ■ Alfisols
- ▨ Andisols
- ▨ Aridisols
- ▨ Entisols
- ▨ Gelisols
- ■ Histosols
- ▨ Inceptisols
- ▨ Mollisols
- ■ Oxisols
- ▨ Spodosols
- ▨ Ultisols
- ▨ Vertisols

Soil layers (below) A vertical section of soil, known as a soil profile, shows the soil's distinct layers, or horizons. The profile shows all the horizons that are possible, but not every type of soil has all these layers.

- Organic debris
- Partly decomposed organic debris
- Mineral materials with fine particles of organic matter
- Mineral materials into which nutrients have moved from above
- Transitional layer
- Transitional layer
- Layers in which most nutrients accumulate
- Transitional layer
- Parent material
- Bedrock

CLASSIFYING SOILS

As rocks weather, they release different kinds of particles. Climate affects the rate of weathering, but it also determines the plants that grow in a specific type of soil and the animals that feed on them. Consequently, the climate and type of rock produce radically different soils, from desert soils that are little more than sand and dust, to the deep but infertile soils of the wet tropics and the dark peat soils found in parts of northern Europe.

The first classification of soil types was attempted in Russia in the 19th century. By the middle of the 20th century many countries had classified the soils within their own territories. Then American soil scientists developed a classification system, called a soil taxonomy, which could be applied to soils anywhere in the world. More recently, the United Nations Food and Agriculture Organization has introduced an alternative international classification based on 30 reference soil groups comprising 170 subunits.

The U.S. classification divides soils into the 12 orders shown on the map above. The orders are then subdivided into 47 suborders, which are again divided into groups, subgroups, families, and soil series. The classification is based on the physical and chemical properties of soils at particular depths, known as diagnostic horizons.

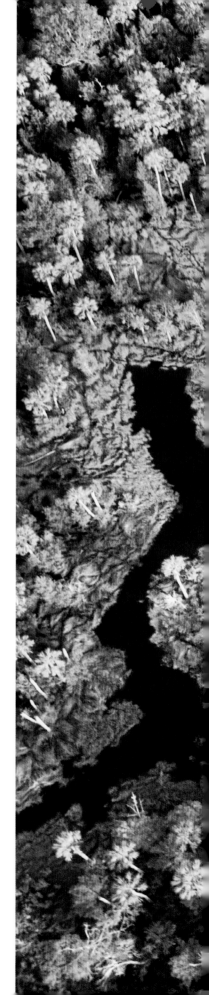

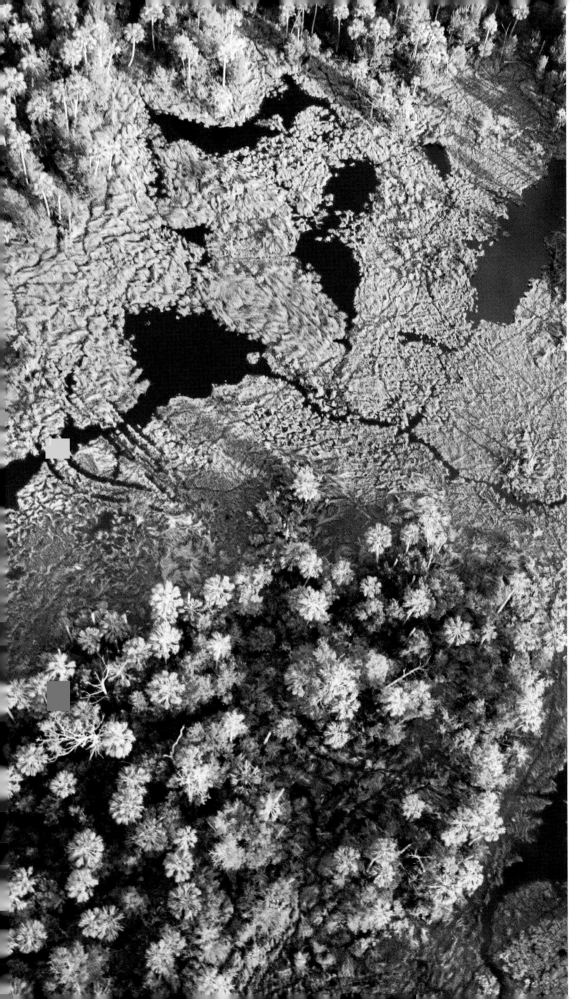

Loess soil (above) This kind of soil consists of particles ground out by glaciers during the ice ages. The particles dried on exposure to the air, and were deposited by the wind. The loess in Shanxi Province, China, is 330 feet (100 m) or more deep. Loess releases nutrients through weathering, making it highly fertile.

Waterlogged soil (left) This swamp in Florida, U.S.A., is covered with shallow water for most of the year. Its soil is permanently waterlogged. The soil is rich in fine silt that has been washed in by rivers that spread out and slow down as they enter the swamp. It also contains much organic material from the luxuriant vegetation. Decomposition is slow and the organic matter slowly compacts to form peat. The waterlogged soil is airless and tree roots absorb oxygen through "knees" that protrude above the surface. In drier areas of the swamp that are flooded only occasionally, the soils are mainly sandy.

■ Entisols: deserts

■ Spodosols: coniferous forests

■ Oxisols: tropics and subtropics

■ Ultisols: seasonal tropics

■ Andisols: volcanic, ash-rich soils

■ Alfisols: savanna grasslands

The World's Soils

Soil consists of mineral particles derived from underlying rock, and mixed with decayed organic matter and fragments of plant and animal material. Rocks vary from place to place, and the climate determines their rate of weathering. Average temperatures and moisture also influence the species of living organisms that are found in each region. Soils are therefore products of their local environment and vary greatly.

■ **Entisols** Soils with little or no layer development, such as disturbed soils or soils formed from river sediments.

■ **Spodosols** Forest soils rich in organic matter, acidic, and sometimes with a dense aluminum- or iron-rich subsurface layer.

■ **Oxisols** Intensely weathered soils, rich in aluminum and iron oxides, with only traces of unweathered material.

■ **Ultisols** Acid soils that have less than 35 percent of total possible nutrients, with clay below the surface.

■ **Andisols** Soils formed from volcanic ash, which are deep, light in texture, and rich in iron and aluminum.

■ **Alfisols** Soils where at least 35 percent of total nutrients have washed to lower layers, where clay has accumulated.

Russian scientists were the first to classify soils, in the 19th century, and many countries have their own classification schemes. The widely used U.S. Soil Taxonomy divides soils into 12 orders, each with further subdivisions.

■ **Gelisols** Soils in tundra regions that have a layer of permafrost within 6.5 feet (2 m) of the surface.

■ **Inceptisols** Soils such as very young soils that contain little organic matter and have weakly developed subsurface layers.

■ **Aridisols** Soils with a subsurface layer that contains calcium carbonate and often salt, which crystallizes when dry.

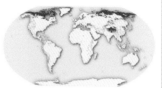

■ Gelisols: tundra

■ Inceptisols: floodplains and deltas

■ Aridisols: dry regions

■ **Mollisols** Grassland and forest soils with a surface layer rich in organic matter, with 50 percent of possible total nutrients.

■ **Histosols** Soils rich in organic matter that must be at least 15 inches (40 cm) deep when overlying mineral soil.

■ **Vertisols** Soils with more than 30 percent clay that swell when wet, and shrink and crack when dry.

■ Mollisols: deciduous forests

■ Histosols: peat bogs and swamps

■ Vertisols: steppes, seasonal tropics

Soil formation As rocks weather, plants establish themselves among the mineral particles, rainwater washes nutrients to deeper levels, and the soil gradually develops distinct layers, called horizons.

Regolith This layer of sand, pebbles, gravel, or other material on bedrock is not yet soil.

Young soil The surface layer is organically rich and subsurface layers are developing.

Mature soil With three or more layers, this recycles mineral nutrients to plant roots.

DOMESTICATED SOILS

Agricultural soils are productive because farmers have domesticated them. They have been cultivated to control weeds and improve drainage, and nutrients removed through cropping have been replaced in the form of manure or fertilizer. Provided they are well managed, these soils will remain fertile indefinitely.

Soil and Living Things

Fungi, animals, and bacteria comprise a large, complex soil community that breaks organic matter down to its constituent molecules, thus recycling nutrients. Plants grow in temperatures above about 43°F (6°C), provided their roots can absorb water containing mineral nutrients. Because nutrients are soluble, rainwater washes them away and old soils become infertile.

THE SOIL COMMUNITY

Life in soil Plants, soil-dwelling creatures, and microscopic organisms interact with one another to maintain the fertility of soil, each playing a role in the decomposition of organic matter and the recycling of nutrients.

Ants Most species live in nests below ground, feeding on a wide range of plant material. Their tunnels and chambers aerate the soil and their wastes fertilize it.

Red velvet mites Living on the woodland floor, the larvae are parasites of other invertebrates, while the adults feed on insect and snail eggs and hunt animals smaller than themselves.

Leaf litter Dead leaves mixed with small twigs and other plant material supply food on which living soil organisms depend.

Roots, nematodes, and fungi When roots die their tunnels remain, allowing air and water to circulate. Nematodes feed on bacteria, algae, and plants, and help to recycle nutrients. Fungi absorb nutrients, some of which they pass on to plants in exchange for carbohydrates.

Protozoa and bacteria These break down large organic molecules into simple molecules that plant roots can absorb. Some protozoa feed on bacteria.

Earthworms Stabilized by a mucus lining, earthworms' tunnels aerate the soil and allow water to flow through it. Worms also feed on decaying matter in the soil, helping to recycle it.

Millipedes These help with decomposition by feeding on decaying plant material. They move through small spaces in the soil or make tunnels, burrowing deeper when the soil is dry or frozen.

Termites Living in colonies, these social insects digest and break down dead wood to use for food and nesting material.

Pseudoscorpions These live among the leaf litter and are about 0.25 inch (6 mm) long. Like scorpions, but without tails, they hunt insects.

Springtails Found in the upper layer of soil, these feed on decaying plant matter. One pint of soil can contain more than 1,100 (2,000 per liter).

Buttercups and grass Through their roots these absorb mineral nutrients that are constantly recycled by the billions of fungi, animals, protozoa, and bacteria in the soil.

Moles Using their tunnel networks as traps, moles feed mainly on earthworms that fall in. Moles aerate and mix the soil, but damage plant roots.

Centipedes Voracious, fast-moving carnivores, centipedes eat nematodes, insect larvae, and even worms, slugs, and snails. Many of their prey are garden pests that damage plants.

Dung beetles These insects collect animal dung, roll it into a ball, bury it, and lay their eggs in it. Burying dung accelerates its decomposition, returning its nutrients to the soil.

FACT FILE

Root systems Plant roots vary with growing conditions. Tap roots reach water deep underground, while fibrous roots spread a more extensive network to collect water near the surface.

Tap roots Swollen tap roots store nutrients for the plant to use as it grows. The tap roots of some plants such as carrots are harvested for food.

Primary tap roots Growing vertically downward, these anchor the plant. Small outward-branching roots absorb water and nutrients.

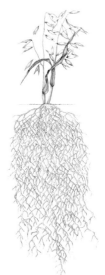

Fibrous roots Typical of grasses, these form a mat just below the surface. The many fibers maximize contact with water and hold the plant firm.

LANDFORMS

Slowly, over millions of years, Earth's crust moves. As it does so, it folds, fractures, and deforms rocks in many ways. Mountain ranges are thrust high into the air, sections of the ground sink, and volcanoes form conical mountains or inundate wide areas with lava. As soon as rocks are exposed to air, they are weathered by wind, rain, ice, and sunshine. Rivers cut channels through them, and glaciers scour them, grinding and depositing loose rock as moraines. These processes shape the surface features, or landforms, of every landscape. Geomorphology is the study of the way they develop and change over time.

LANDSCAPE FEATURES

If Earth lacked an atmosphere, and therefore had no weather, its surface would be a wilderness of rough, bare rock. Weathering by wind, water, ice, and acids dissolved in water, as well as by wind and water erosion, is what transforms the bare rocks into the familiar features of Earth's surface. Earth's crust is made from rigid, moving plates. Collisions between plates raise mountain ranges. These are then slowly eroded by the forces of weather until they eventually become level plains.

Flowing water is a powerful agent. It turns solid soil to fluid mud that can slide down hillsides or cause rocks to tumble. Each slide or fall makes a hill a little smaller and the land at its foot a little higher. Rivers carve valleys, finding their way through the softer rocks and at the same time transporting soil particles to the lake or sea into which they flow. Very deep river valleys eventually become canyons.

Rivers flow across deserts only occasionally, usually following heavy rain. Most of the time their riverbeds are dry canyons, known as wadis or arroyos. When a large river crosses a low-lying coastal plain, it often deposits sediment and divides into many small channels, so forming a delta.

Glaciation is another process that shapes the landscape. Glaciers moving down mountainsides carve wider, deeper valleys, leaving behind piles of loose rocks, or moraines. When glaciers retreat, hanging valleys left by tributary glaciers carry rivers into the main valley as dramatic waterfalls.

Ocean tides, currents, and waves are the forces that shape the coastline. They carve sea cliffs from hills, wash away soft rock to leave resistant rock as headlands, and cut caves into headlands. In some cases, the sea wears right through a headland to form an arch that eventually collapses, leaving behind an isolated column, or stack.

Types of landforms (above) In natural settings specific landscapes are usually very extensive, so only a few landforms can be seen in any one area. The imaginary composite landscape in this illustration stretches from snow-capped mountains across a desert and a fertile coastal plain and ends at the coast. The landscape features represented are as follows: mountain range (**1**), valley (**2**), escarpment (**3**), glacier (**4**), glacial lake (**5**), drainage basin (**6**), desert (**7**), canyon (**8**) mountain peak (**9**), hills (**10**), plateau (**11**), bay (**12**), cliff (**13**), peninsula (**14**), lagoon (**15**), river delta (**16**), isthmus (**17**), and spit (**18**).

Ancient headland (right) Seljalandsfoss Waterfall in southern Iceland thrusts its water down 197 feet (60 m) from the edge of what was once a coastal cliff. The ancient headland was carved into a thick layer of volcanic basalt about 10,000 years ago.

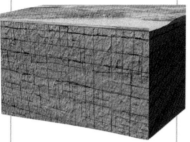

1 Weakly acidic rainwater trickles downward along the joints.

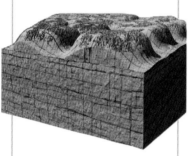

2 The acid dissolves the limestone, widening the joints.

3 The joints continue widening until the blocks are separated by valleys.

4 Seawater may flood the valleys, leaving the limestone peaks still eroding.

Weathering and Erosion

Minerals in rocks close to the surface react with substances in rainwater and dissolve. Rocks at the surface are heated, chilled, and battered by rain and wind. These processes break the rock into ever-smaller fragments. Together, they are called weathering. Erosion is the removal of rock by wind or water.

The Mittens and Merrick Butte Over millions of years, wind and water have carved these sandstone buttes in Monument Valley, Arizona, U.S.A., out of a large plateau.

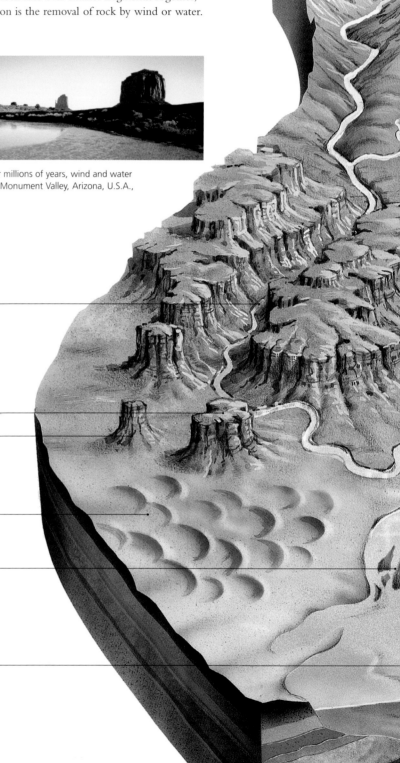

Valley carving Where a river is much higher than the lake or sea into which it discharges, it cuts deep, steep-sided valleys, or canyons, through the rock.

Sedimentary erosion When rivers wear away the less resistant rocks in horizontal sedimentary layers, large, flat-topped hills, known as mesas, are formed

Butte This smaller version of a mesa is formed by continued erosion of sedimentary layers by the river.

Wind erosion Sand grains eroded by the wind from rocks accumulate as sand dunes.

Deposition of eroded material As a river crosses a wide, level plain to reach the sea, it deposits its load of sand and silt to form a delta.

Sea currents Disturbance can make the sediment at a delta mouth slide downhill, producing turbidity currents that erode the seabed. Where material is removed, underwater canyons form; where it settles, plateaus are created.

SHAPING THE LANDSCAPE

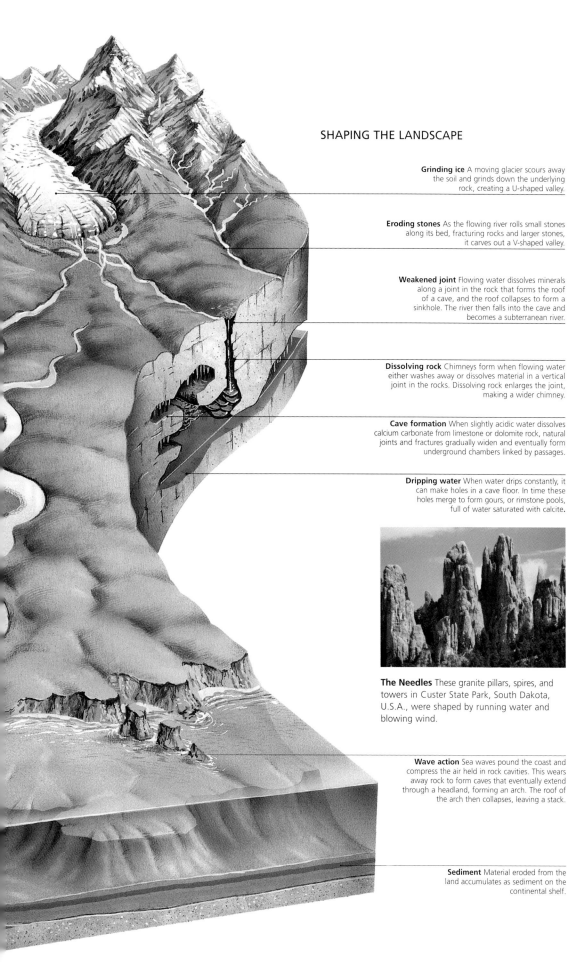

Grinding ice A moving glacier scours away the soil and grinds down the underlying rock, creating a U-shaped valley.

Eroding stones As the flowing river rolls small stones along its bed, fracturing rocks and larger stones, it carves out a V-shaped valley.

Weakened joint Flowing water dissolves minerals along a joint in the rock that forms the roof of a cave, and the roof collapses to form a sinkhole. The river then falls into the cave and becomes a subterranean river.

Dissolving rock Chimneys form when flowing water either washes away or dissolves material in a vertical joint in the rocks. Dissolving rock enlarges the joint, making a wider chimney.

Cave formation When slightly acidic water dissolves calcium carbonate from limestone or dolomite rock, natural joints and fractures gradually widen and eventually form underground chambers linked by passages.

Dripping water When water drips constantly, it can make holes in a cave floor. In time these holes merge to form gours, or rimstone pools, full of water saturated with calcite.

The Needles These granite pillars, spires, and towers in Custer State Park, South Dakota, U.S.A., were shaped by running water and blowing wind.

Wave action Sea waves pound the coast and compress the air held in rock cavities. This wears away rock to form caves that eventually extend through a headland, forming an arch. The roof of the arch then collapses, leaving a stack.

Sediment Material eroded from the land accumulates as sediment on the continental shelf.

FACT FILE

Weathering processes Expansion and contraction due to changing temperatures combine with the action of wind and water to detach fragments from rocks, wearing them away.

Exfoliation When the surface layer of rock is heated, it expands and detaches from the layer beneath.

Block disintegration Crevices widen when salt crystallizes and expands as rainwater dries, detaching fragments that are removed by the next rain.

Frost wedging Water that freezes deep inside crevices reacts with minerals that wash away when the ice melts, widening the cracks.

Pinnacle formation Wind and water erode the soft material from around harder cap rocks, leaving isolated pillars protected by cap rocks.

FACT FILE

Coastal formations Cliffs form when waves erode coastal hills. Erosion sometimes continues to play a major role in shaping coastal features, such as caves, arches, and stacks.

1 When coastal currents erode softer rocks from the face of a headland, a sea cave is hollowed out.

2 Wave action continues to widen the cave and eventually wears through the headland to produce an arch.

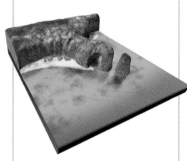

3 The top of the arch then thins out and collapses, leaving a sea stack, which in turn will be worn away by the sea.

HERITAGE WATCH

Simien National Park, Ethiopia This land of high plateaus, broad valleys, and jagged peaks was formed when erosion cut through 10,000 feet (3,000 m) of lava that erupted 40 million years ago. A World Heritage site, it is now endangered by road construction and disturbance of its very rare mammals by humans.

Weathering and Erosion continued

Water and wind are the agents of erosion. Glaciers grind rocks to small particles. Plants with penetrating roots contribute to the weathering of rocks by widening joints, then decomposing and allowing water to enter the crevices. Wind raises sand grains and hurls them forcibly against rock surfaces, sometimes sandblasting them into unusual shapes.

Glacial abrasion (below) The straight parallel grooves, called striations, incised on this limestone rock in Ohio, U.S.A., were made by boulders and other coarse material dragged over it by a glacier.

Biological weathering (top left) Tree roots penetrate rocks and fill cracks and joints. When the roots decompose, they release acids that dissolve the surrounding rock and widen the spaces.

Wind erosion (left) Delicate Arch, in Arches National Park, Utah, U.S.A., has been shaped by the wind, which has worn away the sandstone.

The Shifting Surface

Material that has been eroded from rocks is transported by wind and water and eventually settles to the surface elsewhere, creating distinctive landscapes. For example, the loess soils that cover vast areas of China and the United States consist of wind-blown silt, while sand grains that have accumulated on the seabed are blown into dunes when the sea retreats.

FACT FILE

1. Loess walls At Balatonakarattya, Hungary, loess has been eroded, exposing walls, which are termed reefs. Loess is fine-grained material that was ground from rock by glaciers. It was

deposited when the glaciers of the last ice age retreated, and was then blown by the wind to its new location.

Balatonakarattya, Hungary

2. Desert dunes Saharan dunes are formed from wind-blown sand and shaped by the wind direction. The biggest dunes are up to 1,000 feet

(300 m) high. Sand seas, or ergs, have many large dunes and cover up to 200,000 square miles (518,000 km²).

Sahara Desert, North Africa

3. Mountain sediment The dunes in Death Valley, U.S.A., consist of quartz and feldspar grains from the Cottonwood Mountains. Flash floods

carry weathered particles onto the valley floor, where the sediment dries and is blown into the dune system.

Death Valley, U.S.A.

4. Tombolo Chesil Beach, Dorset, England, is the largest tombolo in the United Kingdom. It is 18 miles (29 km) long, 660 feet (200 m) wide, and 60 feet (18 m) high, and consists of shingle. It has a large lagoon on

the landward side and connects the Isle of Portland, a limestone island, with Abbotsbury on the mainland.

Chesil Beach, Dorset, England

5. Sandbanks Mont Saint-Michel, in Normandy, France, is a granite outcrop 256 feet (78 m) high. It is surrounded by sandbanks and linked

to the mainland by a causeway that has trapped sand, thus raising the height of the sandbanks over time.

Mont Saint-Michel, Normandy, France

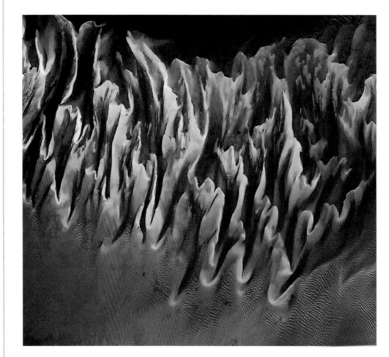

Sculpted seabed (above) At Ocean Sand in the Bahamas, tides and ocean currents have sculpted the sand and seaweed on the seabed into these elaborate shapes captured by the Landsat 7 satellite.

Hidden river (below) Namibia's Ugab River has eroded nearly vertical beds of limestone, sandstone, and siltstone to form its underground channel. It appears on the surface for only a few days each year.

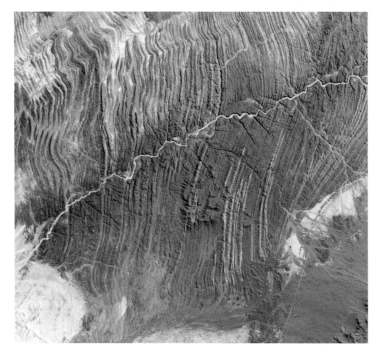

Tombolo formation A tombolo is one or more lines of sand or pebbles connecting an island to the shore. If there are two tombolos, the lagoon between them eventually fills with sediment.

1 Longshore currents carry sand grains along or just above the seabed. Sand settles between the island and shore.

2 The settled sand forms a breakwater. This traps more sand, reducing the water depth and creating a submerged causeway.

3 Sand deposited at high tides and in storms raises the causeway above the surface to form a tombolo.

Moving sands In part of Africa's Sahara Desert, sand blows over rocky outcrops, constantly reshaping the landscape. This satellite image shows an area, about 30 miles (50 km) across, near Terkezi Oasis in Chad.

Rockfalls and Landslides

Cliffs and hillsides that appear stable can collapse suddenly, while most materials are unstable on slopes steeper than about 36 degrees. During prolonged heavy rain or melting snow, water not only streams down hillsides, but moves underground as well, loosening the surface material. Earthquakes can also trigger rockfalls and landslides, as can human activity.

Soil creep This very slow movement of dry soil or rock particles may occur between ice melting and refreezing.

Landslide Earth flow happens slowly if the soil is dry and sandy, but wet clay soils can collapse very rapidly.

Rockfall Blocks of rock become detached from a near-vertical rock face and drop to a lower level.

Rotational landslide In this kind of landslide, a large block of material slides in an outward and rolling motion over a weakness in the bedrock, or failure surface.

Scarp As the surface material moves downslope, it exposes the underlying material as an approximately vertical escarpment, or scarp, near the top.

Crown This is the level ground at the top of a slope, above the level where the surface material has become detached, triggering a landslide.

Rotated block Where a block of moving material passes over a concave failure surface, it is tilted and rotated, and then partly rolls back on itself.

Tension cracks As the landslide begins to move, sections of the material pull away from other sections that move more slowly, producing tension cracks between adjacent blocks.

Failure surface Surface material slides downhill over the surface of more stable rock. The failure surface is the surface from which the sliding material has become detached.

Clay landslide In wet conditions, a mass of clay can quickly become fluid, detaching itself at the top of a slope and flowing rapidly over the failure surface.

Transverse tension cracks Most tension cracks are transverse, developing across the slope at right angles to the direction in which the material is moving.

Main back scarp This almost vertical face at the top of the landslide is the place where the material has become detached.

Minor back scarps Further separation occurs at intervals down the slope, as the material lower down slides away from the material above it.

Original surface The toe of the landslide projects over material that has not moved and buries the original ground surface beneath it.

Failure surface This is the boundary between the underlying stable material, usually bedrock, and the sliding mud.

Toe At the foot of the slope, where the movement is checked, the sliding material accumulates in a rounded heap called the toe.

Lateral shear This is the region between the moving block of material and the stable material on either side of it.

Tension cracks

Toe The sliding material piles up into a large heap, or toe, at the bottom of a landslide, where the slope ends and the material comes to rest.

California mudslide In January 2005, a mudslide swept through the town of La Conchita, California, U.S.A., killing 10 people and destroying 13 homes.

1. Massive rockfall In September 2002, some 350 million cubic feet (100 million m³) of rock fell down a slope of a massif in the Caucasus Mountains. The rockfall virtually

destroyed the Kolka glacier and traveled 12 miles (20 km), causing massive destruction and the loss of 140 lives.

Kazbek, North Ossetia, Russia

2. Multiple slides Padang Municipality, West Sumatra, Indonesia, was struck by several landslides in September 2005, and again in January 2007. In both cases, the landslides

followed several days of heavy rainfall. The rapid mud flow destroyed and buried houses in its path.

Padang, West Sumatra, Indonesia

3. Hundreds displaced In June 2005 at Senahu, in the mountains north of Guatemala City, landslides triggered by heavy rain buried houses in several

districts. A total of 23 people were killed, 40 were injured, and more than 300 families were displaced.

Senahu, Guatemala

4. Unknown trigger In Guizhou Province, China, 39 people lost their lives in December 2004 when a landslide caused severe damage and buried 25 houses at the foot of

a mountain. The weather at the time was good and the cause of the landslide is a complete mystery.

Guizhou Province, China

5. Earth tremors In April 2004, violent earth tremors at Budalyk, Kyrgyzstan, dislodged more than 100 million cubic feet (3 million m³) of wet soil, which was sent sliding

into the village. The uncontrollable mass of soil buried 11 buildings, and at least 33 people were killed.

Budalyk, Kyr gyzstan

Sinking or Rising Land

In some regions, land can subside or be lifted up. The surface may collapse suddenly into a cave or mine, or it may subside gradually due to loss of groundwater. In karst limestone landscapes, subsidence can produce sinkholes, or dolines. Uplift can be caused by the rebound that follows the disappearance of an ice sheet, or by a hot spot below the crust.

Great Salt Lake, Utah, U.S.A. (right) About 70–50 million years ago, compressive forces linked to the rise of the Rocky Mountains lifted this region to its present elevation of about 9,000 feet (2,745 m). Water enters by a river, but as the lake has no outlet, it loses water only by evaporation.

Collapse doline (right)
Limestone caves grow larger as acidic water steadily dissolves and removes calcium carbonate. Eventually the cave may be so large that its roof is not well supported and sections collapse.

1 At the surface a collapse doline is a steep-sided opening into a limestone cave.

2 Rocks become detached along vertical joints in the cave roof and fall in.

3 The cave grows as water dissolves more material, but the poorly supported roof eventually collapses.

1 At the surface, a solution doline is a depression in the rock, with gently sloping sides.

2 Acid water dissolves rock and collects in the hollow, enlarging it by eroding the limestone.

3 The water, saturated with calcium carbonate, drains away through the vertical joints, gradually widening them.

Solution doline (left)
Limestone rocks consist of large blocks separated by vertical joints. Acidic rainwater penetrates a little way into the joints, dissolving rock, widening the joint, and draining into the cave below.

Subsidence doline (right)
Soil lying on top of a layer of limestone rock sinks into a hollow formed when a deep solution doline penetrates the limestone layer.

1 At the surface the doline is a bowl-shaped depression with gently sloping sides.

2 The surface depression does not extend all the way down to the underlying bedrock.

3 Surface material has sunk into a passage dissolved by water along joints in the limestone.

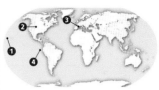

1. The Hawaiian Islands This group of islands in the Pacific is formed from the tops of volcanoes that rise above sea level. The volcanoes grew from the ocean floor when it was uplifted as the Pacific plate crossed a hot spot in the upper mantle of Earth's crust.

The Hawaiian Islands

2. Yellowstone National Park This is set on high plateaus surrounded by mountains built from lava that erupted 2 million, 1.2 million, and 600,000 years ago. The central section later collapsed to form a basin, or caldera, that is 28–47 miles (45–75 km) wide.

Yellowstone, Wyoming, U.S.A.

3. Massif Central This upland region consists of plateaus that were raised 360–250 million years ago during a Paleozoic mountain-building event, and were later tilted. The central Massif landscape is dominated by extinct volcano cones.

Massif Central, France

4. Galápagos Islands These volcanic islands in the Pacific Ocean, close to Ecuador, rise from an uplifted section of oceanic crust. The Galápagos Islands are located at a geologic hot spot above a mantle plume—a place where abnormally hot rock wells up from deep inside Earth.

Galápagos Islands

HERITAGE WATCH

Sarisariñama Tepui The nearly circular dolines in this flat-topped mountain in Bolívar, Venezuela, are about 1,150 feet (350 m) wide and deep, with vertical walls. Some of the plants and animals found at the bottom do not exist anywhere else in the world.

Canyons and Wadis

A canyon, or gorge, is a deep, steep-sided valley that has been carved through a plateau by a river. Abrasive fragments transported by the flowing water wear away less resistant rock, leaving harder rock to form the canyon walls. In karst landscapes, underground rivers also form canyons. A wadi, or desert canyon, is usually dry and carries a river only occasionally, at times of heavy rain.

1 A river, high above the lake or sea into which it flows, begins to carve a valley across a plateau.

2 In a dry climate, rock is baked hard and cannot absorb water, so the fast-flowing river wears it away.

3 As the valley deepens, the river erodes softer rock layers at the sides, which collapse, widening the valley.

Grand Canyon (right) The Colorado River took about six million years to carve this spectacular canyon in northern Arizona, U.S.A. It is 277 miles (446 km) long, 1 mile (1.6 km) deep, and up to 18 miles (29 km) wide.

Bering Canyon (below) Extending for 250 miles (400 km) across the bed of the Bering Sea, this is possibly the world's longest submarine canyon. In places it is 2,600 feet (800 m) deep.

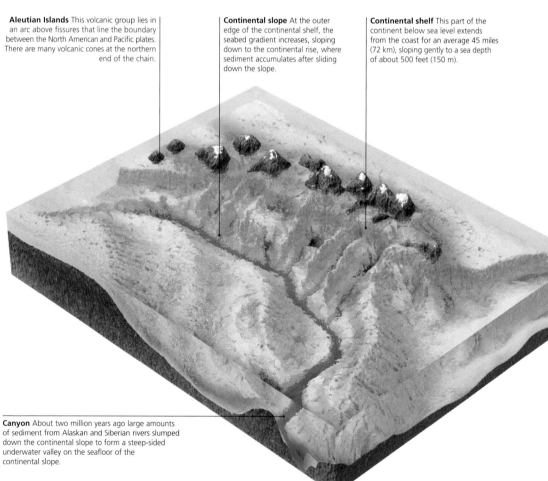

Aleutian Islands This volcanic group lies in an arc above fissures that line the boundary between the North American and Pacific plates. There are many volcanic cones at the northern end of the chain.

Continental slope At the outer edge of the continental shelf, the seabed gradient increases, sloping down to the continental rise, where sediment accumulates after sliding down the slope.

Continental shelf This part of the continent below sea level extends from the coast for an average 45 miles (72 km), sloping gently to a sea depth of about 500 feet (150 m).

Canyon About two million years ago large amounts of sediment from Alaskan and Siberian rivers slumped down the continental slope to form a steep-sided underwater valley on the seafloor of the continental slope.

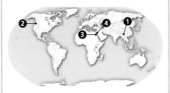

FACT FILE

1. Tsangpo Gorge This is the world's deepest and possibly longest canyon, at about 150 miles (241 km) long. Its river drops from 9,840 feet (3,000 m) at the start of the canyon to 984 feet (300 m) where it leaves the gorge. With its remote and inaccessible location, the gorge has

 been little disturbed by humans. Its unique ecosystem includes many rare species of plants and animals.

Tsangpo Gorge, Tibet

2. Fraser Canyon Crossing Canada's Coast Mountains, this canyon carries the Fraser River from the interior plateau of British Columbia to the Fraser Valley, passing between spectacular mountains that rise more than 3,000 feet (914 m) above the rushing river. Rail lines and the Trans-

 Canada Highway run along the sides of Fraser Canyon, the road passing through seven tunnels.

Fraser Canyon, Canada

3. Wadi Allaqi On the eastern side of Lake Nasser, 112 miles (180 km) from Aswan, Egypt, this dry river valley links the Nile Valley with the Red Sea. The downstream section of Wadi Allaqi is often flooded and supports shrubs. In contrast, farms and drought-resistant plants are found in the drier upstream

 section. The area is a UNESCO Biosphere Reserve, conducting research into arid zone ecology and resource use.

Wadi Allaqi, Egypt

4. Timna Park Located in the Red Sea Desert 18 miles (30 km) north of Eilat, Israel, this U-shaped valley is surrounded on three sides by yellow sandstone mountains and has Mount Timna, an extinct volcano, at its center. Formed by tectonic plate

 movements, the valley is part of the Syrian–African rift and extends over 23 square miles (60 km²).

Timna Park, Eilat, Israel

Disi sandstone These large, solid blocks made from medium-to-large quartz grains have no internal structure.

Umm Ishrin sandstone This consists of quartz grains with scattered thin layers of siltstone and shale containing sheets of mica.

Wadi Rum, Jordan (below) This desert valley was formed by the erosion of sandstone. Its steep sides expose five rock layers. The basement is of granite, above which there is a layer of conglomerates, then three types of sandstone.

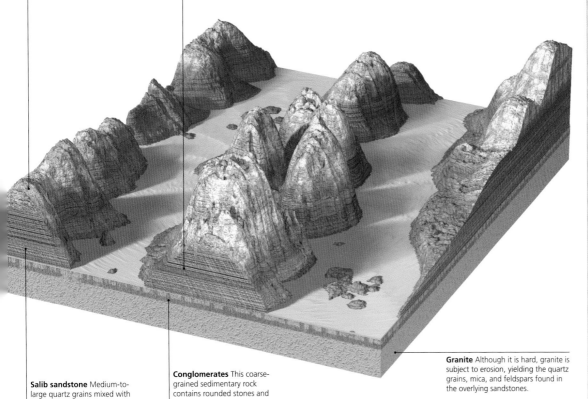

Salib sandstone Medium-to-large quartz grains mixed with feldspars and silicate minerals make up this somewhat crumbly and moderately porous layer.

Conglomerates This coarse-grained sedimentary rock contains rounded stones and is permeable. Water moves through it and emerges as springs on the valley floor.

Granite Although it is hard, granite is subject to erosion, yielding the quartz grains, mica, and feldspars found in the overlying sandstones.

River Deltas

A delta often forms where a large river deposits sediment as it meets the sea. If the sediment is deposited faster than sea currents can remove it, the sediment accumulates, the coastline is extended, and the river divides repeatedly into many channels. The form of a delta is determined by river flow, tides, or waves—whichever is the prinicipal source of the sediment.

River-dominated deltas These tend to produce an indented coastline with one or more protruding river mouths. The coastal area and delta plain are often marshy and there are few sandy beaches.

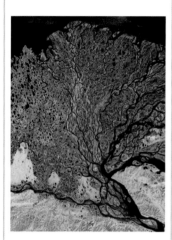

Lena On the Russian Arctic coast, this delta has a plain with features produced by permafrost. The river flows only during the short summer.

Mississippi Several long distributary channels, separated by marshes and mudflats, spread to the sides, giving this delta a "bird foot" appearance.

Eastern Scheldt Delta, Netherlands This is an important wintering ground for aquatic birds. To protect it from seawater in storms without disturbing the ecology, a special dike was built to enclose the delta. A series of steel gates supported by 66 towers create a storm surge barrier that extends for 5.6 miles (9 km).

Wave-dominated (below) Egypt's Nile Delta extends 100 miles (160 km) northward from Cairo. Shaped by wave action, the delta's coastline is smooth and gently arc-shaped, or arcuate, with two slightly protruding river mouths.

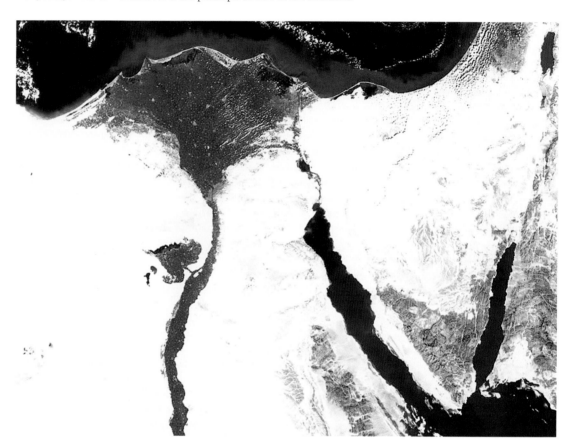

Delta formation (below) This begins with the deposition of coarse material such as pebbles and gravel. Sand sinks farther out, and the finest particles sink where fresh and salt water meet. Pressure compacts the sediments into rock.

1 Only the part of the delta above sea level is visible.

2 Coarse material is dumped first, forming conglomerate rock.

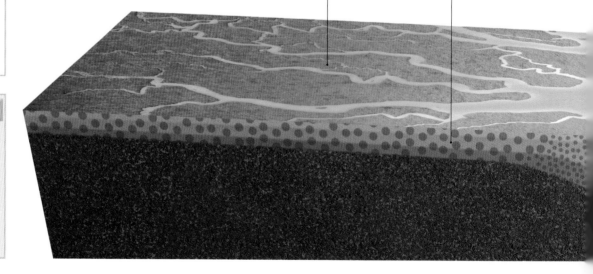

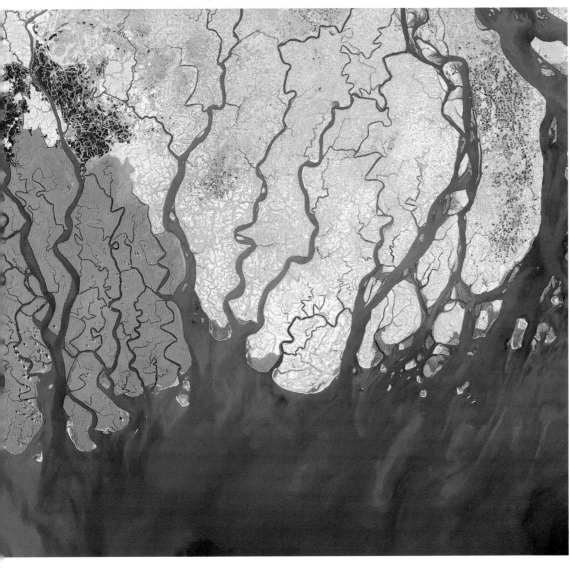

3 Sand grains are deposited farther out, forming sandstone.

4 Fine soil particles sink beyond the sand, forming siltstone.

5 Very fine material is dropped last, forming shale, a slate-like rock.

Tide-dominated (above) The formation of the Ganges Delta is influenced by tides. The world's largest delta, it is 220 miles (354 km) wide at the coast. Its land is so fertile that it is sometimes called the Green Delta. The delta region is extremely prone to flooding.

FACT FILE

1. Nile Delta This extends about 150 miles (240 km) along Egypt's Mediterranean coast and is one of the largest deltas in the world. Its coastline has large sandy beaches, offshore sandbars and sand dunes, salt flats, and lagoons enclosed by sand barriers. The delta's rich soil has been farmed

 for at least 5,000 years, but since the Aswan Dam reduced nutrient supply, fertilizers have also been used.

Nile Delta, Egypt

2. Ganges Delta Stretching between Bangladesh and India, this expansive delta carries the waters of the Ganges (or Padma), Brahmaputra (or Jamuna), and Meghna rivers into the Bay of Bengal. The Ganges Delta extends all the way from the Hugli River, a channel of the Ganges, in the west,

 to the Meghna River in the east, and covers a vast area of more than 40,500 square miles (105,000 km²).

Ganges Delta, Bangladesh and India

3. Lena Delta This is about 250 miles (400 km) wide and extends over 12,350 square miles (32,000 km²). As it crosses the delta, the Lena River divides into 150 channels. The Lena Delta is frozen during the winter months from October to April, but when the ice melts in spring it

 becomes a wetland that is an important wildlife reserve and a significant breeding ground for numerous species.

Lena Delta, Siberia

4. Mississippi Delta This delta covers 4,600 square miles (12,000 km²) of coastal wetlands. About every thousand years one of the distributory channels captures the main river, which then changes course. As it does so, it abandons a lobe of the delta,

 which subsides and erodes. This process has produced a landscape of lakes, bays, and creeks, known as bayous.

Mississippi Delta, U.S.A.

Mountains

A mountain is an area of high ground, with steep slopes, a peak at least 1,000 feet (300 m) higher than its base, and changes in climate and vegetation as elevation increases. It may be an isolated feature, usually a volcano, or part of a mountain range created by movement of Earth's crust along tectonic plate boundaries.

Earth's highest (right) Everest, on the border between Nepal and Tibet, China, in the Himalayan ranges, is the world's highest mountain. The snow on its peak is 29,029 feet (8,848 m) above sea level.

Famous peak (below) The Matterhorn, on the Swiss-Italian border, rises to 14,693 feet (4,478 m). Its sharp, horn-like peak makes it the most recognizable mountain in the European Alps.

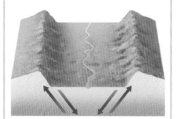
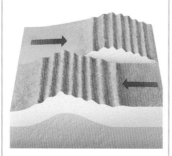
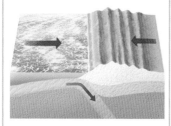

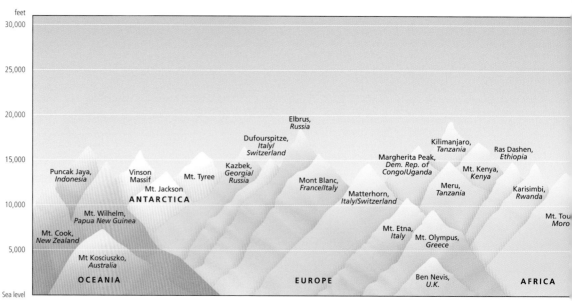

feet
30,000

25,000

20,000

Elbrus, *Russia*

Dufourspitze, *Italy/ Switzerland*

Kilimanjaro, *Tanzania*

Ras Dashen, *Ethiopia*

15,000

Puncak Jaya, *Indonesia*

Vinson Massif

Mt. Tyree

Kazbek, *Georgial Russia*

Margherita Peak, *Dem. Rep. of Congo/Uganda*

Mt. Kenya, *Kenya*

Mont Blanc, *France/Italy*

Meru, *Tanzania*

Karisimbi, *Rwanda*

Mt. Jackson

ANTARCTICA

Matterhorn, *Italy/Switzerland*

Mt. Wilhelm, *Papua New Guinea*

10,000

Mt. Cook, *New Zealand*

Mt. Etna, *Italy*

Mt. Olympus, *Greece*

Mt. Tou Moro

Mt Kosciuszko, *Australia*

5,000

OCEANIA

EUROPE

Ben Nevis, *U.K.*

AFRICA

Sea level

meters

8,000

6,000

4,000

2,000

Sea level

K2,
China/Pakistan

Kangchenjunga,
India/Nepal

Makalu,
China/Nepal

Mt. Everest,
China/Nepal

Lhotse,
China/Nepal

Cho Oyu,
China/Nepal

Annapurna,
Nepal

Qullai
Garmo,
Tajikistan

Mt. Aconcagua,
Argentina

Cerro
Bonete,
Argentina

Nevado
Huascarán,
Peru

Nevado
Sajama,
Bolivia

Nevado Ojos
del Salado,
Argentina/Chile

Volcán
Cotopaxi,
Ecuador

:Kinley,
:.A.

Pico de
Orizaba,
Mexico

Mt. Logan,
Canada

Popocatépetl,
Mexico

Pico
Bolívar,
Venezuela

Mt Ararat,
Turkey

:lias,
:.

Mt. Rainier,
U.S.A.

Mt. Whitney,
U.S.A.

Gunung
Kinabalu,
Malaysia

Mauna Kea,
U.S.A.

Mt. Fuji,
Japan

NORTH AMERICA   **SOUTH AMERICA**   **ASIA**

FACT FILE

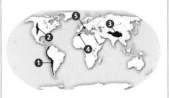

1. Andes This long, high range stretches for 4,400 miles (7,000 km) along the entire western coast of South America, where the Nazca and Pacific oceanic plates are being subducted beneath the South American continental plate. The Andes mountain range began rising about 50 million years ago.

Andes, South America

2. Rocky Mountains Extending 3,000 miles (4,800 km) along western North America from New Mexico to British Columbia, these mountains are made up of several ranges. They formed in three stages from collisions between oceanic and continental plates. The most recent stage took place 70–40 million years ago.

Rocky Mountains, North America

3. Himalaya–Karakorum–Hindu Kush These are the world's highest and youngest mountains. They began to rise about 40 million years ago, when the Indian plate, moving northward, collided with the Eurasian plate. India is still pushing into Eurasia and the mountains are still rising.

Himalaya/Karakorum/Hindu Kush, Asia

4. Atlas Mountains This mountain range extends about 1,500 miles (2,400 km) through Morocco, Algeria, and Tunisia. The highest peak is Jbel Toubkal, which rises sharply to a height of 13,671 feet (4,167 m).

Atlas Mountains, Africa

5. The Alps One of the great mountain ranges of Europe, the Alps stretch across a total of seven countries. The highest mountain is Mont Blanc, at 15,782 feet (4,810 m), on the French–Italian border.

The Alps, France, Italy, Switzerland, Austria, Liechtenstein, Germany, and Slovenia.

The Mountain Environment

Air temperature decreases with height and this produces very different climates at different altitudes. With increasing height the weather becomes colder, wetter, and windier. These climatic changes are reflected in the vegetation, which can vary from tropical rain forest at the base through grassland to tundra, with arctic conditions near the summit.

Mountain zones The vegetation of an equatorial mountain varies with climatic changes at different elevations. Even in the tropics high mountains are capped with snow and ice.

Summit Too cold and windswept for plants to survive, this consists of bare rock with no soil and is capped with ice and snow year-round.

Afro-Alpine Herbaceous plants grow in this zone. Some, such as giant lobelia and senecio, grow to the size of small trees.

Sub-alpine moorland This region has a milder climate and supports taller herbs and shrubs, including in some places tree heath growing 3–10 feet (1–4 m) high.

Bamboo belt Bamboos are the tallest grasses and form dense thickets. Along the lower margin of this belt there are also widely scattered evergreen trees.

Savanna Plants found in this zone include thorn trees, red oat grass, Bermuda grass, and tree ferns.

Montane forest This zone supports evergreen trees and shrubs, including white pear, winged bersama, and fluted milkwood, with herbs in the clearings.

Feet (Met

16,4 (5,00

13,0 (4,00

10,0 (3,00

6,56 (2,00

Table Mountain (above) This plateau, or mesa, overlooking Cape Town, South Africa, is 2 miles (3.2 km) wide and bounded by steep cliffs. It consists of resistant sandstone resting on shale and granite.

Mount Kenya (below) An extinct volcano, this is Africa's second highest mountain. Dry forest around the base gradually changes to bamboo, with alpine meadow above the timberline.

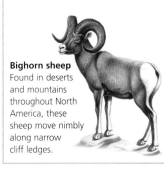

FACT FILE

Valley formation Cascading downhill, rainwater and melted snow carve steep-sided valleys in mountains. Continuing erosion softens the landscape to create gentler slopes.

Young valleys Altai Mountains in Siberia comprise the most northerly region affected by the ongoing collision of India with Asia. The mountains are young, and steep-sided valleys are still being formed.

Gentle landscape Broad, fertile valleys cross the Pennines, a range of hills that runs north–south down the center of northern England and consists of raised blocks of limestone and millstone grit.

Valleys

Most valleys are either V-shaped or U-shaped. Rivers flowing through steep mountains typically wear away deep, V-shaped valleys. At gentler gradients, the shape is more open, and at lower levels the valley bottom may eventually become a broad floodplain. Valleys that have been carved by glaciers are usually U-shaped, with a wide, flat floor and steep sides.

Hanging valley Bridal Veil Fall, in California's Yosemite National Park, drops 620 feet (188 m) from a hanging valley, which was eroded by a tributary glacier as it fed ice into the upper layer of a larger glacier. When both glaciers disappeared, the tributary valley was left high on the side of the main valley.

Typical V-shaped valley Verdon Gorge, in the mountains of Haute Provence, France, is the world's second largest canyon, 12 miles (20 km) long and almost 1,000 feet (330 m) deep. Its steep-sided V shape was formed by the Verdon River as it cut through thick layers of limestone rocks.

FACT FILE

1. Chahkouh Valley This hollow, or dry, valley is at Qeshm Island, a tourist attraction in the Strait of Hormuz, off the coast of southern Iran. Its barren, dusty floor and overhanging walls were formed by the erosion of its limestone rocks, which contain many wells. *Chah kouh* translates as "mountain of wells."

Chahkouh Valley, Iran

2. Valley of the Kings Situated on the west bank of the Nile River in Egypt, this dry valley was carved by heavy rains during the last ice age through a plateau composed of alternating layers of hard sedimentary rock and softer marl. Containing the tombs of many Egyptian pharaohs, it is a world-famous archaeological site.

Valley of the Kings, Egypt

3. Monument Valley Meandering rivers shaped this wide valley in Utah, U.S.A., depositing the sand and siltstone that form its floor. Iron oxide in the weathered siltstone colors the valley a vivid red, while manganese oxide produces blue-gray colors. Erosion has created the mesas, buttes, and spires that give the valley its name.

Monument Valley, Utah, U.S.A.

HERITAGE WATCH

Valley of Mexico Almost entirely occupied by the Mexico City urban area, this basin, located 7,350 feet (2,240 m) above sea level, is encircled by mountains. Aqueducts once ensured a constant supply of water for pre-Columbian civilizations. Today, seasonal lakes have been largely filled in or reduced by the area's water needs. Efforts are being made to tackle serious air pollution, trapped by the natural contours of the basin.

Glaciers

Glaciers cover about one-tenth of Earth's land surface. A glacier forms when snow fails to melt during the summer and accumulates year after year. The snow's weight compresses its lower layers into ice, which then begins to flow. Glaciers vary in size and form from large continental ice sheets and smaller ice caps, to cirque, valley, outlet, and piedmont glaciers.

Outlet glacier Mulajökull Glacier, Iceland, is one of three outlet glaciers that carry ice through from the Hofsjökull ice cap, which rests on a collapsed volcanic caldera. As the glacier reaches flatter ground it spreads out into a rounded piedmont lobe.

Ice formation Glacier ice begins as snow falling on a high snow field. New snow contains plenty of air, but as snow accumulates with fresh snowfalls, its weight squeezes out the air in the layers beneath.

Falling snow

Fresh snowfall

Small granules of ice

Firn

Solid Ice

From snow to ice Snow melts, refreezes, and is compressed into small granules and then into firn, which is ice that survives the summer. When most of the air is gone, blue-colored solid ice remains.

MELTWATER

In summer, surface ice melts briefly, forming pools of water and small rivers. The streams cut channels in the ice and often meander. The water also forms sinkholes, or moulins, and streams that flow beneath the surface.

Types of glacier Ice fields, ice sheets, and ice caps cover large land areas. Their ice flows outward into ice streams and outlet glaciers, which move between ice-free mountain peaks, or nunataks. Cirque glaciers begin in mountain hollows and, together with ice fields, feed ice to valley glaciers. A piedmont lobe sometimes forms when a valley or outlet glacier reaches flatter, lower-lying land.

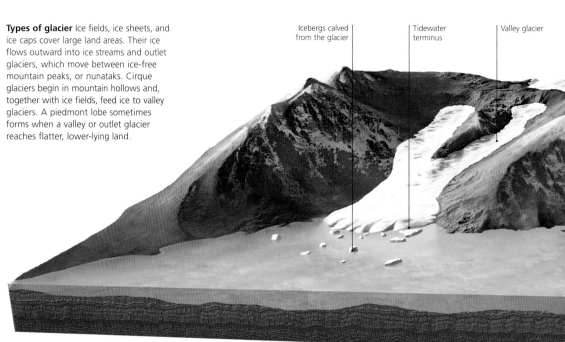

Icebergs calved from the glacier

Tidewater terminus

Valley glacier

Anatomy of a valley glacier Flowing from an ice sheet or mountain ice field, the ice spills down the mountainside. The weight of the ice grinds away all the soil and loose rock from the surface over which it flows, scouring a U-shaped valley. As it does so, it pushes fractured rocks and gravel ahead (terminal moraine) and to the sides (lateral moraine). At its foot the glacier turns upward, forming a snout. Beyond this, melted ice flows as a river or feeds lakes in hollows carved by the glacier before it retreated.

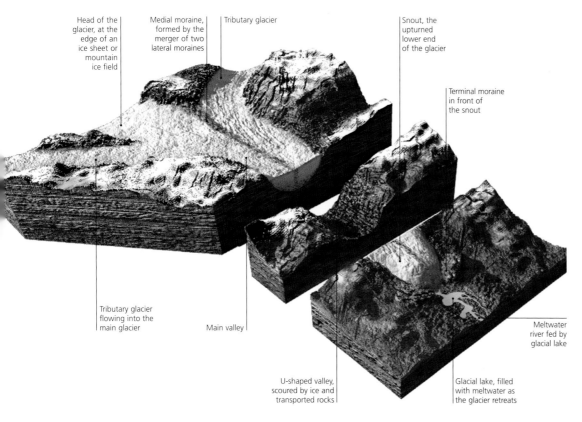

Head of the glacier, at the edge of an ice sheet or mountain ice field

Medial moraine, formed by the merger of two lateral moraines

Tributary glacier

Snout, the upturned lower end of the glacier

Terminal moraine in front of the snout

Tributary glacier flowing into the main glacier

Main valley

U-shaped valley, scoured by ice and transported rocks

Glacial lake, filled with meltwater as the glacier retreats

Meltwater river fed by glacial lake

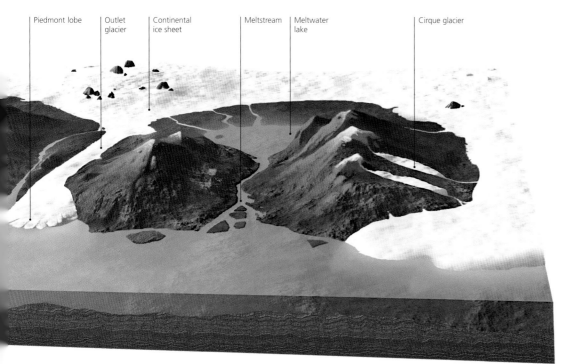

Piedmont lobe

Outlet glacier

Continental ice sheet

Meltstream

Meltwater lake

Cirque glacier

1. Inylchek Glacier This is the largest glacier in the Tien Shan Mountains in Kyrgyzstan and Kazakhstan. At about 37 miles (60 km) long, it is one of the longest in the world and has many

tributaries. The base of the glacier is about 13,000 feet (4,000 m) above sea level. It is not retreating.

Inylchek Glacier, Kyrgyzstan and Kazakhstan

2. Franz Josef Glacier Rising in the ice fields of New Zealand's Southern Alps, this glacier in Westland National Park flows westward for 7.5 miles (12 km) into temperate rain forest. It

has retreated since the last ice age. The glacier advances and retreats in cycles, and at present it is advancing.

Franz Josef Glacier, New Zealand

3. Baltoro Glacier This glacier in northern Pakistan is 35 miles (57 km) long and is one of the longest glaciers outside polar regions. It flows through part of the Karakorum Range, near K2, the second highest peak in the

world. Baltoro is fed by a number of tributary glaciers, and at its center is a large snow field. It is not retreating.

Baltoro Glacier, Pakistan

ILULISSAT ICEFJORD

This World Heritage site on Greenland's coast is where Sermeq Kujalleq Glacier enters the sea, draining the Greenland ice cap. The glacier is one of the world's fastest and most active. It moves 62 feet (19 m) a day and calves 8.4 cubic miles (35 km³) of icebergs a year.

Glaciers continued

Valley glaciers flow from mountain cirques or snow fields above the snowline. While most glaciers move at a steady rate, surge-type glaciers exhibit cyclical variations in the rate of flow over a number of years. In the late 19th century at the end of the Little Ice Age, many mountain glaciers began retreating as snowfall decreased and temperatures rose.

Surge glacier (below) The rate of flow of the Kongsvegen Glacier, Svalbard, Norway, fluctuates as a result of variations in the amount of ice the glacier accumulates from frozen meltwater.

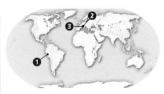

Cirque glaciers (right) These Canadian glaciers were formed when snow accumulated in natural hollows in the mountain's flank, forming ice that widened and deepened the cirques.

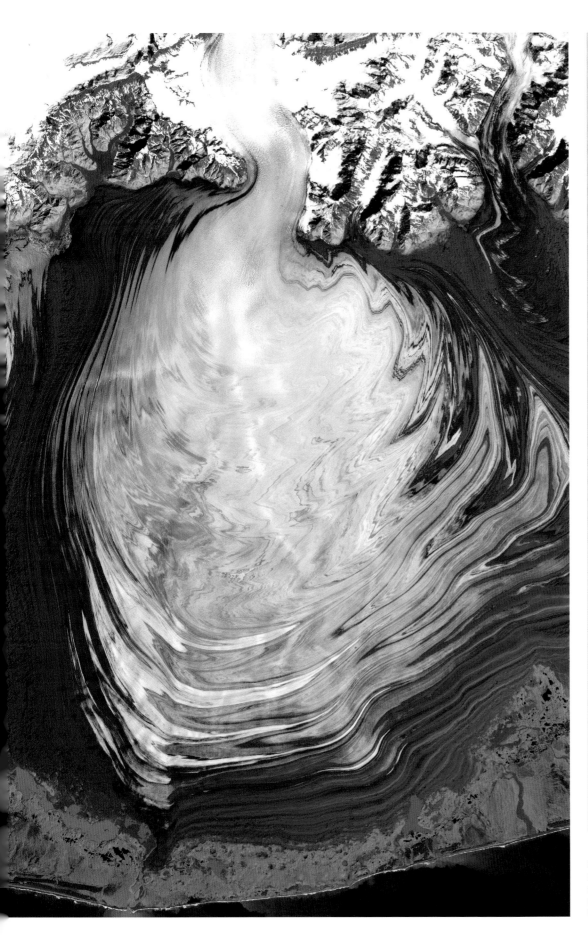

Crevasses These huge cracks in a glacier, with near-vertical walls, are caused by stresses in the ice and can be up to 100 feet (30 m) deep.

Ice peaks, or seracs When ice in the upper layer of a glacier stretches and breaks, pinnacles of ice form on the surface of the glacier.

Kvarken Archipelago Once weighed down by a glacier, the land in this World Heritage site in the Gulf of Bothnia is now rising to form islands.

Piedmont glacier Alaska's Malaspina Glacier covers 1,500 square miles (3,880 km²) and has been melting rapidly since the 1970s. Its tongue is shown in this false-color satellite image.

Glacial cycles Masses of ice lock up large amounts of water. In the Pleistocene period glacial advances and retreats caused sea levels to fluctuate. The weight of the ice also depressed land surfaces.

Extensive ice sheets During the Pleistocene epoch, ice sheets sometimes covered much of Eurasia and North America, and there was a large ice sheet in South America.

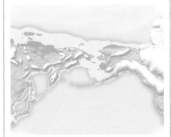

Bering land bridge At times of low sea level, the seafloor between Alaska and Siberia was exposed, allowing humans to migrate on foot from Asia into North America.

Ice weight Franz Josef Land, Russia, is an Arctic archipelago with raised beaches that formed during a past ice age, when the weight of ice depressed the land and the sea level rose.

Vast Expanses of Ice

An ice sheet is a huge glacier that covers 20,000 square miles (52,000 km²) or more. Earth's three remaining continental ice sheets are in west and east Antarctica and Greenland, but the Arctic ice is frozen sea. The weight at the center of a slightly dome-shaped ice sheet forces ice outward. Cold, dense air also moves outward, preventing milder air from entering the area.

Greenland This ice sheet extends over 670,000 square miles (1,735,000 km²), covering 85 percent of the country. The ice has an average thickness of 5,000 feet (1,525 m). Its outlet glaciers, especially Ilulissat, calve many icebergs.

Arctic ice (above) There is no land at the North Pole; the ice is frozen sea, not a continental ice sheet. Ice covers the Arctic Ocean in winter, but partly melts in summer, reducing the ice cover.

Antarctica (below) Two ice sheets cover almost all of west and east Antarctica, separated by the Transantarctic Mountains. The eastern ice sheet is twice the size of the western one.

FACT FILE

1. Scandinavian Peninsula Consisting mainly of Norway and Sweden, this borders the Arctic Ocean. About a quarter of the area lies inside the Arctic Circle. Although it has no ice sheets, there are extensive permanent snowfields and many mountain glaciers.

Scandinavian Peninsula

2. Western Cordillera Extending along Canada's Pacific coast, this comprises several high ranges, including the Rockies. It contains many snow-capped peaks, glaciers, and ice fields, some of which cover 140 square miles (363 km²).

Western Cordillera, Canada

3. Nunataks These bare mountain peaks or ridges protrude above an ice field or glacier, because their sides are too steep to hold ice. In east Greenland, vast fields of nunataks stretch inland from the coast for up to about 60 miles (100 km).

Nunataks, Greenland

ICE WORMS

Worms of the *Mesenchytraeus* genus are 0.5 inch (1 cm) long and live on and inside North American mountain glaciers. Ice worms feed on algae that grow on the surface of glaciers by obtaining nutrients from the dust on the ice.

Glaciated Landscapes

When glaciers melt and disappear, the landscape bears clear evidence of their former presence. Mountain valleys are gouged and broadened into distinctive U-shaped valleys. Hanging valleys are left suspended above the main valleys. Cirques at the head of glaciers remain as hollows that sometimes fill with water, while finger lakes form in glacial depressions.

Fjord valley (right) Valleys such as this one in Alaska occur where a valley glacier meets the sea. The lower part of the glacier has retreated and its valley has been flooded with water.

Lake Wakatipu (below) This finger lake in New Zealand's South Island fills a long glacial trench. The lake is 48 miles (77 km) long, up to 3 miles (5 km) wide, and 1,240 feet (378 m) deep.

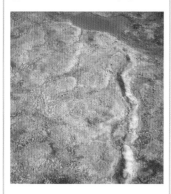
Shaping the landscape (below) Glaciers erode mountains in distinctive ways. When they recede they leave behind valleys with a characteristic U-shape, as well as many other features.

Before glaciation Valleys, carved by fast-flowing streams, are V-shaped with narrow floors and steep, but not precipitous, sides.

Cirque, where snow and ice formed the glacier | Medial moraine left where two glaciers merge

During glaciation Ice enlarges a natural hollow (cirque), then gouges out the valleys. Rock debris (medial moraine) is deposited where two glaciers meet.

FACT FILE

1. Gorner Glacier This Swiss valley glacier is about 9 miles (14 km) in length and is the third longest alpine glacier. During the Medieval Warm

 period it was shorter than at present. It meets several other glaciers at the head of the Mattervisp River valley.

Gorner Glacier, Zermatt, Switzerland

2. Great Lakes These five glacial lakes comprise the world's largest group of freshwater lakes. Their basins were formed from natural hollows that

 were widened and deepened in the last ice age by the weight and scouring action of the Laurentian ice sheet.

Great Lakes, North America

3. Troll's Wall Trollveggen in the Romsdal Valley on Norways' west coast is Europe's tallest vertical rock face. When a glacier retreated, it

 exposed the side of the glacial valley, leaving a vertical wall of gneiss, 3,600 feet (1,100 m) high.

Troll's Wall, Norway

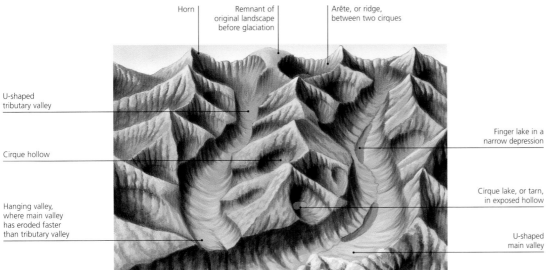

Horn | Remnant of original landscape before glaciation | Arête, or ridge, between two cirques

U-shaped tributary valley

Cirque hollow

Hanging valley, where main valley has eroded faster than tributary valley

Finger lake in a narrow depression

Cirque lake, or tarn, in exposed hollow

U-shaped main valley

After glaciation Valleys are U-shaped, with finger lakes and tarns in deeper places. Cirques and hanging valleys are exposed, and waterfalls abound.

GETTLINGE

Part of the Stora Alvaret World Heritage site on Sweden's Öland Island, this Viking stone ship burial ground used granite moraine material left by ice age glaciers.

MAPPING THE WORLD

When the early explorers ventured into unknown lands, one of their most important tasks was to measure distances and elevations and to draw maps. Today, maps exist of the entire Earth, while orbiting satellites carry instruments that generate accurate three-dimensional images of the land surface below. Satellites can measure the thickness of the ice at the Poles and distinguish types of land surface, and are even used to map other planets. Modern maps contain a wide variety of information, but do not pack in so much detail that they become confusing. Instead, specialized maps are produced to meet the specific needs of different users.

Compass (left) European sailors began using magnetic compasses around 1300. This compass rose, which shows all 32 points of the compass, was added later to a copy of the Agnese Atlas made in 1544, one of several copies published by the Venetian mapmaker Battista Agnese.

EARLY MAP-MAKERS

Travelers need maps to guide them, but people also use maps as pictorial representations of their local area. Maps are so helpful that the very first human tribes may well have used them to show the locations of important resources such as water and to pinpoint hostile territory.

Nomadic peoples used maps to help them skirt obstacles such as deserts, and to find mountain passes and seasonal pastures. The earliest maps were most likely drawn in dust or sand and survived for only a few minutes, but by about 2300 B.C. the Babylonians were inscribing maps on clay tablets. One of the oldest surviving maps of the world, from about 1000 B.C., shows the world as a disk with Babylon at its center surrounded by water.

The ancient Greeks visited all the lands bordering the Aegean, Adriatic, and Mediterranean seas on voyages of exploration, trade, and conquest. They then ventured farther afield to the Caspian Sea and traveled along the coasts of western Europe. Their culture also produced great scholars who measured the globe and determined its shape. It was the Greeks who recognized that Earth is spherical. In about 220 B.C., Greek geographer

Eratosthenes made a map of the then-known world, showing the lands from Britain to India and Sri Lanka, and from north of the Caspian Sea to Ethiopia. Eratosthenes also calculated Earth's circumference as 250,000 stadia. Depending on the stadion value used, this converts to between 23,674 miles (38,092 km) and 28,740 miles (46,243 km), which is very close to the accurate measurement that we have today of 24,902 miles (40,074 km).

One of the most important geographers and cartographers of the ancient world was the Egyptian scholar Claudius Ptolemaeus (A.D. 90–168), better known as Ptolemy. In his eight-volume work *Guide to Geography* he discussed map projection and how to construct a globe, and listed approximately 8,000 places with their latitudes and longitudes. Although Ptolemy made many mistakes, including a recalculation of Earth's circumference that made it much too small, his work laid the foundation for the maps made in Europe during the Middle Ages.

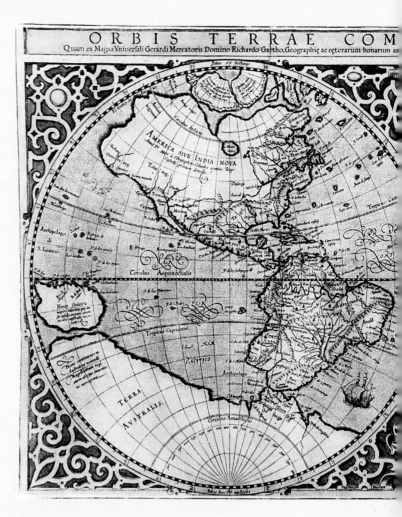

THROUGH THE AGES

7th–6th century B.C. Greek philosopher Anaximander made the first world map, showing the Mediterranean at the center, with Europe, Africa, and Asia.

5th century B.C. Hecataeus of Miletus wrote *Travels Round the Earth*, the first geography book ever written and containing a world map.

Ca 450 B.C. Greek traveler and historian Herodotus drew a fairly accurate map of the world as it was known at the time.

1st century B.C. Marcus Agrippa, a Roman geographer and general, produced a map of the Roman Empire, with roads and distances.

2nd century A.D. Ptolemy wrote his eight-volume *Guide to Geography*, which contained a world map and locations of around 8,000 places.

Sextant (left) A sextant measures elevation—the angle between a celestial object and the horizon. The instrument was invented around 1730 independently by English mathematician John Hadley and Philadelphia glazier Thomas Godfrey. By using a sextant to measure the elevation of the midday sun, navigators could calculate the latitude. The instrument is called a sextant because the length of its scale is one-sixth of a full circle.

World map (below) Drawn in 1587 by Rumold Mercator—based on one made by his father, Gerardus Mercator—this world map depicts the Eastern and Western hemispheres as two disks. It demonstrates the extent of geographical knowledge at the time: the Americas are distorted, but Eurasia and Africa are fairly accurate.

Digital map measurer (left) Journeys by air or sea are easy to measure because the traveler moves along a straight line, but distance is more complicated to determine when traveling on land. A map measurer has a small wheel with which the user traces the route, following all its twists and turns. The measurer multiplies the number of turns of the wheel by the wheel's circumference, then converts this into a distance on the ground.

Satellite view (below) Orbiting satellites have a wide field of view. This false-color image, captured in December 2000, looks eastward over Guinea-Bissau, a West African country, showing it at a scale of 1 inch to 3 miles (1 cm to 1.2 km). Red indicates vegetation and the blue patterns offshore show sediment carried by rivers.

Ca 1300 The Hereford *Mappa mundi* was printed and showed Jerusalem at the center and east at the top.

1585 Flemish engraver Gerardus Mercator published an atlas of the world that had the most accurate maps produced up to that time.

1675 Scottish printer John Ogilby published the first road atlas of Britain. It was plotted by a compass and measuring wheel, and showed roads as strips.

1801 Founded in Britain in 1791, Ordnance Survey published its first sheet map (of Kent) at a scale of 1 inch to 1 mile.

1993 GPS (Global Positioning System) was launched in 1993 and used 24 (now about 30) satellites to pinpoint the positions of GPS receivers.

Floodplain Each time a river overflows its banks, it deposits sediment, which accumulates to form the river's floodplain.

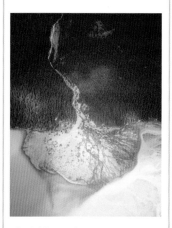

Alluvial fan At the point where a river emerges from a mountain valley onto flatter terrain, the sediment it releases radiates out to form an alluvial fan, one kind of alluvial plain.

Valley plain As a river meanders through a wide valley, it erodes the bank on one side and deposits silt on the other, gradually forming a flat plain across the valley.

Plains

The vast, open expanses of land known as plains owe their origins to several different causes. Floodplains are created when major rivers deposit sediment across wide valleys. A landscape can also become a plain when it is covered by a windblown layer of soil called loess. The widest plains, found in continental interiors, represent the final stage of erosion.

Nullarbor Bordering Australia's Great Australian Bight, this plain was once a seabed. Uplifted by crustal movements 20–25 million years ago, it has eroded to its present flat form. It is the world's largest single limestone expanse and occupies about 77,200 square miles (200,000 km²). While its name means "no tree," it is covered with hardy shrubs.

Serengeti The surface of Tanzania's Serengeti Plain consists of a deep layer of volcanic ash covering igneous rocks. The ash buries all of the low relief, thus forming the vast, level plain, but many house-sized granite outcrops, called kopjes (little hills), protrude through the cover. Serengeti Plain extends over 23,000 square miles (60,000 km²).

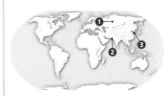

1. West Siberian Plain This extends from Russia's Ural Mountains in western Siberia to the Yenisei River in the east. Covering an area of about 1 million square miles (2.6 million km²), it is considered to be the world's largest unbroken stretch of lowland. It is formed from river sediments and contains extensive peatlands and bogs.

West Siberian Plain, Russia

2. Indus alluvial fan The Indus Valley, running through northern India, Kashmir, and Pakistan, follows the trough between the Karakorum and Ladakh ranges, crossing the Ladakh range twice. As the Indus discharges into the Arabian Sea, it feeds material, mainly from Karakorum, into a vast submarine fan.

Indus Valley, Tikse, Ladakh, northern India

3. Korean coastal plains The western coastline of North Korea is characterized by plains. River valleys descend from mountains that run north–south down the eastern side of the Korean peninsula. As the valleys approach the sea, they merge to form the wide coastal plains that are the country's main cereal-growing area.

Coastal plains, North Korea

GREAT PLAINS, NORTH AMERICA

For approximately 500 million years, North America's Great Plains were under the sea. Layers of sediment 5,000–10,000 feet (1,525–3,000 m) thick accumulated. Uplift raised the land about 70 million years ago.

Altiplano–Puna These two high-altitude plateaus in the Central Andes, 1,120 miles (1,800 km) long and 215–250 miles (350–400 km) wide, were uplifted when Earth's crust thickened.

Yemen Plateau Sediment that was deposited in wadi systems covers parts of this volcanic plateau, much of which rises more than 7,000 feet (2,100 m) above sea level.

Antarctic Plateau Comprising the ice-covered land around the South Pole, this plateau is almost 10,000 feet (3,000 m) above sea level, and is the coldest place on Earth.

Plateaus

A plateau is a fairly flat area elevated above the surrounding land. Some plateaus represent the final stage in the erosion of mountains; others were once seabeds covered by sediment and then uplifted. The Tibetan Plateau was raised when the Indo–Australian and Asian tectonic plates collided, while India's Deccan Plateau was created by layers of volcanic lava.

Tepui, Venezuela (right) This tableland, or tepui, is one of 115 in the Guyana highlands. Tepuis are mesas—the remains of eroded sandstone plateaus—and are among Earth's oldest rock formations.

Utah Valley, U.S.A. (below) Utah Valley is a plateau 4,300–4,700 feet (1,311–1,433 m) above sea level. It was once the bed of the prehistoric Lake Bonneville, of which Utah Lake is a remnant.

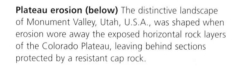

Plateau erosion (below) The distinctive landscape of Monument Valley, Utah, U.S.A., was shaped when erosion wore away the exposed horizontal rock layers of the Colorado Plateau, leaving behind sections protected by a resistant cap rock.

Canyon, a deep, steep-sided river channel

The beginning of erosion (below left) Rivers cut deep channels in the Colorado Plateau as they flowed across its horizontal beds of siltstone and sandstone.

Siltstone and sandstone layers

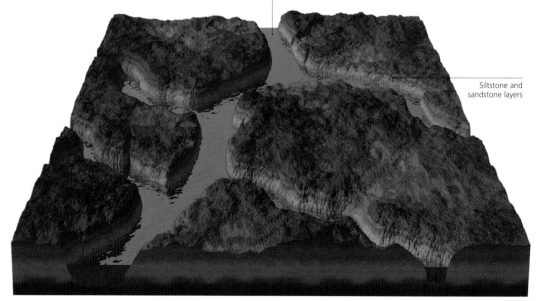

After erosion (below right) Continued erosion widened the channels, leaving sections of the plateau rising above the channels as mesas, buttes, and pinnacles.

Butte, a small, flat-topped hill left after erosion of a mesa

Erosion-resistant cap rock

Pinnacle, the last stage in the erosion of a raised plateau

Mesa, a large raised tableland remaining from the original plateau

FACT FILE

1. Giza This limestone and dolomite plateau on the outskirts of Cairo, Egypt, is famous as the location of the Pyramids and Sphinx. It was formed from seabed sediments and is overlaid

in the south by marls. Two steep escarpments about 90 feet (27 m) high mark the plateau's northern edge.

Giza Plateau, Egypt

2. Columbia River One of world's largest flood basalt plateaus, this covers about 63,000 square miles (160,000 km²). It took shape about

20–25 million years ago as repeated volcanic eruptions released more than 6,000 feet (1,830 m) of basalt.

Columbia River Plateau, western U.S.A.

3. Seychelles The underwater Seychelles Plateau is a microconti- nent—a small section of continental crust that broke away from India and

Madagascar. The inner Seychelles islands, most of them made from granite, sit on the plateau.

Seychelles Plateau, Indian Ocean

4. Mount Roraima Located on the border between Venezuela and Guyana, this is the world's highest table mountain, with an average

elevation of 8,200 feet (2,500 m). It may have been the setting for Arthur Conan Doyle's novel *The Lost World*.

Mount Roraima, Venezuela/Guyana

5. Arnhem Land This rugged sandstone plateau in the Northern Territory, Australia, covers 37,000 square miles (95,800 km²), and is dissected by chasms and gorges.

The plateau rises above a flat landscape that once lay beneath a shallow sea.

Arnhem Land, Northern Territory, Australia

Coasts

Sea and land interact at the coast to create many different landforms and changing shorelines. Deposition of sediment or a falling sea level causes some coasts to extend toward the sea. Others are retreating as the sea level rises or waves erode them. A falling sea level produces an emergent coast, a rising sea level a submergent one, while wave erosion creates coastal cliffs.

Shaping the coast Erosion and deposition constantly reconfigure coastlines, often rapidly. Changing sea level has a more gradual effect, falling to expose new land or rising so that the sea penetrates inland.

Coastal inlet The sea has breached or risen above a barrier and flooded low ground to create this inlet in the Philippines.

Fjords When glaciers melted, the lower ends of valleys were flooded by the sea to form fjords, such as these in Alaska, viewed from above.

Raised beach This former shoreline in Kerry, Ireland, became an emergent landform when sea levels fell at the end of an earlier interglacial period.

Lulworth Cove, Dorset, England (above) A cove with a narrow entrance occurs where the sea has penetrated a band of hard rock lying parallel to the coast and eroded a softer band of rock behind it.

Coastal landforms Vigorous waves and tides cut into rocky coasts, producing cliffs, terraces, caves, arches, stacks, and blowholes. The sea deposits the eroded material elsewhere, building sandbars and spits, and extending beaches.

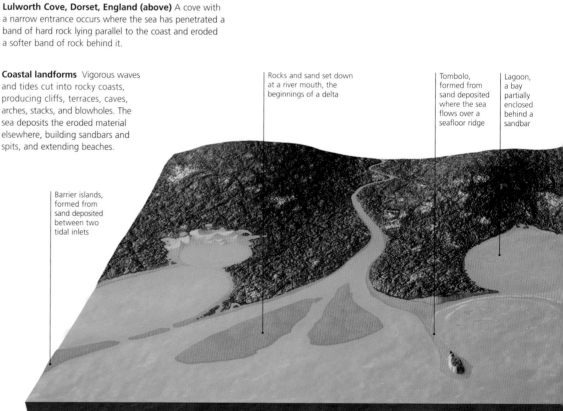

Barrier islands, formed from sand deposited between two tidal inlets

Rocks and sand set down at a river mouth, the beginnings of a delta

Tombolo, formed from sand deposited where the sea flows over a seafloor ridge

Lagoon, a bay partially enclosed behind a sandbar

Low coastline (above) This inlet in North Carolina, U.S.A., is one of many formed by local erosion along a low-lying coastline that is highly vulnerable to a rising sea level.

Sandstone cliffs (above) Along this coast in Portugal, wave erosion has cut into a hill of Cretaceous sandstone, or compressed sand. The waves return the rock to the seabed as sand grains.

Spit, created by deposition of sand where the sea current slows down

Terrace in the cliff, cut by wave action

Blowhole, where the roof of a cave has collapsed

Stack, created by wave erosion at the end of a headland

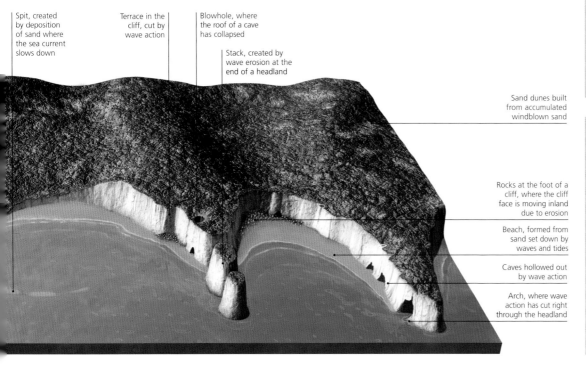

Sand dunes built from accumulated windblown sand

Rocks at the foot of a cliff, where the cliff face is moving inland due to erosion

Beach, formed from sand set down by waves and tides

Caves hollowed out by wave action

Arch, where wave action has cut right through the headland

HERITAGE WATCH

Coastal pollution Coastal waters are subject to pollution by wastes discarded from ships, sewage, industrial effluent, and agricultural runoff carried by rivers. Marine wildlife is put at risk, and beaches are littered by substances and objects that wash up. Antipollution measures have greatly improved the quality of many rivers and it is now an offense to discharge pollutants from ships at sea. Emergency services are skilled at containing oil and chemical spills, but accidents continue to occur.

Caves

A cave is a cavity in rocks large enough for a person to enter. Most underground caves are formed by the action of water. As rainwater seeps downward limestone rock is dissolved, while water flowing along joints and fractures widens them. Other caves take shape when molten rock solidifies, or are formed from spaces between blocks of fallen rock.

1 Growth begins when water saturated in calcium carbonate drips from the roof of a limestone cave.

2 Drop by drop, stalactites grow downward from the roof and stalagmites upward from the floor.

3 After thousands of years, stalactites and stalagmites meet as columns, pillars, spirals, or curtains.

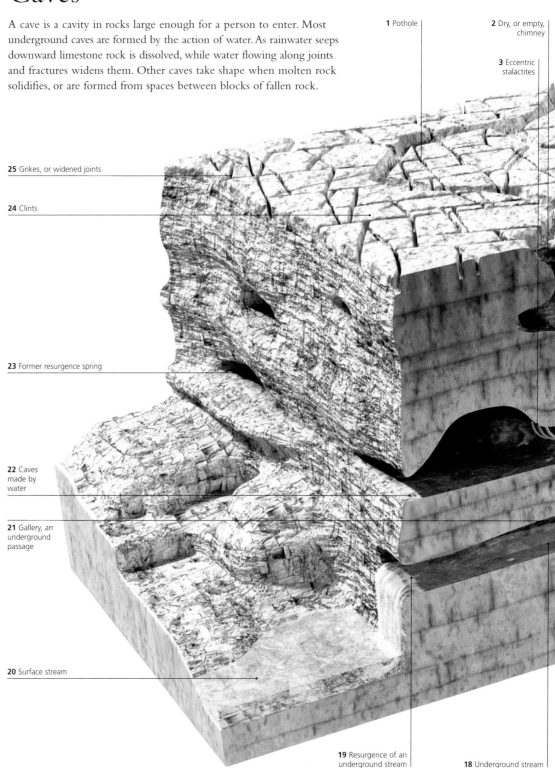

1 Pothole

2 Dry, or empty, chimney

3 Eccentric stalactites

25 Grikes, or widened joints

24 Clints

23 Former resurgence spring

22 Caves made by water

21 Gallery, an underground passage

20 Surface stream

19 Resurgence of an underground stream

18 Underground stream

Limestone cave systems The erosive effect of acidic rain on limestone rocks produces highly complex systems of caves (**22**), galleries (**21**), and underground streams (**18**). Surface streams (**4**) move hard stones that wear away potholes (**1**), then vanish down sinkholes (**9**) and may emerge at a resurgence (**19**, **23**). surface, widened joints form grikes (**25**) that divide the limestone into blocks called clints (**24**) to form a limestone pavement (**6**). Access to some caves is through a narrow opening, or chimney (**2**, **10**), and inside the cave there are often stalactites and stalagmites (**3**, **5**, **17**), columns (**7**), curtains (**14**), and ponds, or gours (**11**).

4 Surface stream

5 Hollow macaroni stalactites

6 Limestone pavement on surface

7 Columns, from roof to floor

8 Abandoned gallery, with empty streambed

9 Sinkhole, or doline

10 Chimney, a narrow opening

12 Boat in the underground stream

11 Rimstone ponds, or gours

13 Blind fish, adapted to cave life

15 Cave art

14 Curtains, a type of stalactite

17 Pinecone and plate stalagmites

16 Siphon, a U-shaped passage

Feengrotte Caves, Saalfeld, Germany The Feengrotte, or Fairy Grottos, are some of the most colorful caves in the world, with dramatic stalactites and stalagmites that have formed from the constant dripping of mineral-rich water.

FACT FILE

Formation of lava tubes These caves are found in areas where there has been volcanic activity. The hollowed underground tubes, often many miles long, were once conduits for lava in an eruption.

1 Hot lava flows along an open depression down the side of the volcano, melting the adjacent rock and enlarging the channel.

2 The surface of the lava loses heat rapidly and begins to solidify, forming a thickening cover beneath which lava continues to flow.

3 The whole upper surface solidifies and forms a tube that insulates the lava, which can flow through it for a long distance.

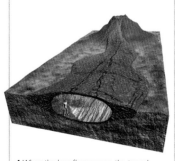

4 When the lava flow ceases, the tunnel empties and leaves a hollow tube that can be larger than a train tunnel.

Caves continued

Caverns deep below ground attract explorers and, once they are declared safe, visitors. They may feature narrow tunnels that open into vast chambers, subterranean rivers and lakes, glittering crystals, and fantastic rock forms. They are places of wonder and often of spectacular beauty. Many large limestone caves are still growing.

Carlsbad Caverns At this World Heritage site in New Mexico there are 300 known caves, of which 113 "rooms" comprise a national park. Formed as acidic rainwater dissolved the Permian limestone, the caves include some of North America's largest.

Cave deposits As molten rocks cool down, the minerals that they contain crystallize. Often brightly colored or with large crystals, these minerals are exposed in caves of igneous or metamorphic rocks.

Crystals Gypsum crystallizes from evaporating seawater. These crystals in the Naica Mine, Chihuahua, Mexico, are up to 20 feet (6 m) long.

Pearls Cave pearls form when water dripping onto sand grains loses carbon dioxide and precipitates calcium carbonate spheres, ovals, or cubes.

CAVE DWELLERS

Many species of bats roost by day and spend the winter in caves, where the temperature remains constant year-round and is warm enough for them to maintain their body temperature. Cave-dwelling bat species will also seek out caves with the best conditions for giving birth and for raising infant bats.

Sea cave (above) Carved over centuries by waves and tides, the flowing shapes in this Patagonian cave, Argentina, were sculpted in the sedimentary rock by currents deflected by the coastline.

Sarawak Chamber, Malaysia (below) The world's largest-known single underground chamber, this cave is 2,300 feet (700 m) long, 1,300 feet (400 m) wide, and 230 feet (70 m) high.

FACT FILE

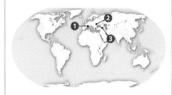

1. Gouffre Berger Discovered in 1953 by Joseph Berger, this cave system in the Rhône-Alpes region of France was for a time the deepest-known system in the world. At its deepest point it lies 3,963 feet (1,208 m) below the surface. The system is 19 miles (31 km) long.

Gouffre Berger, France

2. Maze Cave Also known as Optimistic Cave, this system in Ukraine has up to 143 miles (230 km) of mapped passages that form a dense network on several levels. It extends for 0.8 square mile (2 km²) in a layer of gypsum less than 65 feet (20 m) thick.

Maze Cave, Ukraine

3. Voronya Cave This cave in the Republic of Georgia is the deepest-known in the world and the first explored below 6,560 feet (2,000 m). Its bottom lies 7,051 feet below ground level (2,149 m), with a variation of 30 feet (9 m). It is closed to the public.

Voronya Cave, Republic of Georgia

GLOWING TRAPS

The larvae of the fungus gnat are also known as glowworms. Found in Australian and New Zealand caves, they have adapted to life without daylight. Using light emitted from modified excretory organs, they glow in the dark to attract prey, which they trap in long silken threads dangling from ceiling nests.

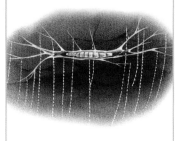

BIOMES

Biogeography is the scientific study of the way plants and animals are distributed. Because climate and soil determine which plants thrive in a particular region, similar types of vegetation, as well as the animals associated with them, occur in places with climates that are similar. These places, occupying large areas and identified by their vegetation types, are known as biomes. For example, the belt of mainly evergreen coniferous forest that runs across Canada and northern Eurasia constitutes a biome known as boreal forest in North America and taiga in Russia. The character of this forest is essentially the same throughout the biome, but the plant and animal species found there vary.

THE WORLD'S BIOMES

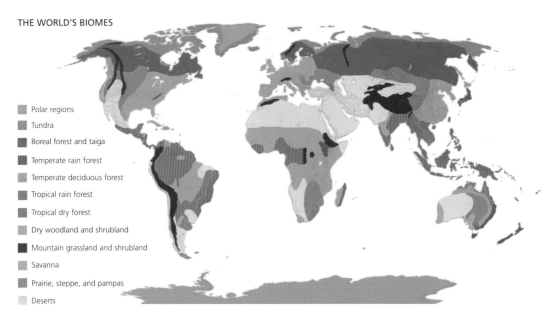

- Polar regions
- Tundra
- Boreal forest and taiga
- Temperate rain forest
- Temperate deciduous forest
- Tropical rain forest
- Tropical dry forest
- Dry woodland and shrubland
- Mountain grassland and shrubland
- Savanna
- Prairie, steppe, and pampas
- Deserts

THE TWELVE BIOMES

Although biomes can be identified by general vegetation types, the vegetation in any biome is, in fact, quite varied because of a number of local differences in land use and environment.

Tropical biomes occur between the tropics of Cancer (north) and Capricorn (south). Temperate biomes can be found in temperate regions, and polar biomes are located near the Poles. Other biomes are more difficult to define precisely, because not all plant communities have clear boundaries. The range of plants in each biome makes it possible to draw the boundaries in different ways. Consequently, not every authority lists biomes in the same way or uses the same names for them.

Twelve distinct biomes are described here and in the pages that follow. Around the Poles, the polar ice biome supports no plant life. The climate is exceedingly harsh and there is neither soil nor liquid water at the surface. Bordering the polar ice is the tundra biome, where the ground is exposed and the temperature

rises above freezing for a short time in summer. Along its edges, tundra gives way to boreal forest or taiga. Tundra and boreal forest are mainly confined to the Northern Hemisphere, because there is little land at the correct latitude in the Southern Hemisphere.

Closer to the equator, deciduous trees become more common among the conifers of the boreal forest. The biome changes and temperate deciduous forest becomes more widespread. This biome is restricted to the continental regions with moist climates, while temperate rain forest is found only in the wettest regions.

As climates grow hotter and drier, the biome changes again. Temperate grassland—the prairies, steppes, pampas, and veld—replace the temperate deciduous forest. In a few parts of the world there is a biome typical of Mediterranean climates, dominated by dry woodlands and chaparral shrublands.

A belt of subtropical deserts lies across both hemispheres. Deserts vary according to their location, with some found along western

coasts and some in the interiors of continents. Where climates are a little moister, subtropical deserts merge into savanna grassland. On either side of the equator there are tropical dry forests and rain forests. The last biome, mountain grasslands and shrublands, is not confined to particular latitudes.

Desert (top left) Sand dunes extend to the horizon in this part of the vast Sahara Desert.
Savanna (top right) Drought-resistant trees and grasses provide food for gazelles, antelope, and other game animals.
Tundra (middle left) Too cold for trees, the shallow soils of the tundra support grasses and scattered small shrubs.
Mountain (middle right) Vegetation changes with elevation, from the forest seen here to tundra and permanent snow.
Tropical rain forest (bottom left) The warm, wet climate supports dense forest with luxuriant vegetation.
Temperate grassland (bottom right) As well as its grasses, the Eurasian steppe features many flowering herbs.

Tundra

The tundra biome extends across northern North America and Eurasia. In these high latitudes the climate is too cold and harsh and the soils too shallow for trees to survive. When the ice and snow melt in spring, the ground is carpeted with mosses, lichens, sedges, grasses, herbs, and low shrubs. Tundra also occurs high on mountains and on subantarctic islands.

Alpine tundra As winter approaches, grasses, sedges, and herbs still clothe stretches of tundra on the slopes of Mount McKinley in Denali National Park, Alaska. The vast reserve is home to a variety of wildlife, including moose.

CLIMATE

The tundra climate is cold and as dry as a desert climate. Winter temperatures are below freezing, and the average summer temperature never rises above 46°F (8°C). Annual precipitation can be as low as 4.2 inches (107 mm).

BARROW, ALASKA

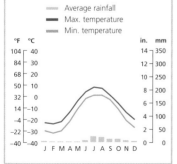

Arctic tundra (above) Summer is brief in the subarctic and herbs all bloom together, competing to attract pollinating insects with their bright, colorful flowers. By fall they have produced seed and die down for the winter.

Glacier buttercup (below) Like all flowering plants in the tundra, this buttercup must complete its life cycle in the brief interval between the spring thaw and the fall freeze. To speed development, it absorbs as much of the weak sunshine as it can.

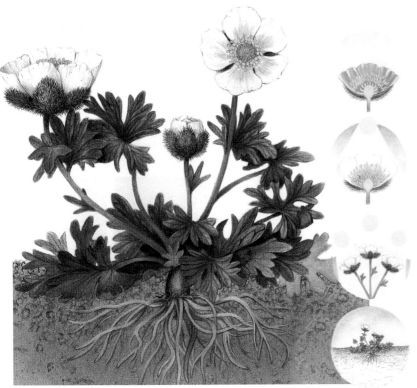

Maximum warmth The central part of the flower, surrounding the reproductive organs, is red. It absorbs the sun's warmth, attracting pollinating insects.

Petal shape The white petals reflect light and heat, but their shape makes them reflect radiation toward the center of the flower.

Angled flowers The plant produces several flowers, angled in different directions. There is always one flower facing the sun as it moves across the sky.

Seed survival Once the plant has flowered and set seed, it dies down. The seeds survive in the soil until the next spring.

Boreal Forest and Taiga

Forests dominated by coniferous trees—larch, fir, pine, hemlock, and spruce—cover a broad swathe of northern North America and Eurasia. In North America this region is known as boreal (or northern) forest and in Russia as the taiga. Conifers thrive in this biome because their needle-like leaves help them tolerate cold and drought better than broad-leaved trees.

Eurasian taiga Near Evje in southern Norway the Otra River flows through a region of old-growth coniferous forest dominated by pine. Timber and wood pulp are commercially important, but the overall forest area in Norway is increasing.

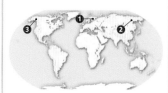
1. Karelia Forest Straddling the border between Finland and Russia, Karelia Forest is composed of pine, spruce, and some birch trees. On the Finnish side the forest is heavily managed, while the Russian side consists mainly of old-growth forest.

Karelia Forest, Finland and Russia

2. Sakha (Yakutia) taiga Coniferous forests cover about 563,000 square miles (1.5 million km²) of Sakha Republic (Yakutia) in Russia, almost half of its area. In the north larch trees predominate, while farther to the south there are also stands of fir and pine.

Sakha (Yakutia) taiga, Russia

3. Yukon This territory in Canada's northwest has 10.6 million square miles (27.5 km²) of boreal forest. White spruce is the predominant species, with many stands that are 200–400 years old. The forest also has trembling aspen and balsam poplar trees.

Yukon, Canada

CLIMATE

The boreal forest and taiga have cool summers, cold winters, and moderate precipitation. Annual average temperatures are relatively low and the climate is quite dry, with snow in winter and a rainfall peak in late summer and early fall.

ANCHORAGE, ALASKA

— Average rainfall
— Max. temperature
— Min. temperature

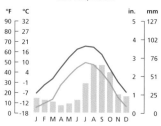

BOREAL FOREST MIGRATION

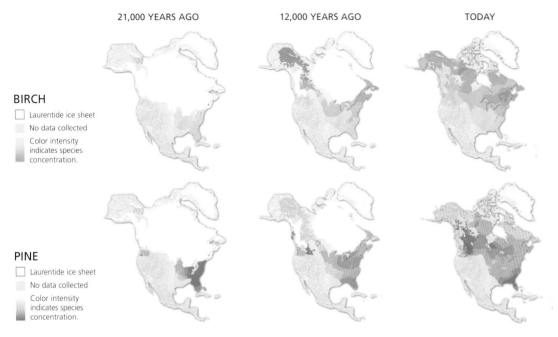

21,000 YEARS AGO   12,000 YEARS AGO   TODAY

BIRCH

☐ Laurentide ice sheet

☐ No data collected

Color intensity indicates species concentration.

PINE

☐ Laurentide ice sheet

☐ No data collected

Color intensity indicates species concentration.

Conifer migration (above) Over the last 21,000 years, birch, pine, and other boreal species gradually relocated farther north as temperatures rose and the Laurentide ice sheet receded.

Tamarack or eastern larch (below) Unlike other conifers, larches shed their leaves in winter and grow them afresh in spring. Young female cones are bright red, turning brown when mature.

Conifer cycle Conifers are self-sufficient when it comes to reproduction, bearing both male and female cones. Pollen released by the male cones is transferred by the wind to the female cones, which contain seeds.

Germination If there is sufficient warmth, moisture, and light, the seed germinates and grows into a new tree.

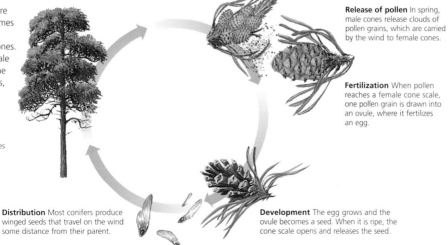

Release of pollen In spring, male cones release clouds of pollen grains, which are carried by the wind to female cones.

Fertilization When pollen reaches a female cone scale, one pollen grain is drawn into an ovule, where it fertilizes an egg.

Distribution Most conifers produce winged seeds that travel on the wind some distance from their parent.

Development The egg grows and the ovule becomes a seed. When it is ripe, the cone scale opens and releases the seed.

FACT FILE

1. Tsitsikamma National Park
Stretching for 50 miles (80 km) along South Africa's southern coastline, this nature reserve receives more

than 300 inches (1,000 mm) of rain annually. Temperate rain forest descends from the mountains to sea level.

Tsitsikamma National Park, South Africa

2. Olympic National Park
Following the Pacific coast for 73 miles (117 km), this park in Washington State, U.S.A., includes temperate rain

forest dominated by spruce, fir, maple, and mosses. It has the highest rainfall in the continental United States.

Olympic National Park, Washington, U.S.A.

3. Yushan National Park
Centered on Jade Mountain (Yu Shan) in Nantou County, Taiwan, this area is mainly subtropical, but temperate rain forest

occurs at higher elevations, with Taiwan cypress, Japanese maple, yew, hemlock, and Taiwan Douglas fir.

Yushan National Park, Taiwan

CLIMATE

Temperate rain forest requires an annual rainfall of more than 50–60 inches (1,300–1,500 mm), warm but not hot summers, and mild winters with temperatures seldom falling below freezing.

KENT, KING COUNTY, WASHINGTON, U.S.A.

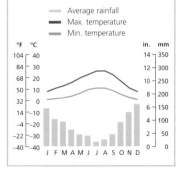

- Average rainfall
- Max. temperature
- Min. temperature

°F	°C		in.	mm
104	40		14	350
84	30		12	300
68	20		10	250
50	10		8	200
32	0		6	150
14	-10		4	100
-4	-20		2	50
-22	-30		0	0
-40	-40			

J F M A M J J A S O N D

Temperate Rain Forest

In temperate regions, rain forest is found close to the coast, where the climate is wet. The rain forest extending along the U.S. Pacific coast from Oregon through to California contains the world's biggest tree species, the coast redwood, which can grow to a height of almost 400 feet (122 m). The temperate rain forest that grows in parts of Olympic National Park, Washington State, U.S.A., is protected and is designated a World Heritage site. Temperate rain forest is also found in parts of Australia, New Zealand, South Africa, and Taiwan. These forests support the highest biomass per area of all the biomes.

Misty forest (right) Patches of temperate rain forest occur in sheltered locations throughout Morton National Park, New South Wales, Australia. Fitzroy Falls shrouds one of these areas in mist, providing the moisture that makes it a rain forest.

Rain forest floor (below) Abundant moisture and mild temperatures provide ideal conditions for the animals, fungi, and microorganisms that feed on dead plant and animal material. In so doing, they recycle the nutrients that allow plants to flourish.

Teeming with life Although dead, a fallen tree on the forest floor is alive with activity, providing food for many living organisms.

Fungi While the fruiting bodies of fungi are on the surface, the part that feeds and grows is inside the dead tree, where fine web-like networks of hyphae break down dead wood cells and extract nutrients.

Bracket fungi Many different species of these shelf-like growths feed on deciduous trees.

Mosses Clinging to the bark, mosses break it down, and create a thin layer of soil.

Hidden decomposers Bacteria break down dead plant and animal material and release nutrients that living plants can absorb.

Animals Rodents and other small mammals feed on seeds and small invertebrates that are found among the plant litter on the forest floor.

Ferns These flourish on the dimly lit forest floor. When they die, they too provide food for other organisms.

FACT FILE

Wildlife With its luxuriant vegetation, temperate rain forest provides food and shelter for a variety of animals. Some, like the raccoon and puma, or mountain lion, also occur in other biomes.

Raccoon This agile animal is a good climber and swims if it must. It is mainly nocturnal.

Green tree frog This native of the Daintree Rain Forest, Queensland, Australia, is active by day and night.

Puma Also called mountain lion and cougar, the puma is a solitary, territorial hunter of deer, hares, and other smaller mammals.

Great spotted woodpecker This bird hammers holes in tree bark with its bill insearch of the insect larvae inside.

HERITAGE WATCH

Diminishing biome Temperate rain forest trees grow very tall, which makes their timber commercially valuable. Half of the world's temperate rain forests have disappeared, and logging is the most serious threat to those that remain. Many of these forests are now protected.

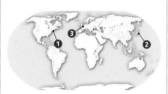

1. Harvard Forest Covering 3,000 acres (1,214 ha), this forest is dominated by red oak, red maple, black birch, white pine, and eastern

hemlock. A research and educational resource since 1907, it is one of the most studied forests in North America.

Harvard Forest, Massachussetts, U.S.A.

2. Ogawa Forest Reserve This beech and oak forest covering 15 acres (6 ha) in Ibaraki, Japan, is surrounded by secondary forest and plantations

on the slopes of the Abukama Mountains. It has been used as a research site since 1987.

Ogawa Forest Reserve, Ibaraki, Japan

3. Veluwe National Park Planted on reclaimed sand dunes and heathland, this park in Gelderland Province is the largest woodland area

in the Netherlands, with 225 square miles (585 km²) of mixed coniferous and deciduous broad-leaf forest.

Veluwe National Park, Netherlands

CLIMATE

Temperate broad-leaf forests require at least 16 inches (400 mm) of rain annually, occurring fairly evenly through the year, and 120 days when the temperature rises above 50°F (10°C).

BERLIN, GERMANY

Average rainfall
Max. temperature
Min. temperature

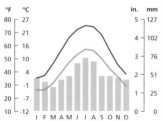

Temperate Deciduous Forest

Deciduous forest occurs in temperate regions worldwide, wherever rainfall is spread evenly through the year and the ground freezes for only a short period. In the northern biome, a dense mix of broad-leaf trees includes oak, beech, and maple. South of the equator, the mixed needle-leaf and broad-leaf forest includes *Araucaria* and *Podocarpus* pines, and southern beech.

The colors of fall The glowing red, orange, and yellow pigments that characterize deciduous forests in fall result from the breakdown of chlorophyll, which is responsible for their green color in spring and summer.

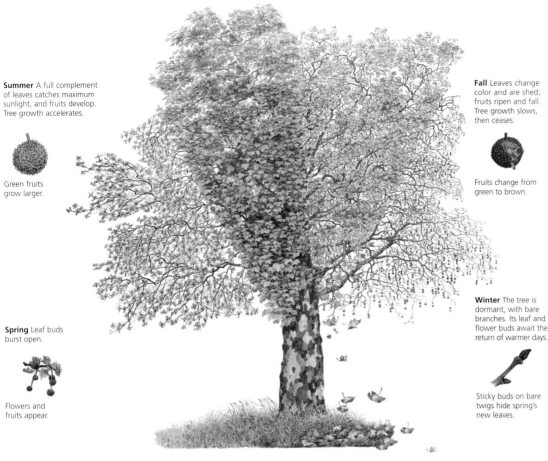

Summer A full complement of leaves catches maximum sunlight, and fruits develop. Tree growth accelerates.

Green fruits grow larger.

Fall Leaves change color and are shed; fruits ripen and fall. Tree growth slows, then ceases.

Fruits change from green to brown.

Spring Leaf buds burst open.

Flowers and fruits appear.

Winter The tree is dormant, with bare branches. Its leaf and flower buds await the return of warmer days.

Sticky buds on bare twigs hide spring's new leaves.

Four distinct seasons (above) Because they grow new leaves every spring and shed them each fall, deciduous trees like this London plane alter their appearance with each season.

In full leaf (below) Deciduous southern beech trees in New Zealand form an open canopy that allows sunlight to dapple the forest floor in summer, encouraging the growth of herbs.

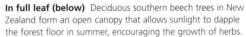

FACT FILE

Wildlife With its seasonal changes and contrasts of light and shade, the temperate deciduous forest provides food, nesting sites, and shelter for more varied wildlife than in any other temperate biome.

Fallow deer
Preferring forests with luxuriant undergrowth, these deer live in large herds, but are shy and mainly nocturnal.

American beaver Seen here with its young, or kit, the American beaver lives beside rivers and uses saplings to build its dams and lodges.

Gray squirrel
This native of North American oak, hickory, and walnut forests is active by day.

Acorn weevil Using its long "snout," or rostrum, this insect drills into acorns to feed on their contents.

HERITAGE WATCH

Fragmentation Temperate deciduous forests in North America were long occupied by Native Americans. Forest cover was cleared by Euro-Americans and reached a minimum in the mid-19th century. For the next century it regenerated in abandoned agricultural areas but since the 1970s it has again been fragmented by urban sprawl.

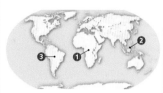

CLIMATE

Tropical rain forests require an annual rainfall of at least 100 inches (2,540 mm), distributed fairly evenly throughout the year, and the temperature must not fall below about 65°F (18°C).

SINGAPORE

— Average rainfall
— Max. temperature
— Min. temperature

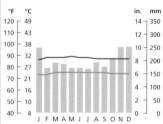

Tropical Rain Forest

The tropical rain forest supports more plant and animal species than any other terrestrial biome. One acre may contain 120 species of trees (300 per hectare). The warm, wet, tropical climate produces a vertical forest structure in which trees of different heights form layers of vegetation and where many animals spend their lives high above the ground.

Borneo Most tropical rain forests develop in the lowlands, especially along the broad valleys of major rivers. This dense forest in Borneo shows the typical vertical structure, with the tallest trees, called emergents, towering over smaller trees and shrubs.

LAYERS OF VEGETATION
IN A RAIN FOREST

Emergents Trees 100 feet (30 m) high or higher
emerge above the canopy and are exposed to
full sunlight. Even leaves that are partly shaded
inside their crowns receive up to one-quarter of
full sunlight.

Canopy This middle layer consists of trees about
65 feet (20 m) high. Their crowns fill most of the
gaps below the emergents and block out most of
the sunlight from the lower levels.

Understory In this layer trees grow to about
30 feet (10 m) high. Among them are saplings
of the canopy and emergent trees that will grow
rapidly to fill any gap appearing in the canopy.

Forest floor Only plants that can survive with little
sunlight grow on this bottom layer. Shrubs, younger
saplings, and small trees reach about 16 feet (5 m).
Below them are seedlings and non-woody herbs,
or forbs, which are about 40 inches (1 m) high.

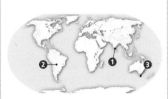
1. East Deccan dry evergreen forest
Bordering the southern coast of Andhra Pradesh and Tamil Nadu, this forest has a dense canopy of low evergreen trees only 33 feet (10 m) high. The taller deciduous trees, once part of the vegetation, have been removed.

East Deccan dry evergreen forest, India

2. Gran Chaco This vast, sparsely populated lowland plain in northwestern Paraguay features thorn forest that comprises more than 500 tree species. Most of these are deciduous, and many of them have medicinal, dyeing, and other industrial uses.

Gran Chaco, Paraguay

3. Tasmanian dry forests These forests include many *Eucalyptus* species, some of which are found naturally only in Tasmania. These are mixed with acacias, myrtle beech, and several coniferous species, including celery-top pine and Huon pine.

Tasmania, Australia

CLIMATE

Tropical dry forests grow where there is a marked seasonal contrast in rainfall. Cloud cover makes temperatures lower in the rainy season than in the dry season, which can be very hot.

ACAPULCO, MEXICO

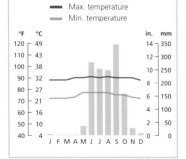

- Average rainfall
- Max. temperature
- Min. temperature

Tropical Dry Forest

Tropical dry forest grows in tropical and subtropical latitudes that have one rainy season and one long dry season lasting weeks or months. The most extreme contrast occurs in monsoon climates. In these seasonal forests, the trees of the upper canopy are deciduous, shedding their leaves in the dry season, while evergreen trees form an understory.

Anjajavy Forest (right) This coastal dry forest in Madagascar provides a habitat for many rare wildlife species. Among the deciduous trees in its canopy are the Madagascar and Za baobabs pictured here, which store water in their trunks.

La Servilleta Canyon (above) Part of the Huasteca Forest in Mexico, this tropical dry forest comprises pines and oaks, as well as West Indian cedars and silk cotton trees, or kapoks.

Monsoon forest (below) In northern India, Dudwa National Park's monsoon climate produces an open forest of mainly broad-leaved, deciduous species, but also including some pine trees.

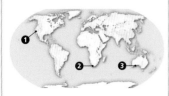
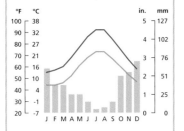
Dry Woodland and Shrubland

In places with a hot, dry summer and a warm, wet winter, many of the trees and shrubs are evergreen and have small, tough, leathery leaves that help them survive the summer drought. This type of tough-leaved, or sclerophyllous, vegetation is found around Mediterranean coasts, and in California, South Africa, and Australia.

Chaparral This typical Californian vegetation consists of thickets of shrubs and trees, 3–12 feet (1–4 m) tall. The chaparral supports approximately 240 species of woody plants, which are densest where conditions are the most favorable.

Regeneration by fire Eucalyptus forest, like many dry woodlands, depends on fire for renewal. Fire not only burns the oil-rich leaves of tall trees and clears the undergrowth. It also makes the trees release their seeds, which then have the space to germinate in soil enriched by ash.

The seeds a tree releases will have to compete with all the plants already growing vigorously in a crowded forest.

Tree seeds germinate in the warm, sunlit ground. As a seedling emerges, it absorbs nutrients from the soil fertilized by ash.

A natural fire destroys the competing plants and its intense heat stimulates the tree to release its seeds.

Banksia in flower (below) Banksia is a shrub that grows on the heaths of southeastern Australia. After flowering, the plant sets seed, but retains the remains of the flower.

Banksia after fire (below) Fire ignites the remains of the dry banksia flower and ruptures the seed cases. The seeds fall to the ground and germinate, but the fire kills the parent plant.

Mountain Grassland and Shrubland

Most trees cannot grow if the average summer temperature is lower than 50°F (10°C). Because air temperature decreases with height, even in the tropics there are many mountains that rise above the climatic limit for trees—the treeline. At these high altitudes the vegetation consists of grasses, shrubs, and herbs.

Alpine flowers Brilliant sky lupines, native to the United States, carpet this alpine meadow on Figueroa Mountain, Los Padres National Forest, in California's coastal ranges. The mountain's alpine flowers attract many visitors.

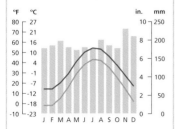

Bale Mountains National Park (above) Set on a high plateau in Ethiopia, this park has the largest area of Afro-Alpine vegetation in Africa. These lobelias take 100 years to grow to 24 feet (8 m).

Krummholz (below) Wind-sculpted trees, or krummholz, grow near the treeline in the Appalachian Mountains, U.S.A. The prevailing wind dries and kills buds on one side of the trees.

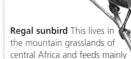

Savanna

Savanna develops where it is too dry for forests, but not dry enough for desert. Its vegetation usually consists of grasses with scattered shrubs and trees. Initially describing the tropical grasslands on Caribbean islands and in Central and South America, the term savanna now also applies to Australian and African tropical grasslands, which are home to many large mammals.

Tarangire National Park Covering 1,005 square miles (2,600 km²), this vast Tanzanian park supports the greatest concentration of wildlife outside the Serengeti ecosystem, including lions, elephants, zebras, and wildebeest.

FACT FILE

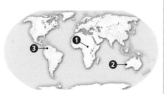

1. Manovo-Gounda-St. Floris National Park This World Heritage site in the Central African Republic has 6,700 square miles (17,400 km²) of

wooded savanna. Its abundant wildlife includes cheetahs, black rhinoceroses, leopards, wild dogs, and buffalo.

Manovo-Gounda-St. Floris National Park, Central African Republic

2. Kalbarri National Park This rolling sandstone plateau in Western Australia covers 707 square miles (1,830 km²). It has hummocky grasses,

small daisy bushes, wattles, banksias, grevilleas, smoke-bushes, starflowers, and other flowering plants.

Kalbarri National Park, Western Australia

3. Llanos, South America The vast plains of the Orinoco Basin have 220,000 square miles (570,000 km²) of grassland, with scattered scrub

oaks and dwarf palms. The wildlife includes ocelots, jaguars, giant anteaters, armadillos, and river otters.

Llanos of Orinoco Basin, South America

CLIMATE

Savanna develops where the average temperature never falls below 64°F (18°C). Rainfall is about 40 inches (1,016 mm) and occurs mostly in summer, with a winter dry season lasting 3–5 months.

N'DJAMENA, CHAD

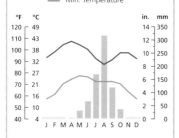

—— Average rainfall
—— Max. temperature
—— Min. temperature

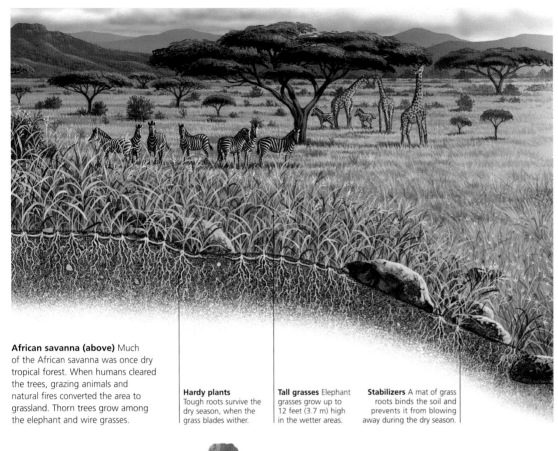

African savanna (above) Much of the African savanna was once dry tropical forest. When humans cleared the trees, grazing animals and natural fires converted the area to grassland. Thorn trees grow among the elephant and wire grasses.

Hardy plants Tough roots survive the dry season, when the grass blades wither.

Tall grasses Elephant grasses grow up to 12 feet (3.7 m) high in the wetter areas.

Stabilizers A mat of grass roots binds the soil and prevents it from blowing away during the dry season.

Termite mounds A striking feature of African and Australian savannas, these mounds can be as high as 20 feet (6 m) and house some two million insects. Ventilation shafts occupy the upper part, while termite activity is concentrated lower down.

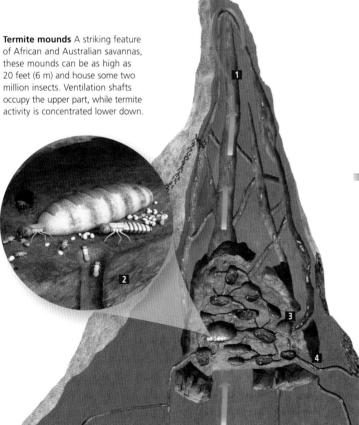

Natural ventilation Fresh air is drawn in through the mound's porous surface on the windward side and stale air is flushed out on the leeward side.

1 Cooling system Hot air rises up the central shaft and down the outer walls, where it cools and filters up through the nest.
2 Royal cell Here the large queen mates with the smaller king and produces thousands of eggs, which workers carry away and tend.
3 Nest Around the royal cell are smaller chambers for storing food, growing fungi and, beneath it, raising larvae.
4 Workers These termites collect plant matter for the fungal gardens they cultivate for the colony's food.

Prairie, Steppe, and Pampas

Temperate grassland—prairie in North America, pampas in South America and steppe in central Asia—occurs mainly in continental interiors, where rolling plains were once covered by vast seas of grasses. Only a relatively small percentage of natural grassland remains today. Grass species vary with conditions: tall grasses grow in moister areas, shorter grasses in drier climates.

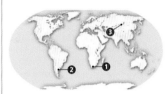

Prairie This extends over the North American plains from southern Canada to Mexico. The surviving natural grassland changes from tall-grass prairie in the east, to mixed-grass, then short-grass, with bunch-grass prairie in the far west.

Steppe Between latitudes 40°N and 50°N, this Eurasian grassland stretches for 3,500 miles (9,000 km) from Hungary to western China. Moving north to south, forest steppe gives way to meadow steppe, then dry steppe, which merges into desert.

Pampas This South American grassland covers an area of 290,000 square miles (751,000 km²) in parts of Argentina and most of Uruguay. In the west it is a dry plain that merges with the desert, while the smaller fertile eastern sector receives more rainfall.

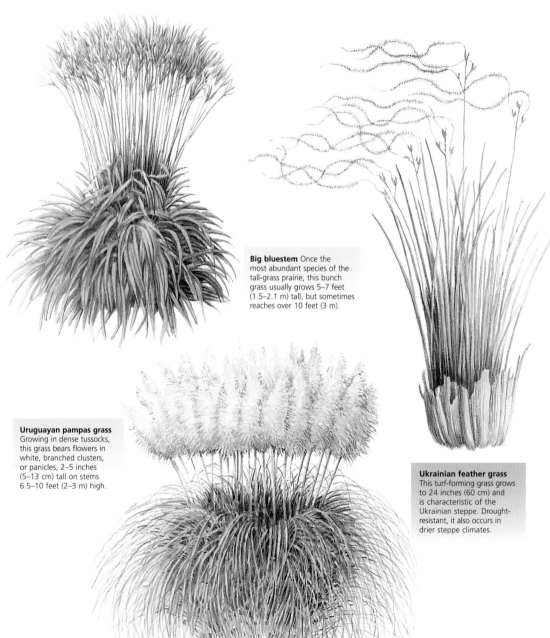

Big bluestem Once the most abundant species of the tall-grass prairie, this bunch grass usually grows 5–7 feet (1.5–2.1 m) tall, but sometimes reaches over 10 feet (3 m).

Uruguayan pampas grass Growing in dense tussocks, this grass bears flowers in white, branched clusters, or panicles, 2–5 inches (5–13 cm) tall on stems 6.5–10 feet (2–3 m) high.

Ukrainian feather grass This turf-forming grass grows to 24 inches (60 cm) and is characteristic of the Ukrainian steppe. Drought-resistant, it also occurs in drier steppe climates.

CLIMATE

Temperate grasslands grow where temperatures in summer rise up to 100°F (38°C), but drop to 10°F (–12°C) or lower in winter. Annual rainfall, mainly in winter, averages 12–40 inches (305–1,016 mm).

SASKATOON, SASKATCHEWAN, CANADA

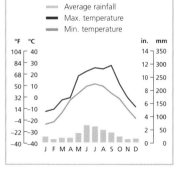

Average rainfall
Max. temperature
Min. temperature

PRAIRIE SHORT GRASSES

Buffalo This grass grows to 2–5 inches (5–13 cm) in clumps that are 6–12 feet (3–4 m) across. Male flowers are panicles; females are clusters of 2–4 short pikelets.

Indian grass Forming bunches about 12 inches (30 cm) across, this species grows up to 8 feet (2.4 m) high. Its flowers are panicles 6–12 inches (15–30 cm) long.

Galleta Also called curly grass, this short, rather coarse grass grows 3–20 inches (8–50 cm) high. Its hermaphrodite flowers, open in July and August, are wind-pollinated.

EASTERN STEPPE GRASSES

June grass Widely distributed, this is also called koeleria and koelersgrass. It grows to a height of 6–8 inches (15–20 cm) and has upright, green-yellow flower spikes.

Lessing's feather grass This grass grows in clumps 40–60 inches (100–150 cm) high. It produces beige flowers and fine leaves that sway in the wind, and tolerates drought.

Crested wheatgrass Common in Siberia, this drought-tolerant bunch grass grows to a height of 18–36 inches (46–90 cm). Its narrow flower spikes are 0.5–4 inches (1.3–10 cm) long.

PAMPAS GRASSES

Puna grass This forms tussocks of narrow, flat or rolled leaves 20 inches (50 cm) high. Its flowers are purple-brown spikes that grow up to 33 inches (84 cm) high.

Wild cane Also known as uva grass, this has stems 16–20 feet (5–6 m) tall. It bears grayish, plume-like flowers that consist of panicles up to 6.5 feet (2 m) long.

Tussock paspalum Green-blue tussocks grow up to 33 inches (84 cm) high and wide. The seed heads rise as high again. Rust-colored flowers grow on elongated axes, or racemes.

FACT FILE

Wildlife Temperate grasslands provide food and shelter for many ground-dwelling animals, as well as for herds of grazing mammals. Where herbivores occur there are also carnivores hunting them.

Secretary bird This inhabitant of African grasslands, including veld, nests in trees but chases its prey on foot.

Bison Millions of these native cattle once lived on the prairies, but were hunted almost to extinction. Numbers are now increasing.

Prairie dogs These highly social animals live in groups called coteries. Several coteries are said to form a township.

Pampas cat Also known as colocolo, this small, stocky animal is probably nocturnal, feeding on birds and small mammals.

HERITAGE WATCH

Natural vegetation The pampas has been largely converted to cattle and sheep ranches, most of the prairies now grow cereals, and the European steppe is farmland. Efforts are now being made to protect those small areas of original vegetation that remain.

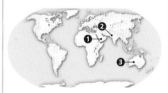
SUBTROPICAL DESERTS

1. Rub' al-Khali Extending from the eastern bank of the Nile River and across the Arabian Peninsula, this desert is the world's largest continuous area of sand, covering 230,000 square miles (595,700 km²). Its name is Arabic for "Empty Quarter."

Rub' al-Khali, Arabian Peninsula

2. Thar Desert Also called the Great Indian Desert, this sandy desert of dunes, plains and low hills covers an area of about 77,000 square miles (199,430 km²). It occupies about half of the Indian state of Rajasthan and a small part of eastern Pakistan.

Thar Desert, India and Pakistan

3. Great Sandy Desert This plain in Western Australia consists of large ergs with red longitudinal dunes. Australia's second largest desert, it stretches over 140,000 square miles (360,000 km²), In summer, temperatures can reach 100°F (38°C).

Great Sandy Desert, Western Australia

SUBTROPICAL DESERT CLIMATE

Temperatures in parts of the Sahara can exceed 110°F (43°C) in summer but can fall below freezing on winter nights. Rainfall is usually less than 10 inches (250 mm).

SALAH, ALGERIA (SAHARA)

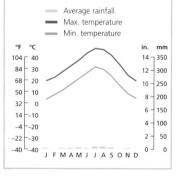

Desert

A desert develops wherever the total annual rainfall is less than the amount of water that would evaporate if there were an unlimited supply. Occurring in all latitudes, deserts may consist of rolling sand dunes, rocky terrain, high plateaus, or flat salt-lake beds. Some are very hot all year round, while others have very cold winters and hot, dry summers. The South Pole lies at the center of the world's driest desert, where the air is too cold to hold water vapor but snow never melts. Hot subtropical deserts form a belt around the world in both hemispheres.

Distance from the ocean makes continental deserts dry, while west-coast deserts like the Atacama are arid mainly because the air that reaches them is dry after crossing a continent. Other deserts such as the Mojave are in the rain shadow of mountains.

Seas of sand The Sahara is a subtropical desert characterized by vast stretches of sand dunes, or ergs. Kerzaz oasis, Algeria, is surrounded by the largest erg, the Grand Erg Occidental, which covers 74,000 square miles (192,000 km²).

CONTINENTAL DESERTS

1. Gobi Desert This vast central Asian desert extends over about 500,000 square miles (1.3 million km²) of southern Mongolia and the Mongolian Autonomous Region of China. Much of it supports some grass and other vegetation, but the center is very arid.

Gobi Desert, Mongolia and China

2. Takla Makan With dunes 300 feet (91 m) high, Takla Makan is one of world's largest sandy deserts and extremely dry. Occupying 105,000 square miles (272,000 km²) of north-western China, it is hot in summer, but bitterly cold in winter.

Takla Makan, China

3. Karakum Desert This sandy desert covering about 70 percent of Turkmenistan, in central Asia, has an area of about 135,000 square miles (350,000 km²). Its wind-formed sand ridges rise up to 300 feet (91 m) high and it supports some plants.

Karakum Desert, Turkmenistan

CONTINENTAL DESERT CLIMATE

The air above the center of a continent has lost most of its moisture and produces a dry climate, with a wide day–night and summer–winter temperature range.

ULAANBAATAR (ULAN BATOR), MONGOLIA

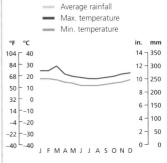

— Average rainfall
— Max. temperature
— Min. temperature

The Desert Environment

In most deserts, winds have blown away dust and sand from large areas, leaving a surface of bare rock or half-buried rounded cobbles called desert pavement. Elsewhere, sand accumulates into dunes that are constantly shaped and moved by the wind. Despite the heat and aridity of this hostile environment, many plants and animals have adapted to survive.

Types of sand dunes (below) Desert dunes are created by windblown sand. The shape of a dune is influenced by the prevailing wind direction and the amount of sand. Basically dunes form either crescent shapes or long, parallel lines.

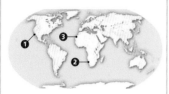

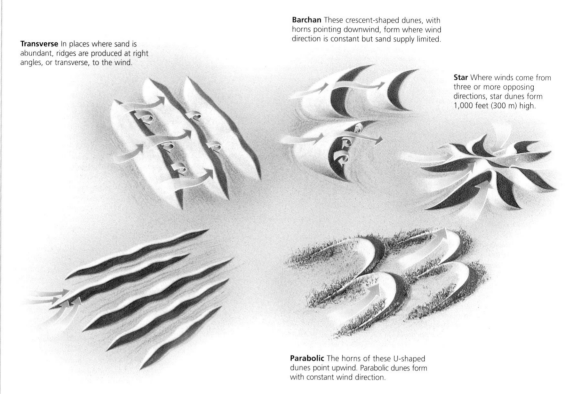

Transverse In places where sand is abundant, ridges are produced at right angles, or transverse, to the wind.

Barchan These crescent-shaped dunes, with horns pointing downwind, form where wind direction is constant but sand supply limited.

Star Where winds come from three or more opposing directions, star dunes form 1,000 feet (300 m) high.

Parabolic The horns of these U-shaped dunes point upwind. Parabolic dunes form with constant wind direction.

Longitudinal (linear) These form parallel to the average wind direction where sand is plentiful and wind direction slightly variable.

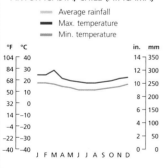
Adapting to desert life (below) Desert plants survive by storing water or remaining mostly dormant, reviving after rain. Many small animals are nocturnal or avoid the daytime heat by burrowing. Larger animals like the camel use water very efficiently.

Cactuses These store water in fleshy stems. Sharp spines lose less moisture than regular leaves and deter animals. Shallow, spreading roots absorb all available water.

Camels Able to retain water, camels can go several days without drinking. Woolly fur keeps them cool and the hump stores food. Broad feet allow them to move easily over loose sand.

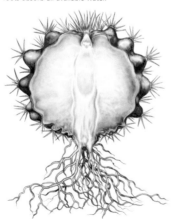

Lizards To minimize contact with the hot ground a lizard raises its body and lifts one leg at a time to cool its feet. It often seeks shelter during the hottest part of the day.

FACT FILE

Saguaro cactus This native of the Sonoran Desert, Mexico and Arizona, U.S.A., grows very slowly, with a spurt each rainy season. A plant may be only 0.25 inch high (6 mm) after one year, but can reach 50 feet (15 m) in 150 years.

10 years 12 inches (30 cm)

50 years 7 feet (2 m)

75 years First branches

100 years 25 feet (7.6 m)

150–200 years Up to 50 feet (15 m)

Thar (top) The vegetation in this sandy subtropical desert consists of scattered shrubs.

Gobi (center) This continental desert has longitudinal dunes, but there is also enough vegetation for nomads' animals.

Atacama (bottom) A west-coast desert, this has almost no rain, but fog that forms on the coast often drifts inland at night.

HERITAGE WATCH

Animals and plants at risk Visitors to deserts, who often drive all-terrain vehicles, disturb wildlife. Hunting depletes populations of vulnerable species. Overgrazing destroys vegetation around oases and waterholes, while trees—dry but not dead—are cut down to use for firewood.

FACT FILE

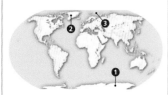

1. Antarctica The fifth largest continent has an area of 4.8 million square miles (12.4 million km²). The Transantarctic Mountains separate East

Antarctica from West. The Antarctic Peninsula projects from West Antarctica toward South America.

Antarctica

2. Greenland (Kalaallit Nunaat)
This large Arctic island has several coastal towns, but its interior plateau lies beneath a dome-shaped ice sheet

that is an average of 5,000 feet (1,525 m) thick and is more than 8,000 feet (2,440 m) thick at its deepest point.

Greenland

3. Arctic lands Northern Alaska, U.S.A, Canada, Greenland, Scandinavia, and Russia all surround the Arctic Ocean, which is completely

covered with ice in winter and partially in summer. The North Pole is on the ocean floor at the center of the Arctic.

Arctic lands

CLIMATE

Temperatures inside the Arctic and Antarctic circles rise above freezing for only a short time in summer, while temperatures on the ice sheets are always below freezing. Precipitation is low.

McMURDO, ANTARCTICA

▬ Average rainfall
▬ Max. temperature
▬ Min. temperature

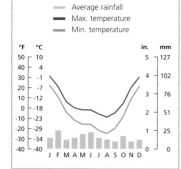

Polar Regions

The lands surrounding the North Pole beyond the far northern tundra and those around the South Pole encircled by the vast Southern Ocean are too cold for plants. Only microbes live on the Greenland ice sheet. Emperor penguins raise their young inland on the Antarctic ice sheet under extremely harsh conditions, but they feed at sea, where life is abundant.

Northern mountains Two ranges run parallel to Greenland's east and west coasts, with the ice sheet between them. The highest mountains are in the east, some rising over 11,500 feet (3,500 m). The central ice sheet fills a basin.

Emperor penguins (above) The largest penguins, these are the only ones that breed in winter, when they make the long trek from the sea to an inland breeding site on the Antarctic ice sheet.

Akpatock, Canada (below) This Arctic island is a limestone plateau whose sheer cliffs rise steeply from the pack ice. It is visited by walruses, polar bears, and birds such as the thick-billed murre.

THE STUDY OF PLANTS

Botany is the scientific study of plants, but its area of interest has grown so wide that the term "plant sciences" is now more commonly used. Plant sciences cover the structure and physiology of plants, their growth and reproduction, and the biochemical processes taking place inside them, which leads to the study of cell processes. Plant scientists are also interested in the evolution, domestication, and genetic modification of plants, as well as in the pests and diseases that attack crops. Plant taxonomists classify plants into species, genera, and higher categories, based on degrees to which different plants are related.

Medicinal plants (below) This illustration of marigolds is from a 15th-century edition of Dioscorides' *De materia medica*. Originally written around A.D. 77, the work was copied many times, with added illustrations and some Arabic and Hindu entries. It remained in circulation until about 1600 and is the precursor to all later herbals and pharmacopoeias. Dioscorides' travels as a surgeon for the Roman army allowed him to examine countless species.

Father of botany (left) Theophrastus (372–287 B.C.) was often called the "father of botany." He studied with Plato and later Aristotle in Athens, and in 335 B.C. succeeded Aristotle as leader of the Lyceum school. His real name was Tyrtamus. Theophrastus, meaning "divine expression," was the nickname Aristotle gave him. His botanical books described many Asian as well as European plants.

HISTORY OF BOTANY

We depend on plants for food, fiber, medicine, building materials, and fuel. Without them, no animal could survive, because only plants can synthesize carbohydrate foods from carbon dioxide and water. Long before the beginning of recorded history, people were learning about plants. They discovered which were edible, which poisonous, which had therapeutic properties, and which were the best for making dwellings, tools, furniture, and clothing.

Formal study began in Greece in the 4th century B.C. In about 300 B.C. Theophrastus wrote *Inquiry into Plants*, the earliest-known work on plant science. It is the first-known attempt to classify plants, describing the appearance, growing requirements, and uses of more than 500 species.

In the 1st century A.D., Greek physician Pedanius Dioscorides wrote *De materia medica*, in which he described about 600 medicinal plants. At about the same time, Roman naturalist Pliny the Elder gathered all that was then known about natural history into the 37 volumes of his *Historia naturalis*.

Most of the books on plants written during Greek and Roman times were rediscovered in the 15th and 16th centuries. Dioscorides' work inspired the authors of many herbal books.

The study of medicinal plants led to an interest in plants of all kinds. In 1623, Swiss anatomist and herbalist Gaspard Bauhin published *Pinax theatri botanica*, which described approximately 6,000 species.

Later in the 17th century, John Ray, arguably the greatest of all botanists, insisted that in plant classification account should be taken of all characteristics. Ray devised a detailed classification and distinguished two groups by their possession of one seed leaf (monocotyledons) or two (dicotyledons). The modern system of plant classification is based not on Ray's work but on that of 18th-century Swedish botanist Carolus Linnaeus.

Parallel to this work of description and classification, other scientists were examining the physiology of plants. Today, plant science concentrates mainly on cellular processes and plant genetics.

THROUGH THE AGES

Ca 300 B.C. Greek botanist Theophrastus wrote the first books on botany, entitled *Inquiry Into Plants* and *Causes of Plants*.

A.D. 40–90 Dioscorides wrote his *De materia medica*, describing nearly 600 plants, including colchicum, water hemlock, cannabis, and peppermint.

16th century Among the most notable herbals written in the 16th century were those by Otto Brunfels, Leonhard Fuchs, Pierandrea Mattioli, and John Gerard.

1623 Gaspard Bauhin published *Pinax theatri botanica*, an attempt at a formal plant classification, relating it to the traditional botanical names for plants.

1650–51 *Historia plantarum universalis* by Jean Bauhin was published after his death. It described more than 5,000 plants and became a standard reference work.

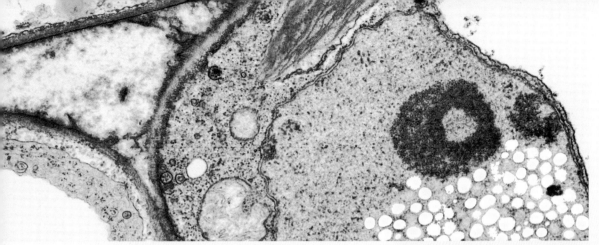

Genetics (left) This image of an *Arabidopsis thaliana* seed was taken through an electron microscope. *Arabidopsis* has been used since the 1940s as a model organism for studying plant biology, and it was the first plant to have its complete genome sequenced. Its genome comprises 27,000 genes on 5 chromosomes, encoding 35,000 proteins. The plant shown here has been genetically modified to synthesize a polymer in its cell nuclei. The polymer can be seen clearly as the yellow spheres in the cell's nucleus.

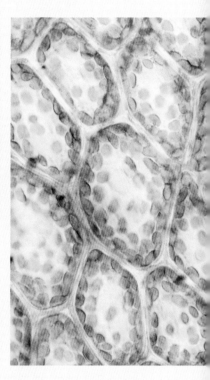

Micropropagation (above) When tissue cultures such as these insectivorous sundew cultures mature in a petri dish, they will grow into genetically identical plants. Tissue culture, or micropropagation, is used to produce plants with particular qualities or to copy genetically modified plants. Many plant cells are capable of regenerating an entire plant. Tissue culture uses small pieces of leaf or, less commonly, root.

Jumping genes (above left) This variety of Indian corn has kernels in many colors, which is the natural condition that is determined genetically. Most commercial varieties have been bred to produce kernels all of one color. Biologists use corn as a model organism. Barbara McClintock won the 1983 Nobel Prize for Physiology or Medicine for her discovery of transposons ("jumping genes") in corn.

Leaf cells (above right) This micrograph shows mesophyll cells immediately below the epidermis, or skin, of a green leaf. The specks are chloroplasts, which contain the green pigment chlorophyll and are the sites of photosynthesis—the process in which carbohydrates are synthesized from atmospheric carbon dioxide and water drawn up from the ground.

Carolus Linnaeus (left) Swedish botanist Carolus Linnaeus (1707–78) collected plants from all over the world and used them to devise a classification system based on their reproductive organs. The binomial (two-name) system he described in his 1735 *Systema naturae* identifies plants by two Latin names (for genus and species) and is still used today.

1665 English scientist Robert Hooke coined the word "cell" after studying thin slices of cork through a microscope. He saw the cell as a hollow space surrounded by solid walls.

1682 English botanist Nehemiah Grew published *The Anatomy of Plants*. He recognized that the stamen is a plant's male sex organ and the pistil its female organ.

1824 Swiss botanist Augustin Pyrame de Candolle began work on his 17-volume classification, but died before finishing it. His son Alphonse completed the task.

1961 Melvin Calvin received the Nobel Prize for Chemistry for his discovery of the route carbon follows through photosynthesis, now known as the Calvin cycle.

2000 The full genome of *Arabidopsis thaliana*, comprising 27,000 genes, was published, making thale cress the world's best-known plant.

AIR

AIR

EARTH'S ATMOSPHERE

Earth is enveloped by a cocktail of the gases nitrogen, oxygen, and argon, with traces of about 15 other gases. These form a band extending from Earth's surface to a height of about 600 miles (1,000 km) above it. At this altitude, the atoms and molecules of the gases are so widely separated that they rarely collide. The atmosphere is divided into five layers, with all of Earth's weather occurring in lowest of these, the troposphere. All weather phenomena result from interactions between solar energy, air, and water vapor carried in the air.

Monsoon rains (left) Clouds over the Indian Ocean with rainbow-like light effects herald the arrival of the monsoon rains over Madagascar. These fall between November and February and are heavier than the winter rain.

Where space begins (right) There is no boundary between the atmosphere and space. Gases simply become less dense. Satellites orbit where the air is so thin that it has little effect on them. Their cameras capture the clouds far below where the biggest storm clouds are no higher than about 10 miles (16 km).

Atmospheric layers (below) Temperature decreases with height up to the tropopause, where it ceases to fall. This change forms a boundary to rising air, above which the temperature increases with height up to another boundary, the stratopause, where it starts decreasing again. This divides the atmosphere into distinct layers.

AIR AND ITS LAYERS

Air is invisible, but its molecules scatter sunlight to produce the sky's blue color. While cloud droplets are also colorless, when large masses of droplets reflect incoming light they create clouds that seem white, gray, or almost black. Cloud patterns are monitored from satellites and meteorologists interpret them to track weather.

Dust particles, cloud droplets, and ice crystals reflect, refract, and scatter light. These effects create red sunsets, rainbows, and a variety of other optical phenomena. The refraction of light as it passes between layers of air at different temperatures also produces mirages.

In the lower layers, the atmospheric gases are well mixed by turbulent winds. At about 62 miles (100 km) above Earth gravitational effects become larger than the turbulent mixing and gases begin to separate based on their mass. A small fraction of the lightest gases, hydrogen and helium, achieve escape velocities and leave Earth.

The lowest layer of the atmosphere, the troposphere, accounts for 90 percent of its total mass. In the middle latitudes, the troposphere's average height is about 7 miles (11 km), but it reaches higher near the equator and is lower close to the Poles. The border between the troposphere and stratosphere, the next atmospheric layer, is called the tropopause.

The stratosphere extends from the tropopause to about 30 miles (50 km) above Earth's surface. It is in this zone that relatively high concentrations of ozone are found, known as the ozone layer.

Temperature in the layers of the atmosphere is determined by height. In the troposphere temperature decreases with altitude. Air in the stratosphere, however, warms with height, varying from about −65°F (−54°C) to 32°F (0°C) at the stratopause. Moving up through the mesosphere, air temperature falls from about 32°F (0°C) to −110°F (−80°C) at the mesopause, at an altitude of about 50 miles (80 km). Air in the thermosphere is very cold, but at the top, near the thermopause, its temperature exceeds 1,500°F (815°C). Temperatures continue to rise in the exosphere, the atmosphere's outermost region, which gradually blends into outer space.

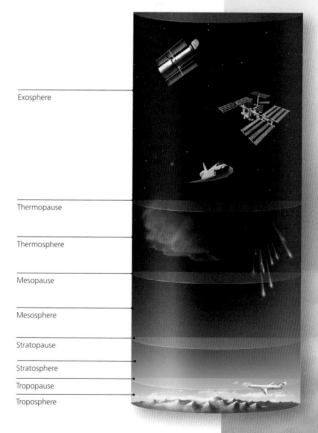

Exosphere

Thermopause

Thermosphere

Mesopause

Mesosphere

Stratopause

Stratosphere

Tropopause

Troposphere

Solar Energy and the Atmosphere

The Sun emits electromagnetic radiation at all wavelengths, but most intensely in the wavelengths we see as visible light. Clouds and pale-colored surfaces reflect about 30 percent of the incoming radiation, clouds and air absorb 19 percent, atmospheric gases scatter 26 percent, and 25 percent travels directly to Earth's surface.

Solar wind The protons, electrons, and other particles streaming out from the Sun, known as solar wind (white), make Earth's magnetosphere (blue lines) pear-shaped. The particles reach Earth at speeds of 186–310 miles per second (300–500 km/s).

FACT FILE

Solar phenomena The intensity of solar radiation varies by a small amount over an 11-year cycle, but from time to time a solar storm or flare may release so much energy that it damages satellites and electronic equipment.

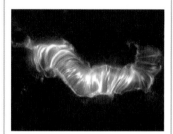

Bastille Day flare A solar storm on July 14, 2000, was one of the most violent ever recorded, releasing a massive cloud of hot, electrically charged gas.

Blue haze This phenomenon, known as limb haze, occurs when sunlight is scattered by air molecules. It is seen here 6–30 miles (10–48 km) above northern Africa.

OZONE HOLE

The ozone layer absorbs the Sun's harmful ultraviolet radiation. Over time pollutants have thinned the concentration of ozone over the globe and most visibly over Antarctica during early spring.

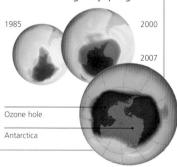

1985

2000

2007

Ozone hole

Antarctica

ENERGY AND THE ATMOSPHERE

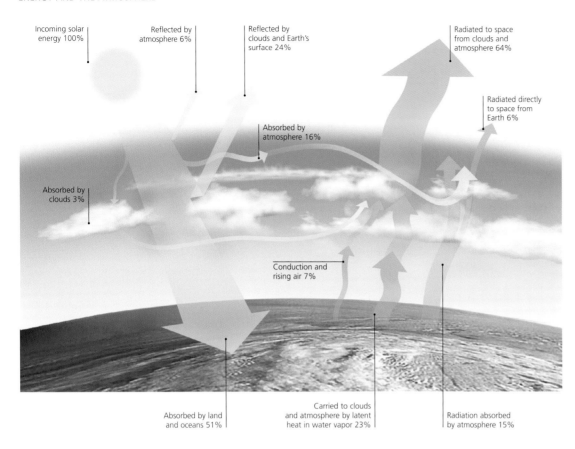

Incoming solar energy 100%

Reflected by atmosphere 6%

Reflected by clouds and Earth's surface 24%

Radiated to space from clouds and atmosphere 64%

Radiated directly to space from Earth 6%

Absorbed by atmosphere 16%

Absorbed by clouds 3%

Conduction and rising air 7%

Absorbed by land and oceans 51%

Carried to clouds and atmosphere by latent heat in water vapor 23%

Radiation absorbed by atmosphere 15%

Where the Sun's energy goes (above) Of all the solar energy reaching Earth, only half reaches the surface. As the surface warms up, it radiates all its absorbed heat back into space.

Auroras (below) When solar wind particles trapped in Earth's magnetic field descend over polar regions, the impact of their collision with air molecules emits light, creating a luminous display.

FACT FILE

Radiation Beyond the waveband of visible light, infrared radiation (heat) is at the red, low-energy end of the electromagnetic spectrum, and ultraviolet (UV) radiation is at the violet, high-energy end.

UV INDEX	
UV category	Time to burn (mins)
0–2	30–60
3–4	15–20
5–6	10–12
7–9	7–8.5
10–15	4–6

UV index The higher the radiation intensity values, the quicker the skin is likely to burn.

Skin damage Sunburn and suntan are levels of skin damage caused by UV radiation. Too much sunbathing can lead to skin cancer.

PLANT GROWTH

Plants need sunlight, but if the light is too bright it can cause chemical reactions that oxidize cell constituents. This is referred to as solarization and it slows the photosynthesis process.

The Troposphere

The troposphere is the lowest level of the atmosphere, extending above the surface an average 10 miles (16 km) at the equator, 7 miles (11 km) in middle latitudes, and 5 miles (8 km) at the Poles. It is in this closest zone to Earth's surface that pressure differences, winds, vertical convection currents, and water evaporation and condensation produce all our weather.

High-altitude living Villagers in Nepal breathe air that is less dense than air at sea level. To compensate, their blood holds more oxygen than the blood of people living at lower altitudes.

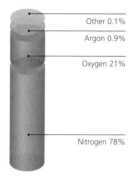
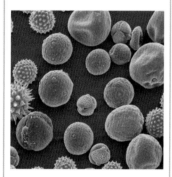

Above the weather (above) Flying near the tropopause boundary at the top of the troposphere, a fighter aircraft is above the clouds and almost all the weather.

Smog (below) Los Angeles, U.S.A., is prone to photochemical smog consisting primarily of ozone, carbon monoxide, nitrogen dioxide, and small particles.

RECYCLING NUTRIENTS

The troposphere plays a role in recycling nutrients, for example in the carbon cycle, together with living organisms, soil, and water.

SAILING THE AIR

A machine can fly by one of two basic methods. It is either filled with a gas that is less dense than air, making it sufficiently buoyant to lift a payload, or it is shaped in such a way that air passing across its surface generates sufficient lift to overcome gravity. Aeronautics is the scientific study of flight. It has led to the design of all types of aircraft, both heavier-than-air, such as gliders, powered fixed-wing aircraft, and helicopters, as well as lighter-than-air machines, such as air balloons, airships, and non-rigid airships called blimps.

The first helicopter (left) Around 1500, Leonardo da Vinci designed a flying machine to be lifted by a spinning, helical wing, driven by the muscle power of its pilot. The device was never built but even if it had been, it would not have flown because human muscles could not have generated enough power to raise it. The hang glider, however, one of da Vinci's other inventions, did fly.

Hot-air balloon (below) In 1782 French brothers Joseph-Michel and Jacques-Étienne Montgolfier were the first to discover that heated air collected inside a large lightweight bag causes it to rise. The first manned flight, as shown here, took place in Paris on November 21, 1783. The passengers were airborne for about 25 minutes and traveled 5.5 miles (9 km).

HISTORY OF AVIATION

For thousands of years, people dreamed of flying like birds, but it was not until the 15th century that Leonardo da Vinci designed an ornithopter, a machine that flaps its wings. Da Vinci also designed a machine with a helical wing, much like a helicopter.

The first device to take to the air was made by the Montgolfier brothers. Normally papermakers, they started experimenting with hot-air balloons in 1782. On September 19, 1783, they successfully sent a balloon into the air carrying a rooster, a duck, and a sheep.

One of history's most famous aircraft builders, German Count Ferdinand von Zeppelin launched his first airship on July 2, 1900. His airship design consisted of a rigid hull covered with a fabric skin. Airships hold their shape because they are filled with gas, usually helium, under pressure.

Meanwhile, other aeronauts were experimenting with heavier-than-air designs. In England, Sir George Cayley began building model gliders early in the 19th century. In 1849 he launched a full-scale glider piloted by a 10-year-old boy. In 1853 he launched a larger model, piloted by his coachman. Cayley's gliders, however, were not easy to control. The pioneer of controlled gliding

was the German engineer Otto Lilienthal.

Efforts turned toward finding a way to power gliders. The first attempts used steam engines. American scientist Samuel Pierpont Langley built flying models of steam-powered aircraft. In 1896 he attempted to launch a full-scale, but unmanned, model by catapulting it from the roof of a houseboat on the Potomac River. The machine was powered by a lightweight steam engine using gasoline fuel. The attempt failed and he tried again on December 8, 1903. That attempt also failed.

December 17, 1903, is remembered as one of the most important days in aeronautics. On this day, brothers Orville and Wilbur Wright made the first controlled, powered flight near the town of Kitty Hawk, North Carolina, U.S.A. The first jet-powered aircraft, the German Heinkel He 178, flew on August 27, 1939, and by the late 1940s jet aircraft were replacing piston-engined machines in military and civilian use.

In 1905, the Wright Flyer III set an airspeed record of 37.85 mph (60.91 km/h). The current record was set in 2004 by a NASA X-43A scramjet, a supersonic combustion ramjet, flying at almost 7,000 mph (11,260 km/h).

Henri Giffard (above) The French engineer Henri Giffard built a three-horsepower steam engine weighing 350 pounds (160 kg). He used it to power his 144-feet- (44-m)-long, hydrogen-filled airship. He flew from the Paris Hippodrome at a speed of about 6 mph (10 km/h) and covered a distance of about 20 miles (30 km).

Airplanes throughout history (below) Since the first powered flight in 1903, aviation design has advanced rapidly. By the 1930s, flying boats were making commercial transoceanic flights, soon followed by land aircraft. Helicopters first flew in 1937 and by the 1950s were in widespread use. Jet airliners entered service in the 1950s. Today, some modern military aircraft fly at several times the speed of sound.

THROUGH THE AGES

1500 Leonardo da Vinci designed the ornithopter around 1500. Powered by its pilot's muscles, his machine was designed to take flight as the pilot flapped its wings.

1783 Jean François Pilâtre de Rozier and François Laurent d'Arlandes conducted the first manned flight of a hot-air balloon.

1849–53 In 1849 Sir George Cayley launched a glider piloted by a 10-year-old boy. Two years later he launched a full-size version piloted by his coachman.

1852 The first flight by an airship powered by a lightweight steam engine was made by Henri Giffard on September 24, 1852, in Paris.

1903 Orville Wright made the first powered flight by a heavier-than-air machine on December 17, 1903. He flew 120 feet (36.6 m) in 12 seconds.

The *Wright Military Flyer* (above) More than 10,000 people gathered on July 27, 1909, to watch Orville Wright complete one of the final demonstration flights for the U.S. Army. The Wright brothers showed that their aircraft could fly for more than one hour at an average speed of 40 mph (64 km/h) and land safely. The brothers sold their aircraft to the U.S. Army Signal Corps for $30,000.

***Spirit of St. Louis* (left)** In 1928, Charles Lindbergh made the first nonstop solo flight of the Atlantic. He took off from Long Island, New York, and landed 33 hours, 30 minutes, and 29.8 seconds later at Le Bourget airfield in Paris. *The Spirit of St. Louis* was a high-wing monoplane powered by a single 223-horsepower, air-cooled engine.

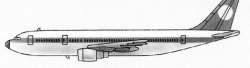

1919 In June, 1919, former Royal Air Force pilots John Alcock and Arthur Brown made the first nonstop crossing of the Atlantic in 16 hours and 28 minutes.

1924 Four biplanes left Seattle, U.S.A., for the first round-the-world flight on April 6, 1924. One crashed in dense fog, but three completed the journey in 175 days.

1929 A Fokker C-2A named *Question Mark* set a world flight endurance record of more than 150 hours. It landed only because of engine failure.

1969 The supersonic airliner called the Concorde made its maiden flight on March 2, 1969. Between 1976 and 2003, Concorde operated flights between Paris, London, and New York.

2007 The world's largest airliner, the Airbus A380, can seat up to 853 people using both upper and lower decks along its length. It entered service in 2007.

Light and Color

Air molecules, water droplets, and solid particles scatter, reflect, and refract light passing through the atmosphere. When water droplets reflect light, isolated clouds appear white, but extensive cloud sheets look gray, and storm clouds are almost black when seen from below. Raindrops and ice crystals reflect and refract light, causing rainbows and other phenomena.

Sunsets (right) The spectacular colors of a sunset are caused by dust in dry air. When the sun is low in the sky, all the blue light is scattered, but the dust particles scatter orange and red in a forward direction.

Sundogs and halos (below) When light is refracted by 22 degrees through ice crystals that are falling slowly, two bright spots (sundogs) are produced on opposite sides of a halo.

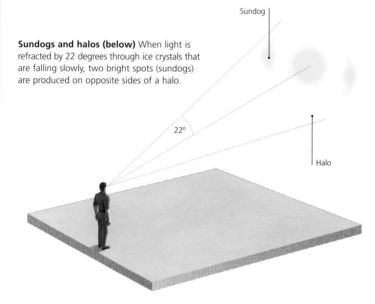

Sundog

Halo

22°

Antarctic phenomenon (below) Flashing sundogs, or parhelia, with their 22-degree halo, are often seen in Antarctica. They are accompanied by a downward-extending shaft of light, known as a sun pillar.

Light effects Light is refracted when it passes between materials of different densities. Air layers at different temperatures refract light, so that hot road surfaces appear to shimmer. Water and ice both refract and reflect light.

Mirages When light passes between warm and cool air, its refraction produces raised or lowered images of real objects.

Sun pillars Usually seen above the sun, but occasionally extending down, these are caused by reflection from the undersides of ice crystals.

Moondogs Mock moons, called moondogs, appear on either side of a 22-degree halo when moonlight is refracted by slowly falling ice crystals. They are identical to sundogs, but much rarer.

Light and Color continued

Water droplets, and sometimes air itself, can act as prisms, refracting light by different amounts according to its wavelength. This breaks white light into its constituent colors. Diffraction has a similar effect, occurring when light passes close to a sharply defined edge. Different light colors then interfere, producing iridescent effects.

Rainbow (below) Raindrops refract sunlight twice, separating the light into the colors of the spectrum. Violet is on the inside, bent at 40 degrees to the sun, and red on the outside, at 42 degrees.

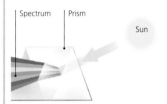
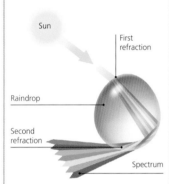
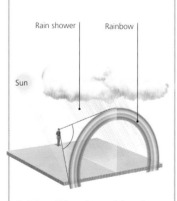

Crepuscular rays When a low sun shines through cloud gaps, sunlight is reflected from dust particles.

Corona Two or more colored rings around the sun or moon occur when light passes through altostratus cloud.

Moonbow In the moonlight, colors are not usually visible in a moonbow, formed in the same way as a rainbow.

Iridescence Bands of color appear on the sea when water diffracts light, breaking it into colors. As the patterns mingle, some colors are lost, leaving just a few.

WIND

Winds are caused by differences in pressure but are modified by the rotation of Earth. Differences in pressure occur because solar radiation warms some regions more strongly than others, and surfaces vary in the extent to which they absorb or reflect heat. Warm air near the equator rises by convection and moves toward the Poles, establishing a system of circulating air that transports heat away from the equator. It also produces patterns of winds, blowing from the east in high latitudes of both hemispheres and in the tropics, and from the west in middle latitudes.

WHAT CAUSES WIND

If air could move in a straight line, the differences between areas of high and low pressure could not arise because air would move immediately to cancel them out. Because Earth rotates on its axis, however, air moves in relation to a surface that is also moving beneath it.

The result of Earth's rotation is an effect that was discovered in 1835 by the French engineer Gaspard-Gustave de Coriolis and is called the Coriolis effect, which is abbreviated as CorF. The CorF deflects moving air, and ocean currents, to the right in the Northern Hemisphere and to the left in the Southern Hemisphere. As air moves toward a low-pressure center, the CorF deflects it, so instead of moving directly to the center, the air flows around it. In the Northern Hemisphere air moves counterclockwise around low-pressure areas but clockwise around high-pressure areas. These directions are reversed in the Southern Hemisphere.

Air flows smoothly around centers of high and low pressure high above the surface. Friction with the surface slows the wind and reduces the amount of CorF deflection, while obstacles alter the wind's direction. Deep valleys and city streets lined with tall buildings can funnel the wind and greatly accelerate it.

Cold air sinking down a mountainside produces what is known as a katabatic wind. In some places the sinking air warms up as it subsides. This can result in a warm wind blowing from the mountains. The chinook wind on the eastern side of the Rocky Mountains in North America is of this type, as is the foehn wind of the European Alps. Effects such as these produce countless local winds. Each has its own name and some have names in several different languages.

Winds that blow across hot deserts carry dust and sand. The dust-laden harmattan is so dry that it can warp wood. At the other extreme, strong winds driving heavy snow produce blizzards.

Cloud shaped by wind (above) A lens-shaped cloud sometimes forms above mountain tops, like this one on the summit of Mount Cho Oyu, behind prayer flags fluttering in the breeze high in the Himalayas on the Chinese–Nepalese border. Lenticular clouds form when a vertical standing wave develops in the wind flowing over the mountain. Water vapor condenses in air rising to the top of the wave, producing the unusual cloud.

Wind-driven fire (top right) Wildfires like those that raged in California, U.S.A., on October 23, 2007, are driven by gale-force winds that feed oxygen to the flames and blow sparks and flaming fragments into the trees ahead of the blaze. The heat is so intense that air spiraling in at ground level to replace the rising air produces firestorms.

Wind at sea (right) Wind experiences less friction over sea than over land, which means it is usually stronger and more persistent. In the moderate storm shown here, wind is driving the water into waves that are probably 18–25 feet (5.5–7.5 m) high, and is whipping away the wave tops as streaks of spray. The wind speed is 38–46 mph (61–74 km/h).

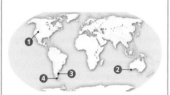

Famous Local Winds

Although winds usually circle centers of low and high pressure, and there are latitudinal belts of prevailing easterly and westerly winds, local topographical conditions produce many variations, each with its own name. Valleys, for instance, can redirect and strengthen winds, while air sinking down a mountainside becomes a warm, dry foehn wind.

Santa Ana (right) Funneled through valleys, this wind brings air at temperatures of up to 90°F (32°C) from the Nevada and Arizona deserts. In October 1996 it fueled destructive wildfires in California, U.S.A.

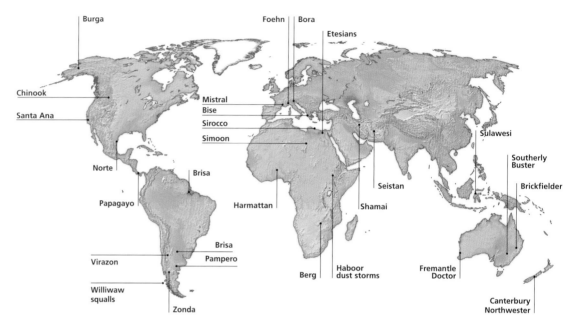

Local names The maps shows just some of the distinctively named winds that occur in every part of the world.

Harmattan (right) This hot, dry, Saharan wind blows only in the daytime and can produce severe dust storms, such as this one in a Tuareg camp in Mali.

Mistral (far right) Huge waves are produced by this cold, northerly wind, which blows at speeds of up to 80 mph (129 km/h) in winter in southern Europe.

1. Foehn Blowing on the northern slopes of the Alps, this strong, warm, dry wind is similar to the chinook and the zonda. Air descends the leeward

mountainsides, most often in spring. As it does so, it warms by compression and accelerates because of gravity.

Foehn, Alps, Europe

2. Barat A strong northwesterly wind, the barat blows over Manado Bay on the northern coast of Sulawesi, Indonesia. It most frequently occurs

between December and February. The barat is linked to squalls and sometimes damages property.

Barat, Sulawesi, Indonesia

3. Bora This is a cold, usually dry northerly or northeasterly wind that blows down from the mountains and across the coasts of countries that

border the Adriatic Sea. At Trieste in northeastern Italy, the bora blows on an average of 40 days a year.

Bora, Adriatic regions (Italy, Slovenia, Croatia)

4. Seistan A hot, extremely dry, dusty northerly or northwesterly wind, the seistan is associated with the monsoon. It blows almost incessantly

from June to September in eastern Iran and Afghanistan at speeds of up to 80 mph (129 km/h).

Seistan, Iran and Afghanistan

HERITAGE WATCH

Nor'easters These storms produce winds of up to hurricane force in eastern North America, most often between September and April. They can bring very cold conditions and heavy snow. Householders need to secure their homes and store emergency supplies in case they are snowed in.

Windblown Dust and Sand

Evolution of a dust devil These swirling columns of wind, dust, and debris occur when high ground temperatures produce a strong uplift of air, and prevailing winds are deflected by natural obstacles.

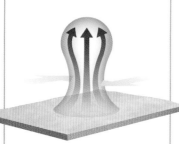

1 Some surfaces absorb heat better than others, and become hotter. The air above is warmed and rises.

2 Air rises in a column, sometimes as high as 300 feet (100 m), before it cools sufficiently to stop rising.

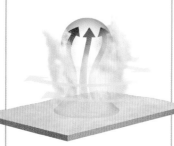

3 Low pressure near the ground draws in surrounding air, which begins to rotate as it warms and rises.

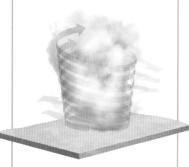

4 The rising, spinning air column picks up dust and debris, but as the ground quickly cools, the dust devil dies.

Deserts are windy places. A wind of more than 15 mph (24 km/h) will lift up dry sand grains to a height of several feet (1–2 m) and drive them horizontally. An even lighter wind will blow dry soil particles into clouds of dust. Windblown dust and sand become storms when they are caught in rising air currents, usually at weather fronts.

Pall of dust (right) Sand from the Sahara Desert can rise to a great height up a cold front. This satellite image shows desert dust streaming across the Atlantic to envelop the Canary Islands.

Clouds of sand (above) In Egypt sandstorms are caused by the khamsin, a frontal wind that blows for some 50 days a year. Severe storms can close airports, damage crops, and make livestock sick.

Dust devil (below) Dust, leaves, and loose scraps of paper spiral upward as warm air rises from a small surface area that is much hotter than its environs. Dust devils occur mainly in arid regions.

CLIMATE

The climate of a particular area is the pattern of weather it experiences day by day and season by season over a long period of time. Some years are warmer, cooler, wetter, or drier than others, but climates remain fairly constant through several decades. Over longer periods of time, however, climates do change. During the Middle Ages the world was probably warmer than today, and during the Little Ice Age, from about 1450 to 1850, it was cooler. At present, we are living in an interglacial, a period of mild weather between ice ages.

THE WORLD'S CLIMATE ZONES

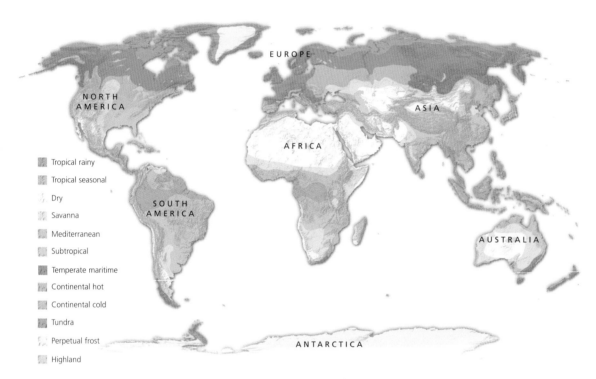

- Tropical rainy
- Tropical seasonal
- Dry
- Savanna
- Mediterranean
- Subtropical
- Temperate maritime
- Continental hot
- Continental cold
- Tundra
- Perpetual frost
- Highland

CLASSIFYING CLIMATE

There are similarities between climates in different parts of the world. All deserts, for example, are dry, while temperate regions near coasts have mild temperatures and rainfall throughout the year. Across northern Canada and Eurasia the summers are short, and winters are long and hard. These similarities, due mainly to latitude and distance from the ocean, allow scientists to arrange the world's climates in groups—that is, to classify them.

Climates can be classified in different ways. The ancient Greek philosopher Aristotle based his system on the elevation of the sun in the sky, dividing the world into three zones. Most modern schemes identify climates either by their effects on plant growth or by the atmospheric conditions that produce them. The scheme devised by the German climatologist Wladimir Köppen (1846–1940) is of the latter type. The climate zone map shown above is based on the Köppen classification.

Köppen divided climates into six principal types, each designated by a capital letter. In tropical rainy climates (A), temperatures never fall below 64.4°F (18°C). Dry climates (B) may be hot or cold. Warm temperate rainy climates (C) have winter temperatures between 26.6°F (–3°C) and 64.4°F (18°C) and above 50°F (10°C) in summer. In cold boreal forest climates (D) winters are colder than 26.6°F (–3°C) and summers warmer than 50°F (10°C). Tundra climates (E) have summer temperatures between 32°F (0°C) and 50°F (10°C). Perpetual frost climates (F) are below freezing all year. There is also a category for highland climates (H). Köppen further qualified these categories according to precipitation and other characteristics.

Mediterranean climate (right) Vineyards thrive in northern Italy's Mediterranean climate, with its hot, dry summers and mild, wet winters.

Climate graphs (bottom) The climate of a place can be summarized visually in a climate graph. Two curves represent maximum and minimum average monthly temperatures, while vertical bars show the average precipitation. Singapore is warm all year, with heavy rainfall in every month. Cairo, Egypt, is warm in winter, hot in summer, and has very little rain. Paris, France, has a temperate maritime climate, with mild winters, warm summers, and rainfall distributed evenly through the year. Churchill, Canada, has a tundra climate. Its summers are mild, but very brief, and its winters are very cold and fairly dry, with most precipitation falling in summer.

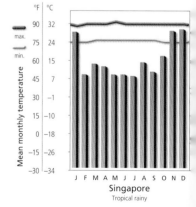

J F M A M J J A S O N D
Singapore
Tropical rainy

Cairo, Egypt
Dry

Paris, France
Temperate maritime

Churchill, Canada
Tundra

in | mm
10 | 254
8 | 203
6 | 152
4 | 102
2 | 51
0 | 0

Mean monthly rainfall

J F M A M J J A S O N D
J F M A M J J A S O N D
J F M A M J J A S O N D

■ 1 Tropical rainy
■ 2 Tropical seasonal

Tropical rainy (1); tropical seasonal (2) These occur between latitudes 23.5°N and S. Temperatures never fall below 64.4°F (18°C). In rainy climates rainfall is spread evenly through the year, but in seasonal climates it is heavier in one season.

□ 3 Dry
■ 4 Savanna

Dry (3); savanna (4) Found just outside the tropics in all the continents, these climates are arid deserts, or have rain in one season. The savanna climate is hot in summer and mild in winter. Arid deserts are hot or cold, depending on location.

■ 5 Mediterranean
■ 6 Subtropical

Mediterranean (5); subtropical (6) Mediterranean summers are hot and dry, averaging around 80°F (27°C) by day. Winters are mild, occasionally below freezing, and wet. Subtropical climates are hot in summer and warm in winter, with a summer rainy season.

■ 7 Temperate maritime

Temperate maritime (7) Mild in winter, these climates seldom have temperatures below freezing. They are warm in summer, with average daytime temperatures around 70°F (21°C). Rain or snow falls in every month of the year.

Climate Zones

The ancient Greeks classified the world's climates into three zones based on latitude—torrid, temperate, and frigid, which correspond to the tropical, temperate, and polar regions of the world. Starting from the 19th century, many more classification schemes have been devised, based mainly on the type of vegetation a particular climate would sustain. The classifications most widely used today are those devised by the Russian-born German climatologist W. P. Köppen between 1900 and 1936 and by the American climatologist

C. W. Thornthwaite between 1931 and 1948.
The Köppen classification followed here divides
climates into six basic types: tropical rainy (1),
dry (3), temperate maritime (7), continental cold
(9), tundra (10), and perpetual frost (11).

CLIMATE CLASSIFICATION

Most modern classification
systems fall into two groups.
Generic systems, such as those
of Köppen and Thornthwaite,
classify climates by aridity and
temperature, and their effect on
vegetation. Genetic systems group
climates by the physical processes
that produce them. No single
system is satisfactory for all
purposes, but generic systems
are of particular interest
to agriculturists and geographers.

A History of Earth's Climate

Earth's climate is constantly changing. The most dramatic changes, between glacial and interglacial periods, were triggered by cyclical changes in Earth's orbit and rotation. More recently, there have been climatic periods known as the Warm Roman, Cool Dark Ages, Medieval Warm, and Little Ice Age. We are now entering the Modern Warm period.

1. Niagara Falls Located on the Canadian–U.S. border, these falls comprise the Bridal Veil, American, and Canadian Horseshoe falls. They carry water along the Niagara River between lakes Erie and Ontario. The falls are eroding the river bed and have retreated 7 miles (11.3 km) since they formed at the end of the last ice age.

Niagara Falls, U.S.A. and Canada

2. Greenland ice sheet This ice mass is possibly the only large remnant In the Northern Hemisphere of the last glaciation during the Pleistocene epoch. It covers 670,272 square miles (1,736,095 km²). At its thickest points the ice is about 10,000 feet (3,050 m) deep. At the present time, it is thinning at lower levels and thickening over the higher elevations near the center.

Greenland ice sheet

3. Canadian Shield This occupies approximately 1.7 million square miles (4.4 million km²) in northeastern Canada, northern United States, and most of Greenland. It is a land of coniferous forests, tundra, and of tens of thousands of lakes filling basins scoured by the ice sheets that have covered it during successive ice ages.

Canadian Shield

Niagara Falls At the end of the last ice age, about 12,000 years ago, these falls formed when glacial lakes filled with water from a retreating glacier and discharged over a high escarpment.

FUTURE ICE AGE

During the last three million years ice sheets have advanced and retreated many times. Today we live in an interglacial period called the Holocene that began 10,000 years ago. The next ice age may begin in approximately 18,000 years.

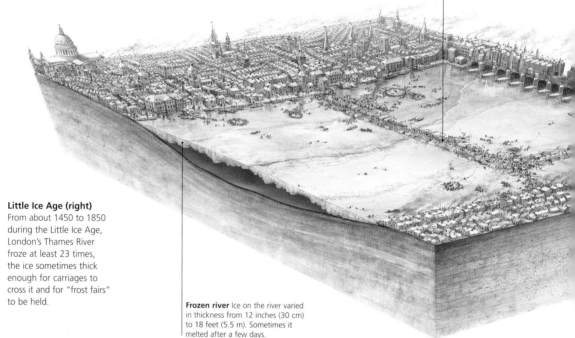

Thames frost fairs The first of these events, held in 1564, was attended by Elizabeth I. The last, in 1813, continued for a month. Stalls were erected on the ice selling food, drink, and souvenirs.

Little Ice Age (right)
From about 1450 to 1850 during the Little Ice Age, London's Thames River froze at least 23 times, the ice sometimes thick enough for carriages to cross it and for "frost fairs" to be held.

Frozen river Ice on the river varied in thickness from 12 inches (30 cm) to 18 feet (5.5 m). Sometimes it melted after a few days.

Timeline of climate change
The graph shows how Earth's atmospheric temperature has risen and fallen throughout the planet's history, measured against the horizontal line representing the average in recent years. Ice ages have become more frequent over the last two million years. The present interglacial period began 10,000 years ago.

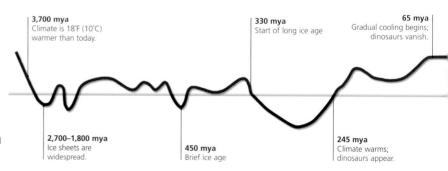

3,700 mya
Climate is 18°F (10°C) warmer than today.

330 mya
Start of long ice age

65 mya
Gradual cooling begins; dinosaurs vanish.

2,700–1,800 mya
Ice sheets are widespread.

450 mya
Brief ice age

245 mya
Climate warms; dinosaurs appear.

Shaped by ice (right) In the Canadian Shield lakes and swamps fill irregular basins in a landscape that was depressed and severely eroded as ice sheets repeatedly advanced across it.

Ancient ice cap (below) Covering 80 percent of Greenland, this huge ice sheet has existed for more than 100,000 years. It is so thick that only bare mountain peaks, or nunataks, protrude above its surface.

The evidence To learn about past climates, paleoclimatologists study the annual growth rings of trees, the chemical composition of ancient corals and seashells, and ice cores drilled from ice sheets.

Tree rings Growing conditions affect the width of tree rings. Wide rings indicate periods of warm, moist weather, while narrow rings form in cool, dry weather.

Corals Over hundreds of years corals build skeletons of calcium carbonate, the composition of which is affected by water temperature. Growth bands can thus provide clues to past climate.

Ice cores These long ice columns record each year's snowfall as a band in the ice. The ice's thickness and its chemical makeup reflect climatic conditions in the past.

1.6 mya Cooling continues; ice ages occur roughly every 100,000 years.

Brief, warm interglacial periods occur between ice ages.

A.D. 900–1100 Warm period called Medieval Climatic Optimum

6,000 ya Warm climate encourages birth of farming.

Present average temperature.

18,000 ya Peak of last ice age

1450–1850 Little Ice Age

WEATHER

Varying conditions make up the weather people experience day by day. Sunshine or cloudy, warm or cold, weather is local and in many parts of the world it is highly changeable. Meteorology is the scientific study of weather, and meteorologists use their understanding of the way weather works to predict its behavior for a few days ahead. Weather is the product of the interaction of sunshine, air, and water. The evaporation, condensation, and freezing of water produce clouds, fog, snow, hail, frost, rain, and dew. Rapidly rising moist air may lead to thunderstorms, occasionally with tornadoes.

Barometer (left) Any change in air pressure can forecast short-term changes in the weather. A barometer measures these variations, so that rain or fine weather can be predicted. The instrument shown here has two dials, but displays three readings. At the top is an aneroid, or non-liquid, barometer for measuring pressure, and the bottom dial clock shows temperature and humidity readings.

Hurricane Katrina (right) The spiral cloud formation is clearly visible in this satellite image. Katrina crossed the Louisiana coast, U.S.A., on August 29, 2005, as a category 4 hurricane with sustained winds of 150 mph (240 km/h). It caused severe damage, nearly demolishing the town of Biloxi, Mississippi. In New Orleans, its heavy rain breached the levees protecting the city, causing widespread flooding.

TYPES OF WEATHER

Air is constantly carried around by the global belts of prevailing winds. Its temperature, density, and humidity equalize at every height, so the characteristics of the air are approximately the same everywhere. A continental (dry) or maritime (moist) air mass may also be polar or tropical according to the latitude in which it is formed.

When two air masses meet, the denser air pushes beneath the lighter air and a front develops. The movement of air along fronts often creates cloud and precipitation of various kinds. Frontal weather systems tend to follow one another, dragged beneath the high-level jet stream. Dew is a kind of precipitation that forms at night when water vapor condenses onto cold surfaces that have lost their heat by radiation. Water freezes as frost. Water vapor can also condense at ground level, producing fog.

Insufficient precipitation can result in drought, while excessive precipitation causes floods. Flooding happens when heavy or prolonged rain falls onto saturated ground that cannot absorb it. The water then overflows riverbanks.

Monsoon rains often cause flooding. The monsoons, which occur in parts of West Africa, Australia, and Asia, result from a seasonal change in wind direction. This brings continental air in the dry winter season or maritime air in the rainy summer season.

Frontal weather is typical of temperate latitudes. The tropics, however, experience disturbances that can develop into tropical cyclones (hurricanes), the most violent of all weather systems. Storms of all kinds often produce lightning. Thunder is the sound of air exploding when lightning suddenly heats it, making it expand violently.

Thunderstorms are common along very active weather fronts and in association with tropical cyclones. They can also occur in isolation—for example, on summer afternoons when the air is moist and the ground is very warm.

Throughout history people have attempted to forecast the weather. Around 100 B.C. the ancient Greeks built the Tower of the Winds in Athens. This structure was decorated with a frieze of figures representing the eight wind gods, and had a sundial, a weathervane, and a waterclock. Modern forecasting began to develop from the middle of the 19th century, when the telegraph allowed data gathered over a wide area to be transmitted rapidly to a forecasting center. Nowadays meteorologists use information from orbiting satellites, surface weather stations, balloons, buoys at sea, ships, and aircraft to predict the weather.

Hurricane Ivan (above) On September 16, 2004, category 5 Ivan hit the coast of Alabama, U.S.A. This radar image shows the rainfall, with black indicating the least, and red the highest amount. At the time, Ivan was the sixth-strongest storm ever to occur in the Atlantic basin.

Winter snow (left) Most rain begins as snow that melts before leaving the cloud. However, if the temperature under the cloud is below about 39°F (4°C), precipitation falls as snow. If the ground is below freezing, the snow will settle.

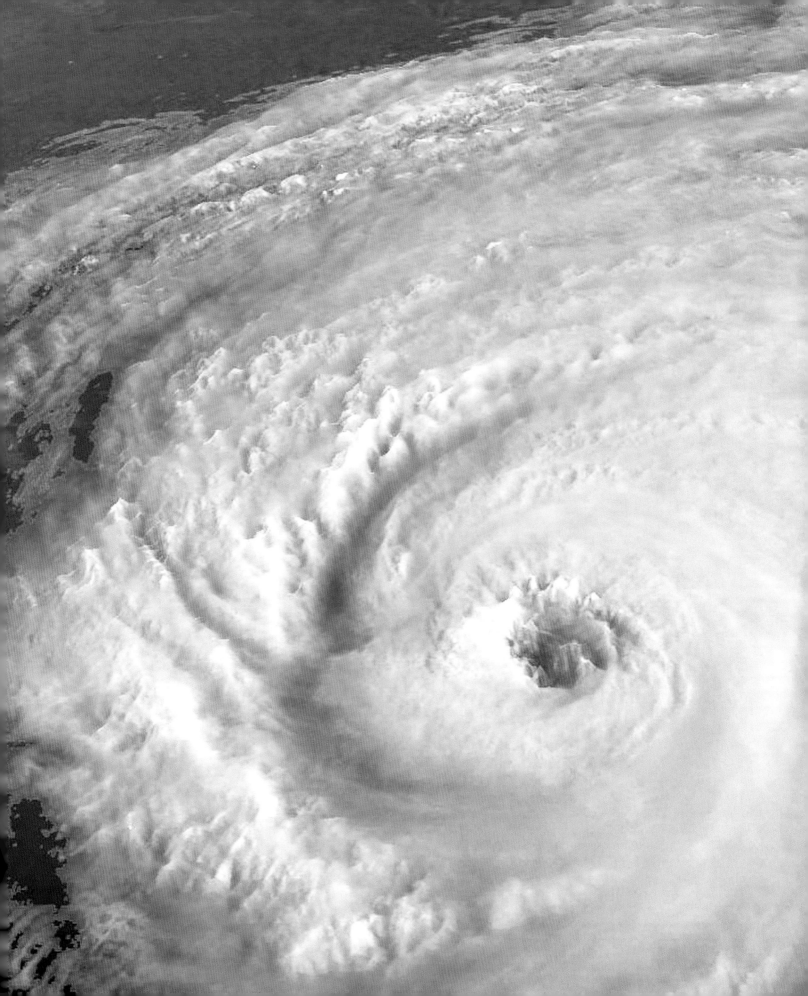

Frontal systems A front is the boundary between air masses that contain air of different densities. Cool air pushes beneath warmer air and raises it. Water vapor then condenses and forms cloud.

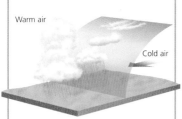

Warm air

Cold air

Cold front This heralds the arrival of cooler air. Layers of cloud that are in warm air ahead of the cold front slowly clear.

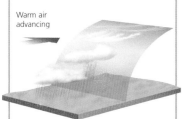

Warm air advancing

Warm front When cooler air pushes underneath warm air, a warm front develops. As the air rises its water vapor condenses, producing cloud.

OCCLUDED FRONT

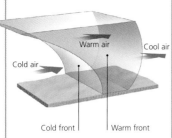

Warm air

Cool air

Cold air

Cold front | Warm front

1 As the cool air advances against the warm air, it begins to lift the warm air.

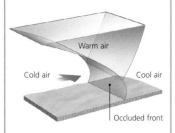

Warm air

Cold air

Cool air

Occluded front

2 The cool air raises the warm air and warm front clear of the surface and the frontal system then dissipates.

Moving Air Masses

When a large volume of air, or air mass, lies over a large continent or ocean for some time, its temperature, humidity, and density become fairly uniform. The region where an air mass forms is known as its source region. Air masses are classified by moisture content as continental (dry) or maritime (moist), and by temperature as arctic, polar, tropical, or equatorial.

Air mass boundary A frontal cloud is a wide band of cloud that marks the boundary between cool and warm air masses. Warm air moves up over the cool air rather than mixing with it.

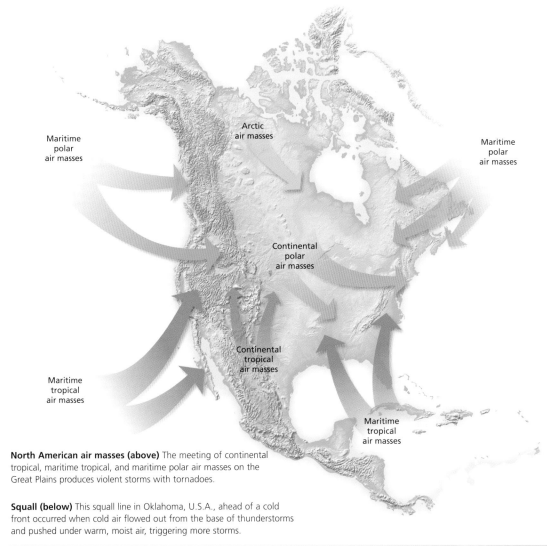

Maritime polar air masses

Arctic air masses

Maritime polar air masses

Continental polar air masses

Maritime tropical air masses

Continental tropical air masses

Maritime tropical air masses

North American air masses (above) The meeting of continental tropical, maritime tropical, and maritime polar air masses on the Great Plains produces violent storms with tornadoes.

Squall (below) This squall line in Oklahoma, U.S.A., ahead of a cold front occurred when cold air flowed out from the base of thunderstorms and pushed under warm, moist air, triggering more storms.

Frontal cycle A frontal system begins with a wave along a front. The wave grows larger and a frontal depression develops around its crest. Eventually the fronts occlude.

1 Cold and warm air are side by side, moving in opposite directions. A curve appears along the front between them.

2 A warm sector separates the cold and warm fronts, and cold air advances against the warm air.

3 The cold air pushes beneath the warm air. Air turning at the wave crest produces a low-pressure center.

4 Cold air raises air in the warm sector clear of the surface. The cold and warm fronts are occluding.

5 The warm air is entirely clear of the surface, the system is dissipating, and the cycle is ready to repeat.

Clouds

The amount of water vapor air can carry depends on the air temperature. When air rises, its temperature falls and some of its moisture may condense into minute droplets or ice crystals, so forming clouds. Gently rising air produces sheets of cloud, while strong air movement produces deep, piled-up shower or storm clouds.

Storm cloud (below) Vigorous convection produced this ominous towering cumulonimbus storm cloud. Any droplets that rise or fall into the dry air outside the cloud instantly evaporate.

How clouds form The temperature of air drops as it moves higher. The height at which water vapor condenses in rising air, known as the lifting condensation level, depends on the moisture content of the air.

1 Air rises by convection over warm ground. With every 1,000 feet (300 m) in height it cools by 5.4°F (10°C/km), and nears the lifting condensation level.

2 Above the lifting condensation level, water vapor condenses into droplets on tiny particles, or cloud condensation nuclei, forming cumulus cloud.

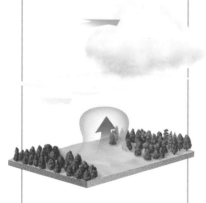

3 The cloud drifts away, carried by the wind. If the ground below remains hot, a new convective cloud may form in the same way.

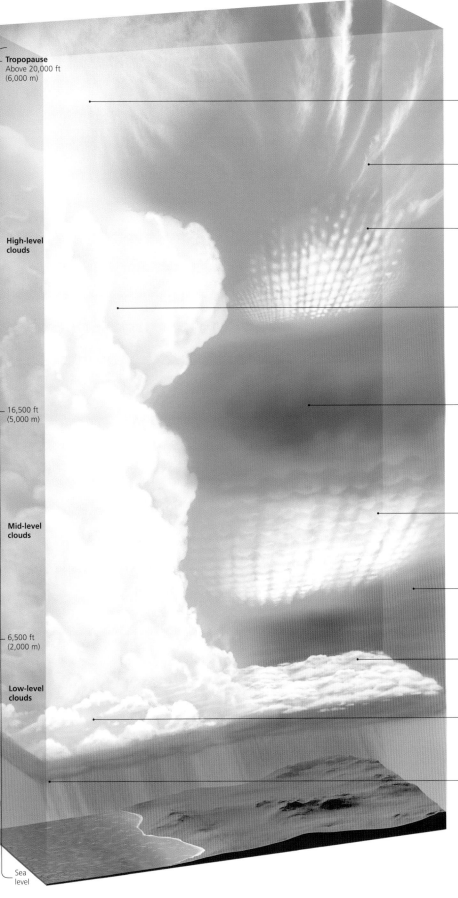

Tropopause
Above 20,000 ft
(6,000 m)

**High-level
clouds**

16,500 ft
(5,000 m)

**Mid-level
clouds**

6,500 ft
(2,000 m)

**Low-level
clouds**

Sea
level

Cloud types Most clouds form in the troposphere, although there are rare cloud types that occur in the mesosphere and stratosphere. The most common cloud types are described below.

Cirrostratus Composed of ice crystals, this cloud is a thin veil across the sky, often at the top of a warm front. It can indicate approaching rain.

Cirrus Forming long, wispy filaments, narrow bands, or white patches, cirrus is always fibrous. A high cloud, it consists entirely of ice crystals.

Cirrocumulus A high, ice-crystal cloud, this forms sheets or masses of small, nearly spherical, puffy clouds that often produce a mackerel sky.

Cumulonimbus This cloud takes shape in air rising by convection. It has a low base but often towers to a great height. It delivers heavy precipitation and sometimes thunderstorms.

Altostratus This middle-level cloud forms a fibrous or featureless sheet on warm fronts and warns of approaching rain.

Altocumulus Occurring at middle levels, this often has a wavy or banded, woolly appearance, but is highly variable. It does not predict coming weather.

Nimbostratus A low, gray cloud, this forms a uniform layer that can often obscure the sun or moon. It delivers continuous rain or snow.

Stratocumulus This low-level cloud occurs in sheets or patches, with gaps through which the sun shines, and with dark rolls or rounded masses.

Cumulus Air rising by convection creates cumulus. If it is small and scattered against a blue sky, it is called fair-weather cumulus.

Stratus This low cloud often forms a featureless gray layer, sometimes thin enough for the sun or moon to be faintly visible.

FACT FILE

Rising air Cloud forms when moist rising air cools to below its dew point temperature, which is the temperature at which water vapor condenses. Air can be forced to rise by convection, as well as by orographic or frontal lifting.

Convection Convection occurs when air is heated by contact with a warm surface. This produces cumulus or the much bigger cumulonimbus cloud.

Orographic When air is forced to rise as it crosses high ground, it is called orographic lifting. This usually produces stratus-type cloud layers.

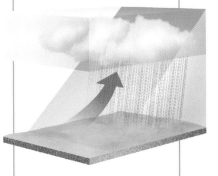

Frontal As cold air pushes beneath warm air at a front, the warm air lifts and produces layers of stratus-type clouds on both warm and cold fronts.

Clouds continued

The names of the basic cloud types refer to their appearance, which is partly determined by the height at which they form. This height depends on how far the temperature of rising air must fall before it reaches its dew point temperature, when it becomes saturated and water vapor starts to condense. The moister the air, the lower the cloud base will be. Clouds are also classified by the height of their bases as high (cirrus, cirrocumulus, cirrostratus), middle-level (altocumulus, altostratus, nimbostratus), and low (stratus,

stratocumulus, cumulus, cumulonimbus). The height limits of these categories are higher in the tropics than at the Poles. High clouds consist of ice crystals, and middle-level and low clouds of water droplets, but cumulonimbus has both ice and liquid water.

CLOUD CLASSIFICATION

The names given to the cloud genera are based on a scheme that was introduced in 1803 by the English meteorologist Luke Howard. He combined appropriate Latin words to coin names that describe cloud properties—*alto* means "high," *cirrus* is "curl," *cumulus* is "heap," and *stratus* is "layer." *Nimbus* is the Latin word for cloud, but Howard used it to mean rain.

READING THE SKIES

Meteorology is the scientific study of the physical and chemical processes in the atmosphere that result in weather phenomena. Routine weather forecasting forms a major part of what meteorologists do, but they also warn of hazardous weather conditions and track the systems producing them across continents and oceans. Information is acquired in many ways. Surface stations on land and at sea measure temperature, pressure, wind, precipitation, and cloud cover, and monitor changes. Satellites photograph cloud formations and gauge atmospheric conditions, while floating buoys keep track of conditions at sea.

Ancient weather vane (left) The Tower of the Winds was built in Athens in the 1st century B.C. Its eight sides were aligned with the points of the compass. At the top of each side a carved figure represented the appropriate wind, one of which is pictured here. At the center of the tower a rod turned with the wind to indicate the wind direction.

Radiosonde balloon (right) This balloon, launched from Antarctica, will rise to 66,000–98,000 feet (20–30 km) and then burst. Instruments that hang 98 feet (30 m) below it transmit data to a ground station. Worldwide, around 500 stations release balloons of this kind every day.

Radio and forecasting (below) Guglielmo Marconi made the first transatlantic radio transmission in 1901. Radio communications eventually allowed meteorologists to exchange data in real time, which greatly improved forecasting.

THE STORY OF WEATHER

The ancient Greeks were the first to formally study the weather. The word "meteorology" derives from *Meteorologica*, the title of a book by the 4th-century Greek philosopher Aristotle. *Meteoros* means "lofty" and *logia* "a discourse or study." In his book Aristotle explained the formation of clouds, hail, wind, rain, and storms, while deriving many of his ideas from Egyptian and Babylonian scholars.

Aristotle's pupil and friend Theophrastus, who is best known for his studies of plants, also wrote two short publications on weather. In *On Weather Signs* and *On Winds* he listed the natural signs that people used to predict the weather. Several other Greek and Roman authors also compiled lists of weather signs and beliefs.

The ancient Greeks and Romans had no instruments to make measurements to help them study atmospheric phenomena. It was not until 1593 that Italian natural philosopher Galileo Galilei invented the first thermometer. Called an air thermoscope, it was highly inaccurate. In 1714 German physicist Daniel Fahrenheit made the first accurate mercury thermometer. Evangelista Torricelli, an assistant to Galileo, invented the barometer in 1643.

In the following years, understanding of atmospheric physics and circulation improved rapidly. Robert Boyle, Edmé Mariotte, Jacques-Alexandre-César Charles, and others discovered the relationship between air temperature, pressure, and volume. In 1735 English meteorologist George Hadley published an explanation of the way air circulates around the world that was almost correct. The major breakthrough, however, occurred with the opening of the first telegraph in 1844. This new form of communication made it possible to collect near simultaneous meteorological data from a wide area so that weather forecasts could be prepared.

THROUGH THE AGES

4th century B.C. Aristotle's *Meteorologica* was the first written attempt to explain weather phenomena as entirely natural.

1643 Italian physicist Evangelista Torricelli invented the barometer by filling a glass tube with mercury and observing the changing height of mercury in the tube.

1662 Irish scientist Robert Boyle published his law stating that the volume of a gas is inversely proportional to the pressure under which it is held.

Ca 1787 French physicist J.-A.-C. Charles published his law stating that, provided a gas remains under constant pressure, allowing it to expand, its volume changes with changes in temperature.

1803 English meteorologist Luke Howard proposed a system for classifying clouds by their appearance and height. The classification used today is based on Howard's system.

Weather imaging (left) Satellite images allow scientists to observe the formation and development of an entire weather system. On April 2, 1978, the Nimbus 5 weather satellite photographed a cyclonic storm as it raged over the Bering Sea, producing the image shown on the left. Hidden beneath the cloud is the Kamchatka Peninsula. A false-color effect has been added to the image on the right, in which red indicates the greatest concentration of water droplets and the heaviest precipitation.

Weather satellite (above) The Television and Infrared Observation Satellite (TIROS), launched on April 1, 1960, was the first weather satellite. In this image, scientists are seen preparing TIROS-1 for launch. TIROS-1 was followed by several other satellites, now termed NOAA-class. These satellites travel in polar orbits, covering every part of the world once every 24 hours. Their instruments transmit images in visible and infrared light.

Predicting electrical storms (left) Lightning is a spark resulting from the separation of positive and negative electrical charges caused by turbulence inside storm clouds. Meteorologists, electrical utilities, and fire prevention services are able to evaluate the likely extent of electrical activity and predict the duration and severity of a storm by using lightning detectors and weather radar.

1805 English naval officer Francis Beaufort proposed his 12-point scale for classifying wind force by its observed effects. The Beaufort scale is still used.

1844 The first telegraph line began to operate between Baltimore and Washington, U.S.A. Soon after, the telegraph was used to link weather stations.

1851 The first weather map, or synoptic chart, displayed at London's Great Exhibition, showed readings taken by instruments at many locations at the same time.

1895 Guglielmo Marconi transmitted the first radio signal. Radio communications are now crucial to weather forecasting.

1926 John Logie Baird demonstrated the first television transmission. This stimulated research, ultimately leading to the use of television in weather satellites.

Fog and Frost

Fog is cloud that occurs at ground level and that reduces visibility to less than 3,280 feet (1 km). It is denser than mist, which reduces visibility to less than 6,560 feet (2 km). Most fog is composed of minute water droplets, but frozen fog is made from ice crystals. Freezing fog forms in air below freezing temperature, so that fog droplets freeze on contact with surfaces.

Advection fog This occurs when warm, moist air crossing a cold surface is chilled to below its dew point temperature, the point at which water vapor condenses.

Radiation fog This kind of fog forms on clear nights when the ground cools rapidly by radiation, chilling the air that is in contact with it.

Fog stratus If the ground warms quickly, fog may clear from the bottom up and create a band of fog just above the ground, known as fog stratus.

Coastal fog Advection fog shrouding the Golden Gate Bridge, San Francisco, U.S.A., is a common phenomenon in summer. It forms when warm, moist air blowing in from the Pacific Ocean crosses the cool water of the California Current, just offshore.

Inland fog When the land surface in inland areas loses heat by radiation at night in clear weather, the layer of air next to the ground is cooled to below its dew point temperature and fog forms. Inland radiation fogs can extend up to 654 feet (200 m) above the ground.

Valley fog In some mountain regions, such as the Austrian Alps, fog often hangs in the valleys between mountain peaks at night. Radiation fog forms when the upper slopes lose heat by radiation. The cool, fog-laden air then sinks to the bottom of the valley.

Rime frost (above) Very cold fog or drizzle droplets freeze on contact with a surface below freezing temperature. As more droplets freeze onto the ice, a white, irregular coating is formed.

Hoar frost (below) If outdoor surfaces fall below freezing temperature at night, water vapor freezes directly onto them, coating them with a thin layer of white crystals.

FACT FILE

Dew and frost Dewdrops and frost crystals form on surfaces, such as leaves, on clear nights. This happens when surfaces lose heat by radiation and chill the air in direct contact with them.

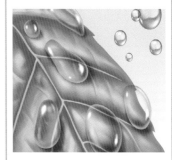

Dewdrops When air temperature cools to a dew point above 32°F (0°C), water vapor condenses in droplets, which collect on surfaces as dew.

Frost When air temperature drops to a dew point below 32°F (0°C), frost forms on surfaces, either from water vapor or from minute liquid droplets.

FERN FROST

If ice crystals form between water droplets and the droplets freeze onto the crystals, frost patterns that are known as fern frost appear on windowpanes.

Odd phenomena Clouds that drift across deserts bring no rain, either because the cloud droplets fail to grow big enough to fall, or because they fall but evaporate before reaching the ground.

Sun showers These occur very rarely. When rain or drizzle is blown away from a cloud, it appears to fall from a cloudless sky.

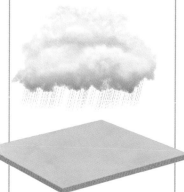

Virga rain Virga rain, or fallstreaks, which hangs like a veil beneath a cloud, is falling rain that evaporates before it reaches the ground.

RAINDROPS

Raindrops, with a diameter of 0.08–0.2 inch (2–5 mm), are much larger than drizzle droplets, which average 0.02 inch (0.5 mm) across. Small raindrops are spherical. As larger drops fall, air resistance deforms them into oblate spheroid shapes, as illustrated below.

Drizzle drop

Oblate raindrop

Raindrop

Spherical raindrop

Precipitation

Precipitation is water that falls from the sky as dew, fog, drizzle, rain, hail, frost, or snow. Water evaporates from the ocean or land surface, is transported as water vapor through the air, and eventually returns as precipitation to the land and ocean. Without precipitation there could be no life on land.

Types of precipitation (right) A large cumulonimbus cloud can produce rain, hail, or snow. Inside the cloud, water vapor condenses and freezes in rising air, then starts to fall. As ice crystals are swirled repeatedly up and down by air currents inside the cloud, they form hailstones. Ice crystals join to form snowflakes, and melting snowflakes become raindrops.

Rain curtain (below) A heavy shower falls like a curtain from a cumulonimbus cloud in New South Wales, Australia, and fleetingly refreshes drought-stricken land.

Rain

At the top The upper part of the cloud contains ice crystals and pellets that grow into hailstones as water freezes onto them.

Middle level Warm upcurrents and cold downcurrents meet about halfway down the cloud, where there is a mix of ice crystals, snowflakes, hailstones, and liquid water droplets.

Lower level If the air under the cloud is below freezing, snow falls. If the air temperature is above freezing, snowflakes melt into raindrops.

Hail

Snow

FACT FILE

1. Birmingham This large city in England's West Midlands receives 26.5 inches (674 mm) of rain annually, falling evenly all through the year. August is the wettest month,

with 2.8 inches (70.1 mm), and February has the least rain, with only 1.9 inches (47.4 mm).

Birmingham, England

2. Tehran Iran's capital city has an average annual rainfall of 9.5 inches (241 mm). The rain falls mainly in winter, with only 2.3 inches (56.5 mm) occurring during the summer months

between April and September. January is the wettest month of the year and September is the driest.

Tehran, Iran

3. Mojave Desert This arid region in western U.S.A. receives an average of only 3.6 inches (92.4 mm) of rain annually. No rain at all falls from the

end of April until the beginning of September. The wettest month is November, with 1.1 inches (28.7 mm).

Mojave Desert, U.S.A.

4. The Sahel Just to the south of the Sahara Desert, this part of Africa is very dry. The city of Timbuktu in Mali is typical, with an average 9 inches

(231 mm) of rain a year, almost all falling in summer. August is the wettest month, with 3.2 inches (81 mm).

Sahel, Africa

5. Quibdó Located in western Colombia, the city of Quibdó is close to the equator. It experiences a very wet climate, with an average annual rainfall of 315 inches (8,004 mm).

August is the wettest month, but rain usually occurs on 22–27 days of every month.

Quibdó, Colombia

Monsoon Rains

The name monsoon derives from the Arabic for season and is used to describe the seasonal winds that affect most parts of the tropics. In the dry winter monsoon, the prevailing winds blow outward from high pressure centered over the continents. In the wet summer monsoon, the pressure and winds reverse as the land warms and bring heavy rain.

Hyderabad, India (right) The sudden heavy downpours in the summer monsoon force pedestrians in the city to run for cover and can flood roads and railroads, making travel difficult.

Summer monsoon This is strongest in South Asia due to the effect of the Himalayas on pressure distribution. It brings warm, moist air from across the Indian Ocean. Cherrapunjee, India, has 323 inches (8,202 mm) of rain between May and August.

Winter monsoon Air flows outward from an area of high pressure over central Asia and loses its moisture as it crosses the Himalaya Mountains, bringing dry weather. Cherrapunjee receives 6 inches (152 mm) of rain between November and February.

Monsoon clouds (above) Viewed from a space shuttle in 1984, storm clouds gather over Brazil before releasing torrential rain. The wet monsoon delivers a large amount of rain in a very short time.

Flooding (below) Monsoon floods often strike Bangladesh, much of which is low-lying. Today few lives are lost and damage is limited because people receive ample warning.

Essential rains Farmers and wildlife in areas that experience monsoons depend on the rains after the dry winter. If the monsoon fails or is late, harvests are poor. If the rains are unusually heavy, floods may destroy the crop.

Terraced soil Flooding is essential for the growth of rice seedlings. These terraced paddies in Bali, Indonesia, are drained to ripen the crop.

Plant adaptation Plants in monsoonal climates become dormant during the dry season and grow rapidly when water is abundant.

Yellow-billed storks The monsoon rains bring plentiful water for these African wading birds that feed on small aquatic animals in open water.

FACT FILE

1. New Orleans On August 30, 2005, heavy rain brought by Hurricane Katrina caused surging floodwaters to breach many of the levees around the shores of Lake Pontchartrain and along canals linking the lake to the

Mississippi River. The catastrophic floods that resulted rendered the low-lying parts of the city uninhabitable.

New Orleans, Louisiana, U.S.A.

2. La Paz Flash floods and mudslides devastated Bolivia's administrative capital on February 19, 2002, after the most destructive storm in the city's history. In one hour the storm delivered almost one gallon of water

to every square foot of land (40 liters/m²), transforming the main street of La Paz into a fast-flowing river.

La Paz, Bolivia

3. Bangladesh Between June and August 2002, widespread major floods inundated northwestern and southern Bangladesh, as well as Nepal and northeastern India. Exceptionally heavy monsoon rains saturated the

ground, and rivers overflowed their banks, while high tides flooded many of the islands in the Bay of Bengal.

Bangladesh

Kenya floods (right) In November 2006, prolonged heavy rain caused Kenya's largest river, the Tana, to overflow its banks, inundating villages and affecting 723,000 people.

Floods

Floods happen when prolonged rain, intense storms, or melting snow release more water than rivers can contain, so that they overflow their banks, usually into surrounding low-lying land. Of all the natural disasters afflicting Earth, floods are the most frequent and are by far the worst in terms of the lives they claim, and the injuries and property damage they cause.

Flash floods (right) When more than double the average summer rainfall swelled China's Yangtze River in August 2002, farmland was protected by embankments. These satellite images show the region before (left) and during (right) the floods.

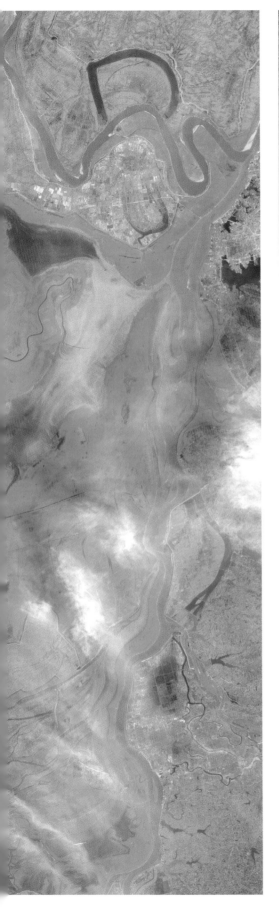

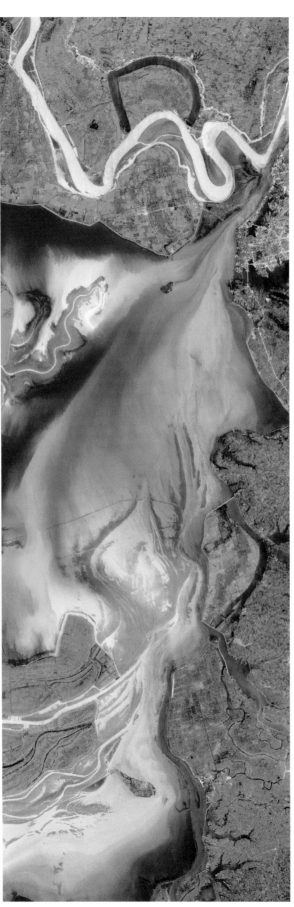

FACT FILE

Flood control The best way to prevent flooding is by providing land onto which rivers can overflow harmlessly. Traditionally levees, barriers, and dams have contained the surplus water.

Levee A raised river embankment is constructed higher than the highest likely river level.

Tidal barrier Built across estuaries, this protects against high tides and surges. Sluices provide normal flow.

Dam Water is held in a lake on the upstream side. Sluices control the gradual release of water downstream.

TEN WORST FLOODS

Year	Location	Fatalities
1931	Huang He, China	1–3,700,000
1887	Huang He, China	900,000–2,000,000
1938	Huang He, China	500,000–900,000
1642	Huang He, China	300,000
1975	Ru River, Banqiao Dam, China	230,000
1931	Yangtze, China	145,000
1099	Netherlands and England	100,000
1287	Netherlands	50,000
1824	Neva River, Russia	10,000
1421	Netherlands	10,000

Snow

As air rises, its temperature drops. If the temperature falls below freezing, water vapor condenses into hexagonal ice crystals that drift upward through the clouds. When crystals collide they freeze together, eventually forming snowflakes that are heavy enough to sink downward. If the temperature rises above freezing, the snowflakes melt and fall as rain, but otherwise they fall as snow.

Year-round snow (right) At high latitudes and elevations, the temperature never rises above freezing long enough for the snow to melt, as in these mountains in the Republic of Georgia.

LAKE-EFFECT SNOW

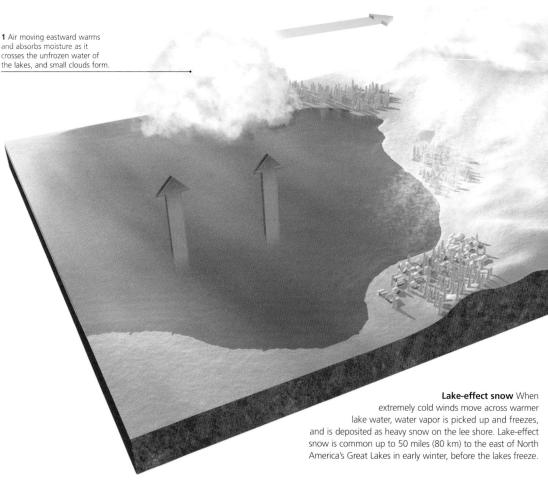

1 Air moving eastward warms and absorbs moisture as it crosses the unfrozen water of the lakes, and small clouds form.

2 When it passes over frozen ground, the moisture condenses into larger clouds and snow.

Lake-effect snow When extremely cold winds move across warmer lake water, water vapor is picked up and freezes, and is deposited as heavy snow on the lee shore. Lake-effect snow is common up to 50 miles (80 km) to the east of North America's Great Lakes in early winter, before the lakes freeze.

SNOWLINE

Temperature decreases with height, and on mountains the freezing level is marked by the snowline, above which there is always snow cover. The height of the snowline varies with latitude and season.

Snowline

3 Heavy snow falls in early winter, ending when the lakes freeze.

Blizzards These severe snowstorms are bitterly cold and occur when a strong wind drives heavy snow. Blizzards can happen almost anywhere snow falls, sometimes producing a whiteout in which people become disoriented.

Avalanches These catastrophic slides of snow can move at 100 mph (160 km/h) or more, and drive an even faster wind. Most are triggered on slopes of 30–40 degrees.

1 Snow accumulates on a slope that is too shallow to shed it immediately and too steep for it to remain stable.

2 A new snowfall, or water flowing under the snow from melting, can detach snow, starting an avalanche.

3 An avalanche can uproot trees, transport large boulders, and bury buildings and people.

Ice

As water freezes, its molecules lock together and form an open structure that is less dense than liquid water, which is why ice floats on open water. Inside clouds where the temperature is below freezing, ice crystals join to form snowflakes. Compaction turns snow into ice by squeezing out the air from between snowflakes.

Ice cave (right) Water flowing through a fissure in or beneath a glacier melts ice to create huge open caves such as this one being explored by an ice climber. These caves are often unstable.

Penguins on ice (below) Adelie penguins crowd on top of an iceberg off the Antarctic Peninsula. Solid ice that has not been in contact with the land is very clean and retains its pristine blue color.

AUFEIS, ALASKA

German for "ice on top," aufeis is a mass of layered ice that forms from flows of groundwater in river valleys in winter.

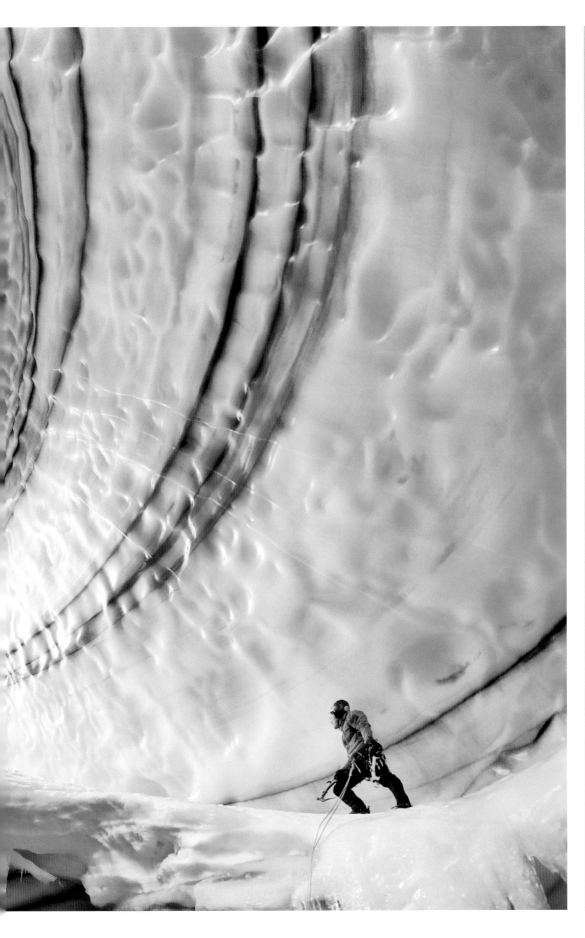

Ice formations Ice can form in different ways according to local conditions, and assume many different shapes. Accumulated ice is heavy and its weight can break branches from trees and bring down power and telephone lines.

Freezing rain When supercooled raindrops fall on a frozen plant they freeze instantly, encasing it in a layer of clear ice that rapidly grows thicker.

Icicles These long spikes of ice grow when the air is below freezing but bright sunshine melts fallen snow. Water trickles downward and freezes.

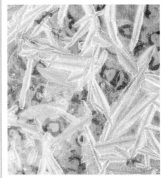

Ice patterns Ice crystals form between liquid droplets of dew that are below freezing. The supercooled droplets freeze onto the crystals in a chain reaction that produces attractive patterns.

Storm cycle Thunderstorms pass through three stages. Most last 30–60 minutes, but as a storm dies its downdrafts may push beneath moist air, causing it to rise and triggering another storm.

1 Moist air rises vigorously and condensation creates a rapidly growing cumulus congestus cloud that resembles a cauliflower.

2 At the peak of the storm, the cloud has grown to a cumulonimbus and produces rain and hail.

3 When the downdrafts have cooled the warm updrafts, suppressing them and depriving the cloud of its moist air, the storm dissipates.

Thunderstorms

A thunderstorm can release as much energy as an atom bomb. It develops when condensation in moist rising air warms the surrounding air so that it continues to rise and produces a towering, moisture-filled cumulonimbus cloud. Thunderstorms occur in hot, humid weather and along vigorous weather fronts. A line of storms may move ahead of a front as a squall line.

Supercell storms (right) These are more intense and last longer than ordinary, or multicell, storms. Updrafts and downdrafts separate, so downdrafts do not suppress updrafts and the cloud continues growing.

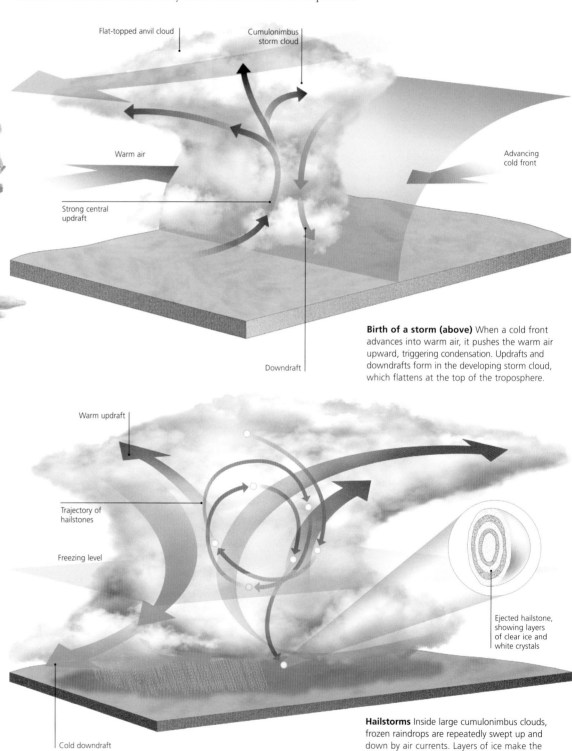

Flat-topped anvil cloud

Cumulonimbus storm cloud

Warm air

Advancing cold front

Strong central updraft

Downdraft

Birth of a storm (above) When a cold front advances into warm air, it pushes the warm air upward, triggering condensation. Updrafts and downdrafts form in the developing storm cloud, which flattens at the top of the troposphere.

Warm updraft

Trajectory of hailstones

Freezing level

Ejected hailstone, showing layers of clear ice and white crystals

Cold downdraft

Hailstorms Inside large cumulonimbus clouds, frozen raindrops are repeatedly swept up and down by air currents. Layers of ice make the hailstones progressively larger until a downdraft expels them.

Lightning and Thunder

In an electrical storm, collisions between rising and falling ice crystals cause particles with a positive charge to gather near the top of the cumulonimbus cloud and those with a negative charge near the bottom. The negatively charged particles induce a positive charge on the ground. Radioactive decay and cosmic radiation then accelerate a cascade of electrons that grows rapidly into a lightning spark, neutralizing the charge. In less than a second, lightning heats the surrounding air by 54,000°F (30,000°C). The air explodes and the shock

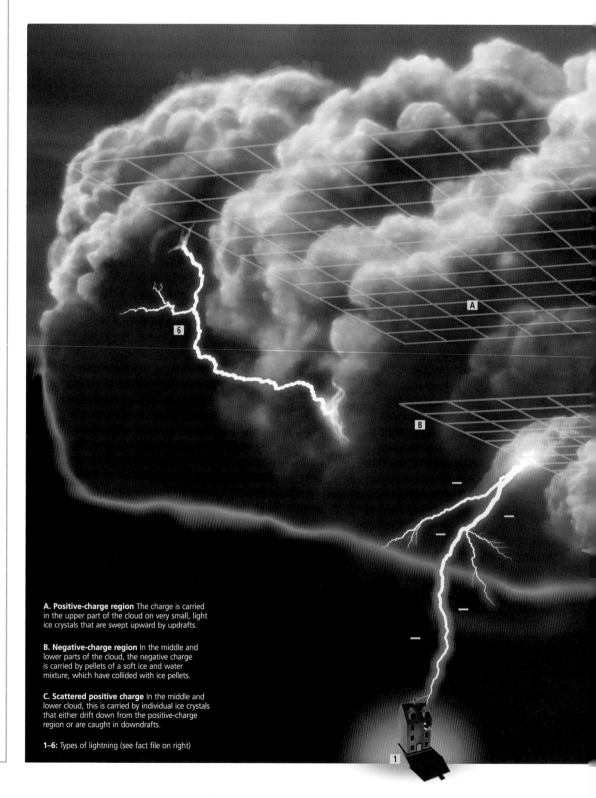

A. Positive-charge region The charge is carried in the upper part of the cloud on very small, light ice crystals that are swept upward by updrafts.

B. Negative-charge region In the middle and lower parts of the cloud, the negative charge is carried by pellets of a soft ice and water mixture, which have collided with ice pellets.

C. Scattered positive charge In the middle and lower cloud, this is carried by individual ice crystals that either drift down from the positive-charge region or are caught in downdrafts.

1–6: Types of lightning (see fact file on right)

wave is heard as thunder. It rumbles because sound travels different distances from the top and bottom of the lightning stroke and arrives gradually. Lightning can flash inside a cloud, between clouds, between a cloud and the ground, or upward from the cloud.

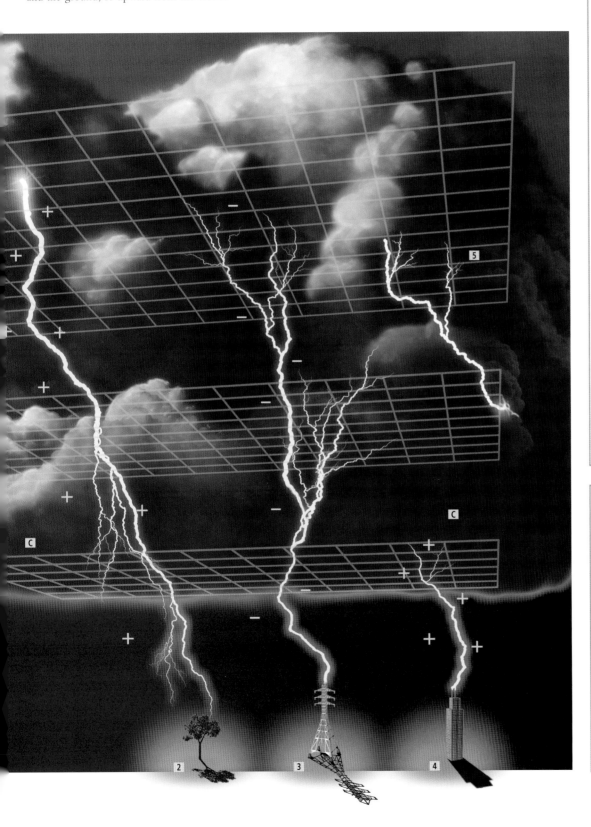

LIGHTNING TARGETS

Most lightning flashes from the ground to the cloud, but cloud-to-ground flashes are the second most common, and the most dangerous. They can cause fatal injuries and considerable property damage.

1 As the rotating mesocyclone extends downward, it becomes narrower and spins faster. Core pressure in the vortex is very low.

2 The vortex emerges from the cloud base. In moist air the low core pressure causes condensation, making the funnel visible.

WATER SPOUTS

Columns of water like this one in Newport News, Virginia, U.S.A., are tornadoes that form over warm, shallow water. They may also begin on land and then move to the coastal waters offshore.

Tornadoes

A tornado is a funnel of air spiraling upward into a cloud and is the most violent of all climatic phenomena. It can extend to 1,200 feet (366 m) across at its base, and the wind can reach speeds of 40–300 mph (64–480 km/h). Tornadoes can strike anywhere, although they are rare in the tropics, while the majority occur in the area of the United States known as Tornado Alley.

Touchdown (right) A funnel becomes a tornado when it touches the ground. Air spirals into the low-pressure vortex, sweeping up and hurling out debris, which forms a dark cloud around the base.

Tornado Alley (below) The Great Plains region of the United States suffers more numerous and more severe tornadoes than any other part of the world. Most occur between May and September.

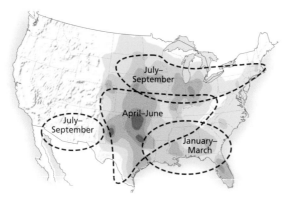

Average number of tornadoes a year per 10,000 square miles (26,000 km²)

☐ < 1	3	7
1	5	9

···· **Peak seasons**

Total devastation (right) A tornado at Paisley, Florida, U.S.A., in February 2007 killed several people and caused widespread damage. Tornadoes are more likely in summer, but can happen any time.

London (far right) On December 7, 2006, a tornado struck the U.K. capital. It damaged about 100 buildings in a 0.25-square-mile (0.6 km²) area and temporarily displaced several hundred residents.

THE FUJITA SCALE		
Category	Wind speed, mph (km/h)	Damage
F0	40–73 (64–117)	Light
F1	74–112 (118–180)	Moderate
F2	113–157 (181–251)	Considerable
F3	158–206 (252–330)	Severe
F4	207–260 (331–417)	Devastating
F5	More than 260 (417)	Incredible

TEN WORST TORNADOES

Year	Place	Death toll	F Scale
1925	Tri-State (Missouri, Illinois, Indiana)	695	F5
1840	Natchez, Mississippi	317	–
1896	St. Louis, Illinois	255	F4
1936	Tupelo, Mississippi	216	F5
1936	Gainsville, Georgia	203	F4
1947	Woodward, Oklahoma	181	F5
1908	Amite, Pine, Purvis, Louisiana, and Mississippi	143	F4
1899	St. Croix County, New Richmond, Wisconsin	117	F5
1953	Flint, Michigan	115	F5
1953	Waco, Texas	114	F5

Hurricane life cycle A hurricane begins as a local disturbance in the pressure pattern over the eastern North Atlantic. As it intensifies, it is progressively termed a tropical depression, tropical storm, and tropical cyclone.

Day 1 When wind speeds exceed 38 mph (61 km/h), the depression is classed as a tropical storm and named.

Day 3 A distinctive spiral structure develops, and there are towering cumulonimbus clouds around the center. Wind speeds are increasing.

Day 6 The storm is now a tropical cyclone. The sustained winds exceed 74 mph (120 km/h) around the warm, subsiding air in the eye.

Day 12 The hurricane continues to widen and intensify. The heaviest rain and strongest winds are in the eyewall around the eye.

Hurricanes

Tropical regions of low pressure generate violent storms, with torrential rain and powerful winds that reach speeds of more than 75 mph (120 km/h). Meteorologists call these storms tropical cyclones, but they are commonly known as hurricanes in the Atlantic and Caribbean, and typhoons in the Pacific and Indian oceans and China seas. Hurricanes develop in late summer.

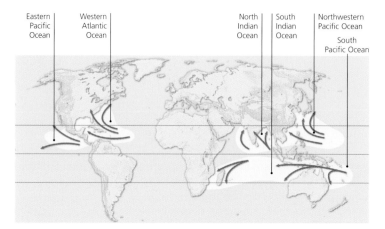

Eastern Pacific Ocean · Western Atlantic Ocean · North Indian Ocean · South Indian Ocean · Northwestern Pacific Ocean · South Pacific Ocean

Tropical Cyclone Diana (right) In a satellite view of this hurricane over Madagascar in January 2002, the structure of the storm is clearly visible, with banks of cloud, thickest in the eyewall, spiraling around the eye, where the air is still and warm.

Distribution and paths (left) Tropical cyclones develop in the North (but not the South) Atlantic, North and South Pacific, and Indian oceans, in latitudes between 5° and 20°, where the Coriolis effect is strong enough to start them turning.

THE SAFFIR-SIMPSON SCALE				
Category	Pressure, mb	Wind speed, mph (km/h)	Storm surge, ft (m)	Damage
1	980	74–95 (119–153)	4–5 (1.2–1.6)	Minimal
2	965–979	96–110 (154–177)	6–8 (1.7–1.6)	Moderate
3	945–964	111–130 (178–209)	9–12 (2.6–3.7)	Extensive
4	920–944	131–155 (209–248)	13–18 (3.8–5.4)	Extreme
5	Less than 920	More than 155 (248)	More than 18 (5.4)	Catastrophic

Low air pressure As air rises it creates intense low pressure, which draws in air from the ocean to feed the storm, and also makes the ocean surface bulge.

Rain clouds Reaching as far as 200 miles (320 km) from the center, whirling bands of rain clouds form, becoming more intense closer to the eyewall.

Eyewall Around the clear, calm eye, the eyewall has the biggest, darkest, storm clouds, producing the heaviest rain and strongest winds.

Spiraling air An upward spiral of warm, moist air drawn into the central area of low pressure brings moisture to sustain cloud formation.

Anatomy of a hurricane (below) A hurricane consists of bands of convective cloud rotating around the clear, calm eye. Convection and heat released by the condensation of moisture fuel the storm.

Storm surge Wind-driven waves strike the coast, heightened by the low-pressure bulge. The surge sometimes coincides with a high tide.

TEN WORST HURRICANES

Year	Name (Place)	Deaths
1998	H. Mitch (Central America)	11,000
1900	No name (Texas)	6,000–12,000
1974	H. Fifi (Honduras)	5,000
2004	T.S. Jeanne (Haiti)	>3,000
2005	H. Katrina (Louisiana & Mississippi)	1,193
1979	H. David (Caribbean, Florida, Georgia, New York)	>1,000
1994	T. Fred (China)	1,000
2004	T. Winnie (Philippines)	1,000 dead or missing
1944	T. Cobra (Philippine Sea)	790
2005	H. Stan (Central America)	725

H = Hurricane, T.S. = Tropical Storm, T = Typhoon

RECORD-BREAKING WEATHER

Climates vary widely, but they can also bring extreme weather. At the South Pole, for example, Vostok Station is 11,401 feet (3,475 m) above sea level in East Antarctica, the world's highest continent. Not surprisingly, Vostok is the world's coldest place. It is also where the world's lowest-ever surface temperature to date was recorded. Other parts of the world with very hot climates are likely to experience record-high temperatures. Records also exist for the driest, wettest, and windiest places, as well as for the largest-ever hailstone.

WEATHER RECORDS

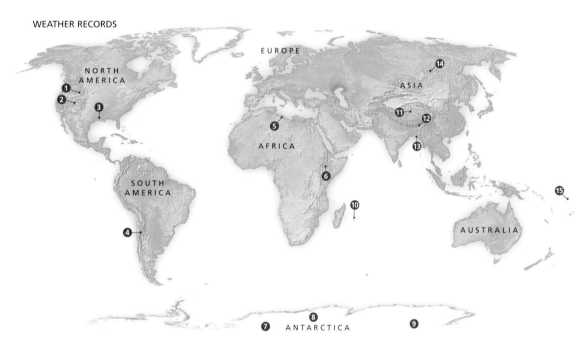

EXTREME WEATHER

Particular combinations of circumstances produce extreme weather conditions. Vostok is exposed to temperatures lower than those found anywhere else on Earth because of its latitude, 78.46°S, and high elevation.

India experiences the Asian monsoons, which bring intense rain during the summer months. The rain falls more heavily in the Himalayan foothills than it does on the plains, and it is there that the wettest place on Earth is found.

The Atacama Desert in Chile is dry because air crosses the South American continent and the Andes before reaching the desert. When the wind reverses direction, air approaches from the ocean and crosses the cold Peru Current.

Other phenomena involve chance. The biggest hailstone that formed inside a towering storm cloud could have developed in any of a number of places, while the strongest winds could blow in any part of the world that is exposed to tropical cyclones.

Weather records (above)

1. Greatest temperature change in one day Browning, Montana, U.S.A. On January 23–24, 1916, the temperature fell from 44°F (6.7°C) to –56°F (–49°C).

2. Deepest snow Tamarack, California, U.S.A. In March 1911, the snow lay 37.58 feet (11.46 m) deep on level ground.

3. Strongest wind Alabama and Mississippi, U.S.A. In August 1969, Hurricane Camille brought winds of 200 mph (320 km/h).

4. Driest climate Atacama Desert, Chile. Arica received an average rainfall of 0.03 inch (0.76 mm) measured over 59 years.

5. Hottest place Al' Aziziyah, Libya, with 136°F (57.8°C) on September 13, 1922.

6. Hottest annual average Dakol, Ethiopia. Between 1960 and 1966 the average temperature was 94°F (34.4°C).

7. Coldest annual average Pole of Inaccessibility, Antarctica. The annual average temperature is –72°F (–58°C).

8. Coldest place Vostok Station, Antarctica. On July 21, 1983, the temperature fell to –128.6°F (–89.2°C).

9. Windiest place Commonwealth Bay, Antarctica, has winds of 50 mph (80 km/h).

10. Heaviest single rainfall Chilaos, La Réunion, Indian Ocean. On March 15–16, 1952, 73.5 inches (1867 mm) fell.

11. Heaviest annual rainfall Cherrapunjee, India, had 905 inches (22,987 mm) in 1860–1861.

12. Highest average annual rainfall Mawsynram, India. Average rainfall over 38 years was 468 inches (11,872 mm).

13. Largest hailstone 2.25 pounds (1 kg) at Gopalganj, Bangladesh, in April 1986.

14. Highest surface air pressure Agata, Siberia, Russia. On December 31, 1968, the pressure was 1083.5 hPa.

15. Lowest air pressure 300 miles (483 km) west of Guam, Pacific Ocean. In October 1979, the pressure fell to 870 hPa.

Extreme cold (top right) Winter in Siberia lasts from October to April. The average temperature rises to 4°F (–16°C) by day, but falls to –12°F (–24°C) at night. This photo was taken on December 11, 2000, near Listvyanka, on the shore of Lake Baikal, 43 miles (70 km) from Irkutsk.

The world's driest desert (bottom right) The Valley of the Moon in Chile's Atacama Desert is part of the world's driest desert. No significant rain fell between 1570 and 1971, and nothing lives there. The constant wind rearranges the sand into a Moon-like landscape.

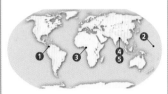

1. Lloro This small town in Colombia, located approximately 520 feet (159 m) above sea level, is the wettest place in South America and certainly one of the wettest in the world. Its estimated average annual rainfall is 523.6 inches (13,299 mm).

Lloro, Columbia

2. Pohnpei Island This Micronesian island receives more than 300 inches (7,620 mm) of rain a year. Pohnpei is the tip of an extinct volcano, lying in the oceanic warm pool, where the water temperature is almost 85°F (29°C).

Pohnpei Island, Micronesia

3. Debundscha Point This is on the coast at the foot of the southwest side of Mount Cameroon, Cameroon, West Africa. It receives an annual average rainfall of 405 inches (10,290 mm), mostly between May and October. The upper slopes of Mount Cameroon are above the clouds and dry.

Debundscha Point, Cameroon

4. Cherrapunjee Located 4,500 feet (1,370 m) above sea level on the windward side of India's Khasi Hills, Cherrapunjee receives monsoon rains that approach across the Bay of Bengal. It has an average annual rainfall of 450 inches (11,430 mm), of which 366 inches (9,301 mm) falls between May and September.

Cherrapunjee, India

5. Mawsynram This village in the Khasi Hills, Meghalaya State, India, reportedly receives 468 inches (11,872 mm) of rain a year. However, this figure is unofficial. As there is no meteorological office, the village cannot claim to be wetter than its neighbor, Cherrapunjee.

Mawsynram, India

Earth's Wettest Places

Rainfall is not distributed evenly around the world. Moist sea air, rising as it crosses mountains, delivers heavy rain to the windward side of coastal ranges. In southern Asia the summer monsoon brings torrential rain, while heavy rainstorms batter islands near the equator. In the future, rising global temperatures may increase the rainfall in such places.

Mount Waialeale, Kauai, Hawaii (right) With an average annual rainfall of more than 460 inches (11,680 mm), this mountain is one of the wettest places on Earth.

World precipitation (below) Rainfall is heaviest near the equator, where convection is vigorous. Regions are driest where air crosses large land areas to reach them.

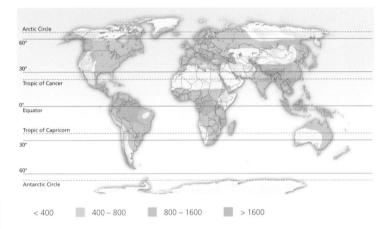

< 400	400 – 800	800 – 1600	> 1600

Measuring rainfall (below) Measurements from different sites are comparable because rain gauges are of standard designs.

Collection An opening 8 inches (20 cm) across collects rain, which is funneled down to the buckets.

Filter A debris-filtering screen ensures only clean water reaches the buckets.

Hatch Held in place by a security chain, this allows access to the electronic equipment for maintenance.

Gauge The mechanism is inside a cylindrical casing.

Pivoted buckets When 0.1 inch (2.5 mm) of rain has dripped into one side, its weight tips the bucket, which empties, and this is recorded electronically. At the same time, the other bucket is positioned under the drip.

Power A solar panel provides power for the electronic equipment.

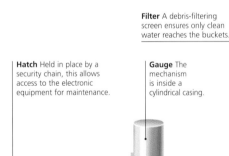

Electronic equipment Housed inside a metal cylinder, this stores and transmits data.

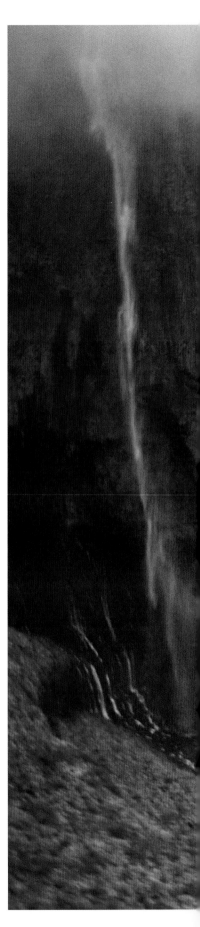

FACT FILE

Mount Waialeale This mountain on Hawaii's Kauai Island, rising to 5,148 feet (1,569 m), receives rain almost every day of the year. Its wet climate is the result of its geographic location and shape.

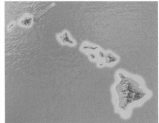

Location The most northerly of the Hawaiian islands, Kauai is exposed to frontal systems that bring rain in the winter months.

Shape The island is round and conical, which means that it is exposed on all sides to moist winds from the ocean, whichever direction they come from.

Height The peak of Mount Waialeale lies just beneath the trade wind inversion, at 6,000 feet (1,830 m), which traps rising air.

Out of reach Mauna Loa is more than twice as high as Mount Waialeale. Rising air cannot penetrate the temperature inversion, so the peak has a dry climate.

Earth's Driest Places

The driest climates are found in large subtropical deserts, continental interiors, and at the Poles. In deserts, dry, subsiding air flows outward at a low level and prevents moist air from entering. Continental interiors are dry because of their distance from the ocean, and polar air is too cold to hold moisture. A warmer climate may increase rainfall in some deserts.

Antarctica (below) Thick ice has accumulated over millions of years on this extremely dry continent. Precipitation is just over 1 inch (25 mm) per year at the geographic South Pole marker, shown here surrounded by international flags.

FACT FILE

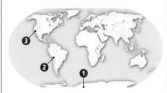

1. South Pole This is a long way from the ocean and the air is too cold to hold much water vapor. Permanently high pressure means surface air flows

outward, producing frequent gales and preventing milder, moister air from penetrating into the interior.

South Pole, Antarctica

2. Arica, Chile In the north of the Atacama Desert, Arica has prevailing winds that blow from the northeast. Before reaching Arica, air crosses the

South American continent and the Andes Mountains, losing its moisture and producing extreme aridity.

Arica, Chile

3. Mojave Desert This arid region lies to the south and east of the Sierra Nevada mountain range and in its rain shadow. As air from the ocean crosses

the mountains, it loses its moisture. As a result, the desert receives 5 inches (127 mm) of rain a year.

Mojave Desert, U.S.A.

OASES

Even in the driest of deserts water flows below ground. In certain places rock strata bring it to the surface as an oasis, which supports palm trees and sometimes crops and other vegetation.

Death Valley (above) With an average annual rainfall of a low 1.5 inches (38 mm), the barren landscape of Death Valley is witness to the extreme aridity of California's Mojave Desert.

Arica (left) With a population of about 200,000, this Chilean city is an important port and tourist center, but must import its water, for its annual rainfall averages only 0.03 inch (0.9 mm) per year.

Living larders (right) In some arid regions of Australia and the United States, honey ants have adapted to survive. Specialized ants called repletes store honey in their abdomens and regurgitate it to others.

FACT FILE

CAM photosynthesis Plants such as cacti and other succulents have adapted to dry climates. Unlike most other plants, they open their stomata at night to exchange gases when the air is cool, and photosynthesize during the day.

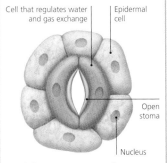

Cell that regulates water and gas exchange

Epidermal cell

Open stoma

Nucleus

At night An open stoma allows carbon dioxide to enter the plant and oxygen to leave. Water also evaporates through the stoma.

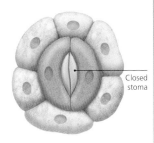

Closed stoma

By day A closed stoma prevents evaporation during the day, conserving water. This is when the plant converts the stored carbon dioxide to food.

ATACAMA CACTUS

Eulychnia iquiquensis is a cactus found in the Atacama Desert. Its swollen structures are not leaves, but stems that store water. The spines deter thirsty animals seeking a drink.

FACT FILE

1. North America, 1246–1305
A drought began in the southwest in 1246, was most intense between 1276 and 1299, and finally ended in 1305. The drought

may have brought about the demise of the prehistoric Anasazi civilization.

North America, 1246–1305

2. England, 1276–1305 This long
period of drought began in 1276 with a very hot, dry summer. Food prices increased and in some years farmers could not produce any hay. The

summers of 1289 and 1294, however, were unusually wet. In 1305 many animals died from starvation.

England, 1276–1305

3. Great Drought of China,
1876–1879 During the deadliest drought in the world's recorded history, no food at all could be grown on 386,000 square miles (one million

km²) of farmland across nine provinces of northern China. An estimated nine million people died.

Great Drought of China, 1876–1879

4. Great Drought, U.S.A. 1930s
Drought affected 150,000 square miles (388,500 km²) of the Great Plains. It triggered the largest migration in the nation's history, putting 2.5

million people on the move as impoverished farming families were forced to abandon their land.

Great Drought, U.S.A. 1930s

HERITAGE WATCH

Farming in droughts Dry-farming techniques have been developed for growing crops under arid conditions. Land left fallow between crops is cultivated to destroy weeds, provide mulch, and store moisture.

Drought

A drought is a prolonged period during which less precipitation occurs than is usual in that place at that time of year. Severe droughts reduce agricultural production, sometimes destroying farm crops. When the rain returns, it may take some time to recharge aquifers, which means that drought conditions continue despite the rain.

Driest continent (below) Severe droughts occur in Australia at roughly 20-year intervals. Many are linked to the El Niño, a large-scale change in pressure distribution across the Pacific Ocean.

LOCALIZED DROUGHT, MARCH–OCTOBER 1954

NOT RELATED TO EL NIÑO, JUNE–DECEMBER 1980

SHORT AND INTENSE: TYPICAL STRONG EL NIÑO, APRIL–FEBRUARY 1983

LONG-LIVED: EL NIÑO RELATED, MARCH–DECEMBER 1995

■ Serious deficiency   ■ Severe deficiency   ■ Lowest on record

Dry river (left) The Amargosa River, in Nevada and California, U.S.A., is often dry. When it flows, it carries water from northwest of Las Vegas into Death Valley, where it disappears below ground.

Lake without water (above) Despite good monsoon rains, drought affected most of the southern states of India in June 2003, completely drying the bed of Osman Sagar Lake on the outskirts of Hyderabad, India.

Disappearing lake Lake Chad, on the edge of the Sahara Desert, was never more than 23 feet (7 m) deep. Agricultural demands and dry weather have reduced the area it covers, but efforts are being made to replenish it.

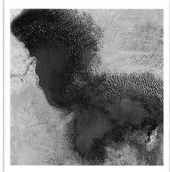

1973 More than 30 years ago, Lake Chad straddled the borders of four countries: Chad, Cameroon, Niger, and Nigeria. The green area surrounding the lake is vegetation growing on its dry bed.

1997 Although it had filled during the 1950s, by 1997 it had shrunk to two small lakes, a state that it had reached only once before, in 1908, when it nearly dried out.

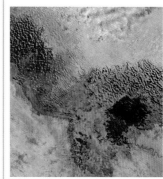

2001 By this date Lake Chad had retreated to a single, small, shallow lake, no more than 5 feet (1.5 m) deep. It may well disappear altogether in the course of this century.

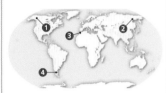

Extreme Cold

Winters are long and dark inside the Arctic and Antarctic circles. Although summer days are long, the sun remains low in the sky and brings little warmth to these regions. Temperatures never rise above freezing and snow accumulates on land to form ice sheets that extend over the sea as ice shelves.

Northern Canada (right) Thick blubber and fur insulate polar bears against the cold, and a short tail and small ears help prevent heat loss.

Antarctica (below) The Antarctic continent is one of Earth's coldest places. This satellite view shows the Transantarctic Mountains, which divide the continent into two unequal parts.

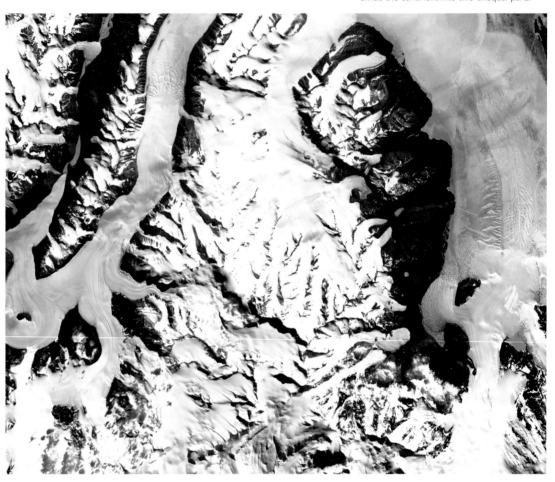

Polar regions Both polar regions are cold because the tilt of Earth's axis means that they receive little solar radiation, but the Antarctic is colder.

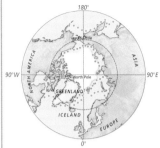

Arctic Basin Despite the Arctic Ocean's permanently frozen center, ocean currents maintain warmer temperatures in the region.

Antarctic The Antarctic is colder because it is a continent, with winter temperatures in the interior ranging from –40°F to –94°F (–40°C to –70°C).

VINSON MASSIF

The extremely harsh and windless conditions of Vinson Massif, Antarctica's highest mountain, rising to 15,257 feet (4,650 m), make its ascent a challenge to climbers.

Siberia Winter transport is by caribou-drawn sleigh in Siberia. On February 7, 1892, the temperature near Verkhoyansk reached a record low of –130°F (–90°C).

FACT FILE

1. Oodnadatta Located in the heart of the desert 628 miles (1,011 km) north of Adelaide, this is the hottest place in Australia. On January 2, 1960, the temperature rose to 123.3°F

 (50.7°C), the highest ever recorded there. It was an important railroad town until the rail was relocated in 1981.

Oodnadatta, South Australia, Australia

2. Dakol This Ethiopian town has the world's highest average temperature, of 94°F (34.4°C). It is located on the Danakil Plain, a depression that in

 places is 380 feet (116 m) below sea level. Air sinking down to it warms by compression as it descends.

Dakol, Ethiopia

3. Death Valley On July 10, 1913, the temperature at Greenland Ranch reached 134°F (56.7°C). Death Valley is the hottest place in North America and has the highest summer average

 temperature of 98°F (36.7°C). It also contains the lowest point in the U.S.A., 282 feet (86 m) below sea level.

Death Valley, U.S.A.

4. Pad Idan Average maximum temperatures are above 100°F (37.8°C) from April to September, but the temperature has been known to reach

 120°F (48.9°C). Though hot in summer, winter temperatures can drop close to freezing at night.

Pad Idan, Pakistan

5. Tirat Tsvi This town in Israel's North District is about 50 miles (80 km) from Jerusalem, near the Jordan border, and is 722 feet (220 m) below sea level. On June 6, 1942, the temperature rose

 to 129°F (53.9°C), the highest ever recorded in Asia. Despite the hot climate, the area is cultivated.

Tirat Tsvi, Israel

Extreme Heat

Equatorial regions are hot, and continental climates far from the ocean experience scorching summers, but the highest temperatures occur in subtropical deserts. In extreme heat, few plants can survive if the temperature of their leaves remains above 113°F (45°C) for more than a short time, while animals die if their body temperature strays far above its normal level.

Highest temperature (right) Al' Aziziyah, a town in Libya surrounded by the Sahara Desert, observed a record high of 136°F (57.8°C) on September 13, 1922.

Surviving the heat (below) The Tuareg are nomads who thrive in the Sahara. Their loose clothing, traditionally dark blue, shades their bodies and traps cool air.

FACT FILE

Coping with heat Animals living in hot deserts seek shelter during the middle of the day, to prevent overheating and to conserve fluid. Some obtain all their water from the food they eat.

Desert travelers Sidewinder snakes, which exist in most sandy deserts, move in loose, hot sand by throwing their bodies in loops.

Gemsbok These antelopes of southern African deserts feed early and late in the day. They can survive for weeks without drinking.

Bilby A marsupial found in Australian deserts, the bilby eats plants and small animals, and does not need to drink, getting all its water from its food.

Close for comfort Camels lie closely side by side to shade one another, and face the sun rather than expose the wide expanse of their flanks to its heat.

1. Europe, July 2006 In this heatwave affecting most of Western Europe, temperatures exceeded 97°F (36°C)

in several countries, breaking records. In the Netherlands 1,000 people died from heat-related conditions.

Europe, July 2006

2. North America, July 2006 Temperatures reached 110°F–115°F (43°C–46°C) in central California,

119°F (48°C) at Los Angeles, 118°F (48°C) at Phoenix, and over 105°F (41°C) in British Columbia.

North America, July 2006

3. North Italy, June 2005 For several days, temperatures remained above 90°F (32°C), exceeding 95°F (35°C) in

Milan, Florence, and Turin, and peaking at 99°F (37°C) in Milan. At least 18 people died from heat and humidity.

Northern Italy, June 2005

4. Arizona, July 2005 Temperatures over 110°F (43°C) for 14 days and up to 100°F (38°C) daily for several weeks

caused more than 20 deaths in Phoenix and more than 20 among illegal immigrants entering U.S.A. from Mexico.

Arizona, U.S.A, July 2005

5. India, May–June 2003 More than 1,900 people died as the temperature rose to 122°F (50°C) in May. The heat

wave lasted longer than usual because the monsoon rains were late, reaching most of India in early June.

India, May–June 2003

Pakistan heat wave The colors on these maps indicate the air temperature before (May, left) and during (June, right) the 2007 heat wave. Dark blue indicates cold cloud- and snow-covered mountainside (–4°F/ 20°C), dark red is 77°F (25°C), and palest pink represents 158°F (70°C).

Heat Waves

A heat wave is a period of at least one day, but more often several days or weeks, when the temperature is higher than usual for the place and time of year. A temperature that would be considered normal in a hotter climate might be termed a heat wave in a cooler one. People can adapt to constant heat, but an unexpected heat wave can make people sick and can even kill.

Cooling off During a heat wave in Pakistan in June 2007, the temperature rose to 124°F (51°C), 30°F (17°C) above the average daytime normal summer temperature, causing people to seek relief in this canal in Lahore.

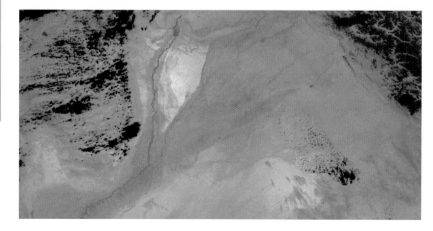

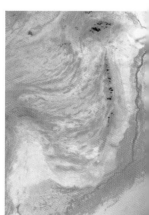

Heat casualties (right) Fruit bats are susceptible to dehydration while roosting in trees by day. Many young bats and their mothers perished during a heat wave in New South Wales, Australia, in 2006.

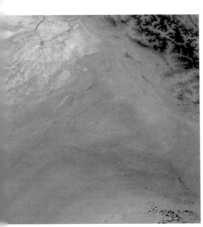

Water replacement Dehydration is a danger in hot weather, when the body keeps cool by sweating. It is important to drink water.

Coping with heat During a July 2006 heat wave in Chongging, China, people had to endure a temperature approaching 104°F (40°C).

HEAT CHART INDEX

Temp.	Relative humidity (%)					
°F (°C)	90%	80%	70%	60%	50%	40%
80 (27)	85	84	82	81	80	79
85 (29)	101	96	92	90	86	84
90 (32)	121	113	105	99	94	90
95 (35)		133	122	113	105	98
100 (38)			142	129	118	109
105 (40)				148	133	121
110 (43)						135

Comfort zone	Risk
80°F–90°F (27°C–32°C)	Fatigue possible with prolonged exposure and physical acitivity
90°F–105°F (32°C–40°C)	Sunstroke, heat cramps and heat exhaustion possible
105°F–130°F (40°C–54°C)	Sunstroke, heat cramps, and heat exhaustion likely; heat stroke possible
130°F (54°C) or greater	Heat stroke highly likely with continued exposure

Actual temperature and humidity are combined to produce a temperature related to physical comfort. For example, 100°F (38°C) feels like 129°F (54°C) in 60 percent humidity.

PERCEPTIONS OF WEATHER

Ancient Greek philosopher Aristotle (384–322 B.C.) taught his followers to seek natural explanations for natural phenomena. He urged them to abandon the belief that winds, storms, floods, and droughts are manufactured by spirits acting on whims that were often seen as malignant. His was an uphill struggle, because until there were instruments to measure atmospheric changes, natural explanations must have seemed implausible. Consequently, in cultures across the world, people attributed each aspect of weather to its own supernatural being and interceded with those beings to produce the weather they desired or needed.

Thunderbird (above) Tribes in northwestern Canada believed that the huge eagle spirit Tseiqami, or Thunderbird, brought thunder with his wings and lightning with his eyes. As the spirit of winter he is celebrated in winter dance ceremonies and is the foe of Qaniqilak (Kumugwe), the spirit of summer.

SKY LORE

In the absence of alternative explanations, it is easy to believe the sky is inhabited by beings who control the rain and wind, and possess the power to reward or punish mortals by making crops flourish or destroying them. Weather gods, some violent and others benign, featured in stories told all over the world.

Most cultures revered gods of thunder and lightning. Among the Kwakwaka'wakw tribes of northwestern Canada, for example, Tseiqami, or Thunderbird, was a giant eagle who ruled the skies in winter. His image adorns many totem poles. On the opposite side of the Atlantic in Europe, the Norse and Germanic Thor, champion of the gods, wore iron gloves and a belt of strength, and wielded a terrible hammer. He would hurl thunderbolts at the heads of those who offended him,

or send a gale to drive their ships onto the rocks. Thursday was named in his honor, being derived from Thor's Day.

Not all weather gods were violent, of course. Lugh, one of the most important Celtic gods, was patron of the harvest festival in Ireland and he may have been a sun god. In Egypt, Satet was depicted as a woman who carried water jars and wore a star on her head. Every year she poured water into the Nile, causing the flood that watered the crops and fertilized the fields with silt.

People did not rely wholly on the whims of the gods. They also observed the sky and learned to recognize signs predicting the weather: a fine day often follows a red sunset, rain early in the morning often clears, and an early mist often heralds fine weather.

The sky has also fascinated artists. J.M.W. Turner (1775–1851), the English landscape painter, was a master at depicting the effects of light, cloud, and mist. Dutch painter Vincent van Gogh (1853–90) was also inspired by the natural formations in the sky in works such as *Landscape Under a Stormy Sky* or *The Starry Night*.

Demonic wind god (right) This 17th-century painting shows Fujin, the god of the wind in the Japanese Shinto religion. One of the oldest of the Shinto gods, he was present when the world was created. He is depicted as a demon wearing a leopard skin and carrying a bag of winds. When he released the winds from his bag at the creation, they cleared away the morning mists, allowing the sun to shine.

Weather gods (left) Ancient Egyptians believed that their weather fortunes were inextricably linked with the moods and actions of their gods. Re-Harakhte, seen here in the center of the solar boat, was a combination of the all-powerful sun god, Ra, and Horus the god of sky, light, and goodness. Every day, the sun god traveled across the sky in the solar boat, creating and nourishing life on Earth.

THROUGH THE AGES

3000 B.C. Ancient Egyptians believed the goddess Satet controlled the annual Nile flood, which began when the star Sirius rose.	**2350 B.C** In Akkadian society, Zu was a god of storms and darkness, as well as an enemy of the great gods.	**1100 B.C.** Zeus was the supreme ruler of Mount Olympus in ancient Greek mythology, but originally he was a weather god.	**800 B.C** In the Etruscan religion, Tinia was a sky god who carried a cluster of lightning bolts and caused storms.	**750 B.C.** For the Germanic tribes, Thor was the god of thunder and champion of the gods. When angered, he blew up gales and hurled thunderbolts.

European folklore (above) "Red sky at night, shepherd's delight," is an old saying that is often true. As the sun sets, dust suspended in dry air scatters the light, making the sky appear red. Dry air produces fine weather and, as weather systems in middle latitudes usually travel from west to east, this will probably arrive by the following morning.

Startling similarities (left) *Diamond Mine* is an example of fractal geometry—computer art created from a huge number of mathematical calculations. Interestingly, fractal geometry is visually similar to naturally occurring phenomena, such as cloud patterns, lightning, and various types of fluid interaction; both feature few straight lines and have many spirals, whorls, and eddies. This picture is similar to satellite images of cloud patterns.

5th century B.C. In ancient Celtic culture, Lugh was a sun god or storm god. His weapon was a rainbow, which he used as a sling.

8th century A.D. The rise of Buddhism in Japan introduced Nikko-Bosatsu as the goddess, or bodhisattva, of sunshine.

8th–11th centuries The Vikings believed the god Njörðr controlled wind and sea, fertile coastal land, sailing, fishing, and seamanship.

13th–16th centuries Tlaloc was the Aztec god of rain, water, and fertility. He wore a net of clouds, carried thunder rattles, and inflicted droughts and floods.

Present Chiuta is the all-powerful god of the Tumbuka people of Malawi. He is believed to control seasonal rains and fertility.

WATER

WATER

OCEANS AND SEAS

Earth, also known as the "Blue Planet," is unique in the solar system because 71 percent of its surface is covered by liquid water. The development of the oceans, in which life probably originated, is a result of our planet's position in relation to the Sun. Earth is far enough away to prevent water from instantly vaporizing, but close enough to prevent most water from instantly freezing solid. Earth's mass generates a gravitational field that retains atmospheric gases, and its rotation ensures that it is warmed more or less evenly. All these factors have permitted the creation of a living water world.

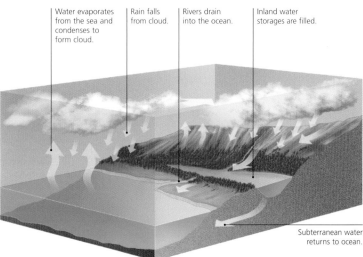

Water evaporates from the sea and condenses to form cloud.

Rain falls from cloud.

Rivers drain into the ocean.

Inland water storages are filled.

Subterranean water returns to ocean.

Water cycle (left) Oceans play a key role in the cycles that move energy and matter around Earth. The hydrological, or water, cycle is a continuous exchange of moisture between the oceans, the atmosphere, and the land. Water vapor falls to the surface as rain or snow. It eventually finds its way back to the sea from rivers, glaciers, or seepage. Seawater evaporates by solar heating, returning to the atmosphere, and the cycle starts again.

Oceanic boundaries (right) The boundary between the Gulf Stream and the surrounding waters is most obvious as it flows north along the Florida coast, U.S.A. The Gulf Stream water is usually warm, clear, and blue because of its lack of nutrients. The water surrounding it is often cloudy and green because it contains phytoplankton.

Wave formation (below) Waves that approach a steeply shelving shore tend to rise much more quickly than those that move over a gently sloping beach. With the rapid rise in wave height, the top of the wave becomes very thin, so that it curls over and topples, creating an air-filled channel, or tube, between the crest and the foot of the wave. Waves of this type provide ideal conditions for surfing enthusiasts around the world.

DISTRIBUTION

We normally think of the world's seawater as being divided into four major basins: the Pacific, Atlantic, Indian, and Arctic, with smaller subdivisions and adjacent marginal seas. However, a world map, particularly when viewed from the South Pole, shows that all the great oceans are interconnected. They exchange water, heat, and organisms, so that oceanographers often refer to Earth's seawater as the "world ocean." The boundaries between the oceans are usually related to the coastlines of the continental landmasses at their margins or by major underwater features such as ocean ridges.

When seen from the South Pole, the Atlantic, Indian, and Pacific oceans appear to be branches of a single system that extends northward from the Southern Ocean and between the major continental landmasses. The Arctic Ocean, however, is nearly landlocked by the Eurasian and North American landmasses. Much of it is covered by permanent ice, within which the geographical North Pole is located. The Southern Ocean has been officially recognized as an ocean since 2000

and its northern boundary has been arbitrarily fixed at 60°S.

The major oceans are subdivided into smaller seas, gulfs, or bays, which are usually defined by obvious geographical boundaries, as are the Mediterranean and Black seas. Some areas are delimited by less obvious features. The Sargasso Sea in the Atlantic Ocean, for example, is defined by the mass of seaweed that accumulates in it. Not all seas are part of the world ocean: some large bodies of salt water, such as the Caspian and Salton seas, are actually salt lakes.

The distribution of land and sea over Earth's surface is not even, and there are marked differences between the hemispheres. More than two-thirds of Earth's land area is found in the Northern Hemisphere, while oceans cover at least 80 percent of the Southern Hemisphere. Many continents and ocean basins are diametrically opposite one another, or antipodal, so that continents are found on the opposite side of the planet from ocean basins. For example, the continent of Antarctica is antipodal to the Arctic Ocean, and the landmass of Europe is antipodal to the southern Pacific Ocean.

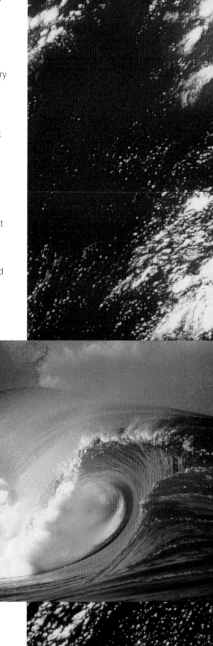

Oceans

The oceans are a complex, three-dimensional environment covering 71 percent of Earth's surface. Huge current systems transport heat and chemicals around Earth, affecting the weather both over the oceans and on the land. Life abounds in the water and on the seafloor, from the seashore down to the deepest trenches.

Ocean basins (below) Ocean basins have a distinct structure. The shelf and slope are continental landmass, but the abyssal plain is formed at the mid-ocean ridge and destroyed at trenches, where there are volcanoes and submarine ridges.

Formation of the oceans Many oceans originated as flooded rift valleys. Rift valleys are formed when two continental plates move apart and magma rises up into the boundary. Oceans develop in three stages, as illustrated below.

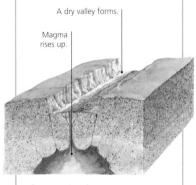

A dry valley forms.

Magma rises up.

Rifting As the plates separate, magma rises up, initially forming a dry valley. The Great Rift Valley in Africa will eventually become an ocean basin.

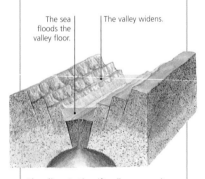

The sea floods the valley floor.

The valley widens.

Flooding As the rift valley grows, its floor eventually breaks through to the sea and is flooded. The Red Sea is a flooded rift valley.

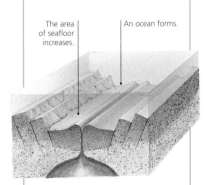

The area of seafloor increases.

An ocean forms.

Spreading The rift valley continues to widen as magma rises up into the mid-ocean ridge, adding up to 0.5 inch (13 cm) of seafloor per year.

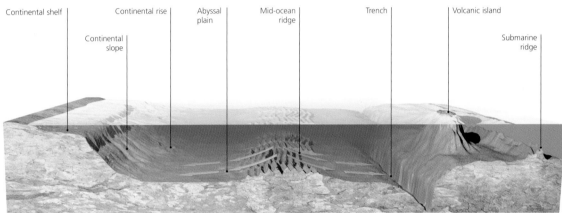

Continental shelf | Continental rise | Abyssal plain | Mid-ocean ridge | Trench | Volcanic island

Continental slope

Submarine ridge

Iceberg (above) At the Poles 12 percent of the ocean is covered by great ice sheets. These break up into pack ice and icebergs, like these in Antarctica.

Temperate zones (right) There are large variations within climatic zones. The Mediterranean Sea, seen here at Amalfi, Italy, is less productive than other temperate zones.

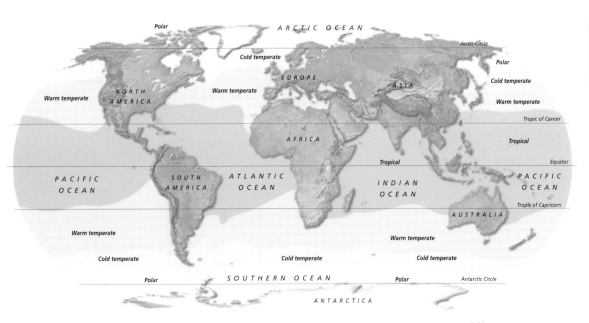

Polar
ARCTIC OCEAN
Arctic Circle
Cold temperate
Polar
EUROPE
Cold temperate
NORTH AMERICA
Warm temperate
ASIA
Warm temperate
Warm temperate
Tropic of Cancer
AFRICA
Tropical
Tropical
Equator
PACIFIC OCEAN
SOUTH AMERICA
ATLANTIC OCEAN
INDIAN OCEAN
PACIFIC OCEAN
Tropic of Capricorn
AUSTRALIA
Warm temperate
Warm temperate
Cold temperate
Cold temperate
Cold temperate
Polar
SOUTHERN OCEAN
Polar
Antarctic Circle
ANTARCTICA

Climatic zones Ocean and geographic climatic zones can differ owing to the effects of ocean currents. For example, cold currents extend up the warm temperate zones of the west coasts of Africa and South America.

Tropical
(over 69°F/20°C)

Warm temperate
(50–69°F/10–20°C)

Cold temperate
(40-50°F/5–10°C)

Polar
(less than 40°F/5°C)

FACT FILE

Distribution of oceans Most of the continents and ocean basins are diametrically opposite each other (antipodal). It follows from this that the continents are found on the opposite side of the planet from the ocean basins.

Northern Hemisphere The Arctic Ocean is almost landlocked by Eurasia and North America. The North Pole lies under the ocean's ice.

Southern Hemisphere The oceans extend northward, like branches of the Southern Ocean, between the major continents.

THE WORLD'S WATER

The oceans contain 97.5 percent of the world's water as seawater. The remaining 2.5 percent is fresh water, which is distributed between groundwater, ice caps, freshwater lakes and rivers, and atmospheric water vapor.

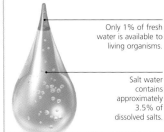

Only 1% of fresh water is available to living organisms.

Salt water contains approximately 3.5% of dissolved salts.

Coral reefs and lagoons Coral reefs and lagoons, as seen here in Moorea, French Polynesia, are found only where average water temperatures are above 70°F (21°C).

Pacific Ocean

The Pacific is the world's largest ocean, covering about one-third of Earth's surface. It is also the deepest, with an average depth of 13,127 feet (4,001 m) and a maximum depth, in the Mariana Trench, of 36,201 feet (11,034 m). At its widest point, it extends for 11,185 miles (18,000 km) and reaches almost halfway around Earth. Sixty percent of the world's fish catch comes from the shallow seas of the North Pacific and from upwelling zones along the coast of South America. Iron and other minerals are extracted from the Pacific, but

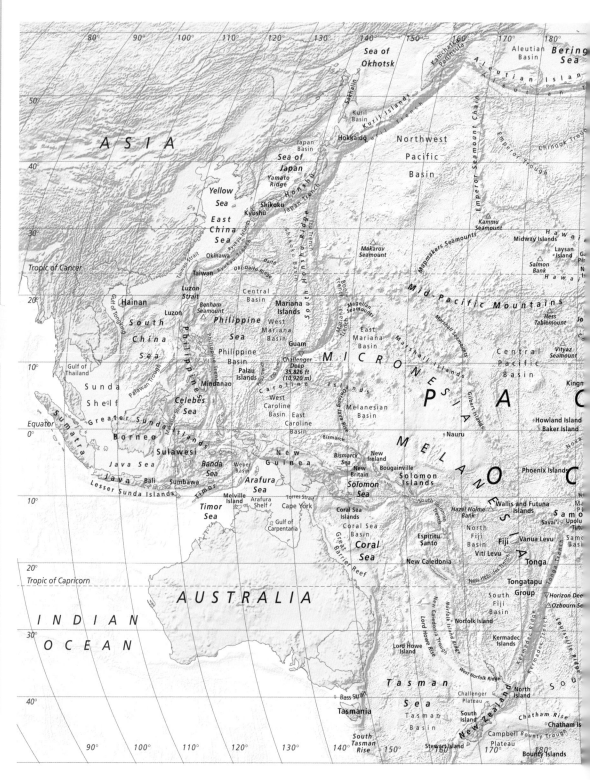

FACT FILE

PACIFIC OCEAN STATISTICS

Area 65.6 million square miles (169.8 million km²)	
Average depth 13,127 feet (4,001 m)	
Maximum depth 36,201 feet (7,455 m)	
Maximum width 11,185 miles (18,000 km)	
Maximum length 8,637 miles (13,900 km)	
Coastline length 84,301 miles (135,663 km)	
Precipitation (per year) 48 inches (121 cm)	
Runoff from adjoining land (per year) 2 inches (6 cm)	
Evaporation (per year) 45 inches (114 cm)	
Ocean water exchange (per year) 5 inches (13 cm)	

NATURAL RESOURCES

- Whales
- Fishing
- Oil
- Gas
- Tourism
- Shellfish
- Precious metals and minerals
- Mining

COMPOSITION

- Rises and ridges 35.9%
- Volcanoes and volcanic ridges 2.5%
- Continental rise 2.7%
- Trenches 2.9%
- Shelves and slopes 13.1%
- Deep ocean floor 43%

SCALE 1:62,500,000
Robinson Projection

0   1500 miles

0   1500 kilometers

there are also enormous fields of metal-rich manganese nodules as yet unexploited on a commercial scale. The recent discovery of oil and gas in the Malay archipelago has stimulated oil and gas prospecting and production right around the rim of the Pacific.

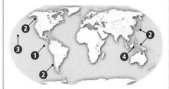
1. Galápagos Islands The more remote islands of the Pacific have been isolated from human activities for a long time, which has produced unique biological communities. Charles Darwin's study of the Galápagos flora and fauna led to his theory of evolution.

Galápagos Islands

2. Andesite Line Between the central Pacific basin and the continental margins lies the Andesite Line. It marks the change in rock type and encloses most of the troughs, submerged volcanic mountains, and oceanic volcanic islands that define the Pacific basin.

Andesite Line

3. Mauna Kea On the island of Hawaii, Mauna Kea is Earth's tallest mountain, measuring 38,184 feet (9,200 m) from base to peak. It rises from the floor of the Pacific Ocean, and is a now-dormant volcano.

Mauna Kea, Hawaii

4. Wallace Line The zoogeographical regions of Asia and Australasia are separated by the Wallace Line. Asiatic species are found to the west of the line, and Australian species to the east. This division was first noticed by English naturalist Alfred Russell Wallace during his travels in the 19th century.

Wallace Line

HERITAGE WATCH

Largest living tortoise The Galapagos giant tortoise is the largest living tortoise species. There are 11 subspecies, all exclusive to the nine islands. One, the Pinta tortoise, seems certain to become extinct on the death of the only known individual, "Lonesome George," if a Pinta female or one with Pinta genes cannot be found.

Atlantic Ocean

The Atlantic is the world's second largest ocean, covering approximately one-fifth of Earth's surface. Its maximum depth is 28,374 feet (8,648 m), in the Puerto Rico Trench. Many of the world's great rivers drain into the Atlantic Ocean: on its north and south American margins, the St. Lawrence, the Mississippi, the Orinoco, the Amazon, and the Río de la Plata; on the west African coasts, the Congo and the Niger; and in the northeast, Atlantic inputs from the Loire, the Rhine, the Elbe, and the great rivers draining into the

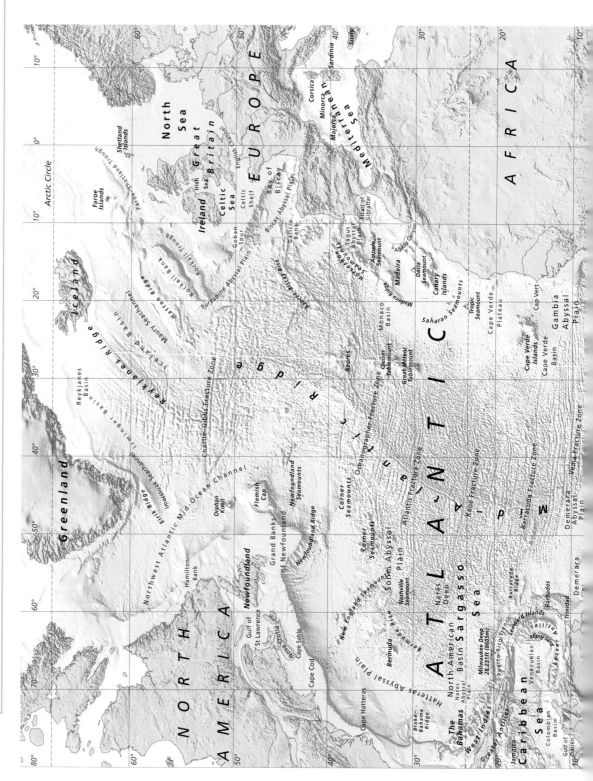

Mediterranean, Black, and Baltic seas. The margins of the Atlantic Ocean are far more stable than those of the Pacific, with broad continental shelves, and in these regions are found major fishing grounds and rich reserves of oil, gas, and other minerals.

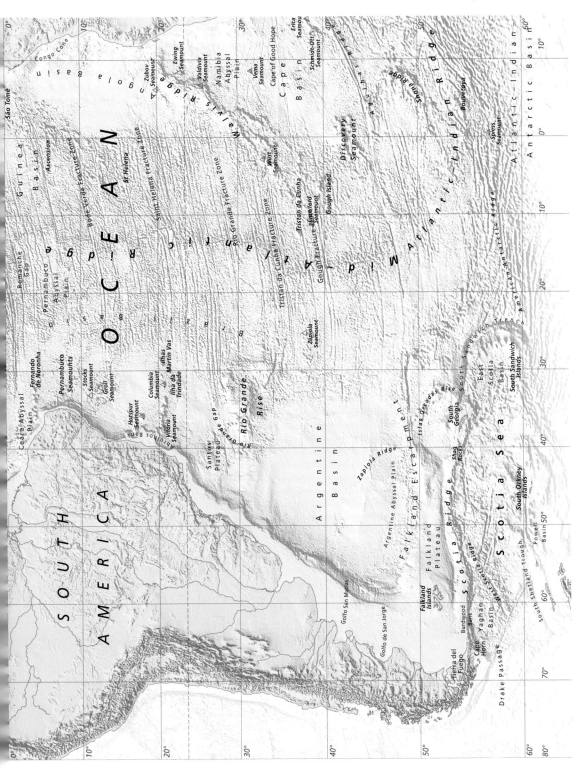

Indian Ocean

The Indian Ocean is the third largest of the world's oceans, occupying just under one-fifth of their total area. Its average depth is 12,645 feet (3,854 m), and at its deepest point, in the Diamantina Trench in the South East Indian Basin, it extends to a depth of

24,460 feet (7,455 m). The current systems in the Indian Ocean are unique in that they change direction twice a year, whereas currents in all other oceans flow in the same direction all year round. In winter monsoon winds force currents to flow toward Africa, and in summer

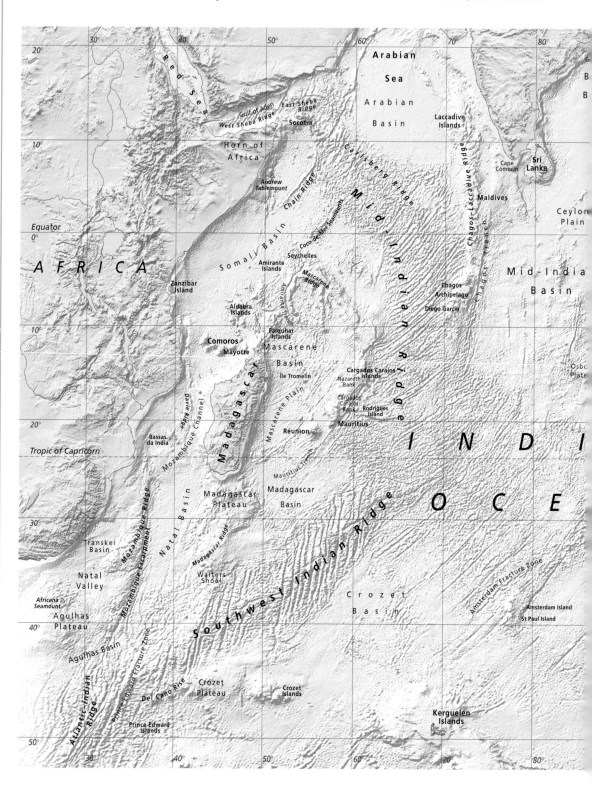

prevailing winds move currents toward India. In addition to the abundant oil and gas fields of the Persian Gulf and off western Australia, the Indian Ocean's mineral resources include manganese nodules and offshore phosphate deposits.

FACT FILE

1. Ganges Fan Otherwise known as the Ganges Cone, the Ganges Fan is the largest submarine deposit of river sediments on Earth. Sediments are carried up to 1,240 miles (2,000 km) from the Ganges Delta, over the floor of the Bay of Bengal, in deep-sea canyons.

Ganges Fan

2. Aceh This was the closest point of land to the epicenter of the massive Indian Ocean earthquake that occurred on December 26, 2004, triggering a tsunami that caused some 230,000 deaths (mostly in Aceh), and great devastation around the Indian Ocean.

Aceh, Indonesia

3. Coelacanth The most famous inhabitant of the Indian Ocean is the coelacanth, a prehistoric fish species thought to be extinct until it was recognized in fish catches in 1938. Further specimens were not found until 1952, when a population was identified around the Comoros islands.

Comoros islands

4. Red Sea A narrow offshoot of the Indian Ocean, the Red Sea is still getting wider because it lies over a spreading ridge. Some of the dense, salty water of the Indian Ocean is initially formed here.

Red Sea

HERITAGE WATCH

Marine turtles at risk Six species of Indian Ocean turtles are particularly endangered from overharvesting (for meat and eggs); destruction of nests and feeding areas; and accidental drowning in fishing nets. The United Nations Environment Programme (UNEP), through the Convention on Migratory Species (CMS), has tried protect these endangered species.

THE ROARING FORTIES

The Southern Ocean is famed for its fierce weather and huge waves. At certain latitudes, waves can travel right around the world.

Southern Ocean

In 2000, the International Hydrographic Organization defined the boundary of the Southern Ocean as the line of latitude 60°S. This closely approximates to the southern edge of the Antarctic Circumpolar Current. This current flows clockwise around Antarctica and effectively isolates the surface waters of the Southern Ocean from those of the oceans to the north. The continental shelf in the Southern Ocean is generally deep and narrow, and is covered by 1,200–1,600 feet (366–488 m) of water, compared with an average shelf depth of 600 feet (183 m) in the Atlantic. It reaches a maximum depth, in the South Sandwich Trench, of 23,736 feet (7,235 m).

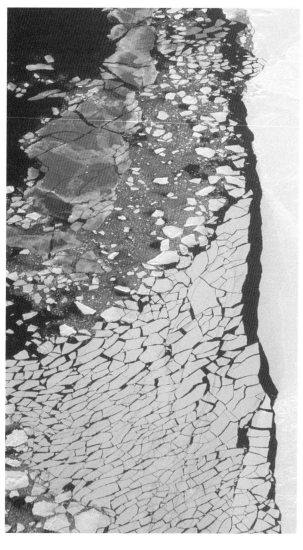

Pack ice, McMurdo Sound Pack ice forms around the Antarctic coastline at the start of the austral winter in March, and gradually thickens and extends until spring. For this period, access is virtually blocked.

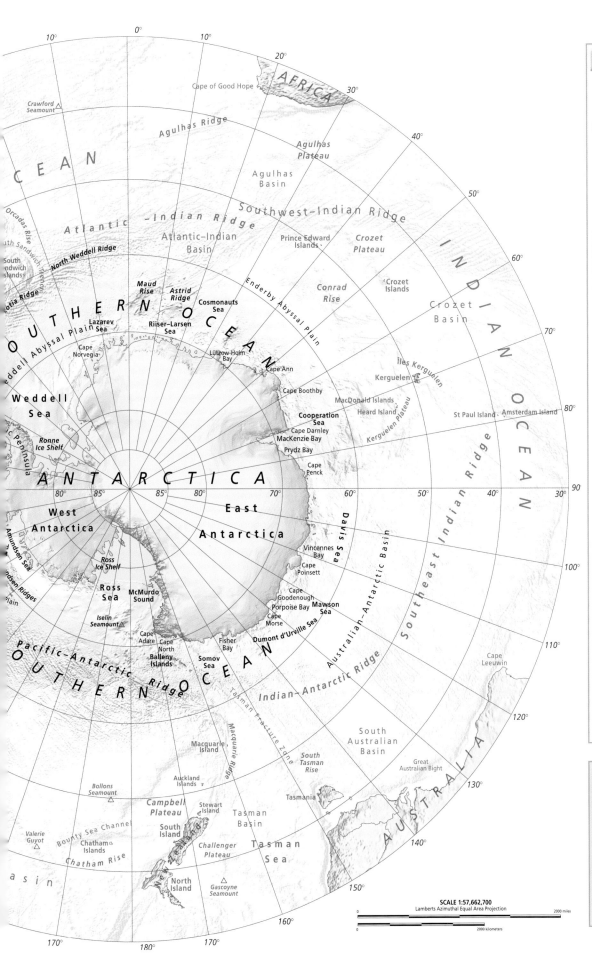

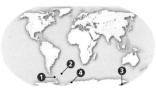
1. Drake Passage At the southern tip of South America, Drake Passage lies between Cape Horn and the South Shetland Islands of Antarctica,

connecting the Atlantic and Pacific oceans. Famed for its bad weather, it is also known for its whales and seabirds.

Drake Passage

2. South Sandwich Trench This is a deep, arc-shaped trench in the South Atlantic Ocean that lies 62 miles (100 km) to the east of the South

Sandwich Islands. Its southern end extends into the Southern Ocean and includes that ocean's maximum depth.

South Sandwich Trench

3. McMurdo Sound Initially an important site for scientific study in the Antarctic, McMurdo Sound has more recently started to attract tourists.

McMurdo Station (U.S.) has been in continuous use and occupation by scientists and staff since 1957–58.

McMurdo Sound

4. Larsen Ice Shelf Situated in the Weddell Sea, the Larsen Ice Shelf consists of three sections called Larsen A (the smallest), Larsen B, and Larsen

C (the largest). Larsen A and C are stable at the present time, but Larsen B disintegrated in February 2002.

Larsen Ice Shelf

HERITAGE WATCH

Threats to marine ecology The Antarctic ozone hole has increased solar ultraviolet radiation. This has reduced the production of vital phytoplankton, which forms the base of complex marine food webs. Illegal and unregulated fishing is threatening fish stocks, and many seabirds are killed by longline fishing methods.

SCALE 1:57,662,700
Lamberts Azimuthal Equal Area Projection

2000 miles

2000 kilometers

NO HIDDEN CONTINENT

In 1958 the nuclear submarine USS *Nautilus* was able to surface through the ice at the North Pole and prove that there was no Arctic continent hidden beneath the ice.

Arctic Ocean

The Arctic Ocean is the smallest and shallowest of the world's oceans and is almost completely surrounded by the landmasses of Eurasia and and North America. The continental shelf in the Arctic Ocean is exceptionally wide, and since the discovery of oil in Alaska in the 1960s it has been the focus of mineral prospecting. The permanent ice of the Arctic Ocean is referred to as polar ice; the ice that forms in winter around its edges is called pack ice; and so-called "fast ice" forms at the margins between the continental shores and joins with the pack ice. In August 2007 the Russian flag was placed on the seabed at the geographic North Pole.

Sinuous curves In this enormous ice sheet near the sea around Baffin Bay, Canada, the tracks of the glaciers are visibly marked by sinuous curves. The white dots in the sea are icebergs that have separated from the glaciers.

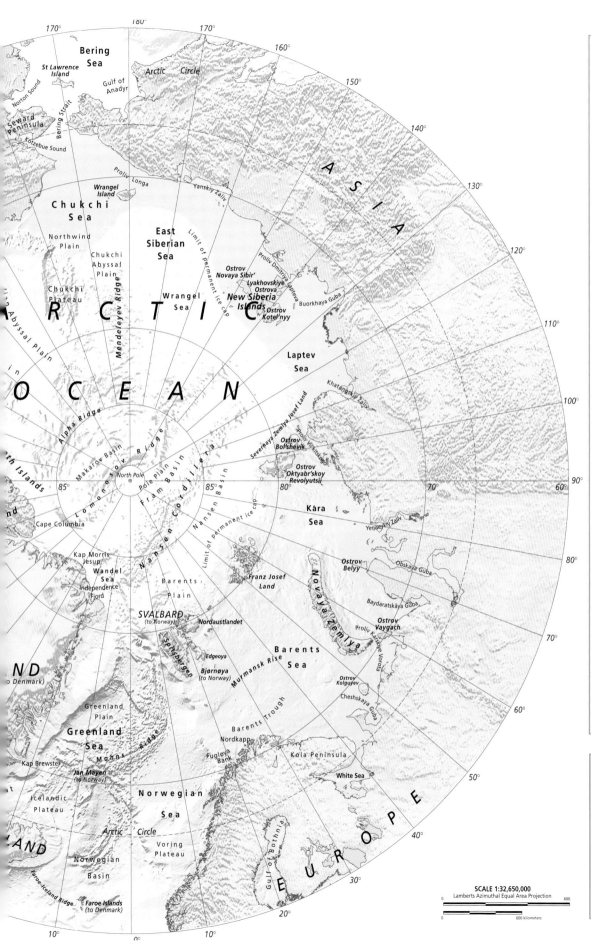

Map Labels

Bering Sea
St Lawrence Island
Gulf of Anadyr
Norton Sound
Seward Peninsula
Kotzebue Sound
Bering Strait
Arctic Circle
Proliv Longa
Wrangel Island
Chukchi Sea
Northwind Plain
Chukchi Abyssal Plain
Chukchi Plateau
Mendeleyev Ridge
East Siberian Sea
Wrangel Sea
Ostrov Novaya Sibir'
Lyakhovskiye Ostrova
New Siberia Islands
Ostrov Kotel'nyy
Yanskiy Zaliv
Proliv Dmitriya Lapteva
Buorkhaya Guba
Limit of permanent ice cap
ASIA
ARCTIC
Abyssal Plain
OCEAN
Alpha Ridge
Makarov Basin
Lomonosov Ridge
North Pole
Pole Plain
Fram Basin
Nansen Cordillera
Nansen Basin
Laptev Sea
Khatangskiy Zaliv
Severnaya Zemlya
Franz Josef Land
Proliv Vil'kitskogo
Ostrov Bol'shevik
Ostrov Oktyabr'skoy Revolyutsii
Kara Sea
Cape Columbia
Kap Morris Jesup
Wandel Sea
Independence Fjord
Nansen Cordillera
Limit of permanent ice cap
Yeniseyskiy Zaliv
Barents Plain
Ostrov Belyy
Obskaya Guba
Islands
Greenland
Cape Brewster
Kap Brewster
SVALBARD (to Norway)
Nordaustlandet
Franz Josef Land
Novaya Zemlya
Baydaratskaya Guba
Spitsbergen
Edgeoya
Bjørnøya (to Norway)
Murmansk Rise
Barents Sea
Proliv Karskiye Vorota
Ostrov Vaygach
Greenland Plain
Greenland Sea
Mohns Ridge
Barents Trough
Nordkapp
Ostrov Kolguyev
Cheshskaya Guba
Kola Peninsula
Kap Brewster
Jan Mayen (to Norway)
Icelandic Plateau
Fugløya Bank
White Sea
Norwegian Sea
Arctic Circle
Voring Plateau
Norwegian Basin
Faroe-Iceland Ridge
Faroe Islands (to Denmark)
Gulf of Bothnia
EUROPE
ND (to Denmark)

SCALE 1:32,650,000
Lamberts Azimuthal Equal Area Projection
0   600
0   600 kilometers

EXPLORING THE OCEANS

Oceanic exploration has a long history. There are records of regular sea trade routes around the Nile Delta in 4000 B.C., while from about 3000 B.C. an increase in the size and speed of ships made longer sea voyages possible. Early explorers had to rely on maps that were more the product of the cartographer's imagination than of geographical knowledge. These early maps had no scale and reflected local cultural perceptions of the world. As navigational ability and instrumentation improved, voyages became longer, and by the 18th century only the inhospitable seas of Antarctica had not been explored.

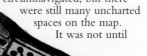

South America (above) In 1499, Italian merchant Amerigo Vespucci and Spanish explorer Alonso de Ojeda explored the north coast of South America. After accounts of Vespucci's voyages were published, the new continent was named "America" after his first name.

Europe (below) Around 300 B.C. Greek navigator Pytheas sailed from the Mediterranean Sea into the Atlantic. He most likely followed the European shoreline to the tip of Brittany. Pytheas also visited other European countries and may have reached the mouth of the Vistula River on the Baltic Sea.

FILLING THE GAPS

In pursuit of knowledge, wealth, and power, humans have always been driven by a desire to find out what lies over the horizon. Today, there is no longer any part of the world map marked "Terra Incognita" (Unknown Territory). Technology has not only made it possible for us to see our own world in its entirety, but has also offered the prospect of exploring other planets.

It has taken millennia of exploration to piece together an accurate map of the world. The first recorded voyages describe the journeys of an Egyptian explorer who traveled to Arabia in 2750 B.C. The Polynesians made long voyages in the Pacific using outrigger canoes and astronomical navigation, and reached Tonga and Samoa by 1000 B.C. In Northern Europe, the Vikings were the first to explore beyond the coastal

waters of Scandinavia. The Norse explorer Leif Erikson landed in North America in A.D. 1001, probably somewhere near the Gulf of St Lawrence, and named the area Vinland. In the east, the Indian Ocean was explored by Arab traders and Chinese trading fleets from about A.D. 200 onwards, culminating in the great voyages of the Chinese admiral Cheng Ho between 1405 and 1433. His fleets visited Africa and may even have reached northern Australia.

In the late 15th century, improvements in ship design and navigational instruments enabled European mariners to undertake long ocean voyages. By the mid-17th century, both coasts of the New World had been visited and the globe had been circumnavigated, but there were still many uncharted spaces on the map.

It was not until the mid-18th century that systematic mapping finally became possible, with the refinement of navigation instruments and, most importantly, the ability to determine longitude at sea using Harrison's chronometer.

The polar voyages and expeditions of the early 20th century filled in the final blank spaces on the map. Today, GPS fixing enables anyone to know their exact position anywhere on Earth to within a few feet.

Ancient boat (above) Most seafaring boats used by the Egyptians were small and simple. They consisted of a rectangular sail and usually one or two rudder oars—similar to the one shown on this 5000-year-old relief. However, records exist describing the construction of a ship that was 170 feet (52 m) long. Later, bigger ships of 70 to 80 tons suited to long voyages became quite common.

Henry the Navigator (right) Prince Henry of Portugal (1394–1460), also known as Henry the Navigator, was responsible for initiating worldwide explorations by Europeans. Although he never went on any voyages himself, he sponsored exploration of the west coast of Africa. He was motivated by curiosity and his interest in testing developments in navigational instruments and ship design.

THROUGH THE AGES

127 B.C. Hipparchus used simple sighting devices to navigate by the stars. He was also able to measure the geographical latitude and time.

1419 Prince Henry of Portugal established the first school of navigation to train mariners and to improve the instruments needed on long voyages.

1642 Dutchman Abel Tasman became the first European to sail to Tasmania, New Zealand, Tonga, and the Fijian islands in a quest to find an "unknown Southland."

1730 Englishman John Hadley invented the octant, enabling sailors to measure the angle between landmarks, or between the horizon and the stars or the sun.

1760 John Harrison presented his H4 marine chronometer to England's Board of Longitude. The instrument was a simple, accurate way to find longitude at sea.

Caravel (above) This type of ship first appeared in the 15th century. The caravel was light, fast, and better able to sail to windward than older ships. It was used by Spanish and Portuguese explorers for long voyages to Africa and the Americas. Two of Columbus' ships from his 1492 voyage, the *Niña* and the *Pinta*, were caravels.

James Cook Exceptional seamanship and navigational skills equipped James Cook (1728–79) to command Royal Navy expeditions. He is mainly remembered for his three voyages to the Pacific Ocean, which took him from the Antarctic ice fields to the Bering Strait, and from North America to Australia and New Zealand.

Oceanic research (below) The first voyage of marine exploration around the world was made by HMS *Challenger* in 1872–76. Scientists made ground-breaking oceanographic observations and collections of specimens that are still being studied, as well as ethnographic records of their shore visits, such as these Fijian dance costumes.

1845 In his Azoic Hypothesis, British naturalist Edward Forbes concluded that the deep sea is lifeless when he observed that the number of animals decreased with depth.

1855 American Matthew Fontaine Maury published *The Physical Geography of the Sea,* which showed sailors how to make best use of ocean currents and winds.

1872–76 HMS *Challenger* carried out the first world-wide oceanographic expedition, under the direction of Charles Wyville-Thompson and John Murray.

1902 The International Council for Exploration of the Seas was founded to work on practical problems and to serve as a forum for all the marine sciences.

1947 Danish anthropologist Thor Heyerdahl set out on his *Kon Tiki* expedition on a balsa wood raft to show how Polynesians spread across the Pacific.

Before

After

HORIZONTAL WATERFALL

The Horizontal Waterfall in King Sound, Western Australia, is produced by tidal movements causing water to bank up against one side of the narrow cliff.

Tides

Since very early times, people have observed the daily rhythm of the sea as it rises and falls along the shore. Tides are generated by the gravitational pulls of the Sun and the Moon on Earth. These forces interact, causing the surface of the oceans to rise and fall—to wash to and fro, as if in a giant bowl. Being closer to Earth, the Moon has more effect on tides than the Sun.

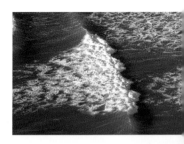

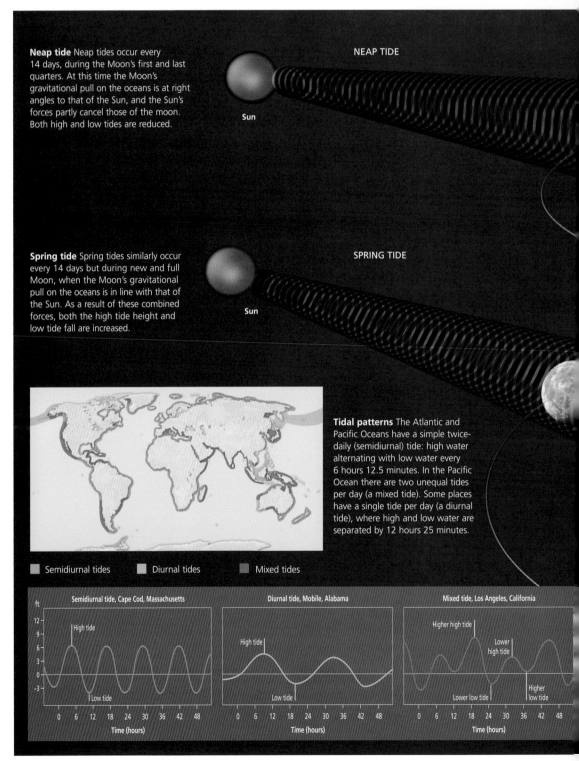

NEAP TIDE

Neap tide Neap tides occur every 14 days, during the Moon's first and last quarters. At this time the Moon's gravitational pull on the oceans is at right angles to that of the Sun, and the Sun's forces partly cancel those of the moon. Both high and low tides are reduced.

Sun

SPRING TIDE

Spring tide Spring tides similarly occur every 14 days but during new and full Moon, when the Moon's gravitational pull on the oceans is in line with that of the Sun. As a result of these combined forces, both the high tide height and low tide fall are increased.

Sun

Tidal patterns The Atlantic and Pacific Oceans have a simple twice-daily (semidiurnal) tide: high water alternating with low water every 6 hours 12.5 minutes. In the Pacific Ocean there are two unequal tides per day (a mixed tide). Some places have a single tide per day (a diurnal tide), where high and low water are separated by 12 hours 25 minutes.

■ Semidiurnal tides   ■ Diurnal tides   ■ Mixed tides

Semidiurnal tide, Cape Cod, Massachusetts

ft
12
9
6
3
0
-3

High tide

Low tide

0 6 12 18 24 30 36 42 48
Time (hours)

Diurnal tide, Mobile, Alabama

High tide

Low tide

0 6 12 18 24 30 36 42 48
Time (hours)

Mixed tide, Los Angeles, California

Higher high tide

Lower high tide

Lower low tide

Higher low tide

0 6 12 18 24 30 36 42 48
Time (hours)

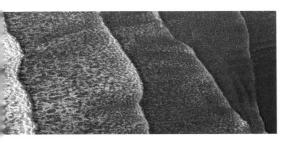

Surf and tides (left) The surf zone moves up and down the shore with the tide. Paradoxically, the tide moves across gently sloping beaches at a faster rate than those with a steeper gradient.

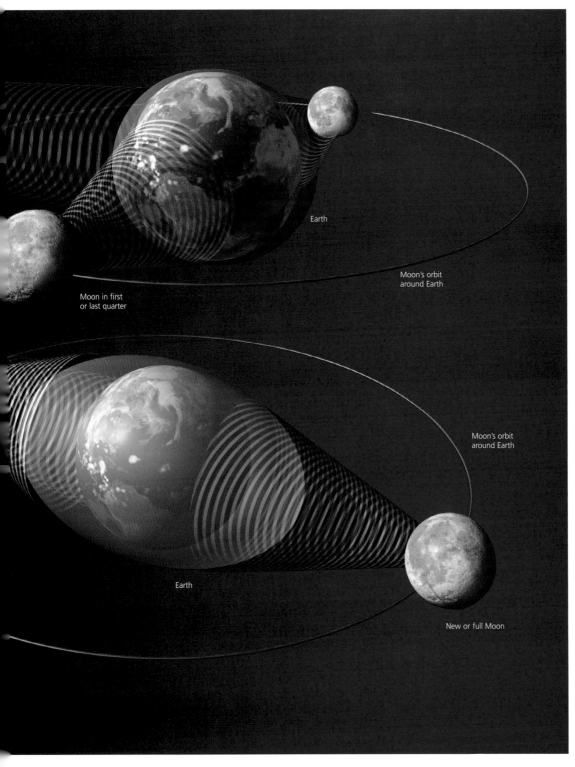

Earth

Moon's orbit around Earth

Moon in first or last quarter

Earth

Moon's orbit around Earth

New or full Moon

FACT FILE

1. Southampton This major port on the south coast of England owes much of its size and prosperity to an unusual tidal pattern. The shape of the coastline gives rise to an extended period of high tide—sometimes incorrectly referred to as a double high. This increases the period during

which large ships can enter and leave the port, allowing it to handle some of the biggest ships in the world.

Southampton, England

2. Bristol Channel Located in southwest England, the Bristol Channel has the world's second biggest tidal range (after the Bay of Fundy): approximately 40 feet (15 m). At certain tide combinations, the rising water funnels up the estuary of the River Severn—part of the Bristol

Channel—giving rise to the Severn Bore, a step-like wave that travels rapidly upstream against the river current.

Bristol Channel, England

3. Moskstraumen The famous tidal current called Moskstraumen, also known as the Lofoten Maelstrom, is the fierce tidal current that flows at speeds of up to 7 miles (11 km) per hour between two of the Lofoten Islands of northern Norway, Moskenesøya in the north and Mosken

in the south. It is one of the world's strongest tidal currents, and its speed creates powerful whirlpools.

Moskstraumen, Norway

4. Mediterranean Sea Tides occur in this sea, but they have a very small range (averaging about an inch, or a few centimeters) and are not usually noticeable. The entrance to the Mediterranean at Gibraltar is too narrow to allow large movements of water, but there is a

tidal oscillation, with water flowing from the East Mediter-ranean to the West and back again.

Mediterranean Sea

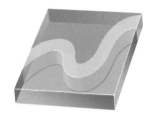

1 The Gulf Stream develops meanders as it flows. These meanders may "bud off" as either cold-water or warm-water core eddies.

2 North-closing meanders trap warm Sargasso Sea water and rotate clockwise; south-closing meanders are cold and rotate anticlockwise.

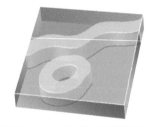

3 Eddies can be up to 200 miles (320 km) across and can last for up to three years before merging again with the main current.

GULF STREAM FLOW

Warm Gulf Stream water, shown orange and yellow in this satellite image, flows at a rate of 1 billion cubic feet (30 million m³) per second, 300 times the Amazon outflow. It flows from the Gulf of Mexico northward along the east coast of North America at 4 miles per hour (6.5 km/h).

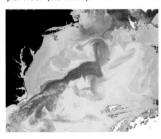

Deep Ocean Currents

Deep ocean currents are not affected by surface winds. They are driven by changes in the density of water produced by variations in water temperature and salinity. Because of this, these currents are usually called the thermohaline circulation, a term that refers to the movement of huge water masses that do not mix easily when they come into contact and can take centuries to complete their circulation around the global ocean.

Thermohaline circulation (right) Seawater becomes denser when it is cold. At high latitudes, cold water sinks and travels slowly away from the Poles as deep currents. These eventually rise and return in the upper layers as countercurrents.

World currents (below) The world's oceans are linked by a deep-water circulation that is often referred to as the Great Ocean Conveyor. This slow-moving system of deep currents takes approximately 1,000 years to complete a single cycle.

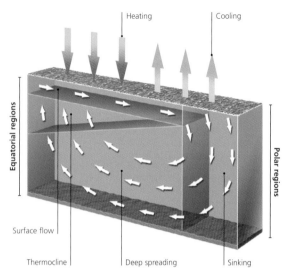

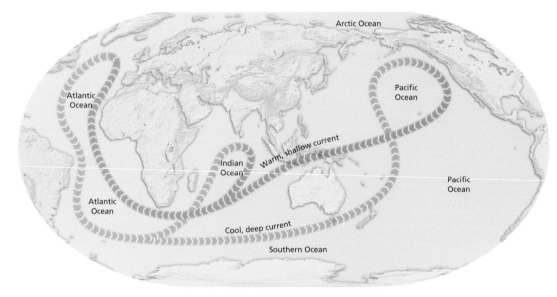

Little Ice Age (left) The Little Ice Age lasted from the 16th to the mid-19th centuries. It is thought have been caused by changes in the deep ocean circulation that caused the oceans to remove more heat from the atmosphere.

Benguela Current (right) The arid Skeleton Coast and Namib Desert of Namibia, in southwest Africa, is an example of the influence of ocean currents on climate. The adjacent cold Benguela current creates cold, dry air at the coast, so little moisture is carried inland.

1. North Atlantic Deep Water North Atlantic Deep Water (NADW) is found in the Atlantic at depths between 3,300 and 13,120 feet (1,000 and 4,000 m). It can be traced from there

into most other ocean basins. The NADW formation process is the driving force of the Great Ocean Conveyor.

North Atlantic Deep Water

2. Antarctic Bottom Water Between 706 and 1,766 million cubic feet (20 million and 50 million m³) of Antarctic Bottom Water are formed every second, mainly in the Weddell

and Ross seas but also at other shelf locations. Antarctic Bottom Water is the densest water in the oceans.

Antarctic Bottom Water

3. Two routes North Atlantic Deep Water flows southward from its point of formation and eventually flows through the Antarctic Ocean Basin and

up around South Africa. One part then flows into the Indian Ocean, the other past Australia into the Pacific.

Routes of North Atlantic Deep Water

TURTLE MIGRATION

Loggerhead turtles from the Caribbean and the Gulf of Mexico are known to migrate out into the Atlantic and to move north in the Gulf Stream. Most are carried south again west of Ireland, at the point where the North Atlantic Drift divides, but some are carried north and end up stranded on the Atlantic coasts of Europe.

A satellite transmitter tracks migration

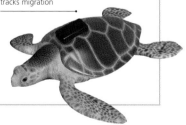

Surface winds and currents Wind-driven currents at the surface of the ocean move at about 2.5–3.0 percent of the wind speed blowing over them. The speed of the water rapidly diminishes in the first 3 feet (1 m) below the surface.

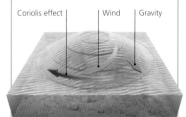

Coriolis effect | Wind | Gravity

Shifting currents Gravity and the Coriolis force deflect surface currents to the right of the wind above the equator and to the left below it.

Atlantic gyres In each hemisphere, the currents flowing east and west interact, creating large circular currents, called gyres, in subtropical latitudes.

WEDDELL SEA CURRENTS

This false-color radar image of the Weddell Sea was taken from the space shuttle *Endeavour*. It shows two large eddies at the northern edge of the pack ice.

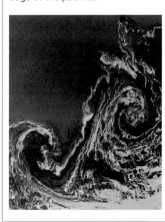

Boundary Currents

The combined effect of wind patterns and the Coriolis force produces gyres (circular currents) in the oceans that move clockwise in the Northern Hemisphere and counterclockwise in the Southern Hemisphere. Earth's rotation from west to east pushes water to the western sides of ocean basins. The excess water is deflected north or south by the coastline as a continental boundary current. Western boundary currents are narrow, deep, and fast-flowing. Eastern boundary currents occur where the edge of the gyre touches a continent's western coast, and are broad, shallow, and slow-moving.

Surface current systems (right) Surface current systems follow the wind. Either side of the equator, the north and south equatorial currents flow westward, following the trade winds, and are separated by an eastward-flowing countercurrent that coincides with the region of relatively calm winds known as the doldrums.

■ Above 86°F (30°C)	■ 50–59°F (10–15°C)	∘∘∘∘ Summer pack ice limit
■ 77–86°F (25–30°C)	■ 41–50°F (5–10°C)	□□□□ Winter pack ice limit
■ 68–77°F (20–25°C)	■ Under 41°F (5°C)	→ Warm current
■ 59–68°F (15–20°C)		→ Cool current

Phytoplankton bloom (below) This satellite image shows a huge mass of phytoplankton bloom (blue-white) off the Irish coast. This phenomenon is often associated with ocean fronts—regions where water masses of different temperatures meet. An upwelling of deep water, which is rich in nutrients, stimulates the growth of phytoplankton on nearby surface water.

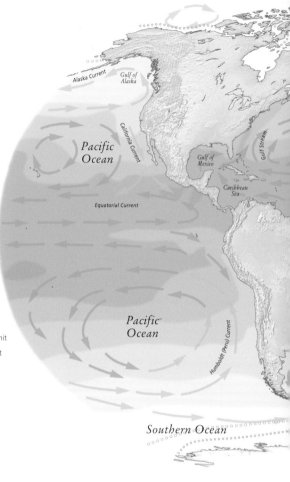

Alaska Current | Gulf of Alaska

Pacific Ocean

California Current

Gulf of Mexico

Gulf Stream

Caribbean Sea

Equatorial Current

Pacific Ocean

Humboldt (Peru) Current

Southern Ocean

Upwelling and downwelling (below) Upwelling occurs where prevailing winds push warm coastal water away from the coast in gyres or convergence zones, or where a deep current is deflected upward. Downwelling occurs where a unit of surface water becomes colder or more saline than the surrounding water; it then sinks or is drawn down.

Major fisheries are associated with the nutrient-rich waters of coastal upwelling zones. The best known is the Peruvian anchovy fishery.

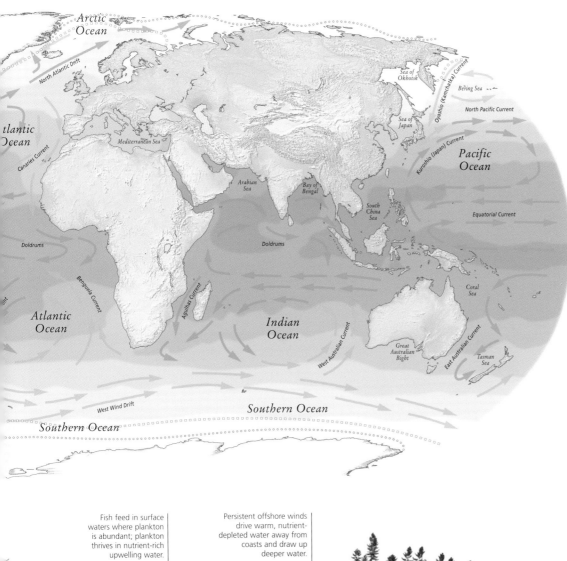

Convergence zones Where two currents with opposite internal circulations converge, deep water is drawn up, causing intense phytoplankton bloom at the surface. Some of this is drawn down at the convergence by downwelling.

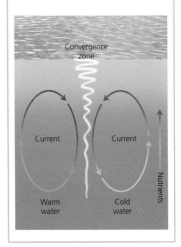

NUTRIENT-RICH RIVERS

These eddies off the coast of northwest America are created by river water flowing into the Pacific. The river water is rich in nutrients, stimulating the growth of phytoplankton. The bloom can be detected by satellite imaging.

Fish feed in surface waters where plankton is abundant; plankton thrives in nutrient-rich upwelling water.

Persistent offshore winds drive warm, nutrient-depleted water away from coasts and draw up deeper water.

Upwelling water will have accumulated phosphate and nitrate, minerals that are in limited supply at the surface.

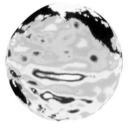
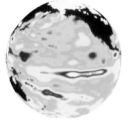

El Niño and La Niña

Trade winds normally drag the warm surface water of the Pacific Ocean westward, away from the west coast of South America, allowing the cold, deep, nutrient-rich water of the Peru Current to reach the surface. Every 3–8 years, however, the winds stop and the currents are reversed. This initiates a period of unusually warm ocean temperatures in the equatorial Pacific, called El Niño, that causes extreme weather conditions globally. It is usually followed by a cool La Niña.

Coral bleaching (right) This bleached coral on the Great Barrier Reef, in Queensland, Australia, was caused by high water temperatures. These resulted from an unusually hot summer linked to an El Niño event.

Peru (below) Following the 1997–98 El Niño event, there were periods of prolonged and exceptionally heavy rainfall over parts of South America. This caused destructive floods, such the one in Peru shown here.

NORMAL CONDITIONS

EL NIÑO CONDITIONS

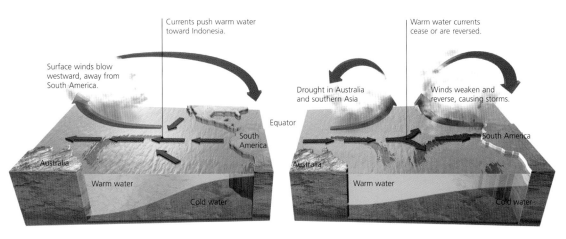

Currents push warm water toward Indonesia.

Surface winds blow westward, away from South America.

Equator

South America

Australia

Warm water

Cold water

Warm water currents cease or are reversed.

Drought in Australia and southern Asia

Winds weaken and reverse, causing storms.

South America

Australia

Warm water

Cold water

From normal to El Niño (above) An El Niño begins when air pressure rises over the Indian Ocean and falls over the Pacific. The trade winds weaken, and coastal upwelling of the Peru Current ceases.

Drought and El Niño (below) The Australian drought that began in 2003 was intensified by the 2006–07 El Niño. Rainfall returned with the onset of La Niña conditions in mid-2007.

FACT FILE

1. Brazil In El Niño years, northern Brazil experiences unusually dry conditions, particularly during the usual rainy season, which normally extends from January to June. Strong El Niños produce severe droughts, which not only cause crop failure, but

have also been linked to epidemics of leishmaniasis, a parasitic infection transmitted by a type of sandfly.

Brazil

2. Southeast Asia The El Niño of 1996–97 caused severe droughts and forest fires across Southeast Asia. Vast areas burned for months, blanketing much of the region in thick haze and

destroying regional economies. The fires also destroyed the habitat of endangered species such as orangutans.

Australia and Southeast Asia

3. China El Niño events have been linked to more frequent warm winters in China, resulting in more rain in the southern parts, and severe drought in

northern China. Some evidence also links El Niño to cool summers in northeastern China and fewer typhoons.

China

4. Mexico In El Niño years, fewer tropical storms affect Mexico, but those that occur are often particularly intense. Higher-than-usual water

temperatures off the Mexican coast in El Niño years can help maintain the strength of storms or intensify them.

Mexico

5. The Americas El Niño has major effects on the proliferation of wildlife along the western coastlines of the Americas. The loss of upwelling off Peru causes a collapse in fish stocks

such as anchovy, salmon, and tuna. This is the basic food supply for seabird colonies, seals, and sea lions.

The Americas

Tube wave Plunging waves like this one rise up quickly as they approach a steeply sloping shore, often forming a "tube" before spilling over.

Back splash spray wave Less steeply sloping shores produce less dramatic, spilling waves, where the crest slides down the face of the advancing wave.

WAVE HEIGHTS

The biggest surface waves are tsunamis, which are created by undersea earthquakes. There are also "rogue" or "killer" waves. It was earlier thought that these had a maximum height of 60 feet (18 m), but a wave of 112 feet (34 m) has been reliably observed.

Biggest tsunami wave
1,720 feet (524 m) high

Biggest storm wave
100 feet
(31 m) high

Average wave
6.6 feet
(2 m) high

Waves

Waves are generated by wind blowing over the surface of the sea. They are not a ridge of water traveling on the sea's surface, but rather show where the wind's energy has been converted into circular movements of groups of water molecules. Tidal and other forces also produce internal waves within the ocean.

Surface waves Surface waves are created by the wind or geologic effects and range in size from small ripples to huge tsunamis.

Internal waves Internal waves occur along the boundary of (but below) the surface layer of water, and move along the interface between water masses of different densities.

Size and power These waves breaking on the shores of Baja California, Mexico, owe their size and power to the distance over which they are generated, called "fetch." In this part of the eastern Pacific, waves can travel distances of up to 7,000 miles (11,000 km).

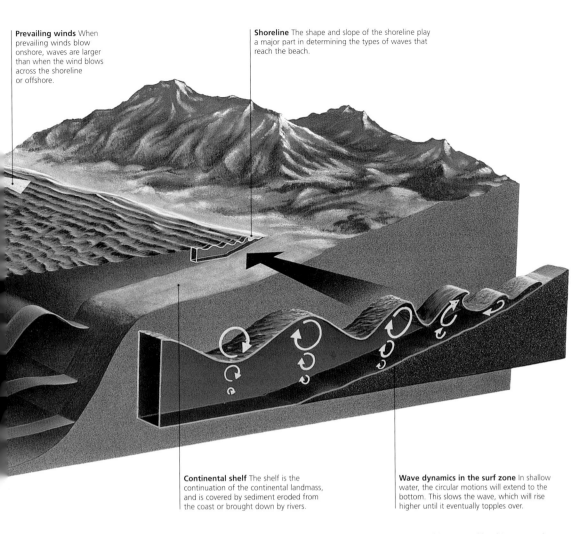

Prevailing winds When prevailing winds blow onshore, waves are larger than when the wind blows across the shoreline or offshore.

Shoreline The shape and slope of the shoreline play a major part in determining the types of waves that reach the beach.

Continental shelf The shelf is the continuation of the continental landmass, and is covered by sediment eroded from the coast or brought down by rivers.

Wave dynamics in the surf zone In shallow water, the circular motions will extend to the bottom. This slows the wave, which will rise higher until it eventually topples over.

Breakers The energy contained in a wave like this one on the Hawaiian island of Maui is dissipated when it breaks on the shore. High-energy breakers stir up sediments, erode rocks, and create bubbles that help to oxygenate the water.

FACT FILE

The filtering shore Some water from waves advancing up a sand or shingle shore percolates into the beach and flows back as the wave retreats, being filtered in the process. Some water remains trapped in the beach.

ADVANCING WAVE

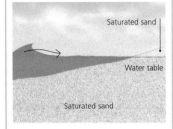

Saturated sand

Water table

Saturated sand

HIGH WAVE

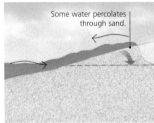

Some water percolates through sand.

RECEDING WAVE

Surface wash slides back to next oncoming wave.

Water filters back.

PARTS OF A WAVE

Wavelength is the distance between crests. Height is the vertical distance between trough and crest. Amplitude is half the wave height. Steepness is the angle between the bottom of the trough and the crest top.

Crest

Wavelength

Amplitude

Steepness

Height

Trough

Seafloor

Shaping the Coastline

The world's coastlines are shaped by the immense power of waves and currents. Waves exert pressures of up 100 pounds per square inch (689 kPa) slowly wearing away the hardest rock, and powerful currents can sweep away beaches. The same forces, however, can also throw up new shingle bars in a few days or slowly create huge coastal mudflats.

Coasts Primary coasts are formed by terrestrial processes, whereas secondary coasts are the result of marine processes. Sandbars and spits are large-scale features of secondary coasts and are formed in three major stages.

1 Longshore drift currents are slowed where they meet a headland. This causes sediments to accumulate on the downstream side, forming a spit.

2 A single spit can close off a bay, but storms or a strong river flow will open up a passage to the sea.

3 Double spits are formed when two dominant wind directions produce longshore drift in two opposing directions along a coast.

Rapid erosion Barrier islands are vulnerable to rapid erosion. Storm waves wash over the top of low islands like this one in Virginia, U.S.A., and heavy rainfall can swell rivers that flood the lagoon and break through the dune.

Sea stacks (right) The Twelve Apostles on the coast of Victoria, Australia, are geologically short-lived features. These distinctive sea stacks will eventually succumb to the power of the sea and become sand on the nearby beach.

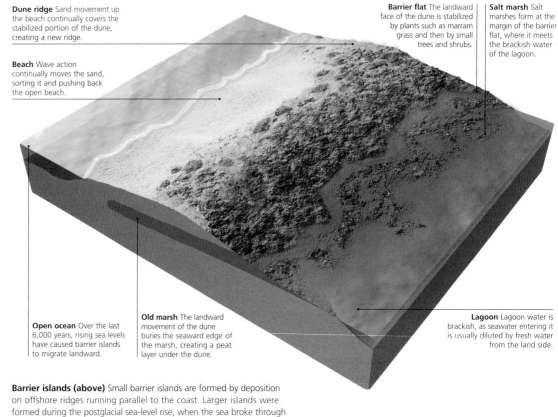

Dune ridge Sand movement up the beach continually covers the stabilized portion of the dune, creating a new ridge.

Beach Wave action continually moves the sand, sorting it and pushing back the open beach.

Barrier flat The landward face of the dune is stabilized by plants such as marram grass and then by small trees and shrubs.

Salt marsh Salt marshes form at the margin of the barrier flat, where it meets the brackish water of the lagoon.

Open ocean Over the last 6,000 years, rising sea levels have caused barrier islands to migrate landward.

Old marsh The landward movement of the dune buries the seaward edge of the marsh, creating a peat layer under the dune.

Lagoon Lagoon water is brackish, as seawater entering it is usually diluted by fresh water from the land side.

Barrier islands (above) Small barrier islands are formed by deposition on offshore ridges running parallel to the coast. Larger islands were formed during the postglacial sea-level rise, when the sea broke through coastal dunes, flooding the land behind.

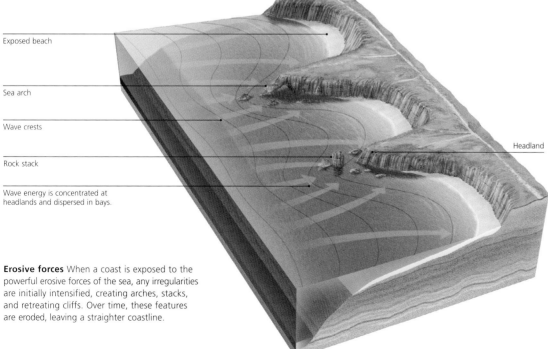

Exposed beach

Sea arch

Wave crests

Rock stack

Wave energy is concentrated at
headlands and dispersed in bays.

Headland

Erosive forces When a coast is exposed to the
powerful erosive forces of the sea, any irregularities
are initially intensified, creating arches, stacks,
and retreating cliffs. Over time, these features
are eroded, leaving a straighter coastline.

FACT FILE

1. Perce Rock This limestone
monolith off the Gaspe Peninsula,
Quebec, Canada, has become isolated
by erosion at its landward end,
although it is still accessible from
the shore at low tide. The rock gets

its name from the
numerous holes
that pierce it—the
largest of these is
98 feet (30 m)
in diameter.

Perce Rock, Quebec, Canada

2. Sea Lions Caves These caves on
the coast of Oregon, U.S.A., were
formed about 25 million years ago.

The main cavern
is the world's largest
sea cave—as high
as a 12-storey
building and as long
as a football field.

Sea Lions Caves, Oregon, U.S.A.

3. Vertical cliff Enniberg (also called
Cape Enniberg), located on the
island of Viðoy, is the northernmost
point of the Faroe Islands. At
2,473 feet (754 m) from sea level
to the top, it is the highest vertical

cliff above sea in
the world. It is
also home to the
most important
seabird colony
in the Faroes.

Enniberg, Faroe Islands

4. Cliffs of Etretat With their needle
and arch formation, these chalk cliffs
at Etretat, on the Normandy coast
of France, are a popular tourist

destination. They
were made world
famous by the
Impressionist painter
Monet, who painted
them in 1883.

Cliffs of Etretat, France

5. Nahant This place in Massachusetts,
U.S.A. gets its name from the Native
American description of the site as
"almost an island." It is an example

of a tombolo—a
spit created by
longshore drift that
connects an island
to the mainland,
or two islands.

Nahant, Massachusetts, U.S.A.

Northern Hemisphere Seas

The majority of the world's landmasses lie within the Northern Hemisphere, and as a consequence there are many small, semi-enclosed, shallow seas on the continental shelves and associated with island arcs at subduction zones along continental margins. These seas are found in all climate zones, from the tropics to polar regions.

Fjords (right) At high latitudes, coastlines are dominated by fjords, as can be seen in this satellite image of the West Fjords peninsulas of Iceland. In fjordic valley bottoms, there is very little flat land suitable for human settlement.

PHILIPPINE SEA

Area 1,776,230 square miles (4,600,000 km²)
Average depth 19,700 feet (6,000 m)
Greatest known depth 34,578 feet (10,539 m)
Length 1,800 miles (3,000 km)
Width 1,200 miles (2,000 km)
Volume 6,622,513 cubic miles (27,600,000 km³)

0   1000 miles
0   1000 km

BAY OF BENGAL

Area 839,000 square miles (2,173,000 km²)
Average depth 8,500 feet (2,600 m)
Greatest known depth 15,400 feet (4,694 m)
Length 1,056 miles (1,700 km)
Width 994 miles (1,600 km)
Volume 1,355,648 cubic miles (5,649,800 km³)

0   500 miles
0   500 km

BERING SEA

Area 884,900 square miles (2,291,900 km²)
Average depth 5,075 feet (1,547 m)
Greatest known depth 15,659 feet (4,773 m)
Length 1,490 miles (2,397 km)
Width 990 miles (1,593 km)
Volume 850,746 cubic miles (3,545,569 km³)

0   1000 miles
0   1000 km

CARIBBEAN SEA

Area 1,049,500 square miles (2,718,200 km²)
Average depth 8,685 feet (2,647 m)
Greatest known depth 25,218 feet (7,686 m)
Length 1,678 miles (2,700 km)
Width 360–840 miles (600–1,400 km)
Volume 1,726,430 cubic miles (7,195,075 km³)

0   500 miles
0   500 km

EAST SIBERIAN SEA

Area 361,000 square miles (936,000 km²)
Average depth 328 feet (100 m)
Greatest known depth 510 feet (155 m)
Length 777 miles (1,250 km)
Width 497 miles (800 m)
Volume 22,459 cubic miles (93,600 m³)

0   500 miles
0   500 km

NORWEGIAN SEA

Area 328,220 square miles (850,000) m²)
Average depth 5,254 feet (1,600 m)
Greatest known depth 13,020 feet (3,970 m)
Length 870 miles (1,400 km)
Width 684 miles (1,100 km)
Volume 326,327 cubic miles (1,360,000 km³)

0   500 miles
0   500 km

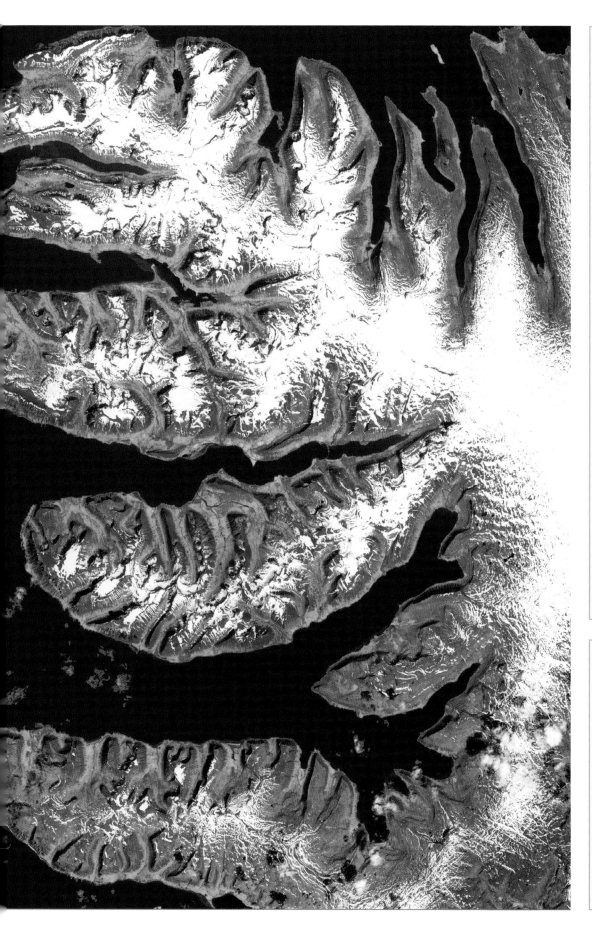

1. Bay of Bengal This bay forms the northeastern part of the Indian Ocean. Its seafloor is covered by the sediments of the Ganges Fan, and its currents flow clockwise between January and October and counterclockwise for the rest of the year— changes associated with the monsoon season.

Bay of Bengal, Indian Ocean

2. Caribbean Sea Some 9 percent of the world's coral reefs, covering about 20,000 square miles (50,000 km²), are found in the Caribbean. They are at risk from periods of unusually warm water temperatures and increasing tourism. Remnants of once-extensive mangroves survive along the coast.

Caribbean Sea

3. Norwegian Sea Part of the North Atlantic, this sea is separated from the main ocean by a submarine ridge that runs between Iceland and the Faroes, and from the Arctic Ocean by the Jan Mayern Submarine Ridge. Warmed by the Norwegian current, a branch of the North Atlantic Drift, it is ice-free.

Norwegian Sea

NORTHERN SEA RESOURCES

The concentration of inhabited landmasses in the Northern Hemisphere has meant that marine fisheries and mineral resources have been exploited for centuries.

RESOURCES

Philippine Sea Fisheries, with some 2,000 species of fish

Bay of Bengal Predominantly prawns

Bering Sea More than 300 species of fish, 25 of which are exploited commercially (including salmon, herring, cod, and halibut)

Caribbean Sea Spiny lobster

East Siberian Sea Thought to have immense hydrocarbon and gas reserves

Norwegian Sea Major fisheries and gas

FACT FILE

1. Greenland Sea Lying south of the Arctic Basin proper, this sea is an arm of the Arctic Ocean and the Arctic's main outlet to the Atlantic. Drifting ice in the northern part makes it

hazardous to shipping, but despite this its rich fishing grounds are worked, mainly for cod, halibut, and herring.

Greenland Sea

2. Kara Sea North of Siberia, the Kara Sea supports a range of wildlife, including bearded seals, walruses, and narwhals. Polar bears hunt for seals on the frozen edge of the sea. Fish,

such as Arctic cod, flat-fish, and smelt, are abundant, but the sea is navigable for only two months of the year.

Kara Sea

3. Baffin Bay This bay lies northwest of Greenland, connecting to the Atlantic through Davis Strait and to the Arctic through several narrow channels of Nares Strait. It is home

to one of the main populations of Beluga whales (also called white whales), which feed on small fish and crustaceans.

Baffin Bay

NORTHERN SEA WHALES

The most abundant of the large cetaceans, beluga whales are threatened by pollution and whaling by indigenous peoples. Gray whales migrate 12,000 miles (1,900 km) between feeding grounds in the Bering and Chukchi seas, to the warm waters of Mexico's Baja Peninsula to give birth.

Beluga whale

Gray whale

Northern Hemisphere Seas continued

The marginal seas of the Arctic Ocean lie on its exceptionally wide continental shelf—it has the widest shelf of all the oceans, covering nearly 50 percent of the total seafloor. These shallow seas are frozen for most of the year. They have been the focus of mineral prospecting since the 1960s discovery of oil in Alaska.

Qaanaaq, Greenland (right) Situated on the northwestern coast of Greenland, Qaanaaq is the world's most northerly town. Most of Greenland's population live on the southwestern coast, where the sea is ice-free throughout the year.

GREENLAND SEA

Area 353,320 square miles (915,000 km²)
Average depth 4,750 feet (1,450 m)
Greatest known depth 16,000 feet (4,800 m)
Length 808 miles (1,300 km)
Width 621 miles (1,000 km)
Volume 318,349 cubic miles (1,326,750 km³)

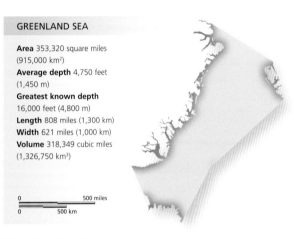

0 — 500 miles
0 — 500 km

KARA SEA

Area 340,000 square miles (880,000 km²)
Average depth 417 feet (127 m)
Greatest known depth 2,034 feet (620 m)
Length 932 miles (1,500 km)
Width 559 miles (900 km)
Volume 26,816 cubic miles (111,760 km³)

0 — 500 miles
0 — 500 km

BAFFIN BAY

Area 266,000 square miles (689,000 km²)
Average depth 6,234 feet (1,900 m)
Greatest known depth 7,000 feet (2,100 m)
Length 900 miles (1,450 km)
Width 68–400 miles (110–650 km)
Volume 314,113 cubic miles (1,309,100 km³)

0 — 500 miles
0 — 500 km

LAPTEV SEA

Area 250,900 square miles (649,800 km²)
Average depth 1,896 feet (578 m)
Greatest known depth 9,774 feet (2,980 m)
Length 528 miles (850 km)
Width 497 miles (800 km)
Volume 90,120 cubic miles (375,584 km³)

0 — 500 miles
0 — 500 km

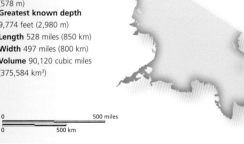

CHUKCHI SEA

Area 225,000 square miles (582,000 km²)
Average depth 253 feet (77 m)
Greatest known depth 7,218 feet (2,200 m)
Length 559 miles (900 km)
Width 435 miles (700 km)
Volume 10,753 cubic miles (44,814 km³)

0 — 500 miles
0 — 500 km

BEAUFORT SEA

Area 184,000 square miles (476,000 km²)
Average depth 3,239 feet (1,004 m)
Greatest known depth 15,360 feet (4,682 m)
Length 684 miles (1,100 km)
Width 404 miles (650 km)
Volume 114,671 cubic miles (477,904 km³)

0 — 500 miles
0 — 500 km

NORTHERN SEA RESOURCES

The broad continental shelves of many Northern Hemisphere seas have supported abundant fisheries. However, mammals such as walruses and whales are endangered. Easily accessible minerals are also found beneath these seas.

RESOURCES
Greenland Sea Cod, halibut, herring
Kara Sea Arctic cod
Baffin Bay Lead and zinc (mined on Baffin Island)
Laptev Sea Salmon (caught at the mouths of rivers)
Chukchi Sea Walruses and seals
Beaufort Sea Oil and gas

COLD-CLIMATE SPECIES

Each year, the Arctic tern flies 24,000 miles (38,000 km) from its Arctic breeding grounds to its wintering grounds off the Antarctic, and then back again. The porbeagle shark is found in the temperate and subpolar waters of both hemispheres, between 30°S and 60°S below the equator.

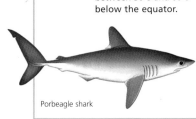
Arctic tern

Porbeagle shark

Southern Hemisphere Seas

In Earth's Southern Hemisphere, there are five continents—Antarctica, Australia, most of South America, parts of Africa, and parts of Asia—and four oceans—the South Atlantic, Indian, South Pacific, and Southern oceans. The balance between land and sea south of the Equator is, nonetheless, in favor of the sea—more than 80 percent of the Southern Hemisphere is covered by water.

Milford Sound, (below) Situated in the Fiordland National Park, on New Zealand's South Island, Milford Sound is a world-famous example of a Southern Hemisphere fjord. The cold, still water conditions at the bottom of the fjord are similar to the conditions found in the deep sea, and some deep-sea species are found there—a phenomenon known as deep-water emergence. By studying such species in these shallow waters, scientists can gain an insight into how less-accessible deep-sea ecosystems work.

CORAL SEA

Area 1,849,000 square miles (4,790,000 km²)
Average depth 7,870 feet (2,400 m)
Greatest known depth 25,134 feet (7,661 m)
Length 1,400 miles (2,250 km)
Width 1,500 miles (2,414 km)
Volume 2,758,421 cubic miles (11,496,000 km³)

TASMAN SEA

Area 1,545,000 square miles (4,000,000 km²)
Average depth 9,023 feet (2,750 m)
Greatest known depth 17,000 feet (5,200 m)
Length 1,243 miles (2,000 km)
Width 1,400 miles (2,250 km)
Volume 2,639,407 cubic miles (11,000,000 km³)

WEDDELL SEA

Area 1,080,000 square miles
(2,800,000 km²)
Average depth
13,124 feet (4,000 m)
Greatest known depth
16,405 feet (5,000 m)
Length 1,200 miles
(2,000 km)
Width 1,200 miles
(2,000 km)
Volume 2,687,397 cubic miles
(11,200,000 km³)

0 — 500 miles
0 — 500 km

GREAT AUSTRALIAN BIGHT

Area 366,830 square miles
(950,000 km²)
Average depth 7,218 feet (2,200 m)
Greatest known depth
14,765 feet (4,500 m)
Length 1,740 miles
(2,800 km)
Width 620 miles
(1,000 km)
Volume 501,487 cubic miles
(2,090,000 km³)

0 — 500 miles
0 — 500 km

ROSS SEA

Area 370,000 square miles
(960,000 km²)
Average depth 656 feet
(200 m)
Greatest known depth
2,625 feet (800 m)
Length 684 miles
(1,100 km)
Width 621 miles
(1,000 km)
Volume 46,070 cubic miles
(192,000 km³)

0 — 500 miles
0 — 500 km

SCOTIA SEA

Area 348,000 square miles
(900,000 km²)
Average depth
10,000–13,000 feet
(3,000–4,000 m)
Greatest known depth
27,651 feet (8,428 m)
Length 870 miles
(1,400 km)
Width 497 miles (800 km)
Volume 755,830 cubic miles
3,150,000 km³)

0 — 1000 miles
0 — 1000 km

SOUTHERN SEA RESOURCES

There is a rich supply of marine life and other resources in seas of the Southern Hemisphere. However, there are relatively few large-scale shelf fisheries in the region. This means that opportunities to exploit resources have been limited.

RESOURCES
Coral Sea Fisheries and oil
Tasman Sea Fisheries and oil
Weddell Sea Antarctic cod
Great Australian Bight Deep–water flathead and Bight redfish
Ross Sea Toothfish
Scotia Sea Antarctic krill

Southern Hemisphere Seas

continued

Climates in the Southern Hemisphere tend to be slightly milder than those in the Northern Hemisphere. This is due to the thermal buffering effect of the oceans, which cover a greater area of Earth's surface than land does. The Southern Hemisphere is also significantly less polluted, because it is less populated, accounting for some 10 to 12 percent of the human population.

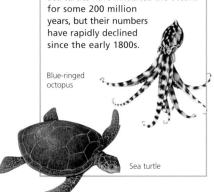
DAVIS SEA

Area 347,520 square miles (900,000 km²)
Average depth 6,562 feet (2,000 m)
Greatest known depth 9,843 feet (3,000 m)
Length 621 miles (1,000 km)
Width 559 miles (900 km)
Volume 431,903 cubic miles (1,800,000 km³)

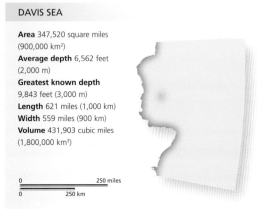

0   250 miles
0   250 km

AMUNDSEN SEA

Area 297,330 square miles (770,000 km²)
Average depth 6,562 feet (2,000 m)
Greatest known depth 9,843 feet (3,000 m)
Length 684 miles (1,100 km)
Width 435 miles (700 km)
Volume 369,517 cubic miles (1,540,000 km³)

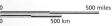

0   500 miles
0   500 km

SOLOMON SEA

Area 278,019 square miles (720,000 km²)
Average depth 14,765 feet (4,500 m)
Greatest known depth 29,988 feet (9,140 m)
Length 621 miles (1,000 km)
Width 497 miles (800 km)
Volume 777,425 cubic miles (3,240,000 km³)

0   500 miles
0   500 km

ARAFURA SEA

Area 250,990 square miles (650,000 km²)
Average depth 230 feet (70 m)
Greatest known depth 12,000 feet (3,660 m)
Length 620 miles (1,000 km)
Width 435 miles (700 km)
Volume 10,918 cubic miles (45,500 km³)

0   500 miles
0   500 km

TIMOR SEA

Area 235,000 square miles (615,000 km²)
Average depth 459 feet (140 m)
Greatest known depth 10,800 feet (3,300 m)
Length 609 miles (980 km)
Width 435 miles (700 km)
Volume 20,659 cubic miles (86,100 km³)

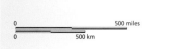

0   500 miles
0   500 km

BANDA SEA

Area 181,000 square miles (470,000 km²)
Average depth 14,765 feet (4,500 m)
Greatest known depth 24,409 feet (7,440 m)
Length 652 miles (1,050 km)
Width 228–330 miles (380–550 km)
Volume 507,486 cubic miles (2,115,000 km³)

0   500 miles
0   500 km

Solomon Islands (above) This archipelago of some 1,000 mountainous islands and low-lying coral atolls lies east of Papua New Guinea and northeast of Australia, in the South Pacific.

Amundsen Sea (below) The ice covering this sea is, on average, 2 miles (3 km) thick. The Amundsen Sea Embayment is one of three major ice drainage basins of the West Antarctic Ice Sheet.

FACT FILE

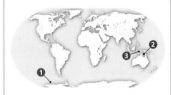

1. Amundsen Sea In March 2002, a huge iceberg, named B-22, broke away from the Thwaites Ice Tongue, which extends into the southern part of Antarctica's Amundsen Sea. The

 iceberg measured 46 by 35 nautical miles (85 by 65 km), with a total area of some 2,120 square miles (5,490 km²).

Amundsen Sea

2. Arafura Sea Although it lies to the east of the Timor Sea, on the Sahul Shelf (which extends from Australia's northern coast to the island of New Guinea), this sea is part of the western

 Pacific Ocean. Its shallow waters are productive shrimp and finfish fisheries, but are threatened by over-exploitation.

Arafura Sea

3. Banda Sea Located south of the Moluccas and north of Timor, this is a marginal sea of the Pacific. It overlies the junction between three tectonic plates: the Eurasian, the Pacific, and

 the Indo-Australian. Powerful undersea earthquakes occur frequently in this region and can generate tsunamis.

Banda Sea

SOUTHERN SEA RESOURCES

Exploitation of the offshore hydrocarbon and mineral reserves in the Southern Hemisphere has been limited by a moratorium placed on prospecting and production in the Antarctic. Rather than allow territorial claims over resources, the treaty favors research in the region.

RESOURCES

Davis Sea Limited fishing

Solomon Sea Minerals such as lead, and fisheries

Timor Sea Oil

Amundsen Sea Limited fishing

Arafura Sea Fisheries and pearls

Banda Sea Shellfish and finfish fisheries

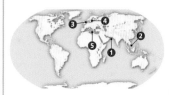
1. Arabian Sea Part of the main sea route between Europe and India, this sea is known for climatic extremes owing to seasonal fluctuations in air and water temperatures and monsoonal rainfall. Its fauna is diverse, including dugongs, turtles, and many species of baleen and toothed whales.

Arabian Sea

2. South China Sea The habitats of this marginal sea south of China include mangroves, seagrass, and coral reefs. They support major shellfish and finfish fisheries, but destruction of the mangrove forests for wood and to create shrimp farms, as well as pollution from land sources, pose serious threats.

South China Sea

3. North Sea Part of the Atlantic, the North Sea lies between Britain and Europe. Its coastal regions are among the world's most diverse, with fjords, estuaries, deltas, banks, beaches, sandbanks, mudflats, marshes, rocks, and islands. Overfishing has seriously depleted its fish stocks.

North Sea

4. Baltic Sea This northern European sea is the world's largest body of brackish water. Marine species inhabit the saltier waters at the western end, while species that are salt-intolerant inhabit the fresh water at the eastern end, which receives river input.

Baltic Sea

5. Mediterranean Sea Dividing Europe from North Africa, this sea is largely populated by species that have entered via the Straits of Gibraltar and adapted to warmer, more saline water than the Atlantic. However, since the Suez Canal opened in 1869, Red Sea species have begun to colonize the Mediterranean.

Mediterranean Sea

Enclosed and Semi-enclosed Seas

A number of seas are either partly or completely surrounded by land. These semi-enclosed seas maintain contact with other oceans of the world through an opening such as narrow straits, the best-known examples being the Mediterranean and North seas. There are also large, fully enclosed bodies of salt water, such as the Caspian and Salton seas.

North Sea oil rig (right) The semi-enclosed North Sea connects with the North Atlantic, and is home to offshore oil and gas production centers. Oil and gas have been extracted from the North Sea since the 1970s, but intense storms in the region make it a difficult working environment. The flare stack on this oil rig burns off excess gases. Not all gases released from the drilled rocks can be used for natural gas supplies, or be liquefied for the petrochemical industry. Several hundred workers live on these platforms for weeks at a time, working to pump out millions of barrels of oil a day.

ARABIAN SEA

Area 1,491,000 square miles (3,862,000 km²)
Average depth 8,970 feet (2,734 m)
Greatest known depth 16,405 feet (5,000 m)
Length 1,243 miles (2,000 km)
Width 1,320 miles (2,200 km)
Volume 2,533,521 cubic miles (10,558,708 km³)

```
0        1000 miles
0      1000 km
```

SOUTH CHINA SEA

Area 895,400 square miles (2,319,000 km²)
Average depth 5,419 feet (1,652 m)
Greatest known depth 16,456 feet (5,016 m)
Length 1,182 miles (1,970 km)
Width 840 miles (1,400 km)
Volume 919,231 cubic miles (3,830,988 km³)

```
0        1000 miles
0      1000 km
```

NORTH SEA

Area 222,100 square miles (575,200 km²)
Average depth 308 feet (94 m)
Greatest known depth 2,165 feet (660 m)
Length 621 miles (1,000 km)
Width 93–373 miles (150–600 km)
Volume 12,974 cubic miles (54,069 km³)

```
0        1000 miles
0      1000 km
```

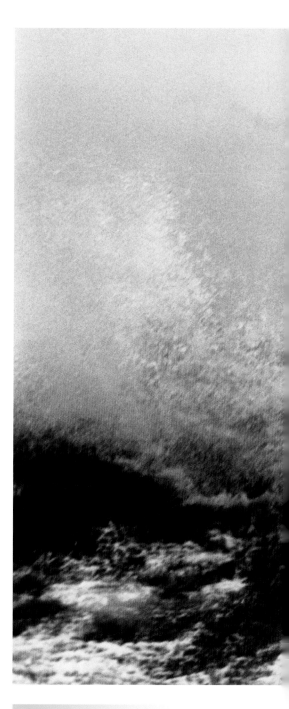

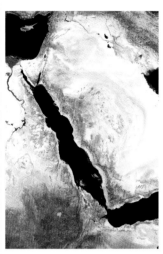

Red Sea A rift valley flooded by the Indian Ocean, the Red Sea was created when Arabia split away from Africa, and is still widening.

Red Sea corals There are 1,240 miles (2,000 km) of fringing coral reefs in the Red Sea. These corals are between 5,000 and 7,000 years old.

BALTIC SEA

Area 163,000 square miles (422,200 km²)
Average depth 180 feet (55 m)
Greatest known depth 1,380 feet (421 m)
Length 795 miles (1,280 km)
Width 24–324 miles (40–540 km)
Volume 5,572 cubic miles (23,221 km³)

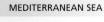

0   1000 miles
0   1000 km

MEDITERRANEAN SEA

Area 969,000 square miles (2,510,000 km²)
Average depth 4,688 feet (1,429 m)
Greatest known depth 16,897 feet (5,150 m)
Length 2,500 miles (4,000 km)
Width 497 miles (800 km)
Volume 860,636 cubic miles (3,586,790 km³)

0   1000 miles
0   1000 km

REGIONAL RESOURCES

The easily accessible offshore oil and gas reserves in this region have largely been exploited, requiring production facilities to be moved into much deeper water.

RESOURCES
Arabian Sea Fisheries
South China Sea Oil and gas
North Sea Oil and gas
Baltic Sea Fisheries
Mediterranean Sea Fisheries and salt

1. Bosporus Strait Less than half a mile (700 m) wide at its narrowest point, this strait marks the boundary between Europe and Asia. The first bridge across the Bosporus was opened in 1973. A second bridge was completed in 1988, and a third bridge and a railway tunnel (the subject of some controversy) are nearing completion.

Bosporus Strait

2. Bering Strait The strait that separates Asia from North America is only 58 miles (92 km) long and has a depth of between 100 and 165 feet (30 and 50 m). During the last ice age, which ended about 10,000 years ago, the drop in sea level turned Bering Strait into a land bridge, allowing people and animals to walk across it.

Bering Strait

3. Gulf of Carpentaria This large, shallow embayment on Australia's northern coast was formed when sea levels rose after the end of the last ice age. It is noted for the cyclones that form here. The gulf is a shrimp fishery, and it also has significant deposits of manganese and bauxite, which have been exploited only since the 1990s.

Gulf of Carpentaria

4. Gulf of Bothnia Bordered by Sweden to the west and Finland to the east, this northernmost arm of the Baltic Sea is very nearly fresh water. The surrounding land cools quickly at the onset of winter, and since fresh water freezes at a higher temperature than salt water, ice formation in the Baltic Sea starts in the gulf.

Gulf of Bothnia

Gulfs and Straits

Gulfs are large bays in the world's oceans and seas, and often have characteristics of their own that distinguish them from other parts of the world's oceans. Straits are narrow strips of water that pass between two landmasses and connect two larger bodies of water. As such, they are of great oceanographic and socioeconomic importance.

Straits of Gibraltar (right) Some six million years ago, the Straits of Gibraltar closed. The Mediterranean Sea dried up, eventually becoming a brackish lake until 5.33 million years ago, when the straits reopened and seawater re-entered.

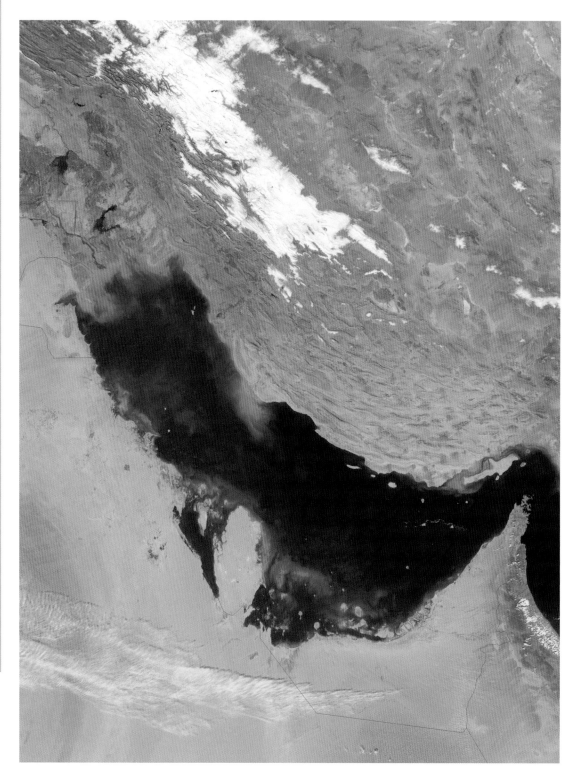

Persian Gulf (right) Once a much larger basin, the Persian Gulf has been infilled with sediments. They have trapped large amounts of organic matter and compressed it to form the vast oil and gas deposits found in this region.

Gulf of Mexico One of the largest semi-enclosed bodies of water in the world, the Gulf of Mexico was probably formed approximately 300 million years ago when the seafloor sank.

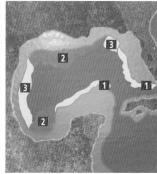

1 Steep carbonate escarpments
2 Areas whose geology and chemistry are influenced by deep salt layers and cold seeps
3 "Normal" deep–water habitats

Gulf basin The basin of the Gulf of Mexico is roughly circular and some 930 miles (1,500 km) in diameter.

Oil production Oil rigs produce up to 1,967,000 barrels of oil and over 16 billion cubic feet (468 million m³) of gas per day from the gulf.

Dead zone Increasingly, river-borne nitrates and phosphates are entering the Gulf of Mexico. These feed the growth of algae, which deoxygenate the water as they decay, killing off all marine life and leaving a "dead zone." The gulf's dead zone is expanding.

THE MARINE ENVIRONMENT

Throughout modern marine science, attempts have been made to classify the marine environment into zones. Early approaches were hampered by a lack of knowledge of the physico-chemical properties of the oceans and the life that was shaped by these factors. As sampling methods have developed, it has become possible to categorize ocean environments according to depth, light, salinity, temperature, latitude, sediment type, and many other physical, chemical, and biological characteristics. The most commonly used classification scheme combines light regime, depth, and location to define marine environmental zones.

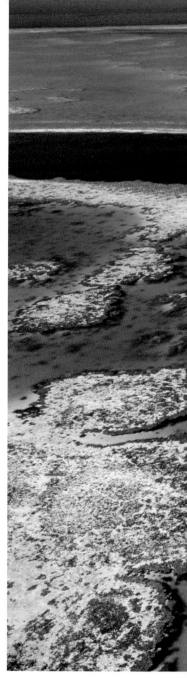

Seaweed (left) Egg wrack is a seaweed that lives attached to rocks on sheltered shores around the temperate North Atlantic. An air bladder along the midline of the fond keeps it floating in the water to maximize the light it receives.

Extensive reefs (right) The Great Barrier Reef is Earth's largest biological entity. It stretches for 1,560 miles (2,500 km) along Australia's northeast coast, and is 95 miles (150 km) at its widest point. It is not a single continuous structure, but thousands of linked segments.

Marine life (below) The energy that fuels most marine life is captured from sunlight by photosynthesis. Marine life is abundant in the surface layers of the oceans but the number of animals declines rapidly with depth. This led early scientists to believe the ocean depths were lifeless.

ZONES AND PROCESSES

The world's oceans are an infinitely complex assemblage of structures and processes. In order to try to make sense of them, some simple divisions are needed.

Oceans occupy depressions, or basins, in Earth's surface. The margins of these basins are an extension of the adjacent land masses. As a result, there is a continental shelf at the margins of ocean basins and this is covered by relatively shallow seas. Most ocean life is found in this zone.

The outermost edge of the continental shelf slopes down steeply to the much deeper ocean floor and the oceanic crustal plate. In this deep part of the oceanic basin, tectonic-plate processes have shaped the topography of the sediment-covered seafloor. This ranges from long, rugged ridges to enormous expanses of flat abyssal plains, with even deeper trenches and arcs of volcanic islands at geologically active margins. Huge current systems, driven by solar heating, transport heat and chemicals around Earth's oceans, and affect the weather over the oceans and on land.

Oceans are a three-dimensional environment and the specific terminology used to describe the different parts of the oceans reflects this. The most basic distinction is between seafloor features and

processes that are described as benthic, and those in the water itself, or water column, which are called pelagic features or processes.

Moving horizontally out from the shore, the only boundary is at the top of the continental slope. The shallower inshore portion is known as the neritic zone, while the zone beyond this point is known as the oceanic realm.

Within the neritic zone, the littoral zone occupies the shore between the tides. This is bordered by the supralittoral above high water and sublittoral below low tide. The zone from high water to the shelf break is the subneritic.

Within the water column, the pelagic zone has several layers. In the surface epipelagic, or euphotic, zone there is sufficient light for photosynthesis. In the mesopelagic zone surface light starts to disappear. In the dysphotic zone, animals can see in the available light, but plants cannot photosynthesize. No surface light reaches the dark bathyal and abyssal zones, or the hadal zone in the deepest trenches.

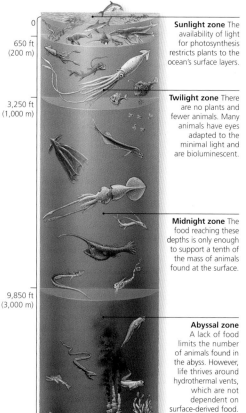

0

650 ft
(200 m)

3,250 ft
(1,000 m)

9,850 ft
(3,000 m)

Sunlight zone The availability of light for photosynthesis restricts plants to the ocean's surface layers.

Twilight zone There are no plants and fewer animals. Many animals have eyes adapted to the minimal light and are bioluminescent.

Midnight zone The food reaching these depths is only enough to support a tenth of the mass of animals found at the surface.

Abyssal zone A lack of food limits the number of animals found in the abyss. However, life thrives around hydrothermal vents, which are not dependent on surface-derived food.

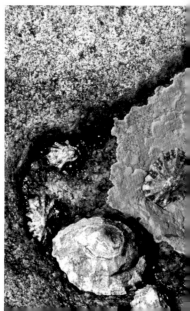

Color and depth (left) White light consists of a spectrum of wavelengths that we see as colors. When light enters the water, the red end of spectrum (longer wavelengths) is quickly absorbed. The green and blue wavelengths can travel farther. The absence of red gives underwater light its blue coloration. All the wavelengths are eventually absorbed. This means that, even in the clearest seawater, the light can penetrate only to a maximum depth of 4,265 feet (1,300 m).

Durable shells (far left) Conditions on the shore can be extremely harsh because there is a daily cycle of immersion and exposure. These limpets have conical shells that help them resist the immense pressure of waves breaking over them and stop them drying out when the tide is out.

Salt Water

Measuring salinity involves a complex calculation. The average salinity of the world's oceans is 35 (salinity is unitless); most vary between 33 and 37. The Red Sea has a salinity of around 40; the Baltic Sea, owing to dilution by rivers, a surface salinity of 7. Marine life has evolved to conserve water, so marine animals have mechanisms for removing excess salt from their bodies.

Salinity (below) For the last 4.3 billion years, rainfall has washed minerals from rocks and volcanic gases, and rivers have carried them to the oceans. There is now a balance between salt inputs and losses, which means that salinity is almost constant.

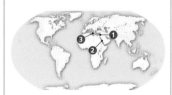

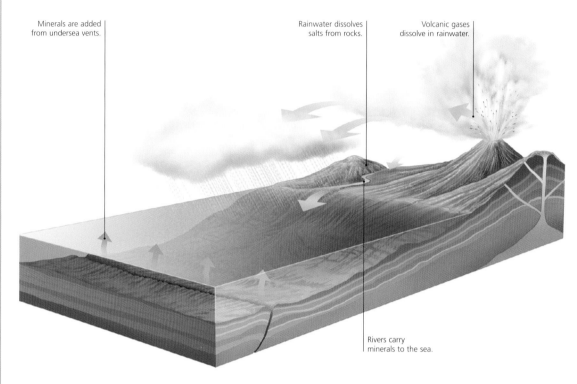

Minerals are added from undersea vents.

Rainwater dissolves salts from rocks.

Volcanic gases dissolve in rainwater.

Rivers carry minerals to the sea.

Antarctic giant petrel These marine birds rely on seawater for drinking. The excess salts they take in are removed by special nasal glands at the base of the prominent tubular nostrils on their beak.

COMPOSITION OF SEAWATER

Sodium and chloride ions make up 85 percent of dissolved sea salts. Most of the rest are calcium, magnesium, potassium, and sulfate.

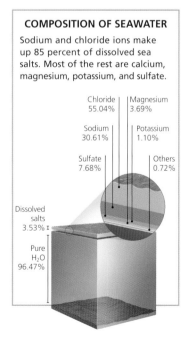

Chloride 55.04%

Magnesium 3.69%

Sodium 30.61%

Potassium 1.10%

Sulfate 7.68%

Others 0.72%

Dissolved salts 3.53%

Pure H_2O 96.47%

Turtles Marine turtles, like this green turtle, have special glands beside the tear ducts that excrete most of the salt they take in from seawater in the form of salty tears. This is why they appear to be weeping when on land.

Sharks The blood of sharks contains large amounts of the waste product urea. This increases the level of dissolved salts in their blood to that of seawater and prevents water being lost by osmosis. Excess salts are removed from the blood by the kidneys.

FACT FILE

Saltwater adaptations Marine bony fishes have to maintain the correct internal balance of water and salt. They lose water by osmosis but take in excess salt by drinking. They have to conserve water and excrete excess salt.

An impermeable skin helps to reduce water loss by osmosis.

Mouth and skin Marine fish constantly take in seawater by drinking. Their impermeable skin also helps them to conserve water.

Gills take in oxygen and also secrete excess salts.

Gills As well as taking in oxygen, the gills of marine fish have special chloride-secreting cells to help get rid of excess salt.

Excess salts are excreted in a concentrated form of urine.

Kidneys and bladder Excess salts are also absorbed in the kidneys in a concentrated form of urine, and then excreted from the bladder.

HERITAGE WATCH

Beluga sturgeon The source of the finest caviar, these fish migrate to the sea as juveniles but return to fresh water to spawn. Overfishing and river-water pollution have reduced their numbers to such low levels that hatcheries have had to be established to stop the decline.

Around the Shore

The margins of the sea are one of the most diverse and challenging habitats on the planet. Shores can range from towering, vertical cliffs to mudflats, all shaped by the immense power of tides and wave–action. The diversity of shore life reflects the dynamic and often harsh conditions found in shore environments.

FACT FILE

At the shoreline Shore animals have to resist wave-action, avoid drying out at low tide, find food, and reproduce. Rocks provide a firm substrate but are exposed to wave-action; sand and mud are unstable but can be burrowed into.

Clams These mollusks bury themselves in mud or sand and filter food from water carried down through siphons extending to the surface.

Seastar These animals fasten themselves to the sides of rocky crevices. They are able to slowly pull mussels apart to feed on them.

Ghost crab Found on tropical shores, ghost crabs sift the sand for food particles brought in on the previous high tide.

HERITAGE WATCH

Too clean? Many sandy beaches are regularly cleaned to remove unsightly and possibly dangerous litter left by visitors, but over-zealous cleaning also removes the natural strandline of decaying weed and dead animals that provides a moist, food-rich shelter for animals such as sandhoppers.

Seaweed in tidal pools (below) Seaweed on rocky shores has to withstand the battering of the waves, but benefits from the increased oxygen in the surf and the nutrients the surf stirs up. Some seaweed can live only where there is strong wave-action.

Life in rockpools (right) Each time that starfish and sea anemones are uncovered at low tide, they have to cope with significant environmental changes—temperature fluctuations (because air and sea temperatures differ), sudden dilution by fresh water in rainstorms, gradual deoxygenation, and fouling of the water by their wastes until the next high tide washes over them.

Sandy beaches (below) Sandy beaches are formed where tides and currents deposit sand brought from rivers or weathered from rocky shores in the subtidal zone, and waves carry these sediments from there to the shoreline. In some places, prevailing onshore winds winnow surface sand off the drier, intertidal parts of the beach at low tide. This sand is carried up the beach and accumulates to form dunes.

Maritime forests Forests develop on dunes that have previously been stabilized by dune shrubs and grasses.

Secondary dunes These dunes are old foredunes that have migrated inland in the direction of the prevailing wind.

Foredunes Initially, dunes build up where onshore winds deposit dry surface sand carried from intertidal areas at low tide.

Beach The finest, lightest sand is deposited at the high tide mark. This dries out and is carried farther up the beach by the wind.

Intertidal zone Waves gather up sediments, depositing them on the beach between the high and low tide marks.

Subtidal zone Here, below the lowest water line, sediments are deposited where tidal currents and longshore drift slow down.

Surface wash

Advancing waves

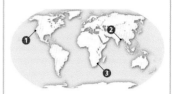
BEACH SLOPE

On most beaches, the size of the sand or shingle particles directly determines the slope of the beach. In general, the finer the particles, the flatter the profile of the beach, as sand binds together less easily than shingle.

Beach particles	Beach slope
Very fine sand	1°
Fine sand	3°
Medium sand	5°
Coarse sand	7°
Very coarse sand	9°
Granules	11°
Pebbles	17°
Cobbles	24°

The Ocean Floor

The area of the seafloor extending from the low tide mark down to the bottom of the deepest ocean trench is called the benthic zone. (The word benthic refers to the bottom of a body of water.) The habitats in this wide-ranging zone are extremely varied, and this is reflected in the many and varied communities of plants and animals that live on or in the seabed.

Crab in sea grass (below) This small crab in a temperate sea grass bed off the coast of British Columbia, Canada, is sheltered by the sea grass and feeds on the snails grazing on the leaf surfaces.

Cerith snails (above) These snails are found in huge numbers on mudflats, gliding over the surface on a broad foot and feeding on films of single-celled algae in the water left by the receding tide.

Benthic communities (below) These include surface grazers such as snails, surface predators like the dog whelk, and buried worms, crustaceans, and bivalve mollusks reliant on food from the surface.

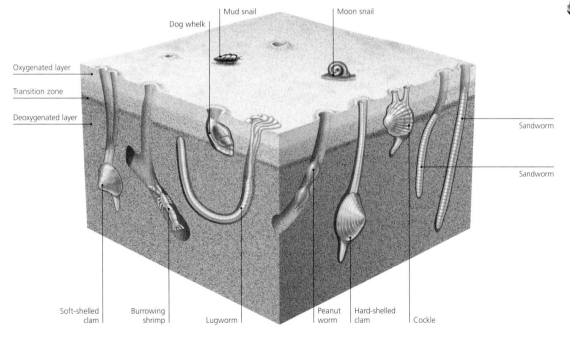

Dog whelk

Mud snail

Moon snail

Oxygenated layer

Transition zone

Deoxygenated layer

Sandworm

Sandworm

Soft-shelled clam

Burrowing shrimp

Lugworm

Peanut worm

Hard-shelled clam

Cockle

Underwater landscape The vast majority of the seafloor consists of featureless mud that covers the abyssal plains of the deep sea. Seafloor topography is more varied in coastal shallows and on mid-ocean ridges.

Black smokers These geyser-like vents emit superheated water that is rich in hydrogen sulfide, which forms a black precipitate on contact with seawater.

Tube worms Bacteria living inside these worms convert the chemicals emitted from black smokers into food for the worms.

Giant clam The largest living bivalve mollusk, the giant clam reaches 4 feet (1.2 m) across and weighs more than 500 pounds (227 kg).

Coastal Shallows

The shallow region of oceans that runs from the shoreline (the low tide mark) to the edge of the continental shelf is called the neritic zone. No more than 656 feet (200 m) deep, it is rich in plankton—the floating or drifting animals and plants that provide the basis of the marine food chain—and supports much larger food webs than the deep sea does.

Australian salmon (below) These fish migrate in large shoals along the south and west coasts of Western Australia, preying on smaller fish. Despite their name, they are not a salmonid species. They are important commercially and for sport.

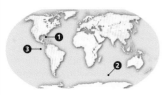

LIFE IN THE DEAD SEA

This photograph of algal bloom in the Dead Sea is unusual, because the surface waters are normally too salty to allow algae to grow and can remain barren for several years until there is above-average river input.

Bull Shark, Bahamas (left) Bull sharks, like this one off the Abaco Islands, are common throughout the world in warm, shallow waters, along coasts, and also far up some large rivers. Unpredictable and often aggressive, they probably account for most inshore shark attacks on humans.

Life in the shallows The abundance of life in shallow water is sustained by the growth of phytoplankton, which forms the basis of complex food webs. Phytoplankton derive nutrients from both the sea and coastal runoff.

Harlequin tuskfish Found in shallow tropical waters, tuskfish have tusk-like teeth and strong jaws, enabling them to dig up and crush bivalves, worms, echinoderms, and small crustaceans.

Squid Shallow water species usually come together in large groups to mate. Squid mate only once; both males and females die after the eggs have been laid and attached to weed or rocks.

Lobster Themselves predators, lobsters are protected from larger predators found in shallow water by their hard exoskeleton, which they shed periodically as they grow.

Purple shore crab Found under stones and among seaweeds on the Pacific coast of North America, from Alaska to Baja California, these crabs feed mainly on algae scraped from stones.

Kelp Forests

Kelp forests are found mainly in cold, nutrient-rich waters on the western side of continents in temperate latitudes—although, unexpectedly, some were discovered in 2007 in warm tropical water around the Galápagos Islands. Below the kelp canopy is an understory of smaller seaweed, and animals shelter among the fronds or attach to the kelp.

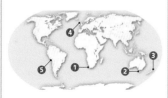

California kelp forest (above) Reserves such as this one off the Catalina Islands play a vital role in protecting their rich marine communities, which are threatened by commercial fishing and kelp harvesting.

Giant kelp (right) This species of kelp reaches lengths of 200 feet (30 m): half comprises the holdfast, and half lies on the surface. The holdfast lives for 4–10 years; individual fronds live for 6–12 months.

Life in the kelp community (above) The food web in kelp forests is complex and easily disturbed. For example, if orcas (**4**) start to eat sea otters (**3**), then sea urchins (**11**) flourish and eat new kelp sporlings, which prevents regrowth of the canopy. Other members of this marine community are ling cod (**1**), garibaldis (**2**), giant kelp (**5**) attached to the rocky seafloor (**8**), California barracudas (**6**), kelp bass (**7**), striped kelpfish (**9**), and sea hares (**10**).

FACT FILE

Structure of kelp Kelp is a large seaweed—the various species are all types of brown algae. It is only distantly related to other aquatic and land plants but is well adapted to life in the sea, growing as much as 18 inches (50 cm) in a day.

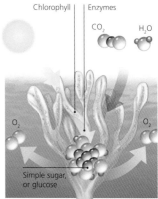

Chlorophyll | Enzymes

CO_2 H_2O

O_2 O_2

Simple sugar, or glucose

Photosynthesis Kelp uses the energy in sunlight to convert carbon dioxide (CO_2) and water (H_2O) into sugars (the fuel used by all living things), releasing oxygen (O_2) as a waste product.

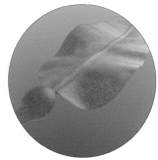

Kelp blade floaters These gas-filled bladders hold up the kelp so that its fronds are at the surface to receive the maximum amount of sunlight.

Holdfast Kelp is firmly anchored to rock by what is called a holdfast. It is not a root, since it does not absorb anything from the seabed.

Coral Reefs

The diversity of life on coral reefs rivals that of tropical rainforests. Reefs are the largest geological structures on the planet that have been formed by living organisms. Reef-building corals (known as hermatypic corals) can grow only where the water temperature does not fall below 70°F (21°C) or rise significantly above this.

Great Barrier Reef (right) Hardy Reef, in Australia's Great Barrier Reef Marine Park, is a platform reef that no longer grows vertically but is extending sideways.

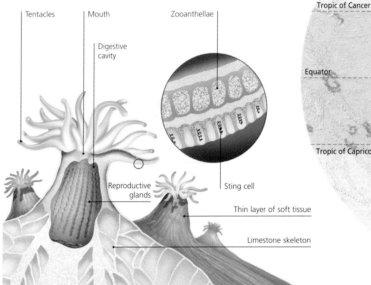

Coral polyps (above) These animals secrete a limestone skeleton, which is covered by a thin layer of living tissue. Tentacles emerge, equipped with sting cells to catch prey and for defense. Polyps derive most of their nutrients, however, from their symbiotic relationship with zooanthellae, single-celled algae that transform sunlight into sugars via photosynthesis.

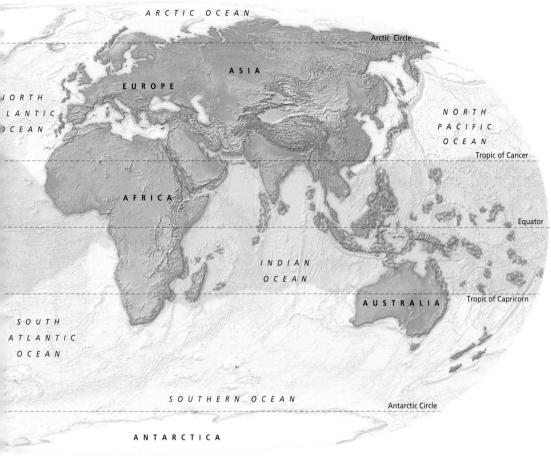

Distribution (above) Most coral reefs are found between the tropics, but some occur around Bermuda, and there are cold-water coral mounds mainly found at higher latitudes.

Deep-water coral reefs
Warm-water coral reefs
Warm ocean

FACT FILE

Reef life The number of species found on a warm-water coral reef is related to the age of the reef. The oldest reefs, with the greatest number of species, are found in the Indo-Pacific region.

Sea squirt Juveniles are like tadpoles, with a precursor to a backbone called a notochord. Adults are filter feeders permanently affixed to a hard surface.

Sea anenome Closely related to corals, these animals have a similar body structure but no hard casing.

Didemnum molle This species of colonial sea squirt is especially common on reefs in the Indo-Pacific region.

Sea fans Close relatives of reef-building corals, sea fans have polyps that raise themselves up on a branched protein skeleton, at right angles to water currents, to catch food particles.

HERITAGE WATCH

Threats to coral Every year reefs are irreparably damaged by sewage and oil pollution, sedimentation, and overfishing. Coral "bleaching" may be a result of global warming. Cold-water corals in temperate zones are threatened by trawling.

Atolls

An atoll is a coral reef that encircles a shallow lagoon. Atolls are usually found in groups; some 300 have been charted to date. The majority are found in the Pacific Ocean, and a number occur in the Indian Ocean (such as the Maldives). The Atlantic has only a few, east of Nicaragua. Atolls occur at all depths on the continental shelf, extending down to the deep ocean.

Bora-Bora, Polynesia (right) One of the Leeward Group, in the Society Islands of French Polynesia, Bora-Bora is an atoll in the early stages of its development—its volcanic origins can still be seen. The twin peaks of Mount Pahia rise 2,385 feet (727 m) above the shallow lagoon and encircling fringing reefs. The mountainous center will gradually subside, and the reef will continue to grow until a mature atoll forms.

Cross section of an atoll (below) Coral islands are formed as coral grows upward from undersea foundations. Here, a typical atoll is forming from barrier reefs surrounding an eroding volcano. Plants grow in the shallow soil from seeds dispersed by birds or washed in by the sea.

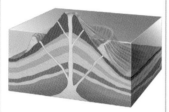
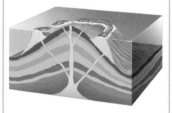
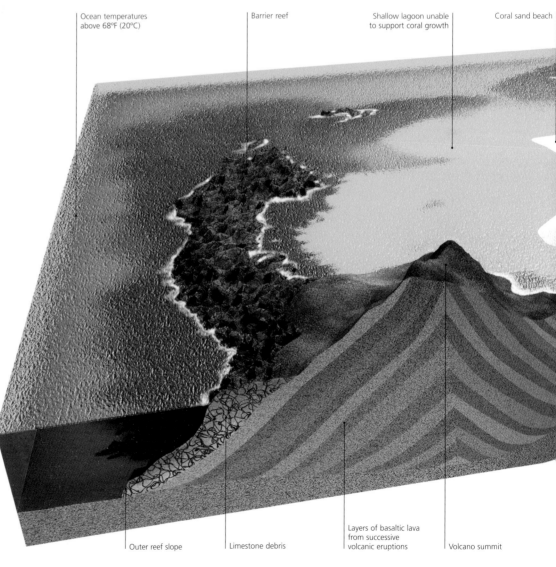

Ocean temperatures above 68°F (20°C) | Barrier reef | Shallow lagoon unable to support coral growth | Coral sand beach

Outer reef slope | Limestone debris | Layers of basaltic lava from successive volcanic eruptions | Volcano summit

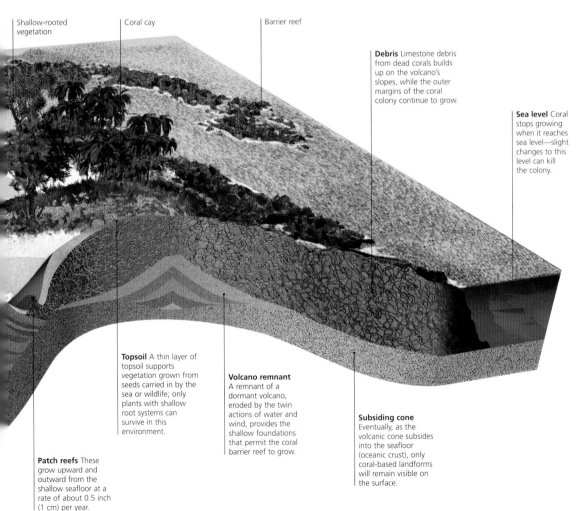

Shallow-rooted vegetation

Coral cay

Barrier reef

Debris Limestone debris from dead corals builds up on the volcano's slopes, while the outer margins of the coral colony continue to grow.

Sea level Coral stops growing when it reaches sea level—slight changes to this level can kill the colony.

Topsoil A thin layer of topsoil supports vegetation grown from seeds carried in by the sea or wildlife; only plants with shallow root systems can survive in this environment.

Volcano remnant A remnant of a dormant volcano, eroded by the twin actions of water and wind, provides the shallow foundations that permit the coral barrier reef to grow.

Subsiding cone Eventually, as the volcanic cone subsides into the seafloor (oceanic crust), only coral-based landforms will remain visible on the surface.

Patch reefs These grow upward and outward from the shallow seafloor at a rate of about 0.5 inch (1 cm) per year.

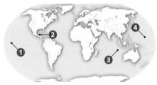

Blue marlin These "blue water" hunters are able to cross vast tracts of the open ocean, feeding on shoals of smaller fish.

Gray whale Migrating between Alaskan feeding grounds and nursery areas in the Gulf of California, gray whales travel up to 6,000 miles (10,000 km).

ELECTRICAL SIGNALS

Sharks are able to sense very weak electrical fields created by the nerve impulses in the bodies of other animals. These fields are detected by a network of jelly-filled pores called the ampullae of Lorenzini, which are concentrated around the shark's snout.

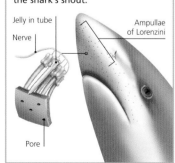

Jelly in tube

Nerve

Ampullae of Lorenzini

Pore

Open Ocean

The open ocean begins at the edge of the continental shelf, where the water depth increases rapidly from about 660 feet (200 m) to around 13,000 feet (4,000 m)—the average depth of all Earth's oceans, which is often termed the "world ocean" by oceanographers. There are more species in the depths, but numbers of individuals are very small.

Life in the open ocean (right) Octopuses (**1**) are predators that live mainly in coastal waters, but a few are found down to 3,300 feet (1,000 m). Anchovies (**2**) are surface-living fish and do not live below 900 feet (300 m). Bonitos (**3**) are fast-swimmers found down to 660 feet (200 m). Sperm whales (**4**) can dive to 9,850 feet (1,000 m) to catch deep-sea squid. Jellyfishes (**5**) float near the surface, grazing on planktonic plants and animals, although some are found deeper. Requiem sharks (**6**) prey on fish, turtles, and sea mammals. Squid (**7**) are found from the surface down to the abyssal depths. At night lanternfishes (**8**) migrate up from 3,940 feet (1,200 m) to 980 feet (300 m). Hatchetfishes (**9**) live at 5,000 feet (1,525 m) but migrate up at night to feed.

Hawaiian green turtle (bottom left) This turtle moves between the open ocean, where it feeds on plant debris, and inshore seagrass beds. It is able to navigate long distances between feeding areas.

Whale sharks (bottom right) Reaching lengths of 60 feet (18 m) and weights of 44 tons (40 tonnes), these sharks feed exclusively on plankton in warm, tropical waters, despite their huge size.

Plankton These small organisms live part or all of their lives suspended in the water column. They are moved horizontally by the movement of the water, rather than being propelled by their own swimming activity.

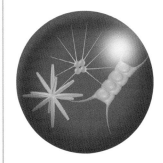

Phytoplankton These single-celled plant-like organisms are confined to the surface layers of the ocean because they need light to photosynthesize.

Zooplankton This kind of plankton consists of small animals that live in the upper ocean, grazing on the phytoplankton and migrating vertically.

COMB JELLY

The comb jelly has a neutrally buoyant gelatinous body that is moved by the beating of the comb rows. It captures its food with its tentacles, which are armed with sting cells. Food is digested in the gut and nutrients are distributed by the vascular canals.

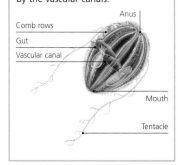

Anus

Comb rows

Gut

Vascular canal

Mouth

Tentacle

The Polar Seas

Polar life is essentially marine. Only a few top predators may be land based. However, there are differences between life found at each of the Poles. The Arctic is a floating island of ice that is accessible to large land predators such as the polar bear, whereas the Antarctic is an isolated continent that no longer has any large, truly terrestrial animals.

Arctic travelers Polar bears can travel hundreds of miles away from land over the frozen Arctic Ocean, following seal migration routes, often drifting on large ice floes and swimming long distances to reach their prey.

Pingos These polar hills that form in the Arctic, subarctic, and Antarctic are mounds of ice covered with earth. They can be as high as 230 feet (70 m) and may measure more than a mile (2 km) across.

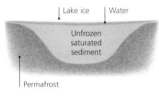

Lake ice | Water

Unfrozen saturated sediment

Permafrost

1 Pingos begin to take shape under the ice of frozen lakes, in locations where there is a core of unfrozen sediment surrounded by permafrost.

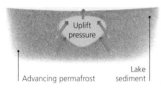

Uplift pressure

Advancing permafrost | Lake sediment

2 Complete freezing of the lake causes the permafrost to advance, creating a lens-shaped mass of saturated sediment that is slowly forced to the surface.

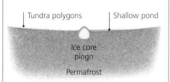

Tundra polygons | Shallow pond

Ice core pingo

Permafrost

3 Eventually a mound of saturated sediment breaks through the surface ice and freezes. Its core becomes a cone of ice within the outer covering of sediment.

Icefish (below right) The blackfin icefish has blood proteins that act as natural "antifreeze," enabling it to survive in the freezing Antarctic waters. It looks pale because it does not need red blood cells, but has excellent blood circulation.

Protecting the Antarctic In 1998 the Protocol on Environmental Protection to the Antarctic Treaty came into force. It provides for the protection of the Antarctic through five specific annexes on marine pollution, fauna and flora, environmental impact assessments, waste management, and protected areas. It prohibits mineral prospecting or extraction, except for scientific purposes.

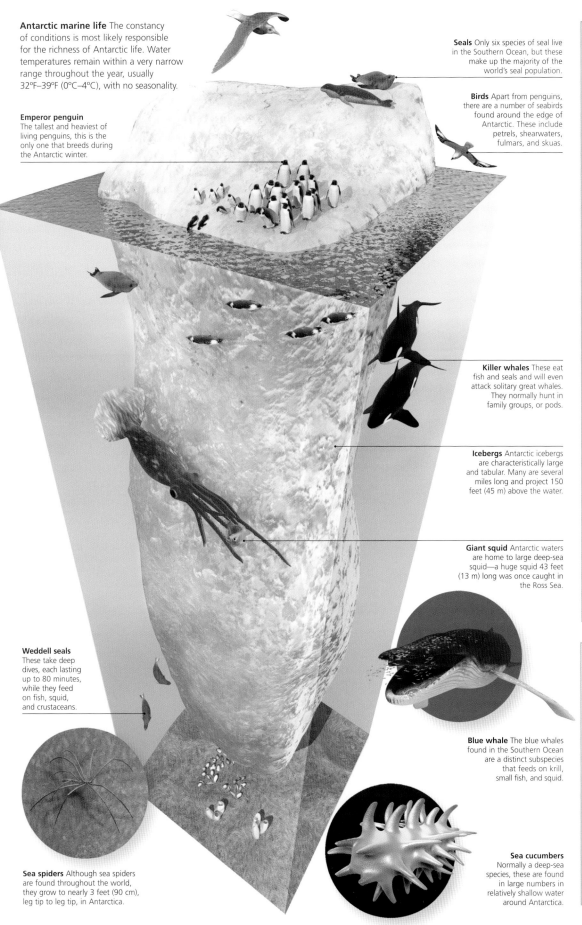

Antarctic marine life The constancy of conditions is most likely responsible for the richness of Antarctic life. Water temperatures remain within a very narrow range throughout the year, usually 32°F–39°F (0°C–4°C), with no seasonality.

Emperor penguin
The tallest and heaviest of living penguins, this is the only one that breeds during the Antarctic winter.

Seals Only six species of seal live in the Southern Ocean, but these make up the majority of the world's seal population.

Birds Apart from penguins, there are a number of seabirds found around the edge of Antarctic. These include petrels, shearwaters, fulmars, and skuas.

Killer whales These eat fish and seals and will even attack solitary great whales. They normally hunt in family groups, or pods.

Icebergs Antarctic icebergs are characteristically large and tabular. Many are several miles long and project 150 feet (45 m) above the water.

Giant squid Antarctic waters are home to large deep-sea squid—a huge squid 43 feet (13 m) long was once caught in the Ross Sea.

Weddell seals
These take deep dives, each lasting up to 80 minutes, while they feed on fish, squid, and crustaceans.

Blue whale The blue whales found in the Southern Ocean are a distinct subspecies that feeds on krill, small fish, and squid.

Sea cucumbers
Normally a deep-sea species, these are found in large numbers in relatively shallow water around Antarctica.

Sea spiders Although sea spiders are found throughout the world, they grow to nearly 3 feet (90 cm), leg tip to leg tip, in Antarctica.

FACT FILE

Polynyas A polynya is an area of open water that is surrounded by sea ice. This term is also used to describe expanses of sea in the Arctic and Antarctic regions that remain unfrozen throughout much of the year.

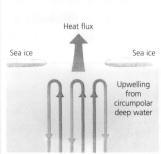

Sensible-heat polynya This type of polynya is found where there is an upwelling of relatively warm water (red) that prevents the formation of sea ice.

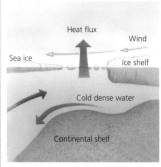

Latent-heat polynya This type occurs at coastlines and the edges of ice sheets, where wind and currents continually push forming ice offshore.

ICEBREAKERS

These ships have specially strengthened hulls and powerful engines that allow them to drive their bows up onto the ice and use the weight of the ship to crack the ice. The broken ice is directed around or under the vessel to prevent it from slowing progress.

FACT FILE

Visual adaptation Many mid-water, deep-sea fish, shrimps, and squid have exquisitely sensitive eyes that can detect the faintest glimmers of light. Some even have yellow filters to distinguish between ambient light and bioluminescence.

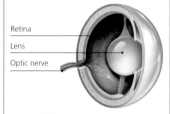

Retina
Lens
Optic nerve

Normal fish eye The lens is large, so that it can gather all the available light and focus it on the retinal rod cells.

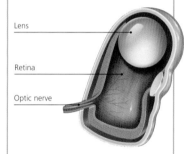

Lens
Retina
Optic nerve

Tubular fish eye Additional lenses and a larger, multi-layered retina make deep-sea fish eyes more sensitive.

The Ocean Depths

The deep sea is divided by oceanographers into the bathyal, abyssal, and hadal zones. These begin at 3,280 feet (1,000 m) and extend down to 19,680 feet (6,000 m). Food, or its inability to reach these zones, is the overriding biological factor that has literally shaped the bodies and biochemistry of deep-sea animals.

Food in the deep Some food is carried into the deep sea by downslope slumps, which bear river and coastal sediments (**1**). The remains of large creatures (**2**), such as whale carcasses, can sustain communities of animals for many years. Large plant remains (**3**) carried out beyond the coastal zone by wind and currents arean important food input to the deep sea. Most of the food supply in the depths is in the form of "marine snow" (**4**)—the slowly sinking remains of plankton produced in the surface layers. Material from the surface also passes down the "ladder of migration" (**5**), where overlapping vertical migrations of predators such as fish (**6**) and squid (**7**) carry food into the lower depths faster than passive sinking.

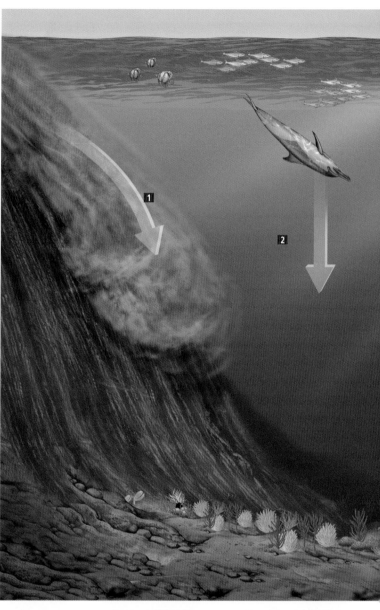

INSIDE A PHOTOPHORE

In bioluminescence, photophores produce light without heat by means of enzyme reactions in the lantern. The light is guided toward the lens, where it is focused into a forward-pointing beam. Any stray light is blocked by the reflective ring in the transparent cap, and pigment around the photophore stops the surrounding tissues from becoming illuminated.

Ostracod (below) Deep-sea ostracods are believed to have the most light-sensitive eyes of any animal. Each eye contains parabolic mirrors that focus light onto a small group of sensitive cells.

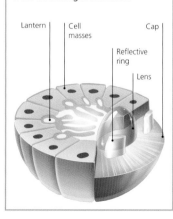

Lantern | Cell masses | Cap
Reflective ring
Lens

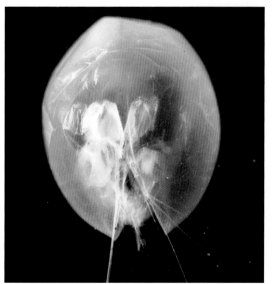

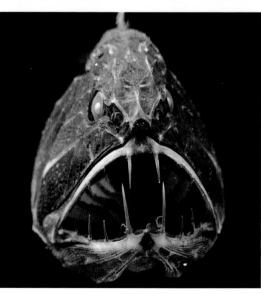

Fangtooth (center left) This ferocious-looking deep-sea fish has fang-like teeth and huge jaws that make sure prey do not escape. The largest two fangs of the lower jaw are so long that they fit into sockets on either side of the brain when the fish's mouth is closed.

Bioluminescent squid (left) This deep-water squid has a semi-transparent body and bioluminescent light-producing organs, or photophores, on its head and tentacles. It is thought that these adaptations help to camouflage the animal from predators, and that the photophores are also used by females to signal to males.

PIVOTING JAWS

Viperfish have jaws that can swing forward and pivot around a specialized neck joint. This increases the gape of the jaws and lets food pass under the sharp fangs without being impaled.

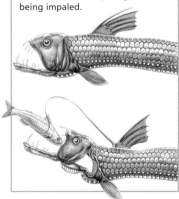

MAPPING THE OCEAN FLOOR

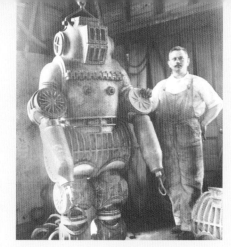

Extended oceanic knowledge has traditionally been hard to accumulate because of problems with position fixing and obtaining information from an alien environment into which humans could not venture. For centuries, mariners had to navigate by the sun and the stars, and rely on sounding leads that could be used only in shallow coastal water. The invention of steel cables in the 19th century enabled the depths of the oceans to be sampled for the first time. Today, marine scientists use remotely operated vehicles (ROV) to see and collect samples from the deepest parts of the ocean, or to receive information from an autonomous underwater vehicle (AUV) thousands of miles away.

TECHNOLOGIES

With the birth of modern navigation in the 18th century, it became possible to map the shapes of the oceans at the surface, often with an accuracy that was not surpassed until the advent of aircraft and satellite imaging in the 1970s. Today, the science of remote sensing with airborne or satellite cameras and other sensors can provide high-resolution visual images. It can also provide other chemical and physical information, such as water temperature, chlorophyll content, the presence of oil slicks, and wave height.

Even "old" technologies have new uses. Airships have proved to be ideal platforms for airborne remote sensors, since they can travel slowly. It is even possible for them to remain stationary, which is something a fixed-wing aircraft cannot do, and they can do it without the disturbance that a helicopter would create. Airborne surveys cover small areas and obtain detailed information that can be used to calibrate satellite sensors. Satellite imaging can follow ocean processes that change with time, something that is not possible with any of the traditional ship-based sampling methods.

Mapping the seafloor and its underlying geological features on a global scale was revolutionized

Early exploration (above) Diving was once the only means of examining and sampling the seabed. To overcome depth limitations, armored suits that remain at atmospheric pressure were tried. Early examples, however, like the 1918 suit above, were prone to leaks and stiff joints.

by the development of seismic and sonar systems. In the 1960s they provided the first detailed information of the structure of the ocean basins. At the same time, the development of deep-diving submersibles enabled scientists to see the deep-sea floor, sample its life, and find features such as deep-sea vents that would not have been found by traditional methods.

Submarines (above) The first practical submarine, launched in 1897, was designed by Irish-American John Holland, pictured above in a submarine hatch. Heavy ship losses inflicted by submarines during World War I stimulated research into sound waves. After the war, sonar detection was used for electrical depth measurement. Similarly, the development of modern electronics during World War II produced instrumentation capable of mapping the seafloor.

Topographical map (right) After World War II, side-scan sonar became available for civilian use. Oceanographers used it to make accurate depth measurements and visualize large swathes of the seafloor. From 1947 to 1977, U.S. geologist Bruce Heezen and cartographer Maria Tharp made a complete topographic map of the world's oceans, using side-scan images collected by survey vessels.

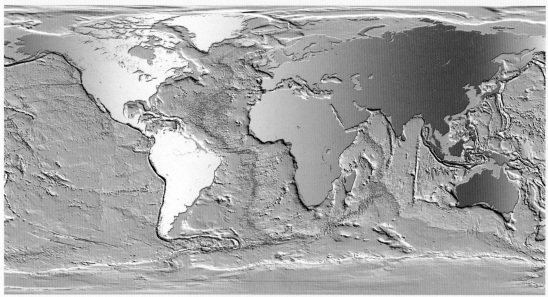

THROUGH THE AGES

1720 The creation of the first official hydrographic department in France recognized that safe navigation was important to a major sea power.

1795 The British Admiralty established a hydrographic survey to chart the world's oceans.

1818 Scottish explorer John Ross collected the first deep-water sediment samples from 1,050 fathoms (1,920 m) during a voyage to Baffin Bay.

1925 The German *Meteor* expedition tested the first echo-sounding system. From 1925 to 1927 it made 14 depth profiles in parts of the Atlantic.

1957 Heezen and Tharp's map of the North Atlantic seafloor showed the presence of the mid-Atlantic ridge, a crucial discovery in modern plate tectonics.

Surveying the seafloor (left) Side-scan sonar uses beams of sound waves sent out from an emitter (**1**) towed behind a ship. Any changes in the reflected sound are processed to give a visual representation of the seafloor. Some side-scan sonars can penetrate into the upper layers of the seabed, showing its structure. However, to map the deeper strata of the seafloor, seismic surveying has to be used. Intense bursts of sound (**2**) are produced by powerful underwater electrical discharges called "sparkers," compressed-air guns, or small explosive charges. The reflected sound is detected by hydrophones (**3**) towed by a ship. Other information can be obtained by unmanned ROVs (**4**) and AUVs, as well from samples collected by grabs (**5**) and dredges.

Armored suit (below left) Divers wearing the armored Newtsuit, seen here with the French ROV *Achille*, can work at depths beyond the range of divers breathing under pressure. A thruster backpack lets the diver move around, and the fluid-filled flexible joints provide dexterity. The suit is designed for salvage and submarine rescue work.

Satellite mapping (below) This image was created from data collected by the ERS 1 satellite that was launched in 1991. Technological advances have increased the sensitivity of height measurements. It is now possible to show the topography of the seafloor by measuring variations in waves on the sea's surface.

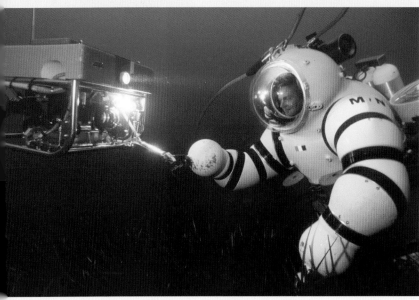

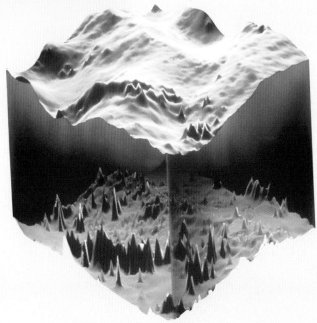

1962 Jacques Piccard and Don Walsh descended 35,814 feet (10,916 m) to the bottom of the Marianas Trench, Earth's lowest point, in the bathyscaphe *Trieste*.

1968 A deep-sea drilling survey begun by the *Glomar Challenger* eventually provided evidence for the seafloor-spreading hypothesis and continental drift.

1977 The *Alvin* deep-sea submersible discovered hydrothermal vents in the Galápagos rift zone. Animals in these unique habitats use vent geochemical energy rather than solar energy.

1995 Japanese ROV *Kaiko* set a depth record for a tethered unmanned vehicle by reaching the seabed at 36,008 feet (10,978 m).

1998 British unmanned submersible *Autosub* began its first mission to collect data using methods that were not possible with normal research ships.

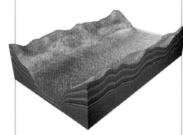
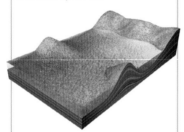
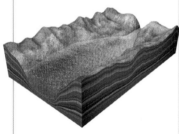
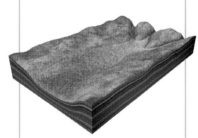
Estuaries

In estuaries, the sea not only meets the land but also mixes with fresh water. This has created environments where highly specialized groups of plants and animals are able to cope with the ever-changing conditions. Estuaries are classified according to how they were formed and the interactions within them between fresh and salt water.

Bar-built estuary (below) Lagoa dos Patos estuary in southern Brazil consists of a long lagoon (174 miles/280 km) separated from the Atlantic Ocean by a sandbar that is 5 miles (8 km) wide.

Glacier-carved estuary (bottom) The extreme depth of Trollfjord in Norway gives some indication of the size and power of the glacier that carved it, leaving sheer rock faces along its shoreline.

FACT FILE

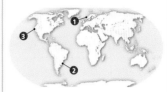

1. Trollfjord This fjord in Norway's Lofoten Islands has little flat land for agriculture, apart from a small delta at its head. As a result, cod fishing is the

mainstay of the local economy. Its spectacular scenery also makes it a destination for summer cruises.

Trollfjord, Norway

2. Lagoa dos Patos The narrow outlet to the Atlantic Ocean reduces the ingress of salt water to this estuary, so that water is brackish for

only a short distance inside the entrance. The water level inside the lagoon is still affected by tidal rise and fall.

Lagoa dos Patos, Brazil

3. San Francisco Bay This is not one bay, but consists of a series of shallow embayments and interconnected

bays. Around their margins there are extensive wetlands, which support a wide variety of plant and animal life.

San Francisco Bay, California, U.S.A.

Tectonic estuary San Francisco Bay, California, U.S.A., began as a depression in Earth's crust between the western San Andreas Fault and eastern Hayward Fault. When sea levels rose after the end of the last ice age, the sea broke through into a canyon at what is now the Golden Gate, forming the bay, seen here from above.

HERITAGE WATCH

Self-cleaning environments
Estuaries are the most polluted of all marine environments, but they also have some capacity to clean themselves. Many pollutants are removed by being adsorbed onto mud particles. Plant life in estuaries removes nitrogen compounds produced by sewage and other sources, as well as scavenging out metals from the water.

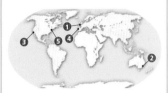

1. Kingsbridge This estuary in Devon, southwest England, is an extreme example of a drowned river valley. It is quite disproportionate to the size of its river because only a number of small streams flow into it, instead of one main river.

Kingsbridge Estuary, England.

2. Broken Bay A drowned valley estuary on the east coast of New South Wales, Broken Bay carries water from the Hawkesbury and Pittwater rivers to the Tasman Sea. Its 3-mile (5 km) wide entrance leads to an interior broken into three small inlets.

Broken Bay, New South Wales, Australia

3. Tijuana This estuary is on the Mexican–U.S.A. border. It is noted for the extensive mudflats and marshland that exist around its margins. It is also one of the most variable estuaries in North America, experiencing peak river flow in March but no flow at all for many months of the year.

Tijuana estuary, Mexico

4. Ria de Vigo On the Galician coast of Spain, this is a classic ria form of estuary created by the inundation of a steep-sided valley. The strong tidal flushing of the lower end of the estuary makes it particularly suited to intensive shellfish culture.

Ria de Vigo, Spain

5. Chesapeake Bay The drowned valley of the Susquehanna River, this is the largest estuary in the United States. It is nearly 200 miles (300 km) long and it salinity ranges from water that is completely fresh at the mouth of the Susquehanna River to full-strength seawater closer to the opening of the estuary into the Atlantic.

Chesapeake Bay, U.S.A.

Drowned River Valleys

Drowned river valleys, also known as rias, are the most common type of estuary and are found all around the world. They are created either as a result of rises in global sea levels or when the land sinks. Valleys that were previously at sea level become submerged, often resulting in a very large estuary at the mouth of a relatively insignificant river.

Whitsundays (below) These islands on the Great Barrier Reef, Queensland, Australia, are not coral atolls, but partially drowned mountain tops dissected by many small drowned valleys.

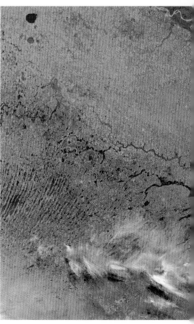

Estuary life Species that tolerate estuarine conditions benefit from the reduced competition for space and food, and fewer predators. Many coastal fish use estuaries as nurseries to protect growing young. In Australia adult barramundi swim downriver after summer rains (**1**) and spawn close to the estuary mouth (**2**). Larvae are carried in on the tide and develop in creeks and swamps (**3**), eventually reaching adult size (**4**), when they swim back upriver. The abundance of invertebrates provides food for the fish and attracts wading birds. Crocodiles and bull sharks prowl the warm waters in tropical estuaries.

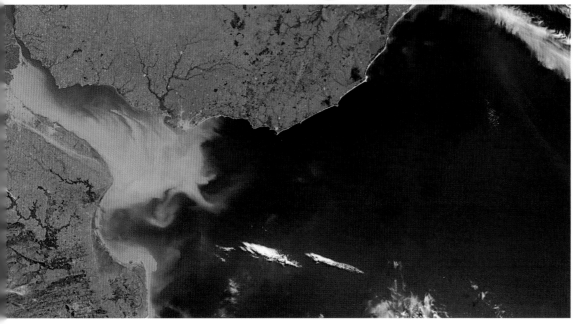

FACT FILE

Large species Not all estuarine species are small. In tropical and subtropical estuaries sharks and saltwater crocodiles are the top predators, and in temperate zones seals and dolphins inhabit the lower ends of many estuaries.

Dugongs These distant relatives of elephants live in shallow tropical waters and estuaries, grazing on sea grasses throughout the Indo-Pacific region, particularly in northern Australia.

Bull sharks Able to tolerate fresh water, bull sharks are found not only in estuaries but can travel far inland. They have been reported 2,220 miles (4,000 km) up the Amazon River.

Río de la Plata estuary This is the widest estuary in the world. At its head, at the confluence of the Uruguay and Paraná rivers, it measures 30 miles (48 km) across and funnels out to 137 miles (220 km) wide at its mouth. The estuary provides a habitat for the rare La Plata dolphin.

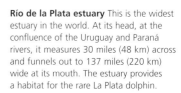

HERITAGE WATCH

Milford Haven This large estuary on the southwest tip of Wales, U.K., is rich in marine life, but it also has oil refineries around its shores. In February 1996, the tanker *Sea Empress* ran aground at the entrance and spilt 73,000 tonnes of crude oil. Despite the initial devastation, monitoring of marine life has shown that it has made a remarkable recovery.

Fjords

Fjords are estuaries created by glaciers that have carved out deep U-shaped valleys. As the glaciers retreated, the valleys filled with seawater. Fjords are found only at high latitudes. In the Northern Hemisphere they occur in Norway, Alaska, and British Columbia in Canada. In the Southern Hemisphere they are found in Chile and on New Zealand's South Island.

Ice-covered fjord (below) Tracy Arm Fjord in Alaska, U.S.A., is more than 30 miles (48 km) long and, because it is at a high northern latitude, about one-fifth of it remains ice-covered throughout the year.

FACT FILE

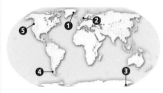

1. Scoresby Sund On the east coast of Greenland, Scoresby Sund is 217 miles (350 km) long and the longest fjord in the world. It is also one of the deepest, reaching depths of more than 4,900 feet (1,500 m) in the central zone of the fjord.

Scoresby Sund, Greenland

2. Sognefjord This is the second largest fjord in the world and the largest in Norway. It is 126 miles (203 km) long and reaches a maximum depth of 4,285 feet (1,308 m). At the fjord's mouth the bottom rises abruptly to form a sill about 330 feet (100 m) deep.

Sognefjord, Norway

3. Skelton Inlet This fjord in Antarctica still has a glacier at its head. The fjord is 38 miles (60 km) long and ranges in width from 10 miles (16 km) at the mouth to about 3 miles (5 km) near the place it meets with the grounded ice of the glacier.

Skelton Inlet, Antarctica

4. Messier Channel Located on the Patagonian coast of Chile, this is one of the deepest fjords in the world. In the northern section of the channel, it reaches a depth of at least 4,226 feet (1,288 m). The Messier Channel has fairly strong subsurface currents, which is unusual for a fjord.

Messier Channel, Chile

5. Burrard Inlet This is a relatively shallow-sided coastal fjord on the southwestern coast of British Columbia, Canada. It was formed during the last ice age. Its shores are occupied by the port area of the city of Vancouver, whose suburbs now occupy both sides of the inlet.

Burrard Inlet, Canada

Sognefjord (left) This is one of the larger fjords on Norway's west coast. Nærøyfjord, a branch of the fjord 12 miles (20 km) long, was declared a World Heritage site in 2005.

FACT FILE

Fjord formation There have been at least four major ice ages in Earth's history. These cycles of glaciation, followed by melting and retreat, have left characteristic landforms, the most obvious of which are fjords.

70 million years ago Earth was passing through a warm phase, with little or no ice, even at the two Poles.

Ice ages The last ice reached its coldest point about three million years ago, covering much of Earth with thick ice sheets.

10,000 years ago At the end of the last ice age, sea levels started to rise as the ice sheets began to melt.

Present As glaciers retreat, the sea has risen over the sills left at the ends of the valleys gouged out by the glaciers.

RIVERS

Rivers are a clear sign of the hydrological cycle, carrying water from upland areas where it was deposited as rain or snow. They have always been essential for humans. The earliest-known civilizations grew around rivers, using them for water, irrigation, sanitation, transport, and the first forms of mechanical power. The modern world is still dependent on rivers for waste disposal, the inland transport of heavy goods, water, and the generation of hydroelectric power. Great strides have been made in some areas to restore the damage done by human activity, but many rivers worldwide are threatened by pollution and water extraction.

FROM SOURCE TO SEA

A river or stream can begin its life in a number of ways: as an outflow from a spring, lake, or marsh, as meltwater from a glacier, or as the gradual accumulation of small flows in an upland area. These areas are usually known as headwaters. The highest stream is regarded as the definitive source, and all flows joining it are tributaries.

The visible flow in a river or stream channel does not always represent the total flow. Often, a substantial volume flows through porous subsurface rocks and gravels that surround the river or stream channel, known as the hyporheic zone. For many rivers in large valleys, this unseen flow may often greatly exceed the visible flow. In extreme cases, particularly where the surface flow is low or strongly influenced by seasonal precipitation, rivers may not reach the sea or another large body of water, but flow underground, sometimes carving out large caverns in limestone areas.

Healthy rivers (left) The health of a river is reflected in its associated wildlife. Otters are now returning to British rivers that were once blighted by pollution.

Near the source (right) Most material that is washed into upland streams is carried downstream, but enough organic debris is trapped between stones and boulders to support aquatic life.

Most rivers will eventually end in a lake or the sea. This endpoint is taken as the lowest point of the river and is called the base level. A river normally carves a valley proportionate to its size, but so-called "misfit streams" occupy valleys that are too large to have been eroded by rivers. Most of these have been enlarged by glaciers, but some are the result of upstream dams or diversions.

Where glaciers have cut across existing river valleys, they leave hanging valleys that end in spectacular waterfalls, although most waterfalls form where there is an abrupt change in rock type.

THE COURSE
OF A RIVER

Youthful In its early stage a river is sometimes called "youthful." Youthful rivers have a steep gradient, which makes them fast-flowing, but carry only small volumes of water. They erode deep, narrow channels. Some never progress beyond the youthful stage, especially if the mountainous area is near the sea or a lake.

Mature stage The gradient of a mature river is less steep than that of a youthful river. Its water moves more slowly than in youthful rivers, but flow rates are often much greater because tributaries greatly increase the volume of water carried. As a result, mature river channels tend to erode laterally, rather than cutting downwards.

Old river A river in its last stage has a shallow gradient and a low flow velocity, which minimizes its erosive power. Old rivers usually meander over floodplains, depositing more sediment than they erode from the banks. When they reach the sea or large lake, they deposit their remaining sediment load in a delta or alluvial fan.

Catchment and Drainage

A catchment area or drainage basin is an area of land that is drained by a self-contained, branching network of channels. Within the catchment area, all the water from rainfall or snowmelt drains from high ground, finding its way down in streams and rivers that join and increase in width as they flow toward either a lake or a sea. Catchment areas are separated from one another by upland ridges, called watersheds.

Self-contained (right) Each of the densely forested islands of the Bissagos Archipelago in the Atlantic Ocean forms a self-contained catchment area. The islands receive about 100 inches (2,500 mm) of rain each year from June to November.

Mount Waialeale drainage basin (far right) Located on the Hawaiian island of Kauai, this is one of the world's wettest places, with an average rainfall of 460 inches (11,680 mm) per year, and a record 683 inches (17,340 mm) in 1982.

Features of a drainage basin (below) Drainage basins share common features, but behave differently because of differences in annual precipitation, land relief, rock type and porosity, soil thickness, vegetation cover, land use, and river channelization.

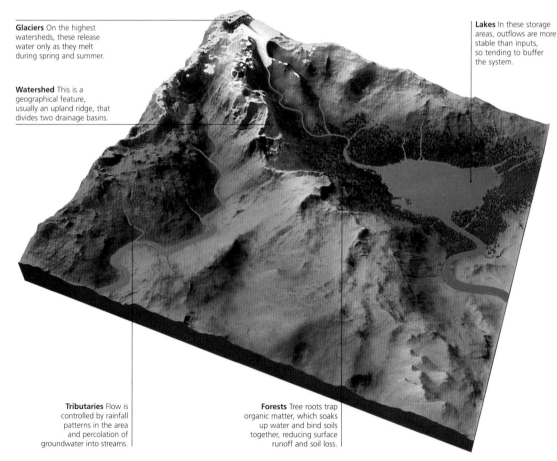

Glaciers On the highest watersheds, these release water only as they melt during spring and summer.

Watershed This is a geographical feature, usually an upland ridge, that divides two drainage basins.

Lakes In these storage areas, outflows are more stable than inputs, so tending to buffer the system.

Tributaries Flow is controlled by rainfall patterns in the area and percolation of groundwater into streams.

Forests Tree roots trap organic matter, which soaks up water and bind soils together, reducing surface runoff and soil loss.

Valley development How a river valley takes shape depends on several factors that vary in relative importance as a river gradually changes from a fast-flowing upland stream to a wider, slower floodplain river.

1 In its early, upland stages near its source, a river is fast-flowing and cuts a narrow but deep channel in the rock over which it flows.

2 In the middle reaches, the valley sides are eroded much faster than the river can cut downwards and the valley widens.

3 As the river slows down a little more in its lower reaches and is joined by tributaries, it widens by further erosion of the valley sides.

4 Finally, a flat floodplain is formed when the velocity of the water is much reduced and the river deposits its load of sediment.

GATEWAY ARCH

The St. Louis Gateway Arch soars 630 feet (192 m) high. It was erected on the banks of the Mississippi River in 1965 to commemorate the role played by the city in the westward expansion of European settlement during the 19th century.

Rivers of North America

The flow regimes of North American rivers are controlled by the climatic differences across the continent. For example, the northward-flowing rivers, such as the Yukon, Mackenzie, Red, and Nelson, as well as the rivers of eastern Canada, freeze in winter, but their upper reaches thaw before the lower sections, often causing flooding.

MISSISSIPPI

Length 2,348 miles (3,778 km)
Drainage area 1,243,700 square miles (3,221,200 km²)
Countries U.S.A.
Source Lake Itasca, Itasca State Park, Clearwater County MN
Elevation at source 1,475 feet (450 m)
Mouth Pilottown, Plaquemines Parish LA
Outflow Gulf of Mexico
Elevation at mouth 0

Major tributaries *Left*: Ohio. *Right*: Missouri, Arkansas

MACKENZIE

Length 1,079 miles (1,738 km), excluding head streams
Drainage area 682,000 square miles (1,766,000 km²)
Countries Canada
Source Great Slave Lake, in Northwest Territories
Elevation at source 505 feet (154 m)
Mouth Mackenzie Bay
Outflow Beaufort Sea, Arctic Ocean
Elevation at mouth 0

Major tributaries *Head:* Finlay, Slave, Peace, Athabasca, Hay. *Left*: Liard, Redstone, Keeler, Arctic Red, Peel. *Right*: Great Bear

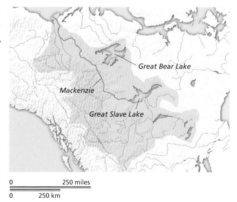

HUDSON

Length 306 miles (492 km)
Drainage area 13,370 square miles (34,630 km²)
Countries U.S.A.
Source Lake Tear of the Clouds, Mount Marcy, Adirondack Mountains NY
Elevation at source 4,322 feet (1,317 m)
Mouth Upper New York Bay
Outflow Atlantic Ocean
Elevation at mouth 0

Major tributaries *Left*: Hoosic. *Right*: Mohawk, Rondout Creek/Wallkill River

Punch Bowl Falls This waterfall is on the Eagle Creek Oregon, a tributary of the Columbia River. The river is confined in a narrow channel above the falls so that it shoots out into a large bowl. In waterfall classification schemes, these falls are used as the type example of a "punchbowl" waterfall.

COLUMBIA

Length 1,243 miles (2,000 km)
Drainage area 258,000 square miles (668,217 km²)
Countries Canada, U.S.A.
Source Columbia Lake, British Columbia, Canada
Elevation at source 2,650 feet (808 m)
Mouth NW of Portland OR.
Outflow Pacific Ocean
Elevation at mouth 0

Major tributaries *Left*: Kootenay, Pend Oreille, Spokane, Snake, Deschutes, Willamette. *Right*: Okanogan, Yakima, Cowlitz

SAINT LAWRENCE

Length 744 miles (1,197 km), excluding head streams
Drainage area 397,683 square miles (1,030,000 km²)
Countries Canada, U.S.A.
Source Lake Ontario
Elevation at source 820 feet (250 m)
Mouth Gulf of Saint Lawrence
Outflow Atlantic Ocean
Elevation at mouth 0

Major tributaries *Head*: St. Louis. *Left*: Ottawa, Saguenay. *Right*: Richelieu

COLORADO

Length 1,450 miles (2,330 km)
Drainage area 242,900 square miles (629,100 km²)
Countries U.S.A., Mexico
Source Grand Lake, Rocky Mountains
Elevation at source 8,372 feet (2,552 m)
Mouth Gulf of California
Outflow Pacific Ocean
Elevation at mouth 0

Major tributaries *Left*: Gunnison, San Juan, Little Colorado, Gila. *Right*: Green, Dirty Devil

---

FACT FILE

1. Columbia A high flow rate and the relatively steep gradient of the Columbia River have made it particularly suited to hydroelectricity generation. With its tributaries it produces about 60 percent of the hydroelectric power generated on the west coast of North America. The largest of its 150 hydroelectric projects are the Grand Coulee and Chief Joseph Dams.

Columbia River, Canada and U.S.A.

2. Saint Lawrence Providing the primary drainage of the Great Lakes Basin, the Saint Lawrence connects the lakes with the Atlantic Ocean. It flows to the northwest and forms part of the provincial boundary between Quebec and Ontario and part of the international boundary between Canada and the U.S.A.

Saint Lawrence River, Canada and U.S.A.

3. Colorado This is the principal river of the southwest of North America. It drains the western slopes of the Rocky Mountains and has carved out the Grand Canyon during the last six million years. However, water is extracted to supply the Imperial Valley irrigation schemes and this now causes the river to dry out before it reaches the Gulf of California.

Colorado River, U.S.A. and Mexico

SALMON DECLINE

The Columbia–Snake Basin was once one of the world's most prolific runs of Pacific salmon, with more than 15 million wild salmon returning each year. Fewer than 10,000 salmon are now recorded. Habitat destruction, poor water management, and dams have caused wild salmon and steelhead populations to decline so dramatically that they are listed under the Endangered Species Act.

Rivers of North America
continued

The drainage pattern of North America is asymmetric. The continent is divided north–south by the Rocky Mountains, but these lie well to the west. Consequently, west-coast rivers are relatively short, but those flowing eastwards are longer, with many tributaries. Eastern rivers were also the first routes followed during European settlement.

CHOKED RIVER

The Rio Grande's natural flow is one-twentieth of that of the Colorado River, and less than one-hundredth of the Mississippi's flow. In some places there is so little flow that water hyacinths (bright red in this near-infrared satellite image) choke the river.

RÍO GRANDE

Length 1,885 miles (3,033 km)
Drainage area 171,585 square miles (444,405 km²)
Countries U.S.A., Mexico
Source San Juan Mountains CO
Elevation at source 12,800 feet (3,900 m)
Mouth Gulf of Mexico
Outflow Gulf of Mexico
Elevation at mouth 0

Major tributaries *Left*: Pecos, Devils, Chama, Puerco. *Right*: Conchos, Salado, San Juan

YUKON

Length 2,300 miles (3,700 km)
Drainage area 321,500 square miles (832,700 km²)
Countries Canada, Alaska, U.S.A.
Source Atlin Lake, Canada
Elevation at source 2,168 feet (661 m)
Mouth Yukon-Kuskokwim Delta
Outflow Bering Sea
Elevation at mouth 0

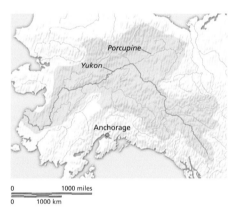

Major tributaries *Left*: White, Tanana. *Right*: Pelly, Stewart, Porcupine, Koyukuk

OHIO

Length 976 miles (1,570 km)
Drainage area 203,900 square miles (546,700 km²)
Countries U.S.A.
Source Confluence of the Allegheny and Monongahela rivers at Pittsburgh PA
Elevation at source 709 feet (216 m)
Mouth Confluence with Mississippi River, Cairo IL
Outflow Mississippi River
Elevation at mouth 279 feet (85 m)

Major tributaries *Head*: Allegheny, Monongahela. *Left*: Kanawha, Kentucky, Cumberland, Tennessee. *Right*: Wabash

Fraser River At McBride in British Columbia, Canada, the Fraser River and its surrounding forested valley are the basis for a thriving tourist industry that has started to develop as the local timber industry has begun to decline.

FRASER

Length 854 miles (1,375 km)
Drainage area 84,942 square miles (220,000 km²)
Countries Canada
Source Near Mount Robson, Rocky Mountains, British Columbia
Elevation at source 6,500 feet (1,981 m)
Mouth Fraser River Delta, Strait of Georgia, British Columbia
Outflow Pacific Ocean
Elevation at mouth 0

Major tributaries *Left:* Quesnel, Thompson. *Right:* McGregor, Nechako, West Road, Chilcotin

TATSHENSHINI

Length 304 miles (490 km)
Drainage area 1,948 square miles (5,046 km²)
Countries Canada
Source Northwest British Columbia
Elevation at source 5,027 feet (1,532 m)
Mouth Confluence with Alsek River
Outflow Alsek River, Pacific Ocean
Elevation at mouth 416 feet (127 m)

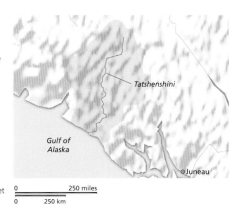

Major tributaries *Right:* Blanchard, Takhanne, Klukshu, Village Creek, Tats Creek

TENNESSEE

Length 652 miles (1,049 km)
Drainage area 40,910 square miles (105,960 km²)
Countries U.S.A.
Source Confluence of French Broad and Holston rivers at Knoxville TN.
Elevation at source 813 feet (248 m)
Mouth Ohio River at Paducah KY
Outflow Ohio River
Elevation at mouth 302 feet (92 m)

Major tributaries *Head:* French Broad, Holston. *Left:* Little Tennessee, Hiwassee, Bear Creek, Big Sandy. *Right:* Clinch, Sequatchie, Elk, Duck, Cumberland

---

FACT FILE

1. Fraser The valley of this river is noted for its rich farmland, and the river itself provides water for numerous pulp mills. However, the Fraser remains a noted salmon river because the main river has never been dammed, so there has been no interference with salmon spawning. The delta is an important stopover for migrating shorebirds.

Fraser River, Canada

2. Tatshenshini In 1993 this river in British Columbia, Canada, became part of the largest internationally protected area in the world. To ensure the preservation of the region's unique tundra ecosystem, the Alsek and its tributary, the Tatshenshini, were given full protection, becoming the only large river drainage system in North America to be so protected.

Tatshenshini River, Canada

3. Tennessee The construction of nine major dams along the Tennessee River was begun in 1933 by the Tennessee Valley Authority to improve navigation, and to provide flood control and cheap hydroelectric power. The works were intended to revive the economy of a region that had been hit particularly hard by the Great Depression.

Tennessee River, U.S.A.

RIVER BRAIDING

The Yukon River in central Alaska is one of the few examples of an extensive braided river system. Braiding is found where there is an abundant supply of sediment, highly variable water flows, and erodable banks.

1. Río Negro This is the largest left tributary of the Amazon and the largest blackwater river in the world. Its dark color comes from leaves and humus that have been washed in from the tree-lined banks. The large quantity of peaty plant detritus in suspension colors the river a tea-like dark brown rather than making it completely black.

Río Negro, Colombia and Brazil

2. Río de la Plata This river is the joint estuary of the Uruguay and Parana rivers. There is a marked difference between its northern and southern shores. The Argentine (southern) side is low-lying and subject to flooding. On the Uruguayan (northern) side it is bordered by rocky shores and high sand dunes.

Río de la Plata, Uruguay and Argentina

3. Colorado The Argentine Colorado River rises in the Andes and flows southeast to the Atlantic Ocean. It crosses large tracts of arid land before reaching more fertile areas in Patagonia. The valley in this area is wooded, and there is flat land suitable for agriculture that is enough to sustain small, scattered rural populations.

Colorado River, Argentina

HOUSES ON STILTS

Since pre-Columbian times stilt houses have been built by native peoples along the tropical river valleys of the Amazon and Orinoco rivers. The massed stilt houses located around Lake Maracaibo inspired the 15th-century Italian explorer Amerigo Vespucci to call the area "Venezuela," which means "Little Venice."

Rivers of South America

The east–west asymmetry of drainage patterns in South America is extreme. All the major basins lie east of the Andes. The close proximity of the Andes to the Pacific coast and the scarcity of rainfall from southern Ecuador to central Chile mean that the rivers are short, and few of them convey any large quantity of water.

RÍO NEGRO

Length 1,860 miles (2,990 km)
Drainage area 278,038 square miles (720,114 km²)
Countries Colombia (forms a section of the Colombia–Venezuela border), Brazil
Source Highlands of Colombia
Elevation at source 790 feet (241 m)
Mouth Amazon River at Manaus
Outflow Amazon River
Elevation at mouth 61 feet (19 m)

Major tributaries *Left:* Casiquiare, Cauaburi, Araçá, Demini, Branco, Jauaperi. *Right:* Içana, Vaupés-Uaupés, Cuiuni, Jaú, Unini

RÍO DE LA PLATA

Length 180 miles (290 km)
Drainage area 1,679,533 square miles (4,349,975 km²)
Countries Uruguay, Argentina
Source Joint estuary of Paraná and Uruguay rivers
Elevation at source 0
Mouth Between Uruguay and Argentina
Outflow Atlantic Ocean
Elevation at mouth 0

Major tributaries *Head:* Joint estuary of Paraná and Uruguay rivers

COLORADO

Length 570 miles (920 km), excluding Grande
Drainage area 155,582 square miles (402,956 km²)
Countries Argentina
Source Andes, formed by junction of the Grande and the Barrancas rivers
Elevation at source 2,881 feet (878 m) at confluence
Mouth 70 miles south of Bahía Blanca
Outflow Atlantic Ocean
Elevation at mouth 0

Major tributaries *Head:* Barrancas, Grande. *Left:* Salado (uncertain river)

Río Negro Shallow offshoots of the main river, called *igarape*, such as this on the Río Negro, are characteristic of Amazonian rivers. They are important communication routes, navigable only by small boats.

AMAZON

Length 4,225 miles (6,798 km)
Drainage area 2,722,000 square miles (7,499,000 km²)
Countries Peru, Colombia, Brazil, Bolivia, Ecuador, Venezuela
Source Apacheta cliff, Nevado Mismi, Arequipa, Peru
Elevation at source 16,962 feet (5,170 m)
Mouth Brazil
Outflow Atlantic Ocean
Elevation at mouth 0

Major tributaries *Head:* Marañón, Ucayali. *Left:* Santiago, Morona, Pastaza, Tigre, Napo, Putumayo-Içá, Caquetá, Japurá, Negro, Urubu, Uatumã, Nhamundá, Trombetas, Curuá, Maicurú Paru, Jarí, Maracá. *Right:* Huallaga, Ucayali, Javarí, Jandiatuba, Jutaí, Juruá, Tefé, Coarí, Purus, Madeira, Paraná-Urariá, Tapajós, Xingú, Anapu, Pacaja, Jacunda, Tocantins (strictly not a tributary).

MAGDALENA

Length 930 miles (1,497 km)
Drainage area 99,091 square miles (256,622 km²)
Countries Colombia
Source Cordillera Central
Elevation at source 6,822 feet (2,079 m)
Mouth Caribbean Sea, near Barranquilla
Outflow Caribbean Sea
Elevation at mouth 0

Major tributaries *Left:* Saldana, Cauca, San Jorge.
Right: Bogotá, Cararé, Sogomobo, César

ORINOCO

Length 1,498 miles (2,410 km)
Drainage area 368,186 square miles (953,598 km²)
Countries Venezuela, Colombia
Source Sierra Parima, Venezuela and Brazil
Elevation at source 3,435 feet (1,047 m)
Mouth Orinoco Delta, Venezuela
Outflow Atlantic Ocean
Elevation at mouth 0

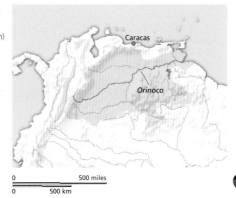

Major tributaries *Left:* Guaviare, Inirida, Vichada, Tomo, Meta, Cinaruco, Capanaparo, Arauca, Apure, Portuguesa, Guarico. *Right:* Ventuari, Cuao, Caura, Caroni, Paragua

---

FACT FILE

1. Amazon Until recent decades the Amazon basin has been sparsely populated. However, the increasingly effective control of malaria, improved diets and sanitation, and the greater ease of transportation have made it more attractive for settlement. Also, increased resource extraction activities have contributed to the exploitation of the Amazon and its vast hinterland.

Amazon River, Peru, Colombia, Brazil, Bolivia, Ecuador and Venezuela

2. Magdalena Colombia's principal river, the Magdalena runs from south to north through the western half of the country. It is navigable through much of its lower reaches and was the main route for exports during the tobacco boom in the region in the middle of the 19th century. It is inhabited by the endangered Magdalena turtle.

Magdalena River, Colombia

3. Orinoco For most of its length, the Orinoco flows through impenetrable rain forest or through the savanna region of the Llanos, which occupies 60 percent of the Orinoco basin north of the Guaviare River and west of the lower Orinoco River and the Guiana Highlands. The savanna has long been used as a vast cattle range.

Orinoco River, Venezuela and Colombia

FLESH-STRIPPING FISH

Red-bellied piranhas are found throughout the Amazon basin. They feed mainly on fish, insects, worms, and crustaceans. In the dry season, when numbers are concentrated in shrinking water holes, schools sometimes converge on large animals, such as anacondas, caimans, birds, and terrestrial mammals, and strip their bones of flesh in a matter of minutes.

Rivers of South America
continued

The drainage basins that lie east of the Andes cover 75 percent of South America and the main rivers flow into the Atlantic Ocean. The largest drainage systems are the Amazon, Río de la Plata, Orinoco, and São Francisco. West of the Andes, the major rivers are the Guayas in Ecuador and the Santa in Peru.

PARANÁ DELTA

The delta of the Paraná River is a huge forested marshland about 20 miles (32 km) northeast of Buenos Aires, Argentina. Large numbers of wading birds make the area a very popular destination for bird watchers.

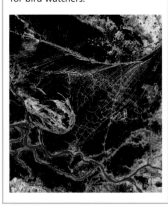

PARAGUAY

Length 1,584 miles (2,549 km)
Drainage area 451,176 square miles (1,168,540 km²)
Countries Bolivia, Brazil, Paraguay, Argentina
Source Serra dos Parecis, south of Diamantino, Brazil
Elevation at source 1,427 feet (435 m)
Mouth Paraná River at Paso de la Patria
Outflow Paraná River
Elevation at mouth 148 feet (45 m)

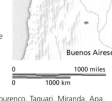

Major tributaries *Left:* São Lourenço, Taquari, Miranda, Apa, Tebicuary. *Right:* Monte Lindo, Confuso, Pilcomayo, Bermejo

MARONA

Length 260 miles (420 km)
Drainage area 6,907 square miles (17,887 km²)
Countries Ecuador, Peru
Source Northeast of Macas, Ecuador
Elevation at source 3,447 feet (1,051 m)
Mouth Marañón River, Peru
Outflow Marañón River, Peru
Elevation at mouth 520 feet (158 m)

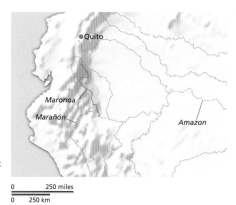

Major tributaries *Left:* Macuma, Cangaime, Situche. *Right:* Cusuhma, Mangosia

PURUS

Length 1,995 miles (3,210 km)
Drainage area 24,391 square miles (63,166 km²)
Countries Peru, Brazil
Source Peruvian Andes
Elevation at source 1,543 feet (470 m)
Mouth Amazon River
Outflow Amazon River
Elevation at mouth 105 feet (32 m)

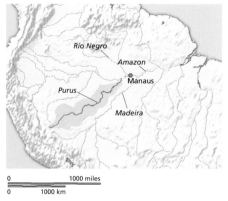

Major tributaries *Left:* Inaiuini, Pauini, Tapauá.
Right: Chandless, Iaco, Acre, Sepatini, Ituxi, Mucuim, Ipixuna

Wetlands The Paraguay River is the primary water supply of the Pantanal wetlands. Studies show that the proposed re-channeling of the river would have a devastating impact on these wetlands.

PARANÁ

Length 1,600 miles (2,570 km), excluding Paranaíba River
Drainage area 997,175 square miles (2,582,672 km²)
Countries Brazil, Uruguay, Argentina
Source Confluence of Paranaíba and Grande rivers, at Aparecida do Taboado, Brazil
Elevation at source 1,100 feet (335 m)
Mouth Río de la Plata
Outflow Río de la Plata, Atlantic Ocean
Elevation at mouth 0

Major tributaries *Head:* Paranaíba, Grande. *Left:* Tietê, Aguapeí, Peixe, Paranapanema, Ivaí, Piquiri, Iguaçú, Corrientes, Gualeguay. *Right:* Sucuriú, Verde, Pardo, Ivinheima, Monday, Paraguay, San Javier, Saladillo, Salado

ESSEQUIBO

Length 600 miles (970 km)
Drainage area 60,817 square miles (157,500 km²)
Countries Guyana
Source Sierra Acaraí
Elevation at source 2,200 feet (671 m)
Mouth NW of Georgetown
Outflow Atlantic Ocean
Elevation at mouth 0

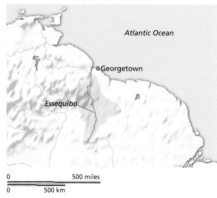

Major tributaries *Left:* Kassikaityu, Kuiyuwini, Rupununi, Pataro, Mazaruni, Cuyuni

CHUBUT

Length 516 miles (830 km)
Drainage area 16,218 square miles (42,000 km²)
Countries Argentina
Source Andes
Elevation at source 4,328 feet (1,319 m)
Mouth Rawson, Argentina
Outflow Atlantic Ocean
Elevation at mouth 0

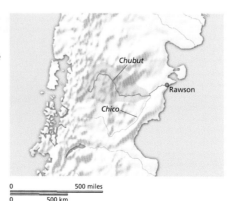

Major tributaries *Right:* Chico

FOREST PROTECTION

The Chubut River flows through the Los Alerces National Park in Chubut Province, Argentina. The park was created in 1937 to protect the alerce forest and other flora from logging. The alerce is one of the longest-living trees in the world.

DISCOVERING RIVERS

Nearly all civilizations can trace their origins back to early settlement around a river or river system. Rivers not only provided water, they were also convenient transportation routes. It is therefore not surprising that some of the first-recorded journeys of exploration were in search of the world's great rivers. In the 5th century B.C. Greek historian Herodotus described one of the earliest-known exploratory expeditions. He wrote about five North African explorers who traveled from south to west across the desert and found a great river flowing west to east, which is now thought to have been the Niger River.

African discoveries (below) Scottish missionary David Livingstone (insert top) traveled to Africa in 1853–56 to expose the evils of the slave trade. During his expedition, he mapped the Zambezi River and became the first European to see Victoria Falls (below). In 1869 Sir Henry Morton Stanley (insert bottom) was sent by the *New York Herald* to find Livingstone. The two men joined forces and discovered a river later shown to be the Congo.

Pinzon and the Amazon (left) One of the three ships of Christopher Columbus' first voyage in 1492 was the *Niña*, commanded by renowned navigator Vicente Pinzon (pictured). In 1500, Pinzon reached the Brazilian coast and sailed along it for four months, entering the Amazon estuary. This is now regarded as the first European sighting of the river.

THREE PHASES

The quest for geographical knowledge of the world has been continuous throughout history, but there have been three periods of intense activity. The first was the exploration of the ancient world, centered on the shores of the Mediterranean, the great river civilizations of the Tigris and Euphrates, and Egypt and the Nile. The earliest-known surviving map, dating from around 2300 B.C., shows Mesopotamian waterways.

The second period of exploration was linked to the increasing economic power of northwest Europe during the late 15th and early 16th centuries, and a search for sea routes to the east. This led to the accidental discovery of the New World. By the mid-16th century, European explorers had traveled along the east and west coasts of the Americas and found the mouths of the continents' great rivers. From the mid-18th century these rivers, particularly those in North America, became the main routes into the interior for European settlers.

The third phase of exploration began in the mid-18th century and reached its peak in the 19th century. Most exploration was focused on Africa and linked with the emergence of European nations as imperial powers, especially with the zenith of British imperialism. British exploration of African rivers began with the Scottish explorer Mungo Park, who mapped much of the Niger. The Zambezi and lower Congo rivers were explored by David Livingstone, who died during an expedition to find the source of the Nile. The source of the Blue Nile in Lake Tana in the Ethiopian highlands had been visited in 1618 by Spanish priest Father Paez and in 1770 by Scottish explorer James Bruce. However, the source of the White Nile was not seen by a European until the Burton and Speke expedition of 1856–58, when the latter discovered Lake Victoria.

Today, satellite imaging allows geographers to become virtual explorers, able follow the smallest streams anywhere on Earth.

THROUGH THE AGES

3800 B.C. The first-known maps were drawn on clay tablets and showed the distribution of Egypt's fertile land and the irrigation channels connected to the Nile.

2300 B.C. Ancient Egyptian governor Harkuf led Nile expeditions southwards into Nubia (modern Sudan) and may have reached the second Nile cataract (now under Lake Nassar).

1541 Spaniard Hernando de Soto was the first European to reach the Mississippi. After a disastrous expedition, he returned to the Gulf Coast via the Mississippi.

1609 English explorer Henry Hudson sought shelter off what is now New York. He found the mouth of a large river which was later named after him.

1828–29 Englishman Charles Sturt traced the courses of several Australian rivers and discovered the Darling. In a subsequent expedition, he discovered the Murray River.

In search of the Nile's source (left)
British army officers Richard Burton and John Speke began an expedition in 1856 to find the source of the Nile. By the time they reached Lake Tanganyika in 1858 (shown here), Burton was so ill he could not walk, and Speke was almost blind. At this point, Burton turned back, but Speke carried on. He reached Lake Victoria later that year, rightly believing it to be a source of the Nile.

Along the Amazon (below) The Amazon and its tributaries, such as the Tigre River pictured here, were the only routes into the interior of South America for early European explorers. From 1541, Portuguese explorer Francisco de Orellana followed the Amazon from the Andes to the Atlantic. In 1743, Frenchman Charles-Marie de La Condamine traveled for four months on a raft down the Amazon, during which time he made geographic and ethnographic observations of the Amazon basin.

1852 Scottish explorer Francis Cadell was the first European to travel the entire length of the Murray River, 1,300 miles (2,092 km), in a canoe.

1855 David Livingstone was the first European to see Victoria Falls. The local people called it Mosi-oa-Tunya, meaning "The smoke that thunders."

1877 Anglo-American journalist Sir Henry Morton Stanley was the first to establish the course of the upper reaches of the Congo River.

2004 The White Nile Expedition, led by South African Hendri Coetzee, became the first to navigate the entire length of the Nile River.

2007 A Brazilian expedition located the most distant headwaters of the Amazon, confirming it to be longer than the Nile.

FLOOD PROTECTION

The Thames Barrier was constructed between 1974 and 1984 to protect London from flooding caused by exceptional high tides associated with storm surges in the North Sea. The barrier is raised an average of four times a year.

Rivers of Europe

Europe has a radial pattern of drainage, with most rivers flowing outward from the heart of the continent, often starting from headwaters that are located close together. The longest European river, the Volga, flows south and discharges into the Caspian Sea, and the second longest, the Danube, flows west to east, discharging into the Black Sea.

THAMES

Length 215 miles (346 km)
Drainage area 5,500 square miles (14,250 km²)
Countries England
Source Kemble, Cotswold Hills, Gloucestershire
Elevation at source 350 feet (107 m)
Mouth East of London
Outflow North Sea
Elevation at mouth 0

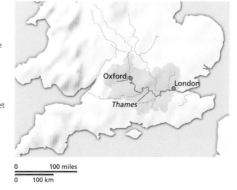

Major tributaries *Left:* Churn, Windrush, Cherwell, Thame, Colne, Lee, Roding.
Right: Ock, Kennet, Loddon, Wey, Mole

RHINE

Length 820 miles (1,320 km)
Drainage area 85,000 square miles (220,000 km²)
Countries Austria, Germany, France, Netherlands
Sources Vorderrhein from Lake Tuma; Hinterrhein from Paradies Glacier
Elevation at source Lake Tuma 7,696 feet (2,346 m); Hinterrhein 8,200 feet (2,500 m)
Mouth Rhine-Meuse-Scheldt Delta
Outflow North Sea
Elevation at mouth 0

Major tributaries *Head:* Vorderrhein, Hinterrhein. *Left:* Aare, Andlau, Ill, Lauter, Nahe, Selz, Mosel, Ahr.
Right: Kinzig, Saalbach, Kraichbach, Neckar, Main, Lahn, Sieg, Rhur, Lippe

SEINE

Length 485 miles (780 km)
Drainage area 30,400 square miles (78,700 km²)
Countries France
Source Northeast of Dijon near Saint-Germain, in the Côte d'Or region of Burgundy
Elevation at source 1,545 feet (471 m)
Mouth Le Havre
Outflow English Channel
Elevation at mouth 0

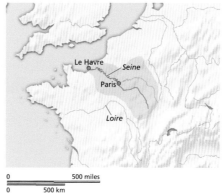

Major tributaries *Left:* Yonne, Essonne, Orge, Eure, Risle.
Right: Ource, Aube, Marne, Oise, Andelle

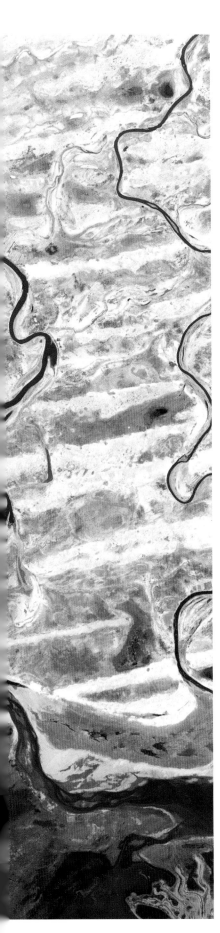

Niger inland delta This unusual feature occurs where the gradient of the Niger suddenly decreases. Sediment deposition creates a region of braided streams, marshes, and lakes the size of Belgium.

NILE

Length 4,132 miles (6,648 km), to source of Kagera River
Drainage area 1,293,000 square miles (3,349,000 km²)
Countries Burundi, Egypt, Ethiopia, Kenya, Rwanda, Sudan, Tanzania, Uganda
Source Confluence of the White Nile and Blue Nile, Khartoum. *White Nile source:* Kagera River, Burundi. *Blue Nile source:* Lake Tana, Ethiopia
Elevation at source Confluence of White Nile and Blue Nile: 1,248 feet (380 m). *Kagera:* 6,300 feet (1,920 m). *Blue Nile:* 5,873 feet (1,790 m).
Mouth Nile Delta
Outflow Mediterranean Sea
Elevation at mouth 0

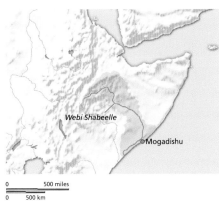

Cairo
Nile
White Nile
Blue Nile
Lake Victoria

0 — 1000 miles
0 — 1000 km

Major tributaries *Head:* Kagera, Akanyaru, Lake Victoria, White Nile, Blue Nile.
Right: Atbara

WEBI SHABEELLE

Length 1,130 miles (1,820 km)
Drainage area 129,976 square miles (336,604 km²)
Countries Ethiopia, Somalia
Source Ethiopian Highlands
Elevation at source 9,766 feet (2,977 m)
Mouth Jubba River
Outflow Jubba River, Indian Ocean
Elevation at mouth 36 feet (11 m)

Webi Shabeelle
Mogadishu

0 — 500 miles
0 — 500 km

Major tributaries *Left:* Ramis, Mojo.

LIMPOPO

Length 1,100 miles (1,770 km)
Drainage area 132,059 square miles (342,000 km²)
Countries South Africa, Botswana, Zimbabwe, Mozambique
Source Krokodil River, Witwatersrand, South Africa
Elevation at source 5,257 feet (1,602 m)
Mouth Southern Mozambique
Outflow Indian Ocean
Elevation at mouth 0

Limpopo
Gaborone
Mozambique Channel
Maputo

0 — 500 miles
0 — 500 km

Major tributaries *Head:* rises as Krokodil River, becomes Limpopo at confluence with Marico River. *Left:* Marico, Shashi, Mzingwani, Bubi, Mwenzi, Changane. *Right:* Mogalakwena, Olifants

CAIRO

Egypt's bustling capital, Cairo, is located on the banks and islands of the Nile River. The city is just south of the point where the river leaves its desert-bound valley and divides into two branches that flow into the low-lying Nile Delta region.

Rivers of Australia

The Great Dividing Range, Australia's main mountain range, runs the entire length of the eastern coastline and then turns west. Rivers to the east flow into the Coral Sea and rivers to the west flow inland to the site of a sea that no longer exists, having disappeared approximately 80 million years ago. Some rivers flow north into the Gulf of Carpenteria.

AUSTRALIAN PELICAN

The Australian pelican is the largest of the world's eight species of pelican and is found living in large flocks or colonies all around Australia, congregating in large numbers wherever there is either salt water or fresh water.

MURRAY

Length 1,609 miles (2,589 km)
Drainage area 415,000 square miles (1,075,000 km²)
States New South Wales, Victoria, South Australia
Source The Pilot (a mountain), south of Mount Kosciuszko in southeastern New South Wales
Elevation at source 5,250 feet (1,600 m)
Mouth Goolwa, South Australia
Outflow Great Australian Bight, Indian Ocean
Elevation at mouth 0

Major tributaries *Left:* Mitta Mitta, Kiewa, Ovens, Goulburn, Campaspe, Loddon. *Right:* Murrumbidgee River, Darling River,

DARLING

Length 1,704 miles (2,742 km)
Drainage area 250,000 square miles (650,000 km²)
States New South Wales
Source Bourke, New South Wales. Source considered to be the Severn River
Elevation at source Darling 354 feet (108 m); Severn 4,108 feet (1,252 m)
Mouth Murray River, Wentworth
Outflow Murray River
Elevation at mouth 112 feet (34 m)

Major tributaries *Head:* Severn, which becomes successively the Dumaresq, Macintyre, Barwon, and, finally, the Darling. *Left:* Bogan. *Right:* Warrego, Paroo

MURRUMBIDGEE

Length 1,050 miles (1,690 km)
Drainage area 32,440 square miles (84,020 km²)
States New South Wales, Victoria
Source Eastern Highlands, New South Wales, 20 miles north of Kiandra
Elevation at source 4,740 feet (1,445 m)
Mouth Murray River, east of Boundary Bend, Victoria
Outflow Murray River
Elevation at mouth 190 feet (58 m)

Major tributaries *Left:* Gudgenby, Cotter, Tumut. *Right:* Yass, Molonglo, Lachlan

Snowy River During the 1990s the low level of water in the Snowy River was a major environmental concern for the State of Victoria. A political campaign was run with the objective of increasing the water level from 1 per cent to 28 per cent of its original flow.

LACHLAN

Length 930 miles (1,500 km)
Drainage area 32,700 square miles (84,690 km²)
States New South Wales
Source Eastern Highlands, New South Wales, 8 miles (13 km) east of Gunning
Elevation at source 2,500 feet (762 m)
Mouth Murrumbidgee River, at Great Cambung Swamp, near Oxley
Outflow Murrumbidgee River
Elevation at mouth 259 feet (79 m)

Major tributaries *Left:* Boorowa. *Right:* Abercrombie, Belubula, Willandra Billabong

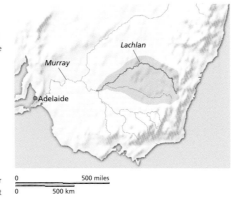

MACQUARIE

Length 590 miles (950 km)
Drainage area 21,814 square miles (61,673 km²)
States New South Wales
Source Confluence of the Campbells and Fish Rivers, near Bathurst
Elevation at source 2,192 feet (668 m)
Mouth Barwon River, east of Brewarrina
Outflow Barwon River
Elevation at mouth 413 feet (126 m)

Major tributaries *Head:* Campbells, Fish. *Left:* Bell, Little. *Right:* Turon, Cudgegong, Talbragar, Castlereagh

SNOWY

Length 270 miles (430 km)
Drainage area 6,093 square miles (15, 779 km²)
States New South Wales, Victoria
Source Snowy Mountains near Mount Kosciuszko
Elevation at source 5,935 feet (1,809 m)
Mouth Bass Straight at Marlo, Victoria
Outflow Bass Strait, Pacific Ocean
Elevation at mouth 0

Major tributaries *Left:* Eucumbene, Bombala. *Right:* Thredbo, Buchan

DAMAGED SYSTEM

The Darling River is seriously polluted by pesticide runoff, and damaged by drought. Clearance of native vegetation and over-irrigation have produced a high salt content, and a rise in the water table has carried salts to the surface, contaminating rivers and topsoil.

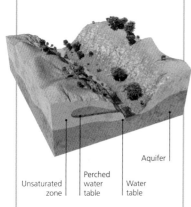

Unsaturated zone | Perched water table | Water table | Aquifer

Shape Rock type and surface define the water table's shape. It is "perched" if impermeable rock lies above the main aquifer but below the surface.

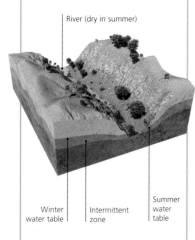

River (dry in summer)

Winter water table | Intermittent zone | Summer water table

Level When rainfall is seasonal the water table rises and falls. This creates a zone between winter and summer levels that has intermittent saturation.

Underground Water

All rocks contain some water, but they have different porosity and permeability characteristics. This means that water does not move around in the same way in all rocks, and underground rivers are confined to particular rock types. Rock formations with large amounts of water that are easily accessible from springs or wells are called aquifers.

Torrent underground Churning rapids and waterfalls await explorers of Ora Cave, Papua New Guinea. One of the world's largest sinkholes, it is nearly a mile (1,400 m) long, half a mile (750 m) wide, and 1,038 feet (317 m) deep.

Surface Alluvial floodplains consist of clays and fine-grained sands that are sufficiently impermeable to allow streams to flow over them.

Stream Some of the stream's water percolates through the bed and dissolves the limestone beneath the alluvial layer.

Limestone While this rock is mechanically quite hard, water can percolate through it and dissolve it, especially if the water is acidic.

Sinkhole Where an underground cave or mine roof has collapsed in the path of a stream, the water either disappears down a sinkhole (doline) or the hole fills to create a circular lake.

Blockage Rubble from the collapse of the underground cave may block drainage, causing the cave to fill with water.

Artesian wells These are found in valleys where less porous rock overlies an aquifer. This causes water in the hills to rise above the lowest point so that it is forced out through any cracks or boreholes.

Less porous rock The capping layers prevent water held in the aquifer beneath from seeping away, so the water rises above the surrounding water table.

Porous rock In the hills, where they are not covered by an impermeable capping layer, water soaks into the porous rock layers.

Artesian well The weight of water held in the hills pressurizes the aquifer and forcing water out through any defects in the capping layers.

Bedrock An impermeable layer of bedrock below the porous rock of the aquifer prevents the water from seeping away into deeper layers.

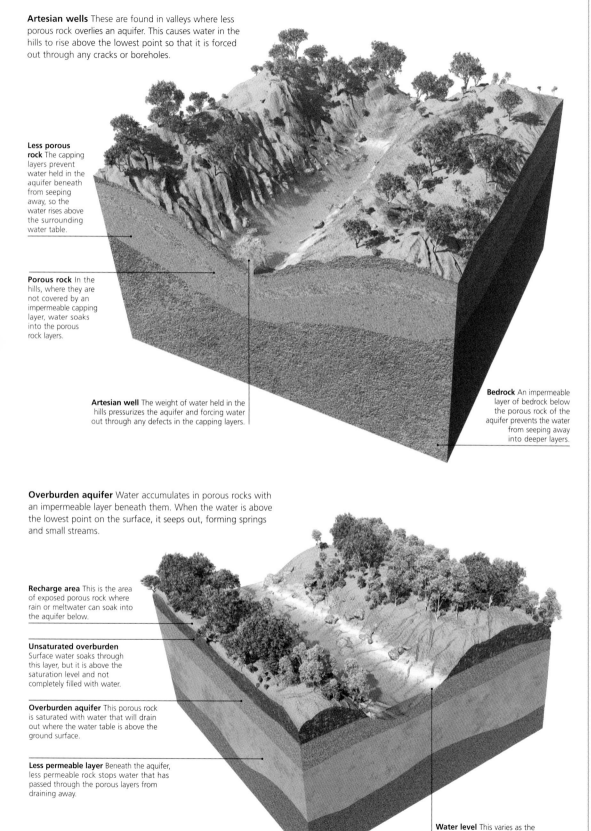

Overburden aquifer Water accumulates in porous rocks with an impermeable layer beneath them. When the water is above the lowest point on the surface, it seeps out, forming springs and small streams.

Recharge area This is the area of exposed porous rock where rain or meltwater can soak into the aquifer below.

Unsaturated overburden Surface water soaks through this layer, but it is above the saturation level and not completely filled with water.

Overburden aquifer This porous rock is saturated with water that will drain out where the water table is above the ground surface.

Less permeable layer Beneath the aquifer, less permeable rock stops water that has passed through the porous layers from draining away.

Bedrock This layer is also impermeable, preventing water seepage to lower layers.

Water level This varies as the balance changes between the amount collected by the recharge area and drainage or extraction.

Waterfalls

Waterfalls are some of the most spectacular natural features on the planet. They occur where there is a sudden break in gradient along a river, often where there is a sharp boundary between rock types. The International Waterfall Classification system groups waterfalls into ten classes of average water flow, using a logarithmic scale.

Formation The slow but irresistible erosive power of flowing water seeks out any weaknesses in the bedrock over which it flows. Waterfalls are formed at suitable "nickpoints" that are eroded by the water.

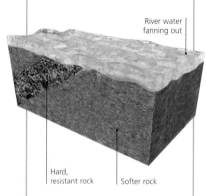

River water fanning out

Hard, resistant rock   Softer rock

1 On a newly exposed land surface, river water fans out. Where there are different rock types, the river eventually begins to cut away the less resistant material.

Hard, resistant rock

Soft rock eroded to create a steep drop

2 Softer rock that lies downstream is eroded away much more quickly than the harder rock upstream, and a sharp drop develops at the junction between the rock types.

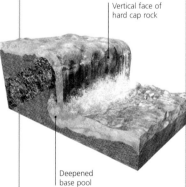

Vertical face of hard cap rock

Deepened base pool

3 With further erosion, the hard cap rock is cut back to a vertical face, and the force of the water cascading down gouges a deep pool in the softer rock at the base.

Waterfall system (above) The Iguazu Falls are a system of 275 waterfalls along a 1.67 mile (2.7 km) section of the Iguazu River, on the Brazil–Argentina border. Their normal flow is 350,000 to 400,000 gallons per second (1,300,000–1,500,000 liters/s) .

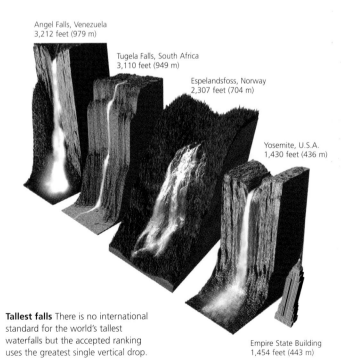

Angel Falls, Venezuela
3,212 feet (979 m)

Tugela Falls, South Africa
3,110 feet (949 m)

Espelandsfoss, Norway
2,307 feet (704 m)

Yosemite, U.S.A.
1,430 feet (436 m)

Tallest falls There is no international standard for the world's tallest waterfalls but the accepted ranking uses the greatest single vertical drop.

Empire State Building
1,454 feet (443 m)

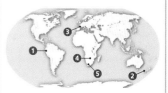

1. Gocta Catarata The exact height of this waterfall in Peru is still disputed, since the existence of the falls has only

recently become widely known. The falls are tiered and drop, in two stages, a total distance of 2,531 feet (771 m) .

Gocta Catarata, Peru

2. Sutherland Falls This waterfall on the South Island of New Zealand forms the outlet of Lake Quill and drops

down three steps in very quick succession: 751 feet (229 m), 815 feet (248 m), and 338 feet (103 m).

Sutherland Falls, New Zealand

3. Grande Cascade de Gavarnie Located in the central Pyrenees, this is the tallest waterfall in France. The falls

are two-tiered, with a total height of 1,384 feet (422 m), and the tallest single drop is 922 feet (281 m).

Grande Cascade de Gavarnie, France

4. Victoria Falls These falls on the Zambesi River are between Zambia and Zimbabwe. They form a single drop of

350 feet (107 m) and have four sections: Devil's Cataract, Main Falls, Rainbow Falls, and Eastern Cataract.

Victoria Falls, Zambia and Zimbabwe

5. Augrabies Falls This is a major waterfall on the Orange River in South Africa. The river divides itself in several channels before dropping 183 feet

(56 m). When it is In full flood, the river nearly fills the gorge below, almost submerging the falls.

Augrabies Falls, South Africa

Angel Falls This spectacular waterfall in Venezuela is the tallest in the world and has the highest single drop. The total height is 3,212 feet (979 m) with a single drop of 2,648 feet (807 m).

WETLANDS and SWAMPS

Wetlands are found in all parts of the world where terrestrial ecosystems meet marine systems. Wetland is currently defined as an area of land that is permanently or seasonally waterlogged or flooded. It is shallow enough to allow the growth of rooted as well as free-floating plants. The meeting of two types of habitat creates biologically varied and productive areas that not only contain plants and animals from the adjacent land or water, but also species unique to the wetland habitat. The world's wetlands are under continual threat from pollution and encroachment to satisfy the demand for land for housing and agriculture.

Wetland reptiles (left) Crocodiles, alligators, caimans, and gharials are large aquatic reptiles that live in rivers, lakes, and wetlands throughout the tropics in Africa, Asia, the Americas, and Australia. Some live in brackish or saltwater mangroves and estuaries. They feed on fish, reptiles, and mammals, as well as invertebrates like mollusks and crustaceans.

Water tupelo (right) This wetland species found in swamps and waterlogged floodplains of the southern United States requires periodic inundation of its root system in order to thrive. Nectar from its flowers is favored by honey producers. Mature trees yield commercial-grade timber that is used to make furniture and crates, as well as by woodcarvers.

FORMATION

Wetlands are among the world's most productive and species-rich habitats, and their biodiversity is comparable with that of rain forests and coral reefs. There are a wide range of types, but many wetlands are also highly variable environments in themselves. Many wetlands are not constantly covered in water, but have wet and dry phases of varying lengths and intensities. Some wetlands are wet for only part of the year, while others have no standing water but, because they are near the water table, remain saturated. Others may dry out completely for long periods, sometimes even for years.

Wetlands have a finite life cycle, beginning with the saturation of a terrestrial habitat and usually ending as a transition back to a fully terrestrial habitat. Many wetlands were formed when glaciers retreated after the last ice age, about 10,000 years ago. The shallow, water-filled depressions left by the ice sheets were quickly filled with sediments and organic debris, and became wetland rather than lakes. Wetlands can also be formed by the overtopping of river banks and changes in sea level that can leave waterlogged areas behind.

Climate, too, plays a key role in the formation of wetlands. High rainfall and poor drainage, for example, can cause the ground to become waterlogged.

Once formed, wetlands are constantly changing as their plant life changes in a process known as succession. For example, one type of floating plant, such as pondweed, begins to fills up a pond or lake. Dead stems and leaves make the water thick, shallow, and slow moving. As a result, plants that need roots in soil, such as reeds and grasses, can then grow. As dead plant remains continue to accumulate, the pond gradually becomes wetland. It is colonized first by low-growing wetland plant species, then by larger shrubs and trees tolerant of wet and acidic soils. As succession continues, the level of accumulated material raises the upper layers above the water table. Soil dries out and fully terrestrial species can colonize the area.

Mangrove forest (below) The Ten Thousand Islands National Wildlife Refuge in Florida is part of the largest expanse of mangrove forest in North America. Approximately two-thirds of the refuge is mangrove, which dominates its tidal fringes and islands, or keys. The northern third of the refuge consists of brackish marsh and is interspersed with ponds and patches of coastal forests of oak, cabbage palms, and tropical hardwoods.

Freshwater Ponds and Wetlands

Freshwater wetlands and ponds are found in areas of poor drainage where the water table is at or close to the surface and covered by vegetation adapted to survival in saturated soils. In the past much effort has been put into draining wetlands and exploiting their fertile soils for agriculture. Over the last two decades, however, such areas have been recognized as important unique and species–rich environments. In addition, it has been realized that wetlands not only play a significant role in flood control by absorbing flood water and then releasing it slowly, but they also help to improve water quality through natural detoxification processes.

Pantanal (right) Covering parts of Brazil, Bolivia, and Paraguay, the world's largest freshwater wetland is home to 3,500 known plant and at least 1,230 animal species. The abundance and diversity of life in the Pantanal rivals that of the Amazonian rain forest.

Walden Pond (below) This pond in Concorde, Massachusetts, U.S.A., is an example of a kettle pond left by a retreating glacier. Winter ice was once harvested at Walden and many other New England ponds, a process immortalized by the writer Henry David Thoreau, who lived on the shores of the pond.

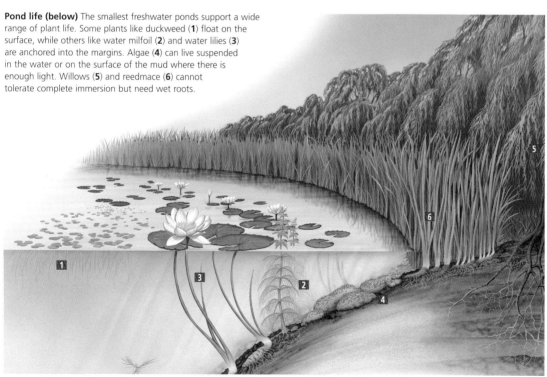

Pond life (below) The smallest freshwater ponds support a wide range of plant life. Some plants like duckweed (**1**) float on the surface, while others like water milfoil (**2**) and water lilies (**3**) are anchored into the margins. Algae (**4**) can live suspended in the water or on the surface of the mud where there is enough light. Willows (**5**) and reedmace (**6**) cannot tolerate complete immersion but need wet roots.

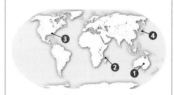

1. Point Riou Spit Extensive marsh and tidal mudflats have formed in the lee of this spit at the mouth of Icy Bay, Alaska, U.S.A. The area is an important feeding ground for

wildfowl. In winter bears, wolves, and wolverines in some numbers scavenge the area for food.

Point Riou Spit, Icy Bay, Alaska, U.S.A.

2. Kazakhlyshor This salt marsh in Turkmenistan is unusual because it is completely landlocked. There is no outlet for its inflows of water, except by evaporation, leading to a build-up

of dissolved salts. Unfortunately, this has also meant that pollutants are carried into it and accumulate.

Kazakhlyshor Salt Marsh, Turkmenistan

3. Long Island Found along the sheltered northern shore of Long Island Sound, U.S.A., this typical northern temperate salt marsh has glasswort in the lowest parts next to

the open mudflats. In much of the mid-marsh there is salt marsh cord grass, with salt meadow grass on drier areas.

Long Island Salt Marshes, U.S.A.

4. The Camargue This national park in France's Rhone Delta is best known for its semi-wild bulls, the huge flocks of pink flamingoes feeding on the rich mudflats, and the unique Camargue

horses that are thought to be closely related to the prehistoric wild horses that once roamed the area.

The Camargue, France

5. Wooloweyah Drainage schemes have destroyed most of the intertidal salt marsh wetlands around the mouth of the Clarence River, Australia. There

are plans to remove the levees and drains, and return the largest area, Wooloweyah, to wetland.

Wooloweyah Salt Marsh,
New South Wales, Australia

Tidal Wetlands and Salt Marshes

Salt marsh is one of the most biologically productive habitats on the planet, rivalling tropical rain forest for biodiversity. This is largely because salt marsh has two sources of nutrients. One of these comes from any freshwater runoff that occurs, and the other from the daily tidal influx of salt or brackish water, which deposits nutrient-rich material around plant roots.

Major site This salt marsh on the Dutch island of Texel is part of the Waddenzee, a shallow inlet of the North Sea. As one of the main wetlands in northwest Europe, much of the area is protected.

1 A heron lures small fish by dropping sticks or leaves on the water surface.

2 The bird follows the swirling twig or leaf downstream, watching to see if it attracts any fish.

Fishing lures The many small inlets in salt marshes are ideal nurseries for coastal and resident fish. The abundance of small fish attracts birds like the green heron, which uses clever fishing tactics.

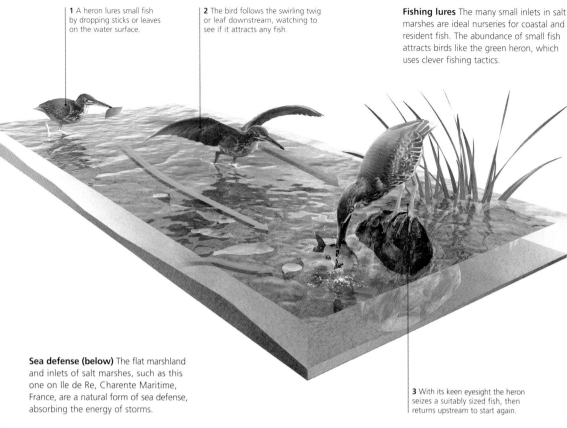

Sea defense (below) The flat marshland and inlets of salt marshes, such as this one on Ile de Re, Charente Maritime, France, are a natural form of sea defense, absorbing the energy of storms.

3 With its keen eyesight the heron seizes a suitably sized fish, then returns upstream to start again.

Wildlife The distinct zones of tidal wetlands support different species. Most invertebrates are found in the mudflats, while the sloping sides of gullies below the high water mark are inhabited by waterfowl and reptiles.

Marsh wren The male marsh wren builds nests in tall marsh vegetation, often creating several unused nests to mark out his territory.

Turtle The diamondback terrapin is the only turtle in North America that lives exclusively in brackish water. It hibernates buried in mud.

Periwinkles These have a kind of biological clock, feeding on the surface of the mud at low tide, then burying themselves before the tide returns.

HERITAGE WATCH

Dieback Sudden wetland dieback, also called brown marsh syndrome, is when salt marsh cordgrass dies suddenly or unexpectedly fails to spread. The cause is not fully known, and there has been a sudden increase in dieback along the east coast of North America.

Mangrove Ecosystems

Found throughout the tropics and subtropics, mangroves are tree-dominated, coastal saltwater wetlands that develop as mud is trapped around the extensive root systems of the trees. There are about 70 species of mangrove trees, but the greatest diversity of species is found in the mangroves of the Indo–West Pacific region.

Mangrove roots Mangrove trees have a complex aerial buttress root system, which supports the trunk in the soft mud. The roots also absorb oxygen from the air, as mud has little or no oxygen.

Life in mangroves (right) The abundance of food sources in mangroves supports many individual animals, but they belong to the relatively few species that are able to cope with the daily cycle of immersion in seawater and exposure to air.

Ghost nippers These shrimps excavate a burrow in the mangrove mud and wait to pounce on passing small prey.

Root colonies The roots of the mangrove are colonized by animals, such as saddle oysters, that need to attach to a firm surface.

Wading birds Large flocks of wading birds sift through the rich mangrove mud to extract small worms, bivalves, and shrimps.

Fish-eaters Mangroves are ideal hunting grounds for fish-eating birds, because vast numbers of small fish live in the shallow water.

Crabs These scavengers eat fruits and seeds from vegetation, as well as small invertebrates and any animal remains.

Blue fish These voracious predators prey on other young fish but they in turn are eaten by birds.

FACT FILE

1. Timonha Estuary Tree species are relatively few in this estuary's pristine mangrove, but animal life is abundant.

 The mangrove and forest are a refuge for endangered animals such as manatees, jaguars, and pumas.

Timonha Estuary, Brazil

2. Florida Mangroves survive along the Florida peninsula because winter is tempered by warm waters on the west

 and east. As Florida is subtropical, the trees tend to be shorter, with smaller leaves than in the tropics.

Florida mangroves, U.S.A.

3. Gazi Bay In these extensive but degraded Kenyan mangroves, seedlings are being planted to help restore the habitat as well as to

 provide wood and fish vital to local fishing communities. Planting will also reduce beach erosion.

Gazi Bay, Kwale District, Kenya

4. Sungai Merbok This forest reserve in Malaysia is known for its diversity of mangrove species and its animal life.

 It attracts bird watchers and wildlife tourism, a sustainable use that contributes to the local economy.

Sungai Merbok Reserve, Malaysia

5. Costa Rica west coast This area's unique type of mangrove is a major nesting site for a number of bird

 species. It also supports the mantled howler monkey, spectacled caiman, and the false vampire bat.

West coast mangroves, Costa Rica

Nursery grounds The tangled roots of submerged mangrove trees make an ideal nursery for many coastal fish species. The young fish have an abundant supply of food and can escape their larger predators by hiding among the roots in spaces too small for predators to follow.

Small Waters

Some of the most ecologically complex freshwater habitats are not large lakes or vast wetlands, but what are known as small waters. These are streams, brooks, and creeks that typically form the headwaters of larger rivers and so are mainly found in upland areas. Small waters can also be outflows from lowland springs.

Ormiston Creek (right) The semi-permanent waterhole at the southern end of this creek in the Northern Territory, Australia, provides water for red wallabies and wallaroos, or euros.

FACT FILE

Meander development Friction between water in a stream and its banks creates horizontal and vertical eddies in the water. These eddies erode sediment from one side of the stream and deposit it on the other.

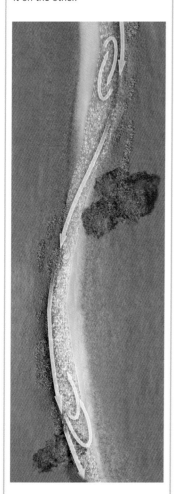

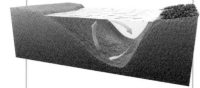

Clockwise eddies When eddies carrying eroded sediment run against the main flow, they are slowed and drop their sediment.

Counterclockwise eddies Eddies that move in the same direction as the main river flow are accelerated and erode sediment.

Fishing bears (above) In the Valley of the Geysers wildlife reserve on the Kamchatka peninsula, Russia, the fish populations of the innumerable streams are a principal food source for bears.

Natural aeration (right) Animal life in small waters depends on adequate oxygen in the water. Fast-flowing streams are naturally aerated where they tumble over boulders, rapids, and small falls.

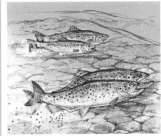

LANDLOCKED WATER

Lakes are large bodies of water that are contained in depressions on land. Nearly all contain freshwater, with the exceptions of the Caspian, Salton, and Dead seas. Even though water in these three is up to six times saltier than seawater, they are true lakes. About 80 percent of all lakes are found at high latitudes in the Northern Hemisphere. This is because of the unequal distribution of landmasses between the hemispheres, and the balance between precipitation and evaporation. Sixty percent of the world's lakes are in Canada, where the last ice age left behind innumerable depressions and an irregular river pattern, producing a "deranged drainage system."

Ponds (left) Pond lilies are found in the shallow margins of ponds and lakes. Ponds can be defined as bodies of freshwater that are much smaller in size than lakes, and shallow enough to allow light to penetrate the deepest parts. This exposure to light allows rooted plants such as the water lilies pictured here to grow anywhere in the pond.

Mountain lake (right) Moraine Lake near Banff, Canada, is 6,183 feet (1,884 m) above sea level, and it receives only a seasonal input of glacial meltwater during the summer months. The meltwater contains rock flour ground away from the surrounding mountains. It is the refraction of light by the tiny rock particles in the lake water that gives it its intense blue color.

Crater lake (below) The Troitsky Crater was formed when the Maly Semiachik volcano on Russia's Kamchatka peninsula erupted around 400 years ago. The volcano remained active and has since erupted several times, the last time being in 1952. The lake is acidic because sulfur from the active volcano saturates the water. Despite its cold surroundings, the lake is hot, and vents, or fumaroles, at its margins reach temperatures of 194°F (90°C).

LAKE FORMATION

Lakes can be formed by a number of processes, causing a depression to fill with water, or to contain water that once flowed freely.

Tectonic forces can create a lake if fault lines are formed. An example of this is the Great Glen fault in Scotland, which contains a number of freshwater lakes, including Loch Ness. Fault lines can widen into rift valley lakes such as Lake Baikal and Lake Tanganyika; these lakes are the oldest and deepest in the world, and may be destined over millions of years to become oceans. Tectonic activity can also cause earthquakes, which trigger landslides that block the ends of existing river valleys.

Glaciation can create lakes by gouging depressions that become water-filled when the ice retreats or by blocking the ends of valleys with moraine. Periglacial lakes form where glaciers prevent water draining away. Kettle lakes form where a block of ice left by a glacier becomes covered by sediments and later melts, leaving a steep, bowl-shaped hollow. Lakes can even form under ice sheets, as in the case of Lake Vostok, where the immense pressure of ice combined with geothermal warming has melted the lowest layers of ice.

Other lakes occupy craters or calderas of extinct or dormant volcanoes and some may be warmed by geothermal activity. Minerals and gases may leach into the lake bed from the magma chamber beneath the crater. If the leached gases are toxic, crater lakes may become a serious hazard. Around 1,700 people were asphyxiated in 1986 by carbon dioxide suddenly released from Lake Nyos in Cameroon.

Rivers can also form lakes. The best known are ox-bow lakes, which are found on floodplains where the meandering of a river has cut off a bend in the main channel. A circular lake can be formed when a river has created a sinkhole in porous rock and the roof of the underground cavern has collapsed as a result.

On a geological timescale, lakes are only short-lived features. They disappear in a few million years after erosion of the basin sides has filled them with sediments.

Lakes

In summer the water of many lakes becomes stratified into a warmer upper layer, called the epilimnion, and a cooler lower layer known as the hypolimnion. This stratification affects the movement of nutrients and dissolved oxygen in the lake. When the lake begins to cool at the end of summer, the cooler surface water tends to sink because it is denser. Eventually this breaks up the stratification and the layers mix in a process called overturn. Lakes that have two seasonal periods of overturn are termed dimictic. The Great Lakes of North America are dimictic because, in addition to the fall overturn, they can also exhibit a spring overturn after the ice cover melts. The Caspian Sea is dimictic in the north but permanently stratified in the south, and Lake Victoria is partially stratified throughout the year.

Chicago, Lake Michigan Chicago developed as a major city because of its strategic position on the Chicago portage—the short overland route linking the Great Lakes with the navigable sections of the Mississippi.

CASPIAN SEA

Length 750 miles (1,200 km)
Maximum width 270 miles (435 km)
Area: 149,200 square miles (386,400 km²)
Drainage area 1,400,000 square miles (3,625,000 km²)
Average depth 604 feet (184 m)
Maximum depth 3,360 feet (1,025 m)
Volume 18,761 cubic miles (78,200 km³)
Elevation –92 feet (–28 m)
Countries Kazakhstan, Turkmenistan, Iran, Azerbaijan, Russia

0   500 miles
0   500 km

LAKE SUPERIOR

Length 383 miles (616 km)
Maximum width 160 miles (258 km)
Area 31,820 square miles (82,414 km²)
Drainage area 49,305 square miles (127,700 km²)
Average depth 482 feet (147 m)
Maximum depth 1,330 feet (405 m)
Volume 2,900 cubic miles (12,100 km³)
Elevation 600 feet (183 m)
Countries Canada, U.S.A.

0   500 miles
0   500 km

LAKE HURON

Length 206 miles (332 km)
Maximum width 152 miles (245 km)
Area 23,010 square miles (59,596 km²)
Drainage area 51,800 square miles (134,100 km²)
Average depth 194 feet (59 m)
Maximum depth 750 feet (229 m)
Volume 849 cubic miles (3,540 km³)
Elevation 577 feet (176 m)
Countries Canada, U.S.A.

0   100 miles
0   100 km

Volcanic lakes Some lakes cover active volcanic vents and are often called volcanic lakes. Their water is typically acidic, saturated with volcanic gases, and cloudy with a strong greenish color.

Lake Toba The eruption that formed what is now Lake Toba in Sumatra was the largest volcanic explosion to occur in 25 million years.

Fertile soils Samosir Island in Lake Toba was formed by the same volcanic eruption, leaving it rich in fertile volcanic soils.

LAKE MICHIGAN

Length 321 miles (517 km)
Maximum width 118 miles (190 km)
Area 22,400 square miles (58,016 km²)
Drainage area 45,500 square miles (118,000 km²)
Average depth 279 feet (85 m)
Maximum depth 923 feet (282 m)
Volume 1,180 cubic miles (4,918 km³)
Elevation 577 feet (176 m)
Countries U.S.A.

```
0        100 miles
0      100 km
```

LAKE VICTORIA

Length 210 miles (337 km)
Maximum width 150 miles (240 km)
Area 26,828 square miles (69,484 km²)
Drainage area 74,500 square miles (193,000 km²)
Average depth 131 feet (40 m)
Maximum depth 276 feet (84 m)
Volume 660 cubic miles (2,750 km³)
Elevation 3,720 feet (1,133 m)
Countries Tanzania, Uganda, Kenya

```
0        100 miles
0      100 km
```

Ecological disaster The Nile perch was introduced to Lake Victoria in the 1950s, but the experiment was an economic failure and an ecological disaster. Nile perch are voracious predators and have driven many of the native cichlid fish species to near-extinction.

Lakes continued

Relatively newly formed post-glacial lakes, such as the Great Bear and Great Slave in Canada, generally contain few nutrients. Described as oligotrophic, they can support only limited plant and animal life. Over time nutrients build up in the lake from river water and rainwater into which they have dissolved from the fallout of dust from the atmosphere, and in association with the sediments that have washed into the lake. Much older lakes, such as Baikal, Tanganyika, and Malawi, eventually acquire high levels of nutrients and are known as eutrophic. Rates of eutrophication are normally relatively slow, but can be accelerated by human activities, which add excessive nutrients in wastewater and the residues of agricultural fertilizers.

Mumbo Island, Lake Malawi Because this island has never had any permanent settlement, it has retained some of the ancient woodland that once lined the shores of the lake.

LAKE TANGANYIKA

Length 418 miles (673 km)
Maximum width 45 miles (72 km)
Area 12,700 square miles (32,900 km²)
Drainage area 90,000 square miles (231,000 km²)
Average depth 1,870 feet (570 m)
Maximum depth 4,823 feet (1,470 m)
Volume 4,530 cubic miles (18,900 km³)
Elevation 2,536 feet (773 m)
Countries Burundi, Democratic Republic of the Congo, Tanzania, Zambia

LAKE MALAWI

Length 363 miles (584 km)
Maximum width 50 miles (80 km)
Area 11,430 square miles (29,604 km²)
Drainage area 40,000 square miles (100,500 km²)
Average depth 866 feet (264 m)
Maximum depth 2,316 feet (706 m)
Volume 3,000 cubic miles (7,775 km³)
Elevation 1,569 feet (478 m)
Countries Malawi, Mozambique, Tanzania

LAKE BAIKAL

Length 395 miles (636 km)
Maximum width 50 miles (80 km)
Area 12,160 square miles (31,494 km²)
Drainage area 216,000 square miles (560,000 km²)
Average depth 2,487 feet (758 m)
Maximum depth 5,371 feet (1,637 m)
Volume 5,700 cubic miles (23,600 km³)
Elevation 1,496 feet (456 m)
Countries Russia

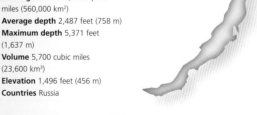

FACT FILE

Highest navigable lake At an altitude of 12,500 feet (3,810 m), Lake Titicaca is the world's highest lake navigable by large vessels. It sits astride the border between Peru and Bolivia and is the second largest lake in South America.

Islands Lake Titicaca has 41 islands, some of which are densely populated. The largest of these is Titicaca Island, located in Bolivia.

Reed boats The traditional totora-reed boats of the Uros people of Lake Titicaca share many features with ancient Egyptian Nile reed boats.

HERITAGE WATCH

Baikal seals The rare nerpa, or Baikal seal, is found only in Lake Baikal. It is not known exactly how the seals found their way into the lake, although they may have entered at a time when a sea passage linked the lake with the Arctic Ocean.

GREAT SLAVE LAKE

Length 298 miles (480 km)
Maximum width 140 miles (225 km)
Area 11,031 square miles (28,570 km²)
Drainage area 376,900 square miles (976,200 km²)
Average depth 240 feet (73 m)
Maximum depth 2,015 feet (614 m)
Volume 502 cubic miles (2,090 km³)
Elevation 512 feet (156 m)
Countries Canada

```
0                    500 miles
0              500 km
```

GREAT BEAR LAKE

Length 200 miles (320 km)
Maximum width 110 miles (175 m)
Area 12,096 square miles (31,328 km²)
Drainage area 44,293 square miles (114,717 km²)
Average depth 236 feet (72 m)
Maximum depth 1,356 feet (413 m)
Volume 536 cubic miles (2,236 km³)
Elevation 610 feet (186 m)
Countries Canada

```
0                    500 miles
0              500 km
```

HUMANS

H U M A N S

A PEOPLED PLANET

Since first appearing on Earth, up to 250,000 years ago, modern humans have spread across the planet to create permanent settlements on every continent—except Antarctica. No other species lives in such a broad environmental range: from the extreme cold of the Arctic, to the intense arid heat of Africa's Sahara Desert; from tsunami-susceptible lowlands around Asia's sprawling river deltas, to elevations above 13,000 feet (4,000 m) in South America's Andes Mountains. In numbers too, the global population is impressive: more than six billion people now inhabit the planet. But for most of human history, the global population has numbered fewer than ten million.

Family unit (left) Most traditional human settlements are based on the family unit, although this can take a variety of forms. The Samburu, for example, of north central Kenya practice polygamy; each adult man usually has several wives. Human settlement size in such arid environments is usualy small, restricted by the limited availability of resources. The Samburu live in groups of no more than a few families.

Blue planet (inset right) One notable feature of the global environment is that most of it is water. More than 140 million square miles (360 million km²) is covered by seawater—a vast blue global expanse of ocean that drives Earth's climate and is intimately linked with the terrestrial stores of fresh water that make the planet habitable.

GLOBAL SPRAWL

The explosive growth that characterizes today's global human population is a recent phenomenon. For thousands of years, deaths and births remained relatively even. The advent of farming around 8000 B.C. triggered the first significant growth in human numbers, although the earliest increases were gradual.

The global population reached 500 million about 3,500 years ago. Agricultural development supported the growth of early settlements and, with shelter and food accounted for, the trappings of civilization began to develop. Our species reached the one billion mark in 1800. Since then, the global population has not only grown to an extraordinary level, but its structure has also been shifting.

As revolutions in both agriculture and industry led to improved living conditions and health care, death rates began to decline during the 18th century in North America and Europe. However, birth rates also stayed high, and in the ensuing centuries populations in these regions exploded. Gradually, birth rates began to decline, and so, too, did population growth rates.

In contrast, the population across much of the developing world is at an earlier stage than that of North America and Europe, and this is where the greatest increases in numbers now occur. Although birth rates have begun to fall in Africa, South America, and Asia, it will be many decades before their populations stabilize. Asia is where most of the world's people now live, and the continent where most of the population growth during the next 50 years is expected to take place.

Africa, which had half the population of Europe in the mid-1900s, now has more people. By 2050, Africa's population is likely to be three times that of Europe.

There is one current trend that is universal across all regions: the global population is, for the first time in history, more urban than rural. Increasing urbanization is a trend that is predicted to continue, ultimately uniting humanity in a way that has never before occurred.

Megacity (top right) A potent symbol of 20th-century population growth, New York, the largest city in the U.S.A., represents a new era of globalization. The trend toward increasing urbanization has transformed it into one of Earth's 20 megacities, each with more than ten million people. The city that never sleeps is a major center for international trade, and most major companies have offices there. Ethnically, New York's population is exceptionally diverse, with more than one-third of its residents born outside the U.S.A.

Distribution (bottom right) City lights beaming into space reveal much about the distribution of the global population. Brightness indicates urbanization, but not necessarily population size. Asia is the most populated continent, with China and India alone accounting for more than one-third of the world's population, and yet the heavily urbanized and industrialized nations of Europe and North America glow brighter and more extensively. Much of Asia is unlit, like much of Africa, partly because many people in these regions lack access to reliable electricity. Japan, which is lit up as much as any country, is a notable exception.

Where Humans Live

People now live permanently on every continent except Antarctica. About 60 percent live in Asia and during the next 50 years more than half the world's population growth will occur there. The greatest increases are expected in densely populated developing nations, and by 2025 one-third of the world's population will live within 60 miles (100 km) of a coastline.

Population distribution (below) Earth's population is distributed very unevenly. The most heavily populated areas tend to be along river valleys and near coastal areas. Africa's Sahara Desert, outback Australia, and Asia's Himalaya Mountains are among the most sparsely inhabited regions.

High density Almost 67,000 people live in every square mile (2.6 km²), of Manhattan. Its Upper West Side is the most densely populated area in the U.S.A..

Low density Just 3 million people live in Mongolia, which has the world's lowest population density of 1.7 people per square mile (2.6 km²).

DOMESDAY BOOK

In 1085, William the Conqueror, who invaded England in 1066, commissioned the Domesday Book. An extensive record of the country's landholders and tenants, and the property they owned and occupied, the survey was compiled to be a register of English subjects from whom taxes could be raised.

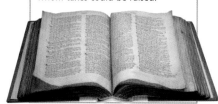

Uninhabited

Fewer than 2.6 people per sq. mile/1 per sq. km

2.6–26 per sq. mile/ 1–10 per sq. km

26–65 per sq. mile/ 10–25 per sq. km

65–130 per sq. mile/ 25–50 per sq. km

130–260 per sq. mile/ 50–100 per sq. km

260–250 per sq. mile/ 100–200 per sq. km

520–1040 per sq. mile/ 200–400 per sq. km

1040–2080 per sq. mile/ 400–800 per sq. mile

More than 2080 per sq. mile/ 800 per sq. km

○ City with 3–5 million people

● City with 5–10 million people

● **Megacity** with more than 10 million people

* Rhein-Ruhr ia an agglomeration of cities including Düsseldorf, Essen, Bonn, and Cologne

Changes and trends (right) Major changes have been occurring in the distribution of the world's population, particularly in Africa and Europe. In 1950, Europe had more than twice the population of Africa. Within 50 years, however, Africa's population was overtaking Europe's, a trend that is expected to continue.

■ Africa
■ Asia
■ Latin America (South America, Central America, and Mexico)
■ Europe (including Russia)
■ North America (U.S.A. and Canada)
■ Oceania

POPULATION DISTRIBUTION 1950

Asia 55.5%

Europe 22%

Africa 9%

Oceania 0.5%

North America 6%

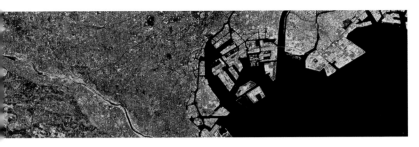

Tokyo rising (left) Japan's capital Tokyo began as a fishing village but now, with a population of 35 million, it is the largest of the world's 20 megacities. These are urban areas with populations greater than 10 million.

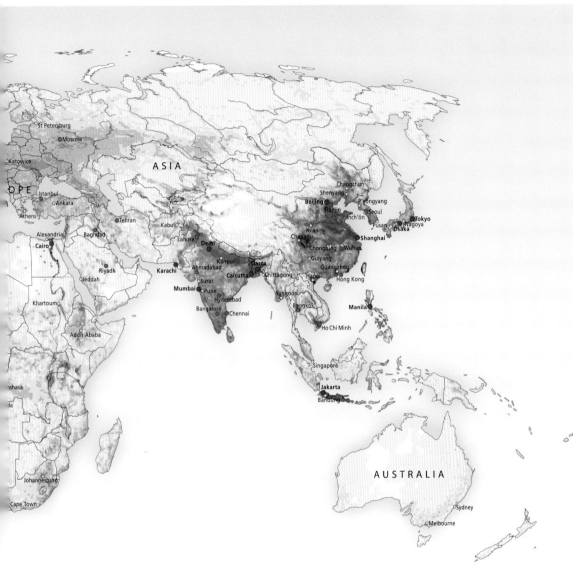

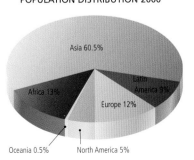

POPULATION DISTRIBUTION 2000

Asia 60.5%
Africa 13%
Europe 12%
Latin America 9%
Oceania 0.5%
North America 5%

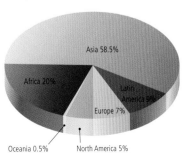

POPULATION DISTRIBUTION 2050

Asia 58.5%
Africa 20%
Europe 7%
Latin America 9%
Oceania 0.5%
North America 5%

1. Monaco With a total land area of 0.8 square mile (2 km²), the tiny European principality of Monaco has a population of almost 33 million, making it the world's most densely populated country. In 2007, the population was continuing to grow at rate of almost 0.4 percent.

Monaco

2. Singapore Every 0.4 square mile (1 km²) of Singapore supports an average of 6,000 people. In 1965, the government introduced a public program to reduce the birth rate. It was so successful that in 2001 a baby bonus scheme was implemented to counter the growing aging population.

Singapore

3. Vatican City Fewer than 900 people lived in the urban enclave of Rome's Vatican City in 2007. The world's smallest state, the Vatican covers an area of just 0.2 square mile (0.4 km²) and is populated almost entirely by clergy from the Roman Catholic Church, most of whom are Italian.

Vatican City

4. Malta Only three of the seven islands of the archipelago that forms the nation of Malta are populated. With a population of just over 400,000 occupying a total area of 122 square miles (316 km²), Malta has the highest population density of any country within the European Union.

Malta

5. Maldives During the late 1980s, the Maldives had a population growth rate of 3.4 percent, among the world's highest; it is currently 1.7 percent. Most of the nation's 1,200 islands are uninhabited with about a quarter of the population living on just one island.

Maldives

1. Mesopotamia Around 3500 B.C., the Sumerians established the world's earliest-known civilization in southern Mesopotamia, between the Tigris and Euphrates rivers. They developed levees and irrigation channels, and also the earliest writing system.

Mesopotamia

2. Indus River valley From about 2500 B.C., the Indus civilization developed around the Indus River, in parts of modern Pakistan and India. Founded on agriculture, it became urbanized and cultured, but disappeared after a few centuries.

Indus Valley civilization

3. Dynastic China By 3000 B.C., Yellow River settlements in northern China were farming, making pottery, spinning silk, and using wheels. From 1766 B.C., the Shang Dynasty was the first of a series of many different clans to rule China until modern times.

Dynastic China

NUKAK PEOPLE

Since their first European contact in 1988, diseases have decimated the Nukak, who live a traditional nomadic hunter-gatherer lifestyle in remote Colombian tropical rain forest. Many have fled colonists growing coca for the cocaine trade.

Human Habitats

The earliest human civilizations—settlements with a well-developed culture and social organization, including a system of government, job specialization, and an established belief system—sprang up around the floodplains of large rivers. At these sites, people found permanent water and fertile soil suitable for horticulture and agriculture.

Communications (right) The pathways and trade routes that developed between the cities of the past were predecessors of today's overpasses, underpasses, and motorways, all of which are, like this Tokyo highway, sophisticated and elaborate feats of modern engineering.

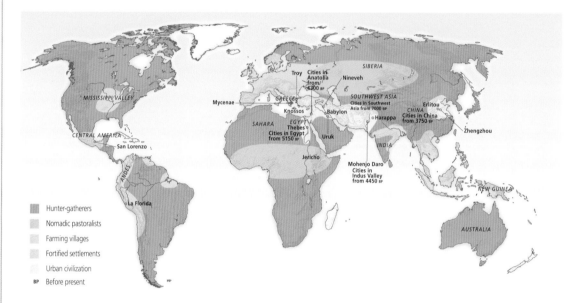

Hunter-gatherers
Nomadic pastoralists
Farming villages
Fortified settlements
Urban civilization
BP Before present

Early civilizations (above) By about 3,750 years ago, civilizations centered on cities had emerged along rivers. Eurasia had more domesticable plant and animal species than any other continent.

Ancient rule (below) Thought to have been a ceremonial and political hub of the ancient Minoan people of the Greek Island of Crete, the expansive palace of Knossos was first built around 2000 B.C.

FACT FILE

1. Welwyn Garden City This English town was a 1920s development designed by British urban planner Sir Ebenezer Howard. Welwyn was part of his vision for new pre-planned slum-free towns of a limited size— towns that combined rural life with access to city-based opportunities.

Welwyn Garden City, UK

2. Palmas One of South America's fastest-growing cities, Palmas was built in the 1980s to help open up Brazil's vast interior. It is located 373 miles (600 km) north of the capital Brasilia. Palmas has a population of around 200,000 and has been the capital of Tocantins state since 1990.

Palmas, Brazil

3. Abuja The new city of Abuja was built in the 1980s to replace the Nigerian capital Lagos, which had the highest population density in Africa. Regarded as relatively clean, safe, and the best purpose-built city in Africa, Abuja has become one of the most expensive African cities in which to live.

Abuja, Nigeria

4. Washington D.C. Designed largely by French-born army engineer Pierre Charles L'Enfant, Washington D.C. was developed on the banks of the Potomac River during the late 1700s as the purpose-built United States' capital. The city has the same boundaries as the District of Columbia, or D.C.

Washington D.C., U.S.A.

Business epicenter (far left) During the late 20th century, Shanghai, now the world's eighth-largest city, emerged as the center of China's rapidly expanding modern economy.

Australian capital (left) American architect Walter Burley Griffin's design for Canberra was selected during the early 20th century through an international competition.

Urban Environments

For the overwhelming majority of human history, most of the world's people have lived a rural lifestyle. However, the global population experienced a rapid urbanization during the latter half of the 20th century, and between 1950 and 2005 the number of people living in towns and cities tripled to more than 3.1 billion people.

Mega-world (below) Densely populated urban concentrations of more than 10 million people are called megacities. In the mid-1990s, 14 cities fitted the description. Today there are 20, three-quarters of them in developing nations. The UN predicts another two by 2015.

FACT FILE

Fringe-dwelling Rapid urbanization has caused a huge worldwide increase, particularly in developing nations, of impoverished settlements within and around cities. Called slums, these typically feature overcrowded conditions and a lack of basic services.

FIVE LARGE SLUM POPULATIONS*

Country	Urban %	Slum %
Sub-Saharan Africa	34.6	71.9
Southern Asia	29.6	59
Eastern Asia	39.1	36.4
Latin America	75.8	31.9
Northern Africa	52	28.2

*Slum populations are percentages of the urban population as a whole.

FIVE SLUM CONDITIONS

1. Inadequate housing Lack of housing made from long-lasting materials that protect against extreme weather.
2. Insufficient living areas Cramped conditions with more than three people sharing one room.
3. Limited water Lack of easy access to a source of clean water at an affordable price.
4. Inadequate sanitation Limited access to a public or private toilet; those available used by many people.
5. Insecure tenure Tenants under the constant threat of forced eviction.

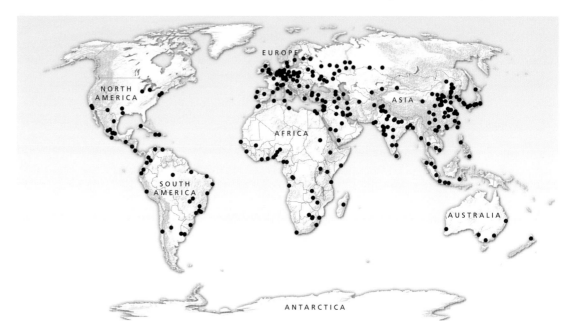

GLOBAL URBAN POPULATION

Population (billions)

1994   2025

■ World total
■ More developed regions
■ Less developed regions
■ Least developed regions

Urban poverty Slums have always existed in Mumbai, India. Now, 40 percent of the city's population of 13 million lives in slum-like settlements called shanty towns.

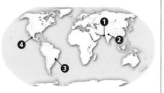
1. Karachi Although estimates vary widely, at least 12 million people probably now live in the city of Karachi, Pakistan's largest city, representing massive growth from fewer than 500,000 during the 1940s.

Karachi, Pakistan

2. Delhi More than 15 million people live in Delhi's greater metropolitan area. Migration has long contributed to the city's expansion, but the huge migration rate now makes it one of the world's fastest-growing cities.

Delhi, India

3. São Paulo The ethnically diverse center of Brazilian trade and industry, São Paulo supports over 11 million people (18 million including the extended urban area), making it Brazil's most populous city.

São Paulo, Brazil

4. Mexico City The extended metropolitan area of Mexico's capital, Mexico City, supports more than 19 million people. This includes the largest single population of American expatriates —between 400,000 and 600,000.

Mexico City

Sprawling metropolis The city section of Brazil's Rio de Janeiro is just 450 square miles (1,165 km²), but its suburban spread covers an area four times larger.

HERITAGE WATCH

Slum cookers A huge problem in slums is rubbish occupying space and spreading disease. In Kibera, one of Kenya's biggest slums, a pilot project to provide a community incinerator is being trialed. It will also supply hot water, cooking facilities, and employment.

GREAT CITIES AND CIVILIZATIONS

The emergence of cities was one of the most significant milestones for human societies and appears to have occurred independently in several locations at a similar time. It began with substantial increases in settlement sizes and huge changes in social organization. Significant developments followed, such as writing, legal codes, metallurgy, mathematics, and engineering principles. All are linked with the early cities of Sumer (now southern Iraq), which appeared on the Mesopotamian plain between the Tigris and Euphrates rivers more than 5,000 years ago.

ENDURING IMPACTS

As Sumer's cities developed, civilization and urbanization hallmarks also emerged in Egypt, East Africa, South Asia's Indus Valley (present-day Pakistan), and China. Sumerians invented the wheel, developed legal and administrative systems, and were early astronomers. Egyptians developed literature and medicine, while people of the Indus Valley became skilled mathematicians and practiced dentistry.

The ancient Greeks had perhaps the greatest influence on modern Western society. They created the democratic political and jury systems, their alphabet was the basis of the English alphabet, and their architectural styles were embraced.

At its peak, the Roman Empire stretched from Syria across much of Western Europe. Many examples of Roman engineering and architecture survive there today, while influences persist worldwide in art, law, literature, and language.

The legacy of the ancient Chinese is also strong. Inventions such as paper, the compass, gunpowder, and printing traveled westwards along what became, from the 5th century B.C., the Silk Road, which ultimately connected China with Rome.

Today, China joins other industrialized nations with natural resources and strong economies, such as the United States and Japan, whose products and philosophies now exert wide cultural influences.

Incan civilization (above right) The Incan city of Machu Picchu was built around 1460 at an altitude of 7,710 feet (2,350 m) in the Peruvian Andes. Its ruins, discovered in 1911, consist of baths, temples, and some 150 houses, and are surrounded by agricultural terracing. About 1,200 people, mostly women, children, and priests, may have once lived there.

Urban dominance (right) In the 1800s, just 3 percent of the global population lived in cities. By 2030, the United Nations estimates that it will be over 60 percent. The world's megacities, including Chicago (pictured), will support 350 million people.

Islamic creativity (above) The early residents of Uzbekistan's Samarkand were skilled artisans and scholars. Their buildings and monuments, such as this blue-tiled minaret, influenced architecture from the Mediterranean to India. The city first prospered 2,500 years ago, thanks to its location on the Silk Road.

Roman architecture (right) Building work on Rome's Coliseum began in A.D. 72. The ancient sporting arena stood over 210 feet (64 m) high, could hold more than 50,000 people, and had 80 entrances to ensure the streamlined movement of audiences. It was used to stage public events such as gladiator and wild-animal fights.

THROUGH THE AGES

Ancient Egypt (3000 B.C. – 7th century A.D.) The great pyramids, built between 2575 B.C. and 2465 B.C., demonstrate the Egyptians' ingenuity and technical prowess.

Ancient China (1600 B.C. –A.D. 906) The skills of Chinese artisans are evident in the terracotta warriors and horses buried with the Emperor Qin Shi Huang in 210 B.C.

Ancient Greece (1200– 323 B.C.) Athens, renowned as a center for learning, philosophy, the arts, and trade, was a core cultural influence.

Ancient Rome (753 B.C.– A.D. 476) Legislation passed by a citizens' assembly and approved by a senate was a fundamental process in Roman democracy. It is still evident in some modern political systems.

Moors (711–12th century) Moors invading from Africa ruled in the Iberian Peninsula. Their influence still exists in Spain and Portugal.

Easter Island (below) A religious and artistic Stone Age culture began when 100 Polynesians arrived in about A.D. 318 at Easter Island, 2,200 miles (3,540 km) west of Chile in the Pacific. The population peaked at about 10,000, but by about 1700 only ruins, artifacts, and giant stone monoliths (pictured) were left. Overuse of natural resources, leading to deforestation, species extinction, and other calamities, were the likely causes of the decline.

British Empire (1500s–1931) Rapidly emerging in the 16th century, the British Empire covered a quarter of the planet's land area by the 1920s.

Modern China (from 1949) The People's Republic of China was established in 1949 under Mao Zedong. It is now the world's fourth-largest economy.

Western nations (after 1945) A key rationale for the official 1945 formation of the United Nations was the reduction of global conflicts.

U.S.A. (from 1945) The global proliferation of U.S. products and philosophies, termed "cultural imperialism," highlights the rise of the U.S.A. as a dominating global culture..

Russia (from 1991) The Russian Federation was formed in 1991, when attempts at social reform precipitated the dissolution of the U.S.S.R. and the end of the Cold War.

Rural Life

In mid-2007, for the first time in history, the global population became less rural than urban, according to U.S. researchers. By 2030, they predict, increasing migration into urban environments will mean that just 40 percent of all people will live in rural areas. The fact that three-quarters of the world's poor live rurally is helping drive the global shift toward urbanization.

Joining forces (below) The British Columbia Rural Network, set up in 2005, is helping small communities across the western Canadian province connect, share resources, and deal with issues affecting rural livelihoods.

New options (right) Some residents of the historic village of Hartsop, in England's Lake District, are rejecting traditional rural livelihoods and moving into other industries, such as tourism, to survive.

GLOBAL RURAL POPULATION

Population (billions)

1994   2025

■ World total
■ More developed regions
■ Less developed regions
■ Least developed regions

FACT FILE

Natural roofing Shelter is one of the most basic of human needs. Traditionally, house design and construction have reflected an area's climate and available natural resources, as well as the cultural beliefs of the local people.

English thatched cottage Thatching with local vegetation is a traditional method of roofing found worldwide. The roofs of rural English cottages were traditionally made of wheat straw.

Chinese farmhouse The Chinese have been thatching the roofs of rural homes for millennia. Materials used vary between districts, depending on what is plentiful in each area.

Nigerian fishing hut Constant maintenance keeps thatched roofs on homes of Nigerian fishermen leak-free. Grass is the most commonly used material for thatching across Africa.

HERITAGE WATCH

Self-determination For many of the world's 350 million indigenous people, a positive future means being able to determine and fulfill their potential on their own land. In Australia, governments are slowly returning land rights to Aboriginal communities, with about 15 percent of the country now restored.

Saami, Lapland (left) Traditionally, the Saami people were nomadic reindeer herders. Now, most Saami live in villages and travel out to their herds on snowmobiles.

Maasai, East Africa (above) Most Maasai still live in traditional villages—groups of mud huts inside thorn-bush fences. At night, the cattle are herded inside the fence for protection.

Mountain Dwellers

The high-altitude environments of mountains are characterized by reduced oxygen levels, elevated ultraviolet radiation, wide temperature fluctuations, and limited natural resources. Despite the hardships, about ten million people live permanently in settlements at altitudes above 13,000 feet (4,000 m), most of them in South America and about one-fifth in Asia.

Partial nomads (below) The herders of the high-altitude Qinghai-Tibetan Plateau have led a partially nomadic existence for many centuries, moving between campsites according to the seasonal availability of resources and descending from higher summertime pastures as winter sets in.

High-altitude empire The Andes town of Cuzco developed into the Incan capital after it was founded during the 11th century. It was rebuilt by the Spanish about 500 years ago, sits at an altitude of 11,500 feet (3,500 m), and has a growing population of more than 300,000. It was recently identified as the location that receives the highest levels of ultraviolet radiation on Earth.

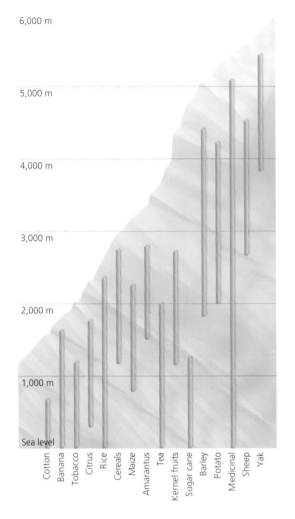
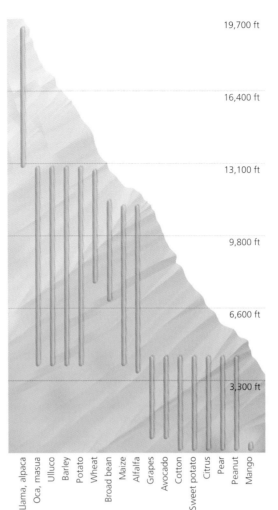

6,000 m — 19,700 ft

5,000 m — 16,400 ft

4,000 m — 13,100 ft

3,000 m — 9,800 ft

2,000 m — 6,600 ft

1,000 m — 3,300 ft

Sea level

Cotton, Banana, Tobacco, Citrus, Rice, Cereals, Maize, Amarantus, Tea, Kernel fruits, Sugar cane, Barley, Potato, Medicinal, Sheep, Yak

Llama, alpaca, Oca, masua, Ulluco, Barley, Potato, Wheat, Broad bean, Maize, Alfalfa, Grapes, Avocado, Cotton, Sweet potato, Citrus, Pear, Peanut, Mango

Mountain economics (above)
The "vertical archipelago" was an agricultural system developed by Andean communities for producing resources along an extreme vertical gradient. They learned to domesticate similarly acclimatized animals and crops. This model has been adapted to suit other mountain areas.

Remote Buddhism (left)
The monastery at Linghset in the Himalayan kingdom of Ladakh dates back to the 10th century. Situated at an elevation of approximately 13,000 feet (4,000 m), it is one of the most sparsely populated and remote locations in India, but it is becoming well-known among tourists trekking in the area.

Fast growth With an annual population growth rate of more than 4 percent, Riyadh, the Saudi Arabian capital, is among the world's fastest growing cities. Its water supply is being increasingly supplemented by Persian Gulf desalination plants.

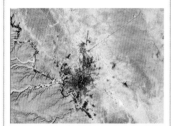

Riyadh 1972 Fuelled largely by the 1950s oil boom, Riyadh's population grew, in little more than 40 years, from 30,000 in 1930 to 500,000 in 1972.

Riyadh 1990 The population reached 1.5 million while the city's area grew more than ten-fold from its 1 square mile (2.6 km²) coverage in the 1930s.

Riyadh 2000 The city had 3.4 million people and covered about 600 square miles (1,500 km²). The population is predicted to reach 11.1 million by 2020.

Desert farming Runoff agriculture, an ancient and continuing practice in arid environments, involves gathering or redirecting wet-season runoff from hillsides and inclines. The water is collected, via natural tributaries known as wadis, in a leveled receiving field and trapped by a retaining wall. This allows it to percolate into the soil profile, while the spillway controls the surplus water.

Life in Arid Regions

About 500 million, or 8 percent, of the world's people live in or along the edges of deserts. Traditionally they survive the wide temperature fluctuations and lack of water, both characteristic of such environments, through cultural and behavioral adaptations. In recent decades, technology has also contributed significantly to easing the hardships associated with life in arid regions.

Parched Africa (right) Much of Kenya's population lives in small villages scattered across a landscape that receives less than 20 inches (500 mm) of rain a year. Members of these settlements are usually related by blood or marriage.

Phoenix (below) Its location in one of North America's largest and hottest deserts, the Sonoran, has not prevented Phoenix from growing into the fifth largest city in the U.S.A., with a population of more than 1.5 million.

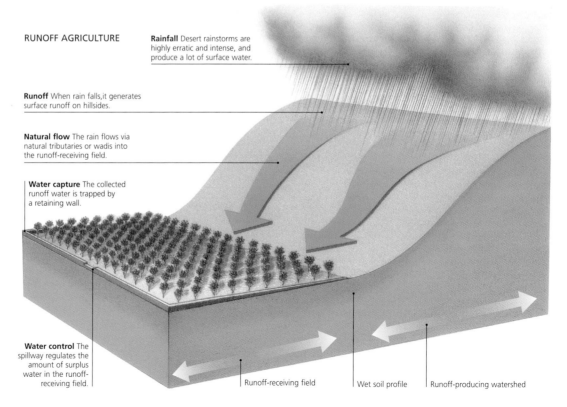

RUNOFF AGRICULTURE

Rainfall Desert rainstorms are highly erratic and intense, and produce a lot of surface water.

Runoff When rain falls, it generates surface runoff on hillsides.

Natural flow The rain flows via natural tributaries or wadis into the runoff-receiving field.

Water capture The collected runoff water is trapped by a retaining wall.

Water control The spillway regulates the amount of surplus water in the runoff-receiving field.

Runoff-receiving field | Wet soil profile | Runoff-producing watershed

Desert design Mauritanian women traditionally wrap their entire bodies in a loose cloak, called a malaffa, which protects them from the desert heat.

ADOBE BRICKS

Built more than 1,000 years ago by Native Americans, New Mexico's Taos Pueblo is famed for its multi-storied adobe residence. Adobe bricks, made of sand or clay mixed with straw or dung, are good insulators and may last centuries.

Surviving Extreme Cold

There have never been any indigenous Antarctic settlements. The circumpolar Arctic, however, supports a population of about four million, including indigenous peoples for whom seasonal nomadism and migration to exploit resources have been traditional survival tactics. Insulating clothing and homes, and the use of fire, are widespread responses to cold.

Arctic nomads (below) The Dolgans, indigenous migrants to north-central Russia during the 1700s, are traditionally reindeer herders who traversed the tundra on dog-sleighs, skis, and bark boats. Anthropologists believe they are ethnically connected to northern Asia's Mongols.

FACT FILE

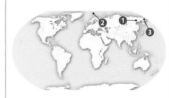

1. Oymyakon Located just south of the Arctic Circle, the Siberian village of Oymyakon, population 1,000, is famed as the coldest permanently inhabited

settlement on the planet. In 1926, the temperature there dropped to a record-breaking -96.2°F (-71.2°C).

Oymyakon, Russia

2. Spitsbergen This is the largest island in the Norwegian Sea archipelago of Svalbard, 600 miles (1,000 km) south of the North Pole. It has a population of

2,500. Fur trapping, whaling, and coal-mining industries; these are now being overtaken by tourism and research.

Spitsbergen, Norway

3. Chukchi The indigenous Chukchi people of the Arctic's Chukchi Peninsula, in eastern Russia, date back to Neolithic times. Traditionally, they

have lived either in coastal settlements and hunted marine mammals, or as semi-nomadic reindeer herders.

Chukchi, Siberia

SEALING IN CANADA

Traditional seal hunting by Inuit in Canada includes waiting at seal breathing-holes in the ice. Seal meat is an important protein source in the Arctic, but hunting is regulated.

Time-honored transport (left) The 650 people of Qaanaaq, Greenland's most northern town, communicate with the rest of the world via satellite. Nevertheless, traditional transport—sleds pulled by huskies—remains the best way to travel across snow and ice.

EARTH'S RESOURCES

People have been growing crops, raising livestock, and extracting minerals from Earth for millennia, but the industrialization and population growth that accelerated rapidly from the middle of last century have seen Earth's resources plundered on an unprecedented scale. Certainly, there are more of us than ever before. In the industrialized world, however, individuals now use more resources than our ancestors ever did: we eat more, use more energy, and travel farther. What is more, as is suggested by the growth in number and size of landfill sites across the planet, we also produce substantially more waste.

WORLD LAND USE AND RESOURCES

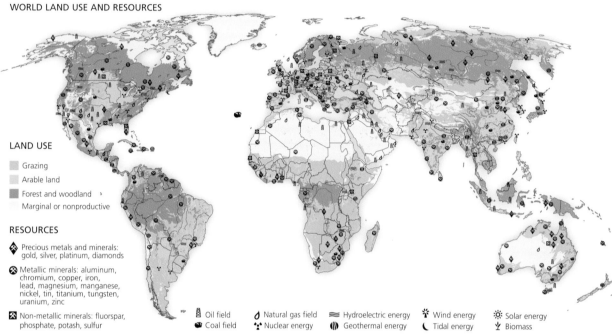

LAND USE

- Grazing
- Arable land
- Forest and woodland
- Marginal or nonproductive

RESOURCES

- Precious metals and minerals: gold, silver, platinum, diamonds
- Metallic minerals: aluminum, chromium, copper, iron, lead, magnesium, manganese, nickel, tin, titanium, tungsten, uranium, zinc
- Non-metallic minerals: fluorspar, phosphate, potash, sulfur

- Oil field
- Coal field
- Natural gas field
- Nuclear energy
- Hydroelectric energy
- Geothermal energy
- Wind energy
- Tidal energy
- Solar energy
- Biomass

SHIFTING ASSETS

Humans have shown great resourcefulness in using Earth's rich resources. As a species, we have exploited the planet's wild food supplies, forests, arable and grazing land, fresh water, minerals, and energy sources. But phenomenal population growth and industrialization have led to a looming resource crisis, particularly in fossil fuels and metals.

Before the industrial revolution in the 18th century, people relied on a range of energy sources, such as human and animal muscle power, wood and other biomass fuels for heating and cooking, and a limited harnessing of wind and water power by sails, windmills, and watermills.

Coal-fired steam engines and oil-fueled internal combustion engines transformed the world, as did natural gas and nuclear power. Much of the planet was electrified, industry boomed, and living standards in industrialized nations rose along with life expectancies. Energy use grew spectacularly, as did pollution caused by fossil fuels, but supply of these fuels is finite, and we face serious energy shortages if alternative sources are not developed.

In our attempt to meet rising demands for food, shelter, and other human needs, the scale of human activities has grown. Almost one-third of all Earth's land has been transformed for agriculture, while some mining operations are so large their scars in the landscape are visible from space. Yet, pressures on resource supplies continue to rise.

Most agriculture is now carried out on an intensive scale. Applications of large quantities of synthetic fertilizers and pesticides aim to coax ever higher production levels from increasingly exhausted and depleted land.

Of all today's resource issues, the scarcity of clean, fresh water may well be the most pressing. During the 20th century, as the need to feed burgeoning populations grew, increasing areas of land were irrigated, consumption increased by as much as six times, and the number of people living without enough water skyrocketed. At least 35 percent of the world's people now suffer from chronic water shortages; many are in developing countries, such as India, Ethiopia, Nigeria, Kenya, and China.

Inequitable distribution (above) Humans have tried to control resources since civilization began, but the global distribution of minerals, arable land, and other assets is uneven. As controls of these resources have shifted, so have the borders of states, nations, and empires.

Age-old staple (right) Wheat is among the world's most important foods. People collected wild wheat relatives before 10,000 B.C., but today's varieties are the product of many years of selective breeding.

Energy option (far right) Wind turbines appear like sentinels of change across the landscape. Wind power is just one of a range of sustainable, emission-free energy options increasingly being put to use. The most rapid uptake is in solar energy.

FACT FILE

Fuel formation Oil and gas develop from marine plant and animal remains, which have been crushed over many years between rock layers. The inland location of many deposits is due to changing sea levels during Earth's geological past.

1 Dead microscopic organisms drop to the ocean floor and are covered by mud and silt layers, which become rock layers.

2 The rock layers pile up and, under the pressure the layers exert, the organisms' organic remnants slowly turn into oil and gas.

3 Oil and gas rise through the layers of rock and pass through lower porous rocks, but are trapped by higher impermeable levels.

4 Under the right conditions, the oil and gas collect in a reservoir. These valuable reservoirs are accessed by drilling.

Earth's Energy Resources

The onset of the industrial revolution in the 18th century marked a significant turning point in human history. Impelled by energy from fossil fuels—first coal, then oil, and later natural gas—it initiated cultural change on a global scale that has been transforming human societies ever since. Today, however, 25 percent of the world population still lacks access to modern energy services.

Coal (top) Formed from plant remains buried in swamps 40–100 million years ago, coal underlies more than half of the U.S. state of Wyoming and is extracted by massive draglines.

Industrial access (bottom) The cargo ports of Hampton Roads, a huge urban area in the U.S. state of Virginia with the world's largest natural harbor, support a permanent presence by most major shipping lines, and hugely influence the nation's economy.

Unequal supply Although the world economy relies heavily on fossil fuels, only a handful of countries govern production: the Middle East controls oil; Russia dominates in natural gas; and the U.S.A. is the biggest coal producer.

COAL RESERVES

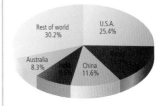

OIL RESERVES

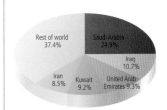

NATURAL GAS RESERVES

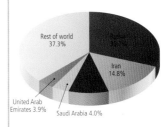

Oil The 1938 discovery of oil at Kuwait's massive Burgan field transformed the Middle East nation into one of the area's richest. It is home to about 10 percent of the world's known oil reserves and 1.1 percent of global natural gas reserves.

FINITE RESOURCES

More than 80 percent of the world's primary energy production currently comes from the burning of fossil fuels. These resources, which took millions of years to form, are being consumed in mere centuries. Inevitably, they will soon run out; some estimates put this at about 50 years for oil, 70 years for gas, and just over 250 years for coal.

FACT FILE

Metal use The first metal widely exploited by humans was gold, from around 6000 B.C. Today, there are 86 known metals. Steel, aluminum, and magnesium are the most frequently used metals in industry and construction.

Steel Steel is an alloy of mostly iron, and is valued for its strength. It was first used in East Africa some 3,500 years ago.

Aluminum Malleable but sturdy aluminum, used in the 1893 Eros statue in London's Piccadilly Circus, is a widely used non-ferrous metal.

Magnesium Magnesium compounds are often used to make high-grade wheels for vehicles, known as "mag" (magnesium) wheels.

Metals and Other Minerals

For thousands of years, people have exploited, mined, and expanded territories searching for natural resources. However, phenomenal population growth and industrialization is now precipitating a looming resource crisis in minerals, as well as fossil fuels. Large-scale recycling of some metals has been one important response to diminishing finite resources.

Scarred landscapes (right) One of the biggest challenges for mining in the 21st century is expected to be the rehabilitation and renewal of sites that have been left barren and unproductive after the large-scale extraction of metal ores.

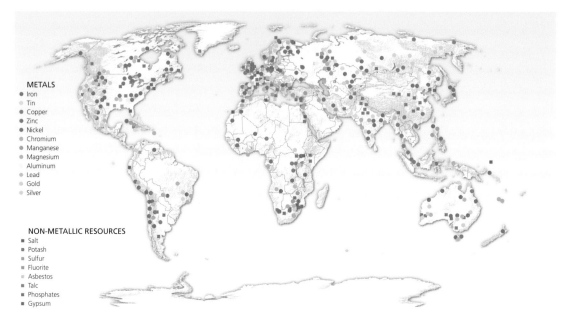

METALS
- Iron
- Tin
- Copper
- Zinc
- Nickel
- Chromium
- Manganese
- Magnesium
- Aluminum
- Lead
- Gold
- Silver

NON-METALLIC RESOURCES
- Salt
- Potash
- Sulfur
- Fluorite
- Asbestos
- Talc
- Phosphates
- Gypsum

Resource spread (above) Productive land, minerals, and energy reserves are distributed unevenly, a fact that accounts for some of the differences in global technological and living standards.

Industrial artistry (below) The Centre Georges Pompidou in Paris, France, features extensive use of metal and glass. Once criticized, it is now regarded as an innovative architectural landmark.

Manganese nodules A major component of deep-sea ocean floors, manganese nodules were first discovered in 1803, but it was only in the 1960s that they were recognized as a new, potentially valuable source of metal ores.

Cross section   External view

Structure The complex concentric formation of a manganese nodule is suggested by its intricate interior structure.

COMPOSITION

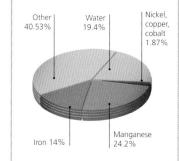

Other 40.53%

Water 19.4%

Nickel, copper, cobalt 1.87%

Iron 14%

Manganese 24.2%

Deep-sea extraction Nodules can contain several metal ores, making them an alternative to declining energy resources. Methods are being developed to lift them from as deep as 19,500 feet (6,000 m) below the sea.

Land Use

Notions of owning and controlling land extend back to the earliest human settlements, and lie at the heart of some of the mightiest battles waged in history. Today, they remain a fundamental premise of modern populations. The world's land area totals about 57,393,000 square miles (148,647,000 km²). It rises from 1,350 feet (410 m) below sea level on the shores of the Dead Sea, to the high altitudes of Mount Everest, 29,029 feet (8,848 m) above sea level.

Land–use imagery (right) This satellite image of the U.S.–Mexico border dramatically highlights differences in land use. The amount of solar radiation reflected back from different surfaces is represented by color. Here, the healthy vegetation of U.S. fields appears red, contrasting with the barren Mexican fields (light blue).

Changing patterns (far right) This 1996 Landsat view of Washington D.C., U.S.A., has been combined with earlier data. Three periods of urban growth are indicated by different colors: growth between 1973 and 1985 is red; growth between 1985 and 1990 is orange; and the yellow areas represent growth between 1990 and 1996

Competing land uses Human activity has shaped huge tracts of the world's terrestrial ecosystems. As the world population continues to grow and development proceeds, protecting the needs of the natural environment will be a major challenge.

Agriculture Almost one-third of the planet's surface has been transformed into agricultural land, and millions of acres are still being converted annually.

Industry The effects of industrialization were initially contained within localized areas. Impacts now include global phenomena such as acid deposition.

Transport The land-use requirements of modern road transport systems make areas converted for roads and motorways virtually unusable for any other application.

Rural landscape The advent of agriculture had a profound impact on much of Earth's natural landscape. By the medieval period, Europe was largely deforested, and farms, villages, and towns dominated the landscape.

Early farming Large tracts of forest were cleared to make space for strip cultivation to provide food for settlements.

Water transport Rivers provided a vital means of transport and helped open up trade routes between settlements.

Water access In medieval times settlements developed next to easily accessible sources of water.

Wind energy Since ancient times humans have harnessed the power of wind, using windmills to grind grain.

Urban landscape Over time, human impact on the land increased and started to dominate landscapes. The development of the steam engine and the industrial revolution led to the rapid expansion of towns and the growth of their populations.

Agricultural revolution After the industrial revolution, farming became largely mechanized and grew dramatically in scale.

Industrial ports Harbors and ports were constructed to handle imports, exports, and transport on a global scale.

High-rise structures In the 1880s, the first multistory structures were built to cater for the increased demand for urban housing.

Mass production In the late 18th century, traditional, small–scale manufacturing was replaced by factory–based production.

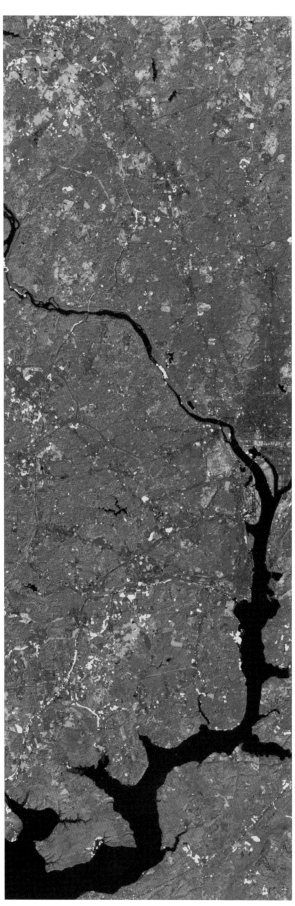

FACT FILE

Land extensions Where dry land is scarce, usable terrestrial areas can be created by reclaiming parcels of land, called polders, from low-lying or submerged earth that is in, or adjacent, to seas, rivers, lakes, and marshes. Polders are used extensively in the Netherlands.

1 The process begins with excavation of drainage channels that are in the low-lying area.

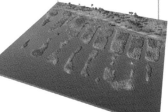

2 The selected areas for polder creation are enclosed within walls, often called dykes or levees, which are designed to keep back encroaching water.

3 Water is pumped from enclosed polders into surrounding water bodies, leaving dry, usable land. In the Netherlands, windmills were traditionally used for pumping.

4 The reclaimed land remains below the water table, so pumps must regulate incoming water, particularly during heavy rain, high tides, and storm surges.

Traditional Farming

The term traditional farming describes types of agricultural systems that have been practiced by human societies for centuries and, in some cases, even thousands of years. Historically, they have been based largely on sustainable methods that rely on natural fertilizers and pest and weed control, and use locally available resources.

Spread of agriculture Farming is believed to have first developed more than 10,000 years ago in the Middle East, near present-day Iraq. Other areas followed, with farming settlements emerging independently around the world at sites with reliable water and fertile soils.

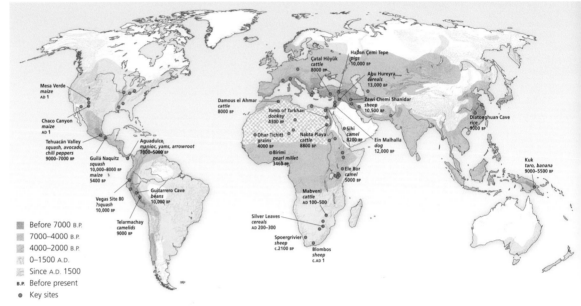

Mesa Verde
maize
AD 1

Chaco Canyon
maize
AD 1

Tehuacán Valley
*squash, avocado,
chili peppers*
9000–7000 BP

Guilá Naquitz
squash
10,000–8000 BP
maize
5400 BP

Vegas Site 80
?squash
10,000 BP

Guitarrero Cave
beans
10,000

Telarmachay
camelids
9000 BP

Aguadulce,
manioc, yams, arrowroot
7000–5000 BP

Damous el Ahmar
cattle
8000 BP

Tomb of Tarkhan
donkey
4300 BP

Dhar Tichitt
grains
4000 BP

Birimi
pearl millet
3460 BP

Nabta Playa
cattle
8800 BP

Ele Bor
camel
5000 BP

Mabveni
cattle
AD 100–500

Silver Leaves
cereals
AD 200–300

Spoergrivier
sheep
c.2100 BP

Blombos
sheep
c.AD 1

Çatal Höyük
cattle
8000

Hallan Çemi Tepe
pigs
10,000 BP

Abu Hureyra
cereals
13,000 BP

Zawi Chemi Shanidar
sheep
10,500 BP

Sihi
camel
8200 BP

Ein Malhalla
dog
12,000 BP

Diaotonghuan Cave
rice
9000 BP

Kuk
taro, banana
9000–5500 BP

Before 7000 B.P.
7000–4000 B.P.
4000–2000 B.P.
0–1500 A.D.
Since A.D. 1500
B.P. Before present
● Key sites

FARMING IN THE MIDDLE AGES

Feudal agriculture During the Middle Ages most people in Europe worked on the land and their lives revolved around the changing seasons. Noblemen were landholders, while peasants were tenants who worked the fields to pay rent and feed their families.

Winter During the quiescent cold months, ditches were dug, wood cut, and manure spread to fertilize fields. Tools were made or repaired, and new fences were built.

Spring Longer days presaged intense activity; fields were plowed and sowed with seed in readiness for a fall harvest, and newborn livestock required attention.

Summer Wheat was harvested as the weather warmed, sheep were shorn of their wool, and grass was cut for hay to feed the cattle over winter.

Fall Pre-winter activity was intense: oats, barley, honey, and apples were harvested. Some livestock was sold or slaughtered, pigs were fattened, and grapes were pressed for wine-making.

FACT FILE

Age-old approaches Today, many indigenous people continue applying traditional agricultural practices. Their usually simple subsistence methods require few external resources and respond to local environmental conditions.

Utilitarian livestock Tibetans use most parts of yak, from hides for boots and saddles to milk and meat for food.

Wheat product Rural Iranians still employ the ancient practice of winnowing grain, in which wind blows the lighter chaff from wheat kernels.

Free-ranging poultry Duck herds in China fertilize rice fields with droppings, eat pests, and provide humans with eggs, meat, and down.

Dry store In Sudan, trees offer good locations for drying and storing maize bales, while keeping them away from pests.

Mechanized agriculture During the 20th century, farming was boosted through the invention and use of machines capable of replacing or improving human labor. Mechanization allows larger areas to be farmed in less time.

Tractors In the early 1900s, the horse-drawn and steam-powered tractors of the 1800s were replaced by tractors with internal combustion engines.

Combine harvesters In widespread use since the 1930s, combine harvesters can perform all aspects of cutting, harvesting, and threshing.

Silage storage Computers and sensors now allow for precise control of the temperature and moisture at which livestock feed is stored and preserved.

Modern Farming

The usually strong ecological ties of traditional agricultural systems have become fractured in the type of farming that now prevails in developed countries. Impelled partly by the increased demand, modern crop and livestock production has come to rely on the application of large quantities of artificial fertilizers, pesticides, and intensive animal husbandry techniques.

Gallic agriculture Like much of France, the gentle slopes and mild climate of Burgundy have helped make the nation one of Europe's most important agricultural producers. About 60 percent of France's land is devoted to cropping and livestock.

Terraced crop (above) Although the rice fields of the Indonesian island of Bali appear extensive, they continue to be worked along mainly traditional lines. The men use water buffalo to plough and prepare fields, and the women harvest the rice by hand with small knives.

Wool production (right) With more than 35,000 flocks of sheep, each with an average of 1,400 animals, New Zealand is one of the world's biggest wool producers. The largest consumers of wool include the U.K., U.S.A., and Japan.

Sea farming Production from mariculture—aquaculture in the oceans—has been growing worldwide at an annual rate of almost 7 percent. Marine life now being farmed includes seaweeds, shellfish, salmon, and tuna.

Mariculture Marine fish farming is playing an increasingly important role in providing protein for the world's rising population.

Oyster production Oysters have been commercially cultivated for pearls since the early 1900s and more recently for food. They require pristine waters.

Trees farming Some farms, such as this one in Orange County, U.S.A., have begun to grow trees alongside crops and livestock. It is a form of agricultural diversification that expands farmers' options: the trees can be harvested for wood or left and sold for carbon credits.

FACT FILE

Refined approach In traditional breeding, plants of the same species with sought-after traits are crossed, the intent being that those traits will pass to resultant seedlings. Modern technology has improved and refined the traditional process.

Dominant traits A pepper that produces large, yellow fruit is crossed with one that produces small, red fruit. Large size and red color are dominant traits and so, according to genetic laws of nature, most offspring plants will produce large red-colored fruit.

Producing hybrids To create new improved hybrid crops, such as large, red peppers, scientists select and cross individuals with desirable characteristics. They repeat the process for the resulting seedlings until a new superior crop variety is eventually produced.

Genetically Modified Crops

Humans have been manipulating crop genetics through traditional plant breeding since farming began. Late last century, however, scientists developed capabilities to precisely alter a plant's genome by removing, inserting, or switching on or off specific genes. The results are genetically engineered or modified (GM) crops, which have the world both enthralled and alarmed.

Selective cropping (below) This GM rape crop in Winchester, U.K., has had a gene added to its DNA to make it resistant to the herbicide sprayed on the field. The herbicide kills all plants except the rape crop.

GENETIC MODIFICATION

Bacteria insertion method Scientists exploit the natural capability of the bacterium *Agrobacterium tumefaciens* to carry new genes into plant cells. *Agrobacterium* is a plant parasite that normally causes plant tumors.

New addition A desirable gene is inserted into *Agrobacterium's* plasmid—an extra, circular-shaped DNA that is common in bacterial cells—in place of the tumor-causing gene.

Transfer maneuver As *Agrobacterium* infects the plant cell it carries with it the new gene. This becomes incorporated into the plant cell's DNA.

Cell with desirable gene

Bacterial cell

New plant cell is infected by bacterial cell.

Plasmid

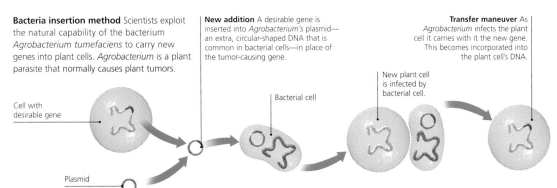

Ballistic method *Agrobacterium* is not suitable for all plants. In cereal crops, for example, an alternative is the "gene-gun," which fires microscopic, heavy metal "bullets" into plant cells. The bullets are coated with DNA that contains desirable genes.

Rapid access Microscopic tungsten or gold particles, coated with DNA containing desirable genes, are fired directly through plant cell walls.

Comfortable merger The process causes no damage to cell walls and, once inside, the foreign DNA becomes naturally incorporated into the cell's own DNA.

Bullets coated with DNA

Modified vegetation The altered plant cells divide rapidly and, in a medium that is rich with nutrients and hormones, they can be coaxed to develop into tiny plants. The new plants are complete with leaves and roots, which contain the modified DNA.

Extra boost An additional "promoter" gene can also be inserted. This activates the transferred gene, switching it on to perform its desired function.

Growth begins In a controled environment, such as a petrie dish, cells develop into plants.

Beneficial features The new plants are clones of one another, and as they grow the trait conferred by the desirable gene is switched on by the promoter and expressed.

Trait test Within the DNA material being transferred, scientists often insert an additional gene—a "marker"—that allows for a quick and easy test to determine whether the procedure has worked. This gene is often resistant to antibiotics.

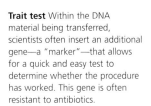

Success indicator Antibiotic resistance, conferred by the marker gene, allows the cells to survive and plants to grow when treated with antibiotics.

Failure sign When cells do not contain the transferred genetic material, they will be killed by the application of antibiotics.

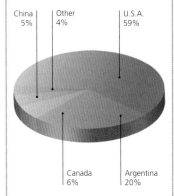
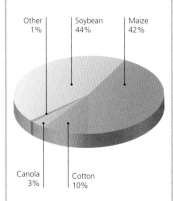
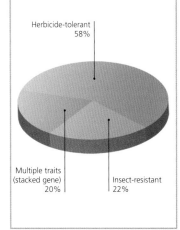

Organic Farming

Concerns about the impacts of intensive modern farming methods on environmental and human health prompted the rise last century of the organic farming movement. The organic approach spurns the use of synthetic chemicals. Instead it relies on traditional practices, such as crop rotation and composting, to improve soil condition and boost harvests.

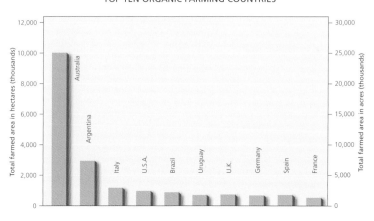

TOP TEN ORGANIC FARMING COUNTRIES

Total farmed area in hectares (thousands) — *Total farmed area in acres (thousands)*

Australia, Argentina, Italy, U.S.A., Brazil, Uruguay, U.K., Germany, Spain, France

Selling point (right) Consumer demand for organic products is underpinning the rapid growth of the movement in Europe. These lettuces, being grown in Devon, England, are likely to attract a premium at market for their organic status.

Targeted control (below) In companion planting, crop plants are grown in direct association with vegetation, such as marigolds, which produces compounds in leaves, roots, or flowers to discourage pests and diseases.

FACT FILE

Growing movement By 2007, almost 650,000 farms in 120 countries had adopted the organic approach— and more than a third of these were in Australia. The fastest growth, however, is occurring in Europe and North America.

SHARE OF GLOBAL AREA UNDER ORGANIC MANAGEMENT

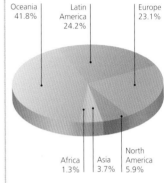

Oceania 41.8%
Latin America 24.2%
Europe 23.1%
Africa 1.3%
Asia 3.7%
North America 5.9%

SHARE OF TOTAL NUMBER OF ORGANIC FARMS IN THE WORLD

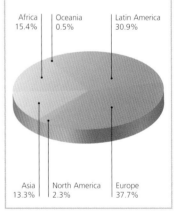

Africa 15.4%
Oceania 0.5%
Latin America 30.9%
Asia 13.3%
North America 2.3%
Europe 37.7%

Community farming Honey Brook Organic Farm in New Jersey, U.S.A., is an example of a Community Sponsored Agriculture (CSA) farm. Shares of the harvest are sold in advance, so that the community has a shared responsibility for the risk of farming.

HERITAGE WATCH

Principal pioneer British botanist Sir Albert Howard became one of organic farming's principal pioneers. In particular, his 1940 book, *An Agricultural Testament*, which drew on 25 years of work as an agricultural adviser in India, helped drive organic farming's rise in the developed world.

Mining

Metal ores and minerals for ceremonial and religious use were the first resources mined by humans. Archaeological excavations reveal, for example, that ocher was mined at locations worldwide many tens of thousands of years ago. Today, most mining relies on modern technology, is conducted on a massive scale, and is mostly carried out by multinational corporations.

Methods Accessibility of an ore deposit influences how it is mined. Open-pit mining excavates minerals located less than a few hundred feet below ground. Ores lying deeper or within solid rock require vertical shafts or angled tunnels.

Deep underground This type of coal mining flourished in the 18th and 19th centuries, driving the industrial revolution, but has an uncertain future.

Hard rock Alaska's underground gold is recovered by hard-rock mining, which involves the excavation of tunnels following veins of the ore through rock.

Open pit About 90 percent of copper ore is extracted by open-pit mining, which requires the removal of surface earth before quarrying beneath.

Massive hole (right) Claimed to be the world's largest human excavation, Bingham Canyon Copper Mine, Utah, U.S.A., has been worked for more than a century, but still annually yields more than one billion U.S. dollars worth of copper, gold, silver, and molybdenum.

Continuous mining People have been digging coal from below Earth's surface for centuries. Today, machines do the excavation and most of the world's coal mines use a method known as continuous mining.

Coal egress Mined material is brought to the surface in the upcast shaft and surface fans suck out stale air from below.

Downcast shaft Miners take the downcast shaft to reach the coal face. Fans at the top provide an air supply below.

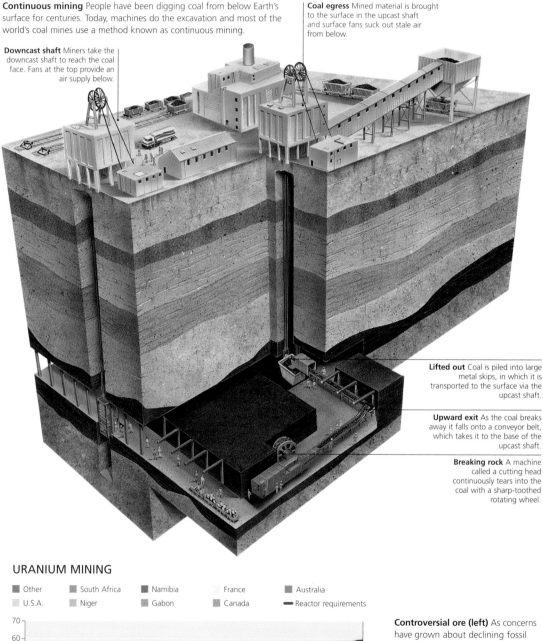

Lifted out Coal is piled into large metal skips, in which it is transported to the surface via the upcast shaft.

Upward exit As the coal breaks away it falls onto a conveyor belt, which takes it to the base of the upcast shaft.

Breaking rock A machine called a cutting head continuously tears into the coal with a sharp-toothed rotating wheel.

URANIUM MINING

■ Other ■ South Africa ■ Namibia ☐ France ■ Australia
☐ U.S.A. ▨ Niger ■ Gabon ▨ Canada ━ Reactor requirements

1,000 tonnes uranium

70
60
50
40
30
20
10
0

1945 1949 1953 1957 1961 1965 1969 1973 1977 1981 1985 1989 1993 1997 2001

Controversial ore (left) As concerns have grown about declining fossil fuel reserves, uranium is one alternative energy source to which the world has been turning. More than 16 percent of the world's electricity is now generated from uranium in nuclear reactors, mostly in Europe. Over half the world's uranium comes from Canada, Australia, and Kazakhstan.

FACT FILE

1. Ashio Copper Mine During the 1890s, the Ashio Copper Mine, north of Tokyo, caused Japanese industry's first environmental disaster. Toxic

emissions killed local woodlands. Effluent that discharged into rivers poisoned farmers and polluted their land.
Ashio Copper Mine, Japan

2. Berkeley Pit Lake This lake in the state of Montana, U.S.A., is the toxic legacy of what was once a lucrative open-pit copper mine. After the mine was closed in 1982,

Berkeley Pit Lake was formed by seeping acidic groundwater, which was polluted with various heavy metals.
Berkeley Pit Lake Copper Mine, U.S.A.

3. Britannia Copper Mine Canada's now abandoned Britannia Copper Mine was one of North America's worst pollution sources for 70 years.

Highly acidic, heavy-metal-contaminated runoff flowed from the mine into nearby waterways until it was treated in 2006.
Britannia Copper Mine, British Columbia

4. Wheal Jane Tin Mine When England's Wheal Jane Tin Mine was closed in 1992, millions of liters of

groundwater became polluted as it rose and flooded the area. It also flowed into nearby Falmouth Bay.
Wheal Jane Tin Mine, Cornwall, U.K.

HERITAGE WATCH

Gems of war Profits from so-called blood diamonds, mined in parts of Africa controlled by armed rebel forces, have funded some of the nation's bloodiest civil wars. Today, more than 70 governments and the world's legitimate diamond industry support the Kimberley Process Certification Scheme, which ensures shipments are conflict-free.

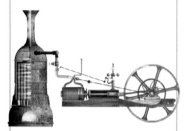

Industrial Land Use

The 18th-century beginning of the industrial revolution initiated a transformation of the world that continues today at an ever-increasing pace. Now, for virtually all of the developed world and growing parts of the developing world, industry has become the basis of economic success. Its requirements and outputs dominate land use across large parts of the planet.

Mechanized workforce (right) The main five producers of the 69 million motor vehicles manufactured worldwide in 2006 were Japan, the U.S.A, China, Germany, and South Korea. Human labor in automobile manufacturing is being gradually supplanted by automated factory lines and robotics.

GLOBAL INDUSTRIAL OUTPUT AS A PERCENTAGE OF U.S. PRODUCTION

- ● 100% U.S.A (> 2 trillion U.S. dollars)
- ● 10%
- • 1%

Global industry (above) In 2005, industrial output was greatest in the U.S.A. The next most productive regions in the world were Europe and Asia.

Specialized economy (below) Hong Kong's economy has thrived through the development of modern financial, trading, and business industries. As a result, its port has become one of the world's busiest.

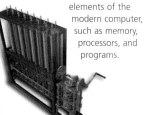

Rag trade (top) While the developed world seeks premiums for its fashion products through value-added elements such as design, much of the production is now outsourced to developing nations.

Leading employer (bottom) The textile and clothing industry has grown to become India's second largest employer after agriculture. It now accounts for 14 percent of total industrial production.

FACT FILE

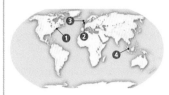

1. Staten Island The Fresh Kills landfill on Staten Island opened in 1947 and closed in 2001. It was the world's largest landfill—

 more than 2,000 acres (810 ha). It grew taller than the Statue of Liberty and was visible from space.

Staten Island, New York, U.S.A.

2. Stockport Adswood Household Waste Recycling Centre, in England's Stockport Borough, had to close temporarily in

 2007 because rotting waste was emitting high levels of methane gas. This highlights a common landfill problem.

Stockport, England

3. Polmont In 2006, Avondale Landfill became the first in Scotland capable of accepting hazardous waste. It

 takes non-reactive hazardous waste from all over the country for isolation permanently in a special waste cell.

Polmont, Scotland

4. Semakau About 90 percent of Singapore's waste is incinerated. The resulting ash, and any waste that cannot

be incinerated, is disposed of at the Semakau landfill site. It opened in 1999, and is located between two islands.

Semakau, Singapore

Solid Wastes and Landfills

The developed world now disposes of more rubbish than ever before. This is not simply because the human population is growing at an unprecedented rate but, as individuals, we each discard more waste than our ancestors ever did. To a large extent the solution to the growing global waste problem is embodied in the simple mantra "reduce, re-use, recycle."

Future playgrounds (right) A 30-year project to transform New York's Fresh Kills landfill began in 2007. Plans feature reclaimed wetlands, parklands, and a memorial to the September 11 Twin Towers disaster.

From wasteland to Olympics (below right) The venues of the Sydney 2000 Olympic Games, promoted as the Green Olympics, were built on former industrial wasteland that included about 317 million cubic feet (9 million m³) of landfill waste.

Problem e-waste (below) The disposal of computers in landfills is discouraged because they take up space and contain toxic components. Recycling programs now operate in many of the developed world's cities.

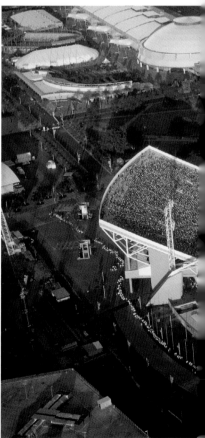

FACT FILE

Waste supply The most affluent nations are the most wasteful. The U.S.A., with less than 5 percent of the global population, produces a quarter of the world's waste. On average, each U.S. citizen annually generates more than 1,600 pounds (730 kg) of trash.

AVERAGE HOUSEHOLD WASTE

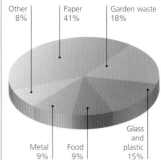

Other 8%
Paper 41%
Garden waste 18%
Metal 9%
Food 9%
Glass and plastic 15%

LITTER DEGENERATION

Type of litter	Time to degenerate
Organic waste	1–2 weeks
Paper	10–30 days
Cotton cloth	2–5 months
Wood	10–15 years
Woolen items	1 year
Tin, aluminum, and other metal cans	100–500 years
Plastic bags	One million years

WASTE PER CAPITA

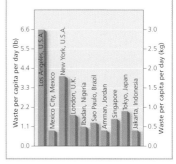

Waste per capita per day (lb) / Waste per capita per day (kg)

Los Angeles, U.S.A.
Mexico City, Mexico
New York, U.S.A.
London, U.K.
Ibadan, Nigeria
Sao Paulo, Brazil
Amman, Jordan
Singapore
Tokyo, Japan
Jakarta, Indonesia

NUCLEAR WASTE

The most problematic of all hazardous waste is high-level nuclear waste, which comes mostly from power plants and decommissioned nuclear missiles. It includes highly radioactive forms of uranium, plutonium, and other elements. Much of it is kept in short-term on-site facilities at nuclear power stations, but a long-term solution is urgently required.

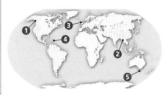
1. Tongass National Forest The world's largest remaining area of temperate rain forest is in the Tongass National Forest. It supports many rare and endangered plant and animal species. Logging began in the 1950s, but today less than 10 percent is set aside for harvesting in the next century.

Tongass National Forest, Alaska

2. Bago Yoma This area supports about 3.8 million acres (1.5 million ha) of different forest types ranging across evergreen, moist deciduous, semi-evergreen, and dry bamboo. Within these are large natural stands of teak. Myanmar has about 86 percent of the world's remaining teak.

Bago Yoma, Myanmar

3. Galloway Forest Park Established as a woodland park in 1947, the area has been logged since the 1930s. It supports many valuable tree species and 500,000 tons (450,000 t) of timber are harvested each year. About 300 square miles (780 km²) are also managed and for outdoor activities.

Galloway Forest Park, Scotland

4. El Yunque National Forest This forest reserve is renowned for its ancient tropical rain forest and high level of biodiversity, including many endemic plant and animal species. It was first set aside as a Crown Reserve in 1876, by the then King of Spain, and managed for more than 100 years.

El Yunque National Forest, Costa Rica

5. Tasmania Forests cover almost half of Australia's island state Tasmania. In response to conflicts arising over forest resources, more than 7 percent of the island's 8,374,895 acres (3,391,832 ha) of forest is now managed as plantations of native and exotic species.

Tasmania, Australia

Forest Resources

The value of the world's forests is truly immeasurable. They are vast repositories of biodiversity and are critical to the health of watersheds, the very air we breathe, and the planet's carbon balance. They provide basic resources, such as food, medicines, building materials, and fuel, and support the livelihoods of an estimated 1.6 billion people.

Diminishing resources (below) Just centuries ago, half of Earth's land surface was swathed in natural forests. Today, forests cover less than one-third and, based on 2005 estimates, 32 million acres (13 million ha) continue to be destroyed each year.

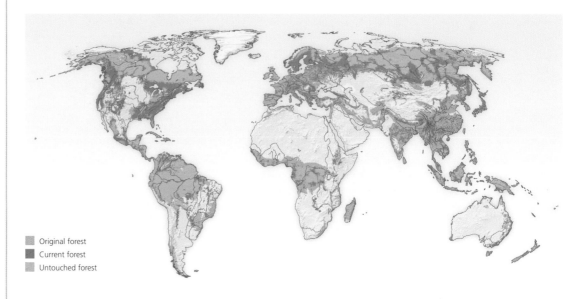

- Original forest
- Current forest
- Untouched forest

Using the forest (below) Indigenous populations have been clearing patches of rain forest for family farms for thousands of years. This does not have the same extensive impact on forest ecosystems as large-scale commercial clearing.

Sustainable ecosytem Virgin rain forest is a self-supporting environment that takes hundreds of years to grow to maturity.

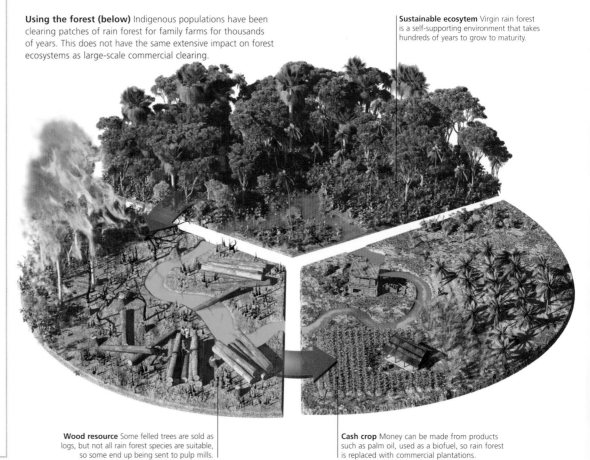

Wood resource Some felled trees are sold as logs, but not all rain forest species are suitable, so some end up being sent to pulp mills.

Cash crop Money can be made from products such as palm oil, used as a biofuel, so rain forest is replaced with commercial plantations.

Green belt (left) The northern end of the planet is wrapped in a continuous band of coniferous cold-temperate forest called the taiga. It accounts for one-third of the world's forested area and covers more than 10 percent of the planet's land area.

Marine Resources

The world's oceans are a rich source of food and minerals. These resources were once regarded as infinite but alarm bells began ringing during the 20th century when many important fish stocks began crashing, a sign of struggling ocean ecosystems. Exploitation over thousands of years, overfishing, pollution, and habitat degradation have been major causes.

Oceanic energy (below) As a solution to dwindling land-based energy supplies, off-shore oil and gas production has already become a multibillion-dollar industry, supporting a vast workforce. Methane hydrates also present growing opportunities.

Fish facts The global wild fish catch is believed to have peaked in 2000 at 96 million tons (87 million tonnes) and has since been falling. The industry generates more than U.S.$80 billion annually.

TOP TEN MARINE CAPTURED SPECIES 2004

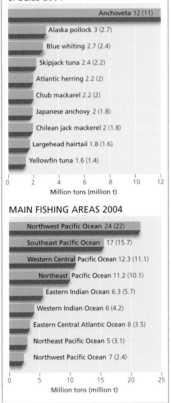

Species	Million tons (million t)
Anchoveta	12 (11)
Alaska pollock	3 (2.7)
Blue whiting	2.7 (2.4)
Skipjack tuna	2.4 (2.2)
Atlantic herring	2.2 (2)
Chub mackarel	2.2 (2)
Japanese anchovy	2 (1.8)
Chilean jack mackerel	2 (1.8)
Largehead hairtail	1.8 (1.6)
Yellowfin tuna	1.6 (1.4)

MAIN FISHING AREAS 2004

Area	Million tons (million t)
Northwest Pacific Ocean	24 (22)
Southeast Pacific Ocean	17 (15.7)
Western Central Pacific Ocean	12.3 (11.1)
Northeast Pacific Ocean	11.2 (10.1)
Eastern Indian Ocean	6.3 (5.7)
Western Indian Ocean	6 (4.2)
Eastern Central Atlantic Ocean	8 (3.5)
Northeast Pacific Ocean	5 (3.1)
Northwest Pacific Ocean	7 (2.4)

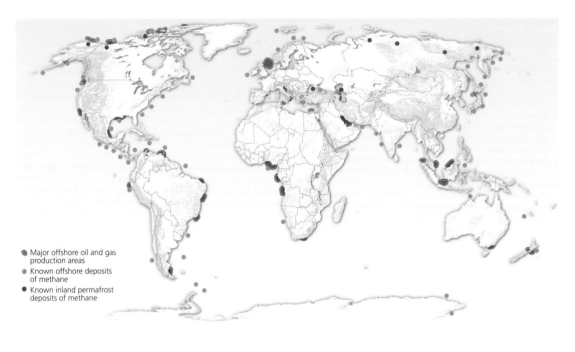

- Major offshore oil and gas production areas
- Known offshore deposits of methane
- Known inland permafrost deposits of methane

MARINE GEMS

Bivalve mollusks produce pearls in response to debris entering their shells. The irritants are isolated within layers of nacre (mother-of-pearl). Today, high-quality natural pearls are found in oyster beds in the Persian Gulf and in the Indian Ocean's Gulf of Mannar.

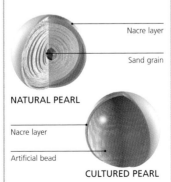

Nacre layer
Sand grain

NATURAL PEARL

Nacre layer
Artificial bead

CULTURED PEARL

Alternative energy (below) Methane hydrates, formed at high pressure and low temperatures in seafloor sediments and Arctic permafrost, contain trapped methane—a potential source of fuel.

Sea salt (right) Today, a third of the world's table salt comes from the sea and production is carried out on an industrial scale. The mineral is often held in giant white stacks before processing.

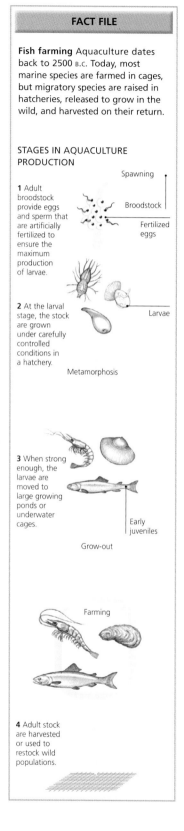

FACT FILE

Fish farming Aquaculture dates back to 2500 B.C. Today, most marine species are farmed in cages, but migratory species are raised in hatcheries, released to grow in the wild, and harvested on their return.

STAGES IN AQUACULTURE PRODUCTION

1 Adult broodstock provide eggs and sperm that are artificially fertilized to ensure the maximum production of larvae.

Spawning

Broodstock

Fertilized eggs

2 At the larval stage, the stock are grown under carefully controlled conditions in a hatchery.

Larvae

Metamorphosis

3 When strong enough, the larvae are moved to large growing ponds or underwater cages.

Early juveniles

Grow-out

Farming

4 Adult stock are harvested or used to restock wild populations.

Job opportunities (left) The global fishing industry grew rapidly in the early 21st century, creating much seasonal employment for factory workers, such as these herring gutters in 1920s England.

DISTRIBUTION OF EARTH'S WATER

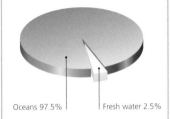

Oceans 97.5% Fresh water 2.5%

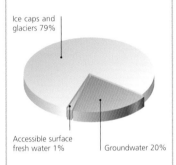

Ice caps and glaciers 79%

Accessible surface fresh water 1% Groundwater 20%

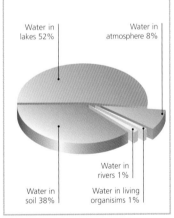

Water in lakes 52% Water in atmosphere 8%

Water in rivers 1%

Water in soil 38% Water in living organisims 1%

Surface Water Resources

More than two-thirds of Earth's surface is covered by water. Globally, the total amount of water remains at a relatively constant level, but it moves between the atmosphere, landmasses, and oceans in a perpetual cycle. It is one of the few resources that can exist in a liquid, gas (as water vapor in the atmosphere), or solid state (as ice or snow), at the range of temperatures that normally occurs on Earth.

Hydrologic cycle (right) Water evaporates from the world's vast expanse of oceans. Some returns directly to the sea as precipitation, but much is carried over land and falls there. Water evaporates from the land and is transpired back into the air by plants. The water that falls on land flows back to the ocean via rivers, streams, and underground channels to complete the planet's water cycle.

Usable supplies (below) Earth's available fresh water is unevenly distributed. Parts of Africa and Asia have the least available water and, as a result, the people on these continents are often highly efficient users of water.

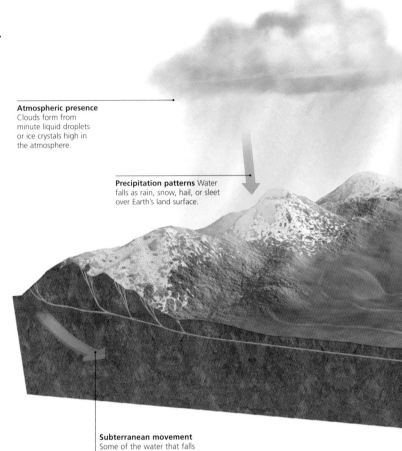

Atmospheric presence Clouds form from minute liquid droplets or ice crystals high in the atmosphere.

Precipitation patterns Water falls as rain, snow, hail, or sleet over Earth's land surface.

Subterranean movement Some of the water that falls over the land seeps deep into the ground and is eventually carried back to the oceans via underground channels.

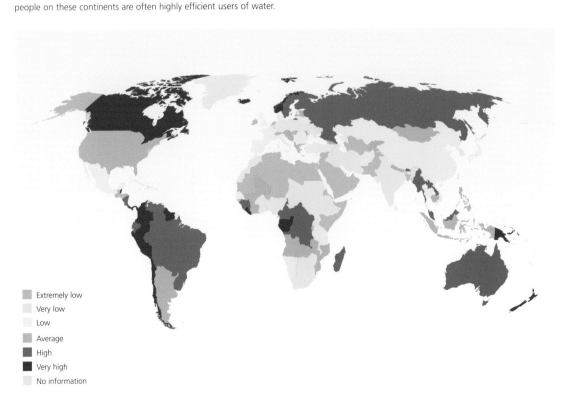

- Extremely low
- Very low
- Low
- Average
- High
- Very high
- No information

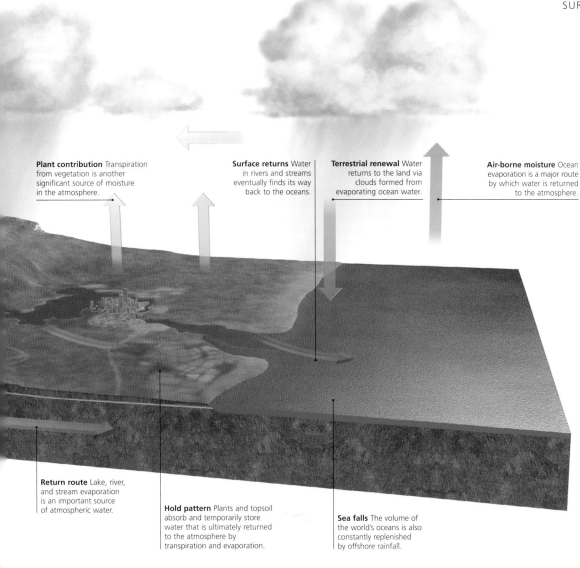

Plant contribution Transpiration from vegetation is another significant source of moisture in the atmosphere.

Surface returns Water in rivers and streams eventually finds its way back to the oceans.

Terrestrial renewal Water returns to the land via clouds formed from evaporating ocean water.

Air-borne moisture Ocean evaporation is a major route by which water is returned to the atmosphere.

Return route Lake, river, and stream evaporation is an important source of atmospheric water.

Hold pattern Plants and topsoil absorb and temporarily store water that is ultimately returned to the atmosphere by transpiration and evaporation.

Sea falls The volume of the world's oceans is also constantly replenished by offshore rainfall.

FACT FILE

1. Finland Fresh water covers 10 percent of Finland's surface. In the 1970s, industry and agriculture, coupled with the area's geology, threatened water quality. Finland resolved this by investing heavily in environmental technology.

Finland

2. Iceland More than 13 percent of the surface area of the island nation of Iceland, in the North Atlantic, is covered by glaciers and fast-flowing rivers. These have been used since the early 1900s as a renewable energy source. Now more than 80 percent of Iceland's power is from hydroelectricity.

Iceland

3. Ireland Pollution of Ireland's surface water, caused mainly by runoff from intensive agriculture, has been a problem since the 1970s. With the introduction of initiatives such as the catchment management plans, Ireland aims to improve surface and groundwater quality significantly by 2015.

Ireland

4. Spain In 2001, semi-arid Spain adopted its controversial National Hydrologic Plan, foreshadowing more than 100 new dams and the transfer of water from the Ebro River to provinces along the country's Mediterranean coastline. It was argued that the plan was contrary to Europe's sustainable objectives.

Spain

Well water (left) In the drought-prone central African nation of Niger, half the population—six million people—does not have access to clean, safe water. Most of Niger's people live a rural lifestyle and many depend on wells dug by hand to access groundwater. Traditionally, the heavy well water is pulled up by women.

Dams

Dams are constructed across rivers to block their flow. Water upstream, held behind the dam wall, creates a lake. It may be released via a pipeline to supply water to downstream towns, into the river below for irrigation purposes, or through hydroelectric power stations. Many modern dams are massive engineering feats that require years to build.

Energy flow (below) Hydroelectric power stations harness mechanical energy created by the rapid flow of water (**1**), channel it through turbines (**2**), and convert it to electricity (**3**). These stations usually involve building a dam across a steep-sided valley.

FACT FILE

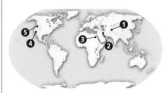

1. Nurek Dam At 884 feet (270 m) tall, Tajikistan's Nurek Dam is one of the world's tallest dams. It took the Russians two decades to build it across a gorge on the Vakhsh River, near the Afghanistan border. It generates power to meet almost all of Tajikistan's needs and also provides irrigation water.

Nurek Dam, Tajikistan

2. Karun-3 Dam One of the largest constructions ever undertaken in Iran, this dam became operational in 2005. Built across a narrow gorge in south-western Iran, the dam's arched shape provides it with the strength to hold back the waters of the Karun River. It provides electricity and stops flooding.

Karun-3 Dam, Iran

3. Aswan Dam The vast Lake Nasser was formed by the 1959–70 construction of the Aswan High Dam across the Nile River, forcing the relocation of more than 90,000 Nubians. Built to prevent flooding and to provide irrigation water, it generates about half of Egypt's power supply.

Aswan Dam, Egypt

4. Hoover Dam Construction of this dam across the Colorado River created thousands of jobs during the Great Depression of the early 1900s. The project began in 1931 and was completed just four years later. The dam provides a reliable water supply and irrigation for southern California.

Hoover Dam, U.S.A.

5. Grand Coulee Dam Although the main construction of the dam was completed in 1941, the generators were not all installed until 1942. The dam is 550 feet (170 m) high and is the largest on the Columbia River. It created the Franklin D. Roosevelt Lake.

Grand Coulee Dam, U.S.A.

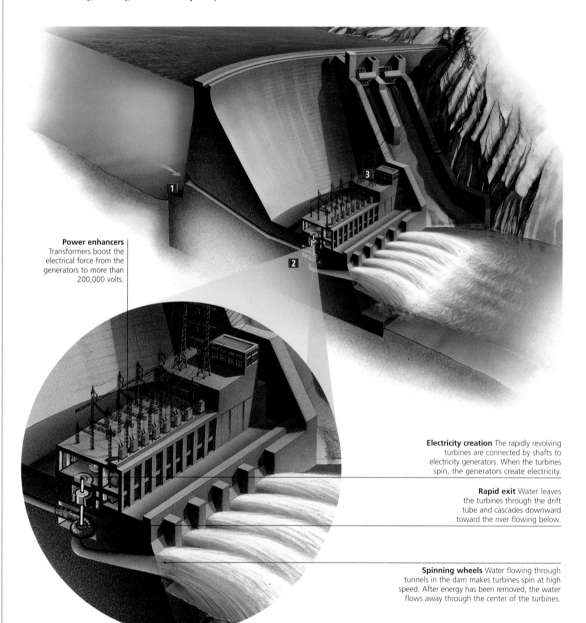

Power enhancers Transformers boost the electrical force from the generators to more than 200,000 volts.

Electricity creation The rapidly revolving turbines are connected by shafts to electricity generators. When the turbines spin, the generators create electricity.

Rapid exit Water leaves the turbines through the drift tube and cascades downward toward the river flowing below.

Spinning wheels Water flowing through tunnels in the dam makes turbines spin at high speed. After energy has been removed, the water flows away through the center of the turbines.

WORLD'S LARGEST HYDROELECTRIC DAMS

*megawatts

NAME	LOCATION	POWER (MW*)	NAME	LOCATION	POWER (MW*)
Itaipu	Brazil-Paraguay	14,000	Krasno-Shushensk	Russia	6,000
Guri	Venezuela	10,000	Churchill Falls	Canada	5,428
Tucurui	Brazil	8,370	La Grande-2	Canada	5,328
Grand Coulee	U.S.A.	6,494	Bratsk	Russia	4,500
Sayano-Shushensk	Russia	6,400	Moxoto	Brazil	4,328

Economic boost (left, below) When the U.S.$13-billion Three Gorges Dam that crosses China's Yangtze River becomes fully operational, its hydroelectric power station will have the largest capacity of any in the world. However, more than 1.3 million people will be displaced by the waters rising behind the dam.

FACT FILE

Tide mills Before the 20th century, tide mills were widely used in many countries to harness the power of tides. They were used to grind wheat into flour, saw lumber, and operate basic machinery before the invention of the steam engine.

1 A sea gate retains high-tide water within the pond in which the mill sits.

2 When the tide in the estuary outside begins to fall, the gate opens.

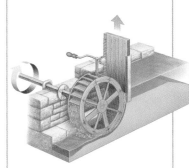

3 The wheel turns as the tide drops, providing power to turn the millstone.

4 The mill keeps going until the tide turns or the pond water runs dry.

Controlling Water

Around 70 percent of available water is used for agriculture. Irrigated areas total almost 1 million square miles (2.6 million km²) and produce 40 percent of the world's food. Irrigation occurs mostly in arid and semi-arid areas, and Asia accounts for about three-quarters of all irrigated land. The future challenge is to limit the environmental impact of irrigation.

Ancient application Human populations began controlling and redirecting water flow at least 8,000 years ago. It was a significant stage in agricultural development, instead of sole reliance on rainfall.

Egypt The ancient Egyptian shaduf featured a long pole balanced on a crossbeam, with a rope and bucket at one end and a weight at the other.

China Ancient Chinese peasants pedaled irrigation machines to raise water from canals and streams where waterway volumes fluctuated.

Greece The Archimedes pump consisted of a screw inside a close-fitting cover. The turning screw raised water from lower levels.

Water conduit (right) Designed by Roman architects and engineers, the Pont du Gard aqueduct in southern France, built 2,000 years ago, carried spring water across the Gard River to the town of Nîmes.

WATER DEMAND IN THE 20TH CENTURY

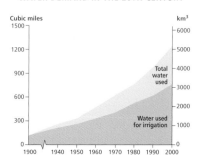

Cubic miles / km³

Total water used

Water used for irrigation

1500 / 6000
1200 / 5000
900 / 4000 / 3000
600 / 2000
300 / 1000
0 / 0

1900 1940 1950 1960 1970 1980 1990 2000

IRRIGATED LAND USE IN THE 20TH CENTURY

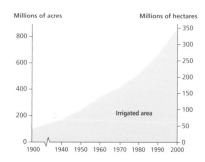

Millions of acres / Millions of hectares

Irrigated area

800 / 350
/ 300
600 / 250
/ 200
400 / 150
200 / 100
/ 50
0 / 0

1900 1940 1950 1960 1970 1980 1990 2000

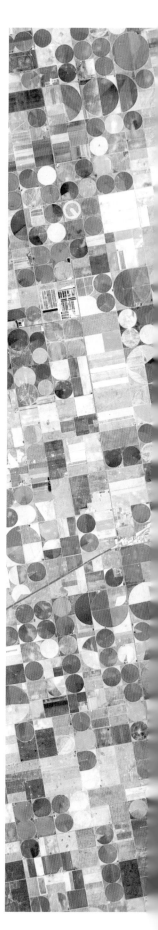

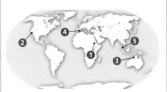

1. Gezira Scheme Sudan's Gezira Scheme is one of the world's largest irrigation systems. Established in the 1920s, it now carries life-giving water from the Blue Nile through 2,700 miles (4,300 km) of trenches and canals to farmland.

Gezira Scheme, Sudan

2. Californian irrigation With just 4 percent of U.S. farms, California produces more than 50 percent of the country's vegetables and fruit, largely thanks to irrigation. The daily water usage is about 305 million gallons (1,200 million liters).

Californian irrigation, U.S.A.

3. Ord River Project Damming of northwest Australia's Ord River during the 1960s, for the purposes of flood control, irrigation, and hydroelectricity, created the country's largest artificial freshwater reservoir: Lake Argyle.

Ord River Project, Australia

4. Ebro River irrigation The flow at the mouth of the Ebro River, the longest river in dry Spain, declined by 22 percent between 1971 and 1994, influenced by extensive extractions along its middle section for irrigation.

Ebro River irrigation, Spain

5. Kerian Irrigation Scheme The first major irrigation system in Malaysia, the Kerian Scheme began in the late 1800s. Today, the country has more than 932 such schemes, which cover more than 840,000 acres (340,000 ha) of predominantly rice paddy fields.

Kerian Irrigation Scheme, Malaysia

Pivot watering (left) The green circles in this satellite image of Kansas farmlands, U.S.A., are crops watered using central pivot irrigation, in which water is distributed in a circular motion via above-ground sprinklers.

HUMAN IMPACT

More than any other species, humans have a unique capacity to modify and manipulate the planet. We have been transforming landscapes and harnessing natural resources on a large scale since the earliest agricultural settlements emerged in southwest Asia. This is where wheat, olives, peas, goats, and sheep were first domesticated more than 10,000 years ago. Today, human agriculture wreaks ecological change on a massive scale across the planet. So, too, do mining and a range of other industries. More generally, the lifestyles that increasing urbanization and industrialization create have been driving irreversible environmental changes that could lead to a global crisis this century.

Not-so-pretty picture (left) As benign as farmlands may appear, they are also a potent symbol of the extensive damage that is caused to the planet by large-scale commercial agriculture. Landscapes are changed physically by land-clearing; water tables shift because of irrigation and the overuse of water; and soil, fresh water, and marine environments are polluted by agricultural chemicals. Methane emissions of livestock contribute to climate change, as do synthetic fertilizers.

A CATASTROPHE UNFOLDS

There is evidence to suggest the use of fire and hunting by humans in the Stone Age may have caused animal extinctions. The potential for humans to cause environmental damage is also seen in the ruins of ancient civilizations. In fact, land degradation caused by intensive agriculture, irrigation, and deforestation is implicated in the declines of great civilizations in Egypt, Greece, Central America, North Africa, Mesopotamia, and China.

We have also been aware for many centuries that environmental degradation has an impact on our own health and well-being. In some parts of medieval Europe, laws were passed to protect forests from the overcollection of wood. In the 1300s, Edward I reportedly restricted the burning of coal in London when parliament was sitting, with the aim of reducing smog.

As the industrial revolution spread from Great Britain to Western Europe, then to the United States, there were increasing signs that we were having a negative impact on the world. At first they seemed isolated, but by the late 19th century, as a litany of environmental catastrophes unfolded across the planet, the warning signs were clear and the potential impacts far-reaching.

In the 1890s, effluent discharged into local rivers from the Ashio copper mine refinery in Japan killed surrounding woodlands, poisoned thousands of farmers, and polluted their land. Millions of Californians were forced off their land during the U.S. dust bowl phenomenon in 1930, caused by poor agricultural practices in the American midwest. In 1952, smog in London claimed the lives of more than 4,000 over four days. In 1984, a chemical spill at the Union Carbide pesticide plant in the Indian city of Bhopal killed up to 5,000. A massive oil spill from the tanker *Exxon Valdez* in 1989 caused unprecedented damage in Alaska's Prince William Sound.

Overgrazing, overcropping, and other poor agricultural practices now play havoc with water tables and have led to the desertification of many millions of acres across the planet. Many millions more are alienated by pollution of the air, water, and land from mining and industry, which has become commonplace. More than half the forests that covered the planet before the industrial revolution have gone. In the oceans, the world's commercial fisheries have been crashing en masse.

The consequences are widespread: food and water shortages; increasing respiratory problems caused by smog and other air pollution; and a loss of biodiversity proceeding on such a massive scale that as many as half the planet's plant and animal species could disappear forever this century.

Exacerbating all of this is the looming specter of climate change. Arguments raged in the late 20th century about whether human-induced emissions of so-called greenhouse gases were causing global

Warning sign (top right) Some scientists believe that 18th- and 19th-century versions of industries, such as this contemporary English steel mill, initiated the enhanced greenhouse effect responsible for global warming. In the 20th century, motor vehicles compounded the problem on a huge scale. Most experts say the main underlying cause is the burning of fossil fuels—coal, oil, and gas. These release large quantities of carbon dioxide and other greenhouse gases that wrap the planet in an atmospheric blanket, keeping in too much heat from the sun.

Refuge (bottom right) Since the 1970s, migrants escaping the Saharan drought—possibly exacerbated by human-induced climate change—have helped swell the population of the once-tiny Mauritanian capital, Nouakchott, to more than two million. Deserted just decades ago, the coast is now regularly fringed by a huge fishing flotilla, as locals turn to the sea for food.

warming. Although the extent to which human activity can be blamed for the phenomenon is still debated, the world's scientists and governments now acknowledge that climate shifts have already occurred. Average temperatures are rising on all continents. Sea levels are rising. Droughts, floods, cyclones, and other extreme weather events are increasing not only in number, but also in severity. The Arctic ice cap is receding at such a rate that it may have disappeared by the century's end. Many of the world's glaciers—thousands of years old—are melting so fast that they are predicted to be gone by the middle of the century.

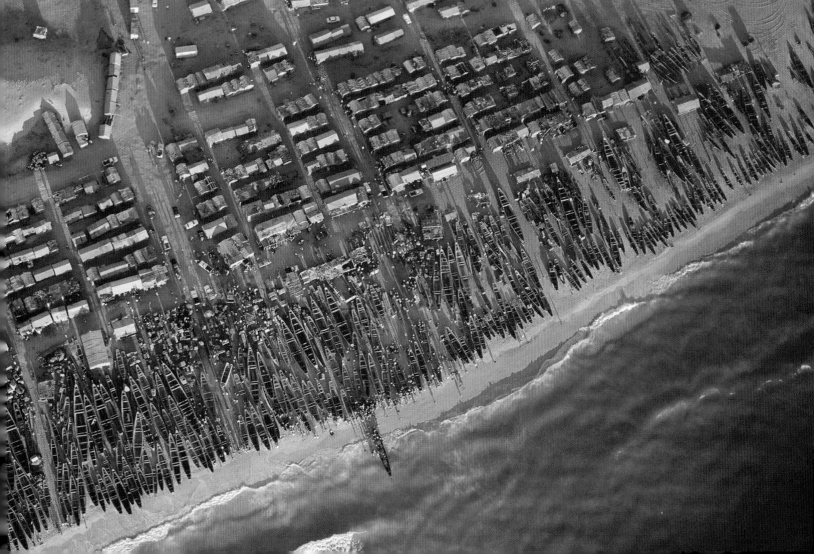

Food Shortage

As global food prices soared to record highs in 2007 and the UN warned that the planet's food supply was dwindling rapidly, more than 850 million people around the world were living in a state of chronic hunger. Each year, ten million people die worldwide from malnutrition-related causes, including six million children aged below five years.

Supply inequities (below) More than 50 countries have inadequate food to nourish their people. An adequate daily dietary energy supply is 2,600 calories (10,900 kJ) per person. Fewer than 2,300 calories (9,600 kJ) indicates hunger and malnutrition.

FACT FILE

1. Sudan More than 70,000 people are thought to have died from the 1998 famine in Sudan. The nation regularly suffers drought, but the international community, who donated U.S.$1

million per day for famine relief as the disaster peaked, also blamed human rights abuses and years of civil unrest.

Sudan

2. Zimbabwe Before the late 1980s, Zimbabwe was known as southern Africa's "bread basket" because of its rich agricultural production. Corruption and government policies led to

economic collapse and a commodities shortage. By 2007, half the population was thought to be malnourished.

Zimbabwe

3. Ethiopia Almost one million people died in two famines that devastated Ethiopia during 1984-85. Crippled by civil war, the country's economy was unable to cope, but the relief response

from developed nations was huge, including more than U.S.$100 million raised by the Live Aid concert.

Ethiopia

4. North Korea Over three years during the mid-1990s, two million people are believed to have died from diseases and famine caused by political change, natural disasters,

and poor economic planning. A 2006 survey found almost 40 percent of the population remained malnourished.

North Korea

5. Cambodia From 1970 to 1980 up to two million people are thought to have died from starvation and malnutrition-related disease. After civil

war came Khmer Rouge policies that included forced starvation of thousands, and a famine in 1979.

Cambodia

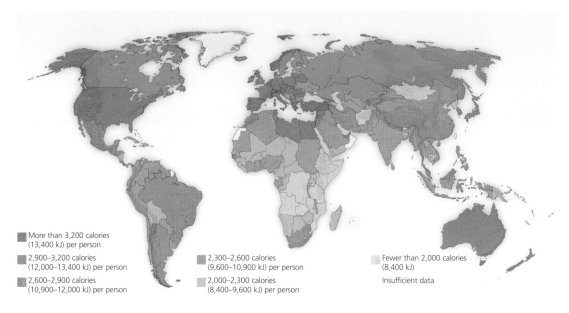

■ More than 3,200 calories (13,400 kJ) per person

■ 2,900–3,200 calories (12,000–13,400 kJ) per person

■ 2,600–2,900 calories (10,900–12,000 kJ) per person

■ 2,300–2,600 calories (9,600–10,900 kJ) per person

■ 2,000–2,300 calories (8,400–9,600 kJ) per person

Fewer than 2,000 calories (8,400 kJ)

Insufficient data

COMPARISON OF UNDERNOURISHMENT

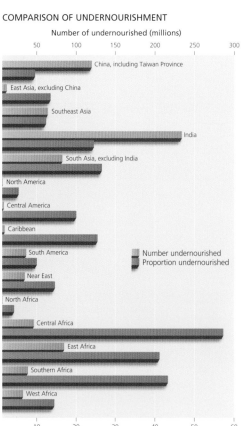

Number of undernourished (millions)

50   100   150   200   250   300

China, including Taiwan Province
East Asia, excluding China
Southeast Asia
India
South Asia, excluding India
North America
Central America
Caribbean
South America
Near East
North Africa
Central Africa
East Africa
Southern Africa
West Africa

Number undernourished
Proportion undernourished

10   20   30   40   50   60
Proportion of undernourished (%)

Supermarket affluence (above) One-third of North Americans are overweight. The gulf between the haves and have-nots is reflected keenly in a comparison of food availability between nations.

GLOBAL FOOD PRODUCTION	
FOOD TYPE	1,000 tons (1,000 tonnes)
Cereals	2,455,928 (2,227,980)
Fruits and vegetables	1,534,696 (1,392,253)
Sugar crops	1,533,272 (1,390,960)
Roots and tubers	784,495 (711,682)
Meat	292,228 (265,105)
Oilseeds and nuts (oil eq.)	146,353 (132,769)
Pulses	68,019 (61,706)
Tobacco	6,565 (5,955)

GLOBAL FOOD CONSUMPTION	
FOOD GROUPS	1,000 tons (1,000 tonnes)
Cereals	1,039,179 (942,728)
Milk	545,393 (494,772)
Roots and tubers	440,316 (399,448)
Meat	268,017 (243,141)
Sugar	173,975 (157,828)
Vegetable oils	76,805 (69,677)

Famine queue (left) In Somalia, where years of conflict and long-term drought have led to enormous food shortages, women wait for life-giving rations provided by international aid and distributed by soldiers.

1. Sudan Average annual rainfall is less than 24 inches (60 cm) in Sudan. Access to water was a major source of tension in 2003, and ignited a conflict in the Darfur region. Potential resolution of the water crisis came in 2007, after scientists discovered a huge underground lake, the size of America's Lake Erie, in the region.

Sudan

2. Iran Just 10 percent of Iran receives enough rainfall to support agriculture. More than 2,500 years ago, Iranians began exploiting the little they have using subterranean channels called qanats, which collect underground water and direct it to surface crops. Iran still has about 50,000 qanats.

Iran

3. Venezuela Pollution has affected Venezuela's freshwater resources for decades. Water shortages due to a lack of infrastructure to treat and transport the resource are common. Many laws aimed at stemming the pollution have been developed, but enforcement has proved difficult.

Venezuela

4. Syria Like more than a dozen nations worldwide, Syria sources most of its water from rivers that cross the borders of countries with which it has tense political relations. It sees water as a resource more valuable than the oil and gas reserves that make many countries in the area so wealthy.

Syria

5. Zimbabwe Rainfall in Zimbabwe is limited and few rivers are perennial. Water is stored for use in the dry months in dams, but supply to major cities often dries up, creating the need for rationing. People also draw water from wells and boreholes across the country.

Zimbabwe

Water Shortage

A looming global water crisis driven by population increases, poor resource management, and environmental degradation began emerging in the late 20th century. According to World Bank reports, the public health and economies of at least 80 countries now suffer from water shortages, while more than two billion people lack access to clean water or sanitation.

Strict ration (right) Many rural Ethiopians survive on a strict daily water ration of less than 1.3 gallons (5 liters). The recommended basic domestic water requirement per person is ten times as much.

WORLD DRINKING WATER

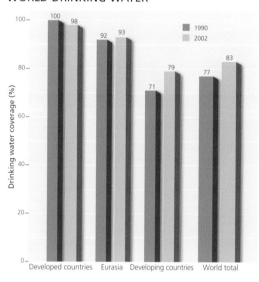

Drinking water coverage (%)

Legend: 1990, 2002

	Developed countries	Eurasia	Developing countries	World total
1990	100	92	71	77
2002	98	93	79	83

Abundant resource (below) In contrast to the limited water supply in developing nations, in developed countries water is readily available for watering recreational areas such as golf courses.

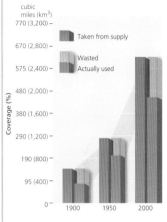
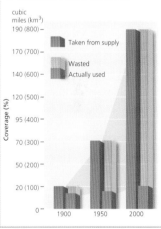
Women's work In many developing nations, water collection and storage is women's work, which often involves hours of daily travel on foot. It is a vital task that prevents many girls from attending school.

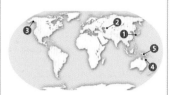

FACT FILE

1. Minemata From the 1930s to 1960s, the Chisso Corporation dumped waste containing methyl mercury into Minemata Bay. Mercury collected in

fish and shellfish that were eaten by the locals, causing widespread neurological damage and death.

Minemata disaster, Japan

2. Aral Sea The volume of this sea has fallen by 90 percent over 40 years because of mismanaged irrigation.

Salt and chemicals have accumulated to create an ecological disaster linked to a rise in disease.

Aral Sea disaster, Eastern Europe

3. Exxon Valdez Recent research confirms direct and ongoing

ecological harm from the huge 1989 oil spill from the tanker *Exxon Valdez* in Alaska's Prince William Sound.

Exxon Valdez oil spill, Alaska, U.S.A.

4. Great Barrier Reef In one of the most visible early impacts of global warming, Australia's Great Barrier Reef

has suffered huge losses in the last 30 years because of coral bleaching caused by oceanic temperature rises.

Great Barrier Reef, Australia

5. Ok Tedi In 1995, Papua New Guinean landholders received U.S.$4 billion from BHP mining giant for heavy-metal pollution of land along

the Fly River caused by the Ok Tedi gold and copper mine. Further legal action was launched in 2007.

Ok Tedi disaster, New Guinea

Natural treatment (right) The duckweed family of flowering plants can "cleanse" waters polluted with excess nutrients such as nitrogen and phosphates, a remedy well-suited to developing nations.

Polluted Water

The world's waters have been deliberate and accidental dumping grounds for society's waste for millennia. Most pollutants on land eventually wash into rivers and oceans. Before the 1800s, isolated impacts were documented, but following the industrial revolution and mass population growth, water pollution now threatens the lives and livelihoods of millions.

Nasty plumes (right) Mining waste, such as the hematite tailings from iron mining creating this discoloration, are often deposited in dams and ponds. Many countries now require the sealing of such sites to prevent pollutants leaching into groundwater.

Oil threat (below) Crude oil is one of the most widespread marine pollutants. Aquatic birds and mammals are particularly vulnerable and die from direct exposure, as well as from the longer-term absorption of toxic chemicals.

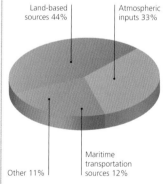

Falling Water Tables

As surface water availability has declined with overuse by the world's ever-growing population, groundwater extractions have increased dramatically. About one-third of the world's people depend on groundwater supplies and, in many countries, volumes removed from subterranean aquifers exceed replenishment rates. Water tables around the world are falling.

Contentious supply (right) Windmills and pumping stations across Texan plains tap underground water reserves that supply 60 percent of the U.S. state's water. The resultant fall in water tables has sparked intense debate over water ownership.

FACT FILE

1. Punjab Underground aquifers supply more than half of India's irrigation water, but water tables are falling in most states, including the nation's main farming areas of Punjab and Haryana.

Thousands of irrigation wells across the country are running dry, creating concern over food shortages.

Punjab, India

2. North China Plain Half China's wheat and one-third of its corn are produced on the country's North Plain, mainly with irrigation water from two aquifers. A 2001 report observed that overextraction is depleting both aquifers. As a result, thousands of wells are drying up and crop yields are falling.

North China Plain, China

3. Northern Mexico Under Mexico's Chihuahuan Desert, one of the world's most biologically diverse arid areas, water tables are falling because of overextraction by irrigators. This makes it harder for small animals and desert plants to access subsurface water.

Northern Mexico, Mexico

4. Israel Quality as well as quantity are issues in Israel. Almost half the supply comes from two aquifers: one along the Mediterranean coastal plain, and the other beneath the central mountain range. Both are in decline, and some wells are salty or polluted.

Israel

Disappearing aquifer The huge Ogallala Aquifer shown on this map underlies parts of eight U.S. states from South Dakota to Texas. Since the first 1911 extraction, the water level has been declining, and today pumping is no longer possible in 6 percent of the aquifer. It may disappear entirely in 25 years.

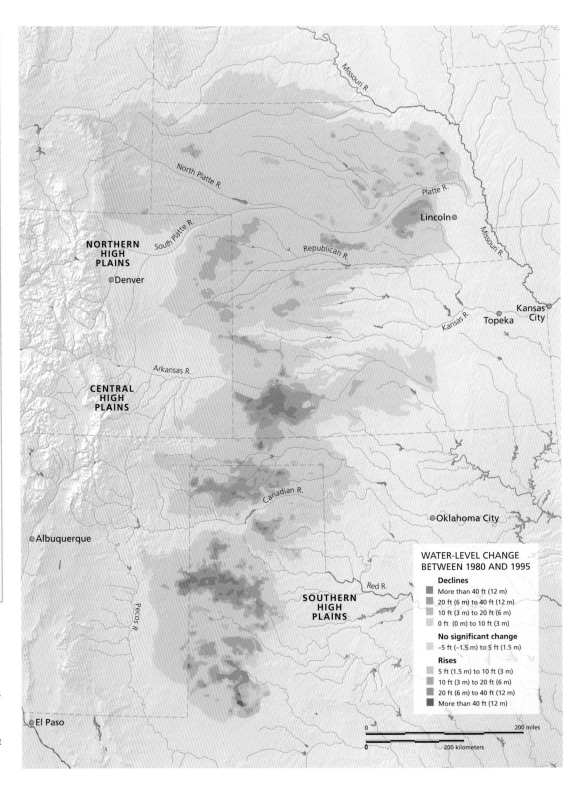

WATER-LEVEL CHANGE BETWEEN 1980 AND 1995

Declines
- More than 40 ft (12 m)
- 20 ft (6 m) to 40 ft (12 m)
- 10 ft (3 m) to 20 ft (6 m)
- 0 ft (0 m) to 10 ft (3 m)

No significant change
- −5 ft (−1.5 m) to 5 ft (1.5 m)

Rises
- 5 ft (1.5 m) to 10 ft (3 m)
- 10 ft (3 m) to 20 ft (6 m)
- 20 ft (6 m) to 40 ft (12 m)
- More than 40 ft (12 m)

Coastal aquifers Extracting too much water from aquifers located near seas and oceans can cause briny, or even salty, water to rise to where it is collected by pumps. This makes it unsuitable for most uses.

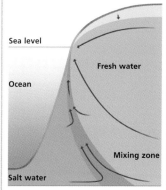

Layered water Because salt water is denser and heavier, it sits below fresh water, with a narrow mixing zone where the two meet.

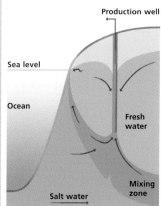

Rising salt Overpumping can cause the water in the mixing zone to expand and intrude into the fresh water, bringing salty water inland.

Sink city Most of Mexico City's water comes from an aquifer beneath the massive metropolis that has been disappearing at a rapid rate since early last century. The water table in some areas has fallen by 33 feet (10 m), and as a result, large areas have subsided. Infrastructure, including the sewage system, is being damaged.

FACT FILE

Disturbing statistics Recent figures show that almost 75 percent of the world's main commercial marine stocks are either fully exploited or overexploited. Nevertheless, annual demand is growing at a rate of 1.5 percent.

COMMERCIAL MARINE STOCKS, 1974

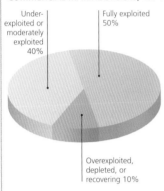

Under-exploited or moderately exploited 40%

Fully exploited 50%

Overexploited, depleted, or recovering 10%

COMMERCIAL MARINE STOCKS, 2002

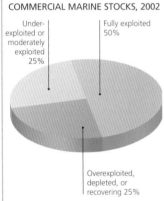

Under-exploited or moderately exploited 25%

Fully exploited 50%

Overexploited, depleted, or recovering 25%

BLUEFIN LOSS

Driven by demand from the Japanese sushi and sashimi market, global populations of all three bluefin tuna species have declined dramatically. The western stock of Atlantic bluefin has fallen 90 percent over four decades, and is now classified as critically endangered. The eastern stock is deemed endangered. Although both species are regarded by scientists as overfished, fishing continues.

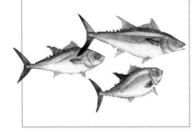

Declining Marine Fish Stocks

At least 20 of the world's most important fisheries have disappeared since the mid-1970s, and many more have been so overfished they are unlikely to recover. Technological advances and increased fishing efforts saw the global marine fish catch rise to a peak of 96 million tons (87 million tonnes) in 2000. However, the catch has not risen since.

Tuna fishing (above left) The bluefin tuna is listed as endangered, but it is still legally fished in several countries. The high prices paid, particularly by Japan, for fish in good condition mean that it continues to be heavily fished.

Whaling (above) A complete ban was placed on commercial whaling in 1985, but Japan, Iceland, and Norway continue to hunt whales under the guise of "scientific whaling." Here, a Japanese harpoonist targets a minke whale.

FISHERIES IN DECLINE

Species	Peak year	Peak catch*	1992 catch*	Decline*	Percent change
Pacific herring	1964	0.7 (0.64)	0.2 (0.18)	0.5 (0.45)	−71%
Atlantic herring	1966	4.1 (3.7)	1.5 (1.4)	2.6 (2.36)	−63%
Atlantic cod	1968	3.9 (3.5)	1.2 (1.1)	2.7 (2.45)	−69%
South African pilchard	1968	1.7 (1.5)	0.1 (0.09)	1.6 (1.45)	−94%
Haddock	1969	1 (0.91)	0.2 (0.18)	0.8 (0.73)	−80%
Peruvian anchovy	1970	13.1 (11.9)	5.5 (5.0)	7.6 (6.89)	−58%
Polar cod	1972	0.35 (0.32)	0.02 (0.02)	0.33 (0.29)	−94%
Cape hake	1972	1.1 (1.0)	0.2 (0.18)	0.9 (0.81)	−82%
Silver hake	1973	0.43 (0.39)	0.05 (0.05)	0.38 (0.34)	−88%
Greater yellow croaker	1974	0.2 (0.18)	0.04 (0.04)	0.16 (0.15)	−80%
Atlantic redfish	1976	0.7 (0.6)	0.3 (0.27)	0.4 (0.36)	−57%
Cape horse mackerel	1977	0.7 (0.6)	0.4 (0.36)	0.3 (0.27)	−46%
Chub mackerel	1978	3.4 (3.1)	0.9 (0.81)	2.5 (2.27)	−74%
Blue whiting	1980	1.1 (1.0)	0.5 (0.45)	0.6 (0.54)	−55%
South American pilchard	1985	6.5 (5.9)	3.1 (2.81)	3.4 (3.08)	−52%
Alaska pollock	1986	6.8 (6.2)	0.5 (.45)	6.3 (5.71)	−93%
North Pacific hake	1987	0.3 (0.27)	0.06 (0.05)	0.24 (0.21)	−80%
Japanese pilchard	1988	5.4 (4.9)	2.5 (2.27)	2.9 (2.63)	−54%
Totals		51.48 (46.61)	17.27 (15.71)	34.21 (30.99)	−58%

*millions of tons (millions of tonnes)

ESTIMATED WHALE NUMBERS 2004

Species	Number
Minke whales	935,000
Blue whales	400–1,400
Fin whales	47,300
Gray whales	26,400
Bowhead whales	8,000
Humpback whales	21,500
Pilot whales	780,000

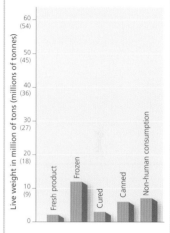

FACT FILE

Global uses The vast majority of the global fish catch is consumed in the developing world, most of it as fresh product. The remainder is frozen, cured, canned, or processed for non-human consumption.

USE OF FISH PRODUCT IN DEVELOPED COUNTRIES

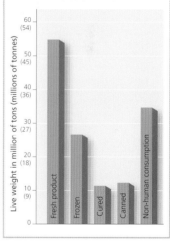

USE OF FISH PRODUCT IN DEVELOPING COUNTRIES

WHALES CAUGHT WORLDWIDE, 1910–2000

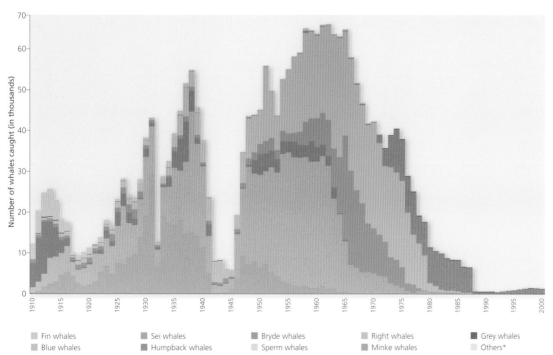

| Fin whales | Sei whales | Bryde whales | Right whales | Grey whales |
| Blue whales | Humpback whales | Sperm whales | Minke whales | Others* |

* Including blue, beaked, bowhead, Baird's beaked, killer, baleen, bottlenose, pigmy blue, and goosebeaked pilot whales

HERITAGE WATCH

Ecosystems at risk According to a ten-year study by German and Canadian researchers published in 2003 in *Nature*, big fish populations have declined by 90 percent since the mid-20th century. Affected species include open-ocean fish, such as tuna, marlin, and swordfish, as well as bottom-dwellers such as cod and flounder. As many are predators at the top of food chains, the decline points to problems in marine ecosystems.

Desertification and Salinization

About one-quarter of Earth's land surface is now at risk of desertification, and more than 15 million agricultural acres (6 million ha) are being transformed annually. Salinization is also growing, with about one-fifth of the world's irrigated land now affected. Both processes are caused by poor land management, transforming once-productive pastures into barren wastelands.

Encroaching desert (below) China has lost 36,000 square miles (93,000 km²) of land to desert since the 1950s. In 2001, the goverment began China's Great Green Wall—a replanting project to hold back the moving sands of the Gobi Desert.

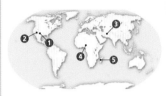

1. Dust Bowl During the 1930s, the Great Plains of North America were devastated by huge dust storms when drought and overgrazing caused large-scale desertification. More than two million people were forced to abandon farms. Today, improved land and water management prevent such disasters.

Dust Bowl, Great Plains, U.S.A.

2. Rio Puerco Just over a century ago the Rio Puerco River basin supported a huge area of productive grasslands. Overgrazing led to desertification, and it is now a bleak place, where the soil is eroded up to ten times faster than it can be replaced. Ecosystems have lost wildlife and suffered weed invasions.

Rio Puerco, central New Mexico

3. Sahel This is a transition zone between the arid Sahara and more lush eco-systems to the south. Population growth was thought to have led to desertification and two decades of famine, which killed one million people and affected millions more, but human-induced climate change is now seen as a major cause.

Sahel, Africa

4. Afghanistan The environment ranges from semi-arid regions to desert. Much of the original vegetation was removed by three decades of conflict, which has led to desertification. Around Kabul, the local people have planted more than one million trees to recreate the once-green zone.

Kabul, Afghanistan

5. Madagascar With 5 percent of the world's biodiversity, Madagascar is a significant repository of life-forms on Earth. Many of these are now at risk as desertification spreads, caused by deforestation after centuries of slash-and-burn agriculture.

Madagascar, Africa

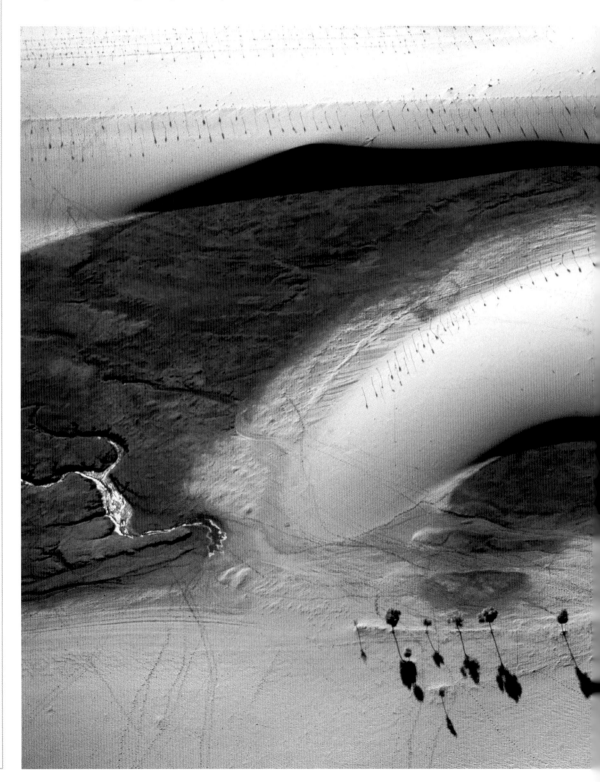

Salinization (left) Soluble salts build up in soil to levels that are toxic to plants in poorly drained semi-arid areas that are subject to drought. All of these conditions have prevailed in China's North Plain, pictured here.

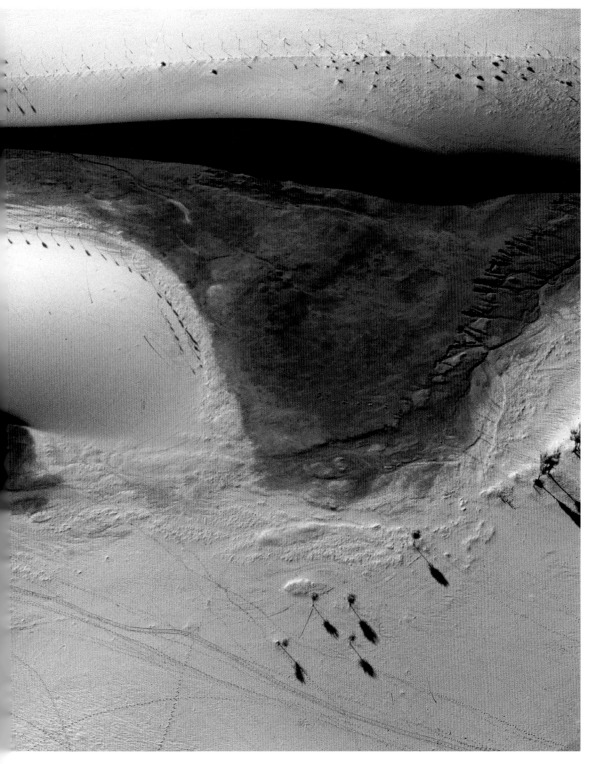

FACT FILE

1. Aral Sea Overpumping in the last century from rivers feeding the Aral Sea has turned much of it into salty soil.

Salinization and desertification have made the area a source of huge dust storms, carried as far as the Himalayas.

Aral Sea, Central Asia

2. Australia Large tracts of farmland in Australia suffer from salinization caused by ancient groundwater laced with salts that has risen to the surface. Deep-rooted native vegetation, now

largely removed, once stopped rain-water from leaking into groundwater and lifting the water table.

Australia

3. China Overgrazing and agricultural mismanagement have caused extensive desertification of native grasslands that stretch 1,800 miles (3,000 km) across China, from the west to the north east.

Resulting dust storms regularly blanket Beijing, and the air-borne pollution reaches as far as Japan and Korea.

China

4. Tunisia About 7.5 million acres (3 million ha) in central and northern Tunisia suffer serious erosion from

desertification, and salinization affects almost 10 percent of the northern African nation's total surface soil area.

Tunisia, Africa

HERITAGE WATCH

Top challenge The United Nations estimates 1.2 billion people face risks from desertification, which annually causes global production losses worth more than U.S.$42 billion. It ranks desertification as a top global environmental challenge and predicts advancing deserts could displace 50 million people in less than a decade.

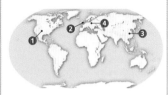
1. Superfund sites The "Superfund" legislation, created in 1980, aims to reduce health and environmental impacts across the U.S.A. caused by toxic waste sites. The fund, which pays for the clean-up of such locations, has a list with at least 1,200 sites.

Superfund sites, U.S.A.

2. U.K. A 2007 analysis of 200 sites across the U.K. found that levels of the carcinogenic group of chemicals known as dioxins held in soil and vegetation had fallen by 70 percent during the past two decades. Strict regulations started in the 1980s.

U.K.

3. China Scientific testing has found that more than 10 percent of China's farmlands are contaminated, mainly through the overuse of fertilizers, application of dirty irrigation water, and dumping of solid wastes. Much of the pollution is in more developed areas.

China

4. Poland The Katowice region is regarded as one of the most ecologically damaged parts of Europe. Past and ongoing industrial activities have left a legacy of heavy-metal contamination that contributes to health problems experienced by people in the region.

Katowice, Poland

Isolated wastelands (above right) Many sites across Russia, such as this heavy-metal-contaminated site in the Urals, have been rendered barren and unproductive by high levels of toxic compounds left in the soil by industrial activities.

From soil to water (right) Unless contained, surface soil contaminants from various light and heavy industrial sources can work their way down through the soil to reach groundwater, causing water pollution.

Contaminated Soil

Industrial, agricultural, and urban activities during recent centuries have created a network of wastelands with contaminated soil across the planet. Impacts such as elevated cancer levels in nearby populations have led to the isolation of many of these. Although laws now limit most of society's outputs, a large number of wastelands will remain toxic indefinitely.

Creating badlands (right) Even when contained to reduce and limit their spread and impact, hazardous wastes can affect both the soil on which they are dumped and the aesthetics and ecological values of wider surrounding areas.

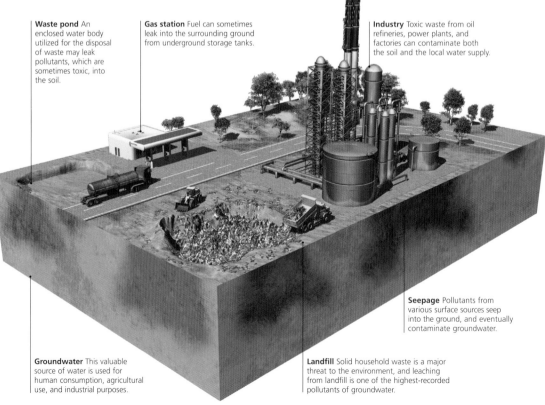

Waste pond An enclosed water body utilized for the disposal of waste may leak pollutants, which are sometimes toxic, into the soil.

Gas station Fuel can sometimes leak into the surrounding ground from underground storage tanks.

Industry Toxic waste from oil refineries, power plants, and factories can contaminate both the soil and the local water supply.

Seepage Pollutants from various surface sources seep into the ground, and eventually contaminate groundwater.

Groundwater This valuable source of water is used for human consumption, agricultural use, and industrial purposes.

Landfill Solid household waste is a major threat to the environment, and leaching from landfill is one of the highest-recorded pollutants of groundwater.

Soil toxins Pollutants can be deposited directly or indirectly into soil, and include both organic and inorganic compounds. Fuel hydro-carbons, pesticides, detergents, and heavy metals such as lead and arsenic are common toxins.

Landfill Unless landfill sites are sealed they release leachates when it rains, carrying both dissolved and suspended chemicals into the soil.

Power emissions Heavy-metal-laden emissions from coal-fired power stations can contaminate local soil. Today, they are usually isolated by a buffer zone.

Dumped waste Industrial waste dumped into waterways is likely to contaminate soil by settling out of the water column and down into sediments.

1. Cairo Decades of unregulated emissions, exacerbated by climate and geography, have led to the air quality in parts of Cairo being up to 100 times worse than acceptable world standards. Levels of cancer-causing particulates, hydrocarbons, and lead have been of specific concern to health authorities.

Cairo, Egypt

2. Delhi The air over the Indian city of Delhi is officially Asia's most polluted. Traffic emissions are the main source of air pollution, particularly from two- and three-wheeled transportation that is powered by two-stroke engines. Coal-based power plants are another cause of considerable air pollution.

Dehli, India

3. Calcutta In 2007, India's Chittaranjan National Cancer Institute reported that about three-quarters of Calcutta's residents suffered respiratory problems because of the city's highly polluted air. The research linked Calcutta's lung cancer rate, the highest of any Indian city, with its air pollution.

Calcutta, India

4. Taiyuan All three major cities in Shanxi, China's leading coal-producing province, have poor air quality, but Taiyuan has the most polluted atmosphere. It has particularly high levels of sulfur and nitrogen oxide, as well as of suspended particles that are of a size that can be inhaled by human lungs.

Taiyuan, China

5. Chongqing Uncontrolled emissions from vehicles and industrial coal burning for electric power have long been sources of pollution in Chongqing. Measures to control pollution, such as banning diesel buses, relocating industry, and planting trees, have been introduced.

Chongqing, China

Polluted Air

Almost 2.5 million deaths annually are attributable to respiratory and related illnesses caused by polluted air. Widespread airborne contamination occurs both inside homes and outside in the open. Anthropogenic sources include vehicular and factory emissions. But some pollution has natural origins, such as particulates and gases from volcanic eruptions.

AVERAGE ANNUAL CONCENTRATIONS OF AIR POLLUTION

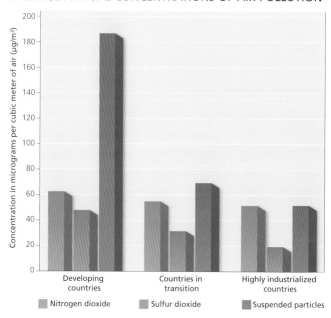

Concentration in micrograms per cubic meter of air (µg/m³)

Developing countries — Countries in transition — Highly industrialized countries

■ Nitrogen dioxide ■ Sulfur dioxide ■ Suspended particles

HEALTH EFFECTS ASSOCIATED WITH AIR POLLUTION

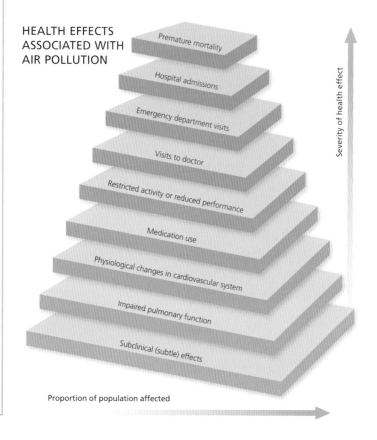

Severity of health effect

Premature mortality
Hospital admissions
Emergency department visits
Visits to doctor
Restricted activity or reduced performance
Medication use
Physiological changes in cardiovascular system
Impaired pulmonary function
Subclinical (subtle) effects

Proportion of population affected

Mexico City (above) Less than 30 years ago Mexico City was considered one of Earth's cleanest cities. Today, it is one of the most polluted. A thick layer of smog regularly covers the metropolis, obscuring volcanoes that dot the horizon.

Unhealthy traffic (right) Exhaust fumes from motor vehicles contain a complex mix of potentially pathogenic chemicals that are created by petroleum combustion. These chemicals can enter the bloodstream via inhalation, and include benzene, nitrogen dioxide, sulfur dioxide, polycyclic hydrocarbons, and formaldehyde.

City smog Smog is caused mainly by chemical reactions involving airborne pollutants from vehicular exhausts and industrial emissions. As cities are often centers of such activities, many suffer smog effects.

Smog filter This traffic officer in Kolkata, India, wears a face mask to reduce the amount of chemicals he inhales from smoggy city air.

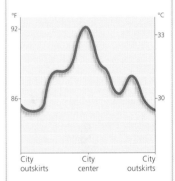

Heat trap Concrete traps daytime heat, making cities warmer at night than surrounding areas. This effect contributes to higher air pollution levels.

ELEVATED PERSPECTIVE

Astronauts report that when seen from space, Earth looks blurred and less blue than it used to because of smog effects. Other air pollution, such as smoke from the 1990s fires that devastated Indonesian forests (below), is also visible from space.

FACT FILE

1. Hubbard Brook In 1963, researchers at the Hubbard Brook Experimental Forest, in New Hampshire's White Mountains, documented acid rain in North America for the first time. In 2001,

they published new evidence showing acid deposition remains a threat for the continent's ecosystems.

Hubbard Brook, New Hampshire, U.S.A.

2. Black Forest A 1983 survey found air pollution had damaged one-third of West Germany's forests. Half of the Black Forest's fir and pine stands had been harmed by acidic fog, cloud,

and mist caused by industrial emissions. However, European legislation since the 1990s has helped the forest's recovery.

Black Forest, Germany

3. Beijing One-third of China's land area was affected by acid rain in 2005, when the country discharged more than 25 million tons (23 million tonnes) of sulfur dioxide, making it the world's

largest producer of the pollutant. Beijing introduced reduction measures ahead of hosting the 2008 Olympic Games.

Beijing, China

4. Scandinavia Degraded forests and thousands of "dead lakes" that have no life because of lowered pH levels occur throughout Scandinavia. Much of the pollution that creates the acid rain comes from other countries,

with Britain being a major contributor. In Norway, more than 90 percent of sulfur fallout comes from other countries.

Scandinavia

5. Poland Sweden and Norway claim airborne pollutants carried from Poland cause much of their acid rain, so

Poland is pioneering technology to remove acid-rain pollutants from emissions. It relies on its vast coal stores for electricity.

Poland

Acid Rain

Although noted scientifically in the mid-1800s, acid rain was not recognized as an environmental problem until the 1960s. Caused mainly by atmospheric chemical reactions involving air pollutants—chiefly sulfur dioxide and nitrogen oxides from motor vehicle and industrial emissions—it was among the first environmental issues to be addressed at a regional level.

Cause and effect (below) Air pollutants, sunlight, and other atmospheric components combine to create acidic precipitation. Acid rain falls over land and sea, harming wildlife and natural environments, and accelerating building decay in urban landscapes.

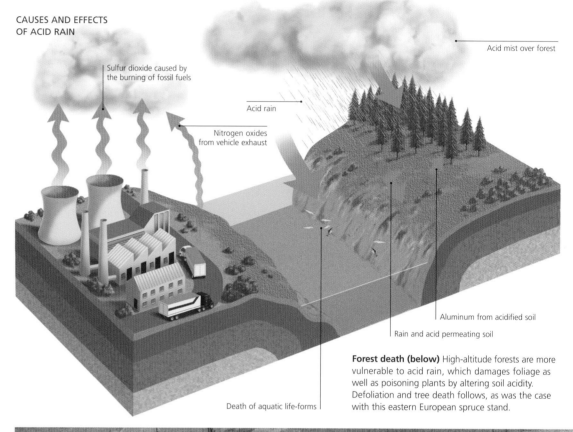

CAUSES AND EFFECTS
OF ACID RAIN

Acid mist over forest

Sulfur dioxide caused by the burning of fossil fuels

Acid rain

Nitrogen oxides from vehicle exhaust

Aluminum from acidified soil

Rain and acid permeating soil

Death of aquatic life-forms

Forest death (below) High-altitude forests are more vulnerable to acid rain, which damages foliage as well as poisoning plants by altering soil acidity. Defoliation and tree death follows, as was the case with this eastern European spruce stand.

FACT FILE

Aquatic impacts Acid rain can devastate freshwater environments. Altered acidity and aluminum released into water by acid rain can cause the death of freshwater plant and animal species.

Snail damage The availability of calcium in the environment is reduced significantly by acid rain, potentially affecting mollusk shell growth.

Fish poison High acidity and aluminum levels caused by acid rain in fresh water are toxic to fish.

Amphibian tolerance Although frogs can cope with higher acid levels than most fish, their food supply can disappear.

Asia's future (left) As scenes such as this Bangkok traffic jam might suggest, the rising use of motor vehicles in Asia is one reason why increasing acid rain events are expected in the region during the coming decades.

NATURAL POLLUTERS

On average, volcanic eruptions emit about 13 percent of sulfur added to the atmosphere each year. Sulfur is also released by biological processes on land, in wetlands, and in oceans, mostly as dimethyl sulfide.

Vanishing Forests

Today, forests cover 10 billion acres (4 billion ha), or one-third of all the land on Earth, half the area they covered at the dawn of civilization. The decline is largely due to 20th-century agricultural and urban clearing, logging, and pollution. Linked to massive biodiversity declines and climate change, forest loss is now one of the planet's principal environmental issues.

Land-use shift (below) Forests (red) cover half of Bolivia, which until the 1990s had low annual deforestation, as the 1975 satellite image suggests. Since 1990, deforestation has more than doubled, mainly because of clearing to grow cocoa and soy beans.

GLOBAL FOREST LOSS

Much of the loss of Earth's forests has occurred since 1960 and the destruction continues at an annual global rate of 32 million acres (13 million ha). About half of this is the destruction of virgin forest. Early losses occurred mostly in Europe and North America, but South America and Africa now suffer the most substantial declines.

DECLINE IN NATURAL FOREST COVER

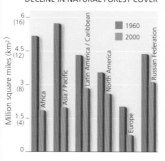

SANTA CRUZ DE LA SIERRA REGION, BOLIVIA, 1975

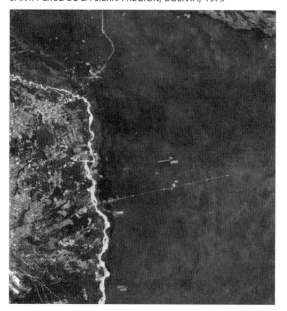

SANTA CRUZ DE LA SIERRA REGION, BOLIVIA, 1992

SANTA CRUZ DE LA SIERRA REGION, BOLIVIA, 2000

1. Siberia Russian taiga accounts for one-fifth of the planet's forested land and half of all evergreen forest. Since the 1990s, Russia has encouraged logging. Other forest threats are mining and pollution. Each year, 46,000 square miles (120,000 km²) of taiga disappears.

Siberia

2. Afghanistan War has destroyed much of Afghanistan's forests, which now cover just 1 percent of the country, and deforestation continues. With the country's power infrastructure also debilitated by war, local people plunder the forests for firewood. Illegal logging is another serious concern.

Afghanistan

3. Indonesia Indonesia's annual rate of deforestation is arguably the worst in the world. Each year, 4.4 million acres (1.8 million ha) of the forest disappears. In some years, the destruction may also be responsible for as much as 10 percent of global greenhouse gas emissions.

Indonesia

4. Vancouver Island Environmentalists and the forestry industry have been at odds for years over attempts to log old-growth rain forest at Clayoquot Soud. In 1993, 12,000 protesters blockaded the site for months, leading to more than 850 arrests. Renewed logging plans were announced in 2006; conflict continues.

Vancouver Island, Canada

New menace (left) Madagascar is one of the poorest nations, but biologically it is one of the richest, with 5 percent of the world's total biodiversity. Clearing for rice paddies and logging activities, particularly since the 1950s, has destroyed about 80 percent of the country's original forests. The remainder now face an additional threat following the recent discovery of rich rainforest deposits of alluvial sapphires.

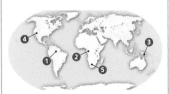
1. Amazonia Threatened largely by deforestation for farming, the Amazon rain forest covers more than 1 billion acres (400 million ha) and includes parts of Brazil, Venezuela, Peru, Colombia, and Ecuador. It is home to more than half of the world's species, estimated at more than 10 million different species.

Amazonia

2. Congo Geographic isolation and political instability have helped preserve much of the vast biodiversity in the Congo, which holds the world's second-largest area of tropical forest. The Congo supports 10,000 plant, 1,000 butterfly, more than 140 reptile, 140 amphibian, and 270 mammal species.

Congo

3. New Guinea This Pacific nation boasts about 5 percent of the world's biodiversity. Coastal and lowland areas are damaged by land clearing, but isolation and inaccessibility have helped preserve much of the highland's rain forests, where new animal species are still discovered.

New Guinea

4. North American deserts The Mojave, Great Basin, Chihuahuan, and Sonoran deserts lie in western North America. The Sonoran may be the most biodiverse of any desert. All have areas that suffer from cattle grazing, urban sprawl, falling water tables, and the introduction of alien animals and plants.

North American deserts

5. South Africa Its range of climate and topography make South Africa one of the planet's most biologically diverse nations. Covering 1 percent of all land, it has 10 percent of Earth's plant, bird, and fish species, and 6 percent of all mammal and reptile species.

South Africa

Global Loss of Biodiversity

Since the 1990s, the world's scientists have warned that a massive global loss of life-forms is under way. Current extinction rates, up to 1,000 times higher than during the past 65 million years, represent a biodiversity catastrophe that could cause widespread ecosystem collapses and lead to dire agricultural consequences that would threaten food supplies for millions.

Tropical loss (right) Destruction of tropical rain forests, such as this one in French Guiana, may cost the planet more than 130 plant, animal, and insect species per day, totally 50,000 a year. Many of these could be sources for new pharmaceuticals.

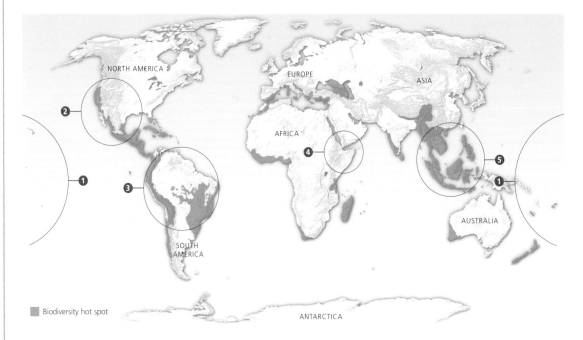

Biodiversity hot spot

Biodiversity hot spots (above) More than 50 percent of plant and 42 percent of terrestrial vertebrate species are endemic to 34 threatened biodiversity hot spots. Together, they once accounted for 15.7 percent of Earth's surface; they now cover just 2.3 percent.

Pacific Islands (**1**): Island species often evolve in isolation from the predation and competition pressures of mainland areas. As a result, many unique birds and plant species, in particular, occur only on individual islands.

North America (**2**): The California Floristic Province is the U.S.A.'s largest avian breeding ground. Amphibians thrive in Mesoamerica's forests, while a quarter of Mexico's plant species exist in the Madrean Pine-Oak Woodlands.

South America (**3**): For its size, the tropical Andes is the Earth's most biodiverse region. Only one-fifth of Brazil's coastal forests and inland savannas remain. Most have been cleared to cultivate sugar cane.

Africa (**4**): With its grasslands overgrazed and rich mineral resources exploited for centuries, less than 5 percent of the Horn of Africa is untouched. Africa is also home to most of the world's last wild ape populations.

Asia (**5**): New species are still discovered in Southeast Asia's hot spots, where habitats are cleared by loggers, often for farm expansion. The area is home to the world's two orangutan species, both endangered.

ANIMAL GROUPS IN DANGER

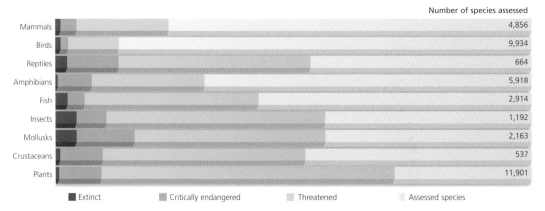

Number of species assessed

Mammals	4,856
Birds	9,934
Reptiles	664
Amphibians	5,918
Fish	2,914
Insects	1,192
Mollusks	2,163
Crustaceans	537
Plants	11,901

■ Extinct   ■ Critically endangered   ■ Threatened   ■ Assessed species

Loss of Biodiversity—Land and Air

Many scientists regard climate change as the 21st century's single largest threat to terrestrial biodiversity, because of its overarching influence on all ecological functions. It exacerbates environmental damage caused by habitat destruction, pollution, and hunting, and has already interfered with season-dependent biological events, such as migration, which affects distribution.

Habitat holes (right) Even traditional small-scale agricultural clearing, such as this slash-and-burn operation in virgin lowland tropical New Guinean forest, creates small, isolated terrestrial "islands" that cannot support animal and plant life.

Orangutans Both species of orangutan face the imminent threat of extinction, mostly because of the destruction of their forest habitat by logging and mining operations.

Polar bear U.S. scientists forecast the world's polar bear population will be just one-third of its present size by mid-century because of global warming.

Tigers Of the nine tiger subspecies, three are already extinct and six are endangered, mainly because of destruction of their Asian habitats.

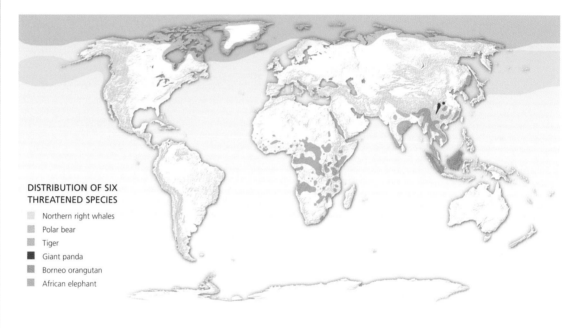

DISTRIBUTION OF SIX THREATENED SPECIES

- Northern right whales
- Polar bear
- Tiger
- Giant panda
- Borneo orangutan
- African elephant

Species at risk (above) Biodiversity is not evenly distributed across the world. Species diversity tends to increase toward the tropics and decrease at higher latitudes. The most biodiverse terrestrial habitats are tropical forests. Deserts, tundra, and boreal forests have the lowest levels of biodiversity. Species restricted to small geographic areas or those that can only survive in a specific, limited habitat are called endemic. The distribution of six threatened species is shown on this map.

Vulnerable panda (right) A naturally low reproductive rate and highly specialized dietary requirements make China's giant panda particularly vulnerable to the destruction of its high-altitude bamboo forest habitat. This, and hunting, have forced numbers down to below 1,000 in the wild.

Extinction candidates Biologists estimate that 32 percent of amphibian, 23 percent of mammal, and 12 percent of bird species now face extinction. For plants, 25 percent of conifers and 52 percent of cycads face an uncertain future.

Haven destruction Deforestation in the migratory monarch butterfly's Mexican wintering grounds has caused a recent, dramatic decline in numbers.

Bird loss Australia's yellow-tailed black cockatoo faces several threats, including the agricultural clearing and fragmentation of its breeding and foraging habitats.

Agricultural conversion (left) In prehistoric times, fire use and hunting by early hominids led to the extinction of some animal and bird species, but it was 20th-century agricultural expansions that triggered a rapid rise in global species extinctions.

VICTIM AND SURVIVOR

Land clearing for agricultural and urban expansion has been a major contributor to the extinction of North American animals, such as the carrier pigeon (left). However, species such as the raccoon (below) have adapted well to human development, prospering by foraging in trash cans and pet bowls.

FACT FILE

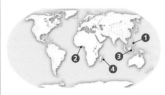

1. Philippines It is estimated that three-quarters of the ecologically unique reefs in the Philippine islands are already damaged or destroyed. Pressures stem largely from the need to feed the nation's growing population, and include illegal, destructive fishing methods, such as the use of explosives.

Philippines

2. Gulf of Guinea The threatened reefs in the waters surrounding the Gulf of Guinea islands of Annobón, Bioco, São Tomé, and Príncipe, off West Africa, face particular pressures from land development. Waters are often clouded by runoff laden with sediment from urban developments and logging.

Gulf of Guinea

3. Sunda Islands The coral reefs of Indonesia's Sunda Islands suffer heavily from collecting for the North American and European aquarium trade. The particularly destructive use of sodium cyanide to stun fish is widespread. About half of the species captured like this die before they reach the marketplace.

Sunda Islands, Indonesia

4. Southern Mascarene Islands Located in the southwestern Indian Ocean, the reefs off the islands of Mauritius, Rodriguez, and Réunion Islands cover 390 square miles (1,000 km²). Major threats come from growing coastal populations and polluted runoff from farming, particularly from sugar cane.

Southern Mascarene Islands

Loss of Marine Biodiversity

Until recently, it was believed that the great expanse of oceans—covering more than 70 percent of the planet—could safely absorb and dilute any human impact. The 20th-century crashing, en masse, of commercial fisheries warned otherwise. So, too, do somber predictions of a possible permanent loss, by 2020, of three-quarters of Earth's coral reefs—the oceans' rain forests.

THREATENED HABITATS		
HABITAT TYPE	THREAT	QUANTIFIABLE LOSS
Shelf-seas seabed	Commercial trawling	The estimated coverage of powered trawlers is 1.4 billion square miles (3.6 billion km²) per year.
Seagrass beds	Land reclamation	15% of seagrass beds were lost between 1993 and 2003.
Cold-water corals	Commercial trawling	4.4 tons (4 tonnes) of cold-water coral is removed in the northeast Atlantic each day.
Warm-water corals	Bleaching, dynamiting	In 2003, 65% of reefs showed some form of damage from trawling. This is estimated to rise to 95% by 2030.
Mangroves	Aquaculture	In 2000, just 50% of all mangroves were still intact, the losses mostly because of coastal development. A further loss of up to 95% is predicted by 2040.
Temperate wetlands	Land reclamation	50% of all temperate wetlands have been lost since 1900. Estimates suggest 31% of salt marshes and 37% of coastal lagoons will be lost by 2050.

Marine turtles (right) Six of the seven marine turtle species are threatened. Large numbers die as commercial fishery by-catch, and they also suffer from destruction of nesting sites and marine pollution, particularly floating debris such as plastic bags.

Black death (right) Oil spills annually render millions of water birds unable to swim, fly, or thermoregulate. Many that survive initial exposure die later from internal organ damage caused by ingesting the pollutant while preening.

PROTECTING THE PLANET

The realization that our use of Earth's resources and ecosystems might require restrictions and guidelines slowly emerged in the mid-1800s. Isolated pollution events, species losses, and habitat destruction began hinting that human activity could cause irrevocable environmental harm with widespread effects. Initial responses were fragmented, but by the end of the 20th century, conservation and environmental movements operated globally. Environmental issues are now of major concern in most countries, involving the highest levels of government, industry, and the judiciary.

A century of safeguards (right) The U.S.A.'s Grand Canyon has been protected for more than a century from development and destruction. In 1908 it was proclaimed a national monument under federal legislation, and in 1919 a national park covering an area of 1,900 square miles (4,900 km²). International protection came in 1978, when it was included as one of the first sites on the World Heritage List.

Rachel Carson (left) In her 1962 book *Silent Spring*, U.S. marine biologist Rachel Carson highlighted the deleterious effects of pesticide use. This brought environmental concerns to a wide public audience, and led to a U.S. (and later worldwide) ban on pesticides such as DDT.

Worldwide protection (right) The 1987 inclusion of China's Great Wall (pictured) on the World Heritage List helps ensure the wall's long-term protection. By 2006, 184 nations had ratified the convention and the list included 851 sites.

WORLDWIDE RESPONSE

Early calls for environmental protection came from 19th century naturalists and biologists, but it was the simple urge to protect natural beauty that inspired the establishment of the world's first national parks: America's Yellowstone in 1872, and Australia's Royal National Park in 1879. In 1903, U.S. president Theodore Roosevelt established Florida's Pelican Island as the first stage in the now massive U.S. National Reserve System.

Widespread public interest in conservation was first sparked when the last passenger pigeon died on September 1, 1914. Once North America's most common bird, the species had been decimated by hunting and habitat destruction.

In both Europe and America, early conservation was marked by the formation of charitable organizations dedicated to the cause, many of which ultimately spread their work to include Asia and Africa. The largest of those organizations today is the World Wide Fund for Nature (WWF), also known as the World Wildlife Fund. The WWF was established in Switzerland in 1961 by two Britons, scientist Julian Huxley and environmentalist Peter Scott, and others. Supported globally by over five million people, it now runs 15,000 projects in more than 90 countries.

When it became clear that environmental issues are not bound by borders, 20th-century conservation was impelled by international treaties and agreements. Now ratified by 172 countries, the 1975 CITES (Convention on International Trade in Endangered Species of Wild Fauna and Flora) has one of the largest memberships.

However, the world's most far-reaching agreement on the environment and sustainable development is the 1997 Kyoto Protocol. Designed as the vital first step in a global scheme to reduce greenhouse gas emissions responsible for climate change, it came into force in 2005. By 2007 it had been ratified by 174 countries.

THROUGH THE AGES

1905 America's National Audubon Society was established. It was one of the first organizations in the world dedicated to species' protection.

1936 The last Tasmanian tiger, the world's largest marsupial carnivore, died in Australia's Hobart Zoo. The species is thought to have been hunted to extinction.

1948 The World Conservation Union (IUCN) was founded to conserve nature and promote sustainable development. Its Red List of Threatened Species was created in 1963.

1949 In response to a war-time rise of interest in conservation, the Nature Conservancy was formed in the U.K. It highlighted the importance of science in conservation.

1968 The group Zero Population Growth was formed by U.S. biologist Paul Ehrlich and others to draw attention and find solutions to the problems of human overpopulation.

Protest (left) The first *Rainbow Warrior*, operated by the international environmental organization Greenpeace, was sunk in 1985 by explosives set by the French foreign intelligence agency. The ship was playing a lead role in protests against French testing of nuclear explosives in the Pacific. Dutch photographer Fernando Pereira was killed in the attack.

Attenborough (below) In the 1950s Sir David Attenborough began using television to inform audiences worldwide about the wonders of Earth's animals, plants, and ecosystems. The nature documentary format he pioneered has since become one of the environmental movement's most valuable educational tools.

1971 Greenpeace, noted for its front-line conservation activism, was founded. Its first campaign was against U.S.-government nuclear tests in Alaska.

1972 The United Nations Environment Programme was established, with the aim of promoting the sustainable development of global environments.

1994 The European Environment Agency began operating as a monitoring body and adviser on issues such as air and water pollution and land use in Europe. By 2007 it had 32 members.

1995 *The Sixth Extinction*, written by paleontologist Richard Leakey and science journalist Roger Lewin, alerted the public to an emerging biodiversity catastrophe.

2006 Former U.S. Vice President Al Gore's documentary *An Inconvenient Truth* brought climate change issues to mainstream audiences.

Greenhouse Gases

Greenhouse gases are a normal atmospheric component and a major reason why Earth supports such rich biodiversity. Because of their molecular structure, greenhouse gases absorb solar infrared radiation (heat) and trap it, like glass panes in a gardener's greenhouse. Without this natural effect, Earth's average temperature would be about 63°F (35°C) colder. Greenhouse gas levels have fluctuated through Earth's history, but in recent centuries have risen rapidly. Scientific evidence now shows that much of this rise is because of human activity.

FACT FILE

Growing gas The main greenhouse gases are water vapor, carbon dioxide, methane, and nitrous oxide. Carbon dioxide levels have risen by about a third since pre-industrial revolution levels. Methane levels have at least doubled.

CARBON DIOXIDE, 1400–2000

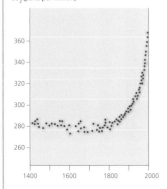

CO_2 (parts per million)

METHANE, 1400–2000

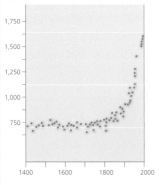

CH_4 (parts per billion)

NITROUS OXIDE, 1400–2000

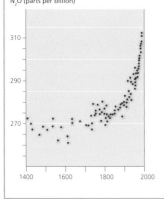

N_2O (parts per billion)

BREAKDOWN OF GREENHOUSE GASES

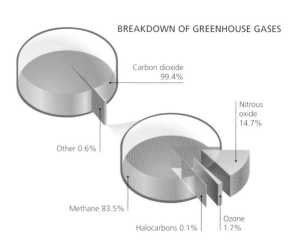

Carbon dioxide 99.4%

Other 0.6%

Nitrous oxide 14.7%

Methane 83.5%

Halocarbons 0.1%

Ozone 1.7%

The human effect (below) The enhanced greenhouse effect refers to the human contribution to global warming. Various human activities, such as burning fossil fuels, release greenhouse gases into the atmosphere. As the amount of greenhouse gases increases, more heat is trapped in the atmosphere. This speeds up the natural greenhouse effect and causes Earth to get hotter.

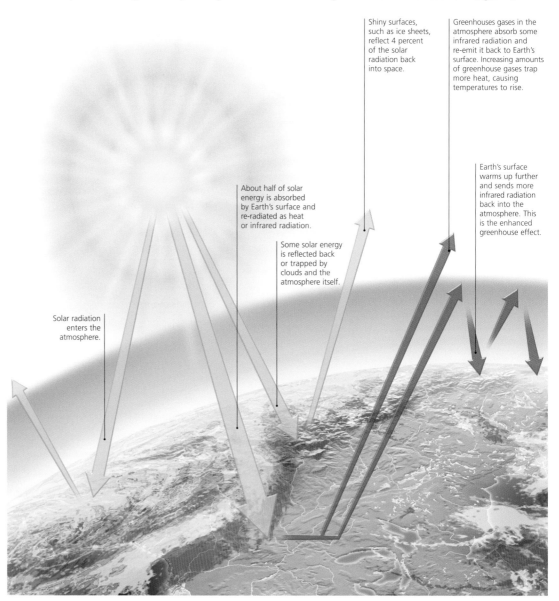

Shiny surfaces, such as ice sheets, reflect 4 percent of the solar radiation back into space.

Greenhouses gases in the atmosphere absorb some infrared radiation and re-emit it back to Earth's surface. Increasing amounts of greenhouse gases trap more heat, causing temperatures to rise.

About half of solar energy is absorbed by Earth's surface and re-radiated as heat or infrared radiation.

Earth's surface warms up further and sends more infrared radiation back into the atmosphere. This is the enhanced greenhouse effect.

Some solar energy is reflected back or trapped by clouds and the atmosphere itself.

Solar radiation enters the atmosphere.

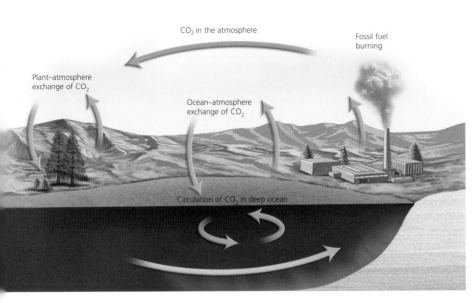

CO₂ in the atmosphere

Fossil fuel burning

Plant–atmosphere exchange of CO₂

Ocean–atmosphere exchange of CO₂

Circulation of CO₂ in deep ocean

Carbon circulation (left)
A finite amount of carbon cycles on the planet. It is found in the atmosphere as the greenhouse gas carbon dioxide (CO_2); absorbed by plants during photosynthesis; absorbed and released by natural oceanic processes; and released when fossil fuels burn.

Safe storage (below)
Forests lock in large amounts of carbon. When they die, the carbon escapes into the atmosphere as CO_2. This means that deforestation contributes to rising greenhouse gas levels.

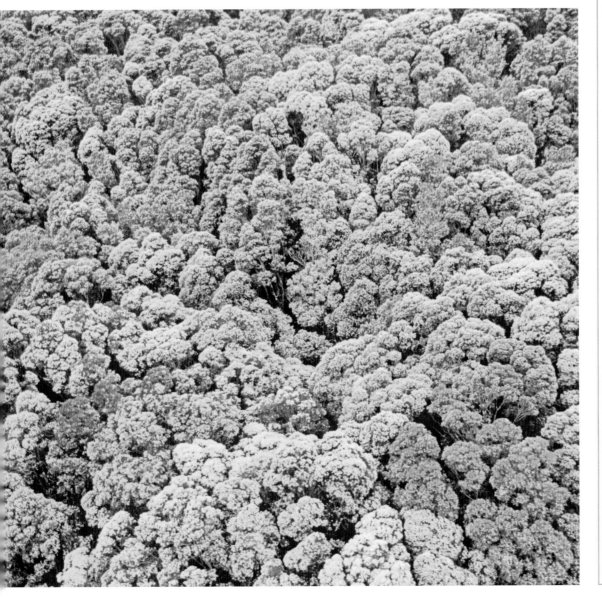

Methane As much as 10 percent of global warming is caused by atmospheric methane. Much of this highly potent greenhouse gas is produced by plants and animals. It is also released by garbage as it rots.

Wood eaters Termites produce some 20 million tons (18 million tonnes) of methane each year, generated by gut bacteria that break down matter.

Livestock Herds of livestock, such as cattle, sheep, and goats emit about 100 million tons (90 million tonnes) of methane annually from gaseous burps.

Paddy pollution Large quantities of methane enter the atmosphere from rice paddies. The gas is produced as a bacterial by-product in stagnant water.

A Shifting Global Climate

Average global temperatures have risen by 1.3 degrees (0.7°C) since 1900, coinciding with worldwide changes in drought and flood patterns; increased polar ice melting and sea-level rise; ocean acidification; shifts in the timing of seasonally related biological events; an increase in extreme weather events; and a rise in greenhouse gas emissions. Scientists predict that mid-21st-century atmospheric carbon dioxide concentrations will be double pre-industrial levels, leading to a rise of as much as 10.4°F (5.8°C) by the end of the century.

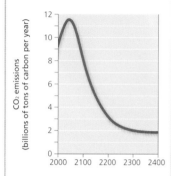
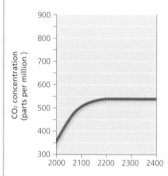
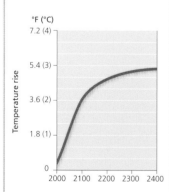
Global transformation (right) Scientists have already recorded climate-related changes at continental, regional, and ocean basin scales. They include Arctic temperature rises, more floods and droughts, and extreme weather, such as heat waves, wildfires, and cyclones. This map shows some of the areas already affected.

Worst drought (left) Record high temperatures hit Australia in 2002, causing one of the nation's worst-ever droughts. About 60 percent of the country had little rain for nine months, and in the state of New South Wales Lake Burrendong nearly vanished. This lake was photographed in 2002 (left) and 2003 (right).

Melting glaciers and ice

Rising sea levels

Heatwaves, droughts, and fires

Storms and flooding

Coral reef bleaching

Plants and animals under threat

Spread of mosquito-borne diseases

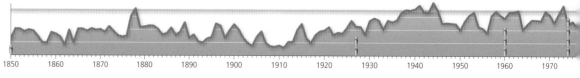

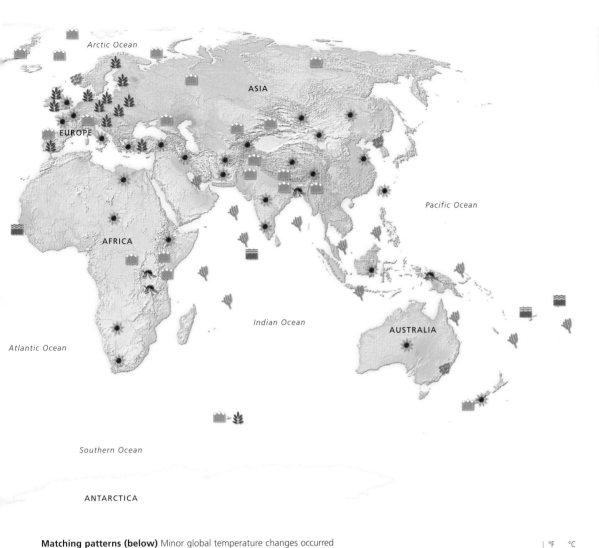

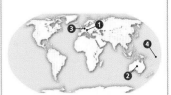

1. Austria Mid-1990s Austrian and Swiss Alps research confirmed alpine plant ranges are moving upward to escape rising temperatures. The area's average temperature rose last century by 1.8–2.7°F (1–1.5°C). Plant distribution shifted up by 12 feet (3.5 m) a decade.

Alpine plants, Austria

2. Australia 2001 projections by the Australian research organization CSIRO forecast a temperature rise of between 1.8°F and 10.8°F (1–6°C) by 2070 for the world's driest inhabited continent. Climate models warn of a marked rise in drought occurrence and severity.

Drought, Australia

3. Northern Europe By the 2040s, U.K. climate researchers predict most European summers will be more extreme than the 2003 heat wave—the hottest recorded European heat wave, which contributed to 15,000 deaths.

Heat waves, Northern Europe

4. Tuvalu Rapidly rising king tides and seawater encroachment of croplands on the tiny, low-lying island nation of Tuvalu back predictions that the nation could be submerged within five decades. This would force the entire population of 11,800 to evacuate their islands and relocate elsewhere.

Rising seas, Tuvalu

Matching patterns (below) Minor global temperature changes occurred in the 1800s as a result of the industrial revolution. Significant rises appear in the wake of the explosive increase in global population that began in the mid-20th century. More people means that more fossil fuels are burned, and as greenhouse gas emissions increase, so does Earth's temperature.

AVERAGE GLOBAL TEMPERAURE

- World population (in billions)
- Actual temperature measurements
- Baseline temperature: 59.5°F (15.3°C)

TEMPERATURE PROJECTIONS: THREE GLOBAL SCENARIOS

- Rapid economic growth, rapid introduction of cleaner technologies, and heavy use of fossil fuels. Population peaks in 2050, then declines.
- Slower and more regional economic growth. Population continues to increase.
- Rapid switch to service and information economy, which uses fewer resources and cleaner technologies. Population peaks in 2050, then declines.

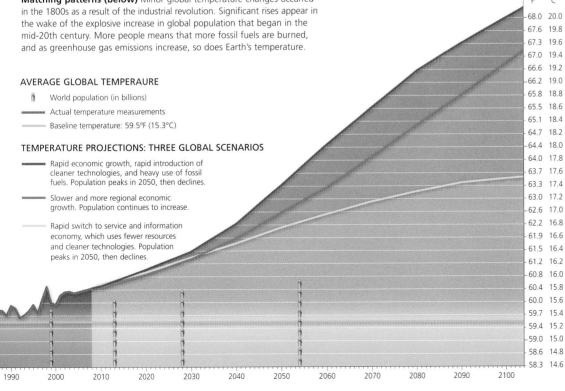

GLORIA The Vienna-based Global Observation Research Initiative in Alpine Environments (GLORIA) was created in 2001 to oversee an international network of more than 40 high-altitude experimental sites studying ecological impacts of global temperature rise. Periodic readings and comparisons are planned to continue indefinitely.

FACT FILE

1. Greenland About 8 percent of the planet's ice is held in the Greenland Ice Sheet. Its southern and eastern edges have thinned by an average annual rate of more than 3 feet (1 m), since the early 1990s.

Melting Greenland ice significantly contributes to Earth's annual sea-level rise.

Greenland

2. Antarctica About 90 percent of Earth's ice is in the Antarctic. Scientists debate if the vast ice sheet is shrinking, because as the coastal fringes melt, snowfall adds mass over the sheet's center. A 2006 study based on NASA

satellite data found that an annual melt of 36 cubic miles (150 km³) causes a rise in sea levels of 0.2 inch (5 mm).

Antarctica

3. Andes Since the mid-1970s, the Andes Quelccaya glacier, the largest in the tropics, has shrunk by one-third. Its annual retreat rate was 10 feet (3 m)

until 1990, but increased ten-fold during that decade. It is the main water source for Lima, the Peruvian capital.

Andes, Peru

4. Glacier National Park The glaciers in this park in the Rocky Mountains are shrinking. Since 1850, the park's total number of glaciers has dropped from 150 to just 35. Scientists warn that if

global warming continues at its current rate, the remaining glaciers could disappear completely by 2040.

Glacier National Park, U.S.A.

5. Himalayas The Himalayan glaciers, a principal water source for the Indus, Ganges, Yangtze, and other major Asian rivers, are believed to be retreating by

up to 49 feet (15 m) each year. Within three decades, the area covered by glaciers is likely to shrink by 20 percent.

Himalayas

Melting Ice

In what is widely acknowledged as one of the strongest signs of human–induced climate change, Earth's ice cover is shrinking at a faster rate than ever before recorded. The loss has already had widespread ecological impacts, and is expected to increase global warming rates, raise sea levels, and lead to widespread and unpredictable flooding around the world.

Ice retreat (below, left and right)
These photos were taken in 2002 (left) and 2003 (right). In just one year, the tongue of Switzerland's Triftgletscher glacier had retreated almost completely. Water from melting ice filled the basin, which was once filled by glacial ice.

Antarctic break-up Part of the large, floating Larsen B ice shelf began shattering and separating from Antarctica in the 1990s. By 2002, it had lost about 60 percent of its area—2,200 square miles (5,700 km²). These images are from January and February, 2002.

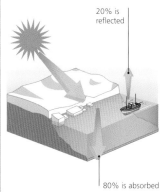

Rising Seas and Rivers

Sea levels rose during the past 100 years by 4–10 inches (100–250 mm) and experts anticipate that, on average, they could rise by another 20 inches (500 mm) this century. Predicted impacts include increased coastal erosion and submersion of low-lying islands. Widespread flooding, particularly of Southeast Asia's coastlines, could threaten the lives of millions.

Saturated cities (below) If the worst prediction eventuates and sea levels rise 3 feet (1 m) this century, parts of some megacities will disappear. Areas of New York (left) and Mumbai (right) that would be inundated are shaded green.

FACT FILE

1. Lohachara Island Since the 1980s, four Indian islands in the Sundarban Delta have become permanently flooded. Lohachara was the first of these. When its final submersion was reported in 2006, it became the first inhabited island to be claimed by rising seal levels caused by climate change.

Lohachara Island, India

2. England At least 62 English sites, including some of the U.K.'s largest wildlife areas, have been designated as having "Special Scientific Interest," and are threatened by sea-level rise. Along the shoreline alone, an estimated 32,000 acres (13,000 ha) are expected to disappear in the next two decades.

England.

3. European Alps A glacial lake outburst flood occurs when millions of gallons of water bursts at high speed down a mountainside. Alpine Europe, where glacial melting has risen by as much as 20 percent, is one of several regions expected to see increases in these floods during coming decades.

European Alps

4. Gulf Coast A sea-level rise of 8–20 inches (20–50 cm) by the century's end is forecast for southern U.S.A.'s Gulf Coast region. The relative sea rise could even be as much as 44 inches (110 cm) in places because the area is so flat, and has extensive shoreline developments and existing subsidence.

Gulf Coast Bay, U.S.A.

5. Shishmaref Relocation is the only long-term protection from climate change effects for the tiny Alaskan village of Shishmaref. The permafrost below it is melting, as is sea ice that helps to weaken storm surges, and erosion is causing the shoreline to recede.

Shishmaref, Alaska

NEW YORK

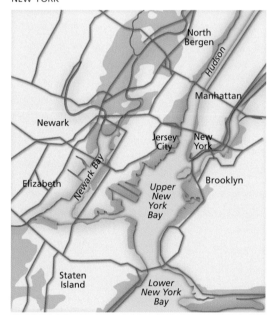

MUMBAI

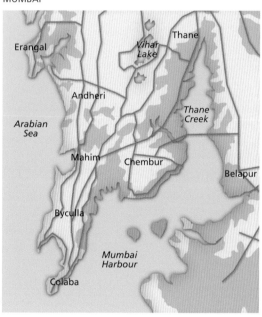

Why sea levels change (right) Melting ice has caused about 20 percent of the recent global sea-level rise. Most of the rise is due to thermal expansion—the volume increase that occurs as water warms—created by heat transfer from the land and lower atmosphere.

Terrestrial impacts
Some water is captured in dams and reservoirs; river flows can change over time; and groundwater can seep into aquifers.

Increased extraction
Population growth increases demand for groundwater extracted using wells.

Land on the move
River delta subsidence, land movement, and the movement of tectonic plates can affect flows of water into the ocean.

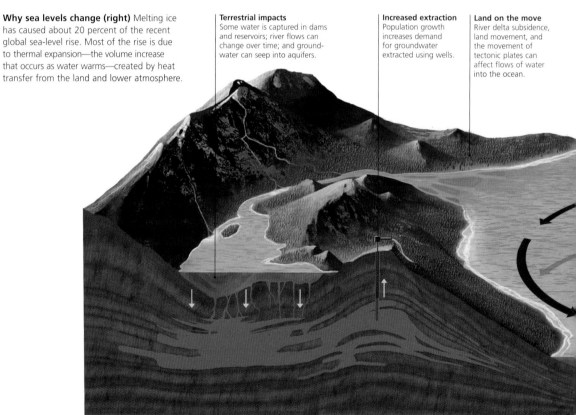

Thermal expansion Water volume increases when warmed by air and nearby land.

Current changes Shifts in circulation of deep and surface level currents can affect warm- and cold-water flows.

Ice reduction Warmer temperatures cause icebergs to break off and enter the sea.

Melted water Water stored on land returns to the sea via glacial, ice, and snow melts at the Poles and in alpine areas.

Bleak outlook (above) More than 42 million people live along Bangladesh's 440 mile (710 km) coastline, much of which is already barely above sea level and prone to cyclones, storm surges, and floods. All are predicted to increase.

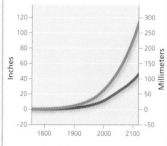

FACT FILE

Acidity measure On the pH scale, 7.0 is neutral, higher is alkaline and lower is acidic. Seawater is usually alkaline; its average pH value has been around 8.16 for some 300 million years, until recent years.

pH SCALE, ACIDIC TO ALKALINE

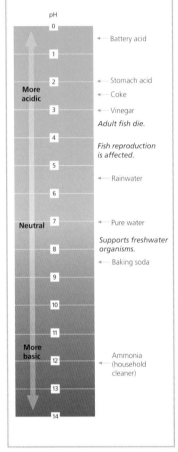

pH	
0	
1	← Battery acid
2	← Stomach acid
More acidic	← Coke
3	← Vinegar
	Adult fish die.
4	*Fish reproduction is affected.*
5	← Rainwater
6	
7 Neutral	← Pure water
8	*Supports freshwater organisms.*
	← Baking soda
9	
10	
11	
More basic 12	← Ammonia (household cleaner)
13	
14	

Acidified Oceans

The oceans absorb one-third of the carbon dioxide emitted by human activity. The process by which this occurs has potentially huge negative ecological consequences because it produces carbonic acid, which causes the acidification of seawater. Since the industrial revolution, ocean pH has dropped by 0.1 units and could fall another 0.5 by 2100.

Chain reaction (right) All marine life is connected ecologically through the ocean's complex network of food webs. Solar energy (**1**) drives the marine food web —plants (**2**), phytoplankton (**3**), and zooplankton (**4**) trap energy from the sun. Marine food webs are usually based on phytoplankton, which are tiny plants in surface waters. These are food for zooplankton, a microscopic menagerie on which many larger marine creatures ultimately feed. Small fish graze on zooplankton (**5**); seabirds (**6**) and large fish (**7**) feed on small fish. Seals, in turn, feed on large fish (**8**), and killer whales (**9**) feed on large fish and seals. As ocean acidification increases, research indicates that many zooplankton species will be unable to produce their protective shells and external skeletons. This would lead to zooplankton declines; then losses of all species that feed both directly and indirectly on zooplankton would follow.

Phytoplankton (right) Like terrestrial plants, phytoplankton—seen here greatly magnified—uses carbon dioxide to photosynthesize, but research shows that phenomena linked to global climate change are harming its productivity.

HERITAGE WATCH

Controversial remedy Despite oceanic acidification, some scientists believe the vast expanse of the oceans could still help alleviate the planet's greenhouse gas problem. It was suggested in 1977, that huge quantities of atmospheric carbon dioxide could be temporarily isolated by direct injection into deep cold ocean layers; studies continue.

Loss of life There is evidence that calcium carbonate, which forms the structures of many marine organisms, is vulnerable to dissolution in more acidified oceans. The full ecological impact is still unknown.

Marine organisms Oceanic acidification reduces the carbonate in seawater that marine organisms use to produce their calcium carbonate structures.

Crustaceans The external skeleton of many marine animals, including crustaceans such as shrimps is composed largely of calcium carbonate.

Industry decline Shell-building rates by mussels and oysters also decrease as pH falls, with potentially huge consequences for mollusk aquaculture.

Testing time (left) Ocean acidification adds to the problem of coral bleaching, which is caused by ocean temperature rise. Experiments such as this assess implications for the future of reefs.

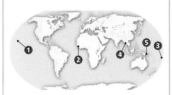

1. Mount Waialeale At 5,148 feet (1,569 m) above sea-level, this peak on the Hawaiian island of Kauai has one of Earth's highest average rainfalls—more than 460 inches (11,684 mm) per year.

Hawaii receives less rain in El Niño years, and this oceanic-atmospheric event is expected to exert increasing influence.
Mount Waialeale, Hawaii

2. Monrovia Climatic shifts in Liberia's capital may signal changing weather patterns farther afield. Researchers have linked rainfall in West Africa with the intensity of Atlantic hurricanes that

develop during the following season. Intense hurricanes appear to follow above-average African rainfall.
Monrovia, Liberia

3. Pago Pago The capital of American Samoa, in the South Pacific Ocean, has always been exposed to the destructive wrath of typhoons. The area is expected to face an increase in frequency and

voracity of these tropical storms as a result of climate change. Sea-level rises have already affected the region.
Pago Pago, American Samoa

4. Moulmein Southeast Asian coastal cities such as Moulmein could suffer increasingly wild and unpredictable weather. For a combination of reasons, climate change might affect Southeast

Asia more than other areas. Melting Himalayan glaciers could cause down-stream river flooding, followed by drought.
Moulmein, Myanmar

5. Lae Increased erosive oceanic forces related to sea-level rise could affect coastal towns like Lae, in tropical Papua New Guinea. Glacial melting in the

island's peaks indicates that temperatures are rising. A more extreme El Niño cycle may also affect the island's weather.
Lae, Papua New Guinea

Changing Weather Patterns

By 2100, the global mean temperature is expected to have risen by 2.5°F to 10.4°F (1.4–5.8°C) since 1900. One troubling anticipated consequence of this rise is an increase in erratic weather patterns, which it appears to have already begun. Droughts, floods, and storms of escalating frequency and intensity have been documented at an increasing rate on all continents during the past few decades.

INCREASE IN FLOOD EVENTS

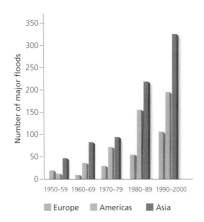

Number of major floods

■ Europe ■ Americas ■ Asia

Hurricane hell During six months that broke almost all previous records, the 2005 Atlantic hurricane season caused more than 2,200 deaths and in excess of U.S.$128-billion-worth of property damage. There were an unprecedented 27 named storms: 15 were hurricanes, of which four were category 5 including Wilma, the Atlantic's most intense hurricane on record, and Katrina, which devastated New Orleans.

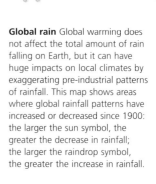

Global rain Global warming does not affect the total amount of rain falling on Earth, but it can have huge impacts on local climates by exaggerating pre-industrial patterns of rainfall. This map shows areas where global rainfall patterns have increased or decreased since 1900: the larger the sun symbol, the greater the decrease in rainfall; the larger the raindrop symbol, the greater the increase in rainfall.

Emily This category 5 hurricane caused damage from Jamaica to Mexico's Yucatan Peninsula, and even Texas. Six people were killed. Emily was the second catastrophic storm to occur before the end of July 2005.

Irene Reaching peak strength on August 14, Irene was the fourth hurricane of the 2005 Atlantic season. It formed near the Cape Verde Islands and remained at sea, so did not cause any damage on land.

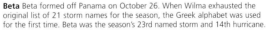

☀ −50%　☀ −40%　⊙ −30%　⊙ −20%　○ −10%

💧 +10%　💧 +20%　💧 +30%　💧 +40%　💧 +50%

Ophelia In early September, this slow-moving storm traveled up the east coast of the U.S.A. It moved over land and dumped heavy rain on North Carolina before turning back out to sea.

Beta Beta formed off Panama on October 26. When Wilma exhausted the original list of 21 storm names for the season, the Greek alphabet was used for the first time. Beta was the season's 23rd named storm and 14th hurricane.

Impacts on Human Health

In 2005, the World Heath Organization reported that human-induced climate change annually leads to more then 150,000 deaths worldwide. Death and injury from extreme weather events, such as heat waves and floods, are rising, and the spread of infectious diseases, particularly those transmitted by blood-sucking invertebrates, is likely to change and, in many cases, increase.

Rising demand (right) The limited resources of Africa's health clinics, such as this one in Kenya, are destined to become stretched even further if diseases like malaria and cholera increase because of the impacts of climate change.

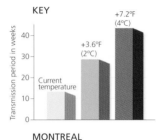

KEY

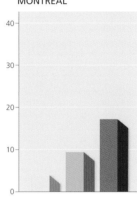

MONTREAL

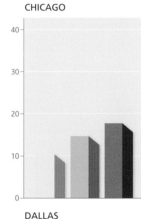

CHICAGO

DALLAS

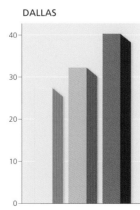

HEALTH IMPACTS OF CLIMATE CHANGE

EFFECTS OF CLIMATE CHANGE

THERMAL STRESS — Cardiovascular and respiratory morbidity and mortality

VECTOR-BORNE DISEASES — Such as malaria, dengue fever, and schistosomiasis

MARINE-BORNE DISEASES — Toxic algae and cholera

FOOD PRODUCTIVITY — Malnutrition

AIR POLLUTION — Asthma and cardiorespiratory disorders

WEATHER DISASTERS, SEA-LEVEL RISE — Deaths, injuries, damage to health infrastructure, increased risk of infectious diseases

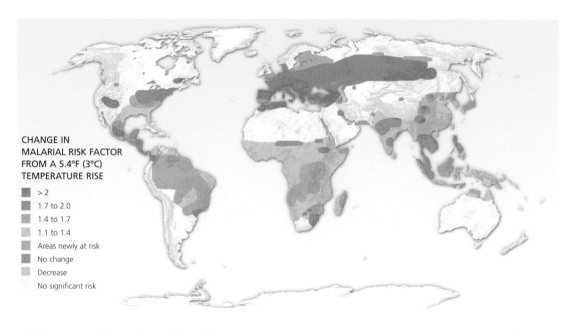

CHANGE IN MALARIAL RISK FACTOR FROM A 5.4°F (3°C) TEMPERATURE RISE

- \> 2
- 1.7 to 2.0
- 1.4 to 1.7
- 1.1 to 1.4
- Areas newly at risk
- No change
- Decrease
- No significant risk

Malaria Up to 500 million people annually are infected by malaria. The parasites causing it are temperature-dependent, and predictions warn that a 5.4°F (3°C) increase in average global temperatures could mean millions more infections.

FACT FILE

1. Ross River fever In Australia, experts warn that this mosquito-borne viral disease, prevalent in the tropics, may be more common in temperate areas as temperatures rise. In 1994 it occurred in Tasmania, thousands of miles south of the tropics, and in 2002, Tasmania recorded Australia's largest ever outbreak.

Ross River fever, Australia

2. Dengue fever Mosquito-borne dengue-fever viral infections occur throughout the tropics. Research suggests climate change may already be affecting its distribution and life cycle. One study found a 5.5°F to 7.2°F (3–4°C) rise could double the viruses' reproductive rate, causing cases in Indonesia to triple.

Dengue fever, Indonesia

3. Malaria Mosquito control measures and improved treatments have reduced malaria in Malaysia since the 1960s, when more than 400,000 infections were reported annually. A warmer climate could expand suitable breeding areas for mosquitoes carrying the malaria parasite, and increase this health threat.

Malaria, Malaysia

4. Tick-borne encephalitis This disease could be increasing in Scandinavia because of rising average temperatures. In Sweden it appears the distribution of disease-carrying ticks extended northward between 1980 and 1994, in line with a changing climate. Norway reported its first case in 1997.

Tick-borne encephalitis, Scandinavia

5. West Nile disease This disease was reported in the U.S.A. for the first time in 1999, when it infected 62 people in New York, killing 7. It has spread to every U.S. state and most Canadian provinces, and there is speculation that climate change could increase transmission.

West Nile disease, U.S.A.

GLOBAL CONSERVATION

Legislation, technology, education, and activism have formed a framework for the world's response to environmental degradation since the late 1800s. Developments in the first three areas during recent decades have reduced the need for activism as the planet's environmental woes have moved to front-and-center of the world's political stage. Environmentalists now wear suits and ply their message in the world's boardrooms and seats of government. There is, however, and perhaps always will be, a need for individuals with a passion to protect the planet's natural environment by lying down in forests in the paths of bulldozers, or by defending the ocean's last whales in high-sea scuffles.

Inspirational leader (top) Former U.S. vice-president Al Gore became the international face of efforts to address climate change through his work on the 2006 documentary *An Inconvenient Truth*. He has worked politically on the issue since the 1970s, and in 2007 his decades of work were recognized when he and the IPCC were jointly awarded the 2007 Nobel Peace Prize.

Historic pact (bottom) Governments at a 1997 UN climate change conference in Kyoto, Japan, agreed to reduce greenhouse gas emissions by 2008–2012 in developed nations by at least 5 percent below 1990 levels. The agreement, called the Kyoto Protocol, has been ratified by 174 nations. In early 2008, the largest producer of greenhouse gases, the U.S.A., was the major exception.

UNIFIED RESPONSE

Legislation to reduce environmental degradation began appearing across the world from the 1950s. Today, most developed nations, and some developing countries, have legal acts aimed at reducing water, soil, and air pollution, as well as government departments, such as soil conservation services and environmental protection agencies to oversee implementation.

While these laws are important to local and regional issues, they have been backed internationally by a spate of environmental treaties, conventions, agreements, and pacts. These include the 1971 Ramsar Convention for protecting wetland habitats, and the 1973 Convention on International Trade in Endangered Species, which has helped reduce the smuggling and poaching of endangered wildlife. The best known and perhaps most powerful international environmental treaty is the Kyoto Protocol, aimed at reducing global warming.

While many blame technology for the problems now besetting the planet, it is also seen as a critical part of the global response. Scientists around the world are working on methods to remediate polluted land and waterways, and to reduce damaging atmospheric emissions from motor vehicles and power stations. They are also searching—backed by billions of government funds—for new, non-polluting, sustainable energy sources to power the planet.

The world's scientists also play a crucial role in monitoring and documenting the evidence and impact of climate change. The results of their work are regularly brought together, distilled, and distributed to the public via the Intergovernmental Panel on Climate Change (IPCC), established in 1988 by the United Nation's Environment Program and World Meteorological Organization.

As simple as it might sound, education is a key way for scientists and research bodies to address climate change. Demystifying the problems, and explaining their consequences and solutions to the general public is critical to the planet's future.

Lesser evil (right) Environmentalists who once actively protested against nuclear power now see it as an ecologically friendly energy compared to fossil fuels. As a result, huge nuclear power plant cooling towers are appearing at a rising rate around the globe. The technology is virtually emission-free, but still produces radioactive waste.

Architectural future (below) Nicknamed "The Gherkin," this is one of the tallest but least environmentally damaging buildings in London. It is known for its unorthodox and innovative layout, and environmentally responsible design and construction.

BY SOURCE

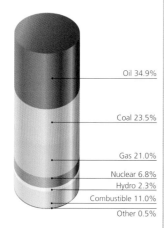

- Oil 34.9%
- Coal 23.5%
- Gas 21.0%
- Nuclear 6.8%
- Hydro 2.3%
- Combustible 11.0%
- Other 0.5%

BY COUNTRY

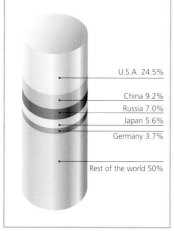

- U.S.A. 24.5%
- China 9.2%
- Russia 7.0%
- Japan 5.6%
- Germany 3.7%
- Rest of the world 50%

Beyond Fossil Fuels

The mid-1970s oil crisis led many countries to investigate alternative energy sources. Reliability of supply and low environmental impacts were early prerequisites. Hydropower, the source of about two-thirds of all renewable energy, is by far the most widely exploited alternative supply. Seven percent of renewable energy comes from solar power and 5 percent from wind power.

Canadian oil (right) The Athabasca Oil Sands in Alberta, Canada, are a massive surface deposit of crude bitumen, rich in oil. Estimates of recoverable oil from these sands put Canada's proven reserves behind those only of Saudi Arabia.

ENERGY PEAKS AND DECLINES

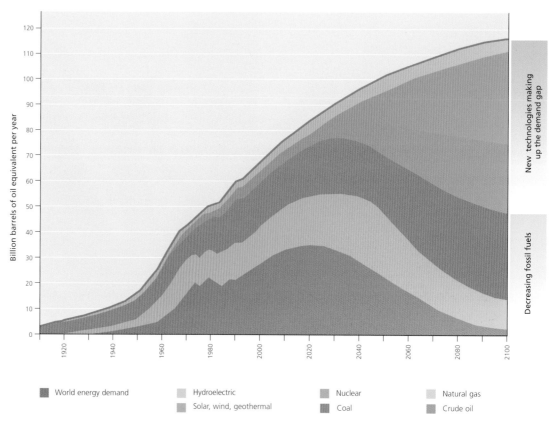

Billion barrels of oil equivalent per year

New technologies making up the demand gap

Decreasing fossil fuels

- World energy demand
- Solar, wind, geothermal
- Hydroelectric
- Coal
- Nuclear
- Crude oil
- Natural gas

NATURAL RESOURCES

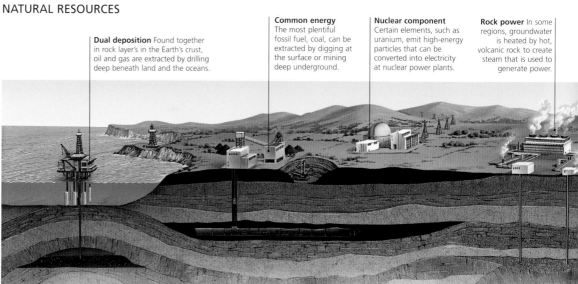

Dual deposition Found together in rock layer's in the Earth's crust, oil and gas are extracted by drilling deep beneath land and the oceans.

Common energy The most plentiful fossil fuel, coal, can be extracted by digging at the surface or mining deep underground.

Nuclear component Certain elements, such as uranium, emit high-energy particles that can be converted into electricity at nuclear power plants.

Rock power In some regions, groundwater is heated by hot, volcanic rock to create steam that is used to generate power.

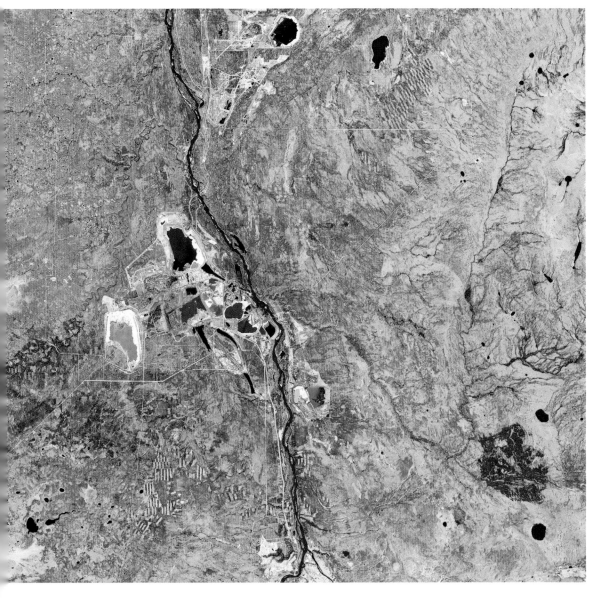

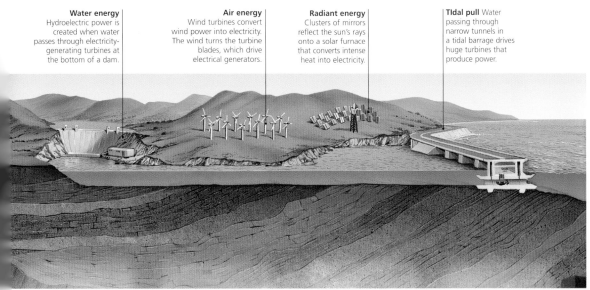

Water energy Hydroelectric power is created when water passes through electricity-generating turbines at the bottom of a dam.

Air energy Wind turbines convert wind power into electricity. The wind turns the turbine blades, which drive electrical generators.

Radiant energy Clusters of mirrors reflect the sun's rays onto a solar furnace that converts intense heat into electricity.

Tidal pull Water passing through narrow tunnels in a tidal barrage drives huge turbines that produce power.

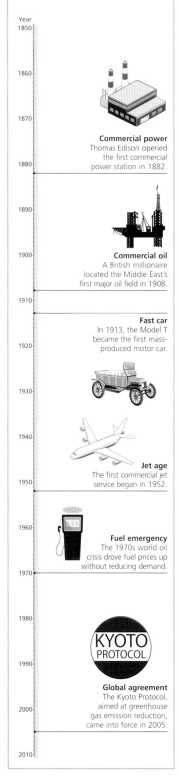

FACT FILE

Burning issue Oil, gas, and coal release energy when burned, a process that also releases harmful gas emissions into the atmosphere. These emissions have been rising since the industrial revolution.

Year

1850

1860

1870

Commercial power
Thomas Edison opened the first commercial power station in 1882.

1880

1890

Commercial oil
A British millionaire located the Middle East's first major oil field in 1908.

1900

1910

Fast car
In 1913, the Model T became the first mass-produced motor car.

1920

1930

1940

Jet age
The first commercial jet service began in 1952.

1950

1960

Fuel emergency
The 1970s world oil crisis drove fuel prices up without reducing demand.

1970

1980

KYOTO PROTOCOL

1990

Global agreement
The Kyoto Protocol, aimed at greenhouse gas emission reduction, came into force in 2005.

2000

2010

Nuclear Energy

About 17 percent of the world's electricity is now produced by nuclear energy. Because nuclear power plants generate no greenhouse gas emissions, they are increasingly regarded as more environmentally friendly alternatives to plants that burn fossil fuels. They do, however, produce small but potentially deadly volumes of hard-to-dispose-of solid radioactive wastes.

Pressurized water reactors (right) Pressurized water reactors, such as this one in the U.K, are now the most common type of nuclear reactor. There are more than 230 pressurized water reactors involved in electricity production located around the world.

Nuclear production (below) A nuclear fuel pellet of enriched uranium just 1 inch (25 mm) in length, and about half the width, can generate as much electricity as 1.6 tons (1.5 tonnes) of coal. The diagram below shows the process of energy production in a nuclear power plant.

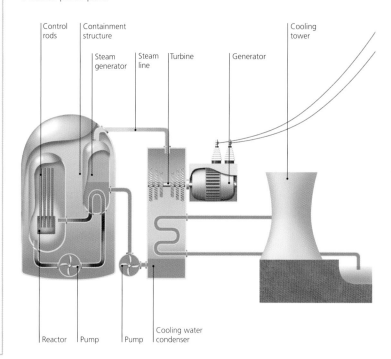

Control rods | Containment structure | Steam generator | Steam line | Turbine | Generator | Cooling tower

Reactor | Pump | Pump | Cooling water condenser

FACT FILE

1. Pakistan The country's first nuclear power plant opened in 1971. Pakistan now has two plants that produce just 2.5 percent of the nation's electricity, but sees nuclear power as crucial to meeting its rapidly growing energy demands. The government has announced plans for at least four more nuclear plants by 2020.

Pakistan

2. India Although India currently produces just 3 percent of its electricity from nuclear power, it has been identified—along with China, Japan, and South Korea—as being at the center of the current global nuclear power expansion. India plans to increase its production of nuclear power eight-fold by 2022.

India

3. Australia Despite being one of the world's biggest exporters of uranium, which is used in the production of nuclear energy, Australia has no nuclear power stations. Instead, it relies mainly on coal for electricity production. A 2006 report found that 25 reactors could meet one-third of the country's 2050 electricity demand.

Australia

Emission-free option (right) France now has 59 nuclear reactors like this one. Nuclear and hydro power produce about 90 percent of the country's electricity, so its carbon dioxide emissions are very low.

HERITAGE WATCH

Nuclear accident Fear of a catastrophic accident was initially a strong deterrent against nuclear energy. In 1986, poor design and management led to an explosion at the Chernobyl power plant, Ukraine. It caused such severe radioactive contamination that the site still has a 19 mile (31 km) exclusion zone.

1. U.S.A. The U.S.A. has 103 nuclear power plants that supply one-fifth of its electricity. No new plants have been built since the 1979 partial meltdown of a reactor core at Three Mile Island,

Pennsylvania. Interest has now been renewed by potential environmental, economic, and political benefits.

U.S.A.

2. France The French Government expanded the country's nuclear power capacity following the mid-1970s oil crisis. More than 75 percent of its electricity is now produced by nuclear

energy, more than any other country. It sells surplus electricity and exports reactors, fuel products, and nuclear services.

France

3. Japan Japan's first nuclear power plant began operating in 1966. It now has more than 50, providing about one-third of its electricity. Having limited fossil fuel reserves, Japan imports most

of its energy resources. For this reason, and to reduce emissions, there is wide local support for nuclear expansion.

Japan

4. Russian Federation From 1992 to 2000, the proportion of Russian energy generated by nuclear power plants rose from 11 to 15 percent, and the government plans to lift the proportion

to 40 percent by 2010. At present, Russia's nine nuclear power stations have 29 reactors between them.

Russian Federation

5. Republic of Korea With no oil or gas reserves in South Korea, support for nuclear power to fuel its industrial and economic growth is strong. Its first plant

began operations in 1978, and by 2015 South Korea aims to generate 45 per-cent of its electricity from nuclear power.

Republic of Korea

Water and Wind Power

Rapidly declining fossil-fuel reserves and the need to slow climate change have increased world interest in environmentally friendly, sustainable power sources. About one-fifth of all electricity comes from hydroelectricity, the largest source of renewable energy. Although wind power generates just 1 percent, global production has risen at least four-fold since 2000.

Hydroelectricity (below) Although power production from hydroelectric plants is emission-free and fundamentally renewable, development of the necessary infrastructure, such as huge dams, can damage to the environment.

FACT FILE

Enduring supplies Renewable resources generate 13 percent of the world's primary energy production. With appropriate technological development, however, the global potential is massive.

RENEWABLE ENERGY PRODUCTION

- Biomass
- Geothermal
- Wind
- Solar

Total energy production in gigawatt hours

U.S.A. 33,107

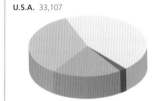

Germany 22,274

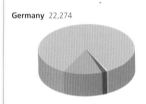

Spain 12,874

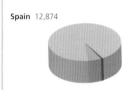

Japan 5,259

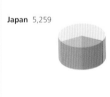

U.K. 4,907

Surf power The U.S.A.'s first commercial power plant that harnesses the energy of ocean waves is located off the northern California coast. In 2012 it is set to begin generating electricity.

Tidal power (above) Energy created by tidal ebbs and flows is harnessed by turbines. Functioning like underwater wind turbines, they exploit the push and pull of tidal currents to turn rotors, which in turn generate electricity.

Bird bane (left) The potential for birds to be killed by turbines on wind farms mistakenly placed in their flight paths was an early environmental concern. However, research shows that losses are negligible.

ENERGY AND HEAT PRODUCED

Installed capacity (gigawatts)

- Small-scale hydro: 61
- Wind: 50
- Tide, wave, ocean: 0.3

Solar and Geothermal Energy

Solar and geothermal energy each produce less than 1 percent of the world's electricity. Solar systems convert sunlight into electricity while geothermal power comes mostly from natural underground supplies of hot water and steam. Demand is growing, and solar systems are a particularly good option for the world's two billion people currently without a reliable energy supply.

Ray power (below) Although climbing from a low base, solar energy demand has grown globally at an annual rate of about 25 percent in recent decades. Annual growth in demand for fossil fuel energy is usually less than 2 percent.

FACT FILE

1. Japan Since 1997, Japan has been the world's largest solar electricity producer. It has more than 40 percent of the world's installed solar cells, including more than 140,000 residential systems. Japan's technology uptake has been driven by government incentives since the mid-1990s.

Japan

2. European Union In the last decade, the European Commission has invested more than 200 million Euros into solar-energy research, development, and demonstration projects. Europe is the world's second largest manufacturer of photovoltaic cells, accounting for more than 24 percent of total production.

European Union

3. U.S.A. Although the U.S.A. is a major producer of photovoltaic cells, it sources just 1 percent of its electricity from solar power. Most is produced in California, where rows of solar panels in the Mojave Desert supply solar thermal power plants that generate electricity for more than 350,000 homes.

U.S.A.

SOLAR CELLS

The basic unit of most solar energy systems, the photovoltaic cell, converts sunlight into electricity and is usually made of silicon. These emission-free devices now provide electricity to more than one million homes worldwide.

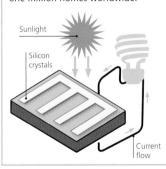

Sunlight

Silicon crystals

Current flow

Working plant (left) The PS10 solar thermal tower plant, located outside Seville, Spain, Europe's first commercial operation of its type, began operating in 2006. Mirrors track the sun and direct rays to the top of a tower, visible at the top of this image, where solar energy converted into steam turns turbines and produces electricity for 6,000 homes.

Geothermal energy In hot-rock geothermal power systems, water is pumped under high pressure into holes that are drilled into permeable hot rocks deep underground. The superheated water is returned to the surface to produce electricity.

Transformer

Generator

Turbine

Power station loop

Heat exchanger

Production loop

Distribution to grid

To scale, each tick represents 0.6 miles (1 km).

Insulating sedimentary rock

Permeable zone of hot, dry, and fractured granite

Water flows through hot, fractured rock.

Cold water is pumped underground.

Superheated water returns to the surface via wells.

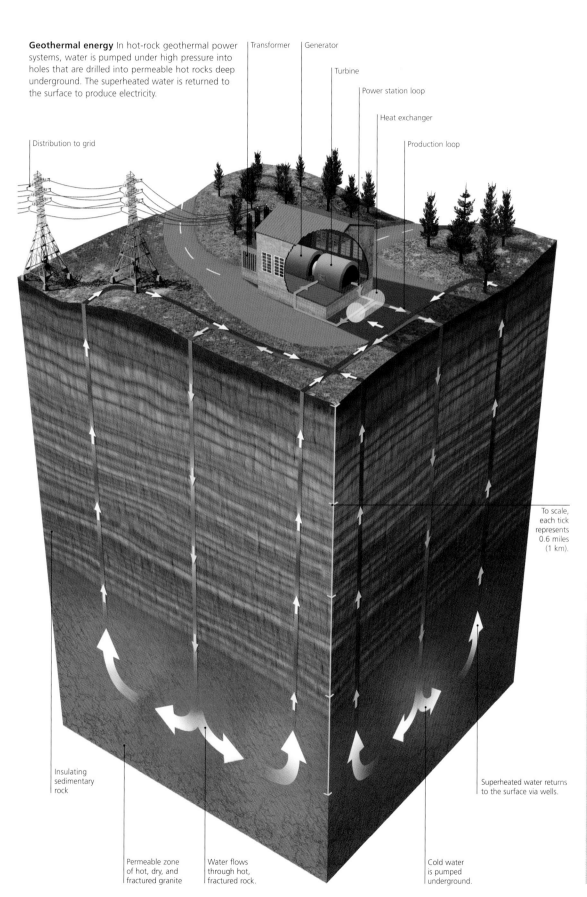

FACT FILE

1. Gut Erlasee Solar Park Located in southern Germany, adjacent to gently rolling agricultural land, this is the largest solar-electric power plant of its kind in the world. It began operating in 2006 and covers 190 acres (77 ha). It supplies power to 1,000 homes in the nearby town of Arnstein.

Gut Erlaree Solar Park, Germany

2. Pecs Although Hungary is said to have the greatest potential in Europe for geothermal energy, it does not yet have a power plant that exploits this renewable energy resource. However, in 2008 exploration began around the southern city of Pecs for a suitable site for geothermal electricity production.

Pecs, Hungary

3. The Geysers This geothermal power plant complex covers 30 square miles (78 km²), and is located 70 miles (110 km) north of San Francisco. It exploits energy from natural steam reservoirs produced by volcanic activity. The Geysers complex generates enough electricity to power 750,000 homes.

The Geysers, San Francisco, U.S.A.

SOLAR AND GEOTHERMAL ENERGY USE

Installed capacity (gigawatts)

Solar	Geothermal	Biomass
4	8.9	39

Cleaner and Greener Transportation

Motivations to make transportation more environmentally friendly are huge. Motor vehicles produce more than 15 percent of fossil-fuel-based greenhouse emissions. These have risen dramatically since the 1950s, when globally there were 70 million vehicles. Today, there are more than 500 million vehicles. The air pollution they create annually claims more human lives than road accidents.

Aviation rise (right) British aviation carbon emissions could rise between four and ten times their 1990 levels by 2050, because annual passenger numbers are forecast to rise from 200 to 470 million by 2030.

Green transportation (left) Because this bus runs on hydrogen instead of gasoline or diesel, it does not produce any greenhouse gas emissions. Iceland was the first country to test hydrogen-powered city buses.

Wasted crop (below left) Once hailed as an alternative fuel source with low carbon emissions, biofuel made from corn (maize) and rapeseed has been found to produce higher emission levels than other fuels.

Hybrid car (below) A hybrid car releases no greenhouse gases when fueled by electricity that is generated by wheel motion. However, emissions rise as soon as a switch to the regular fossil-fuel-powered engine occurs.

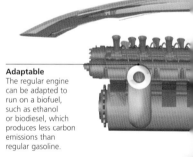

Adaptable The regular engine can be adapted to run on a biofuel, such as ethanol or biodiesel, which produces less carbon emissions than regular gasoline.

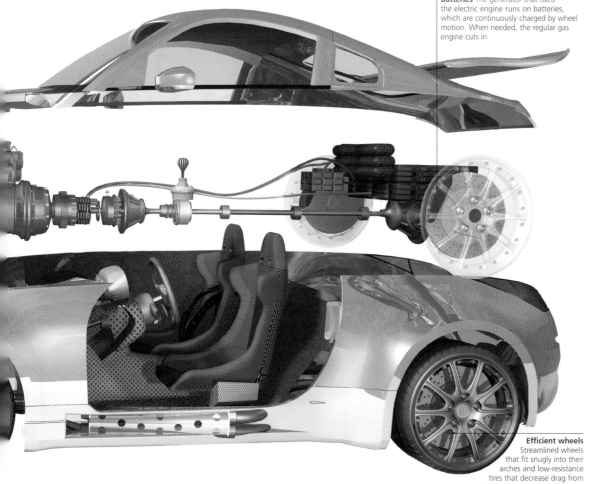

Batteries The generator that fuels the electric engine runs on batteries, which are continuously charged by wheel motion. When needed, the regular gas engine cuts in.

Efficient wheels Streamlined wheels that fit snugly into their arches and low-resistance tires that decrease drag from the road increase fuel efficiency.

FACT FILE

Carbon trading Many industries set maximum emission targets, with members allocated carbon quotas to ensure they reach their target. They can often trade these between themselves, as long as the industry's total is not exceeded.

PROJECT-BASED CARBON EXCHANGE

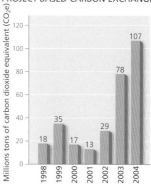

Millions tons of carbon dioxide equivalent (CO₂e): 18 (1998), 35 (1999), 17 (2000), 13 (2001), 29 (2002), 78 (2003), 107 (2004)

KINDS OF TRADING PROJECTS

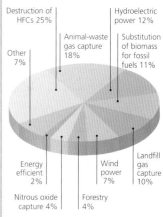

- Destruction of HFCs 25%
- Hydroelectric power 12%
- Animal-waste gas capture 18%
- Substitution of biomass for fossil fuels 11%
- Other 7%
- Landfill gas capture 10%
- Wind power 7%
- Forestry 4%
- Nitrous oxide capture 4%
- Energy efficient 2%

TRANSPORTATION IMPACT

Different transportation methods produce different CO_2 amounts per person per mile. Cars are the least efficient. Buses and planes use more fuel but carry more passengers, so their emissions per person are lower.

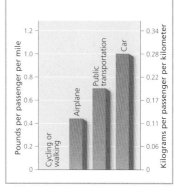

Pounds per passenger per mile / Kilograms per passenger per kilometer: Cycling or walking, Airplane, Public transportation, Car

Conserving Water and Improving Its Quality

Legislation, technology, and social change have dramatically improved water quality and conservation in many parts of the developed world. However, developing nations still suffer from the affects of chronic water shortages and pollution, particularly through raw-sewage contamination. Anticipated increases in floods and droughts due to global warming will compound the problems.

River clean-up (right) After dying out in the 1830s owing to poor water quality, salmon were re-introduced into London's River Thames in 2007. It is hoped the fish species will resume breeding within 10 years.

Restoration project (below) The regular sampling of Walnut Creek, U.S.A., to monitor water quality began during the mid-1990s as part of a program to restore the area's watershed to native prairie.

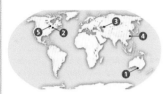

Water change The conversion of salt water to fresh water via desalination is used increasingly in arid areas and where demand outstrips freshwater resources. Arabian Peninsula desalination plants support huge population growth.

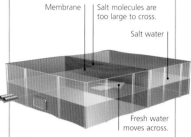

Membrane | Salt molecules are too large to cross.

Salt water

Fresh water moves across.

1 Fresh water separated from salt water by a semi-permeable membrane is drawn toward the higher salt concentration by the natural process of osmosis.

Fresh water | Head of salt water stops osmosis.

2 The process would normally continue until both sides have the same salt concentration—called osmotic equilibrium—but applying pressure to the sea water side stops it.

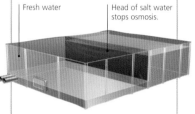

Fresh water | Pressure forces water through the membrane, leaving salt behind.

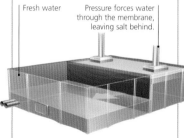

3 During desalination, pressure on the saltwater is increased, forcing it back through the membrane without its salt in reverse osmosis.

DEAD ZONES

A UN Environment Program report found that ocean "dead zones" increased by about 25 percent from 2004 to 2006. There are now about 200 of these mostly lifeless expanses, which can cover thousands of square miles. They are caused by algal blooms that remove oxygen from water as they thrive on high nitrogen levels in sewage and fertilizer-laden agricultural runoff. Untreated effluent is partly to blame.

1. Coon Valley Agriculture from the 1850s left Coon Valley exposed to severe erosion and by the 1930s it was a wasteland. The U.S. Soil Conservation Service moved in to help recover the land as a test-ground for a new, holistic land management approach. The area is now ecologically and agriculturally healthy.

Coon Valley, Wisconsin, U.S.A.

2. Peru Peruvian farmers have used agricultural terracing for at least 500 years to successfully grow potatoes on the steep slopes of the Andes Mountains without causing erosion. About 5 million acres (2 million ha) of fields in Peru are covered by such terraces; most are now abandoned.

Peru

3. Three Gorges Dam Erosion causing landslides, riverbank collapses, and water quality issues have plagued China's Three Gorges Dam project since construction began in 1994. A 2007 government report highlighted these problems, warning of a potential catastrophe if they were not addressed.

China

4. New South Wales Each year, New South Wales loses about 187 million tons (170 million tonnes) of soil from erosion. Excessive clearing of native vegetation, overgrazing, overcropping, and other inappropriate practices are responsible. They have also raised water tables, causing soil salinity problems.

New South Wales, Australia

4. Machakos Colonial farming and land-use changes near this town caused severe erosion until a soil and water conservation campaign began in 1979. Most of the arable land is now bench-terraced to stop erosion, and new land management practices have renewed productivity.

Machakos, Kenya

Saving the Soil

Earth's soils suffered profoundly during the 20th century because of poor agricultural management, urban clearing, and pollution. Consequences, such as large-scale accelerated erosion and human health declines linked to contaminated sites, may continue for decades. Today, sites are being remediated as efforts continue to reverse damage and prevent its recurrence.

Reversing damage (below) Mining operations worldwide are increasingly expected, both legally and morally, to rehabilitate the land they exploit, so as to restore its productivity and prevent its ongoing erosion.

Original terrain It is almost impossible to reach large, underground mineral deposits without affecting local biodiversity. Forests are clear-felled and top soil is often loosened by explosives.

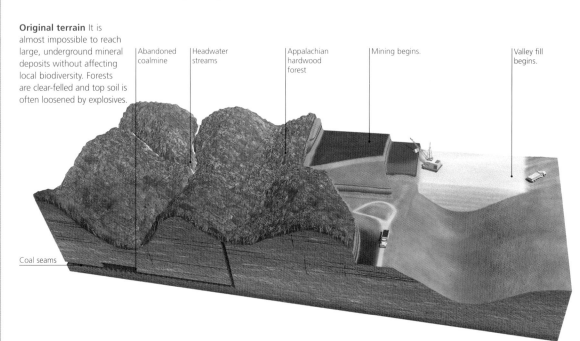

Abandoned coalmine

Headwater streams

Appalachian hardwood forest

Mining begins.

Valley fill begins.

Coal seams

Restored land Site rehabilitation begins by filling in excavated areas and sealing off or removing the contents of tailings dams. Natural rises and falls of the land are followed as much as possible. Fast-growing, non-native vegetation is often a first choice for groundcover. Some companies follow up by replanting areas with locally indigenous plants.

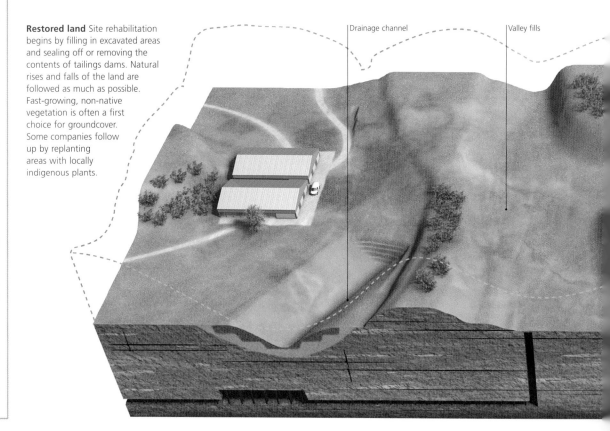

Drainage channel

Valley fills

Toxic pond (right) Copper mines produce millions of tons of debris held for treatment and containment in secure dams and ponds. Characteristically acidic, with high heavy-metal concentrations, this tailings waste is lethal to most life-forms.

Mining in progress Erosion is an inevitable problem, caused by vegetation removal and movements by large mining machinery. Tailings dams are often built to hold mining wastes.

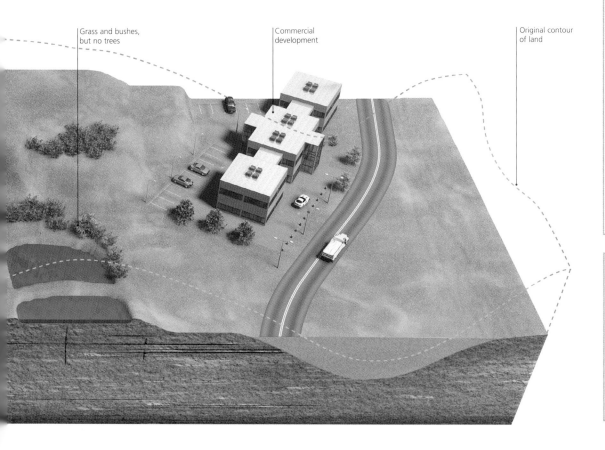

Exposed coal seam

Valley fill

Tailings dam

Valley fill in progress

Terracing valley fill deposits

Grass and bushes, but no trees

Commercial development

Original contour of land

OUR ROLE in CONSERVATION

Many developed nations had a defining moment when grassroots conservation became a powerful political force. In the U.S.A., this milestone occurred on April 22, 1970, when 20 million Americans—angry about smog, polluted water, and disappearing forests—gathered in schools, colleges, and community centers across the country for the first Earth Day. The event led to the passage of landmark antipollution legislation, and continues to be a focus for environmental change.

Solar-powered car (left) The first solar-powered car was invented in Britain in 1960 by Dr. Charles Alexander Escoffery. He fitted a 10,000-cell solar panel on a vintage 1912 Baker. Ten hours of sunlight enabled the car to drive for one hour at 20 miles per hour (32 km/h). The car was highly regarded at the time, not for its low emissions, but for its low noise output.

Energy saving lightbulb (below) Invented by General Electric engineer Ed Hammer during the early 1970s, the compact fluorescent lamp (CFL) uses up to 70 percent less energy and can last 10 times longer than a traditional incandescent lightbulb.

Bike sharing (right) The high emissions of transportation have created growing interest in pedal power. The Worldwatch Institute reports that government support for bicycles is increasing. European cities, including Berlin, Paris, Barcelona, Brussels, Vienna, and Stockholm, have already implemented bicycle-sharing programs.

Green homes (below) Interest in sustainable architecture has been a global phenomenon since the 1990s, when governments worldwide introduced codes for construction that aimed at reducing greenhouse emissions. Green architecture uses sustainable building materials and exploits design that works with surrounding environments and local climates to reduce the use of heating and lighting. It also incorporates waste-reduction technologies, such as gray-water systems and solar power.

THE PERSONAL APPROACH

Grassroots conservation has always been strongly influenced by the NIMBY (Not In My Back Yard) phenomenon. It is the same personal desire to create a safe and healthy place to live, work, and relax that fuels protests against developers threatening town commons in England, acid rain polluting lakes in Scandinavia, whaling in the Antarctic, and poachers hunting wildlife to extinction in Africa.

On average, each person produces 1.4 tons (1.3 tonnes) of carbon emissions. However, Earth's capacity to absorb carbon is only 0.7 tons (0.6 tonnes) per capita—achieved by only a handful of nations, all of them developing. Industrialized countries are well above that level, and the top four polluters are the United States, Australia, Saudi Arabia, and Canada.

To decrease individual carbon footprints, populations in the developed world are encouraged to change their lifestyles through education and incentives to choose green energy suppliers, trade gas-guzzling SUVs for hybrids that use emission-free electricity, and reduce water use through low-flow shower heads, faucet aerators, and time-limited showering. As the U.S. Earth Day experience showed, the personal approach has strength when populations band together. One compelling recent example occurred in Sydney, Australia, when on March 31, 2007, more than two million residents simultaneously turned off their lights and appliances for just 60 minutes. Called Earth Hour, the event led to a 10.2 percent drop in energy use across the city, representing a carbon dioxide reduction that is equivalent to taking almost 50,000 cars off the road for one hour. The Earth Hour event went global in 2008.

THROUGH THE AGES

1892 American environmentalist John Muir founded the Sierra Club organization, and is involved in protecting key U.S. wilderness sites, such as the Yosemite Valley.

1916 The American National Park Serviice was founded by U.S. President Woodrow Wilson to protect natural surroundings for future generations.

1948 The Severn Wildfowl Trust was founded by British conservationist Sir Peter Scott, who also co-founded the World Wildlife Fund and designed its famous panda logo.

1962 One of the world's oldest environmental lobby groups, the Campaign to Protect Rural England, was formed.

1970 More than 20 million people participated in the first Earth Day, held in the U.S.A. In 1990, it became an annual international event.

People power (far left) Our planet has been experiencing enormous population growth since the mid-20th century. The combined power of individuals to create change cannot be underestimated. While gentle protests such as this continue to have their place, personal conservation in the 21st century is focused on adapting sustainable practices to modern lifestyles.

Waste recovery (left) Switzerland, a world leader in recycling, has bottle banks at all supermarkets, paper collections in every town, and special depots for a range of other recyclable material. The country's 80 percent recycling rate for plastic PET bottles is twice the European average.

1972 The United Tasmania Group, the world's first green political party, is formed in the Australian state of Tasmania.

1973 The Chipko movement is formed in India. Influenced by Mahatma Gandhi, the movement's peaceful resistance to deforestation involves hugging trees, leading to the term "tree hugger."

1989 Australian Ian Kiernan launched the Clean Up Sydney Harbor campaign, followed by Clean Up The World, started in 1993. More than 35 million people in 120 countries now participate.

1992 The U.N. Earth Summit concluded that answers to Earth's environmental woes would require a transformation of attitudes and behaviors.

2006 The death of the passionate wildlife documentary maker Steve Irwin provoked a worldwide outpouring of grief.

INTO THE FUTURE

O̲ur unparalleled ability to alter and exploit Earth's environments has been pivotal to our success as a species. The same ability, however, may also have set us on a path to our demise.

The impacts of human activity are now felt right across the planet, even in remote and uninhabited locations. Pollution and degradation of Earth's land, water, and air have been occurring on such a massive scale that dire predictions for the planet's future are now signaled daily in headlines worldwide. Although much of the damage is almost certainly irreversible, much also can still be done to correct past mistakes and prevent future damage.

There is still time to halt the ecological calamity that appears to be unfolding across Earth. However, hope comes with a caveat that crosses cultural, ethnic, political, and spiritual boundaries. To salvage Earth, the human species will need to communicate and cooperate globally like never before.

Drum circle A rabana is a traditional Sri Lankan drum played at major celebrations, such as New Year or religious ceremonies. Drums have been used for hundreds of years in Sri Lanka, and remain an important means of communication. Here, Sri Lankan children create sounds together, sharing an experience and a purpose. Humans have a special gift for communication and cooperation—a gift that we must nurture on our increasingly crowded planet.

GLOSSARY

ablation The removal of snow and ice by melting and direct vaporization.

abyssal plain The smooth, almost level, deep ocean floor, located between the *continental slope* and the mid-ocean ridge.

abyssal zone The part of the ocean that lies between 13,120 and 19,680 feet (4,000–6,000 m) deep.

acicular Of mineral crystals, having a slender needle-like shape.

acid rain An acidic form of rain that occurs when chemicals produced by the burning of *fossil fuels* mix with water vapor in the air.

algae (sing. alga) Simple, plant-like organisms lacking a stem, leaves, or roots, but containing chlorophyll and performing *photosynthesis*.

alluvial fan or plain A fan-shaped, level area covered by river sediment deposited where the gradient of the river bed decreases abruptly.

amplitude Of an ocean wave, the vertical distance between the midpoint and the peak or the trough (bottom).

angiosperm A flowering plant.

anticline An arch-shaped fold in layers of *sedimentary rock*.

apparent temperature The temperature a person senses when the effects of wind-chill and humidity are taken into account.

aquifer Porous rock through which water is able to flow.

archipelago A group of islands or an area that contains many small islands.

asteroid Also called a minor planet, a small stony and/or metallic object with a diameter of less than 600 miles (1,000 km) orbiting the Sun, usually in the Asteroid Belt.

asthenosphere A layer in Earth's upper *mantle*, below the rigid *crust*, that is semi-soft, like modeling clay.

atmosphere A layer of gases around a planet or moon held there by gravity.

atoll A coral reef surrounding a central lagoon, often around the rim of an extinct underwater volcano.

atom The smallest unit that can be called a chemical element.

aurora Colored lights in the sky seen in high latitudes.

barchan dune A crescent-shaped sand dune with the horns of the crescent pointing downwind.

barometer An instrument that uses air, water, or mercury to measure

variations in air pressure, making it possible to anticipate weather changes.

barrier island A ridge of sand, or gravel, that lies parallel to a coast.

barrier reef A coral reef around islands or along coasts, with a deep lagoon between the reef and the coast.

basalt A dark, fine-grained, *igneous rock* that covers about 70 percent of Earth's surface.

batholith A large body of *igneous rock* formed under Earth's surface by the intrusion and solidification of *magma*.

bathyal zone The part of the ocean that lies between 660 and 13,000 feet (200 to 4,000 m) deep.

bathymetric zonation The division of the deep ocean's *water column* into different zones according to depth and the amount of light present.

bedrock The solid mass of rock lying beneath the ground surface.

benthic zone The seabed.

Big Bang According to our best cosmological theory, the event that marked the birth of the *universe* about 13.7 billion years ago.

biodegradable Describes material that can be broken down by bacteria, insects, or other natural substances.

biodiversity The variety of plant and animal species found in a habitat.

biofuel A fuel that is produced from biological sources, usually plants, rather than from *fossil fuels*.

biogeography The study of the way plants and animals are distributed.

bioluminescence The generation of light by living organisms using the enzyme luciferin.

biome A large area defined by climate and vegetation and having a distinctive community of plants and animals.

bioremediation A process that makes use of natural materials, such as *microorganisms* or green plants, to cleanse a polluted area.

biosphere reserve A conservation area designated by UNESCO as part of a global network of protected areas representing all major vegetation types.

black hole An object in space whose gravity is so powerful that nothing, not even light moving at 186,000 miles per second (300,000 km/s), can escape from it.

blocky Block-shaped.

blocky lava A type of basaltic lava made of broken, block-shaped pieces.

blowhole A hole on the top of a coastal cliff caused by the collapse of a cave roof and through which spray is forced when waves crash into the cave.

bog A *wetland* with a plant community in which high acidity slows the rate of decomposition, favoring the accumulation of *peat*.

boreal Pertaining to the colder parts of the Northern Hemisphere.

botryoidal Of mineral crystals, having a *habit* resembling a bunch of grapes.

braided river A river system consisting of a network of small channels that are separated by small and often temporary islands.

butte A small, isolated, flat-topped hill, the remains of a heavily eroded *mesa*.

caldera The roughly circular *crater* at the top of a volcano, formed by the collapse of a *magma* chamber.

canopy Of a forest, the upper layer composed entirely of trees.

canyon A deep, steep-sided valley formed by river erosion.

cap rock A hard, impervious rock that forms a layer above another rock and, as a result, seals it.

carbon footprint An estimate of the impact of one person's activities on the environment, measured by the amount of *greenhouse emissions*.

carbonic acid The acid formed when carbon dioxide dissolves in water.

cave pearl An almost-spherical body of calcite (calcium carbonate) that forms in a pool of water in a cave.

chaparral A type of vegetation found in parts of California and other regions with a similar climate, dominated by plants adapted to hot, dry summers.

chatoyancy An optical reflectance effect causing a thin, bright line of light across a gemstone's polished surface, as seen in tiger's eye and chrysoberyl.

chimney In limestone, a narrow, vertical shaft formed when rock dissolves along joints and fractures.

chlorophyll The green pigment present in all green plants, and some bacteria. It absorbs sunlight and releases the energy that drives the process of *photosynthesis*.

chloroplast In plant cells and eukaryotic *algae*, a structure that conducts *photosynthesis*.

chromosphere The thin layer of the Sun's atmosphere just above the *photosphere* and below the *corona*.

cirque On a mountain, a half-open hollow formed by glacial scouring.

cleavage The tendency of certain minerals to break along set planes of weakness that are related to their crystal structure.

clint A section of approximately horizontally bedded limestone bounded by joints.

cloud forest Tropical forest on mountainsides at an elevation where atmospheric water vapor condenses, shrouding the vegetation in mist.

cluster In astronomy, a group of stars or galaxies held together by gravity.

cold front A boundary between two air masses of different temperatures. As the front passes, cold air replaces warmer air.

cold pole The place that has the lowest average temperature in a hemisphere or on a continent.

collapse doline A *doline* created by the collapse of the overlying rock into a cavity that has formed where rainwater has dissolved the rock.

comet A small astronomical body composed of ice and dust that orbits the Sun on an elongated path.

compact fluorescent lamp (CFL) A fluorescent lightbulb lined with phosphor that uses much less energy than traditional lightbulbs.

compound mineral A rock type that consists of a chemical combination of two or more elements.

conglomerates Coarse-grained rocks that contain many rounded stones.

continental crust The rocks that lie above Earth's *mantle*, but beneath the surface of continents. .

continental drift The slow movement of continental plates caused by convection currents in the *mantle*.

continental rifting The process of splitting continental plates. Upwelling *magma* pulls the continent apart; as the rift widens, water floods in to form a new ocean.

continental rise The ocean floor beyond the edge of the *continental slope*.

continental shelf The edge of a continent below the ocean surface.

continental slope The steeply sloping area of ocean floor between the *continental shelf* and *continental rise*.

convection A heat-driven process that causes hotter material or air to move upward, while lighter matter sinks.

convergence A flow of air moving from different directions toward a central point.

convergent boundary A boundary between two *lithospheric* plates that are moving toward each other.

coral bleaching The loss of color affecting coral reefs when the algae that live in them are killed or forced out.

cordillera A system of mountain ranges with their plateaus and basins.

core The centermost part of Earth, consisting of a solid inner core surrounded by a liquid outer core.

corona The high-temperature, outermost atmosphere of the Sun that is visible from Earth only during a full solar eclipse.

coronal mass ejection A massive eruption of material from the Sun's *corona* over a period of several hours.

corundum An aluminum oxide mineral that is, after diamond, the hardest-known natural substance. Its colored varieties are the gemstones sapphire and ruby.

crater A circular depression caused either by volcanic activity (volcanic crater) or by the impact of a meteorite (impact crater).

craton The old, thick, stable part of continental interiors that has not been affected by mountain building for more than one billion years.

crevasse A deep fissure in a *glacier*.

crust The outer layer of Earth, consisting of solid rock averaging 3 miles (5 km) thick beneath the oceans and up to 40 miles (64 km) thick beneath mountain ranges.

crustacean A mostly aquatic animal, such as a lobster, crab, or shrimp, that has a hard external skeleton.

crystal A solid mineral with a definite geometric shape.

cubic Of a mineral crystal, having three axes all of equal length and at right angles to one another.

dark matter A form of matter that does not emit light or any other radiation. Dark matter far outweighs normal, visible matter in the *universe*.

deciduous A plant or tree that drops its leaves in fall, winter, or the dry season, and grows new leaves in spring.

delta A layer of sediment deposited at the mouth of a slow-moving river and protruding beyond the coastline.

dendritic Of a mineral, having a branched, fern-like shape.

deranged drainage system A disorganized series of streams, lakes, and wetlands formed in a recently glaciated area.

desertification The process by which fertile land turns into desert as a result of decreasing rainfall.

diagnostic horizon In U.S. soil *taxonomy*, a soil layer that possesses characteristics used to define soil type.

dichroism The different colors seen when a mineral is viewed from different angles.

dike An embankment, or artificial earthen wall, built to prevent nearby lowland from flooding.

dimictic lake A lake where the warmer upper and cooler lower layers of water mix twice a year.

dip Of rock layers, the degree of inclination of one or more layers beneath the horizon.

divergence A flow of air that moves outward from a central point.

divergent boundary A boundary between two *lithospheric* plates that are moving away from each other.

doline Found in limestone areas, a steep-sided depression in the ground surface that may lead to a cave system.

dolomite A rock-forming calcium-magnesium carbonate mineral, or a sedimentary rock that is formed when limestone (calcium carbonate) changes to calcium-magnesium carbonate.

dominant Of a species, one that has the greatest influence on the composition and character of a certain plant or animal community.

dust devil A twisting wind that raises a column of dust. It resembles a tornado, but is smaller and less violent, and is not associated with a storm.

dwarf planet A spherical object orbiting the Sun that, unlike a true planet, has not cleared its vicinity of competitors; for example, Pluto.

dysphotic zone The upper part of the ocean where there is some light, but not enough for *photosynthesis*.

ecosystem A community of living organisms and the environment in which they live.

electromagnetic radiation Energy that propagates through space as waves traveling at the speed of light. The shorter the wavelength, the greater the energy the radiation possesses.

electron An elementary particle that carries a negative charge.

elemental mineral A mineral type that is made up of a single element, such as native copper.

elliptical galaxy A sphere-shaped *galaxy* with a smooth appearance, consisting mostly of aging stars.

El Niño A change in the strength, and sometimes direction, of the trade winds in the tropical South Pacific. It happens every two to seven years and brings changes in weather over a wide area.

emergent A forest tree that is taller than those around it.

endorheic system A drainage basin, usually inland, that has no direct connection to the ocean.

epicenter The point on Earth's surface that is directly above the hypocenter, or starting point, of an earthquake.

epilimnion The warmer upper layer of water in a lake.

epipelagic zone The top ocean layer down to 660 feet (200 m).

equilibrium line The line across a glacier separating the region of ice accumulation from that of ice loss.

era A division of time in Earth's history. Geologists divide eras into periods, epochs, and then ages.

erg An extensive area in a hot desert that is covered by gently sloping sand dunes, also known as a sand sea.

erosion The breaking down and removal of rock and soil by wind, water, and ice, as well as by mass movements such as landslides.

erratic A rock that has been transported by a *glacier* and deposited in an area that has a different type of rock.

escarpment A cliff or steep slope next to level or gently sloping ground.

esker A long, steep-sided ridge with a narrow crest, made of sand and gravel, that was deposited by meltwater from a *glacier* or *ice sheet*.

estuary A partly enclosed area of coastal water that is open to the sea and into which a river flows.

ethnography Detailed description of the culture of a particular society; called ethnology in Europe.

eutrophic lake A lake that, over time, acquires high levels of nutrients.

exfoliation The separation of surface layers from a rock due to weathering, also known as onion-skin weathering.

exosphere The outermost region of the *atmosphere*, 300 to 450 miles (480–725 km) above the surface.

fault A fracture in Earth's crust along which two sections of crust have moved in relation to each other.

feldspar A member of a range of rock-forming silicate minerals.

Fennoscandian ice sheet The *ice sheet* that covered Scandinavia and parts of Russia and western Europe during the most recent ice age.

fetch The distance over water in which waves are generated by a wind that has constant speed and direction.

fissure A fracture in the ground. In volcanic areas, eruptions may occur as a line of vents along a fissure.

floodplain Part of a river valley that is covered with sediment deposited by a river overflowing its banks.

fog Cloud at ground level that reduces general visibility to less than 0.6 miles (1 km).

forb A herbaceous flowering plant that is not grass; for example, clover, sunflower, and milkweeds.

fossil fuels Carbon-based materials, such as oil, coal, and natural gas, formed from the fossils of ancient plants and animals, and burned to produce energy and electricity.

fossil soil Soil that has been buried and sealed from outside influences for a long time. It contains biological material from which information about the past environment can be obtained.

fringing reef A coral reef that forms around the shore of an island and gradually extends outward.

frond The leaf-like part of a seaweed.

front In meteorology, a boundary between two air masses of different temperatures. See also *cold front* and *warm front*.

frontal system The interface between air masses of different temperatures and humidities where the most significant weather tends to occur.

fumarole A vent in a volcanically active area that emits steam and/or other volcanic gasses.

fynbos Drought-resistant vegetation that is adapted to hot, dry summers, found in parts of Cape Province, South Africa. It is similar to *chaparral*, but its plant species are different.

galaxy A huge gathering of stars, gas, and dust, bound by gravity and having a mass ranging from 100,000 to 10 trillion times that of the Sun.

gale A wind between forces 7 and 10 on the Beaufort scale, blowing at 38 to 63 miles per hour (60–100 km/h).

gas giant A planet whose composition is dominated by hydrogen and helium, such as Jupiter and Saturn.

geographic pole One of the two points where Earth's rotational axis intersects its surface.

geomorphology The study of the way landscapes develop and change over time.

geothermal warming Warming of water by contact with the hot rocks beneath Earth's surface.

geyser An opening at Earth's surface from which a fountain of hot water periodically spouts upward.

glacial trench A channel that is scoured by a *glacier*.

glaciation The effect of a moving ice mass on a landscape, resulting in erosion, the gouging of U-shaped valleys and fjords, and the deposition of ridges and sheets of rock debris.

glacier A mass of ice that moves over the underlying surface.

global climate models (GCM) A computer simulation that reproduces global weather patterns and can be used to predict changes in the weather.

Global Positioning System (GPS) A system that enables users to determine location, speed, direction, and time via detailed satellite information.

global warming An observed increase in the average temperature of Earth's atmosphere, leading to climate change and other effects.

globular cluster A large star cluster, shaped like a ball, that contains up to a million stars. Clusters are found on the outskirts of many *galaxies*.

Gondwana The southern supercontinent fragment comprising New Zealand, Antarctica, Australia, South America, Africa, and India. It existed as a separate landmass from 650 million years ago and began to break up only 130 million years ago.

gour A shallow pool surrounded by a raised edge of calcium carbonate, also called a rimstone pool. The rim forms from calcium carbonate that is precipitated when water evaporates.

granite A common and widespread type of coarse-grained *igneous rock*.

gray water Used water drained from baths, showers, dishwashers, or washing machines that is recycled in order to reduce water use in the home.

greenhouse effect The retention of heat in the *atmosphere*. Sunlight reaching Earth's surface is re-radiated as heat, which is then absorbed, trapped, and re-radiated back to Earth by certain gases, such as carbon dioxide.

greenhouse emissions Substances released into the air by machines or natural processes, contributing to the greenhouse effect; often used to describe gases released from car engines and power stations.

grike A deep vertical cleft in limestone caused when rainwater dissolves rock along joints.

groundwater Water that moves through the spaces between rocks below the ground.

gymnosperm A seed plant in which the ovules, from which seeds develop, are borne naked on the cone scales.

gypsum A calcium sulfate mineral that is deposited from evaporating seawater.

gyre A circular motion in a body of water.

habit Of a mineral, the exterior shape of a single crystal or a group of crystals of the same mineral.

hackly Of a mineral, describing a type of fracture that displays sharp edges, jagged points, and depressions.

hadal zone The ocean zone that is below 19,680 feet (6,000 m).

hanging valley A valley that emerges high on the side of a much larger valley and from which a waterfall often descends. A hanging valley occurs in a glaciated landscape at the point where a tributary *glacier* once joined a main glacier.

hardwood The wood of a broad-leaved, or *angiosperm*, tree.

heathland A lowland plant community dominated by dwarf shrubs, especially heathers.

heat wave A period of at least one day, but more usually several days or weeks, during which the air temperature is unusually high for the time of year.

helium The second most common element after hydrogen. It was created in the *Big Bang*, and it is also made inside stars during nuclear reactions.

herb A small, non-woody, seed-bearing plant that is used for cooking or in medicine.

herbivore An animal that eats only plant material, such as leaves, bark, roots, and seeds.

hot spots In volcanology, local areas of high volcanic activity that do not occur at the edges of *tectonic plates*.

hybrid car A vehicle that combines a standard internal combustion (gas) engine with a rechargeable and battery-powered electric motor.

hydroelectric power A form of renewable energy, based on converting the movement of water into electricity. Dams capture river water and direct it past turbine generators at high speed.

hydrogen The most common and lightest substance in the entire *universe*. Stars and *gas-giant* planets are made mostly of hydrogen gas with *helium*.

hydrological cycle The endless cycling of water between land, ocean, and *atmosphere*.

hypolimnion The cooler lower layer of water in a lake.

hyporheic zone The ground around a stream or river where there is an exchange between *groundwater* and flowing water.

ice age A cold phase in the climatic history of Earth during which large areas of land were covered by ice.

iceberg A mass of ice that has become detached from a *glacier* or *ice shelf*, and floats in the sea.

ice cap A layer of ice stretching over land less than 20,000 square miles (52,000 km²) in area, but thick enough to bury underlying landscape features.

ice field An almost-level layer of ice that develops where the land surface is high enough, or level enough, for ice to accumulate.

ice giant A planet whose composition is similar to that of a *gas giant*, but includes a large proportion of rock and slushy ice.

ice sheet The largest type of *glacier*, sometimes also called an *ice cap*.

ice shelf An area of floating ice, once part of a *glacier*, that is still attached to land.

igneous rock A rock that has formed from cooled, hardened *magma*. Earth's first rocks were igneous rock.

inversion Of temperature, a region in the atmosphere in which the temperature increases with height, instead of decreasing.

ionization The loss or gain by an *atom* of one or more *electrons*, resulting in the atom having a positive or negative electrical charge.

irregular galaxy A galaxy that has no visibly consistent shape or form, unlike a *spiral* or *elliptical galaxy*.

island arc A series of seabed volcanoes tall enough to project above the surface as islands. They are associated with an oceanic trench.

joint Of rocks, a fracture where there has been little or no movement along the plane of the fracture, but some movement at right angles to it, so that the fracture has widened.

karst Describes a region with underlying limestone rock that has weathered to produce a variety of distinctive features, including *dolines* and cave systems.

kettle lake A lake in a deep depression formed by the melting of ice left by a retreating *glacier* or *ice sheet*.

kopje (koppie) A small, isolated, steep-sided hill about the size of a house, often with an irregular, castellated outline.

krummholz Gnarled and stunted trees, most no larger than a bush, that grow on mountainsides between the edge of the forest and the *treeline*.

Kyoto Protocol A 2005 agreement between world governments that aimed to limit or reduce *greenhouse emissions* to slow climate change.

labradorescence The optical reflective effect of the gemstone labradorite. The colors change according to the angle of light refraction, and may be blue, green, yellow, and pink.

laccolith A mushroom-shaped body of volcanic rock that is formed when rising *magma* pushes *sedimentary rock* layers upward.

lagoon A coastal area of shallow water that is almost completely enclosed by land, with only a small conection to the sea.

lahar A mudflow that is created by a volcanic eruption.

lake-effect snow High snowfall that occurs on the lee side of a large, unfrozen lake that is entirely enclosed by land.

land bridge A connection between two large landmasses.

landslide The rapid movement down a slope of material that has become detached from the underlying surface.

La Niña Periods of unusually cold ocean temperatures in the equatorial Pacific that occur between *El Niño* events. An episode of La Niña brings these conditions for a minimum of five months.

Laurentian ice sheet A thick layer of ice that covered eastern Canada and the northeastern United States during the Pleistocene ice ages.

lava Hot, liquid rock, or *magma*, that has risen up from chambers deep within Earth and erupted onto Earth's surface from a volcano.

lava tube A hollow passage under solidified *lava*, through which hot lava once flowed.

lichen A compound organism consisting of a fungus and an alga or cyanobacterium.

light-year The distance that light travels in one year, about 6 trillion miles (9.5 trillion km).

lignotuber A starchy swelling on an underground stem or root (tuber).

limestone A *sedimentary rock* consisting mainly of calcium carbonate and/or dolomite.

limestone pavement An extensive area of horizontally bedded *limestone* that has been exposed by *erosion*.

lithosphere The outermost solid layer of Earth, comprising the *crust* and the brittle top part of the *mantle*.

Little Ice Age A period of relatively low average temperatures that affected the whole world and lasted from the 16th century to the late 19th century.

littoral zone The seashore between high-tide and low-tide marks.

loess A loose sediment, consisting mainly of very fine particles, that is deposited by wind.

longitudinal dune A long sand dune that is aligned with the direction of the prevailing wind.

longshore current A sea current that flows parallel to the shore; it is produced by the oblique angle at which waves approach.

longshore drift Movement of beach material parallel to the coastline, driven by the action of wind and waves.

lunar mare A plain of congealed *lava* on the surface of the Moon, darker than the surrounding areas.

macaroni stalactite A long, narrow hollow formation that descends from the roof of a cave.

magma Hot liquid rock and crystals below Earth's surface. When magma erupts onto the surface, it is called *lava*.

magnetic field A region surrounding a magnetic object, within which an iron-rich body will experience a magnetic force.

magnetic pole The north or south pole of Earth's *magnetic field* with which magnetic compass needles align. The magnetic pole is some distance from the *geographic pole*.

magnetosphere A region of space around a planet or star dominated by that body's *magnetic field*.

mallee A scrub community found in southern Australia that consists mainly of drought-resistant shrubs, most belonging to the genus *Eucalyptus*.

mangrove Flowering shrubs and trees tolerant of salt water, found on low-lying tropical and subtropical coasts and estuaries.

mantle The part of Earth that lies between the underside of the *crust* and the outer edge of the outer *core*. It is about 1,430 miles (2,300 km) thick.

mantle plume Hot material rising through the *mantle* that is hypothesized to occur beneath *hot spots*.

mariculture The cultivation of marine organisms such as fish or oysters for food and other products.

marl (marlstone) A lime-rich mud that contains variable amounts of clays and calcium carbonate.

marsupial A type of mammal whose young are born before they are fully developed. The embryo crawls into a pouch where it attaches itself to a teat and continues its development.

massif A large landscape feature consisting of rock that is more rigid than the surrounding rock.

mass wasting The movement of surface material down a hillslope.

megacity An urban area with a population greater than 10 million.

mesa A flat-topped, steep-sided hill, characteristic of arid environments, formed from horizontally bedded rocks that have been uplifted and exposed by the erosion of surrounding rock.

mesopause In Earth's *atmosphere*, the boundary, located about 50 miles (80 km) above Earth's surface, between the *mesosphere* below and the *thermosphere* above.

mesopelagic zone The ocean layer between the depths of about 600 and 3,000 feet (180–900 m) .

mesosphere The layer of the *atmosphere* above the *stratosphere*, from about 30 to 50 miles (50-80 km) above sea level.

metamorphic rock Rock that is formed by the transformation of pre-existing rock as a result of extreme heat and/or pressure.

meteorite The name given to any piece of interplanetary debris that reaches Earth's surface intact.

microcontinent A *lithospheric* plate that is composed of continental crust, but which is too small to be considered a continent.

microorganism An organism too small to be visible to the naked eye.

micropropagation The growing of tissue culture in an artificial environment, such as a laboratory.

millstone grit A coarse *sandstone* consisting of sand grains and small stones deposited in deltas. It was formerly used to make millstones.

mineral A naturally occurring substance with a characteristic chemical composition and crystal structure. Rocks are made of minerals.

monocline In rock, a one-limbed fold that is bounded on both sides by horizontal strata.

monoclinic Describing a mineral crystal system with three axes of unequal lengths, one of which is perpendicular to the other two (which are not perpendicular to each other).

monsoon A seasonal wind that produces heavy rain in tropical and subtropical zones, especially in Southeast Asia.

moraine Rock and gravel that has been removed and ground by glacial scouring and then deposited at the side or terminus of a *glacier*.

moulin A shaft leading to a system of tunnels made by water in a *glacier*.

nappe A folded body of rock in which the fold limbs and axes are approximately horizontal.

natural selection A natural driving force that allows the modification of animals and plants to best suit their environment.

neap tide A tide with a much smaller range than a spring tide. This occurs when the gravitational pulls of the Sun and Moon on the oceans work against each other.

nebula A cloud of gas or dust in space that may appear dark or luminous.

neritic zone The ocean zone between the high-tide mark and the edge of the continental shelf.

neutron star A massive star's collapsed remnant, consisting almost wholly of very densely packed neutrons. It may be visible as a pulsar.

North Atlantic drift The less well-defined portion of the Gulf Stream that moves eastward from Cape Hatteras across the North Atlantic.

notochord The stiff rod of tissue that becomes the backbone in vertebrate animals.

nucleus A nucleus can be the center of an *atom*, the heart of a *comet*, or the center of a *galaxy*.

nunatak A rocky mountain summit that protrudes from an *ice sheet*.

oasis A local area in a desert where the water table is close enough to the surface to allow plants to flourish.

obduction The process of emplacement of a piece of oceanic *lithosphere* on continental lithosphere, usually by sub-horizontal displacement. This occurs at *convergent boundaries*.

oblate A shape that is circular when seen from above, but elliptical when viewed from the side, its width being greater than its height.

ocean basin A large depression in Earth's surface that contains one of the five great bodies of seawater: the Pacific, Atlantic, Indian, Arctic, or Southern oceans.

oceanic crust The rocks that form the *ocean basins*, creating a layer averaging 3 miles (5 km) in thickness.

oceanic realm The part of the ocean deeper than 660 feet (200 m).

oligotrophic lake A lake that can support limited plant and animal life.

oölite An ovoid or spherical crystalline deposit. Most are composed of calcium carbonate, but some may also be iron carbonate, silica, calcium phosphate, or iron oxide.

oölitic Of a mineral, pertaining to a *habit* where it tends to form as small spheres or *oölites*, as typically seen in bauxite, ironstone, and some limestones.

open star cluster A group of young stars, from dozens to a few hundred in number, that are bound together by gravity.

ore A mineral or rock that contains a particular metal in a concentration that is high enough to make its extraction commercially viable. Hematite and iron ore are examples.

ornithopter An aircraft that can fly by means of flapping its wings.

orogeny An episode of mountain building by the upward folding of Earth's *crust*.

orthorhombic Describing a mineral crystal system with three axes of unequal length, all at right angles to one another.

outlet glacier A *glacier* that drains ice from an *ice sheet* or *ice cap*.

overturn The loss of the stratification of the *water column* in deep lakes, bringing bottom water to the surface.

ovule The part of a plant that develops into a seed after fertilization.

ox-bow lake A crescent-shaped lake formed from a single loop cut off from a meandering river or stream.

ozone A type of oxygen in which the molecule consists of three atoms rather than two.

ozone hole A region of the *ozone layer* over Antarctica, and to a lesser extent over the Arctic, where the amount of ozone is depleted.

ozone layer A region of the *stratosphere* 12 to 20 miles (20–32 km) above sea level where the *ozone* concentration is higher than elsewhere.

pack ice Drifting sea ice that has become packed together to form a large mass.

pampas A vast area of level grassland in Argentina and Uruguay, extending from the Atlantic coast to the Andean foothills and bounded by the Gran Chaco and Patagonia.

Pangea The ancient supercontinent that once contained all of Earth's continents. It began to break up about 200 million years ago into Gondwana and Laurasia.

panicle A flowering plant structure that consists of several *racemes*.

parabolic dune A crescent-shaped sand dune in which the horns of the crescent are close together.

peat A soil that contains at least 65 percent organic material by dry weight and that has a surface horizon at least 16 inches (40 cm) thick.

pedogenesis The process in which soil is created; also known as soil evolution.

pelagic zone Earth's entire body of water from the surface to the bottom.

peninsula A strip of land that is bordered on three sides by the sea.

periglacial lake A lake that has formed where the natural drainage of the topography has been blocked by *moraine* or a *glacier*.

period In geology, a specific division of geological time. Periods are further broken down into epochs and ages.

permafrost Ground that has remained frozen for at least two successive winters and the intervening summer.

photophores Luminous organs on some deep-sea fishes.

photosphere The visible surface of the Sun or any other star.

photosynthesis The process by which plants produce their own nutrients, in the form of sugars, using daylight, water, and carbon dioxide. Plants give off oxygen during *photosynthesis*.

photovoltaic cell The basic unit of most solar energy systems.

phreatic zone An area of soil and rock saturated with groundwater.

piedmont glacier A lobe of ice that forms when a valley glacier emerges from the mountain and spreads out onto the plain.

pinnacle A tall, narrow structure, found especially in arid areas, that is formed by the erosion of a *butte*.

planetary nebula A shell of gas blown off by a low-mass star when it runs out of fuel in its core.

planetesimal A small, rocky or icy body that is coalesced to form a planet.

plankton The plant (phytoplankton) or animal (zooplankton) organisms that float or drift in the open sea.

plate tectonics The theory that Earth's *crust* consists of a number of plates that float on top of the *mantle* and move in relation to one another.

plateau An area of high, level ground.

platy Describing a mineral crystal that is plate-like, or short and flat.

play-of-color An optical effect seen in opal that is caused by light refracting. It creates patches of color that change with the angle of the light.

pluton A mass of *igneous rock* that rose buoyantly in molten form from deep under Earth's surface, intruding and cooling near surface rocks as a balloon-like body.

pollen Spore-like structures produced by plants that contain male sex cells.

prairie An area of level or rolling grassland, especially found in central North America, that has few trees, and generally a moderately moist climate.

precipitation Water that falls from the sky as dew, fog, mist, drizzle, rain, hail, frost, or snow.

predator An organism that obtains energy by consuming and usually killing another organism (the prey).

proton An elementary particle that carries a positive charge.

pyroclastic flow A mixture of volcanic gas, ash, and rock fragments that travels down volcanic slopes.

quartz A widely distributed rock-forming mineral made from silica.

quasars Short for quasi-stellar radio source, quasars are thought to be the active nuclei of very distant *galaxies*.

raceme A flower cluster in which a main axis continues growing while flowers are produced on side branches.

radiation Energy radiated from a source as wavelengths or particles.

rain forest A type of forest that develops in regions with high rainfall or frequent fog throughout the year.

rain shadow A certain reduction in precipitation that eventually produces a dry climate on the lee side of a mountain barrier.

raised beach A former beach that is now above the shoreline owing to falling sea levels or earth movements that raised the land.

recumbent fold In rock, a tight fold in which nearly parallel limbs are laid over a nearly horizontal axial plane.

recycle To keep, process, and reuse materials in order to save energy and reduce waste.

red giant A large, cool, red star in a late stage of its life.

reforestation Planting new trees to replace or re-stock forests.

refraction Bending of a light ray when it passes into a medium with a different optical density.

regolith A layer of loose rock fragments, gravel, and mineral grains lying on the surface of solid *bedrock*.

relative humidity The amount of water vapor present in air expressed as a percentage of the amount needed to saturate air at a prevailing temperature.

renewable energy Energy from natural sources, such as sunlight or wind, that do not run out.

reniform Describes a kidney-shaped mineral *habit*, such as that of hematite.

rhizome A horizontal underground plant stem that bears roots and leaves.

Richter scale An open-ended scale that rates the magnitude of an earthquake based on the amount of energy released. Each number on the scale represents an increase ten times greater than the number below it.

rift A split between two bodies of rock that were once joined. Parallel *faults* may allow the section between them to sink, forming a rift valley.

Ring of Fire A region of high volcanic activity surrounding the Pacific Ocean.

salinity A measure of the amount of dissolved salts in water.

sand Mineral grains that are 0.002 to 0.08 inch (0.0625–2.0 mm) in size.

sandbar A low ridge of sand in shallow water close to a shore.

sandstone A *sedimentary rock* formed from sand grains that are packed and cemented together.

sandstorm A wind storm that raises sand grains from the surface, often to a considerable height, and transports them, often for a long distance.

satellite Any small object orbiting a larger one, although the term is most often used for rocky or artificial objects orbiting a planet.

saturation The condition in which air (or another medium) contains as much water vapor as it is capable of holding.

savanna A type of tropical vegetation, dominated by grasses with varying numbers of bushes and trees, that is adapted to an annual dry season.

scavenger An animal that feeds on dead organic material.

sclerophyllous Applied to evergreen plants that have thick, hard, leathery leaves that allow them to survive a prolonged hot, dry summer.

seamount A steep-sided circular or elliptical seafloor projection more than two-thirds of a mile (1 km) high.

seasonal precipitation *Precipitation* associated with seasonal changes.

sedimentary rock Rock formed by extreme compression from pieces of other rocks, often with plant and animal remains included.

sediments Fine particles of mud, sand, and organic debris that are carried by rivers and currents, and settle at the bottom of a pond, river, or ocean.

seismogram A graph that depicts Earth tremors as wavy lines. It is produced by a seismograph.

serac A pinnacle or block of ice on a *glacier*, formed by the glacier's intersecting *crevasses*.

sextant An instrument used in navigation that measures angular distances between a celestial object and the horizon.

shale A fine-grained *sedimentary rock*.

side-scan sonar A technique that gives visual representation of the seafloor by beaming sound waves from an emitter.

sill A sub-horizontal band of *igneous rock* that is formed when *magma* intrudes and solidifies between different parallel rock layers.

siltstone A *sedimentary rock* formed from silt-sized particles of 0.0002 to 0.002 inch (0.004–0.0625 mm).

sinkhole A circular, often funnel-shaped depression in the ground that is formed when the roof of a cavern collapses; also known as a *doline*. It is usually found in areas of limestone rock.

soil horizons Layers of soil in the ground.

solar wind A ceaseless, but variable, high-speed stream of charged particles flowing out into space from the Sun.

snout The upturned terminus of a valley glacier.

snow field An extensive, level area covered by snow or ice.

snowline The lower edge of the snow that remains on a mountain throughout summer.

softwood Wood of a coniferous tree.

soil The natural layer of mineral particles and organic material that lies above weathered bedrock.

soil creep The slow movement of soil down a slope due to gravity.

solar storm A violent explosion in the solar atmosphere, usually occurring close to a *sunspot*, that emits *radiation* and a stream of charged particles.

solar wind A stream of high-energy and charged particles emitted by the Sun, and traveling at hundreds of miles per second.

solution doline A *doline* that is formed where slightly acid rainwater has dissolved limestone along a joint.

Southern Oscillation A periodic change in the distribution of surface air pressure over the South Pacific Ocean that is associated with *El Niño* events.

speleothem A deposit of calcium carbonate that is formed in caves where calcite has precipitated from dripping water.

spiral galaxy A type of large *galaxy* that is flat, resembling a disk, but that has a bulge in the center. The disk includes a spiral pattern traced out by young stars.

spire A tall, narrow tower of rock that is the result of erosion of the softer surrounding rock.

spit An elongated accumulation of sand or gravel that projects outward from a coast.

spring tide A tide that occurs when the gravitational forces of the Sun and Moon act together.

stack A pillar of rock that stands offshore, formed when wave action erodes a cave through a headland, producing an arch that later collapses.

stalactite A long *speleothem* that descends from the roof of a cave.

stalagmite A pinnacle of *speleothem* that rises from the floor of a cave.

star A globe of gas that shines of its own accord because of energy released by nuclear reactions in its core.

star dune A sand dune that consists of arms radiating from the center.

stolon A plant stem that grows horizontally along the ground surface.

stoma (pl. stomata) A pore in a leaf surface through which the plant absorbs carbon dioxide and releases oxygen and water vapor.

stratopause The boundary, about 30 miles (50 km) above Earth's surface, between the *stratosphere* below and *mesosphere* above.

stratosphere An atmospheric layer that lies above the *troposphere* and below the *mesosphere*.

stratovolcano A cone-shaped volcano that occurs at a *subducting* plate boundary where the downgoing plate melts, allowing andesitic *magma* to rise and pierce the overriding plate.

strike-slip fault A vertical or near-vertical *fault* in which the main rock movement is horizontal and parallel to the direction of the fault.

subduction The pulling of one *lithospheric* plate beneath another at the boundary between them.

sublimation The changing of water vapor into ice or the reverse, without it passing through the liquid phase.

subsidence doline A surface depression that is formed when loose surface deposits are washed downward by rainwater.

subtropics The region that lies approximately between latitudes 35° and 40° in both hemispheres.

sunspot A dark, highly magnetic region on the Sun's surface that is cooler than the surrounding area.

supercluster Also referred to as "a cluster of clusters," a supercluster is a vast assemblage of entire clusters of *galaxies*.

supernova The explosion of a massive star, which can briefly outshine entire

galaxies, that occurs when the star reaches the end of its fuel supply.

surge glacier A glacier that flows at varying speeds, sometimes accelerating and then slowing.

suture A linear belt of highly deformed rocks at the boundary between two collided masses of crust.

symbiosis The close beneficial feeding relationship between two species.

syncline A basin-shaped fold in layers of *sedimentary rock*.

taiga The Russian name for the belt of coniferous forest that lies across northern Eurasia.

taxonomy The practice and science of classification.

tectonic forces The forces in Earth's crust that change the shape of rock strata and produce earthquakes.

tectonic plates The *lithospheric* plates that form Earth's *crust*. There are continental and oceanic plates.

temperate Neither very hot nor very cold. Temperate areas have four distinct seasons.

thermocline A zone in the *water column* of a lake or ocean where the present temperature decreases rapidly with depth.

thermohaline circulation Water movement caused by differences in density produced by changes in temperature and/or salinity.

thermopause The boundary, at an altitude varying between about 310 miles (500 km) and 620 miles (1,000 km), between the *thermosphere* below and *exosphere* above.

thermosphere The layer of the *atmosphere* that extends from the *mesopause* about 50 miles (80 km) above the surface, to the *thermopause* at 310 to 620 miles (500–1000 km) above Earth.

terrestrial planet A planet with a mainly rocky composition: Mercury, Venus, Earth, and Mars.

tetragonal Describes a mineral crystal that has three axes, all at right angles to one another, with two axes of equal length and the third axis either longer or shorter.

tidal bore A step-like or high-breaking wave that advances up an estuary and the lower reaches of a river. It is created by the funneling of a *spring tide* into a small area.

tide The regular rise and fall of the sea due to the gravitational attraction of the Moon and, to a lesser extent, the Sun.

tombolo A spit that links an island to the mainland or to another island.

tor A mass of exposed *bedrock*, typically granite, standing above the surrounding land.

trade-wind inversion An *inversion* associated with subsiding air on the side of the Hadley cells farthest from the equator.

trade winds The winds that blow toward the equator from the northeast in the Northern Hemisphere and from the southeast in the Southern Hemisphere.

transform fault boundary A type of *strike-slip fault* at the boundary of two *lithospheric* plates that are sliding past each other with a horizontal motion.

transposons DNA sequences that move around to different positions within the genome of a single cell; also known as "jumping genes."

transverse dune A long sand dune at right angles to the direction of the prevailing wind, with the gradual slope on the side facing into the wind.

trench A deep depression in the ocean floor, often thousands of miles long.

tributary A secondary river or *glacier* that eventually flows into another main river or glacier.

triclinic Describes a mineral crystal with three axes of unequal lengths, and not at right angles to one another.

trigonal Describes a mineral crystal with three axes of equal length intersecting at 120 degrees to one another and a fourth axis of different length at right angles to the other three.

tropopause The boundary, about 11 miles (18 km) above Earth's surface, between the *troposphere* below and *stratosphere* above.

troposphere The lowest layer of the *atmosphere*. This is the layer in which we live and in which about 99 percent of Earth's weather occurs.

treeline A line marking the latitudinal or altitudinal limit of tree growth.

tundra A treeless plain found in Arctic and some Antarctic regions where the predominant vegetation consists of grasses, herbs, shrubs, and trees.

ultramafic Describes *igneous rocks* with silica content below approximately 50 percent by weight.

ultraviolet (UV) radiation *Electromagnetic radiation* with a wavelength of 4 to 400 nanometers, located in the spectrum between violet visible light and X-rays.

unconformity A discontinuity in rock sequence where erosion has separated two rock masses of different

ages, showing that the deposition of sediment was not continuous.

understory The forest trees that form a canopy below the main *canopy*.

universe Everything that exists around us, including space, time, energy, and matter.

vent A pipe inside a volcano through which *lava* and gas move from the *magma* chamber deep within to erupt on the surface.

vertical archipelago Agricultural system developed by Andean communities for producing resources along an extreme vertical gradient.

volcano A landform created by the buildup of *lava* flows and ash. Volcanoes are typically cone-shaped.

wadi The Arabic name for a river channel in a desert. It is usually dry, but carries water occasionally.

warm front A boundary between two air masses at different temperatures that advances with the warmer air behind it.

warm pool The deep layer of warm ocean water that lies in the region of Indonesia, except during *El Niño* events, when the pool is depleted.

water column The conceptual model of a body of water from the surface to the bottom.

water table The upper level of *groundwater* in an *aquifer*.

wavelength Of a wave, the distance between the crest or trough of one wave and another wave's crest or trough.

weathering The breaking down of certain rocks and minerals as a result of the freezing and thawing of ice; the action of chemicals in rainwater; or the force of extreme pressure and/or heat deep underground.

wetland Land that is covered for a part of the year with fresh or salt water. It has vegetation adapted to life in saturated soils.

winnow Of winds blowing across sand or dry soil, to separate and transport light particles.

World Heritage site An area of outstanding international natural or cultural importance that is designated by the World Heritage Committee of the United Nations Educational, Scientific, and Cultural Organization (UNESCO) in order to conserve it.

world ocean The interlinked network of oceans and seas covering 71 percent of Earth's surface.

zooanthellae Single-celled plant-like organisms that live in a symbiotic relationship inside coral polyps.

INDEX

t=top; l=left; r=right; tl=top left; tcl=top center left; tc=top center; tcr=top center right; tr=top right; cl=center left; c=center; cr=center right; b=bottom; bl=bottom left; bcl=bottom center left; bc=bottom center; bcr=bottom center right; br=bottom right

AFP = Agence France-Presse; AGI; = American Geological Institute; AM= Australian Museum; AMNH = American Museum of Natural History; AUS = Auscape International; BE = Brian M. England; BTA = Bernard Thornton Artist UK; CBT = Corbis; COML = Census of Marine Life; GI; = Getty Images; iS = istockphoto.com; JF = Jesse Fisher; MEPL = Mary Evans Picture Library; MP; = Minden Pictures; MRP = D. Malin/Royal Observatory Edinburgh Planetarium; N_V = Visible Earth; NASA; = National Aeronautics and Space Administration; NHM=Natural History Museum; NOAO = National Optical Astronomy Observatories; NPL;=naturepl.com; PD = Photodisc; PL= Photo Library; SCA = Scala Archives SH = shutterstock SW = Stuart Wilensky; USGS = United States Geographical Society; WF = Werner Forman Archive

PHOTOGRAPHS
Front cover SH

1cr GI; 2-3c CBT; 4r AUS; 6c MP; cl SPL; cr CBT; 7c, cl, cr CBT; 8c CBT; 12-13c NASA; 14c NASA; cl ESA; 15cl PL; cr NASA; 16bcr NASA; 17c ESA; 19r NASA; tl SPL; 20bl, cl, l, tcl NASA; c Robert Gendler 21tcr NASA; 22cl SPL; 23br, cr SPL; tl, tr NASA; 24cl CBT; 25bl, r, tl NASA; 27tr PL; 28bc bl MRP; br NASA; 29cl MRP 30bl NASA; 31b ESA; bcl SPL; tcl NASA; 32bl NASA; 33b, bcl, tcl NASA; 34bl NASA; 35cl CBT; r SPL; 36bc SPL; 37br, tr tl SPL; 38l SPL; 39tcl GI; tl MP; 42r CBT; tcl PL; 43c PL; cr iS l AUS; t SH; 44cr CBT; 45bcl, tr SPL; br, cl SH; cr CBT; 46bl GI; c CBT; c SPL; 47br, cr tl GI; cr, tr SPL; tl CBT; 48bc, cl, tl PL; tc SPL; 49bc AUS; 50bc, cr PL; tcl AUS; 52bl GI; l CBT; tr PL; 53bcl, bcr, c, tr PL; 54bl GI; 55cr AUS; tr 56tl CBT; 57cl PL; 58bl PL; 64bc, bl SH; c iS cl 65c CBT; 67c PL; 68bc PL; c SH; 69bc, tr SPL; br AAP; 70bc, c, l PL; bl SH; 71cr AAP; tr CBT; 72bl PL; 73bcl PL; 74c PL; 75tl PL; 76cl GI; 77bcl GI; bcr, tc, tl PL; 78c CBT; 80l CBT; r GI; 81t PL; 82cr PL; 83b MP; t PL; 85bcl CBT; r, tcl SPL; tcr JF; 86bc PL; tc AUS; 87cl PL; 90b, c, t iS; 92bcr, c, tc SH; 94bc iS c, tc SH; 96b, t iS; c SH; 98b SH; c PL; t iS; 100b, c, t iS; 102b, c, t iS; 105bl CBT; tcl GI; 106cr PL; 107c CBT; 108tcl PL; 110br CBT; 111cl GI; 112br CBT; 113l PL; 114bc CBT; l MEPL; r PL; 115r PL; tl NASA; 116c CBT; 118c PL; 119l PL; 121t NASA; 122cl PL; tcl CBT; 123br MP; tl GI; 124c PL; 126bc NASA; c CBT; 127c CBT; 128b PL; 129c PL; 130c CBT; 131tl GI; 132c GI; 133b, t PL; 134bcr, l PL; 135bcl, bcr, br PL; tl GI; 136c CBT; 137cl GI; 138c MP; 139c PL; 141c, cr, tcr PL; 142b AUS c SH; 143cl GI; 145tl GI; 146c PL; 147c NOAO; 148r PL; 149b PL; t COML 150c CBT; 152cl, cr SH; 153cr GI; 155c CBT; c, cr, l Ad-Libitum 157br iS tl GI; 158bcr, br, cr JF tcr, tl BE 159bcl, cl, cr PL; bl, l, r SPL; bl GI; br, tcl, tl CBT; tcr, tr JF tl PD 160c GI; 162r SH; br, cr Robert R Coenraads; br PL; tcr, tr CBT; 163 SPL; bl, br, cr, l, r, tl SH; br JF; tcl, tl, tr PL; tl CBT; 164tr CBT; 165c, tc PL; 166bcr CBT; bl, cr, tcr, tl, tr SH; br, l iS br PL; 167bcl, bl BE; bcr, br, r, tcr PL; cl, l, tcl, tl SH; cr, tr SPL; 168br NHM; br PL; c, l AMNH 169bcl GI; bcr SW bl JF; br PL; c CBT; 171cr, r, tcr SH; b PL; tc GI; tl iS 172bc NHM; br, tc, tcl, tcr, tl SW; c GI; cr PL; 173bl NHM; br AMNH; c 175cr GI; 176bc, br, c, cl, cr, tl SW; bcl, bl, cl, l, tcl, tl AM cr, r NHM; 177bcr, br NHM; bl, br, tl SW; c PL; 178bc, br, c, cl, cr, tcr SW; 179br, bl JF c BE; 180bc, bl, cr, r PL; br AMNH; c, tcr JF; l AM l Ad-Libitum l, tc, tcr, tr SW; 181bl, br JF; bl, br, t SW; c BE; c SH; 182b, bc, c, tr JF; br NHM; c PL; cr, tc, tcl SW 183bl, br SW; bl NHM; c SH; c PL; 184bc, bcr, br SW; c NHM; cl SH; 185bl NHM bl AGI; br SW t PL; 186bc, br, cr, tc, tr SW; br, r WF; c SH; tc NHM; 187bcr CBT; bl AGI; br SW c, cr PL; 188b, bc, br, c, cl, tc, tcr, tr SW c PL; cr, r JF; 189bc, bcl, br, tc, tcl, tcr USDA; bl JF br SW l The Art Agency t, tc PL; 190bc, cr SW; bl NHM br SH; c JF; cl, tcr, tr PL; tc ALA; tcl, tl Jim Frazier; 191bl NHM br SH; br SW; cl PL; tc GI; 192bc CBT; br NHM c, cr GI; c, tc JF; l J. Scovil tcr, tr SW; 193bl, c PL; br NHM 194bc, bcl JF; bl, cl, tcl, tl BE; br, c, tc, tcl, tcr, tl SW; r AGI; 195c NHM; 197cl CBT; tr PL; 199bc, bcl, bcr, tc, tcl, tcr USDA; 203c CBT; 204tcl 205cr 206b cr PL; 207tl SH; 208b, cl NASA; 209c NASA; 211bcr PL; 213cl PL; 215tcl CBT; 216cl, tcr, tl NASA; 217tl NASA; 218c iS 219tcl GI; 221bl AUS; tcl iS 222bc, bl, tl SH; 223cl GI; 224bl iS c GI; 225br PL; 226br MP; c PL; 227br, cr cl NASA; tr SH; 228bc PL; bl CBT; 229bl, tl PL; br CBT; 230bl, c, cl, tl PL; 231br SH; 232tl, tr PL; 233br USGS c SPL; cl PL; 234bc, bl, tl AUS cl MP; 235cl GI; 236bl GI; c CBT; cl, tl PL; 237tcl PL; 238bl, c, cl SH; tl AUS 239tc, tl PL; 241bl iS 242bl Corel Corp.; cl GI; cr PL; tl PJ 243bl, tl CBT; 245bl CBT; br, tr SH; cl, cr, tl PD 246cr PL; 247tl PL; 248cr GI; 249cl PL; 251tl AUS 252cr SH; 253bl SH; 254cr MP; 256bcr, cr PL; 257cl NPL; 258cr PL; 259bl iS 260cr CBT; 261bcl, tcl PL; 262cr GI; 266cr GI; 269bl, cl CBT; tl PL; 270cr CBT; 271bl NASA; tl GI; 272cr CBT; tl PL; 273bl SPL; c, cl, cr, tl PL; 274c CBT; 276cl NASA; cr MP; 277c iS 278cl CBT; 279c PL; 280bc SH; bl, c, tl NASA; cl PL; 281br iS cr CBT; 282bl iS c PL; 283bcl PL; br SH; tl CBT; 284cl PL; cr SPL; 285cl, t PL; 286bc CBT; bl PL; 287bcl PL; br CBT; tcl SPL; tr SH; 288bc CBT; c iS; 289br CBT; cl MP; cr PL; tr iS 290cl GI; 291b GI; t CBT; 292bc PL; c DS; 293br GI; br, cr, tr CBT; cl SH; 294bc CBT; 295bcr SH; tcl CBT; 296bc GI; tc SH; 297br, cr, tr CBT; cl NASA; 299c CBT; 300bl, br, tcl, tr iS; cl CBT; cr AUS; 301br, cl, cr, tl iS tr SH; 302c SH; 303c SH; tcr PL; 304bl CBT; cr SPL; tl 305c PL; 306c AUS; 307bcl GI; 308c GI; 310bcl MP; bcr, tcr PI; tcl CBT; 311bcl, tcl SPL; bcr, cr PL; tcr MP; tr JO; 312cl GI; tr PL; 313c, r, tc, tl PL; 314bc, tc SH; c 315bc COR; br SH; tc GI; 316bc AUS 318bc AAP; 319bcr GI; br, cr, tr SH; cl NASA; 320c AAP; 321cl NASA; 323bc SH; cl iS 324bcl AUS; bl SH; tl PL; 325br, cr SH; cl GI; tr CBT; 327br USA; cl, tr PL; cr iS 329cr CBT; 330bl AAP; 331bcl, bcr AAP; cl PL; cr, tr NASA; 333cr SH; tcl NASA; tr GI; 335b, t GI; 337cl PL; 338bl, tc GI; 339bcr, tcl MP; br CBT; 340cr GI; 341br, cr, tr NASA; c AAP; 342bc PL; tc SPL; 343bcl, tcl GI; br PL; 344bcl GI; 345bcl, tc GI; 346bcl, br NASA; cr GI; 347c, cr, tr GI; 348bl, tl CBT; 349bcl PL; tl CBT; tr GI; 350c PL; 352l SH; r CBT; 353t CBT; 354bcr GI; 355c CBT; 356bc GI; br PL; 357bl CBT; 364bcl CBT; bl GI; 366bc SPL; bl GI; 368bl SCA; tcl PL; 369bc, cl, tr GI; br PL; tl CBT; 370bl AUS; cl SH; tl GI; 371tl SPL; 372bc GI; bl NASA; 373tl MP; 374bcl ESA bl NASA; 375br NASA; 376bc CBT; bl, tl SPL; tr AUS; 377bc SH; 378bcr MP; cl, tl SH; 379bcl MP; 380b PL; 381tl AUS; 383c NASA; 385cl GI; 386br CBT; 389bl GI; t CBT; 391cl GI; cr SH; tr PL; 392c N_V; 393c CBT; cr GI; 394cl PL; 395bl PL; t AUS; 396c AUS; 397c PL; tl GI; 400b NPL; c MP; 401t CBT; 402bl NASA; bl N_V; cr GI; 403br, tl PL; 404c MP; r PL; 406b AUS; 408c CBT; 410bcr NPL; 411bc AUS; 412bcr PL; c GI; 414bcl NPL; br GI; 415bl CBT; 416c, l PL; tr CBT; 417bcl PL; bcr CBT; 418bc GI; c NASA; 419cl NASA;

420c iS; 421bl PL; 424l CBT; 425c CBT; cl PL; tl GI; 426tr ;PL; 427cl PL; 428r, tr PL; 429l PL; 430bl NASA; r GI; 431br PL; 432bl bl SH; cr GI; 434bl USGS r CBT; 435br CBT; 436bc, c, cl PL; tl CBT; 437c, l CBT; t PL; 438bl, cr, r SH; 439br GI; l SH; 440bl SH; r CBT; 441l CBT; 442r USGS 443br SH; l USGS 444r PL; 445br iS l PL; 446c SH; 448tc GI; 449l AUS 450bl CBT; cl SH; 451c CBT; 452bc PL; 453tl CBT; 454br PL; tc MP; 460bc PL; cl MP; 461c PL; 463cr, tcr PL; tl GI; 465r, tcr SH; tl GI; 466c CBT; 468cl AAP; cr PL; 469cr CBT; 470l CBT; 471b NASA; tc GI; 472bc GI; 473cl CBT; 474bl CBT; cl SH; tl iS 475tl PL; 476bc PL; bl AAP; 477bcr PL; bl, tl CBT; 478bc PL; 479cl GI; 480bc PL; l iS 481bcl, tl PL; r CBT; 482bc CBT; 483bcr CBT; bl PL; tcl GI; 484bcr, tc GI; 486c PL; tl NASA; 487bcl, tcl GI; 488bl CBT; cr PL; 489cr SH; tl, tr PL; 491c CBT; 492bc, c CBT; 493cl GI; 494bc GI; bl, cl, tl SH; 495cl, tr PL; 498bc GI; 500bcl GI; bl, cl SH; cr CBT; tl iS; 501bl, c, tr CBT; br SH; 504bc PL; tl PL; 506bl, cl SH; tl iS; 507cl PL; 508bcr CBT; 509bcr, cr CBT; br iS tl PL; 513c, r, tcr PL; 515b, tl CBT; 517bl PL; 519c GI; tl NASA; 520bcr GI; 521c NASA; 522cl CBT; 523b CBT; t PL; 524br CBT; 525cl GI; 526b SH; tr PL; 527cl PL; 528br, c GI; 529tl GI; 531l PL; 532c AFP tr Jeremy Sutton-Hibbert 534-535c PL; 535tl GI; 536c CBT; 537br, r iS c PL; tr SH; 539bc, tl GI; br NASA; tr AAP; 540-541b PL; 541br SH; tcl GI; 542c PL; 543c MP; 545br, r, tr SH; c PL; 546br MP; 547b, c NMR; 548bc CBT; 549l CBT; 550r CBT; tl GI; 551bl, br GI; t CBT; 553bc CBT; br iS r, tr SH; 554bc PL; bcl AAP; 556c PL; 557c, tl PL; 559cr, tl GI; cr SH; 560bc PL; 561bc PL; 562bc, br N_V 563bc, bl N_V; 565cl GI; 566bcr GI; cl CBT; 567c PL; 569c PL; 570bc PL; 571c PL; 572b, c CBT; 573bl iS; 573t AAP; c CBT; 576bc, c PL; 577t PL; 578b PL; 579c PL; 581r SH; tc, tcr CBT; 582b iS; br PL; tl GI; 583bcr SH; c, cl GI; t CBT.

ILLUSTRATIONS

Susanna Addario 498cl, 499cr; **The Art Agency** 38tcl tl, 41cr r, 65bcl, 88bc, 178l, 182l, 186l, 302tcr, 303br tr, 321r, 323r, 401tcr, 455tcl, 514bl, 514bl; **The Art Agency/Robin Bouttell** 45c tc, 54cr; **The Art Agency/Richard Bonson** 117br, 123cr tcr tr, 356bl cl tl; **The Art Agency/ Robin Carter** 66bc; **The Art Agency/Tom Connell** 372tl tr; **The Art Agency/Barry Croucher** 240cr; **The Art Agency/Marc Dando** 400l tcl; **The Art Agency/Sandra Doyle** 257r; **The Art Agency/Jane Durston** 264c, 265bcl cl tcl; **The Art Agency/Kate Green** 201br cr tr, 221cr, 386b, 547cr, 37b; **The Art Agency/David Hardy** 16cr, 29bcr, 36c; **The Art Agency/Steve Kirk** 66c, 161, 221br, 205br, 265br, 382bl, 546bcl, 547br; **The Art Agency/ Tim Loughhead** 73tr; **The Art Agency/Terry Pastor** 22c, 27c, 28cl, 32cl, 40tcl, 41bcr tcr, 56c cl, 64tl, 68bl, 75cr tr, 84bl cl tl, 156bl, 162bl cl l tl, 165br l tr, 209cr tr, 218bl cl tl, 259cl cr tc, 269tr, 336bc, 337br cr tr, 339cr, 374cl, 375tr, 380bcl cl tl, 393tcr, 531cr tr, 540c, 570c; **The Art Agency/Mick Posen** 39tr, 40bl cr l, 48tr, 49tcr, 50tr, 58cl, 60bl, 82l, 84c, 89c, 91c, 97c, 113r, 120b, 125c, 127r, 132t, 137br cr tr, 138l, 143bcr br cr tr, 144b c, 145b, 149tcr, 156c, 157l, 161tlc, 174c, 196bl, 204bl l tl, 205cl, 206bl cl tl, 210l, 214bl cl tl, 216bcr, 225cl, 228tl, 240bl cl tl, 255c, 271tr, 318cl tc, 322bc, 373br, 379br, 384bl, 397r, 398cl tcl, 399b, 404bc, 405bcr r, 408c, 411cr tr, 413bcr bl cl cr, 415tr, 418bl cl tl, 421c tl, 448bc, 517c, 580b c, 581c; **The Art Agency/Steve Roberts** 253bcr, 263br; **The Art Agency/Chris Turnbull** 421cr; **The Art Agency/Steve White** 58c, 429bc, 547cr; **The Art Agency/Jurgen Ziewe** 202c, 427br cr tr, 446b cl tl, 447b t, 448l, 536b; **Amadeo Bachar** 210cr, 211tcr; **Jane Beatson** 265tr; **Anne Bowman** 58tl, 247bl; **Peter Bull Art Studio** 44l, 60cl tl, 129bcr r, 148bcl, 205r, 241r, 251br, 269bl, 281cl, 286c cl tl, 288l, 296l, 306bl cl tl, 308l, 309r, 315cr tr, 316bl tl, 322bl tl, 326bc tc, 330cl tl, 333bcl, 354cl, 356tc, 357br, 374tl, 375bl, 377tc, 381b, 395bcr, 396bl c, 401b, 405tcr, 406c, 408l, 411br cl, 415br, 417t, 485r, 512b, 515r, 519r, 552b, 553tl, 560c, 579r; **Leonello Calvetti** 46cl l tl; **Karen Carr** 62bl cl tl; **Chuck Carter** 200cr l, 201tl, 212br cl tr; **Marjorie Crosby-Fairall** 388bl, 403cr r tr; **Fiammetta Dogi** 119tr, 265r, 332l; **Encompass Graphics Limited** 228cl, 509cr tr; **Simone End** 259br cr; **Chris Forsey** 117r tr, 119cr r r, 140b, 154b, 204cr, 492bl cl tl, 506c; **Lloyd Foye** 561r; **Dr. Mark A. Garlick** 18cr tl, 21cl r, 22tl, 26b bcl, 27br cr, 28c tl, 29tr, 32bcr c cr t tcl, 34cr, 36bl tl, 38t, 39br, 87cr tr, 108l, 109cl, 156bc br, 161b c tc, 224bc tl, 236bcr, 237bc, 238bc, 278bcr, 309cl, 316bl, 317c cr, 329cl, 380c, 423tr, 424b, 425br cr, 426bc, 470c, 558b, 575c; **Jon Gittoes** 104c, 255br cr r; **Jon Gittoes/Mike Gorman/Oliver Rennert** 378tr; **GODD.com** 499bc c tc; **Mike Gorman** 379tr, 412tl, 413tr, 486bc; **Gabrielle Green** 574bl; **Ray Grinaway** 104cl, 172bl l tl, 180l, 253cr, 410tl, 444bl, 483br cr, 498bl tl, 499br tr, 549tcr, 561tcr; **Gino Hasler** 410bl; **Tim Hayward/BTA** 249c; **Steven Hobbs** 263bcl bcr bl; **Robert Hynes** 257br; **Frank Ippolito** 220cr; **Janet Jones** 520bcl; **Contact Jupiter/Alain Salesse** 214bcr, 215bcl; **Suzanne Keating** 28cl, 29br, 31cr r tcr, 33br cr r tcr; **Dr. David Kirshner** 55br, 57br, 66cl, 230bc, 249br r, 253tr, 255tr, 257cr r, 259r, 261cr, 265cr, 283cr tr, 345br cr, 421tr, 433br, 541cr, 546l, 547bcr, 549bcr; **Frank Knight** 221r, 251cr, 261br, 30bcr c cr t tcl; **Martin Macrae/FOLIO** 250bc; **James McKinnon** 60c, 62c, 64tr, 263cr tr; **Stuart McVicar** 568l; **© MagicGroup s.r.o. (Czech Republic) - www.magicgroup.cz** 22bl, 247bcr cr, 249tr, 251r, 271cr, 303cr, 382bl, 400cl, 407cr, 407b, 455cr tl, 549br; **Moonrunner Design** 16cl, 24tcr, 132bl l tl, 370cr, 386bcl, 508bl cl tl, 577bl; **David Moore/Linden Artists** 104bl; **Lionel Portier** 552tr, 557r; **Tony Pyrzakowski** 247tr, 261r, 441br; **Trevor Ruth** 263tcl, 345tr, 401r; **Oliver Rennert** 104tl, 268cr, 326bl cl tl, 361c; **John Richards** 69bcr, 71bcl, 73cr; **Barbara Rodanska** 268bc, 561bcr, 130b; **Claudia Saraceni** 221r, 243br, 251tr, 401r; **Michael Saunders** 57r, 61tr, 164b bc br, 165b bl, 249b bcr bl, 487br; **SeaGen** 574bc; **Peter Schouten** 68bcl; **Shane Marsh/Linden Artists** Ltd 520cl; **Mark Sofilas** 520tcl; **Marco Sparaciari** 388bl; **Kevin Stead** 61br cr, 261tr, 452l, 453b; **Roger Swainston** 398cl, 403br, 407bcr r; **Guy Troughton** 61cr, 66tl, 68bl, 247cr, 268br, 442bl, 546tcl; **Glen Vause** 314bl cl tl; **Genevieve Wallace** 253r; **Rod Westblade** 284b; **Ann Winterbotham** 117bcr, 253cl tc, 259tr, 384bl, 410, 483tr, 532bl, 541tcr tr, 549cr; **David Wood** 307r; **Murray Zanoni** 428bl.

MAPS/GRAPHICS
All maps by **Andrew Davies/Creative Communication** and **Map Illustrations**.

INDEX
Puddingburn

The publishers wish to thank Jasmine Crea, Jesse Fisher, Christina McInerney, Lachlan McLaine, Glenn Murphy, Juliana Titin, and Stuart and Donna Wilensky for their assistance in the preparation of this volume.